New Challenges New Tools

for Defense Decisionmaking

Stuart E. Johnson   Martin C. Libicki   Gregory F. Treverton

Bruce W. Bennett   Nurith Berstein   Frank Camm
David S.C. Chu   Paul K. Davis   Daniel B. Fox   James R. Hosek
David Mussington   Stuart H. Starr   Harry J. Thie

RAND

This research in the public interest was supported by RAND, using discretionary funds made possible by the generosity of RAND's donors, the fees earned on client-funded research, and independent research and development (IR&D) funds provided by the Department of Defense.

Library of Congress Cataloging-in-Publication Data

New challenges, new tools for defense decisionmaking / edited by Stuart Johnson,
  Martin Libicki, Gregory F. Treverton.
    p. cm.
    "MR-1576."
    Includes bibliographical references.
    ISBN 0-8330-3292-5 — ISBN 0-8330-3289-5 (pbk.)
    1. United States—Military policy—Decision making. 2. National security—
  United States. 3. United States—Defenses. 4. World politics—21st century. I.
  Johnson, Stuart E., 1944– II. Libicki, Martin C. III. Treverton, Gregory F.

  UA23 .N374 2003
  355'.033573—dc21

                                                                        2002190880

RAND is a nonprofit institution that helps improve policy and decisionmaking through research and analysis. RAND® is a registered trademark. RAND's publications do not necessarily reflect the opinions or policies of its research sponsors.

Cover design by Peter Soriano

Published 2003 by RAND
1700 Main Street, P.O. Box 2138, Santa Monica, CA 90407-2138
1200 South Hayes Street, Arlington, VA 22202-5050
201 North Craig Street, Suite 202, Pittsburgh, PA 15213-1516
RAND URL: http://www.rand.org/
To order RAND documents or to obtain additional information,
contact Distribution Services: Telephone: (310) 451-7002;
Fax: (310) 451-6915; Email: order@rand.org

PREFACE

This book contains thirteen papers that, collectively, provide a wide variety of perspectives on future defense decisionmaking. The topics range from the global security environment, to tools for assessing both military manpower and information systems, to general techniques for gauging the adequacy of military forces, to specific techniques for improving defense decisionmaking, especially under conditions of uncertainty. The papers were originally delivered as lectures in a short-course series, "Defense Analysis for the 21st Century," that was sponsored by the RAND Graduate School and held in RAND's Washington, DC, offices.

The rethinking of defense planning will continue apace, spurred in particular by September 11, 2001, and the war against terrorism; but many of the ideas and conclusions presented here will retain their relevance for years to come. While no attempt has been made to develop a monolithic "RAND view" on the many challenges defense planners face, readers will see in this collection themes and methodologies characteristic of RAND's recent defense planning work. It is hoped that these will be of interest to a broad class of individuals in government, military service, universities, and industry. The intention has been to provide papers that both describe enough of the research and analytic reasoning to convey a sense of how the work was done and present findings that should be useful for some time to come.

Most of the research underlying the papers in this book was conducted in RAND's three national security federally funded research and development centers (FFRDCs): Project AIR FORCE, the Arroyo

Center, and the National Defense Research Institute (NDRI). These three centers are sponsored, respectively, by the Air Force, the Army, and the Office of the Secretary of Defense and the Joint Staff.

RAND's National Security Research Division oversaw the preparation of this book for distribution within the defense analysis community. This activity was made possible by funding from RAND's continuing program of self-sponsored independent research, which is derived, in part, from the independent research and development provisions of RAND's contracts for the operation of its three U.S. Department of Defense FFRDCs.

CONTENTS

Part I. New Challenges for Defense

Part III. New Tools for Defense Decisionmaking

Chapter Nine
EXPLORATORY ANALYSIS AND IMPLICATIONS FOR
MODELING
Paul K. Davis   255

Chapter Ten
USING EXPLORATORY MODELING
Daniel B. Fox   285

FIGURES

TABLES

ACKNOWLEDGMENTS

Only editors can know how much help it takes to produce a book like this. The authors, first and foremost, suffered, more or less patiently, through delays and revisions, some of them extensive, in the interest of converting a clutch of good ideas into a relatively coherent volume. Bob Klitgaard, dean of the RAND Graduate School, had the idea for the book and was its sponsor throughout. We received, in RAND fashion, reviews that were both detailed and frank from Ted Harshberger, Tom McNaugher, and Michael O'Hanlon. One of us, Greg Treverton, started as a reviewer but was then challenged to put a contribution where his critique had been. He met the challenge.

We had the good fortune to have Jeri O'Donnell as editor and Janet DeLand doing the final page composition. If important analytic concepts are seen to emerge from complicated prose, that is a tribute to their fine work. Last, but hardly least, Rachel Swanger shepherded the book to final completion with grace and persistence.

To all these good people, we express our appreciation. We also repeat the usual disclaimer that while they can take credit for what is good in these pages, only we and the authors should be held responsible for any gremlins that remain.

ABBREVIATIONS

A&T	Acquisition and Technology
ABAT	Army brilliant antitank
ACAV	air-cushioned amphibious vessel
AFQT	Armed Forces Qualification Test
APOD	airport of debarkation
ASD	Assistant Secretary of Defense
ASVAB	Armed Services Vocational Aptitude Battery
ATACM	Army's Tactical Missile System
AWACS	Airborne Warning and Control System
BAT	brilliant antitank
BCP	best commercial practice
bps	bits per second
BRAC	base realignment and closure
BW	biological weapons
CAIV	cost as an independent variable
CAPE	C4ISR Analytic Performance Evaluation
CBW	chemical and biological weapons
CCD	charge-coupled device
C-Day	day on which U.S. forces begin mobilizing
CD-ROM	compact disk—read-only memory
CEC	cooperative engagement capability
CFATF	Caribbean Financial Action Task Force

CFE   Conventional Forces in Europe
C4   command, control, communications, and
                    computers
C4ISR   command, control, communications, computers,
                    intelligence, surveillance, and reconnaissance
CICA   Competition in Contracting Act
CINC   commander in chief
CMOC   civil-military operations center
COBP   code of best practice
CONOP   concept of operations
CONUS   continental United States
CPO   chief purchasing officer
C3   command, control, and communications
C3I   command, control, communications, and
                    intelligence
C2   command and control
CVBG   carrier battle group
CW   chemical weapons
DAB   Defense Acquisition Board
DCAA   Defense Contract Administration Agency
D-Day   day on which war begins
DEPTEMPO   tempo of deployments
DMSO   Defense Modeling and Simulation Organization
DoD   Department of Defense
DoN   Department of the Navy
DOS   disk operating system
DOTML-PF   doctrine, organization, training, materiel, leadership
                    and education, personnel, and facilities
DP   dimensional parameter
DRB   Defense Resources Board
DRID   Defense Reform Initiative Directive
DSD   Decision Support Department
DVD   digital versatile disk

EELV	Evolved Expendable Launch Vehicle (U.S. Air Force)
EMS	electronic meeting system
EPCRA	Emergency Planning and Community Right-to-Know Act
EU	European Union
FAIR	Federal Activities Inventory Reform
FAR	Federal Acquisition Regulations
FCS	Future Combat System
FEMA	Federal Emergency Management Agency
FinCEN	Financial Crimes Enforcement Network
FY	fiscal year
FYDP	Future Years Defense Program
GCC	Gulf Cooperation Council
GCCS	Global Command and Control System
GCSS	Global Combat Support System
GIG	global information grid
GNP	gross national product
GPS	global positioning system
HLA	High Level Architecture
HPM	high-power microwave
HTML	hypertext markup language
HUMINT	human intelligence
ICBM	intercontinental ballistic missile
IFFN	Identification Friend Foe or Neutral
IPT	integrated process team
IRA	Irish Republican Army
ISO	International Standards Organization
ISR	intelligence, surveillance, and reconnaissance
IW	information warfare
JCS	joint chiefs of staff
JDAM	Joint Direct Attack Munition
JFCOM	Joint Forces Command

JICM	Joint Integrated Contingency Model
JPEG	Joint Photographic Experts Group
JSF	Joint Strike Fighter
JSIMS	Joint Simulation System
JSOW	Joint Standoff Weapon
JSTARS	Joint Surveillance Target Attack Radar System
JVB	Joint Virtual Battlespace
JWARS	Joint Warfare System
km	kilometer
Kt	Kiloton
LAN	local area network
M&S	modeling and simulation
MCES	Modular Command and Control Evaluation Structure
MEMS	micro-electromechanical system
MIT	Massachusetts Institute of Technology
MLRS	multiple-rocket launcher system
MOA	mission oriented approach
MOE	measure of effectiveness
MOFE	measure of force effectiveness
MOM	measure of merit
MOOTW	military operations other than war
MOP	measure of C2 system performance
MORS	Military Operations Research Society
MRM	multiresolution modeling
MRMPM	multiresolution, multiperspective modeling
MTW	major theater war
NATO	North Atlantic Treaty Organization
NBAT	Naval brilliant antitank
NCO	noncommissioned officer
NGO	nongovernmental organization
NIPRnet	joint Internet for unclassified work

NPS	Naval Postgraduate School
NRL	Naval Research Laboratory
OFW	Objective Force Warrior
OMB	Office of Management and Budget
ONR	Office of Naval Research
OOTW	operations other than war
OPM	Office of Personnel Management
OSD	Office of the Secretary of Defense
PEM	personal-computer model
PGM	precision guided munition
PO	petty officer
POM	program objectives memorandum
PPBS	Planning, Programming, and Budgeting System
PSYOP	psychological operation
QDR	Quadrennial Defense Review
RAM	random access memory
R&D	research and development
RMA	revolution in military affairs
ROTC	Reserve Officers Training Corps
RSTA	reconnaissance, surveillance, targeting, and acquisition
SADARM	sense and destroy armor munition
SALT	Strategic Arms Limitations Treaty
SAM	surface-to-air-missile
SARA	Superfund Amendments and Reauthorization Act
SAS	Studies, Analysis, and Simulations
SBA	Small Business Administration
SBCT	Stryker Brigade Combat Team
SCAV	Sea Cavalry
SEAD	suppression of enemy air defenses
SFW	sensor fused weapon
SINCGARS	Single Channel Ground and Airborne Radio System

SIPRnet	joint Internet for secret material
SIW	strategic information warfare
SLBM	submarine-launched ballistic missile
SOF	special operations force
SPOD	seaport of debarkation
SROC	Senior Readiness Oversight Council
SSC	smaller-scale contingency
SWA	Southwest Asia
TACCFS	Theater Air Command and Control Simulation Facility
TBMD	theater ballistic missile defense
TCO	transcontinental criminal organization
TCP/IP	transmission control protocol/Internet protocol
TDA	table of distribution and allowance
TOC	tactical operations center
TOC	total ownership cost
TOE	table of equipment
TQM	total quality management
TRI	toxic releases inventory
UAV	unmanned aerial vehicle
UCAV	unmanned combat air vehicle
VV&C	verify, validate, and certify
WMD	weapons of mass destruction
XML	extensible markup language

INTRODUCTION

Stuart E. Johnson, Martin C. Libicki, and Gregory F. Treverton

It is commonplace to say, but still easy to underestimate, how much the collapse of the Soviet Union and the end of the Cold War transformed the task of U.S. foreign and defense policymaking. And the terrorist attacks of September 11, 2001, have opened yet another era, one whose shape and dimensions are yet to be understood. This volume addresses the new challenges of this changed world, the difficulties for defense planning that these challenges engender, and new analytic techniques that have been developed at RAND and elsewhere for framing particular problems.

During the Cold War, the Soviet threat provided the benchmark for both foreign policy and defense: containing that threat was the overriding purpose of policy, and the threat provided the organizing principle for shaping U.S. military forces. If U.S. forces could deter or, if need be, defeat the Soviet military, they could handle other threats as "lesser included cases."

In this context, defense planning was dominated by "force-on-force" comparisons of U.S. and Soviet forces. While the United States spent billions of dollars trying to learn the specific numbers and capabilities of Soviet weapons, overall the Soviet threat changed only gradually and fairly predictably. What Moscow would have tomorrow could generally be predicted to be bigger and slightly better than what it had today. The Soviet defense establishment might float on a sea of shoddiness in the rest of the Soviet economy, but the Soviets could be presumed willing and able to spend what it took to keep pace with the United States.

All of this changed with the end of the Cold War. In place of (albeit sometimes terrifying) predictability, the world became very unpredictable. In place of a single overriding threat that could be used as a benchmark for measuring everything else, a number of possible threats arose, some of them potentially very dangerous if not, ultimately, in a league with the Soviet threat. In place of the threat of force-on-force engagements with a strong foe, there were now "asymmetric" threats from potential U.S. foes much weaker than the United States. Such foes would not be foolish enough to take America on directly (as Saddam Hussein did), instead pursuing the ancient art of strategy long obscured by a bipolar U.S.-Soviet competition. They would look for U.S. vulnerabilities, ways not to defeat U.S. power but to render it irrelevant.

In one respect, defense decisionmaking has not changed. From hot war to cold, to a time of terrorism, the U.S. Department of Defense (DoD) has remained one of the world's largest and most complex organizations. It employs upward of 2.4 million people (military and civilian) and contracts for the direct services of another 400,000. It runs a budget of $400 billion and an accumulated capital stock (real property and equipment) of more than $4 trillion. Managing an organization of this magnitude is a daunting job. Decisions affect multibillion-dollar programs, tens of thousands of people, and, most important, the security of the nation itself.

FROM OLD CHALLENGES TO NEW

During the long Cold War, from the 1950s into the 1980s, RAND, often working with other analytic organizations, played a key role in developing techniques to inform decisionmaking and guide the development of national strategy. Notable RAND contributions to techniques for defense decisionmaking include

- The marrying of blast physics, ballistics, and guidance technology to determine "how much is enough" to hold the Soviet economy and population at risk so as to deter the Soviets from launching a nuclear first strike.

- The application of game theory to determine the appropriate size and configuration of U.S. strategic nuclear forces.

- The application of "armored division equivalents" to clarify the strengths and weaknesses of NATO strategy to defend Western Europe.

- The development of the strategy-to-task methodology to provide a framework for weapon systems evaluation.

These and other techniques were disseminated widely and gained broad acceptance within the defense analysis community. They provided a common framework in which debates over budget allocations, investment strategy, and doctrine development could take place. Although far from perfect in predicting future requirements, these techniques, when broadly shared, managed to carry the debate beyond "strongly held opinion." Positions now had to withstand the test of objective, systematic, and (where possible) quantitative analysis.

The practice of using analytic techniques to illuminate the options available and to provide a framework for such far-reaching decisions began in earnest with Robert McNamara, who served as U.S. secretary of defense from 1961 to 1967 under Presidents John Kennedy and Lyndon Johnson. McNamara brought together a cadre of analysts, led by several RAND researchers, to establish the Office of Systems Analysis as the focal point for changing the basis of DoD decisionmaking from "strongly held views" to objective, thorough analysis. This office had, as all new institutions do, its ups and downs, its supporters and detractors. But as it began to influence important decisions—affecting, for example, the number of U.S. intercontinental ballistic missiles (ICBMs) or the size and disposition of U.S. forces committed to the North Atlantic Treaty Organization (NATO)—the value of an analytic basis for debating decisions became clear. Before long, the Air Force and then other military services and the joint chiefs of staff (JCS) established their own enhanced analytic capability.

In the 1980s, as attention turned to serious arms control negotiations, analytic techniques were adapted to provide a strategic framework for U.S. negotiators in, successively, the Strategic Arms Limitations Talks (SALT) and Strategic Arms Reduction Treaty (START) negotiations over strategic nuclear forces. Similarly, when the United States and the Soviet Union, along with their respective allies, began to discuss in earnest the size of conventional forces in Europe, U.S. negotiators were well informed about which Warsaw Pact forces posed the greatest threat and which NATO forces were most critical to maintaining a stalwart defense of NATO territory. The resulting treaties strengthened the U.S. position and enhanced strategic and conventional stability. Indeed, the START II and Conventional Forces in Europe (CFE) treaties remain, even today, important tools in U.S. national security policy.

These analytic techniques were developed for the specified Cold War requirement: face a large military capable of challenging the United States across the globe and throughout the escalation ladder—from local conflicts involving proxy forces to a strategic nuclear exchange. In this context, the techniques led to measures of military effectiveness (such as armored division equivalents), simulations of large conventional force-on-force engagements, probabilities of killing a missile silo, and simulations of a nuclear exchange.

After Moscow abandoned superpower competition with the United States and the Cold War ended, the requirement that dominated U.S. defense planning changed: to prevail in two nearly simultaneous major theater wars (MTWs). Planning documents typically cited aggression by Iraq or North Korea against its neighbors, attacks that have been the subject of considerable analysis, modeling and simulation, intelligence research, and war gaming. Because such operations would entail large formations of classical military forces, analyses of them have drawn heavily on techniques developed during the Cold War. But even this application of Cold War analytic techniques is losing its utility. Iraq's armed forces suffered from obsolescence as a decade of economic sanctions and lack of access to modern military equipment took its toll. The armed forces of North Korea fared even worse.

As it is, the global security environment is profoundly changed. Preoccupation with the daunting though well-ordered Cold War threat has been replaced by the far different set of challenges cited by recent defense secretaries, challenges driven home by the tragedy of September 11:

- Countering terrorism

- Countering the spread of weapons of mass destruction (WMD)

- Peace enforcement

- Crisis response

- Enforcement of economic and military sanctions

- Combating narcotics trafficking

The task of meeting these challenges is critical to maintaining the economic prosperity and free exercise of democratic governance valued by the United States and its allies. This task is not advanced by naïvely applying analytic and planning techniques developed and refined in the Cold War and appropriate to dealing only with large-scale, cross-border aggression. Planners require different tools. To be sure, even conventional adversaries can inflict serious damage on U.S. and allied forces and interests, but adversaries are likely to turn to other means of challenging us—employing WMD or terrorism. This poses a dilemma for decisionmakers: the analytic tools at their disposal credibly address a problem of declining probability, even as they do little to illuminate the challenges U.S. forces are increasingly being called on to respond to.

During the dozen years since the dissolution of the Soviet Union, the research staff at RAND has worked intensively to adapt traditional defense analysis techniques to today's security environment and to develop new techniques as necessary. These techniques address today's key questions:

- How can the United States set requirements in the face of an uncertain future?

- How can the nation plan for flexibility and program it into our forces?

- How might rapid advances in commercial technologies help the armed forces?

- How has the profile of skills needed by the armed forces changed? And what needs to be done to recruit, train, and retain the required cadre of skilled personnel?

Taken together, the chapters in this volume provide a new portfolio of tools to frame decisions, to solve problems, and to analyze alternatives.

HOW THIS VOLUME IS ORGANIZED

This book comprises thirteen chapters organized into three parts:

I. New Challenges for Defense

II. Coping with Uncertainty

III. New Tools for Defense Decisionmaking

Part I begins with a chapter describing the questions that any nation must answer about its defense—how much, what, and how?—and provides an overview of the structures, especially inside the Pentagon, that the United States has developed to answer them. Chapter Two assesses the challenge of chemical and biological weapons as one class of "asymmetric" strategies a U.S. adversary might employ. The logic of that approach translates to terrorism, in many respects the ultimate asymmetric strategy of the weak against the strong. The subject of the third chapter is the "information architecture" needed for U.S. defense. The rise of the information age coincided with, indeed probably hastened, the collapse of the Soviet Union, and the United States now confronts the challenge of how to structure itself to best take advantage of the continuing revolution in information technology.

Part II of this book takes up the driving challenge of uncertainty. The first chapter is based on the premise that while the future is unknowable, it is not a complete mystery. Broad trends are discernible, one being the continuous improvement in information technology, which suggests that future warfare will be information based, with huge amounts of information from various sensors integrated to build a picture of the battlespace. The second chapter here describes "uncertainty-sensitive planning." Cold War planning may have been based on threats, but the future cannot be, for there is simply too much uncertainty, too many diverse threats. Planning needs to aim at building a portfolio of capabilities designed not just to confront future threats but also to hedge against them and to shape the environment so they do not develop.

The next two chapters in Part II are on planning the human resources for tomorrow's defense. RAND research was the analytic basis for the U.S. shift from conscription to an all-volunteer force in the 1970s and has contributed to the great success that force has been. These chapters outline visions of the future soldier, specify the factors critical to attracting and retaining the talent needed for a volunteer force, and describe a planning mechanism for shaping the force. The final chapter looks at the challenge of adopting best commercial practices from the business world into the apparently similar but actually quite different world of defense planning and management.

Part III begins with a chapter on exploratory modeling, a tool growing out of new techniques in modeling and the computer power that now exists. The technique fits well with capabilities-based planning in that it permits analysts to move far beyond a few canonical scenarios to examine a wide array of variables, looking for key uncertainties and key drivers across a wide range of possibilities. The second chapter in Part III is a more concrete illustration of how exploratory modeling can be employed. The third chapter chronicles the long effort to assess how much information systems contribute to effectiveness in conducting military missions—a quest, needless to say, that has been reshaped by the Cold War's demise and the diversity of future missions.

The penultimate chapter's subject is the "Day After" gaming technique that RAND developed to examine strategic issues. Essentially, this technique entails playing out a scenario and then working backward to see how better decisions at an earlier stage might have improved the outcome by mitigating threats or providing more options. The chapter explains and illustrates the technique. The final chapter then describes another tool, electronic meeting systems, and elaborates with an example of its use—the U.S. Navy preparing for the 1997 Quadrennial Defense Review—that led to interesting, perhaps unconventional results.

An Afterword concludes the book. It suggests some of the implications of the current war on terrorism and homeland security for the challenges that lie ahead. These challenges will require RAND and its fellow organizations to reshape, once again, analytic approaches that improve defense and the national security decisionmaking.

PART I. NEW CHALLENGES FOR DEFENSE

INTRODUCTION TO PART I

Defense planning during the Cold War was dominated by the threat from the Soviet Union. It was, in that sense, threat based. It also was, to a great extent, symmetrical, based on force-on-force calculations for U.S. and Soviet armored forces, fighter jets, and the like. In these circumstances, the U.S. planning structure within the Pentagon became increasingly centralized, seeking to maximize the benefits from various investments in ways to better cope with the Soviet threat.

All the practices that made considerable sense during the Cold War badly need to be rethought now. Soviet strategy may have been more creative than it was usually given credit for, but it was relatively slow moving. By contrast, today's threats—and still more tomorrow's—are many and very uncertain. While none may be in a class with the Soviet threat, the attacks of September 11, 2001, drove home how lethal even "lesser" threats can be. Moreover, U.S. military power has given rise to a paradox: the United States is so dominant in its ability to fight a conventional armored war that it is not likely to have to fight such a war. Realizing the futility of a conventional face-off with the United States, would-be adversaries will instead aim to confront the United States where it is weak or can be surprised—posing what are called *asymmetric* threats. Terrorism, the strategy of the weak against the strong, is quintessentially an asymmetric strategy.

This change from a fairly predictable, symmetrical threat to the myriad unpredictable, asymmetrical threats possible has profound effects for defense planning. It impels a shift from threat-based planning to capabilities-based planning and suggests that a "portfolio" approach to these capabilities—i.e., trying to build breadth and flexibility in the hope that capabilities can be brought to bear across a spectrum of unpredictable threats—would be the most useful type. It also presses the United States to draw on advantages where it has them, particularly in harnessing information technology to identify threats, link shooters tightly to sensors, and manage a flexible, fast-moving campaign. And it hints at the value of decentralizing Pentagon management so as to encourage the innovation needed to produce a real "revolution in military affairs" (RMA).

In the first chapter here, "Decisionmaking for Defense," David S.C. Chu and Nurith Berstein argue that any military organization must ask itself four questions: what forces should be fielded, how should they be trained, how should they be equipped, and what tempo of operations should they maintain? The two questions on force structure and equipment are likely to dominate in the next decade. The debates over the size and structure of military forces that were not fully joined in the 1990s will have to be faced squarely, particularly in light of strains placed on the current force by the pace of operations, all the more so with the war on terrorism. Moreover, the urgent need to recapitalize the present generation of equipment places this issue near, perhaps atop, the agenda. In this regard, a central issue is the degree to which new investment should shift from modernizing existing capabilities to procuring quite different capabilities, ones geared to a different vision of what future military forces might look like. The more decisionmakers lean toward a new vision, the greater the challenge they will pose to how "legacy" systems—including some still under development—are treated. Such fundamental issues are never settled once and for all or even for very long.

In Chapter Two, "Responding to Asymmetric Threats," Bruce Bennett explains why U.S. conventional military superiority has forced adversaries to pursue asymmetric strategies—i.e., those designed to attack such vulnerabilities as U.S. and allied will, host nation support, and basing infrastructure. Potential adversaries have developed weapons of mass destruction (WMD), information warfare, and simple countermeasures such as sea mines as part of their asymmetric threats, and they use camouflage, concealment, and deception to hide their capabilities and strategies. Part of the danger of asymmetric threats stems from the surprise they can achieve, which undercuts U.S. response preparation, leaving the United States at a disadvantage. Asymmetric threats can affect U.S. and allied forces, civilians, and interests in diverse ways that are difficult and expensive to counter. The threat of retaliation, alone, is insufficient to deter their use in at least some cases. What is needed is an integrated defense effort that includes three elements: understanding the threats, protecting against them, and threat management. Understanding the threats is key to addressing them, protection is necessary to reduce any gains the adversary may be seeking, and threat management seeks to deter the spread of such threats and discourage the development of new ones. The United States must institutionalize its response efforts within its own military; it must also internationalize them, coordinating with allies to provide a common defense.

Chapter Three, "What Information Architecture for Defense?" by Martin Libicki, is a plea for planners to recognize the choices, deliberate or not, that underlie enterprise-level information technology systems and thereby shape how they are used. One office networking system may be much like another, but the Pentagon's requirements for information will vary depending on whether it is planning for a strategic campaign (putting a premium on analytic skills to determine enemy strengths and weaknesses), a conventional campaign (with its need for mass force coordination), modern high-technology warfare (which requires that targets be found and prosecuted in real time), or a low-intensity conflict (which requires that warfighters be enabled with subtle but detailed portraits of their environment). Information architectures may be described by how they collect, present, display, circulate, maintain, secure, standardize, and integrate information. Each of these eight dimensions involves choices that the Pentagon must make if it is to make best use of U.S. advantages in information technology.

Chapter One

DECISIONMAKING FOR DEFENSE

David S.C. Chu and Nurith Berstein

Defense is, for all nations, at the heart of national security. All nations face a common set of choices—what decisions must be made, who will make them, how resources will be allocated, and what investments will be made. At one level up, nations have to decide what principles and style of decisionmaking are appropriate for them, and, importantly, what structure will govern the process of defense decisionmaking. This chapter discusses these choices and reviews the issues that must be addressed in devising a governance structure for making them, drawing on U.S. experiences over the last half century. It concludes with a short discussion of alternative approaches and styles before looking briefly to the future.

America's experiences may have lessons for others even if their circumstances dictate a different set of governance arrangements for defense decisionmaking. Equally important, the United States is now at a point in its history when it must reconsider—if only to reconfirm—its own governance structure. The Cold War that motivated so much of the U.S. defense establishment and shaped its decisionmaking mechanisms has been replaced with a much different set of security challenges. The technological assumptions on which so many of DoD's current choices rest also must be reconsidered. Thoughtful defense analysts argue that a "revolution in military affairs" (RMA) is, and should be, under way. In short, should the United States in the early 21st century continue to make defense decisions the way it did in the latter half of the 20th?

DECIDING WHAT DECISIONS MUST BE MADE

Every defense establishment faces a set of interrelated decisions that it must make and that its governance structure should be designed to confront:

- What set of forces should the country maintain? How should forces be organized? Under what command structure?

- What training should forces receive? How ready should they be, and for what?

- With what equipment should forces be armed? In what condition should equipment be maintained?

- What tempo of operation should forces be prepared to maintain? What stock of consumable items and spare parts should be stockpiled to support this tempo? What ongoing maintenance capability is needed to sustain this pace of operation?

These decisions govern what the defense establishment delivers, but they should be guided by the *outcomes* desired by the national leadership. For the past 25 years, DoD has translated these outcomes into scenarios against which U.S. military forces are measured. During the late Cold War, the planning scenario focused on global conflict with the Soviet Union (on two fronts, Europe and Southwest Asia). After the Cold War, this scenario was replaced by a requirement to conduct two nearly simultaneous major theater wars (MTWs) while also conducting operations other than war (e.g., peacekeeping in the Balkans). When pressed for specificity, DoD posited the two MTWs as being on the Korean peninsula and in Southwest Asia.

When the Cold War ended, DoD tried at one point to formulate a new structure in which to make decisions about U.S. military forces—forces would be judged not against specific scenarios but against a set of military capabilities the country should maintain. DoD wanted to move away from a single scenario; its military leadership was concerned that no single scenario would be compelling. The shortcoming of the capabilities approach, as articulated in testimony by then Secretary of Defense Les Aspin, was that it did not yield defensible, specific criteria against which to judge military forces. To define such specific criteria, DoD tried generic "illustrative planning scenarios." The lack of geographic specificity in these scenarios, however, when applied in the debate over the acquisition of the C-17, proved their undoing. DoD reverted to the concrete illustrations of conflict in the Persian Gulf and Korea, from which the notion of two nearly simultaneous MTWs eventually developed.[1]

DECIDING WHO MAKES THE DECISIONS

A notable feature of the American political landscape is the U.S. Congress's salient role in defense decisionmaking, which is spelled out plainly in the Constitution. In enumerating the powers of the Congress, Article I gives it the authority to declare war, to raise and support armies and provide and maintain a navy, and to establish rules for the governance of the military. Indeed, of the 18 congressional powers enumerated in Section 8 of Article I, five explicitly deal with the military.[2]

The creation of a Secretary of Defense in 1947 reflected a balance between the prerogatives of the individual military services and President Truman's desire for a central executive to coordinate and rationalize their separate activities. The first secretary, James Forrestal, resigned after a largely unsuccessful struggle to orchestrate the activities of the National Military Establishment (as it was then called), frustrated by his limited powers as secretary. The 1949 amendment of the National Security Act addressed some of these limitations. It created the Department of Defense, subordinated the military departments to the secretary, and strengthened the staff supporting the secretary. Amendments enacted in 1958 further enhanced the secretary's role, thus paving the way for the far-reaching changes Robert McNamara imposed on the department. But DoD governance retains a tension between the centrifugal, competitive forces reflected in the responsibilities of the individual military departments (in whose well-being Congress takes a deep interest) and the centralizing responsibilities of the defense secretary.

---

[1]Early in the Clinton administration, DoD leadership considered a posture of preparing for one MTW while checking a second opponent until resources could be mobilized or released to deal with it ("win—hold—win"). The resulting political uproar convinced the administration to endorse the two-MTW standard.

[2]The important (but often neglected) role of Congress is discussed usefully in Charles A. Stevenson, "Bridging the Gap Between Warriors and Politicians," paper for the 1999 Annual Meetings of the American Political Science Association, Atlanta, GA.

There is a further division of authority within the military departments, the one between civilian political appointees and the uniformed military hierarchy. This split is reflected in the fact that the separate civilian secretariat reports to the secretary of the military department, whereas the uniformed staff reports to the chief of staff. Much of the statutory authority wielded by a military department is actually held by that department's secretary, even though the uniformed staff is much larger than the civilian secretariat and typically exercises de facto control of the day-to-day agenda.

The Goldwater Nichols Act of 1986 changed the division of defense authority in three important ways. First, within the military departments, it strengthened the hand of the civilian service secretariats by formally subordinating the uniformed officers previously responsible for weapons acquisition and budget execution to their civilian counterparts rather than to the service chief of staff. For several decades, acquisition authority in the military departments had been divided between a civilian assistant secretary and a military deputy chief of staff assigned that function. Likewise, each military department had a military comptroller who reported through the chief of staff rather than to the civilian counterpart in the Office of the Secretary of Defense (OSD) responsible for financial matters. The Goldwater Nichols Act required that these military officers report to the civilian counterpart.

Second, Goldwater Nichols ratified the expanded authority of the commanders in chief of the unified and specified commands (CINCs), who, to the discomfit of the military departments, had been invited by Secretary Caspar Weinberger in 1981 to play a significant role in DoD's resource allocation processes. Goldwater Nichols further reinforced the CINCs' authority by requiring that all military units be assigned to one of their commands. Moreover, the CINCs were explicitly made responsible for the preparedness of their commands to carry out assigned missions. These changes solidified the CINCs' role as "customers" of DoD and, especially, of the military departments. The Act also underscored the future importance of joint operations as the way U.S. forces would be employed in the field, and thus the way in which planning for them should be conducted, including planning undertaken by the military departments. One example of this increased emphasis on "jointness" is that the

annual DoD budget proposals submitted to Congress include a separate item for joint exercises undertaken by the commands.

Third, Goldwater Nichols further empowered the chairman of the
joint chiefs of staff (JCS) and joint staff. In the years following World
War II, that position had gradually evolved into one clearly seen as
the nation's senior military officer. Although the chairman is not
legally part of the chain of command—which runs directly from the
president through the secretary of defense to the CINCs—his advice
is often treated with the same deference as that of the defense secretary, especially by Congress. In these ways, the Goldwater Nichols
Act strengthened the chairman's advisory role, causing considerable
concern within the military departments that his responsibilities importantly infringe on what they believe should be their responsibilities.

The Act also produced, in combination with the distinctive events of
the last 15 years, a new central actor, the joint staff, which is in tension with the military departments because of its perceived intrusion
on their authority (reminiscent of that produced by the "whiz kids"
of Secretary McNamara's staff in the 1960s).

Divided authority could be a formula for bureaucratic gridlock and
inaction, with many having the right to say "no," but no element
strong enough to see a program proposal through to approval and
successful execution. One of the mechanisms that DoD has used in
this circumstance, both to secure a wide circle of advice and to forge
consensus on the best course of action, is the advisory board—i.e., a
formal body that gives many if not all parties a "voice" in the process
while allowing final decisionmaking authority to remain in the hands
of the board's chair. The most powerful senior-level boards are

*   The Defense Resources Board (DRB), chaired by the deputy sec-
    retary of defense. Advises the deputy secretary on major resource
    allocation decisions.

*   The Defense Acquisition Board (DAB), chaired by the under sec-
    retary of defense for acquisition and technology (A&T). Advises
    the under secretary (A&T) on major acquisition programs and
    acquisition policies and procedures.

- The Joint Requirements Oversight Council, chaired by the vice chairman of the joint chiefs of staff (who also serves as the vice chairman of the DAB). Validates mission needs developed by the CINCs and by planning elements of the joint staff, reviews performance parameters and requirements, and develops recommended joint priorities for those needs.

- The Senior Readiness Oversight Council (SROC), chaired by the deputy secretary of defense. Advises the secretary of defense on readiness, oversees readiness-related actions, reports on relevant readiness questions, and coordinates DoD positions on readiness for outside audiences.

Each board was created by the direction of, or with support from, a particular secretary of defense, although succeeding secretaries have used and shaped them in accord with their styles. Thus, while the formal roles of these boards often change little over time, their real roles and authority respond to the style of each secretary, giving each secretary considerable latitude in how the department is managed.

Notably absent from this description of who makes decisions on defense issues is the U.S. president and his immediate staff. Designated by the Constitution as the commander-in-chief, the president could, in principle, take a detailed role in defense decisionmaking. The president and his staff typically do take an active role in formulating national security strategy, thus setting the basic course for the defense establishment, and the president usually makes the key operational decisions in times of crisis. But, otherwise, the American practice has been to leave most department managerial decisions to the defense secretary, although the president does set the budgetary constraint within which the department must live.

In the Kennedy administration, a concerted effort was made to involve the president early in key defense decisions. It was felt that securing the president's guidance early in the decisionmaking cycle would help the department formulate better policies. Draft presidential memoranda were prepared as vehicles for raising issues with the president. But when the first of these was presented to President Kennedy, he indicated that he was not prepared to make choices so early. The memoranda lived on for a period as a useful way to conduct policy debates within DoD, but they were never more than drafts and were never again sent to the president.

DECIDING HOW TO ALLOCATE RESOURCES

Budgets in bureaucracies are typically created one year at a time and are based disproportionately on expenditure patterns of the prior year. A group of analysts at RAND in the 1950s developed an alternative approach to budget preparation, one based on the idea that the proper way to begin was by setting long-term objectives. Codified under the cumbersome title Planning, Programming, and Budgeting System (PPBS), Robert McNamara brought the ideas behind this approach to the Pentagon in the 1960s when he hired Charles Hitch as comptroller from his prior post as head of RAND's Economics Department.[3]

The planning phase of the PPBS sets long-term goals. The secretary of defense announces objectives for the department in what is now called the Defense Planning Guidance. The Guidance is ultimately the secretary's document, although his own staff, the military departments, and the chairman and his staff all participate, reflecting the multiple centers of authority within the department. The document includes a variety of ways to measure progress toward the secretary's goals, including a set of illustrative scenarios describing the military events the secretary believes should guide key decisions of the department.

As administered since the late 1960s, the programming stage of the PPBS consists of the three military departments preparing a set of fiscally constrained proposals to meet the secretary's goals. These program objectives memoranda, or POMs, extend six years into the future. The secretary's office reviews the POMs to ensure they conform with the guidance provided by the secretary in the planning phase. Changes are made as required. Although the programming phase is a debate about means—which program choices best achieve the stated goals—it often reopens the debate about those goals, revisiting choices made in the planning phase.

---

[3]The spirit of the Government Performance and Results Act distinctly parallels that of the PPBS.

Once decisions about the six-year program are made, the material in the POMs is consolidated into the Future Years Defense Program (FYDP), and the department is then ready to formulate its budget for the next fiscal period. The department's constituent elements prepare budget estimate submissions based on the program decisions, reflecting latest pricing and execution experience. These are reviewed by the secretary's office, in a joint process with the Office of Management and Budget (OMB), and consolidated in the president's budget request.

The sharing of authority in PPBS reflects the reality of DoD's divided authority. It gives each element of DoD (most especially the military departments) a chance to fashion its future course within the parameters set by the secretary of defense and subject to his review and final decision. But the parameters are debated with the many elements before they are set, and the reviews of both the program and the budget include the affected parties, which are allowed wide latitude to argue their cases before the secretary makes final decisions.

Nonetheless, PPBS gives the secretary of defense the essential tool to control the department's key decisions, each of which requires resources to implement: the structure of forces, their training and readiness, the equipment with which they are armed, and the provisions set aside to sustain them in operations. At the same time, both the 1969 decision to give each of the department's constituent elements the right to prepare the first draft of the resource plan (the POM) and subsequent decisions to give each element a real voice in the process have made PPBS the vehicle these elements use to define themselves and their futures. Indeed, a military department will often speak of its "POM position" as discourse proceeds about alternatives: It is the POM position that defines where that service's leadership has decided to go and how it is going to get there, thereby providing the starting point for the debate of alternatives.

The fact that the secretary of defense can begin the process with a reasonably clean sheet of paper gives him wide latitude to reshape the department as circumstances dictate, albeit at the expense of established programs and priorities. And because the service secretaries run a similar process within their areas of responsibility (as do the heads of the defense agencies, to a lesser extent) they, too, enjoy considerable latitude. From the perspective of the individual program manager, however, this wide latitude can lead to unwelcome turbulence as resources are reshuffled by senior decisionmakers to meet new needs within a relatively fixed budget. Thus, while senior administrators see their ability to shift resources as a strength of the process, operating elements sometimes see this as a serious problem.

Perhaps the area in which this issue arises most sharply and generates the greatest debate is investment, especially the procurement of new articles of equipment. Investment program managers continually complain about the instability and uncertainty PPBS creates for them. A variety of attempts have been made to address this issue, including reviewing stability as an explicit issue in the programming phase, and pilot efforts to manage investment programs through streamlined processes that would (at least in theory) expose them less frequently to review.

One idea DoD has considered would actually promise some programs protection from resource reallocation between development milestones. "Milestone budgeting" would give each program a budget total at each milestone sufficient to carry it to the next milestone (even if several years away), the underlying reason being that these totals can best be estimated at the milestone junctures. Between milestones, these programs would be "off limits" to resource reallocation. From the perspective of the military department secretaries and the defense secretary, milestone budgeting would reduce their flexibility and could lead them to use the operating accounts as a source of funds to meet unanticipated needs. From the perspective of those responsible for the investment accounts, milestone budgeting would promise welcome stability for programs selected (if potentially greater instability for those excluded). It would increase the risk faced by investment managers, however, because it would severely limit their ability to secure added funds between milestones if they found they had underestimated the requirements or if they encountered unexpected technical or other difficulties.

Whatever milestone budgeting's merits, the fact that it is being debated illustrates PPBS's flexible nature and potential ability to shift resources in response to changing circumstances. Because it is a process under the defense secretary's control, it can easily be changed to adapt to new problems or to try new solutions to old problems. This inherent flexibility and adaptability may be why the system has endured for over a generation. Indeed, a careful examination would demonstrate that in each cycle PPBS has been administered, it has been administered somewhat differently than in the prior cycle. Sometimes the differences have been substantial and dramatic (e.g., the introduction of POMs in the late 1960s, and the inclusion of CINC advice in the early 1980s), which is why today's system is very different from the one Secretary McNamara introduced so many years ago.

DECIDING WHAT INVESTMENTS TO MAKE

One of the important clarifications that the 1958 amendments to the National Security Act made in the powers of the secretary of defense related to investment decisions. While these had traditionally been the prerogative of the military services, the amendments confirmed that Congress ultimately held the defense secretary responsible for the department's investment portfolio. Secretary McNamara capitalized on this clarified authority to impose a centralized review of weapons decisions.

Characteristics of that review process included formal documentation of decisions and their rationale, and the use of cost-benefit analyses to weigh the pros and cons of alternative courses of action. Originally resisted by the uniformed leadership, these characteristics are now widely accepted within the defense community—much more so than elsewhere in the federal government.

For major systems—i.e., those exceeding a threshold value for either development or production—the process now begins with a mission needs statement drafted by the responsible party. The system proceeds through a series of milestones, overseen by the Defense Acquisition Board (DAB), which is chaired by the under secretary of defense for acquisition, technology, and logistics with representatives from the military departments and the joint staff. The DAB's approval is required to enter each milestone phase (concept and technology development, system development and demonstration, and production and deployment).

David Packard, deputy secretary of defense from 1969 to 1971, began the practice of gathering advice on milestone investment decisions through an organized board, creating the Defense Systems Acquisition Review Council (the DAB is its contemporary successor). Packard also initiated the concept of independent cost estimates being produced by the secretary's office as a check on what he considered the too often optimistic views of program managers. DoD's reasonably good record in estimating future costs of technologically ambitious systems (which is much better than that of most federal agencies, and better than that of many large-scale private undertakings) owes a great deal to this innovation.

Perhaps the most important milestone decision for DoD is whether to proceed with production. Development expenses are usually a modest fraction (typically 20 percent) of a system's total acquisition cost. Thus, the financial burden of a development decision does not loom nearly as large as that of a production decision. Moreover, in development there is always the hope that further research will resolve any difficulties the system has encountered. The production decision involves an acceptance of the article as worth the department's investment funds. For these reasons, and because of its long-standing distrust of DoD's decisions to proceed with systems, Congress mandates that systems pass an independent test before procurement in quantity begins.[4]

DoD completely separates development from operational testing. Such tests are expensive, however, so the department is typically reluctant to spend the funds necessary to achieve high confidence in the test results.

Before and during World War II, a substantial amount of weapons production took place in government factories—arsenals or shipyards. This is no longer the case. Government-operated shipyards and depots are still responsible for much of the maintenance work on military systems, including major overhauls, but weapons systems are produced by private companies (sometimes using facilities and/or equipment still owned by the government).[5] Thus, one of DoD's important managerial decisions is how—if at all—it wishes to intervene in the marketplace to shape the set of suppliers that bid on its work. Similarly, the contractual relationship between the govern-

---

[4]This requirement was initiated by Congress in the 1970s.

[5]Congress mandates the minimum proportion of maintenance work that must be carried out in government-owned and -operated facilities (currently 50 percent).

ment and the private contractor is a critical DoD administrative decision.

Defense contracting takes place under the Federal Acquisition Regulations (FAR), a regulatory code that governs all procurement by the U.S. government. A key philosophical tenet of this code is full and open competition, a factor that has an important bearing on the incentives faced by contractors, the way in which procurement is carried out, and the government's ability to intervene directly to shape the marketplace. The FAR also embodies a variety of social policy decisions that the federal government insists be reflected in its acquisition practices, most notably support to small business and special consideration for the disadvantaged entrepreneur.

Private contractors (rather than government labs) also typically carry out the development of major systems. The U.S. military acquisition system has evolved such that the firms that undertake development also undertake production. It is difficult to compete in the procurement of a system developed by another contractor,[6] so, in general, the competition for development effectively becomes the competition for production.

Development of a system that pushes the technological frontier is risky, and private firms understandably wish to limit their exposure to such risks when undertaking development contracts. Private firms thus seek cost plus (or similar) contracts for development, while promising in various ways to hold down the costs of production. As a practical matter, this leaves the government bearing not only most, if not all, of the risk, but also the embarrassment if the risks prove greater than the contractor's estimate. In several periods, DoD attempted to limit its risks (total package procurement in the 1960s, fixed price development contracts in the 1980s), but each attempt was abandoned after being perceived as creating problems worse than the ones it was meant to solve.

All this has left DoD in an unsatisfactory situation. Competition at the development stage, when so little is known, encourages contractors to overpromise on performance, especially because they know

---

[6]Difficult but not impossible. In the 1980s, DoD ran several production competitions, called "second sourcing."

that securing the development contract virtually guarantees them the production contract, where most of the profit potential resides. Then, when the government recognizes that the promises were inflated, it usually must face one of two unpalatable choices: delay the program substantially to switch to another provider, or accept a substantial restructuring of the program with the current contractor.

And firms overpromise not just on performance; they often overpromise on schedule, as well. Schedule delays plus the additional time consumed by program restructurings to resolve performance shortfalls can produce substantial delays in fielding relative to initial expectations. From the contractor's point of view, the federal government can be a capricious client, changing the performance specifications in the midst of development and thus necessitating contract renegotiations and program restructuring.

A different difficulty is created because of industry's belief that research and development (R&D) is not profitable:[7] the extent of research not directly funded by the government itself is sharply limited, and thus so is the set of choices available to DoD. Cold War budgets could support a large government-funded R&D program; but even though R&D has been somewhat protected in the post–Cold War drawdown, the budgetary appetite of a few large programs has limited the investment in innovation.

These recurring acquisition difficulties explain the perennial call for acquisition reform. The Clinton administration was no exception; nor is the current Bush administration likely to be so.

The Clinton administration's approach to acquisition reform was led off by Secretary of Defense William Perry's 1994 paper, "Acquisition Reform: A Mandate for Change." In it, Perry emphasized the loss to DoD from its alleged inability to acquire state-of-the-art commercial technology, which, he asserted, reflected the difficulties created by

---

[7]Indeed, it appears that many of the big R&D contracts of the Cold War earned, at best, subnormal profits, and some R&D competitions explicitly stipulated a company "investment" (e.g., the F-22) that was to be repaid through production profits. Thus, one important academic economist characterizes U.S. weapons procurement as a competition for "production prizes," with firms vying to subsidize the R&D phase (see William Rogerson, "Economic Incentives and the Defense Procurement Process," *Journal of Economic Perspectives*, Vol. 8, No. 4, Fall 1994, pp. 65–90).

the FAR and by DoD practices for doing business with commercial companies. The administration helped develop the Federal Acquisition Streamlining Act of 1994, which encouraged the purchase of commercial products whenever possible and eliminated government-unique certification and accounting requirements, especially for smaller purchases. The Act did not, however, change the principle of fair and open competition.

One of the most significant steps taken to create a more commercial environment was the decision to replace military specifications and standards. The traditional procurement process had typically relied on government-unique specifications and standards, but by 1997, several thousand military specifications and standards had been canceled or replaced by performance specifications or, when practicable, nongovernment standards.

Moving beyond these steps, the Clinton administration's second under secretary of defense for acquisition and technology, Paul Kaminski, sought to directly attack the related problems of how long it takes to acquire a system and how much systems cost. Two innovations particularly sought to change the governance of defense acquisition:[8]

- Cost as an independent variable (CAIV). The aim of this innovation was to reduce life-cycle costs by making cost a driver in system design (replacing the Cold War emphasis on performance). The CAIV picks a cost objective and focuses on cost-performance tradeoffs to achieve savings.

- Advanced concept technology demonstrations (ACTDs). The purpose of ACTDs was to shorten the acquisition cycle (and improve performance) by moving directly to fieldable prototypes. Evaluations were to take place in the field and were to be carried out, in part, by the users of the technology, who could explore how new capabilities might be used and recommend adjustments to improve system performance before a full acquisition decision was made.

---

[8]For a full view of Kaminski's efforts, see his prepared statement for the House Committee on National Security, "Defense Acquisition Reform," February 26, 1997, DoD Testimony, 105th Congress, first session, 1997.

These innovations were the latest in a long series of acquisition re-
forms that began in the Hoover commissions (1949 and 1955) and
continued through the Fitzhugh commission (1970), the Commission on Government Procurement (1972), the Grace commission
(1983), and the Packard commission (1986).[9] Indeed, it can be argued that defense procurement has steadily improved over the past
five decades, as measured by acquisition results (e.g., the performance of equipment in combat operations). But further improvement is still highly desirable, as can be seen in the call of Kaminski's
successor, Jacques Gansler, for DoD to concentrate on cutting in half
the time it takes to acquire weapons systems.[10] Perhaps acquisition
reform is best seen as an evolutionary, rather than revolutionary, set
of changes.

DoD has also taken advantage of "other transactions" procurement
authority, increasing its flexibility because fewer regulations apply to
"other transactions." This form of procurement authority was originally granted to the Defense Advanced Research Projects Agency
(DARPA) by the 1994 Defense Authorization Act; it was then extended to all of DoD on a trial basis by the 1997 Act. Major weapons
systems that have benefited from this initiative include the Navy's
Twenty First Century Destroyer Program (DD21) and the Air Force's
Evolved Expendable Launch Vehicle (EELV). The hope is that the
flexibility of "other transactions" authority will translate into lower
costs, but it is too soon to tell yet.

ALTERNATIVE APPROACHES TO DECISIONMAKING

Ever since McNamara's tenure as defense secretary, DoD has emphasized the principle of optimization in making decisions. Optimization requires a clear statement of objectives against which the
benefits and costs of alternative courses of action are weighed. The
Cold War was well suited to this decisionmaking paradigm. Not only
was the opponent well known, but the threats the opponent posed

---

[9]For a useful summary of these earlier reform recommendations, see Defense Policy
Panel and Acquisition Policy Panel, House Committee on Armed Services, *Defense
Acquisition: Major's Commission Reports*, Committee Print No. 26, U.S. Government
Printing Office, Washington, DC, 1988.

[10]*Defense News*, 6 September 1999, p. 1.

were well specified. Scenarios could be devised that allowed planners to optimize their forces and programs against the threats the Soviet Union presented. Indeed, it can be argued that the U.S. success in winning the Cold War with a defense effort that represented a gradually shrinking economic burden (relative to the output of the U.S. economy) is a tribute to the effectiveness of optimization as a decisionmaking principle: it allowed available resources to be used wisely.

With the end of the Cold War, however, the decisionmaking environment changed significantly. It was no longer clear who would challenge the United States in a way that would require the use of military force, and it was no longer clear what scenarios should be used to judge the effectiveness of future forces. For the greater part of the Clinton administration, DoD focused on having to conduct two nearly simultaneous MTWs—one in Iraq and one in North Korea—as a useful benchmark. But the threat of Iraq or North Korea invading its neighbor began to appear less likely (and their forces less capable) over the course of the 1990s. Regardless of the ill intent of these two countries (and others), however, it was becoming clear that optimizing U.S. forces to fight two nearly simultaneous MTWs was impeding what was really needed: a transformation of U.S. forces to enable them to cope with the wide variety of new, often unpredictable challenges they were facing. Thus, the question became: Given great uncertainty about what opponents the United States might face in the future, and about the location and nature of the conflicts U.S. forces might face, should classic cost-benefit optimization still be the guiding principle for decisionmaking?

Cost-benefit analysis came out of an effort by social scientists to apply the tools of economics to Cold War military problems, and the same tool kit may also yield instruments suited to the uncertain post–Cold War world.

One of the basic principles of economics is that diversification of one's portfolio—i.e., hedging against a variety of possible outcomes—is the appropriate investment strategy when faced with uncertainty. To apply this principle to contemporary defense problems, one must identify the set of possible situations—i.e., the set of possible futures, or even future scenarios—for which the United States should be developing hedges. Since the forces and programs appropriate for one future will not necessarily be appropriate for another, it is only with the greatest good luck that a program optimized for one future will reasonably cover the bets that need to be made. The issue thus becomes how many bets to make and how large they should be, not which is the best single wager.

Warning and the rapidity with which U.S. military forces respond to unforeseen (and currently unforeseeable) circumstances form another approach to an uncertain security environment. If warning can be sufficiently timely or forces are sufficiently flexible in responding to the unexpected, a single programmatic solution to the defense problem might once again be appropriate. Improvement in the ability to discern and act on warning and in the flexibility with which forces respond to unforeseen circumstances can substitute for some of the "portfolio diversification" of the capabilities resident in U.S. forces that would otherwise be required to handle the uncertainties of the post–Cold War world.

ALTERNATIVE DECISIONMAKING STYLES

Decisionmaking gradually became more centralized, consistent with the Cold War emphasis on optimization and with the strengthening of the defense secretary's powers that the 1949 and 1958 amendments to the National Security Act brought. The trend accelerated during Secretary McNamara's tenure, in the 1960s. The secretary of defense's office took control of the defense program, raised issues concerning service plans, and forged a set of decisions that emphasized rationalization of defense efforts in accord with optimizing criteria.

Central planning as a decisionmaking style was well suited to the challenge posed by the Cold War. It also solved the decisionmaking problem of any organization operating in a nonmarket environment in that it created a way to produce coherent and internally consistent decisions when there were otherwise no "signals" to guide the organization's constituent elements. That said, however, central planning can also be stifling. In the uncertain post–Cold War world, it could restrict the very innovation needed to generate alternative options with which to hedge DoD's bets.

As an alternative, the central actors in the department would set the "rules of the game" governing decisions about future forces, their training, their equipment, and their preparations for sustained operations, but would then leave much of the decisionmaking about particular choices to the department's constituent elements. Such decentralization would be a significant shift in the managerial paradigm, but not as significant as might first be perceived. Training decisions remained largely decentralized even in an era of centralized decisionmaking, and in many ways the POM process has already operated in a decentralized manner since the late 1960s. But it would be a significant change for the management of investment decisions.

While a more decentralized decisionmaking approach might encourage innovation, it is not without its own problems. It could restrict the ability of central actors to redirect the department's activities in response to fast-changing circumstances. If authority is decentralized, so is responsibility, which may be inconsistent with Congress's preference to hold the top leaders of the department accountable for the department's actions.

Decentralization would also run up against the question of how to manage the defense agencies. Created over many years (starting in the 1950s), these agencies typically arose because of the perception that it would be more efficient (or at least more effective) to have a consolidated organization carry out certain functions than to permit each military service its own capability. Many of DoD's intelligence, research, and support functions were being carried out by these centralized organizations, and that structure would have to be reconsidered in any serious effort to decentralize.

A very different management issue relates to the time focus of decisionmakers' attention. Especially since Secretary McNamara's tenure, the defense secretary's focus has been on the future, on looking ahead and planning how DoD should best cope with future events. Surprisingly little attention is paid to how well the department executes the plans it has on the books. Such attention as is paid to execution is disproportionately concentrated in the very top of the department and focuses on programs that are "in trouble." The routine monitoring of program execution is largely left to the secretary's assistants, and to the military departments and defense agencies—in essence, a style of management by exception.

This is, of course, a sweeping generalization, and there are exceptions. Secretary Weinberger, in the early 1980s, instituted a series of secretarial performance reviews in which each military department reported directly to him on the performance of major programs once a month. He used these to monitor such issues as the health of the All-Volunteer Force and the president's strategic nuclear modernization program. In the late 1980s, Deputy Secretary William Taft experimented with a biennial POM process, using the off-year to conduct an execution review. Neither innovation survived much beyond its creator's tenure.

It is often observed that the troops on whom the boss checks frequently are the troops who do the best. Especially if a future secretary were to move to a more decentralized decisionmaking style, it would be useful to balance that style with increased attention to program execution. Such attention would have the added benefit of helping DoD more promptly resolve problems that arise—for instance, the concerns over reduced readiness due to reduced resources that existed before the Bush administration's major increases in defense spending. It would also help the department understand how the results of experiments and real-world operations inform decisions about the very uncertain future DoD faces in the years ahead.

LOOKING TO THE FUTURE

Looking to the early years of this century, two of the four enduring decisions any military organization must make are likely to continue being the focus of debate. First, despite the sharp increases in the defense budget that the Bush administration has made, the size and the structure of U.S. military forces are once again likely to be debated. Indeed, this issue has never been fully joined, despite the several major reviews conducted in the 1990s. The current force structure therefore represents more of an evolution than a definite choice geared to the realities of the present era. The strains placed on the current force by contemporary operations, plus the new missions in counterterrorism and homeland security, only add to the pressure to consider this issue explicitly.

The second enduring focus of debate is the nature of equipment that should be used to arm the U.S. force. The urgent need to recapitalize the present generation of equipment has put this decision high on the department's agenda. In short, the new century brings to the fore a critical set of specific defense decisions that must be made, and with them comes the opportunity to consider afresh *how* those decisions will be made. It will be a fascinating period for both students and practitioners of defense decisionmaking.

Chapter Two

RESPONDING TO ASYMMETRIC THREATS

Bruce W. Bennett

As Chapter One indicates, Cold War planning dealt largely with "symmetric" threats—strength-on-strength planning vis-à-vis the Warsaw Pact, especially in central Europe. Warfighters find it easiest to address such threats, ones they understand thanks to the Cold War experience. But America's ability to prevail handily against symmetric threats has forced U.S. adversaries to pursue asymmetric threats. In one sense, strategies often include asymmetric components in that they seek to exploit the other side's vulnerabilities, but the Cold War's image of two broadly similar superpowers obscured that fact.

The 1997 Quadrennial Defense Review (QDR) identified asymmetric threats, or "challenges," as a major issue for the U.S. military.[1] Previous RAND work[2] defined asymmetric threats as those that attack vulnerabilities not appreciated by the target or that capitalize on the target's limited preparation against the threat. These threats usually rely on concepts of operation (CONOPs) that differ from the target's and/or from those of recent history.[3] The U.S. military understands

---

[1]William S. Cohen, *Report of the Quadrennial Defense Review*, Department of Defense, May 1997, in particular pp. 4 and 49–51, but also pp. vii, 12, 13, 19, 41, and 43.

[2]Bruce W. Bennett, Christopher P. Twomey, and Gregory F. Treverton, *What Are Asymmetric Strategies?*, DB-246-OSD, RAND, 1999.

[3]Additionally, asymmetric threats can serve political or strategic objectives not shared by the victim. For example, in 1941, U.S. economic sanctions against Japan were intended to coerce Japan into stopping its aggression in East Asia. But the Japanese, having different strategic objectives, responded with an asymmetric strategy: a strike against Pearl Harbor that sought to neutralize the U.S. Pacific Fleet and thereby to convince the United States to disengage from East Asia.

its own strengths and tends to focus on them even when it does not see comparable preparations by a prospective adversary, assuming that warfare will be largely symmetric in character. This failure to adequately recognize asymmetric threats is neither new nor unique to the U.S. military.[4] However, given that asymmetric threats are now the greatest threats to the U.S. military and U.S. society (as the terrorist attacks of September 11, 2001, drove home), the subject requires particular attention in U.S. military planning.

This chapter characterizes asymmetric threats and outlines steps the U.S. military needs to take to counter them. It starts with a general introduction to asymmetric threats, explaining why and how they would be wielded. It also addresses the importance of adversary surprise and anonymity, as well as the nature of challenge and response cycles. It then focuses on threats based on chemical and biological weapons, which are a significant element of the current threats to the United States and its allies.

FROM THE COLD WAR TO THE PRESENT

The two principal arenas for Cold War military confrontation with the Soviet Union—the NATO Central Front on the inter-German/Czech border, and strategic nuclear conflict—were perceived by the United States as symmetric confrontations, creating a culture of expectation for strength-on-strength combat. Yet even these Soviet threats included many elements that were asymmetric. On the Central Front, armor faced armor in a contest of maneuver, and both sides depended on artillery, aircraft, and naval forces. U.S./NATO strategy eventually focused on developing technologically superior weapons to provide an asymmetric advantage for NATO. Meanwhile, the Soviets relied on quantity and strong CONOPs, including the heavy use of special forces and chemical and biological weapons (CBW); artillery disruption leading to breakthroughs, especially against the weaker forces of some NATO allies; and penetration concepts, such as operational maneuver groups.[5]

---

[4]Comparable historical concepts have included the writings of Sun Tzu, maneuver warfare, and centers of gravity.

[5]An operational maneuver group was a corps-sized heavy maneuver force designed to penetrate an operational breakthrough (the collapse of at least part of a NATO corps

Despite the efforts of some military specialists, however, the extent of asymmetry in the Soviet threat was not well comprehended in the United States.

Each side's strategic nuclear forces consisted of a triad: intercontinental ballistic missiles (ICBMs), submarine-launched ballistic missiles (SLBMs), and bombers. Many in the United States argued that stability was maintained by the assured ability to destroy opposing urban/industrial areas even after suffering a first strike against strategic weapons. The United States planned a nuclear response to a major Soviet conventional force breakthrough in NATO, and proposed a doctrine of limited nuclear operations to control the escalation from such nuclear weapons use. After the Cold War, the United States learned that the Soviets had taken asymmetric approaches to many of these U.S. concepts and did not accept the primacy of assured destruction. For example, the Soviets created vast production capacities for and stockpiles of such biological weapons (BW) as anthrax and smallpox and planned to use them against the United States.[6]

This perception of symmetry led many U.S. analysts to conclude that quantitative measures of military hardware, units, and warfighters were the key metrics for evaluating the military capabilities of the United States and the Soviet Union. Analysts compared the numbers of U.S./NATO tanks, artillery pieces, combat divisions, military manpower, and fighter aircraft to Soviet/Warsaw Pact equivalents.[7] Strategic analysts counted ICBMs, SLBMs, bombers, and warheads, and assessed mixed quantitative/qualitative measures such as equivalent megatons and countermilitary potential.[8] Analysts and de-

---

sector) and overrun targets behind the front, including headquarters, airfields, major storage depots, and even political targets. The hope was that by so doing, these groups would expedite the strategic collapse of NATO's defenses.

[6]See Kenneth Alibek, "Biological Weapons," presented to the USAF Air War College, November 1, 1999. It refers to Soviet storage of anthrax in excess of 100 tons, with an annual production capacity of thousands of tons; it also says that the Soviets had stockpiles of plague and smallpox that were each roughly 20 tons.

[7]See, for example, *NATO and the Warsaw Pact: Force Comparisons,* NATO Information Service, 1984; and William P. Mako, *U.S. Ground Forces and the Defense of Central Europe,* The Brookings Institute, 1983.

[8]See, for example, Paul Nitze, "Considerations Bearing on the Merits of the SALT II Agreements as Signed at Vienna, *The Congressional Record—Senate,* July 20, 1979, pp.

cisionmakers talked in terms of a "military balance," as if roughly equal force quantities were stable and greater quantities conferred military advantage.[9] In practice, most comparisons concluded that because the Soviet Union had more military equipment, personnel, and units, it held a military advantage, though there were some uncertainties even about these quantities. These comparisons were largely strength-on-strength comparisons and thus tended to ignore other key characteristics and relative vulnerabilities—the essence of asymmetric threats.[10] In addition, these analyses seldom considered whether U.S. and allied forces could perform their missions or meet their operational requirements.

Today, military leaders and analysts, trained during the Cold War, are tempted to apply similar methods in discussing U.S. conventional and nuclear superiority over potential adversary states.[11] Figure 2.1 shows how U.S. conventional and nuclear capabilities overwhelm the conventional capability of most prospective adversaries,[12] especially the "rogue states," such as Iraq, North Korea, and Libya. And the addition of weapons of mass destruction (WMD) by these rogue states is not seen as providing sufficient "strength" to offset U.S. ca-

---

S10070–10082; and Robert L. Leggett, "Two Legs Do Not a Centipede Make," *Armed Forces Journal International*, February 1975, pp. 30–32. A critique of these methods is contained in Bruce W. Bennett, *Assessing the Capabilities of Strategic Nuclear Forces: The Limits of Current Methods*, N-1441-NA, RAND, June 1980.

[9]See, for example, arguments on the Conventional Forces in Europe (CFE) negotiations in James R. Thomson and Nanette C. Gantz, *Conventional Arms Control Revisited: Objectives in the New Phase*, N-2697-AF, RAND, December 1987.

[10]These comparisons acted as if the relative quality of military personnel or command-and-control or intelligence or even (in many cases) hardware quality did not matter in the overall assessment. The Soviets included qualitative force multipliers in their assessments, as discussed in Allan S. Rehm and Joan F. Sloan, *Operational Level Norms*, SAI-84-041-FSRC, SAIC, April 24, 1984, especially Section 3.

[11]Most military analysis is still fixed on repelling ground force invasions. Neither the diversity of other U.S. military engagements nor the differences in each side's vulnerabilities and force requirements get much attention. Although such threats as ballistic missiles are recognized, conflicts that entail their use per se (rather than as ancillaries to an invasion) are downplayed.

[12]The United States explicitly wishes to avoid becoming an adversary of the world's other great powers. "The United States is committed to expanding its network of friendships and alliances with the aim that eventually all of the world's great powers will willingly cooperate with it to safeguard freedom and preserve peace" (Donald H. Rumsfeld, *Guidance and Terms of Reference for the 2001 Quadrennial Defense Review*, June 22, 2001, p. 1).

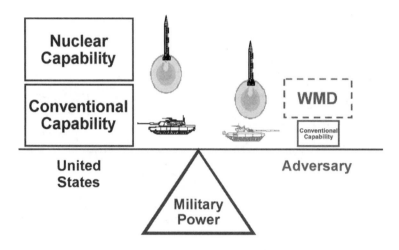

Figure 2.1—Symmetric View of Military Power

pabilities. During the Cold War, many smaller states accepted this imbalance because the Soviet Union counterbalanced U.S. strength. But now they face the United States on their own and cannot afford the U.S. level of military capabilities.

U.S. conventional military superiority remains focused on its traditional threats: armored and air assaults over relatively open terrain to conquer territory of a U.S. ally. In the 1990s, theorists spoke of a revolution in military affairs (RMA) that would allow the United States to use technology to overwhelm such a threat. "An RMA . . . renders obsolete or irrelevant one or more core competencies of a dominant player."[13] Indeed, the United States has made most opposing forces of armor, aircraft, and ships obsolete in symmetric conflicts against it.

Figure 2.2 suggests that because adversaries cannot achieve a military balance with the United States using symmetric approaches, they have been induced to find other ways to undermine U.S. mili-

---

[13]Richard O. Hundley, *Past Revolutions, Future Transformations*, MR-1029-DARPA, RAND, 1999, p. 9.

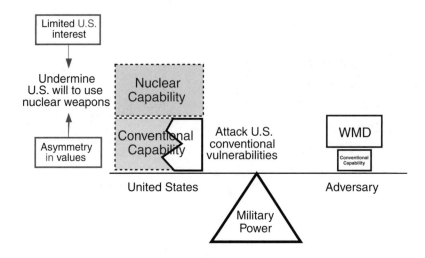

Figure 2.2—How Adversaries Might Use Asymmetric Threats

tary power—by attacking U.S. military vulnerabilities or America's will to use its military might.[14] Any of the approaches could remove a significant part of U.S. strength from the balance, giving adversaries a chance to prevail.

Few U.S. adversaries now contemplate a conventional force invasion of a neighboring territory, especially one allied with the United States, but they have still sought to improve their military capabilities.[15] They are also pursuing asymmetric approaches to achieve their objectives, such as standoff coercion, guerilla warfare, subversion, and information warfare. The little "RMAs" that play a role in the pursuit of these approaches include cover, concealment, and deception to prevent the United States from recognizing threats or

---

[14]This very simple depiction ignores the role of U.S. allies and U.S. forward basing. Figure 2.3 extends this simple approach.

[15]One exception, North Korea, may yet invade its neighbor, South Korea, using conventional forces. Its asymmetric "facilitating force," which would remove or suppress many U.S. and South Korean defenses, includes artillery with chemical shells that would be used against U.S. and South Korean ground forces; special forces and ballistic missiles armed with CBW to suppress airfields, ports, command, control, communications, and logistics; and cruise missiles and aircraft to sustain CBW contamination.

countering them; new delivery means, such as ballistic and cruise missiles or unmanned aerial vehicles (UAVs) that are inexpensive and difficult for the United States to counter; and WMD to affect military operations or coerce neighbors.

EXAMPLES OF ASYMMETRIC THREATS

Examples of asymmetric threats might include the following:

- Computer hackers use e-mail viruses to destroy U.S. military personnel records and the software used to process them, thereby seeking to delay U.S. force deployments and mobilization.

- Terrorists explode bombs against civilian targets in New York City.[16]

- Adversary special forces fire handheld surface-to-air missiles (e.g., SA-16s) against U.S. cargo aircraft, tankers, and command-control aircraft taking off from theater airfields.

- Operating from fishing ships, Iraqi special forces spray BW upwind of U.S. Navy ships in the port of Jabal Ali in the United Arab Emirates. (Jabal Ali is the largest port in the Persian Gulf.)

- Seeking to split the U.S.-led coalition against Iraq, Saddam Hussein claims that U.S.-sponsored sanctions are starving Muslims in Iraq.

- North Korea uses chemical weapons (CW) against the Republic of Korea.

- China threatens a nuclear attack on U.S. cities if the United States interferes in its actions against Taiwan.

These threats may employ novel weapons but need not do so; the weapons can be similar to those of the target. What makes threats asymmetric is the difference in CONOPs and that such threats are used against the target's unexpected vulnerabilities. The target is usually surprised, and the stun effect may delay a response—all of which amplifies the impact. It takes years to build appropriate mili-

---

[16]This example was in the first draft of this text, which was prepared well before September 11, 2001.

tary forces and capabilities to counter such threats. Asymmetric threats are relative; some are more asymmetric than others.

HOW WOULD ADVERSARIES SHAPE ASYMMETRIC THREATS?

Figure 2.3 refines the concepts of Figure 2.2. September 11 notwithstanding, most of the possible conflicts in which the United States will want to intervene will be far from U.S. shores. Hence, the United States must project military power into a region, which requires military means, U.S. will, and the will and support of regional allies that will allow U.S. force and logistics basing and often fight alongside the Americans. U.S. discussions of asymmetric threats usually focus on adversary operations against U.S. military capabilities, such as Scud missiles with chemical warheads being fired at airfields to degrade aircraft operations or disrupt the flow of combat aircraft and their support into the theater. Airfields and other combat support facilities make good targets because they are far more vulnerable than combat aircraft themselves. The United States tends to concentrate its military resources in a few locations in the theater (e.g., airfields, ports, and command facilities) to minimize costs and coordination efforts, but such "massed" facilities make excellent targets for WMD, as well as for conventional weapons delivered by special forces.[17] Despite the recent U.S. focus on protecting these facilities, they remain vulnerable to at least some asymmetric threats.

However, adversaries may find it easier and safer to undermine the will and support of key U.S. regional allies than to attack U.S. military capabilities. Allies understand that their military forces and civilians tend to be more vulnerable than U.S. deployed forces. Their interests frequently differ from those of the United States, especially if they are not the immediate targets of an adversary's invasion. In 1990, when Iraq's invasion victimized only Kuwait, other countries in the Persian

---

[17]An adversary's military culture may lean toward asymmetric threats. For example, because most of North Korea's political and military leadership came out of the special forces Kim Il Sung operated in World War II, North Korea has emphasized special forces operations. By contrast, most U.S. military analysis expresses concern over special forces operations but largely ignores the damage they can do and thus devalues potential actions to counter them.

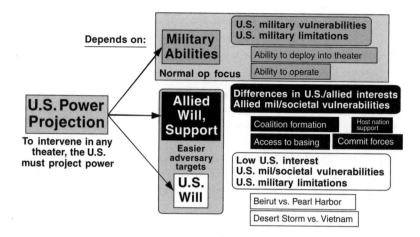

Figure 2.3—U.S. Requirements for Military Power Projection

Gulf were initially uncertain about how much access and support to give the United States. Each worried about its vulnerability to Iraq, fearing that allowing U.S. forces to attack Iraq from its soil might lead to Iraqi retaliation. That is, in fact, what happened: Iraq responded with Scud missiles.

Even when the United States can gain access to regional states, to operate it needs "host nation support"—workers for docks and airfields; power, water, communications, and transportation infrastructure; and so on. Unless these workers are protected against WMD threats by either the host nation or the United States, they may become casualties or flee. Either would degrade U.S. deployment and operations.

U.S. will is especially at risk because U.S. interest in recent and prospective regional conflicts far from home has been limited. U.S. military casualties caused a collapse of U.S. will in the Beirut, Lebanon (1983) and Mogadishu, Somalia (1993) interventions. Some foes contemplate how the U.S. will to intervene, especially in offensive roles, such as in Kosovo, can best be defeated—by posing a strategic threat to the United States[18] or by simply raising the cost of U.S. involvement so that it exceeds the advantages to be gained in interventions of low U.S. interest.

Yet calculating the effects that asymmetric threats or attacks will have on U.S. will is no easy task for would-be adversaries. The 1983 attack on the Marine barracks in Beirut led to a U.S. withdrawal from Lebanon. U.S. interest was very low, and the imposed cost—several hundred soldiers killed—was moderate, with the result that the United States decided to discontinue the intervention. However, the 1941 Japanese attack on Pearl Harbor drove the United States into World War II. The United States perceived its interest in Hawaii to be so vital that Japan was unable to impose too high a price for U.S. intervention. Instead, America felt compelled to remove Japan as a threat to U.S. national security. Getting the threat just right requires imposing costs large enough to prevent U.S. intervention but not so large as to trigger a U.S. change in objectives and/or a demand for revenge.[19] After September 11, there was continued concern about losing too many American lives, but there was no doubt that the United States would do what was required to overturn Afghanistan's Taliban regime and attack Al Qaeda.

The statement of a North Korean sympathizer evokes the dilemma would-be adversaries face: "Which is better prepared for nuclear exchange, North Korea or the USA?. . . The DPRK can be aptly described as an underground fortress. . . . For their part, the North Koreans are

---

[18]See, for example, Northeast Asia Peace and Security Network, "DPRK Report #19: The Importance of NK Missiles," August 9, 1999, http://www.nautilus.org/pub/ftp/napsnet/russiadprk/dprk_report_19.txt. In addition, in an article in the *New York Times*, Michael R. Gordon quotes Chinese official Sha Zukang as saying, "Once the United States believes it has both a strong spear and a strong shield, it could lead them to believe that nobody can harm the United States and they can harm anyone they like anywhere in the world. There could be many more bombings like what happened in Kosovo." Gordon then goes on to say, "He [Sha Zukang] made plain that China's fear was not that the United States would launch a surprise attack on China, but that a missile shield would lead American politicians to believe that the United States was so powerful and well protected that it could act with virtual impunity." (Michael R. Gordon, "China Looks to Foil U.S. Missile Defense System," *New York Times*, April 29, 2001, p. 6.)

[19]Because the United States has learned that many adversary's threats are idle, an adversary may be tempted to demonstrate its capabilities to make its threats credible. Such a demonstration, especially if carried out within the United States, would almost certainly be escalatory.

highly motivated candidate martyrs well prepared to run the risk of having the whole country exploding in nuclear attacks from the USA by annihilating a target population center."[20] Arguably, even the current U.S. interest in Korea would not justify risking a single nuclear attack on the U.S. homeland. But the very first North Korean nuclear attack on U.S. soil would challenge U.S. survival, likely making the United States prepared to withstand great losses to eliminate the North Korean threat.

It is also tempting to think of adversaries posing only a single asymmetric threat—i.e., just one of the examples cited here—even though adversaries may plan some diversity and combination of threats. Then, because U.S. military power requires a combination of many factors, damage to any one of those factors could degrade U.S. combat capability. According to Mark Mateski, the Provisional Irish Republican Army (IRA) once warned Margaret Thatcher, "We only have to be lucky once—you will have to be lucky always."[21] Osama bin Laden might have said the same thing.

THE IMPORTANCE OF SURPRISE AND ANONYMITY

Asymmetric threats target unappreciated vulnerabilities, and they tend to result in surprise. Attacking at unexpected times or in unexpected ways heightens the surprise; so does hiding the preparations or misleading the victim about one's objectives, strategy, capabilities, and deployments. Adversaries that avoid having attacks attributed to them may achieve many objectives *and* avoid retaliation. According to CIA Director George Tenet, "More than ever we risk substantial surprise. This is not for a lack of effort on the part of the

---

[20]Kim Myong Chol, "The Future of the Agreed Framework," Northeast Asia Peace and Security Network, Policy Forum Outline (#23C), November 24, 1998, http://www. nautilus.org/pub/ftp/napsnet/special%5Freports/pf23c%5Fkim%fFon%5Fagreed%5F framework.txt.

[21]Mark Mateski, "The Policy Game," *Red Team: The Journal of Military Innovation*, August 1998, http://www.redteamjournal.com/issuePapers/issue_paper2.htm. In the same article, Mateski says, "And while we spend our strength chasing Bin Laden, each potential adversary will continue to prepare to fight us on its own terms, whatever terms suit it best. For Iraq, the preferred way of war may be another ground assault supplemented with chemical and biological weapons. For North Korea, it may be a massive frontal onslaught. For China, it may be a cat-and-mouse maritime contest. In any case, we must be prepared for them all."

Intelligence Community; it results from significant effort on the part of proliferators."[22]

The possibility of surprise is increased by the fact that U.S. planning and analysis remain so dominated by high-end, largely symmetric threats that resemble those of the Cold War. Most defense policymakers and analysts lack a strategic appreciation for asymmetric threats (such as CBW threats in Korea before 1997), as well as a tactical/operational appreciation for them. They may have known, for instance, that terrorism was a threat in Saudi Arabia before the bombing of Khobar Towers in 1996, but not when and how the towers would be struck. Why the failure?

- U.S. threat-based planning is very susceptible to adversary deception. As a result, the United States mischaracterizes and often underestimates the adversary's threat and thus feels increased surprise when the threat is carried out.

- Analysts tend to "mirror image" an adversary when intelligence on the adversary's strategy and CONOPs is thin.

- Large bureaucracies, plagued by groupthink, have trouble accomplishing the "thinking outside the box" needed to understand how an adversary would employ a threat in novel ways. This also stifles projections of the effects an asymmetric threat may have and thus limits options for changing operations and forces to respond to them.

- Resource constraints tend to focus on force modernization in terms of traditional weapons, such as fighter aircraft, destroyers, and artillery. Less attention is paid to developing and fielding the

---

[22]"Text: DIA Director Tenet Outlines Threats to National Security," U.S. Department of State, International Information Programs Internet Site, Washington File, 21 March 2000. Tenet then cited four reasons why: "First and most important, proliferators are showing greater proficiency in the use of denial and deception. Second, the growing availability of dual-use technologies is making it easier for proliferators to obtain the materials they need. Third, the potential for surprise is exacerbated by the growing capacity of countries seeking WMD to import talent that can help them make dramatic leaps on things like new chemical and biological agents and delivery systems. . . . Finally, the accelerating pace of technological progress makes information and technology easier to obtain and in more advanced forms than when the weapons were initially developed."

equipment and forces required to respond to "unproven" asymmetric threats.

Without adequate preparation, the United States will lack the people and equipment it needs to counter new threats, and responding to such threats takes time.[23]

Most adversaries would like to defeat the United States without having to pay for it. They may attempt to avoid reprisal by hiding their strategy and CONOPs and, perhaps, by carrying out attacks covertly. They may not need to claim credit for the damage done, depending on their objectives. If the United States cannot attribute an attack to an adversary, it may lack the will to retaliate. Thus, deterrence will not work well against an adversary that thinks it can avoid attribution.

CHALLENGE AND RESPONSE CYCLES

As the United States and potential adversaries pursue new military capabilities, "challenge and response cycles" result.[24] Thus, as adversaries' threats create new challenges for the United States, the issue becomes one of how quickly the United States can respond. For example, in the Cold War the Soviet Union used the threat of a massive armored invasion to challenge the United States and its NATO allies. Their response was to seek higher-technology armored forces and, especially, air forces that could interdict Soviet armor. The quality of the U.S. response was inadequate until the late 1980s. As it turned out, this anti-armor response developed for the Soviet threat defeated Iraq's 1990 challenge in the Persian Gulf.

This U.S. anti-armor response challenged other potential adversaries, however. Many responded by developing CBW, thus posing

---

[23]Adversaries often fail to understand asymmetric operations and thus fail to exploit them. See, for example, the discussion of Germany's treatment of chemical weapons in World War I in Kenneth F. McKenzie, Jr., "An Ecstasy of Fumbling: Doctrine and Innovation," *Joint Forces Quarterly*, Winter 1995–96, pp. 62–68. Such failures may reduce the overall effect of the operations, but considerable damage may still be done (e.g., Germany's CW attacks in World War I).

[24]Sam Gardiner and Dan Fox originally described this cycle in unpublished RAND work on RMAs.

a new, asymmetric challenge to the United States, which has renounced the use of CBW. The United States counterresponded by threatening reprisals, which succeeded in deterring Iraq in 1991, and it has also worked on better defenses against CBW. But these responses have lagged adversaries' CBW challenges—even today, the United States remains relatively vulnerable to CBW attacks. And CBW is only one among a diverse set of asymmetric threats.

Worse, in today's relatively short wars (often only weeks or months long, as opposed to years), each side largely brings to the conflict the forces and capabilities it has prepared beforehand. If U.S. adversaries fight differently and the United States lags too far in the cycle, it may be leaving itself particularly vulnerable.

Its focus on threat-based planning has caused the United States to lag in many challenge and response cycles. Planning that is threat based requires an established threat. When adversaries hide the details of their threats, it can take years or even decades (if ever) to uncover the details, which puts the United States behind its adversaries.

The capabilities developed as part of the U.S. RMA also introduce new military vulnerabilities. For example, U.S. use of a global positioning system (GPS) allows precise weapons delivery—unless an adversary finds ways to jam the GPS in the area. In addition, many U.S. weapons that attack ground forces by scattering warheads over a broad area—a single CBU-97, which contains 40 sensor-fuzed weapons and covers an area of 15 acres,[25] or a SADARM (sense and destroy armor munition), which covers 20 acres[26]—may work well in deserts or behind adversary lines, but they can cause great collateral damage to friendly military vehicles or civilian vehicles intermixed with adversary forces (e.g., at the battlefield front, along adversary penetrations, or in urban areas). If adversaries focus on creating intermixed environments (a "nonlinear battlefield"), they can make it difficult for the United States to use its "superior" weaponry.

---

[25]Glenn W. Goodman, Jr., "Nowhere to Hide," *Armed Forces Journal International,* October 1997, p. 59.

[26]Goodman, "Nowhere to Hide," p. 61.

THE CHALLENGE OF WEAPONS OF MASS DESTRUCTION

A particularly fearsome class of asymmetric strategies involves WMD—nuclear, radiological, biological, and chemical weapons. These weapons can hurt military forces and civilians in great numbers and are thus a significant element of adversaries' threats. Not surprisingly, President Bush focused on WMD in his 2002 State of the Union Address: "Our nation will continue to be steadfast and patient and persistent in the pursuit of two great objectives. First, we will shut down terrorist camps, disrupt terrorist plans, and bring terrorists to justice. And, second, we must prevent the terrorists and regimes that seek chemical, biological or nuclear weapons from threatening the United States and the world."[27]

President Bush specifically identified North Korea, Iran, and Iraq as states with WMD and as being part of an "axis of evil." A CIA report immediately after the president's speech also identified Russia and China as key suppliers of WMD technology, and Libya, Syria, Sudan, India, Pakistan, and Egypt as states acquiring technology relating to WMD and advanced conventional munitions.[28] It has been widely reported that North Korea possesses 2,500 to 5,000 tons of CW, that Iran possesses thousands of tons, and that Russia has had some 40,000 tons of CW and potentially thousands of tons of biological agents.[29]

Although often discussed as if they were a single category of weapons, the various WMD differ greatly, as Table 2.1 indicates. Many of their effects are a function of the wind blowing fallout or CBW aerosols. Some BW are incapacitating but not lethal; others, such as anthrax (which was spread by letters in the wake of September 11), are quite lethal. Many BW, especially those dispersed as sprays, are neutralized in minutes or hours by sunlight and rain; others (e.g., smallpox) are contagious and spread from person to person. Some CW (e.g., VX) persist in liquid form on the ground and become a protracted vapor and contact hazard until they evaporate or are ab-

---

[27]See http://www.whitehouse.gov/news/releases/2002/01/20020129-11.hmtl.

[28]See http://www.cia.gov/cia/publications/bian/bian_jan_2002.htm.

[29]See, for example, Office of the Secretary of Defense, *Proliferation: Threat and Response*, January 2001, pp. 56–57.

Table 2.1

Comparing Weapons of Mass Destruction[a]

Weapon Type	Size	Lethal Effect	Time to Effect	Area Covered	Potential Fatalities
Nuclear	100 Kt	Blast	Seconds	35 km^2	100,000–320,000
		Fallout	Hours to weeks	~800 km^2	100,000s
Biological (anthrax)	100 kg	Disease	Days	45–300 km^2	100,000–1,000,000+
Chemical (sarin)	1,000 kg	Nerve damage	Minutes	0.7–8 km^2	3,000–80,000

[a]See Office of Technology Assessment, *Proliferation of Weapons of Mass Destruction: Assessing the Risks*, August 1993, pp. 53–54. This reference assumes that nuclear blast effects in excess of 5 psi overpressure are, on average, lethal. The anthrax and sarin areas were offered for three different weather conditions. Based on other sources, these were apparently the areas of 50 percent lethality; some lethality would occur at far greater distances, especially for anthrax. The fallout area was estimated from Samuel Glasstone and Phillip J. Dolan, *The Effects of Nuclear Weapons*, 1977, pp. 427–430. From their table on p. 430, the downwind distance and maximum width were estimated for a 100 rads/hr dose with a 100-Kt weapon; these were then multiplied by each other and by 0.7 to reflect the actual character of the pattern. Potential fatalities are calculated assuming no treatment and 3,000 to 10,000 people living in each kilometer affected, though the fallout and BW effects will likely go well beyond the range of a city and thus much of the area covered will not have a high population density.

sorbed into the ground (after which they can come back out of the ground over a long period of time). Their persistence varies with temperature, wind conditions, and surface absorption rates.

Because of the large areas they affect, these weapons can be force multipliers. To reduce WMD effects, defenders must employ various protections (reasonable ones exist for CBW, but nuclear weapons are harder to defend against). All of these protections reduce the defending force's effectiveness, but adversaries that deploy CBW risk contaminating areas where their own forces are positioned or need to go, which could cause casualties among their own personnel or degrade performance for their forces.

U.S. threats of retaliation against WMD use, such as that made against Iraq in the Persian Gulf War, are often enough to deter adversaries—at least if those adversaries are not more worried about regime survival than about the U.S. threat. However, the large CW inventories in several countries suggest that some adversaries see using CBW as an operational necessity.[30] They would likely use CBW early, to maximize surprise and devastation, rather than using WMD only to avert final defeat. BW are best employed before an invasion begins because of their long incubation periods; early use (e.g., at D–2) would sicken defenders around the time of D-Day. BW could also be used to cause disruption in a crisis, the adversary seeking to wreak damage while avoiding attribution and thereby escaping retaliation. Yet most adversaries are risk averse, so even a small potential of attributing WMD use to them, associated with the expectation of serious U.S. retaliation, should be sufficient to deter BW use in most circumstances.

A FRAMEWORK FOR RESPONDING TO ASYMMETRIC THREATS

Asymmetric threats pose a quandary for the United States because they threaten U.S. and allied forces, civilians, and interests in diverse ways that are difficult and expensive to counter. This section proposes a framework for responding to asymmetric threats, focusing on responses to CBW threats as an example of the more general problem. The framework is based on two response approaches identified in the 1997 QDR: institutionalizing and internationalizing.[31]

To be effective, responses must be institutionalized. This would require the military to recognize and address all forms of policy—doctrine, strategy, and CONOPs preparation; force structure and equip-

---

[30]For example, North Korea is reported to have 2,500 to 5,000 tons of CW (South Korean Ministry of National Defense, *Defense White Paper, 2000*, p. 86), and Iran apparently has several thousand tons of CW (CIA, *Unclassified Report to Congress on the Acquisition of Technology Relating to Weapons of Mass Destruction and Advanced Conventional Munitions*, January 1 through June 30, 2000). These inventories are far greater than would be needed for strategic deterrence and regime survival. Because the U.S./South Korean plan for war calls for defeat and destruction of the North Korean regime as well as military conquest of the country, any war would be a total war from the North Korean perspective. As such, North Korea would have little incentive to withhold weapons early in a campaign. See "KBS Reports Plan to Topple Kim Il Sung," *Washington Times*, March 25, 1994, p. 16; and Ranan R. Lurie, "In a Confrontation, 'North Korea Will Definitely Be Annihilated,'" *Los Angeles Times* (Washington ed.), March 24, 1994, p. 11.

[31]William S. Cohen, *Report of the Quadrennial Defense Review*, 1997, p. 49.

ment development; and personnel management and training—something DoD does not do well today. There is no single solution to CBW threats, no "silver bullet" that defeats even any individual threat component, let alone the totality.[32] Responses to even the related CW and BW threats often differ greatly, complicating DoD's ability to institutionalize responses to such threats. Instead, an integrated defense effort must include two elements of response institutionalization: institutionalization through protection and institutionalization through threat management. It must also include internationalization, which entails extending the two elements of institutionalization so as to coordinate with U.S. allies and coalition partners. These three parts of an integrated approach are described in the following sections.

Institutionalization Through Protection

Protection against CBW effects has four components: attack operations (destroying delivery systems before they can be launched), active defenses (destroying delivery systems and their payloads en route), avoidance (maneuvering around contamination or working from places not contaminated), and passive defenses (protecting from contamination). As shown in Figure 2.4 and discussed next, these four components of response currently have limited effectiveness for defeating CBW.

Most adversary CBW and delivery vehicle stocks are so large that attack operations, especially in the face of adversary cover, concealment, and deception efforts, would take a long time to make a large dent in them. Active defenses work well against some CBW delivery means, such as combat aircraft and naval ships. Yet very short-range ballistic missiles (e.g., the CSS-8) can fly under current defenses, and longer-range ballistic missiles (e.g., the NoDong) descend at angles and speeds that pose problems for current systems.

---

[32]That an anthrax vaccine suffices for that specific threat may be largely true (even if some share of the victims still die). But this "solution" ignores the challenge and response cycle: eventually, someone may well defeat the anthrax vaccine. Therefore, the United States needs to seek redundant, robust defenses.

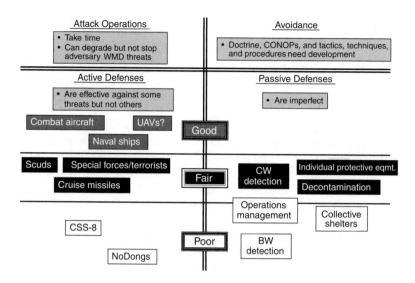

**Figure 2.4—Shortcomings of Today's Means of Force Protection
Against CBW**

Although CBW contamination avoidance can help, the related doctrine, CONOPs, and procedures need more work. Passive defenses
against CBW threats provide a fair degree of protection, but only in
some cases. Note that attack operations and active defenses work together with avoidance and passive defenses by reducing the amount
of chemical and biological material that arrives in the area being
defended. The United States is improving its capabilities in all these
areas.[33]

All military personnel need to be trained in how to operate in CBW
threat and contaminated environments. Today's training is hampered by inadequate doctrine, CONOPs, and procedures; it deals
with very short-term chemical threats and tends to neglect biological
threats and longer-term chemical threats (partly be denying the latter
will take place). Training needs to be broadened to cover the range of
CBW threats and to become more universal (all personnel should be

---

[33]See, for example, the description of the new U.S. protective suit technology in Curt
Biberdorf, "CB Protective Field Duty Uniform," *CB Quarterly*, March 2001, pp. 17–18.

trained) so that military personnel think in terms of fighting in a CBW environment.

Similar limitations apply in the case of other asymmetric threats. Protecting against the use of nuclear weapons is even more difficult; it is also difficult to protect against terrorism or attacks on information systems.

Attack Operations. One way to reduce CBW threats is to attack their delivery systems, although large CBW stockpiles and large numbers of delivery systems mean that eliminating them takes time. Destroying CBW on the adversary's territory at least makes the foe suffer most of the consequences, but successful attacks require capable munitions and good information about the threats: what and where they are, and how best to destroy them while controlling collateral damage. Attacking CBW preemptively is difficult because of the risk of collateral damage that can occur in areas surrounding CBW facilities. U.S. planning normally anticipates that attack operations against adversary CBW will not start until the adversary has used some CBW, but this approach requires that the CBW attack be correctly attributed. The United States needs to show that the adversary is, in the end, responsible for the damage because it used CBW first.

For example, say the United States plans to use radar to follow ballistic missile tracks back to their launchers, the goal being to kill launchers before they can pack up and move on. Since most missile launchers have in storage five to 20 missiles, destroying launchers means potentially preventing the launch of multiple missiles. If each launcher in a 50-launcher force has a 20 percent risk of being killed each time it launches (a high level of effectiveness), after 10 launches each (over five to 10 days?), the force will be cut down to five (which is enough to still do some damage). Thus, attack operations take days or weeks to have much effect; they do little to attrite the threat early unless there are only a few launchers and they are left out in the open. Still, anything that reduces launch rates relieves pressure on active defenses (and limits the odds of their being saturated).

Active Defenses. The next component of response against CBW threats is interception of CBW delivery systems en route. Active defenses can include ballistic missile defenses, air defenses, naval defenses, border guards, and custom agents. They must be matched to the threatening delivery system(s).

The key determinants of an active defense are saturation (how many delivery means can be engaged at one time) and leakage (what percentage get through short of saturation). For example, a Patriot battery with eight launchers (and four missiles per launcher) would be able to engage up to 32 missiles and/or aircraft (the saturation threshold) before reload is needed; if it used two missiles per incoming vehicle, the saturation threshold would be 16 vehicles. If each Patriot missile had a 50 percent probability of killing an opposing ballistic missile, leakage would be 50 percent if only one Patriot were fired per adversary missile, and roughly 25 percent if two Patriots were fired per missile, assuming the kill probabilities were independent of one another.

Beyond saturation and leakage, defenders face other concerns in the challenge and response cycle. A special forces team can more easily destroy a Patriot missile battery than an inaccurate Scud missile can. Adversaries are likely to use combined arms against active defenses, so the United States and its allies need to protect their active defenses. Doing so should let them remove a large fraction—but not all—of the threat.

Avoidance. Force operations can be changed to reduce their vulnerability to adversary CBW threats, even after the United States and its allies develop enhanced defenses. Avoiding contamination is one of the three doctrinal approaches to reducing U.S. vulnerability.[34]

Consider the following analogy. In World War II, the Soviets massed their forces—up to 600 artillery tubes per kilometer—in a breakthrough sector to maximize their ability to penetrate German lines. But in the Cold War, as their vulnerability to U.S. nuclear weapons became clear, the Soviets adjusted their massing factors, eventually settling on artillery densities of about 100 tubes per kilometer in breakthrough sectors. Such a reduced force density complicated breakthrough efforts but prevented a dramatic failure if the opponent targeted the massed forces.

---

[34]Joint Chiefs of Staff, *Joint Doctrine for Operations in Nuclear, Biological, and Chemical (NBC) Environments*, Joint Pub 3-11, July 11, 2000, p. III-6.

To avoid contamination, eight basic adjustments can be made to force operations:

1. *Density reduction.* Forces can be spread out in depth, more reserves can be provided (to replace forward-most forces suffering serious damage), and fires rather than forces can be massed. Density in the rear can be reduced by spreading forces across more bases.

2. *Standoff.* CBW effects can be avoided if forces perform their missions from bases outside the adversary's range.

3. *Dispersal/evacuation.* Forces and personnel, especially those associated with fixed facilities, can be moved away from likely targets (preemptive dispersal/evacuation), and targets already contaminated (remedial dispersal/evacuation).

4. *Relocation.* CBW effects can be reduced or avoided if forces en route to contaminated bases are rerouted to uncontaminated ones.

5. *Avoiding CBW contact.* All forces can try to be indoors during the 30-plus minutes a cloud of aerosolized CBW is passing through. Forces near or in contaminated areas can use reconnaissance to locate and then avoid or decontaminate such areas. Ground forces can maneuver around contaminated terrain.

6. *Threat avoidance.* Ground forces can mount substantial reconnaissance efforts well in front of advancing forces (perhaps 100 km or so) to discover CBW and their delivery systems and destroy them before they are used.

7. *Sequencing operations.* Standoff operations can be used at the start of a conflict to interdict CBW and their delivery means. Once this task is almost finished, forces can enter the theater in greater numbers to complete operations without facing as high a risk.

8. *Quarantine/travel limitations.* Quarantines prevent or limit the spread of contagious BW. Travel limitations imposed during the incubation period of all BW can prevent the appearance that BW were also used elsewhere (i.e., the limitations keep persons exposed at the original site from appearing to have become infected at another location).

Passive Defenses. The final component is passive defenses, which aim to prevent damage from CBW use or to mitigate CBW damage that has occurred. Preventive measures include detection, protective clothing, collective protection shelters, cleanup of residual effects, and consequence management (medical care, personnel replacements, and public information). Figure 2.5 summarizes the current approaches to passive defense, illustrating differences between the CW and BW approaches. The following paragraphs discuss the various elements of the passive defense process.

CW detectors can detect the threat in time to avoid it, but BW detectors cannot currently do so. Thus, passive defense against CW "detects to protect," though CW effects could occur without detection, especially among a civilian population. The persistence of many CW agents also requires reconnaissance and decontamination to finish the job. Passive defense against BW "detects to treat," in part by determining when and by what agent(s) victims have been affected so as to start treatment as soon as possible. Because BW detectors are few and far between, most BW attacks will be detected only by disease surveillance when victims show up at hospitals and clinics.

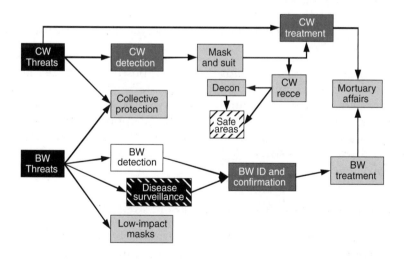

Figure 2.5—Current Passive Defense Efforts

Collective protection keeps CBW out of buildings; it helps those who work indoors avoid exposure. Recent seminars have suggested that it be required in all new construction within potential combat zones. A recent initiative seeks to develop masks that would have less operational degradation than today's CW masks and yet protect against BW (recognizing BW detection limitations) after BW have been used in a theater. CBW medical treatment would be helped by agreements with other governments to provide supplies and specialists, as needed.

Because no single protection suffices, efforts must be combined across them to provide protection packages. Collective protection, for instance, is an ideal defense against CBW for forces that work indoors. If such facilities also have CBW detection, people can be warned to stay indoors when threats loom. By contrast, ground forces in forward units rarely have collective protection against CBW. Masks and suits would be their principal line of defense (plus CBW detection to tell them when to put this equipment on). To avoid overloading their masks and suits, forward units would also maneuver around any contamination they detect by CBW reconnaissance. Reducing the density of forces decreases their value to the adversary as a target and provides reserves to fill holes created by successful adversary attacks. As mentioned earlier, far-forward reconnaissance screens are needed to detect CBW delivery systems and destroy them first.

Although some people working in airfields, ports, and logistics facilities work indoors and can benefit from collective protection, the many people who work outdoors require masks, suits, and CBW detection. In addition, they would be best supported by the use of substantial active defenses—provided by air, missile, naval, and special operations forces (SOF)—to reduce the burden on their passive defenses.

Institutionalization Through Threat Management

The second element of institutionalization is to try to manage asymmetric threats by inhibiting their development in the first place, deterring their use, and mitigating the damage that adversaries seek from them. This element needs to combine prevention, dissuasion, preemption, deterrence, and information operations. While the focus here is on WMD and, specifically, CW and BW as examples of asymmetric threats, in many ways it will be easier for the United States to manage these threats than other asymmetric threats.

Prevention. It is best to prevent asymmetric threats from being developed or, if this is not possible, to get countries to reduce or destroy them. Most prevention strategies are based on arms control; they assume that agreements can be made and enforced to limit or remove certain classes of threats, as was accomplished by the Strategic Arms Limitations Treaty (SALT) and CFE agreements. It is difficult to enforce or verify agreements covering WMD and ballistic missiles even in the case of signatories, however, and many countries are not signatories. The history of Iraqi resistance to WMD-related sanctions suggests that sanctions are no panacea either.

The Bush administration's emphasis on preventing WMD threats runs into obstacles, in particular the "demand" for WMD:

- *Strategic demand.* While the United States has agreed to give up CBW, it still feels it must possess a significant number of nuclear weapons for legitimate national security reasons, including the threat of reprisals. Many other countries appear to feel the same way, though most have focused on CBW because they are less expensive than nuclear weapons. For many of these countries, WMD are the ultimate guarantor of regime survival. They also stand as a symbol of national power while providing some level of coercive power. The United States has not recognized most countries' possession of WMD as legitimate for these purposes.

- *Operational demand.* A number of countries apparently view possession of WMD as an operational military advantage. This is most obvious in countries such as North Korea and Iran, whose inventories of thousands of tons of CBW are difficult to justify for strategic purposes alone.

It is extremely difficult to get countries with these interests to renounce and destroy all their WMD. The United States has not found alternatives for these strategic and operational needs in most cases, making arms control very difficult, especially with regard to countries already possessing these capabilities.

The United States also has arms control concerns on the "supply" side:

- *Moving to "zero" supply.* While the United States has "done away with" all its BW, it still maintains small stocks of many biological agents for defensive development purposes. Recently, it was revealed that even in the United States, the government construed such defensive purposes to include fairly significant biological production efforts to see what a terrorist or other group might be able to produce.

- *CBW breakout.* With BW, most countries prefer to keep primarily small "seed stocks" because of the dangers of storing large quantities and because large quantities can be grown from smaller ones in days or weeks (it takes longer to weaponize the resulting products). Thus, even if a country accepts a "zero" supply, it may be able to produce a substantial wartime capability within months, given adequate expertise and appropriate facilities. Most CBW production facilities have dual civilian and military purposes. Most or all of their production in peacetime might be for civilian purposes, but this could change with little or no warning and few (if any) observables if the decision to prepare for conflict were made.

- *CBW inspections.* Inspections of potential production and storage facilities are a key means for catching countries that are violating WMD restrictions. But since BW production can be done quickly and covertly, it is extremely difficult to catch violators. (Indeed, the UN experience with Iraq after the Persian Gulf War suggests how difficult this process can be.) Moreover, countries are reluctant to enter agreements requiring inspections because they thus open themselves to espionage against key new bioengineering industries. Concerns in this regard have caused the United States to reject the proposed inspections protocol for the Biological and Toxin Weapons Convention.

If all countries were to move to "zero" WMD, a potential adversary could quickly and with little or no notice produce significant quantities of CBW (especially BW) to create an unacceptable coercive or warfighting advantage. Arms control of WMD thus provides only a limited ability to prevent WMD threats. Looking beyond WMD, arms control has even less potential for success with other asymmetric threats such as information warfare and terrorism.

Dissuasion, Intelligence, and the Planning Framework. U.S. efforts to dissuade adversaries from developing or possessing certain asymmetric threats depend on an early understanding of the potential threats, the principles of the challenge and response cycle, and the willingness to invest in capabilities that nullify the threats. If, for example, the United States, anticipating that the smallpox virus has been developed for use against U.S. forces, develops and deploys a smallpox vaccine, few if any adversaries will see utility in further virus development, production, or use. But if the United States does not develop, much less deploy, a vaccine until it has firm evidence that several countries already have weaponized smallpox, it loses the opportunity to prevent this threat, and must instead turn to countering it (which also depends largely on the smallpox vaccine).

Traditional defense planning has been threat-based planning, which copes poorly with asymmetric threats. The defense policy and planning community and the U.S. intelligence community have traditionally required confirming evidence of threats before those threats are included in intelligence estimates.[35] The time it often takes to acquire such confirming evidence means that traditional intelligence estimates lag most adversary capabilities by several years; and they lag adversary asymmetric threats by more years because of a lack of emphasis coupled with the normal difficulties of observing such threats. For example, the production and weaponization of BW agents produces very few of the observables that intelligence agencies usually pursue. Even if BW were observed, the United States would have little information about how they might be used. And since U.S. R&D programs have historically been justified based on such established threats, the United States has tended to seriously lag in the challenge and response cycle associated with asymmetric threats.

---

[35]Ironically, DoD usually ignores the opposite requirement: to confirm that an adversary is *not* developing such a threat before excluding the threat from planning.

The answer for DoD is to try to understand the spectrum of potential asymmetric threats and U.S. vulnerabilities to them.[36] Only then can the United States identify potential threats, search for related adversary developments and strategies, and respond to them. This is the essence of the "capabilities-based planning" proposed in the 2001 QDR. The United States can refine this spectrum of threat alternatives based on cultural and other details of the potential adversary.[37] Planning would then seek to respond to a reasonable threat spectrum.

In essence, the dissuasion strategy element calls on DoD to recognize potential threats and to jump on the leading edge of the challenge and response cycle (rather than being on the trailing edge). It takes the threat spectrum identified in capabilities-based planning, prioritizes it based on threat likelihood and seriousness, and focuses on preventing the top priority threats. To prevent serious threats, the United States must be prepared to invest significantly in developing and fielding appropriate threat counters (such as the smallpox vaccine) well before intelligence can confirm the existence of the threats. The United States must then be prepared to describe the counter to the world in order to convince potential adversaries that the related threat is no longer of use.[38]

Preemption. An alternative to two of the forms of prevention, arms control and dissuasion, is preemption—destroying the threat before it can be used or soon after an early use. Many who heard the 2002 State of the Union Address believe that the United States is threatening North Korea, Iran, and especially Iraq with preemption of their WMD if they do not accept WMD arms control. The U.S. national

---

[36]A focus on known threats leaves the United States open to developing threats. Adversaries would logically start military planning from objectives and develop strategies to achieve them—in part by exploiting perceived U.S. vulnerabilities. Planning of U.S. counters would logically start from a similar perspective. Because the United States may not recognize its own vulnerabilities, this effort must be pursued in part by experts who understand U.S. operations and what can be done to counter them.

[37]One example would be North Korea's interest in special forces and weapons they could use effectively (such as BW), as noted above.

[38]The United States should exercise some care in doing so, as the counter it has developed may, in turn, become the focus of adversary searches for vulnerabilities.

security strategy published in September 2002 included strong support for preemption.

Preemption is akin to attack operations, but would be undertaken as a U.S. offensive action before a war existed with the country in question. Nevertheless, such a preemption would likely begin a war; indeed, North Korea has claimed that President Bush's 2002 State of the Union Address was "little short of declaring a war" on North Korea.[39] In the end, the United States would need to (1) justify to the world that the WMD threat warranted a war, and (2) prove to the world that the preemption largely or entirely removed the WMD threat. To satisfy most countries with regard to the first point, the United States will most likely have to do much more in the way of information operations (many countries do not think WMD threats warrant even President Bush's accusations). And as described earlier, in the discussion on attack operations, the United States will have difficulty entirely destroying the WMD (it will take days or weeks, and may not be possible at all). Moreover, attacks on adversary WMD may well force the adversary into a "use it or lose it" mode in which it responds to preemption with WMD use—for which the United States may then be blamed.

Deterrence. Because protection cannot prevent all losses to asymmetric attacks such as CBW, the United States must deter specific CBW uses.[40] Many equate deterrence with an ability to impose unacceptable damage on the adversary (a reprisal), but the 2001 QDR makes it clear that deterrence by denial (preventing CBW attacks from being effective) is the essence of the new U.S. strategy. Deterrence by denial overlaps very heavily with protection, as discussed above. Still, reprisals do have a role, as do post-conflict sanctions. Because reprisals and sanctions with penalties require that a CBW attack be attributed, the United States needs to prepare plans for achieving attribution in the more difficult cases, such as covert use of BW.[41] And because reprisals and sanctions are escalatory, the United

---

[39]Quoted in David R. Sands, "North Korea Assails 'Axis' Label," *The Washington Times,* February 1, 2002, p. 1.

[40]See Donald H. Rumsfeld, "Toward 21st-Century Deterrence," *Wall Street Journal,* June 27, 2001.

[41]Sometimes attribution is easy. Ballistic missiles, for instance, can usually be traced back to their source (though the country's leadership could claim that they did not

States will need an ability to control escalation, as well as clear knowledge of the price that it and its allies are willing to pay to resolve an adversary's CBW threats.

Inasmuch as no country today is using CBW against the United States, deterrence may be said to be working. The risks of CBW use may far exceed the gains to be achieved, given the probability that those gains can be achieved. But terrorists may feel exempt from such assessments. And if state adversaries begin to feel desperate, their deterrence calculation may change. For instance, if the North Korean regime feared that it was going to be overwhelmed by internal opposition, it might invade South Korea to unify its own citizens; CBW might be an integral component of this invasion. Deterring the desperate from using CBW or other asymmetric threats is hard. The United States can try to prevent desperation through aid, and it can try to convince countries that warfare and CBW use will not solve their problems, or even permit them to achieve what they might want. Potential adversaries should be convinced that the more likely outcome from a CBW attack will be disaster from U.S. reprisals and international economic and political penalties.

Information Operations. Any WMD use would be major international news. Adversaries might seek to ward off penalties, such as international sanctions, in many ways: by denying responsibility, by claiming they are responding to earlier WMD use by the United States or its allies, by depicting themselves as David against the U.S. Goliath, and/or by hindering news coverage of the attack. In using WMD against third countries, they may not even need to pursue these approaches. For example, Iraq's use of CW in its 1980s war with Iran provoked little international response.

---

authorize the launch and will punish the perpetrators). But proving the origins of special forces, terrorist groups, or even cruise missiles is difficult. Without confirmation, the United States may be wary of attacking the wrong party and suffering embarrassment and thus may not act. Adversary deception makes attribution even harder. Given, say, a CBW attack against a U.S. base in the Persian Gulf while Iran is acting militarily against U.S. interests, the United States may well assume Iran did it. But Iraq may actually have done it, hoping the United States would blame and then hurt its archenemy, Iran, in reprisal. The resulting change in the regional balance of power may well be worth the risk for Iraq. Better U.S. capabilities for attribution are needed, and a doctrine of presumed responsibility should be considered, as discussed below.

In peacetime, the United States needs to "prepare the information battlefield." It needs to do so by demonstrating that it and its allies have no plans to use CBW and no deployed capabilities (U.S. CBW has been or is being destroyed), and that U.S. adversaries do have substantial CBW stocks, which they plan to use in wartime and which can inflict a level of damage that easily justifies U.S. and allied protection/defensive efforts. Patriot and weapons systems like Patriot need to be clearly characterized as defenses against serious adversary threats even though some countries' psychological operations (PSYOPs) describe missile defenses as offensive systems.

To justify reprisals, the United States needs to prove that U.S./allied forces were attacked by WMD, convincingly demonstrate the attacker's identity, and show that the United States and its allies have not used CBW and thus are not responsible for whatever CBW casualties occurred in the context of U.S. operations. Otherwise, global nonproliferation efforts will be jeopardized. The United States must clearly describe the damage (especially civilian damage) that resulted from the adversary's CBW use if it is to justify not only the post-conflict sanctions needed to remove the CBW threats, but also the U.S. reprisals—especially if these were carried out with nuclear weapons.

Achieving these objectives in the face of enemy propaganda will be challenging. It will be critical to set international expectations for wartime objectives. Absent clear attribution of adversary CBW attacks, the United States may have to implement a doctrine of "presumed responsibility" that places the burden of proving innocence on regional adversaries with large CBW inventories.

Finally, consequence management requires that the United States be prepared to describe the character and anticipated consequences of a CBW attack, as well as the procedures (e.g., evacuation, medical treatment, and psychological operations to reduce panic) that need to be undertaken after the event.

Internationalization

The United States must also internationalize its response to asymmetric threats, because it will invariably need the support of allies in future conflicts. DoD must prepare itself to fight alongside allies against asymmetric threats, sharing equipment and CONOPs with allies until the latter can meet U.S. standards, which most cannot do yet. Current U.S. efforts offer the opportunity to involve allies in formulating CONOPs and equipment R&D, thereby involving them and potentially reducing U.S. costs. Unfortunately, many U.S. efforts to develop counters to asymmetric threats are pursued on a "U.S.-only" basis, constraining and often directly thwarting U.S. efforts to internationalize the results. This is particularly true with regard to the development of new technologies.

Internationalizing the U.S. approach to CBW threats involves the following five elements:

Understanding the Threat. The United States will need to help its allies understand the CBW threat. Much U.S. information is acquired through technological means; the United States can gain much from the human intelligence (HUMINT) and cultural awareness of its regional allies (especially relative to terrorism). The United States must exchange this information with allies systematically and comprehensively, taking into account all concerns about sensitive sources and recognizing the potential unreliability of such information. The United States and its allies might disagree on the relative likelihood of elements across the threat spectrum, but the spectrum itself should be an easy basis for the consensus needed to establish a common background for strategy and planning.

Synchronizing Operations. Most allies lag the United States in developing CONOPS for CBW threats. Once allies appreciate such threats, they generally welcome U.S. ideas for reducing force vulnerabilities, especially when those vulnerabilities can be reduced merely by adjusting CONOPS. Because U.S. allies lack many of the protections against CBW threats, the United States needs to field phased sets of CONOPs that cover situations from minimal protection through well-developed protection. For example, the first thing all airfield workers should do after a CW attack is get indoors and turn off the ventilation systems that could bring in contamination from the outside. Those who have protective clothing should then put it on; those without protective clothing may not be as well protected, but they will survive better indoors than out.

It is important to set operational norms. For example, in a serious CBW environment, forces ought not be committed to frontline roles without protective clothing. Having this restriction mandated in combined planning would help allies see that acquiring such clothing is a priority if their forces are to be included in desired operations.

Sharing Protections. The United States leads most of its allies in developing protections against CBW. Some of these have been made available to U.S. allies,[42] but not all of them have, so most allies will have inferior protection or none at all. The United States should share as many of its protections as it can in order to facilitate combined operations and promote the use of similar tactics, techniques, and procedures. DoD also needs to appreciate how leaving allies less well protected may lead to sharp criticism of the United States in the foreign media. Until allied protection comes up to U.S. levels, the United States should balance the protections—e.g., offer active defenses (such as Patriot) for key allied facilities that have little or no passive defenses. Such acts will strengthen combined efforts and help to secure allied involvement in difficult conflicts.

Coordinating Destruction. In targeting adversary CBW supplies, there must be clear coordination of U.S. and allied military planning to reduce duplicated effort, avoid collateral damage, and minimize contamination that would impair future maneuver or other operations. Such concerns would be particularly important if U.S. nuclear weapons were used in attack operations. Because most CBW are stored underground, U.S. nuclear attacks on them would rely on ground bursts, which generate fallout. Cleaning up this fallout would be expensive and time consuming. Thus, nuclear weapons should be used against targets only where fallout can be avoided or under wind conditions that would deposit fallout in less sensitive areas. Also, the destruction of BW could lead to a spread of contaminants that would require U.S. and allied efforts to quarantine or control travel in the

---

[42]There are various reasons for not sharing protections with allies: (1) other allies may have helped to develop a protection and may thus be in a position to disapprove its release; (2) a protection that is understood can be countered, so sharing information about a protection with allies makes it more likely that adversaries will find out the details; and (3) some U.S. protections are just too expensive for allies to purchase in sufficient quantity.

affected areas. Finally, because special forces are often the best way to find and destroy CBW stocks and delivery systems, counter-CBW roles for allied special forces need to be developed.

Cooperating to Prevent and Dissuade. Given how hard it is to prevent the development of CBW and their delivery systems, such a task is almost always best performed as a coalition. It is hard for the United States, even as a superpower, to dictate terms to other countries.

Cooperative prevention requires the United States to share with allies a common understanding of CBW threats and their implications. The United States then needs to reach agreements on appropriate objectives for prevention efforts: Can CBW development be completely stopped? If not, what limits are achievable? What must be done to achieve these objectives? How well can prospective adversaries hide or otherwise conceal their CBW efforts? In this regard, the U.S. experience with Iraq is discouraging and suggests that it will be difficult to prevent CBW developments without some degree of cooperation from the countries under suspicion.

CONCLUSIONS

Adversaries are unquestionably pursuing asymmetric threats to counter U.S. and allied military power. U.S. and allied responses are limited by adversary efforts to conceal these developments, forcing the United States to deal with a very uncertain threat spectrum. Dealing with such threats requires an approach having many dimensions—not least of which are forces and CONOPs to sustain military operations against asymmetric threats and to prevent or counter the surprise and operational disruptions that adversaries will seek to achieve.

Because asymmetric threats are diverse and ever-changing, challenge and response cycle analysis seeks to keep U.S. responses ahead of the cycle's curve. Finally, key capabilities, such as the ability to attribute attacks and control escalation, need more attention from U.S. planners.

Chapter Three

WHAT INFORMATION ARCHITECTURE FOR DEFENSE?

Martin C. Libicki

We live amidst an information revolution, which is to say, a revolution in the capabilities of information technologies and infrastructures. The quality and quantity of the information we receive have greatly increased, but for information to be truly useful, it must improve the quality of our decisions, which, in turn, are judged by the quality of the resultant actions.

Two-thirds of all personal computers and almost all networks and databases are used for business, not recreation. Plausibly, therefore, most decisions that information technology supposedly improves are those made in an organizational context. They result, one way or another, from interactions among people and their machines. As such, the quality of the decisions an organization makes is increasingly related to how it constructs its information systems. These architectures are often faithful reflections of the tacit assumptions about power and purpose held in these organizations. Architecture and organization are linked. An organization's tendencies shape its architecture; its architecture, in turn, helps shape its culture.

The theme of this chapter is how organizations respond to the opportunities and challenges that come from giving everyone access to rapidly increasing amounts of information and corresponding tools, such as analysis and communications. Should sensors be few and commanded from up high, or many and commanded from the trenches? Should information be pushed to the user based on what is deemed necessary, or should users be able to pull information and subscribe to data-flows they feel they need? Can information be arranged and rearranged by users to best fit their intuitive grasp of the matter, or does one display fit all? Will bandwidth constraints limit the information and services users can access, or can a robust menu of alternatives be employed to expand or work around such obstacles? How much should be invested in providing the capability needed to discover information in realms ostensibly far from one's learned domains? Must security be enhanced by limiting what warfighters can know of the battlespace? Should interoperability be good enough to permit users to seamlessly skip from one domain to another, plucking what they need from what they can see? Will users come to feel they own their tools?

WHAT IS ARCHITECTURE?

A common-sense definition of architecture holds it to be the relationship of a system's components to each other. But since people are elements of almost all information architectures, architectures involve human participation. Like any policy structure, architecture reflects power relationships. Unlike many policies, though, it can alter the social underpinnings of power relationships.

The subject of information architecture has more of a future than a past. All organizations have an information architecture, but before there were information systems, the fundamental principles of an organization's information architecture directly reflected (1) command relationships and related functional responsibilities, (2) geographic distribution of personnel, (3) the distribution of clearance levels and related physical access privileges (e.g., keys, safes), and (4) personal relationships. In other words, information architectures were a direct reflection of management and institutional relationships and could be almost completely studied in that context.

The development of the telephone and telegraph altered this formulation by removing some of the geographical impediments to communications. Complex machinery with its sensors and controls possessed its own information architecture, but it was generally internal to the machine itself. Rarely were these machines instruments of an organizationwide architecture. Prior to World War II, the percentage of all workers with phones at their workstations was low, and the ability to control machinery remotely was negligible.

The entry of automated data processing systems in the 1950s created specific work flow paths for certain types of information—e.g., payroll processing and inventory management. Most people accessed computers through special-purpose terminals that limited their interactions to predetermined processes. General access to corporate information was rare except within top levels of management. Indeed, for the first few decades of their existence, computers tended to have a centralizing effect in that they permitted management to harvest much more information about its enterprise.

The development of recognizably modern information architectures began not much more than a quarter-century ago, when sophisticated measurement and control systems were coupled with workstations cheap and robust enough to proliferate outside computer rooms. Widespread personal computing in the workplace is no more than 20 years old; networking, no more than 15; and general Internet connectivity, no more than 10 (universities being the primary exception). The advent of pervasive information systems has so greatly changed the quantity of information available to people that it has changed the quality and hence the nature of the architectures.

Organizational information architectures are still evolving. Office workers in most modern Western organizations have workstations with intranet and Internet access. Most production and paperwork processes are monitored throughout their journey and have their minute-by-minute information logged. These data are widely, but not necessarily generally, available. Corporate America is in the midst of switching from phone and paper to the Internet as its primary link to suppliers, collaborators, and customers.

The next decade or two should bring further complexity and richness in organizational architectures, thanks to several trends:

- Access to both the Internet and organizational intranets through initially low-bandwidth and always-on small-screen mobile devices, cell phones, or cousins of the Palm Pilot VII™.

- Greater systemization of institutional knowledge bases to the point where such knowledge can be analyzed with data mining and other forms of logic processing.

- The growing ubiquity of small sensors and smart radio-frequency bar-coding both in process industries and in public,[1] and in quasi-public settings (e.g., hospitals, schools).

- Further increases in the extraction of usable knowledge about customers and the overall environment from external sources both public (the Web) and quasi-public.

- The granting to suppliers, collaborators, and customers of deeper access into one another's corporate knowledge bases.

The Global Information Grid

DoD's interest in information architecture is clear. Joint Vision 2010 and Joint Vision 2020 are paeans to the importance of information superiority to military superiority. Many of the technologies used to construct information systems were developed by or for DoD. For a long time to come, DoD's information architecture will revolve around mobile devices and sensors of the sort that corporate America is only starting to see. But the levels of automation within DoD vary greatly, partially because capital turnover is slower there; large parts of DoD are more digitized than is corporate America. It is a cliché to note that DoD has no information problems not shared by private enterprise, but there are real differences between the two.

DoD is beginning to contemplate an enterprise architecture for itself. It already has bits and pieces under way within service systems (e.g., the Army's nascent Force XXI initiative and the Navy's IT 21 project), joint internets (NIPRnet for unclassified work, SIPRnet for secret material), and its software suites, the Global Command and Control System (GCCS) and the Global Combat Support System (GCSS). The term *global information grid* (GIG) is often used to describe the anticipated agglomeration, variously known as the global grid (the 1992 JASON study), the system of systems (former Joint Chiefs of Staff [JCS] Vice Chairman Admiral William Owens, but also former

---

[1]The events of September 11, 2001, are likely to sharply increase the use of identification cards, such as proximity cards, for automatic logging of entries and exits.

Army Chief of Staff General Gordon Sullivan), and the battlespace infosphere (U.S. Air Force scientific advisory board).

How far along is DoD on its architecture? DoD typically divides architecture into *systems architecture* (what is "wired" to what), *technical architecture* (how interfaces are defined), and *operational architecture* (how data flow to carry out missions). Systems architecture exists, by definition, at every point, but whether it accords to its specifications is a different matter. In practical terms, the shortfall between how DoD's networks are configured and how they ought to be configured given equipment constraints is probably modest. Technical architecture also exists, but the persistence of legacy systems means that the actual state of interoperability falls far short of where it would be if all systems complied with the joint technical architecture, which, itself, covers only a small fraction of what it ultimately has to.

Operational architecture remains largely undocumented, although there are calls to make it more formal. Systems architects could determine where to make investments if they knew where the data were supposed to flow; technical architects could determine where interoperability was most critical if they understood where information had to be exchanged and understood. So what is the hang-up? Operational architecture sounds easy, but it is about such elemental issues as who talks to whom and which processes need what data— which is to say that it is about power, and power is extremely difficult to negotiate and codify in peacetime. Moreover, the nagging feeling persists that, to echo Von Moltke, no operational architecture will survive contact with the enemy. War generates surprise. Many systems fail in combat; others succeed brilliantly but are too few in number.

Yet all three forms of architecture somehow fail, even in combination, to capture the essence of architecture, the constructs under which people exchange information. Physical architects enter school believing that architecture deals with the arrangement of structural elements; they leave school understanding that its subject is really the arrangement of spaces within which people interact. And so it is for information architecture.

Need There Be Architecture?

One approach to architecture posits a hierarchy of tasks.[2] Physical architecture begins with a statement of requirements (the "bubble drawings" that rough out room arrangements) that is successively refined through architectural drawings, construction plans, subcontracting processes, and bills of material. Information systems are, likewise, successively broken down from task requirements to implementation along three parallel paths: data structures, algorithms, and communications networks.

The Internet was built on entirely different principles, even if few people remember that its first purpose was to share computing power too expensive to duplicate everywhere. Data structures (except for addressing), algorithms, and even routing are now entirely beside the point. The Internet does not *do* anything. It is an infrastructure used by a great many people to do a wide variety of things. The Internet does have a straightforward and explicit set of rules that govern how networks become members and format their message envelopes. Otherwise, if architecture is defined as who-can-say-what-to-whom, the Internet has very little of it.

The Internet works famously, so why bother with architecture at all? Why not simply let everyone make information according to their abilities and take it according to their needs? Why limit the resulting conversation? There are several reasons.

First, the Internet is primarily a transport mechanism and hence only part of an information system. To accomplish specific tasks within specified parameters, organizations have had to impose an information architecture on top of it. Even the research community, where the ideals of the Internet are most fully realized, has architectural elements embedded into its culture, such as how material is published.

Second, the Internet's survival for most of its life has been based on shared norms and the kindness of strangers. As it has opened itself up to literally everyone over the past five years, it has faced tough

---

[2]J. A. Zachman, "A Framework for Information Systems Architecture," reprinted in *IBM Systems Journal*, Vol. 38, No. 2, 1999, pp. 454–470 (originally printed in 1987).

problems in privacy protection, intellectual property rights, spamming, and poor security.

Third, even if the principles of the Internet and World Wide Web are the goal of an information infrastructure, such ideals must be made manifest in a world where truly open organizations are rare. Yet not every organization has an information architecture per se. RAND does not have one for its research, although it does have a culture. RAND's ability to get work done depends on researchers acquiring information from outside the corporation and analyzing it using tools they know very well. In effect, RAND rides on the information architectures of its clients and the research community.

Architecture Follows Culture?

How cultural norms affect people's participation in the information era is a big and well-studied subject. But it helps to point out some general questions that suggest there are large variations in how different cultures use information. Intuition says that cultural factors can help or hurt an organization's use of information systems—especially people's willingness to trade information, seek out potential disquieting knowledge, undertake honest analysis, and base decisions on the results of that analysis. Other factors, such as the tradeoff between horizontal and vertical flows, between public and private credibility, and between oral and written communication, ought to affect information system design as well. Part of what DoD (or any organization) ought to do in developing an enterprisewide information architecture is to examine its own cultural assumptions and the ways in which they may feed into architectural decisions—a process akin to warmup exercises before undertaking a long run. To understand any given culture, one should ask

- Are people more likely to hoard and then trade information than they are to share information based on trust?[3]

- Are people more likely to believe what they get from public sources or what their friends tell them?

---

[3]Frank Fukuyama argues that cultures can be characterized as high- or low-trust. See his *Trust: The Social Virtues and the Creation of Prosperity*, The Free Press, New York, 1995.

- Does more information flow vertically or horizontally? Is vertical collaboration accorded the same weight as horizontal coordination?

- Is information passed via the written word or the spoken word? Which form conveys more authority, granted that this often depends on personal preference?

- Is there a bias for acting and letting the facts flow from the results rather than undertaking analysis before acting?

- Must decisions be justified by facts and arguments, or do authority, experience, and/or charisma suffice? To what extent are formal credentials taken seriously as a source of status?

- Will people seek out knowledge even when it may contradict their earlier judgments—especially publicly offered judgments?

Underlying the premise that information systems based on sound architectures can help an organization is the requirement that an organization be sound and coherently organized. A few test questions to make this determination might be:

- Is the organization in the right line of work? Is it looking to the right customers and solving the right problems? (Solving the wrong problems more efficiently is of only modest benefit.)

- Is the achievement of organizational goals accorded a higher priority than the achievement of any one faction's goals? of personal goals?

- Is honesty accorded respect? Can the organization accept bad news without shooting the messenger or inventing fantasies?

If the answers are affirmative, information and thus a good information architecture can help. DoD seems to score above average on all three questions.

DoD as an Institution in Its Own League

DoD differs from other institutions, so many of the issues raised concerning its architecture may be of less consequence to those other institutions. The differences are many.

DoD is a hierarchical organization that relies on command-and-control (especially in the field) irrespective of the distribution of knowledge, and it is likely to remain so regardless of how technology evolves. Warfighting puts people at personal risk, giving individuals a potential motivation that can be at great odds with their organization's motivations. Militaries are built to engage in contests and to serve the national will. Most other organizations, by contrast, respond to whoever will pay them; most customers are individuals. DoD has multiple layers, each with its own assets and requirements, and each strongly biased toward owning its own information sources.

Because DoD needs to know the whats and wherefores of uncooperative foes, information collection is expensive and problematic. Sensors are expensive, deception is the norm, and militaries are obsessed about information security. Businesspeople at least can rely on the force of law to inhibit mischief by competitors; militaries work in an anarchic milieu and thus cannot.

Because DoD works outdoors, it relies heavily on radio-frequency links, often established in austere regions (e.g., at sea). Nodes are often at risk of destruction; communications is ever subject to jamming, so transmission and reception equipment must be hardened. Bandwidth constraints pinch DoD more than they typically pinch commercial enterprises. Combat communications are often urgent, and many of those who have most need of information have limited attention to give to what they see or even hear.

Finally, DoD cannot rely on outside sources for all of its education or institutional learning. Much of what it teaches has no outside counterpart, at least in this country, and often not anywhere. Bill Joy, the cofounder of Sun Microsystems, once observed that regardless of who you are, most of the smart people in the world work for someone else. DoD can occasionally be the exception to this observation. Most of the people who best understand, say, stealth technologies work for DoD either directly or indirectly. This also means that if the state of the art in areas of DoD's interest is to advance, those areas must be deliberately resourced by DoD itself.

Perhaps the most interesting facet of DoD's unique requirements is its imperative to optimize not efficiency, but adaptability—particularly now, when it is so difficult to make reliable statements about where or against which foe the U.S. military will have to practice its craft next (as September 11 and its aftermath have once again proven). To illustrate this point, Table 3.1 categorizes warfare according to whether mass or precision matters more, and whether the United States gets to fight from standoff range or has to move close in. Every square holds a different form of war, each of which demands different features from DoD's architecture.

For the historic, conventional type of warfare—close-in mass operations—commanders need data from the field to build and share almost-instant situational awareness. This information fosters command dominance, which, in turn, permits its possessors to execute decisions faster than enemies can react. The military, however, requires an even larger quantity of *internal* data to exercise its core competence of conducting highly complex maneuvers. Carrier battle groups, theaterwide air tasking orders, and maneuvers in corps are all examples of how the U.S. military can orchestrate the actions of 10,000 to 100,000 individuals better than any other entity can.

For strategic warfare—standoff mass operations—commanders need a more analytic and synoptic understanding of the enemy's pressure points. One method is to learn how the enemy's economy, political structure, and infrastructures (both military and civilian) are wired so as to be able to identify the nodes. This invariably becomes a large modeling exercise.

For hyperwar (DoD's preferred mode), the most pressing problem is to locate, identify, and track mobile targets so that they may be struck quickly from afar. The important qualities are the ability to scan large battlespaces, sift the few interesting data points from the mass of background, sort the targets of potential by priority, and strike those targets while they are still visible. This search for in-

Table 3.1

A Two-by-Two Categorization of War

	Close In	Standoff
Mass	Conventional conflict	Strategic conflict
Precision	Mud warfare	Hyperwar

formation is akin to finding the classic needle in a haystack—or, because targets continually move, finding the snakes among the worms.

Finally, if despite everything DoD is stuck in mud warfare and working within dense milieus, it needs a precise understanding of its environment so that it can distinguish the malevolent from the irrelevant. A precise situational awareness also permits threat patterns to be perceived.

These are, admittedly, gross generalizations. But they illustrate the wide range of functions that DoD's information architecture must satisfy. They also illustrate the potential folly of building the GIG architecture from the top down. If the U.S. military cannot be sure of when, who, or how it will fight, should not its architecture be optimized less for any specific scenario and more to accommodate the fluidity of a real-time, high-density, rapidly changing and restructuring world?

For instance, is the GIG to be understood as a command, control, and communications (C3) system that ties people to each other (and, incidentally, to some interesting services) or as an intelligence, surveillance, and reconnaissance (ISR) system that uses communications to accommodate a distributed workforce? The two facets ought to be two sides of one coin, but the cultures they support differ greatly. Communicators like to share information; intelligence types tend to hoard it. Communicators want to know who talks to whom; intelligence types want to know what information is fused with what.

Who is the ultimate customer: the White House or the foxhole? The intelligence community has been facing this question since the Cold War ended. Initially, both urgency and the scarcity of good information oriented intelligence to the U.S. president. Now, with the Cold War over and open-source information more available, intelligence oriented to the foxhole makes more sense—but how much, and how fast? This question is felt with great keenness in peace operations. Is the primary point of military operations to generate an outcome consistent with U.S. interests or to serve clients (e.g., those who live in an erstwhile war-torn land)? The answer sets up a broader question: Should such a system be designed to spread information down and around or to filter it up?

The issue of who owns information raises command and control (C2) issues. Ownership duly and dually implies both responsibility and control. But is the responsibility to collect information logically connected to the right to control not only who gets to see the information, but also the form in which it is released? That case is hard to make in the age of the Internet and the Web. It would seem that information should be generally releasable, subject to no-more-than-necessary security constraints, broadly accessible, and formatted in the most interoperable way—which often means with the least amount of unnecessary processing. But can potential users counter the collectors' argument that data cannot possibly be released to the rest of the world without being subjected to thorough and time-consuming analysis?

ELEMENTS OF ARCHITECTURE

In this context, eight categories can be used to describe architectural issues related to information: (1) collection, (2) access, (3) presentation, (4) networking, (5) knowledge maintenance and management, (6) security, (7) interoperability, and (8) integration. Each is discussed in turn.

Collection

How an organization gathers data depends on technical considerations as well as its judgment about what kind of information is needed by whom.

What, for instance, should be the mix between hunters and gatherers? Hunters define information requirements and then collect in accordance with them; their questions are specific, and their tools are often focused and may be used intermittently. Gatherers collect large amounts of data and then thresh through what they have for anomalies, telltale changes, and other interesting tidbits; their tools tend to be general and used continuously. The intelligence community has both types of users. The imagery business tends to be filled with hunters, with tools that are continuously busy (e.g., reconnaissance satellites) and tools that are employed only in discrete missions (such as U-2s). The signals intelligence business tends to be filled with gatherers.

Is information to go up or down the logic tree—the oft-cited path connecting data to information to knowledge, understanding, and wisdom? Some use induction, starting with examples and winding up with generalizations. Others prefer deduction: they start with rules and then exploit them to develop differentiations. The first approach is good for figuring out the enemy's doctrine, the second for distinguishing an enemy from a bystander. Inductors start their postprocessing late in the game; deductors early.

What integration metaphor should be exploited? One approach (and many may be needed) is scan-sift-and-sort, which is particularly useful for engaging mobile targets amidst clutter. Another challenge is building a synoptic picture from the coordination of distributed sensors. Managing by maintaining parameters (e.g., the odds that a district is secure, the likelihood that the enemy will do X under stress) requires that new facts be consistently integrated into old equations.

How are data validated and reconciled? The Army says the village has 100 enemy holed up, the Marines say 50—which number goes in the database? What criteria are used to point users toward one or another estimate? What metrics are used to label facts as being of greater or lesser validity?

For DoD, many of these questions are arising as its GIG becomes more deeply networked and more inundated by sensor data. The greater the bit flow of any one phenomenology, the greater the logic to move from hunting to gathering successively lower-grade ores simply because it can be done. Many of the more intractable problems of warfighting, such as tracking targets in clutter or mobile emitters, are problems of gathering. Issues of data integration and validation arise as the volume of data grows apace and such techniques as cue-filter-pinpointing, automatic sensor coordination, systematic parameter maintenance, and even the computer-aided marriage of scattered knowns and needs all become more feasible.

For DoD, data collection is increasingly an issue of sensor deployment and management rather than, say, human reconnaissance.

For instance, should sensor systems be designed to collect broad knowledge and to cue weapons that then find the target, or should sensors collect knowledge precise and timely enough to guide weapons to their target? As Chapter Four, "Incorporating Information

Technology in Defense Planning," suggests, the choice between man-guided, seeker-guided, and point-guided weapons is not simply one of engineering, but of empowerment as well. A third party given man-guided weapons has to be operationally competent to make use of them. Given seeker-guided weapons, the third party can do what it wants. With point-guided weapons, it will have to depend on those who supply the points and tracks, so if that "who" is the DoD, the United States retains a great deal of leverage over how the weapons are used.

A parallel question is whether DoD should lean toward using a few expensive sensors (such as billion-dollar spy satellites, Aegis radar, Joint Surveillance Target Attack Radar System [JSTARS]) or many cheaper ones (such as micro unmanned aerial vehicles [UAVs]) or disposable unattended ground sensors. If expensive sensors are used, there will be contention over who gets to use their capacity. A system of cheaper but more numerous sensors lets all operators have their own capability, but what happens when there are more sensors than humans can manage? How far can and should the sensors be designed to manage themselves?

Finally, should sensors output (1) raw data, (2) data cleaned up by some automatic and semi-automatic processing, (3) only data that are completely exploited and have passed quality-control tests, or (4) only data that have been fully fused with all other comparable data? How close should the coupling be among sensors, sensor data storage, sensor post-processing, and sensor data display?

Access

Over the last half-century, management attitudes on information have shifted from need-to-know to right-to-know. Many companies, for instance, have found labor unions to be more tractable if workers are shown detailed information on the company's financial performance. As a general rule, the military has lagged on this issue, although DoD is gradually giving people more access to its information both internally and externally.[4] For example, the end of the Cold War reduced many classification levels to Secret.

Many reasons have been offered for limiting information. Two of them—the cost of making legacy systems interoperable, and limited bandwidth—have technical solutions. The security argument is a shibboleth to the extent that almost all career military personnel are cleared to the Secret level; *operational* information is rarely classified higher unless sources and methods are involved, but they can usually be scrubbed out of the data.

That leaves one real reason for restricting information: it might be distracting. DoD has gotten great mileage out of warfighters with modest education by carefully developing a hierarchy of task structures to which operators are closely trained. Information requirements are then carefully generated for these tasks. Unfortunately, the narrow task specialization that pervades the national security establishment (only 1 percent of all the intelligence community's workers are all-source analysts) is increasingly at odds with how information is handled elsewhere: workers are given an increasingly broad view of their task within an organizational context.

Another possible reason is that warfighters would not risk their lives in dire circumstances if they understood how bad things really were. Such a logic may apply to other militaries, but the U.S. military takes public pride in the competence and professionalism of its warfighters, who expect to be told the truth and take responsibility for keeping focused.

What gets shared beyond DoD? Many of the arguments made against sharing data with coalition partners follow the logic above. For longtime partners, such as Britain and Canada, this argument rings hollow. For those who are made coalition members for political rather than military reasons (e.g., Syria in the Gulf War), a certain hypocrisy that separates the promise to share from the actual information supplied can be expected. How much of DoD's information should

---

[4]After September 11, 2001, however, public access to civilian information appears to have been restricted because of the fear that terrorists could use it to prepare attacks; see Ariana Eunjung Cha, "Risks Prompt U.S. to Limit Access to Data," *The Washington Post,* February 24, 2002, p. A1.

be publicly accessible? In the last five years, DoD Websites criticized as too revealing have cut back. "Guarded openness"[5] may permit U.S. forces to acquire the cooperation and facilitate the coordination of third parties, or at least to get their input for intelligent preparation of the battlefield.

Presentation

In many cases, information flows and needs cannot be matched unless they are formatted in some standard way, which, in turn, means they must be encapsulated and categorized according to some semantic and cognitive structure.

The choices information providers face regarding how to forward information to the field are rich ones. E-mail, pop-up alerts, and monitors are examples of push processes; Websites and query capabilities typify pull processes. A mix of the two types of processes is possible. In a guided tour, for instance, a broad request yields a linked set of answers, elements of which can be invoked based either on the user's interests or on abilities made explicit by the user. A more sophisticated version would infer what the user wishes to know and push selected information (both stored content and news as it develops) based on the specific inquiry, past inquiries, and perceived user habits.

Information architects endlessly repeat the mantra "the right information to the right person at the right time," also adding "with the right presentation and the right security." But who is to judge what is "right"? Some analysts believe that military missions and tasks can be decomposed so that the right information pops up as needed, much like an automobile navigation system builds trip routes and flashes left or right arrows as key intersections are encountered. Users of good operating systems, such as that of the Palm Pilot[TM], may delight in having the system bring up the right menu of choices whenever one or another action has taken place. There is an ele-

---

[5]Carefully vetting what is released, but then releasing it without restrictions. See John Arquilla and David Ronfeldt, "Information, Power, and Grand Strategy: In Athena's Camp—Section 2," in John Arquilla and David Ronfeldt (eds.), *In Athena's Camp: Preparing for Conflict in the Information Age*, MR-880-OSLVRC, RAND, 1997, pp. 413–438.

gance to good design; this is why people hire architects and try not to draw their own maps.[6] It helps eliminate clutter; it also permits information providers to draw out implicit narratives from media, such as maps, which only the skilled can navigate. Pushing information at users relieves them from having to make explicit choices. It can be valuable when users are overworked or under stress.

To the user, *how* information is presented is a critical adjunct to what information is presented. Simply by highlighting certain information or certain relationships among data elements, a person or program can push everything else to the cognitive background. In a complex environment, data that are not highlighted might as well not exist. But who decides? "Shared situational awareness" is one thing if it means that everyone can access the same information. But should there be a standard method of presentation? If there is, how easy should it be for users to redraw their own map, so to speak, if they can even do so at all? The Common Operational Picture (a GCCS application that indicates the presence of major units on a battlefield map that everyone shares), for instance, permits certain predesignated layers of information to be highlighted or hidden, but it provides no macro language that lets intelligent users (or their information aides) manipulate data fields of unique importance to them. People do, after all, see information in different ways. Having everyone see everything alike has two advantages: it promotes efficiency in conducting complex operations, and it minimizes complaints such as "How come I can't see this?"

But what if the problem is not complex coordination but complex recognition, as may be the case for modern warfare against an elusive and well-hidden foe? Users might usefully be allowed to peer into the weeds in multiple ways on the theory that it may take only one person's burst of insight to find the elusive foe or make everything fall in place for everyone else. Free play exploits the vast differences in how people perceive the world. Making everyone look at the world the same way may not hurt those whose perspective is sufficiently near the official norm, but it may reduce the contribution of those who think differently. Even if people thought similarly, there

---

[6]See Edward R. Tufte's *Envisioning Information*, Graphics Press, Cheshire, CT, 1990; *The Visual Display of Quantitative Information*, Graphics Press, 1992; or *Visual Explanations: Images and Quantities, Evidence and Narratives*, Graphics Press, 1997.

might still be a point to having them learn how to manipulate their perspective on their own until the world comes into focus. They may learn more about perception and pattern recognition for having discovered as much on their own. In an era of information overload, simply going through the exercise of determining which few features of an environment together tell the story is a valuable lesson in recognizing the essential. So presentation, like its close cousin access, also depends on who decides.

Networking

Access often depends on how much bandwidth is available. In a world of thin 9,600 bits-per-second (bps) lines (the top speed of the new Single Channel Ground and Airborne Radio System [SINCGARS]), warfighters can demand neither imagery nor access to databases. Since compression of one sort or another has to take place at the information source, or at least at the last cache before the fiber ends, the prejudice against user choice is easy to explain away as a technology-driven requirement. But is it?

Mobile and fixed access to the Internet differ sharply. Europeans have taken to mobile phones faster than Americans, in part because they settled on digital cellular standards earlier. The race is on to serve them Internet and Web access through small phone screens, although Palm VII™-like devices may be part of the mix. Because cell phones know where they are (to within roughly 300 m), investors are excited about tailoring content to location (pass an ice cream shop, and a pop-up message about new flavors appears on the screen). Americans, by contrast, are more likely to surf while sitting still; they have more screen space and bandwidth to match. Content cannot be presented the same way to both the desktop and the handset. Presentation for the latter must be more parsimonious, favoring text over images, sound over sight, and voice over tactile input.

The differences in information accessibility for mobile versus immobile users are critical for the U.S. Army. Division XXI, the Army's digital initiative, provides a rich array of information devices from the corps headquarters down to the battalion tactical operations center (TOC) using million bit-per-second connectivity for systems that support intelligence, maneuver control, and fire support.

Beyond the battalion TOC, however, soldiers are linked, at best, at 9,600 bps via an Appliqué—a limited terminal to which some information is pushed and from which certain numbered queries can be sent. If the ability to wield power is enhanced both by being close to the field and by being able to access information, the digitized Army appears to pivot around the battalion TOC commander, who alone has a good enough view of both worlds. Is this what the Army really wants? Is this necessarily the optimal configuration for the sorts of wars the Army is likely to fight? Urban combat, peace operations, and new theories of swarming[7] may demand that control be exercised by company commanders, one full level down. The Marines pivot around the squad and the platoon. Will reifying Army doctrine in the hard-to-change hardware and software of its information systems promote jointness or the ability to carry out combined operations with overseas counterparts?

Perhaps the issue is less bandwidth than how bandwidth scarcity is managed, for there are choices other than limiting the functionality of terminals to fit bandwidth limitations. Appliqués could be full-fledged clients that accommodate reduced bandwidth by squeezing information flows, transmitting images with less clarity, less color, less detail, and/or fewer updates, or even abjuring imagery in favor of symbolic transmission. Or, each radio's capability could be enhanced but bandwidth managed explicitly as a battalion-shared resource, so as to use more bandwidth for each radio but employ explicit contention mechanisms to allocate spectrum.

A similar architectural issue comes from the breakdown between the field headquarters and those back home who have copious access to information. If the major source of battlefield information comes from space, and space information comes in gigabytes, will there be an inevitable shift from the field toward those with sufficient access to see everything coming in from space? How will the nascent shift from space to field-supported UAVs affect this balance?

Traditionally, C2 was the metric for distributing bandwidth. Fat pipes connected the commanders in chief (CINCs) with the United States, and these pipes grew successively, if inconsistently, smaller as they

---

[7]For background, see Sean Edwards, *Swarming on the Battlefield: Past, Present, and Future*, MR-1100-OSD, RAND, 1999.

skittered down the ranks. Actual commands or reports are unlikely to overfill the pipes as much as imagery will, but the demand for imagery is not very correlated with rank. The current thinking tries to take operational architecture (who says what and how much to whom) as its foundation, but the calculations have proven vexing. The STU-3 (a telephone handset for making secure phone calls) was said to be the great weapon of Desert Storm because it allowed direct contact between the Pentagon and the field, and, in many ways, circumvented traditional routes of influence. There may be understandable reluctance to accord a patched-up set of relationships equal status with wiring diagrams on paper.

Knowledge Maintenance and Management

Knowledge tells one how to carry out tasks. But in a military context, knowledge also includes broad estimates of reality (e.g., this village is or is not safe) and operational rules of thumb (e.g., a village with few young men visible is generally a hostile one). In deciding how analytic judgments (such as how safe the village is) are to be maintained, one must decide who will have authority over what variables. If automatic processes rather than people maintain judgments, the choice of which variables are fed in and how becomes important.

In any complex environment, there will be many newly discovered facts, including new events, and parameters that change to reflect those facts. The methods used to feed new facts to parameters (and the algorithms by which new facts are ingested) are thus important. Sensors, for instance, may pick up new jeep tracks, a finding that could be used to update the odds that an adversary is working in the area, the specific equipment the adversary has, perhaps how much equipment, and maybe even the adversary's doctrine for using it (why were no efforts made to hide the tracks?).

Many computer specialists are starting to think about how parameters may be maintained by software agents—i.e., processing components passed among machines to perform functions for their owners. To use a biological metaphor, an agent (for a parameter: in this case, evidence of a country's interest in nuclear weapons) may wander among nodes that have receptors for various kinds of events—say, the hiring of engineers with nuclear specialties, market reports of certain chemical sales, and suspicious travel patterns. A match might cause the agent to emit signals that stimulate other agents to activity (to review where the country is sending its graduate students) or lull others into relative inactivity (giving less weight to the country's acquisition of fertilizer plants).

Agents may be similarly used to generate alerts. News that a pilot has been shot down, for example, may trigger a requirement for local intelligence, spur greater liaison with friendly forces behind the lines, allocate more channels for the pilot's signals, prepare for undertaking search and rescue as well as medical evacuation, and establish stay-away zones for certain operations. Some second-order effects may need to follow automatically (e.g., telling rescue teams which substances the pilot is allergic to).

Engineering a system for agents raises difficult questions. How are they authenticated, made safe for circulation, and kept free from contamination? What access to databases, processor time, and bandwidth are they granted? How explicitly should their logic be documented? Under what circumstances can they trigger other processes, and how can their influence be overridden?

Knowledge management is the search for ways to transfer knowledge. Traditionally, analysis determined the one right way to do things, and that method was then fed to everyone. Although this made sure everyone worked to standards, it stifled initiative, demoted the acquisition of tacit knowledge, and left organizations inflexible to change from the bottom, acquired, in part, through frontline contact with new realities. A contrasting approach would be to liberate everyone to learn the best way to do things for him/herself, but this would lengthen learning curves, retard the diffusion of new knowledge, and lead to problems when skilled workers and engineers retire.

Enterprise architectures are also being asked to support knowledge management—i.e., the art of circulating know-how. Knowledge management was a key factor, for instance, in the U.S. Navy's ability to chase U-boats from the East Coast in 1942.[8] Each commander's

---

[8]See Eliot A. Cohen and John Gooch, *Military Misfortunes*, especially "A Failure to Learn: American Antisubmarine Warfare in 1942," Free Press, New York, 1990, pp. 59–94.

contacts were collected and used to build a database of enemy tactics and successful countertactics. What mechanisms are there to tell those with specific knowledge of problems about acquired knowledge? Writers on knowledge management emphasize the human factors (e.g., trust, random interactions) and the sense that the transfer of tacit knowledge requires physical contact.[9]

Can militarily relevant information be systematically organized? After all, its domain is limited (compared to knowledge as a whole) and routed through well-understood task structures. Much information is generated solely to do specific jobs and can be inculcated through training. Those who repair C-17 engines, for instance, can be handed all the information they need. Nevertheless, modern militaries are continually hiving off more specialized offices, few of which are sufficiently well defined to be exclusively self-contained. Even well-established entities generate new information sources as they wander afield from their original tasking. Also, not every useful data point is contained within the manual; the Web has revealed the power of horizontal communications as a device for getting advice, perspective, and solutions to unique facets of problems. If and as defense systems resemble their commercial counterparts—a clear trend in command, control, communications, computers, intelligence, surveillance, and reconnaissance (C4ISR) equipment but less so elsewhere—a growing share of knowledge on how to manage them will be outside DoD. Finally, open-source intelligence is growing as a percentage of all intelligence. Warfighting is an outside activity often in and among third parties. The ability to ferret information from the environment may come to depend on foraging through a thickening forest of digital data. The ability to harvest such information—regardless of its mixed quality—may provide insights denied to those who abjure such disorganized chatter.

To circulate information intelligently, one needs a way to find where it resides, which gets harder as complexity complicates the task of pigeonholing information into predefined categories. If information is organized in many ways (and much information can only be categorized and catalogued approximately), the possession of a reli-

---

[9]See, for example, Thomas Davenport, *Working Knowledge,* Harvard Business School Press, Boston, MA, 1998; and Nancy Dixon, *Common Knowledge,* Harvard Business School Press, Boston, MA, 2000.

able discovery mechanism is important. Although there are many philosophies for building and maintaining such engines for finding random information (especially machines that can be taught to extract meaning from text), the explicit tagging of a document's subject and key data appears to be growing popular.

Security

Information systems have security architectures that govern

- Who can read from or write to which files (or invoke which processes);

- How legitimate users are authenticated;

- How files and processes are protected from mischief;

- What procedures are used to detect when a system is under attack, respond to limit the damage, and recover functionality when control is restored.

Security's first question is, as always, How much? Systems with insufficient security necessarily depend on the kindness of strangers. But excess security costs money, hassles users, often denies service to the legitimate, and is prone to failure if users react by subverting its rules. Systems that deal with the public (e.g., e-commerce sites) must begin by assuming all users to be legitimate, only rejecting such claims after seeing bad behavior. This rule makes them heir to a flood of messages that are individually benign but collectively choking (e.g., the February 2000 distributed denial-of-service attack). Because DoD systems rarely need open themselves to others, they, presumably, can be locked tight. But collecting information from third parties, winning their cooperation, and coordinating everyone's activities with theirs may sometimes require that at least some military systems become transparent and accessible to those third parties. Barriers will then be needed between those systems and the more closed components of the GIG.

At the second level of protection, the question is one of compartmentation. What topics should be walled off or compartmented? What is the cost of inhibiting the cross-fertilization of ideas? Who decides these questions? Convenience and custom let data owners choose, but is that always best? Should certain types of information have a shelf life, and, if so, by what means can the shelf life be imposed without impeding the interoperability of fleeting data with more conventionally permanent information?

Coerced insecurity creates a third set of questions. What if field operatives with a live tap into the GIG find themselves on the wrong end of an AK-47? Soldiers may be instructed to disable their units prior to capture, but they may not always be able to. Adversaries, unimpressed by the Geneva Convention, can credibly threaten people who shut down their access after capture. Do architects therefore limit what such terminals can access? If so, it is then difficult to see how to develop new warfighting techniques, such as swarming, that require warfighters to be fully and minutely informed about the location, activities, and plans of their colleagues—a prerequisite to tight and time-sensitive coordination of fires and maneuver. Another approach may be to make the GIG's servers sensitive to and thus unwilling to answer people who display the biological indicators of stress that being captured might induce. But might not the stress of combat alone then induce a cutoff of information? And what about giving users alternative passwords (as has been mooted for ATMs)? Will they remember to use them without hesitation? What kind of alternative information can be served up that is realistic enough not to anger the captors and put the captured at risk but that also does not reveal compromising details? How can adversaries be shown deceptive data without our own forces being fooled?

Trust is the fourth question. Should people be vouched for centrally or through intermediaries who presumably know for whom they vouch? Should access to the system by its components be predicated on the diligence with which they defend computers? If so, how can such diligence be effectively measured? Should architecture be transparent so that users can understand it, or opaque so that foes cannot?

Interoperability

Interoperability is needed on several levels. At the bottom is the ability to pass bits physically. Next is syntax, the ability to format bits into discrete manipulable chunks (e.g., TCP/IP, HMTL, JPEG). Its faults notwithstanding, DoD's Joint Technical Architecture has pointed the way for interoperability at the physical and syntactic levels. The invention and widespread acceptance of XML as the markup language has resolved the syntax problem of and thus set the stage for the third level: domain semantic standards—the ability to refer to the things and concepts of the real world in mutually understood ways. DoD has endorsed a clutch of semantic standards for e-commerce, message traffic, and mapping symbology, but many domains have no standards, and others have far too many that conflict with each other. Numerous databases use similar terms in incompatible ways, a problem informed but hardly solved by the ongoing conversion from database schemas to XML schemas. The fourth level deals with process semantics: standard ways to express intentions, plans, options, and preferences so as to support negotiations.

The quest for semantic interoperability has architectural ramifications. Behind every semantic structure is an implicit data model of the world, one that makes some things easier to express and other things harder. How the structures of *human* language influence thought is a long-standing issue in linguistics, with some seeing great influence.[10] Whether similar semantic structures exist for digital data is even less clear. Computers are less flexible than people and are thus more in thrall to their limited vocabulary. But to what extent will people take their cognitive cues from their machines' semantics?

The standards *process* within an organization also reflects the organization's distribution of power. Standards can help consolidate the current GIG, which is composed of stovepipe systems managed by disparate owners. Open systems can also help DoD share information with coalition partners and their systems. Can stocking the GIG with interesting information and useful applications that use standard semantics induce others to pick up such standards for their own interactions? Or, alternatively, will various semantic constructs bubble up, with interoperability generated through explicit negotiation over what terms mean or the implicit use of inference?[11] Should

---

[10]An example is the appendix to George Orwell's *1984*. Also see Steven Pinker, *The Language Instinct*, Harper-Collins, New York, 1995; or Noam Chomsky, *Aspects of the Theory of Syntax*, MIT Press, Cambridge, MA, 1965.

[11]See Tim Berners-Lee, *Weaving the Web*, especially Chapter 13, "Machines and the Web," Harper-Collins, New York, 1999.

there be a common framework for referring to real-world objects, or should there be multiple frameworks, each called out by name?

Interoperability issues arise in great force when coalitions are being formed with partners that can build their own global information systems. How should the architecture of something akin to a NATO integrated system be developed? There are no easy choices. Having the United States and Europe build separate systems and merge them as they mature ensures that end-of-cycle integration will be long and hard. The United States could supply the global components (such as long-lines, satellites, and long-endurance UAVs) and make these the background against which local (and thus often coalition-supplied) components sit. Or the United States could supply an architecture in sufficient detail to make European systems plug-and-play. Both are technically feasible approaches, but the Europeans are unlikely to be happy playing second fiddle. Having the United States and Europe build a NATO architecture together from scratch could delay the U.S. architecture by five to 10 years. Standard, or at least explicit, interfaces in planning the U.S. GIG cannot hurt—regardless of which of these four choices is made.

Can access to DoD's GIG be used to induce third world nations to become allies? Although technical issues may be less daunting in linking systems in this case—DoD will give, third world allies will take—trust issues are more salient. Today's friends may not be friends tomorrow, so the case for giving them deep access is hard to make. What are the terms of the relationship? What will such friends be shown, with what restrictions, and in exchange for what? Should the United States applaud or even seek to induce changes in these partners' information systems (e.g., their forgoing the purchase of potentially competitive C4ISR systems or their adopting an architecture and thus viewpoint similar to DoD's)?

Indeed, how deeply should one nation's military information system penetrate another's? Take Walmart's relationship to Proctor and Gamble, one of its major suppliers. Walmart could have chosen to collect data on its own sales, in-store, and warehouse inventories and then calculate the restocking schedules and hand the resulting orders over to P&G. Instead, it makes intermediate data directly available to P&G and leaves P&G responsible for scheduling production so as to optimize Walmart's inventory of P&G products. In deep partnering relationships, all partners can write to the files of the others—much as several doctors may enter information on a patient who is under the primary care of a specific physician—and can trust imported information enough to automatically fuse it with their own. Partners may contribute to a library of codes and subroutines to be liberally passed around. A further step could be for partners to populate a jointly accessed architecture with applets, servlets, agents, or knowledge rules, each capable of successively transforming raw information. When systems seek mutual intimacy, their success may depend on having a transparent architecture.[12] But all these are explicit policy choices.

Integration

Systems must work together. But designing an architecture to make them functional on day one at the expense of everything else is a recipe for growing obsolescence on day two and beyond. How and when should capabilities be added? Is it better to have everything up on day one, or is it better to introduce capabilities (or at least major components thereof) serially, shaking out the bugs one stage at a time? The second of these, incrementalism, has two problems. First, a tool such as a grammar checker must reach some threshold of capability before it is worth using at all. Switching has costs, and users forced to switch too often will simply balk. Second, incrementalism can lead to a hodgepodge. Legacy features (such as DOS and the four-byte address space of IP, not to mention two-digit years) may be hard to eradicate. Conversely, projects that aim to have everything up all at once force users to wait a long time. Only a third of all complex systems arrive on time, and failure can be devastating. And even success can be accompanied by great weariness and hence a wariness of change, or can mean a structure so finely tuned to today's problems that it resists conversion to tomorrow's. All-at-once complex systems are increasingly ill adapted to a world that is always moving on.

---

[12]For example: to provide targeting guidance to a topside gun on an Italian frigate, data from a British UAV's electro-optical sensor is linked through a U.S. network to readings from Dutch microphones, the data flows being fused with the help of a French-hosted software agent and being compared to a German-provided database of marine templates.

Another key issue is whether users feel the systems are theirs, in the sense of being a tool they understand how to use and apply to their problems. Tools, as often remarked, should feel like a natural extension of the body or mind. Good carpenters or musicians take proprietary and personal interest in the tools they use, up to the point, sometimes, of not allowing others to touch them. Tools that are balky, arbitrary, fussy, and unreliable are less likely to be used and, if forced on people, less likely to be mastered or maintained. Will the GIG be perceived by users as friendly and trustworthy enough to entrust their lives and time to? Will they come to "own" their piece of it, seeing it as something they have control over and therefore will step up to feeding and caring for?

THE NEED TO THINK NOW

Information systems reflect the organizations that buy, run, and embed them in an architecture. The architectures reified in computer and communications devices tend to replicate, with some mix of conscious design and unexamined assumptions, relationships that exist among people. But architectures also have a funny way of molding these relationships. Information systems are a tool of amplification and disenfranchisement and inevitably alter the balance of power in any organization they enter.

In their dawning, computers were strange creatures, each seemingly programmed with its own language and conventions. As computers became standardized in the 1960s around the IBM 360 mainframe, the popular expectation was that they would become instruments of top-down control. Data would be entered at the bottom, collated, organized, drawn upwards, and used to give top-level managers a much finer picture of their enterprise. The autonomy of middle managers, which was based on their possessing knowledge too variegated to be effectively amalgamated, would thus end, as would the workers' freedom of action, which was based on their being able to make their own decisions. Computerization into the 1980s did, indeed, encourage the amalgamation of disparate enterprises into conglomerates managed "by the numbers" alone.

However, when the proliferation of personal computers in the workplace that began some 15 years ago combined with the privatization and rapid spread of the Internet that began in 1992, a revolution from the bottom was sparked. Once again, there is an expansion of approaches and a sense of great change, with considerable disagreement about what these all mean for human contact. Will this prove permanent or temporary? Again, the disenfranchisement of middle management appears imminent. In all this flux, it seems right to empower everyone to search for the new best way or at least the best way for him or her.

It is too early to tell whether this empowerment represents a revolution from which there is no going back or simply the blooming of a thousand flowers before a new reconsolidation. But it is not too early to think clearly about the situation. DoD has had, does have, and will continue to have an information architecture, regardless of whether it knows or admits as much. This architecture is driven in large measure by policy choices; it is not solely a consequence of information technology. These policy choices should be made explicit and maybe open in most cases. Otherwise, DoD may either unconsciously make choices it does not like or subconsciously opt for immediate efficiency over longer-term adaptability.

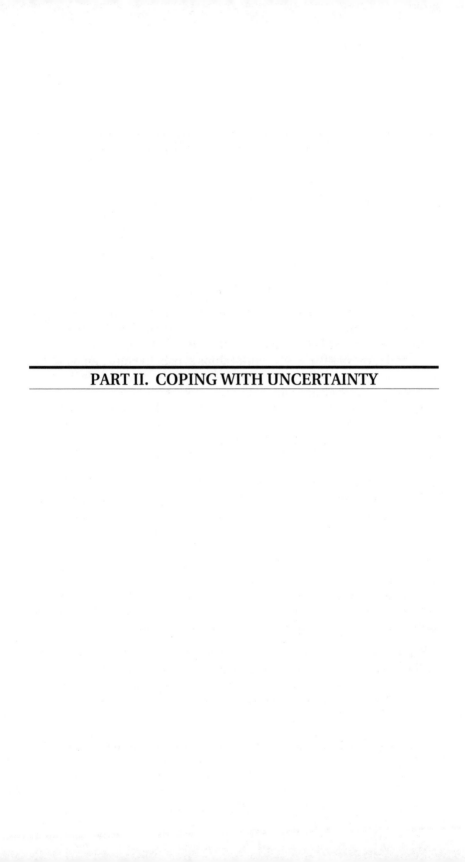

PART II. COPING WITH UNCERTAINTY

INTRODUCTION TO PART II

Defense planning involves a host of factors that interact with each other over a time period often measured in decades. The first M-1 tanks and the first F-16 aircraft entered the force more than 20 years ago, and most of the Navy's capital ships stay in the force for 30 years or more. The longer the time horizon, the harder it is to know the parameters of a decision with any precision. At any point, there are "knowns"—things people know they know; "known unknowns"—things people know they do not know; and "unknown unknowns"—things people do not know they do not know. The deeper the reach into the future, the more the unknown unknowns dominate.

Like all humans, defense planners exercise what is called "bounded rationality."[1] In other words, they lack complete knowledge and anticipation of the consequences of their choices and can think through only a few alternative courses of action on their own. They cannot anticipate future consequences without actively using their imagination, and the imagination of any individual is limited. Faced with complexity and uncertainty, individual planners risk becoming comfortable with familiar mind-sets or illusions. Group decision-making, in turn, risks producing "safe" decisions as members march down the path of "groupthink" to shore up their positions.

No one denies that uncertainty is important and that planners should deal with it as best they can, but the full extent of the problem of uncertainty is not often appreciated—even by planners themselves. Like most of us, planners seldom go back to compare as-

---

[1]A term associated most notably with Nobel-prizewinning economist Herbert Simon.

sumptions they made years ago with what actually happened. Instead, they just go on, vaguely aware of having adapted to circumstances but not at all aware of the extent of their adaptation. Large organizations may be even less aware of adaptations that have proven necessary and even less humble when laying plans for the future. This failure to look uncertainty in the face is perhaps less evident now because of the shock September 11's events brought to U.S. foreign policy and defense planning. Everyone is well aware of uncertainty at this point. In the longer run, however, the tendency to sweep it under the rug will reappear. It is, after all, a natural human tendency.

Moreover, rarely will any one defense planner or decisionmaker possess all the kinds of knowledge and experience needed to face uncertainty and still make good choices. The quest for good decisions thus drives planners and decisionmakers to find tools that can help them cope with the many conditions of uncertainty.[2] Fortunately, there are techniques that can help test the robustness of the knowns, put some bounds on the known unknowns, and discover and even illuminate the unknown unknowns.

The first chapter in Part II, Martin Libicki's "Incorporating Information Technology in Defense Planning," starts with the premise that while the future is not knowable, neither is it a complete mystery; a few educated guesses about the future can go a long way to help planners. Even though many decisions, such as those about force levels, can be reversed in the short term, the future matters precisely because of the long shadows cast by decisions about weaponry or research and development (R&D) or precedents that might be set by policy. One good starting point for the analysis is broad trends that *are* discernible, such as demographics and the continuous improvement in information technology. Libicki works through what this trend in technology means for future conventional combat and information warfare. Improvements in information technology, for instance, suggest that high-intensity conventional warfare could entail

---

[2]For more detail, see Aaron Wildavsky, "The Self-Evaluating Organization," *Public Administration Review*, No. 32, September/October, 1972, pp. 295–365. Also see Paul R. Kleindorfer, Howard C. Kunreuther, and Paul J.H. Schoemaker, *Decision Sciences: An Integrative Perspective*, especially Chapter Six, "Group Decision Making," Cambridge University Press, New York, 1993.

feeding copious amounts of sensor-derived information to a common picture, which, in turn, would be used to determine what to shoot at. Moreover, increasing dependence on information technology does not necessarily make information warfare more attractive for an adversary. Indeed, the very multiplication of information sources makes users less vulnerable to attacks on any one source.

Chapter Five, "Uncertainty-Sensitive Planning," by Paul Davis, begins with a method first developed a decade ago for going well beyond conventional wisdom in contemplating the future. It identifies not only a "no-surprises future," but also various types of possible uncertainties, and then develops plans to cover some contingencies explicitly and to hedge against others. The method also emphasizes environment shaping, based on the argument that the future can be shaped to some degree by U.S. actions. Davis combines this idea with the handling of multiple objectives to define a portfolio-management framework for high-level defense planning. He then applies this framework to the problem of developing capabilities for a wide range of political-military scenarios and operational circumstances.

The post–Cold War focus on one or two illustrative planning scenarios for defense decisionmaking is no longer consistent with today's goals of flexibility, adaptiveness, and robustness. Moving toward such goals requires that alternative force postures be evaluated in an explicit "scenario-space framework" wherein their value can be measured by the variety of circumstances in which they would be effective. This approach to capabilities-based planning is sharpened by the discipline of working within a budget. It thus forces choice. The last part of the chapter describes an analytic framework for combining the portfolio-management construct of overall defense planning with the results of capabilities-based analysis and economics.

In Chapter Six, "Planning the Future Military Workforce," Harry Thie addresses manpower, personnel, and training issues. How are personnel managed—directly, through assignments, or indirectly, through incentives (such as compensation)? How are skills to be transmitted and behaviors to be inculcated? How large a force should be raised? What should its grade, skill, and experience composition be? What are the best ways to procure, enter, train, develop, assign, advance, compensate, and remove people? The key manpower issues have shifted with America's changing security circumstances. As America entered World War II, the issue was how to procure a large force immediately. During the Cold War, it was how to manage a large inventory of people with military experience. External events, societal concerns, missions, organization, technology, budget, and demographics, in turn, shape particular subissues: recruiting, training, retaining, promoting, compensating, and retiring. Against this background, Thie inquires about the personnel and training policies that might best achieve a force that is big enough, qualified, stable, experienced, and motivated. Some policy choices can be applied servicewide; others apply to military units or to individuals. The chapter illustrates how both controllable and uncontrollable variables give rise to complexity and conflicts among competing objectives, as well as to potentially unwanted outcomes.

In Chapter Seven, James Hosek describes how during the past 30 years, the experience of an all-volunteer force has led to a remarkable accumulation of knowledge about the importance of personnel quality for military capability, and about the policies for getting, keeping, and managing such a force—what Hosek calls "the soldier of the 21st century." The U.S. military has been at the forefront in recognizing the value of human capital, and RAND has systematically explored alternative policies for efficiently managing human resources. In the future, the value of people and of the knowledge and skills they possess will become even greater. The story of the 21st century soldier is thus not only about understanding why high-quality personnel are vital to the U.S. defense capability and what can be learned from the history of the volunteer force, but also about what considerations are key in the seemingly mundane, yet fundamentally crucial, task of setting personnel management and compensation policies.

The last chapter here is Frank Camm's "Adapting Best Commercial Practices for Defense." Best commercial practices are those that lead to better, faster, and cheaper products in the companies where they exist. DoD can turn to these practices in determining requirements, designing processes, selecting and making use of external sources, and managing ongoing performance. But to identify those practices with potential for DoD use, DoD personnel must systematically compare the department's performance with that of exemplar organizations of all kinds. As DoD thinks about adapting a specific practice, it must remember that the differences between the commercial setting where the practice was observed and the DoD setting where the practice may be used are crucial. Differences in organizational culture, priorities of stakeholders, and the structure of major management systems affect outcomes. Once DoD understands these differences, it can examine the barriers they present and adapt the practice to overcome them for the DoD setting. DoD should then approach the adaptation of a best commercial practice as a variation on organizational change, addressing all issues likely to arise when any new practice enters an organization. From this perspective, DoD will find that *how* it pursues a best commercial practice is often more important to success than *which* practice it pursues.

Chapter Four

INCORPORATING INFORMATION TECHNOLOGY IN DEFENSE PLANNING

Martin C. Libicki

Inherent in the human condition is the fact that although we will live the rest of our lives in the future, every decision we make is based on what we have learned from the past. For defense planners, this is more than a nominal or philosophical conundrum. Those who plan defense programs face the very real possibility that the world in which these programs reach fruition will be different from the one in which they were planned.

This chapter introduces some guidelines for, if not predicting the future correctly, then at least coming closer to a correct prediction than do those who unconsciously assume the future to be equal to the present. We can think logically, but only time will tell how correctly, about the future. This fact is demonstrated by taking something that can be predicted—the information revolution—and thinking through its likely effect on conventional warfare and the extent to which new forms of warfare, such as information warfare, make sense.

MODEST PROPOSITIONS ABOUT THE FUTURE

Those who fear error should avoid forecasting. Many an expert has been famously wrong about prospects of one or another technology. Yet defense planners are called on to make decisions that will depend on the world's state 10, 20, and 30 years out. Undertakings that bear fruit years hence—long-lived investments, promises hard to back out of, self-reinforcing institutions, standards, and visions—are examples of long-range decisions that have yet-to-be-determined outcomes.

Forecasters make mistakes, it is true. But the effort of forecasting is still valuable if it makes *explicit* statements about the future that are closer to reality than the *implicit* assumptions that too often guide long-term policies. But how is this to be done? Naive forecasters are heir to three clichés: that change is linear, that the pace of change is accelerating, and that complexity is thus increasing.

Not all trends run forever. The rapid progress that characterized aerospace, from Kitty Hawk to the moon landing, was universally expected to continue; it was commonplace for equipment deemed revolutionary upon its introduction to be scorned as obsolete 10 years later. Yet this was not what happened. People did not have an exceptional need for great speed, and by the late 1960s there were few radical technologies that had not yet been discovered. So progress slowed down. The SR-71, the F-15, the Boeing 747, the Concorde, and the Saturn may have been surpassed, but not by very much even *30 years later*.[1] Yet *technical* progress made through 1970 still echoes in terms of *social* and *economic* changes. Pacific air travel, for example, still doubles every seven years because cheaper, faster travel has fostered global institutions and linkages that, in turn, drive the demand for more travel.

Information technology has now become hot, but it is easy to forget what has cooled in the meantime. Today's office environment would be unrecognizable to someone arriving fresh from 1979, but many of the computer systems that most affect our lives—for business management, financial transactions, process control, and transportation scheduling—have been around for twice as long. Indeed, in many ways, overall change may be decelerating. Boomers born in the 1950s and 1960s had a different childhood than their kids are having, but the differences between boomers and their parents are greater— whether measured by income, education, transportation, mass media, or the likelihood of reaching age 60. And the social impact of the

---

[1]The same can be said for plastics (see *The Graduate*, 1968). Every bulk plastic in use today had already been invented by then. Within 10 years, growth rates in demand had fallen from 10 percent to 3–4 percent—just slightly faster than the overall economy.

birth control pill, introduced in 1963, has yet to be exceeded by anything in biotech.

The reason the past often appears simpler than the present is that great issues, once resolved, lose their complexities. In some ways, life is simpler now. Today's personal computers are easier to use than those of the mid-1980s, which, in turn, were far simpler than those of the mid-1970s. Automatic transmissions are simpler than stick shifts. Airline schedules are easier to understand than train schedules.

Having shed the clichés of naive forecasters, the next step is to wring as much as possible from domains where the future is clear, only then moving to the speculative. A fruitful path from easy to hard starts with demography and works through technology, the environment, and economics before chancing the social and political realms. Such a flow follows causality. Technology changes society, but society can only modestly alter the vector of technology. After all, technology must obey physical law.

Demography is a good place to harvest the unexpected from the inevitable. Clearly, for instance, the number of 30-year-olds in the year 2025 cannot exceed the number of 8-year-olds alive today (2003). Better yet, because most 8-year-olds have a high likelihood of reaching 30, and most will mature in the country where they are born, the number of 30-year-olds in 2025 can be forecast with some confidence. This simple generalization suggests that greater Europe, which had four times the population of the Middle East in 1978, will have fewer 30-year-olds come 2025. Even if the long-standing birth dearth in Europe and Japan ends, the size of the productive age group will shrink unless there are large immigration flows—inconceivable in Japan, and possible only at the expense of great change in Europe.

In *technology*, the most fundamental theme over the past 25 years has been the shift from ever-larger to ever-smaller as the driver of change. Progress used to mean size: world-scale factories to serve global markets, taller buildings, heavier supertankers, wider roads, longer runways, gigantic rockets, and multimegaton warheads. Circa 1975, energy shortages, pollution, integrated circuits, and scanning tunneling microscopes heralded a new direction. Today's new factories, buildings, supertankers, roads, runways, rockets, and warheads are not particularly larger than they were 25 years ago. Progress since then has come from the ability to engineer features and to control defects at the micro scale: microelectronics, microbiology, and micro-electromechanical systems (MEMSs).

Microelectronics—measured via processor speeds, communications throughput, and storage capacity, all now doubling every two years or faster—should continue to make progress. Personal devices will continue to be the prime beneficiary, especially with improvements in untethered energy sources: efficient batteries, miniature fuel cells, and photovoltaic devices. Major appliances may soon be network-ready right out of the box, perhaps even looking to link to any network they can find.

As for microbiology, with the human gene now being read and its mapping into folded proteins to follow, scientists are learning a great deal about how life works, how life fails, and the pathogenic and genetic correlates of disease. Easier and earlier disease detection will yield more effective treatments. Research on the human stem cell suggests that organs for transplant will be grown rather than acquired. Such techniques are close to what human cloning requires, making it a near-certain event.

Microstructures are apt to proliferate and become more useful. MEMSs, whose structural features are similar in scale to prior-generation electronic chips, are useful for detecting movement as well as subtle visual, thermal, acoustic, and biochemical features of the environment. Microwatt transmissions from small devices have been demonstrated. So have very small combustion chambers that yield power devices with 10 times the energy density of batteries.

All of these technologies can be used in sensors that have potential military applications: small cheap microphones, electro-optical charge-coupled devices (CCDs), biochemical detectors, and pocket radars for security, biomedical, and controller applications. Sensors the size of pennies may be littered across the battlefield, coupled with MEMS-aided transmitter-receivers that can operate in a remote area for weeks or months. Biosensors on chips or natural sensors on insects may find suspicious chemicals in the air or on surfaces. This confluence suggests that sensors will be key to what tomorrow brings.

Technological vectors have underlying causes. The ability to scale up physical devices reflected steady improvement in knowledge, which, at some point, reached diminishing returns. Nothing so important, one is tempted to conclude, is likely to be realized from macro-scale technologies. No such diminishing returns are apparent from the trends toward miniaturization. Cheap electronics, for instance, fed a global demand for communications, which spurred the launch of communications satellites, which faced a primary constraint of spectrum, which is being relieved through techniques such as beam forming and phased array antennae, which led to a secondary constraint of power radiation, which is spurring the next generation of 25-kW satellites. If technology favors small things, it will favor many of them, and the problem of controlling multitudes will loom. With only a dim prospect of radical advances in the writing and debugging of software, complexity theory, which posits that the right rules can induce complex behavior, can prove its value for simulation and control.

REAL REVOLUTIONS ON THE PHYSICAL BATTLEFIELD

So are there fundamental changes under way in warfare? And, if so, what are their essential characteristics and limits? In 1978, Under Secretary of Defense William Perry noted that DoD would very soon have the ability to see everything of interest on the battlefield, hit everything that could be seen, and kill everything that could be hit.[2] "Very soon" always has to be taken with a grain of salt, but Perry *was* on to something important.

Hitting What Can Be Seen

What does precision mean? Although a tank within 3 km of its target is a precise weapon, attention has rightfully focused on the precision guided munitions (PGMs), which come in three basic types, distinctions among which show how information technology may influence warfare.

---

[2]From Philip Morrison and Paul F. Walker, "A New Strategy for Military Spending," *Scientific American*, Vol. 239, No. 4, October 1978, pp. 48–61. For another early treatment, see "The New Defense Posture: Missiles, Missiles, Missiles," *Business Week*, August 11, 1980, pp. 76–81.

Man-guided PGMs require that the targeter be within visual range and thus a few kilometers of the target. Examples include the TOW (tube-launched, optically tracked, wire-guided) antitank missile, and laser-guided artillery shells and bombs (which date from the end of the Vietnam War). Although the reliability of the PGMs is usually good, their accuracy is only as good as the targeter (who can be distracted by being shot at).

Seeker-guided PGMs find targets using their own sensors. Early types included radar-guided anti-aircraft missiles, heat-seeking missiles, and acoustic torpedoes. The United States has PGMs for acquiring and tracking many types of signatures, and these weapons can usually be fired from standoff ranges. But only so much sensor capability can be put in a small package, and miniaturization that exceeds what is commercial practice tends to be costly. As a result, PGMs are expensive and thus, under current doctrine, available only for use against high-value targets.

Point-guided PGMs, directed to a specific location in real space, include ballistic missiles that rely on inertial guidance, terrain-following cruise missiles, and, more recently, PGMs guided to a specific latitude and longitude by reference to global positioning system (GPS) signals (the Tomahawk [Block IV] cruise missile and the Joint Direct Attack Munition [JDAM]). DoD supposedly lacks munitions that go to a moving point on a map, but there is no technical reason why they cannot be produced. It helps that the United States is working hard to map every object to within 5 or 10 m in absolute coordinates and 1 m in relative coordinates. GPS satellites make it possible for a receiver to know its location to within 18 m, and far closer relative to reference points. If the locations of the target and the PGM seeker are known, the seeker's course can be programmed so that it hits the target.

Why belabor these distinctions? Because they have everything to do with where the "smarts" must reside within the system. Does the sensor go in with the targeter, inside the weapon, or remain external? Giving PGMs their own sensors makes them more robust and shortens the sensor-to-weapon loop. But with limited sensor capability, thanks to cost and carriage factors, they are more vulnerable to deception and have difficulties acquiring targets at long range. The use of off-board sensors to generate target tracks not only provides improved range, tracking, and identification, but also complicates strategies for PGM deception. But point-guided PGMs need a reliable link to both sensor information and the overall command-and-control (C2) system.

Ironically, this technical disadvantage—the need for a reliable link—has political advantages. For instance, the United States supplied surface-to-air missiles (SAMs) to the Afghan rebels in the 1980s and, by doing so, lost control over them. When the Soviets left, the United States started worrying that the SAMs would appear as terrorist weapons.[3] Had these weapons needed externally generated flight track information to work, the United States could have removed this information to devalue them. With self-contained PGMs, power rests with the operator; with point-guided PGMs, it rests with those who control the intelligence system. PGMs, notably point-guided PGMs, also shift the locus of power internally. It is a simple fact of war that if one can kill everything one can see, it pays to see as much as possible of the other side and, equally important, to keep oneself hidden. This ability to seek and to hide, more than the ability to mobilize forces and deploy them into battle, determines outcomes, and thus determines which job contributes more to military outcomes. Here is an application of exponentiation. The existence of precision weapons creates a need for precision information.

The process of seeing is transformed by the growing profusion of sensors in space, on aircraft both manned and unmanned, on and under water, and on the ground. The first effect of using many sensors rather than relying on one super-sensor is the potential for great flexibility in deployment. A penetrating aircraft can survive if it flies below radar, but if microphones are placed under the aircraft's probable path, defenders can detect where the aircraft was flying and perhaps even track it. Flexibility permits one to adapt to the operational challenge of conflict. If the nature of conflict and of the enemy changes, sensors ought to change as well. The variety of sensors becoming available makes it more likely that the battlefield can be made so transparent that the first part of Bill Perry's vision can be realized. Yet transparency will vary greatly. On water and in the

---

[3]The SAM aimed at a commercial airplane flight out of Kenya (November 2002) was actually a Russian model.

desert, nothing large can be hidden for long; on plains and chaparral, some cover is available. Forest and jungle, and finally cities, are progressively more opaque. But in cities, the searching, while more difficult in some aspects thanks to greater cover and the presence of civilians, can be partly accomplished by friendly residents who supply eyes to do much of the work.

The second effect of quantity is that it has its own quality. DoD has many sensors that can illuminate the battlefield with a high degree of precision. Satellites in low earth orbit can take very accurate photographs, conduct strategic reconnaissance, and chart static formations, but they cannot track and target moving objects. If acuity requirements can be forsworn, the purchase and use of many satellites would permit continual, perhaps continuous, target tracking from space. And unmanned aerial vehicles (UAVs) can provide both accuracy and continuity. The Clementine spacecraft, launched by the U.S. Naval Research Laboratory (NRL), proves that many good sensors can be placed on a $50-million satellite. In theory, hundreds of cheap satellites could, along with UAVs, provide continuous coverage for spotting and tracking fleeting targets, at least under favorable weather and lighting conditions.

Another effect of using many small sensors (and one that may ultimately prove to be the most decisive factor) is that it offers better survivability. Having many small sensors rather than a few large ones lessens sensor vulnerability as would-be foes become able to see the battlespace better—an example of how two-sided change carries far different implications than does one-sided change. JSTARS (Joint Surveillance and Target Attack Radar System) and AWACS (Airborne Warning and Control System) are extremely capable sensors, easily the best in their class. But both are mounted on large and not terribly stealthy aircraft. They survive by flying behind front lines, which works only until enemy missiles can range hundreds of kilometers, or enemy shooters can penetrate front lines in the air or on the ground.

A constellation of UAVs would be more able to survive. An individual UAV is not as capable as either of the two aircraft, but UAVs could collectively illuminate the skies. UAV suites include the electro-optical, infrared, synthetic aperture radar, passive millimeter wave, and light detection and ranging sensors. Similarly, although an Aegis cruiser can see surface targets tens of kilometers away and air targets perhaps ten times farther, it is, compared to aircraft, even less stealthy, more complex, and costlier, and it may some day compete with buoy-hosted sensors that individually are less capable but collectively could be less vulnerable. Ground sensors—microphones, remote cameras, and other sensors that can measure seismic, gravitational, biochemical, or magnetic phenomena—may be the ultimate in distributed searching. Some of the detectors coming out of the medical field are small, precise, and intelligent. Ground sensors in development are expensive, but commercial technology suggests that far lower costs are feasible. The wholesale cost of a PC-mounted camera is, for example, about $10; the wholesale cost of a microphone is well below that of its batteries.

The fourth effect of using many sensors is that it puts a premium on data coordination, correlation, and fusion. One sensor may excel at locating an object but not at identifying it. Another may be able to distinguish whether an object is a pickup truck or a tank but not be able to find the object precisely. Using different sensors not only reduces the uncertainty of where the object is, but also helps identify it more confidently. With the importance of sensor coordination across not only phenomenologies but also media, there is no good alternative to thinking about battlefield illumination in a joint context. Jointness is not simply a matter of warfighters with different-color uniforms working together; it now includes asking their machines—which are a good deal more finicky and far less clever—to do so.

If one can see from afar, why shoot from up close? Targets can be hit from 20 km with air-launched munitions, unattended remote-controlled weapons, or pop-up, or even shoot-and-scoot, platforms that are hard to shoot back at. Targets can be hit from 200 km with weapons such as the Army's Tactical Missile System (ATACM), stealth aircraft, and UCAVs; and they can be hit from 2,000 km with ballistic and cruise missiles. Are PGMs too expensive for most warfare tasks? Today's cruise missile costs $600,000. The United States fought the Vietnam War as a war of attrition (wisely or not), spending $1.2 to $1.5 million to kill each enemy soldier. If, as is typical in aerospace manufacturing, each doubling of quantity lowers unit costs by 20 percent, cruise missiles purchased at the rate at which enemy soldiers were killed in that war would cost $100,000 to $200,000 each. Using even expensive weapons to kill three people around a campfire hardly adds to war's costs. Reaching farther than the enemy can reach back is a comparative advantage even—especially—in a perfectly transparent world. And the ability to build long-range propulsion systems is likely to be something the United States and its allies can do well and likely adversaries cannot.

The need for standoff range illustrates today's strategic asymmetry between the United States and its likely opponents. In a slugfest where dollar is traded for dollar, the United States will come out ahead—it can expect to enjoy ten, and more typically, one hundred times more gross national product (GNP) than any of its likely opponents for a long time to come. But if the United States finds itself trading life for life, it will lose.

From Contingency to Necessity

What is suggested when one puts sensors and weapons together is that modern militaries should wage war by using sensors to find targets and using PGMs to prosecute them. But *should* does not imply *will*. The United States and its allies can also go to war in the old-fashioned way—mobilizing force against force—and still do fairly well, as Desert Storm illustrated. But for how long? Which is to say, how great a divergence can arise between what technology promises and what its users grasp?

In Desert Storm, the coalition went to war against Saddam Hussein, an enemy who was fairly blind to what information technology could do. Previous RMAs (such as the dreadnought, blitzkrieg, and nuclear weapons) were built on items not found at local stores, but the current RMA is based on what comes from commercial sources as well as what comes from military labs. What if an adversary opened a checkbook and bought PGMs from the French or the Russians; UAVs made by any of 20 countries, plus digital cameras or digital video-cameras (particularly after the successful advent of high-definition television with its thousand-line resolution) to put on them; space-based imagery, terrain data, and software to meld the two into fly-through quality virtual reality sets; digital video disks (today's 4.7 gigabyte drives can hold an image of all of Yugoslavia accurate to 2 m); portable personal computers; palmtop cellular phones; access to global communications; GPS receivers-on-a-chip; and night-vision goggles—all to provide a fine ground-level complement?

Now take Desert Storm and run it against this enemy, which, armed with these information technology tools, is far more sophisticated than Iraq was. The coalition did three big things to win in Desert Storm: ship in a mountain of material, take out Iraq's C2 capability, and run free over the battlefield, first in bombers and then in armor. The same war fought the same way against a sophisticated adversary—maybe not rich but smart enough to wire itself up in advance—may work poorly, for the following reasons.

First, having to ship in a mountain of material is a recipe for disaster, because most of the elements of the logistics infrastructure—ports, bridges, ships, airlifters, and logistics piles—are highly vulnerable and poorly hidden. Logistics can be attacked by volleys of PGMs.

Second, the coalition could cut Iraq's ability to talk because Iraq used centralized systems such as mainframe computers and central office switches. The world today is moving toward cellular phones and local area networks (LANs), a more distributed architecture and one far harder to knock out.

Third, although maneuvering is more attractive than sitting and dying, maneuver entails moving, and moving disturbs an environment, creating signature and thus making one a target for destruction. Walking into Desert Storm II against a sophisticated enemy could mean a great deal of trouble—and this is without even considering weapons of mass destruction (WMD) being used against massed forces.

This raises the question of platforms—a question that is an unintended but logical result of the information revolution. Today, platforms rule: the Air Force is built around aircraft; the Navy, around ships; and four of the five Army combat branches (artillery, tanks, air cavalry, and air defense), around platforms. Platforms have grown more capable, but only by also growing more complex and costly. As they become more costly, fewer are bought; with fewer in the inventory, owners want them better protected. Self-defense systems are thus needed, raising costs further. As the number of acquisition programs under way declines, each community in DoD becomes more desperate to get its requirements adopted in the new platforms—which retards the acquisition cycle, meaning that fewer can be started at any one time—hence, two vicious circles. Norm Augustine, before becoming CEO of Lockheed-Martin, observed that current trends would leave the U.S. military with one aircraft by the middle of the next century: an aircraft flown three days by the Navy, three days by the Air Force, and on Sundays by the Marines.[4] By contrast, UAVs can be cheaper for owners to replace than for adversaries to shoot down.

Distributed sensors and weapons that are redundant and overlapping are not worth risking lives for, because they are built on civilian specifications and thus benefit from great economies of scale. Although it is harder to deal with a mosaic of smaller pictures than with one big one, only computer power stands in the way of converting the one into the other, and computer power is getting cheaper every day.

The Coming Architecture of Military Organization

Information technology suggests that it may be logical to convert from a platform-based to a knowledge-based military (see Figure 4.1). In the former, operators, local sensors, weapons, and self-protection are all bundled as platforms that work together but are each essentially an autonomous fighting unit. They are given intelligence, but once in combat they usually work with data they collect themselves.

In a knowledge-based military, fused data from networked sensors go into creating a shared knowledge base of the battlefield. All of the battlefield appears in low resolution, and some parts of it appear in high resolution; the two views come in and out of focus as need dictates. Such knowledge, in turn, feeds the weapons, because it generates the targets and tracks they are aimed against.

This architecture permits the separation of information and operations, so those who find the target need not be those with the trigger. Such a separation offers opportunities to build vertical coalitions, in which the United States supplies to local allies information they can use to conduct a war. Why build such coalitions? First of all, they

---

[4]Norman R. Augustine, *Augustine's Laws and Major System Development Programs* (rev. and enl. ed.), American Institute of Aeronautics and Astronautics, New York, 1983.

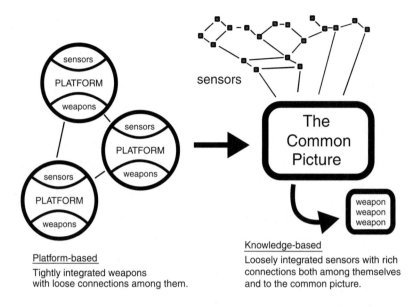

sensors

PLATFORM

weapons

sensors

PLATFORM

weapons

sensors

PLATFORM

weapons

sensors

The Common Picture

weapon
weapon
weapon

Platform-based

Tightly integrated weapons
with loose connections among them.

Knowledge-based

Loosely integrated sensors with rich
connections both among themselves
and to the common picture.

Figure 4.1—The Move from Platform-Based to Knowledge-Based Warfare

would enable the United States to avoid some of the many disadvantages associated with its going to war. For example, the large logistics infrastructures its force structure requires are, as noted, vulnerable, and the large fingerprints left by U.S. operations often work against its political interests. Moreover, if the United States can outfit its friends with PGMs (some have them already), and then provide the requisite information on targets and other enemy dispositions, the friends could prevail in what otherwise would be an evenly matched contest. As an illustration of how this would work, replace "weapons" (lower right corner) with "friends" in Figure 4.1. The United States gives its friends the common picture.

Vertical coalitions also offer other opportunities for altering the nature of the U.S. role and presence. During the Bosnian conflict, NATO was eager to bring Serbians to the bargaining table, but the Serbians would not quit as long as they believed they were militarily superior to the Bosnian and Croatian forces. By presenting the latter with a usable picture of the battlefield, NATO could have tipped the balance against Serbia without setting foot in the Balkans.

In the 1970s, as Egyptian and Israeli forces disengaged, the Sinai was wired to give both sides early warning of an invasion. In the future, DoD could fashion technology to generate not only early warning, but targeting information as well, creating an effective no-man's-land between the two combatants. Violators would show up as targets, putting them at immediate risk.

Information can be the glue behind security arrangements. Countries joining NATO could get a jump-start on interoperability if their C4ISR (command, control, communications, computers, intelligence, surveillance, and reconnaissance) infrastructures and NATO's were compatible beforehand. Were, for instance, Poland and its border areas well illuminated, Poles could feel better about their security without necessarily having to arm themselves heavily or see large numbers of troops deployed on their soil. Information can reassure friends of the United States who eye each other with suspicion. Were Asia better illuminated, each nation could justifiably feel confident that it could see something coming or conclude that nothing was. Belligerence could be further dampened if access to such illumination depended on how each nation behaved and thus postured its military.

The ability to flood the battlefield in lights also carries great implications for force structure. DoD has traditionally scaled its forces for warfare according to enemy strength. But what if the real question is what it takes to illuminate the battlefield, and then how many weapons it takes to shoot the foes? Most of the sensing infrastructure, notably satellites, is not expended but, rather, an investment. Expendable sensors ought to be cheap. Munitions, if bought in quantity, are also cheap; at the height of the 1980s buildup, PGM procurement accounted for only one of every 40 defense dollars. As for platforms and their units—the traditional metric of power—their job would be to haul sensors and weapons closer to the battlefield. Costs, as it turns out, would depend little on how many enemies exist, or how many tanks, planes, and soldiers enemies have. Instead, they would more likely depend on an adversary's sophistication and experience at deception; these two factors would indicate how much redundancy is needed in sensors and weapons.

Conventional War, Hyperwar, and Mud Warfare

Traditional warfare à la Desert Storm, hyperwar, and mud warfare place fundamentally different demands on military information systems because each has its own set of problems that information must be used to solve. To generalize, in traditional combat, what and (broadly speaking) where the enemy is are known. In this case, information systems need to generate data to provide situational awareness to operators. Complexity must be mastered to conduct large operations, and speed helps because it permits action before the adversary can react.

Conventional warfare pits superior force against force. The new logic of warfare, at least for the United States, is to scan the battlefield, sift through fields of data looking for targets, sort them by priority, and then strike those worth hitting. This approach has broad potential for stopping an approaching military and then wearing it down so that more-traditional combat approaches can be used to eventually push it back by successively occupying territory. In some cases, land occupation may not be necessary. If it is, successive attrition makes the job far easier—and, as noted, land forces need not wear U.S. uniforms.[5] Even in nonlinear combat, the ability to illuminate the battlefield can inhibit the enemy from massing forces and thereby from carrying out operations that require doing so. Since everyone makes mistakes, the ability to spot and exploit those mistakes quickly enough permits one to take advantage of them. It may be possible to know which locations the enemy is paying no attention to and thus where friendly forces can operate. Illumination allows supplies to be interdicted more successfully and permits the battlefield to be divided into smaller and smaller cells, each of which can then be attacked.

This capability is a goal and, as NATO operations in Kosovo imply, not yet a reality. Post-war analyses suggest that military assets were hidden in forests and villages and were not easily detected if they

---

[5]This presumes that the interests of the United States and its allies are sufficiently similar. Such is not always the case, as Operation Anaconda revealed. The United States was far more interested in destroying Al Qaeda than its Afghan allies were.

were not moving at the time. That noted, rendering them immobile might have been half the battle won. Unfortunately for the United States, it is precisely the prospects of such warfare that may compel adversaries to think of war in other terms—an example of how innovation for one can spark counterinnovation for others.

One response, termed mud warfare, is likely to be characterized by operating in dense environments, hiding in clutter, wielding civilian-looking material, taking hostages, and using terrorism. Mud warfighters have to learn what to look for and then where to look. Information plus training should prepare warfighters to distinguish patterns of hostile activity from everyday backgrounds. They must know where to intervene quickly when order is tipping over to chaos or enemy control. Because mud warfare features small unit operations, the locus of command is best moved down.

In hyperwar, warfighters know what to look for but not exactly where to find it. Complexity is associated with picking high-value targets from the clutter. Speed is necessary to track and engage such targets while they are visible. The availability of global information and the ability to bring any and all weapons within an ever-larger radius into simultaneous play tend to move command up.

Table 4.1 suggests how the three types of warfare affect C4ISR requirements. Paradoxically, while mud warfare appears crude, the information architecture required to conduct it is, in fact, much more complex than that for hyperwar. Such is the ability of future technology to shape competition that, in turn, reshapes the requirement for technology.

Table 4.1

C4ISR Requirements for Conventional War, Hyperwar, and Mud Warfare

	Conventional War	Hyperwar	Mud Warfare
Environment	Knowns	Known unknowns	Unknown unknowns
Purpose	Data/imagery	Information	Understanding
Complexity	Running ops	Finding things	Sensing patterns
Speed	Gain cycle-time edge	Find fleeting targets	Preempt tipping points
Command	Today's mix	Moves up	Moves down

FALSE REVOLUTIONS ON THE VIRTUAL BATTLEFIELD

If the real revolution in information technology lies not in its continual improvement but in the *form* that its improvement takes—distributing processing power into smaller packages and amalgamating it, in turn, into more powerful networks—does war follow commerce into cyberspace, pitting foes against one another for control of this clearly critical high ground? Does this comparison have a basis in tomorrow's reality, much less today's?

The Defense Science Board seems to believe it does:

> The objective of warfare waged against agriculturally-based societies was to gain control over their principal source of wealth: land. . . . The objective of war waged against industrially-based societies was to gain control over their principal source of all wealth: the means of production. . . . The objective of warfare to be waged against information-based societies is to gain control over the principal means for the sustenance of all wealth: the capacity for coordination of socio-economic inter-dependencies. Military campaigns will be organized to cripple the capacity of an information-based society to carry out its information-dependent enterprises.[6]

What Is Information Warfare?

The purpose of information is, was, and always will be to inform decisions; if not, it is just entertainment. Prior to World War II all these decisions were made by people. With the advent of digitized information systems, an increasing share of decisions—choices made among alternative actions—are made by machines. But they are decisions nonetheless.

Because conflict has always involved decisions, information has always been a part of conflict. Information warfare can thus be defined as the actions taken to influence the enemy's decisionmaking processes so that its decisions are bad or too late or good for your side (e.g., deciding to stand down rather than fight). Seen in this light,

---

[6]*Report of the Defense Science Board Task Force on Information Warfare—Defense,* Office of the Under Secretary of Defense for Acquisition and Technology, Washington, DC, November 1996, p. 2-1.

quintessential human activities such as deception, propaganda, and targeting the other side's commanders are hardly new to warfare.

What is new is that many of today's decisions are made using more information, and that information is richer, generally more timely, and often more widely disseminated. At first glance, this tendency supports a belief that information has become a center of gravity for military operations—and, as such, more deserving of attack. Attack methods, it would seem, now merit greater resources. At second glance, however, the logic is a bit odd. It is as if to say that the task of toppling someone sitting on a stool is more likely to call for breaking the stool's legs if they number eight rather than if they number three. Sound strategy requires looking not only at an opponent's *demand* for information but also at its *supply*. The latter is determined by long-term trends in technology, and these trends are not especially conducive to information warfare. The exception is computer warfare: because computers are everywhere and connected, defending them is harder.

To demonstrate as much requires that information warfare be decomposed. Consider the following information flow: Information is gathered by sensors, relayed to decisionmakers through the electromagnetic spectrum, and reaches the command center, where it is entered in a computer for further processing, the results of which inform decisionmakers. Figure 4.2 shows the primary related forms of information warfare: attacks on sensors, electronic warfare, C2 warfare, computer (hacker) warfare, and psychological operations. Note, again, that with the recent exception of the computer, and the half-century exception of the spectrum, none of this is particularly new, especially if sensors are considered today's version of yesterday's cavalry pickets.

What does the future tell us about the efficacy of information warfare? Modern militaries *are* increasing their dependence on the ability to generate and use information gathered and exploited from well over the horizon. But the industrial-era paradigm of concentrating value in a few machines of increasing complexity may have peaked and, with it, the vulnerability of modern systems, even military systems, to information warfare. Again, computer warfare is an exception, one dealt with below.

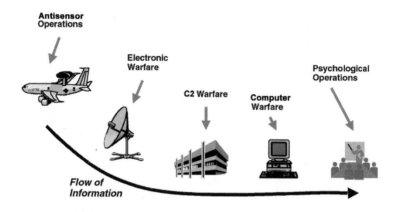

Figure 4.2—Five Types of Information Warfare

Antisensor Operations

The flow of good information into sensors can be disrupted in one of three general ways: (1) destroy the sensor itself, (2) use arcane electronic methods to spoof the sensors into seeing the wrong set of bits, and (3) use cover, concealment, and deception to fool those who interpret these bits into not seeing what is really there (or into seeing what is not there). The second method is specific to electronic equipment (notably radar-based equipment); the other two clearly predate electronics. The primary reason antisensor warfare may be more attractive today is that sensors are more important to warfare than ever before; the growing ability to hit targets at a distance depends on being able to detect and identify them from comparable distances.

The vulnerability of U.S. sensors to attack depends on the attacker. The primary long-range sensors in the U.S. inventory include reconnaissance satellites, aircraft (e.g., JSTARS, AWACS, Rivet Joint, Cobra Ball, the U-2), large radars (e.g., the Aegis system), and UAVs. So far, only Russia can attack a reconnaissance satellite (although China may soon have some capability). Similarly, aircraft and ships can be protected by operating 100 km or more behind the lines and using a protective screen (e.g., F-15s) to keep adversaries at bay.

Twenty years out, the survival of such assets may be dicier, especially against an opponent that determinedly invests to neutralize a decisive source of U.S. advantage. Reconnaissance satellites are expensive, few in number, and fly rather close to the earth. A spruced-up Scud-like rocket on direct ascent may be able to intercept their orbits, and lasers may be employed to blind at least the optical sensors on such spacecraft. Radar-based aircraft are large, hard to maneuver, easy to detect by watching for their energy output, and not at all stealthy. If they have to track deep targets or if front lines are poorly held or defined, they may be vulnerable, particularly to very long range missiles. The Aegis cruiser is at risk because naval fleets are developing increasingly sophisticated defenses against cruise missiles but usually lack the stores to completely counter a sufficiently large attack volley. UAVs are somewhat better protected due to their stealthy characteristics, their ability to fly high, and their small size.

UAVs, however, foretell the coming futility of direct antisensor operations. As electronics get cheaper, the prospect of putting formidable electro-optical capabilities on increasingly smaller and less-expensive UAVs suggests a long-term strategy of employing such sensors in large profusion. Sufficiently cheap but increasingly sensitive UAVs cost less to replace than to destroy. Finally, if unmanned ground sensors approach the low cost of consumer electronics (e.g., microphones, digital cameras) they can provide an even more robust method of collecting signatures.

The fate of electronic spoofing follows a similar logic. It is far easier to spoof a single sensor of known phenomenology (e.g., radar, electro-optical, hyperspectral, passive millimeter wave, acoustic) than to fool a suite of sensors that are in multiple locations and use various phenomenologies to produce readings that can be correlated to develop an increasingly detailed view of the battlespace.

This leaves the opponent with the age-old techniques of making the hostile appear benign (e.g., putting troops in vehicles normally assigned to hospitals) and feeding the preconceptions of adversaries so as to persuade them to classify the normal as threatening. These techniques, in large part, predate technology.

Electronic Warfare

Can messages be stopped, corrupted, or intercepted between nodes in the system? Jamming, message spoofing, and interception—all were the stuff of the so-called Wizard Wars conducted between Britain and Germany in the early 1940s.

One form of jamming works by putting an emitter between two enemy communications devices so that the noise blocks the message. As a general rule, the cost of transmitting a signal of given strength (being largely a matter of power chemistry) may not change very fast. However, the adroit use of digital waveforms, the ability to exploit spread-spectrum and frequency-hopping to hide a narrowband message within a wideband slice of spectrum, and the reduced cost of making receivers are lengthening the edge enjoyed by message senders over message blockers. Tomorrow's phased-array receivers should be able to focus on a transmitter of known location and tune out interference from the side. Thus, if the jammer does not sit between the receiver and the transmitter, it can get in the way only by generating far more power. Phased-array receivers may well become commercial items (the increasingly scarce spectrum can be reused if receivers can be pointed at a specific transmitting antenna to the exclusion of others around it).

Radar jamming still has some life, however, because the source of the signal, as it were, is the reflection off the target, near which the jammer can fly, sail, or stand. The nearness of jammers and targets obviates the line-of-sight defense available to communicators. Radars may instead emit constantly changing pulsed digital waveforms and collect an electronically unique signature, coupling that with mathematical techniques that help separate signal from noise.

As for spoofing and interception, any message as long as a short paragraph may be protected with cryptographic techniques. Transmitters equipped with a private digital key can add a signature tag to a message; this tag can authenticate the transmitter's identity and the fact that the message has not been corrupted.[7] (If the message is

---

[7]The message is mapped into a unique 128-bit hash, which is then processed together with the private key to form a signed block. The receiver takes the public key, reverse-processes the block, extracts the hash, and checks for consistency between the

time-stamped, it cannot be echoed deceptively, either.) Encryption is a well-known defense against eavesdropping. Until recently, encoding everything would have been computationally burdensome, but cheap electronics have ended that problem. Barring some unforeseen mathematical breakthrough or the development of quantum computers of sufficient size (unlikely before 2020), the time required (even by a palmtop) to encode a message will fall—regardless of whether corresponding advances in supercomputers require longer keys to preserve message confidentiality.

In sum, while electronic warfare has always been a seesaw affair, developments over the next 20 years will continue to favor the bits getting through and will generally favor their being read.

Command-and-Control Warfare

The third target for information warfare is the command center itself, using shot and shell to disable the commanders, destroy the command apparatus, or sever the wires and fibers to fielded forces. Electronics are also vulnerable to such soft-kill techniques as microwave bursts and electromagnetic pulses. Apart from the obvious ability to put a precision weapon anywhere within an identified command center, the really new feature of C2 warfare is the modern military's dependence on keeping information systems going—a dependence whose importance, in some respects, even surpasses the importance of keeping individual commanders safe from harm.

But here, again, the vulnerability of command centers may have already peaked because of the proliferation of digital electronics. The traditional architecture of information systems involved large, complex central office switches and mainframe computers. But trends everywhere are toward dispersion. Central office switches are being replaced by routers of decreasing size and increasing number; fixed routing is being replaced by packet switching, thereby permitting every packet to take a different route. Network trees can be replaced by network meshes. Large computers are being replaced by conglom-

---

message and the hash. A time-stamp confounds problems that could arise if the interceptor were to echo the original message back. Similar techniques using private and public keys can be used to exchange other keys that permit more-efficient and harder-to-break symmetric code breaking to be performed.

erations of smaller ones. Fixed storage is being replaced by redundant arrays of independent disks capable of being distributed throughout a network. From late 1993 to late 2002, for instance, the cost of hard storage fell by a factor of 1,000, a drop roughly twice as fast as that for the cost of processors (as measured in dollars per instruction/second). Although the cost of laying a line of fiber is unlikely to decline much, the capacity of that fiber is nearly limitless. If redundant lines are paid for and used, only one line need survive to support all the traffic needed, as long as increasingly sophisticated routing algorithms can redirect traffic at a moment's notice. Finally, dispersed power sources, such as photovoltaics and fuel cells, promise to make information systems at least somewhat independent from the still-vulnerable power grid.

Technology even offers a way to protect the command hierarchy. Given the growing realism of videoconferencing, the utility of whiteboarding[8] tools, and shared access to databases, people no longer need to be physically drawn together for command conferences. This limits the vulnerability of a force's leadership to a lucky strike. And so, the bottom line remains the same. Whereas modern militaries are increasingly dependent on information systems, the technological advances that have made dependence so attractive are also available to protect such systems with increasing confidence.

Psychological Operations

What of decisionmakers themselves? Here the ancient truism comes to the fore: to make adversaries yield, it helps if they are convinced that the benefits of cooperation are high, the cost of resistance is destruction, and that they are operating against the will of the heavens. As a general rule, the dependence of militaries on human factors is no greater than it always has been.

Psychological operations may be defined as the use of information to affect human decisionmaking. They range from attempts to influence the national will, to deception against the opposite commander, to propaganda against opposing forces. The broader term, *psy-*

---

[8]Whiteboarding is the ability to put a word, picture, etc., on a screen that then appears on all screens of all people in a session.

chological warfare, refers to all aspects of combat that affect the willingness of people to fight above and beyond any physical harm that befalls them. Ultimately, however, there is no form of warfare that is not, to one degree or another, psychological warfare.

Some aspects of psychological operations perforce vary with specific circumstances and power relationships (e.g., among politicians, military officers, and military forces). Other aspects reflect pervasive trends. One such trend is the growing openness of societies to external influences—from cable television, direct broadcast television and radio, and the Internet. Over the next 10 years, the proliferation of space-based multimedia broadcast satellites, the continual spread of fiber optic lines, decent language-translation software, the proliferation of remote sensing satellites in commercial hands, and the possibility of agents and bots that can transfer satisfying answers to vaguely worded questions should increase permeability much further.

Will technology make psychological operations more rewarding? Citizens, soldiers, and commanders will be subject to a vast array of data sources, making it harder to cut them off from what the world is saying and to cut the world off from what they are saying and seeing. Further, media dominance by a handful of major networks is moving toward an era of 500-channel television and into Me-TV, where the low cost of creating a video feed and the ability to mix and match sources mean that everyone's news sources are different. The more the potential sources of information cover any one incident (think the random videotaping of the Rodney King incident), the harder it becomes to put out a single effective story line.

The saving grace for the information warrior who wishes to deceive others is still the human tendency to jump to conclusions, willingly consuming supporting evidence, and filtering out everything else. A case in point is Hitler's certainty that the Allies would invade Europe at Calais. Here, too, the evolution of information technology is of little help to tomorrow's information warrior.

The Ghost in the Machine

The most insidious form of information warfare, and the one that has garnered the most media and high-level policy attention, is the ability to get inside information systems in order to render them dysfunctional. If subverted in this way, an information system may work poorly or collapse, permit the entry of corrupted information, or reveal its secrets. Possible hacker entryways include surreptitiously inserting code into the machine at birth (e.g., through deliberately queered circuitry) or later (e.g., viruses), and assuming the identity of an authorized user—or, better yet, a systems administrator—and issuing malicious commands.

For this type of information warfare, cost factors that lead to a proliferation of nodes work against defenders. The more nodes on a system, the more doors for a hacker to try and the more difficult to find the hacker's entryway and where the corruption actually lies. The ability of one node to transfer instructions or control to another permits, among other things, very agile routing around damage, but it also permits vicious viruses, bad bots, and aggravating agents to spread quickly throughout a system.

Clearly, therefore, hacker warfare is more likely to be effective in at least the near future than it has been in the past. But does that mean that hacker warfare can be anything more than a minor annoyance or the source of random damage? That was the case for the April 1999 Chernobyl virus and the October 2001 Code Red Worm, even though both caused hundreds of millions of dollars of damage.

In gauging the effectiveness of future hacker attacks, it is useful to classify information systems into castles and agoras. *Castles* are a nation's critical infrastructures—military C4ISR systems, funds transfer, safety regulation, power plants and similar industrial facilities, telecommunications switching systems, and energy and transportation control points. They are, or should be, generally self-contained units, access to which can and ought to be restricted. *Agoras* are the great consumer marketplaces of cyberspace, in which increased vulnerability to malice, accident, and dysfunction is the price paid for the dense interactions and potential learning experiences that contact with strangers permits. It is as hazardous to use the rules of the agora to govern the castle as it is constricting to enforce the castle's norms on the agora.

In the short run, predicting the course of information security almost requires predicting where the next set of mistakes will be made.

Complexity seems to swing the advantage toward the hackers, who know that finding just a single breach may open the floodgates. But complex systems need not necessarily be insecure. You, the readers, who are several orders of magnitude more complex than any man-made system, are proof of that. No combination of bits that you can read right now could wreak havoc in your operating system. I, the author, have no authority to make you do stupid things. You process these words not as instructions to be obeyed but as data to be analyzed.

Processing inputs as information is the key here. As systems grow more sophisticated, they are likely to become more humanlike. They will be able to absorb data from beyond themselves, filter those data, and analyze them with a sophistication that grows with everything learned—just as humans do. True, critical castle systems can and probably should still be isolated. But the agora systems are fair game. And so, information systems will be heir to the more subtle faults. A computer that analyzes intelligence on a country, for instance, may absorb the content of Web-based newspapers, police reports, crop statistics, tax records, and local bulletin boards to draw conclusions.

These conclusions may, for their part, be influenced by what others—often self-serving and sometimes hostile—post, and computers will have to filter out the chaff to get the nuggets. Learning systems, such as neural nets and knowledge engineering devices, may be corrupted by bad information introduced at an unknown time, the discovery of which may leave administrators wondering how much good learning has to be erased to remove the bad learning. But this is essentially no different from what humans do, and, so far, humans have coped. The result is that hacker activity will express itself not as looming catastrophe, but as the certainty of at least some level of pollution. And pollution is not warfare.

THE LESSON OF SEPTEMBER 11

Peter Schwartz, founder of the Global Business Network, once observed that even futurists consistently underestimate the effects of technological inputs on the course of history.[9] What is underestimated is not the extent of change—i.e., seeing 1, forecasting 2, and realizing 4—but its breadth and depth. Were the problem a question of extent, the fix would be easy: double everything. But insufficient breadth and depth come from not seeing the variety of change, a failure that an overactive imagination cannot easily fix.

The events of September 11 remind us of the inevitability of surprise. Suicide bombers, the use of airplanes to attack symbolic monuments,[10] the anti-American sentiments held by fundamentalist Muslims, and the special animus against the World Trade Center—none of these was particularly new on that day. One prominent futurist who asked what the worst thing a terrorist group could do to America was, was repeatedly told by security experts that it could crash a 747 into the World Trade Center. He thus learned to dismiss this scenario as a cliché. But the event, itself, was still a surprise. Had something of this magnitude taken place in cyberspace rather than in real space, several information warfare gurus would have proclaimed, "I told you so." But they are not right, yet.

The success of the U.S. campaign against the Taliban regime validated, at least in that context, the hopes of believers in the current RMA. While neither the Taliban nor Al Qaeda is assuredly destroyed for all time, precision warfare, carried out in concert with willing if initially less-powerful allies, did in three months what the Soviet Union could not complete in 10 years.

---

[9]Peter Schwartz, *The Art of the Long View: Planning for the Future in an Uncertain World,* Doubleday, New York, 1996.

[10]Several years earlier, French security forces forestalled a plot to launch a jet into the Eiffel Tower.

Chapter Five

UNCERTAINTY-SENSITIVE PLANNING

Paul K. Davis

Consider some of the major strategic surprises that affected national security in past decades.[1] Some of these were negative; some were positive:

- Cuban missile crisis

- Sadat's peace mission to Israel

- Fall of the Shah of Iran and resulting hostage crisis

- Disintegration of the Soviet Union

- Peaceful reunification of Germany

- Iraq's invasion of Kuwait

- East Asian economic collapse of the late 1990s

- India's nuclear testing and Pakistan's response

- Terrorist attacks on the World Trade Center and Pentagon

Now consider some purely military surprises of the past 50 years:

- Torpedoes in U.S. submarines fail to detonate (World War II)

- Early air-to-air radar-guided missiles fail (Vietnam War)

- Egypt launches a surprise attack across the Suez canal (1973)

---

[1]The intelligence community provided what is called "strategic warning" in a few instances (i.e., warning days or weeks before the events).

- Israel's air force is stymied by surprisingly effective SA-6 batteries
- Israel achieves an astounding exchange ratio in air war over Lebanon's Bekka Valley
- Deployment to the Persian Gulf begins a week *after* the attack (Desert Storm, 1990)

These surprises form a long list because they have not been occasional annoyances in a generally predictable world but, rather, quite common. This chapter begins by discussing why addressing uncertainty is so important and difficult. It then discusses analytic methods for dealing with uncertainty in broad, conceptual strategic planning; in doing capability-based analysis of future forces; and in making choices within a budget. Some of these methods are now in use in the Pentagon and elsewhere; others are candidates for future implementation. Resisting the tendency to give short shrift to uncertainty requires both discipline and knowledge of the past. Conscious methodology can help provide some of that discipline.

WHY SO MANY SURPRISES?

Early in World War II, U.S. submarine commanders were horrified as their torpedoes—launched after dangerous approaches—passed harmlessly by their targets. The torpedoes had worked in laboratory testing; their failure in the field was so unexpected that the commanders' reports were initially not believed. In the Vietnam War, early radar-guided air-to-air missiles failed because engagements occurred in circumstances other than those planned for. Faith in the missiles had been so great that most aircraft were designed without backup gun systems. Both of these failures were, in a sense, "merely" technical and analytic, but they had major consequences for the prosecution of war.

Nor have historical surprises all been American. When Egyptian units seized the east bank of the Suez Canal early in the 1973 Yom-Kippur war, the Israeli Air Force was stymied by surprisingly effective SA-6 anti-aircraft batteries. In later years, the Israeli Air Force destroyed scores of Syrian aircraft over the Bekka Valley without losing a single aircraft, thanks to asymmetrically capable command and control (C2). This may not have been a surprise to the Israelis, but it certainly got the attention of militaries worldwide, including that of the Soviet Union, which supplied the Syrians.

In more modern times, there have been different surprises. Even though official U.S. planning scenarios had almost always assumed that U.S. forces would be able to deploy well before the day war would begin, or D-Day, the Desert Storm deployment began six days after D-Day. More recently, in the war over Kosovo, NATO heads of state were reportedly surprised when Slobodan Milosevic was not brought to his knees immediately by NATO's bombing. Their confidence was so great that they prohibited the development of contingency plans involving ground-force operations until late in the campaign. To make things worse, the Yugoslavs did not "play fair," usually keeping their air-defense radars turned off. Destruction of their air defenses thus proved impossible, constraining operations, reducing their effectiveness, and increasing the mass of air forces needed. Serbian military forces dispersed in the woods and emerged from the war with little damage. The United States was badly stretched while prosecuting a one-sided war against a third-rate regional rogue. Ramifications of this unscheduled "small-scale contingency" echoed throughout the entire force structure (particularly for the Air Force, which bore a particularly heavy burden in this conflict).[2]

Why do so many predictions fail and surprises occur? The reasons include the constant competition of measures and countermeasures, the tendency to keep weaknesses out of mind only to have them attacked by the adversary, rather prosaic failures of design or execution, and a failure to appreciate the frictions of war celebrated in the 1832 writings of Clausewitz.[3]

The scientific way to look at uncertainty is to acknowledge that wars and military competitions are "complex adaptive systems," and that, as a result, even small events can and often do have large effects. Further, the "system" is not a constant for which one can prepare

---

[2]As usual, not everyone was equally surprised. Some military leaders were pessimistic from the outset about the effectiveness of bombing conducted with the severe political constraints that applied in the early weeks of the campaign.

[3]Carl von Clausewitz, *On War*, translated by Peter Paret, Everyman's Library, Alfred Knopf, New York, 1993.

straightforwardly. Rather, it includes human beings and organizations that think, behave, and adapt to events in myriad ways.[4] Because of such complications, an accurate prediction of the course of events is sometimes not even feasible.[5] That is, uncertainty is not only ubiquitous and large, but also impossible to get rid of it by merely working hard to do so.

So what do we do about this burden of uncertainty? Do we just wring our hands? In a phrase, we should get on with business—learning to plan in a way that includes the expectation of surprises and the need for adaptations. Until recently, this admonition seemed radical to defense planners, but it is old hat in many other endeavors, ranging from professional sports to U.S. business.[6] It is also quite familiar to warfighters.

CONCEPTUAL STRATEGIC PLANNING

Uncertainty-Sensitive Strategic Planning

Strategic planning can be expensive, tedious, and counterproductive or lean, stimulating, and insightful.[7] The uncertainty-sensitive

---

[4]For an excellent semipopular discussion of complex adaptive systems, see John Holland, *Hidden Order: How Adaptation Builds Complexity*, Addison Wesley, Reading, MA, 1995.

[5]The degree of unpredictability depends on circumstances and what is being predicted. If a massive opponent attacks a much smaller opponent in an "open field," the outcome is determined. When dealing with complex adaptive systems, a key is knowing the "envelope of circumstances" within which control is possible. For a sample discussion on the control of nonlinear complex adaptive systems, see Appendix B of National Research Council, *Modeling and Simulation*, Vol. 9 of *Tactics and Technology for the United States Navy and Marine Corps, 2010–2035*, National Academy Press, Washington, DC, 1997.

[6]For earlier discussions that seemed more radical at the time, see Paul K. Davis (ed.), *New Challenges for Defense Planning: Rethinking How Much Is Enough*, MR-400-RC, RAND, 1994, Chapter 3, and Paul K. Davis, David C. Gompert, and Richard L. Kugler, *Adaptiveness in National Defense: The Basis of a New Framework*, IP-155, RAND, 1996. Planning for adaptiveness is now well accepted by Department of Defense (DoD) leadership (Donald Rumsfeld, *Report of the Quadrennial Review*, Department of Defense, Washington, DC, 2001).

[7]For an excellent but caustic review of failed strategic planning efforts, mostly in the business world, see Henry Mintzberg, *The Rise and Fall of Strategic Planning*, The Free Press, New York, 1994. Some of Mintzberg's criticisms of elderly strategic planning processes apply well to DoD's planning, programming, and budgeting process (PPBS).

planning method is designed for taking an occasional fresh look at the future's challenges and possible strategies—for rethinking matters such as grand strategy and higher-level defense planning. Variants of this method have been used at RAND since the late 1980s, as the Cold War was ending.[8]

Figure 5.1 indicates the basic ideas of uncertainty-sensitive planning. The first step is to characterize the "core" environment, sometimes called the *no-surprises future*. The next step is to identify uncertainties of two types related to *branches* and *shocks*.

Branches represent uncertainties that are taken seriously and monitored and that will be resolved at some point once events take us down one path rather than another. These uncertainties can be dealt

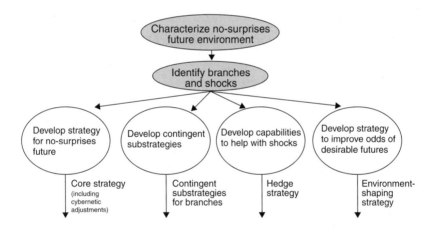

Figure 5.1—Uncertainty-Sensitive Planning

For an informal survey that discusses more strategic methods than can be mentioned here, see Paul K. Davis and Zalmay Khalilzad, *A Composite Approach to Air Force Planning*, MR-787-AF, RAND, 1996.

[8]For more details, see Davis, *New Challenges*, Chapter 6, which summarizes work done some years earlier in collaboration with Paul Bracken. James A. Dewar et al. (*Assumption-Based Planning: A Planning Tool for Very Uncertain Times*, MR-114-A, RAND, 1993) articulate well a variant method, assumption-based planning, that is especially useful for critical reviews of existing plans. It has been refined and applied extensively and James Dewar has recently published a book on the subject (James A. Dewar, *Assumption-Based Planning*, Cambridge University Press, Cambridge, UK, 2002).

with by in-depth contingency plans. Shocks, in contrast, involve plausible (i.e., not impossible) events that are heavily discounted by best-estimate wisdom and are given lip service, at best. Nonetheless, at least some of them will occur—even if they are individually unlikely. When they do occur, they will be disruptive, and there will be no detailed contingency plans for dealing with them. As suggested by the examples listed at the beginning of the chapter, such events not only occur, but occur frequently.

As of early 2002, some illustrative future branches for current U.S. strategic planning included whether

- Al Qaeda is eradicated.

- The U.S. takes military action to force a regime change in Iraq.

- Korea is unified.

- China engages in military actions against Taiwan.

- NATO expands to the Baltics.

- The long-term Chinese military buildup continues.

Some of the many shocks currently regarded as unlikely might be

- U.S.-China conflict arising from a Chinese attack on Taiwan.

- Revolution in Saudi Arabia.

- Collapse of Iran's Islamist government and movement toward normalization (or the opposite, a resurgence of virulent anti-American Islamist-driven actions).

- Disintegration of extremist Al Qaeda-like movements.

- Resolution of the Arab-Israeli conflict and emergence of a Palestinian state.

- Japan going independent.

- Russia moving against Baltic states, Ukraine, or Poland.

As Figure 5.1 shows, planners are to develop a broad strategy consisting of the no-surprises strategy, a series of contingent substrategies to deal with branches, a set of hedging actions laying the groundwork for more ad hoc adaptation to shocks when they occur, and an environment-shaping strategy to affect favorably the odds of various futures. Three particular themes are crucial here:

1. *Operational adaptiveness* is the ability of U.S. forces to deal, at a given time, with a diversity of political-military scenarios and detailed circumstances—some of which can be planned against in detail and some of which will arise as shocks.

2. *Strategic adaptiveness* is the ability to change military posture quickly and easily in response to shifts of the geostrategic environment or national strategy. "Quickly" relates to the time scale of changes in the environment (years); "easily" relates to budgets and effectiveness. Again, some possible shifts can be anticipated and planned against; others will be surprises.

3. *Environment shaping* is influencing the future—e.g., by promoting international stability, economic integration, and universal democratic principles; controlling or mitigating international instabilities; and underwriting general deterrence through commitments, relationships, and credible military forces.

Planning for adaptiveness is more easily said than done, but the United States appears to have often been rather good at it when viewed through the lens of what has been called effective "muddling through."[9] In the real world, the best that can be done is to move in the "right direction" and to adapt routinely without falling prey to the illusion that more precise planning is possible.

Environment shaping is perhaps best understood by considering its opposite: treating the future as an exogenous variable over which one has no influence. Doing so is common in strategic planning activities that spin alternative futures.[10] But the future obviously is not exogenous, or given—especially for a superpower. Humility about shaping efforts is one thing (such efforts can surely fail or be counterproductive), but just waiting to see what happens is quite another.

---

[9]Charles Lindbloom, "On the Science of Muddling Through," *Public Administration Review,* Spring, 1959.

[10]A caricature here is a scenario-based approach that includes a rosy scenario, a bad scenario, and a no-surprises scenario. Sometimes participants emerge with few insights other than that they prefer the rosy scenario.

Surely, the United States should seek ways to improve the odds of favorable developments and circumstances.

Shaping has a positive side, such as seeking to expand the zone of peace; it also has a side that forestalls the negative, as in establishing general deterrence in a given region. It is here that environment shaping connects with the classic strategic concepts of *realpolitik*. Even an optimist about the arrow of human progress has to recognize that military vacuums do arise, malevolent leaders exploit them, and wars still occur. It is far better to deter such events by maintaining a manifest capability to deal with them should they occur, than to have to actually fight future wars. The shaping concept has become increasingly important over the last decade. It seems now to be well established in U.S. national strategy, although terminology changes with each administration, as does the relative emphasis on carrots and sticks.[11] As of late 2002, the United States was considering preventive war against Iraq. Such a war would likely have major longer-term shaping effects, for good or ill.

Operationalizing Strategic Planning in Portfolio-Management Terms

Conceptual strategic planning, then, can address uncertainty in the way suggested in Figure 5.1. The next issue, however, is how to move from that to something more formal, structured, and actionable—i.e., to seeing defense planning as an exercise in portfolio manage-

---

[11]The first official embrace of the "environment shaping" idea was that of Secretary of Defense Dick Cheney, in 1993 (Dick Cheney, *The Regional Defense Strategy*, Department of Defense, Washington, DC, 1993). The early Clinton administration dropped the terminology, but embraced the related concept of engagement. The concept of preventive defense (Ashton B. Carter and William J. Perry, *Preventive Defense: A New Security Strategy for America*, Brookings Institution, 2000) is about certain types of environment shaping. The broad concept of environment shaping per se was reintroduced to official documents in 1997 (William S. Cohen, *Report of the Quadrennial Review*, Department of Defense, Washington, DC, 1997). For a region-by-region discussion of what environment shaping may involve, see Institute for National Strategic Studies (INSS), *Strategic Assessment 1998*, National Defense University, Washington, DC, 1998. The Bush administration referred early to a strategy of dissuading, deterring, and defeating enemies and of reassuring allies (Rumsfeld, *Report of the Quadrennial Review*). The implications of such a strategy clearly include what is called environment shaping here.

ment. The intention of this construct, when first proposed in 1996 as background for the 1997 Quadrennial Defense Review (QDR), was to

- Promote capabilities-based planning for diverse contingencies, both large and small.

- Give environment shaping and strategic adaptiveness the same visibility and status as warfighting.

- Emphasize the need for hedge capabilities permitting future adaptiveness.

- Deal with the potential synergy of and conflicts among portfolio components.

In this construct, planning is about judging how best to allocate investments across the three components of the portfolio. Figure 5.2 suggests schematically what this can mean.[12] The left component

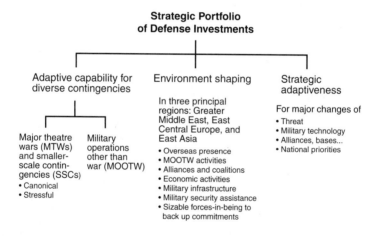

Figure 5.2—Defense Planning in a Portfolio-Management Framework

---

[12]Adapted from Davis, Gompert, and Kugler, *Adaptiveness in National Defense,* which also discusses similarities and differences between this type of portfolio management and that of the business world.

highlights capabilities planning, since that is DoD's core mission; the subsequent components deal with environment shaping and hedging activities to achieve strategic adaptiveness designed to prepare for an uncertain future.

Portfolio management has its limits. As in the investment world, actually doing portfolio management is by no means straightforward, but it is a coherent way to deal with inherent uncertainty and multiple objectives. Choices must be made because there are conflicts. Maintaining near-term readiness can conflict with building future-year capabilities. Worldwide shaping activities can shortchange modernization and transformation of U.S. military forces. Overzealous transformation efforts can mean low readiness until forces, doctrine, and the personnel system adjust.

Subtleties also abound. For example, many military capabilities (first component in Figure 5.2) add or subtract from environment shaping. Thus, environment-shaping investments are investments to *further* increase U.S. effectiveness beyond that stemming from capabilities. Similarly, many activities to enhance both conflict capabilities and environment shaping can add or detract from strategic adaptiveness (e.g., by creating options for using nations' ports and airfields in the future as others become unavailable or undesirable).

Another subtlety is that merely labeling some activity with a positive, such as "increased presence improves environment shaping" may confuse intent with reality. A forward presence can have negative effects when it is too intrusive and runs afoul of independence, sovereignty, or pride. So it was that the United States lost its base in the Philippines. Similar problems have arisen in Korea, Okinawa, and the Persian Gulf. It would not be surprising if the U.S. presence in Saudi Arabia were significantly reduced in the years ahead.

As Chu and Berstein observe in Chapter One, the DoD has, in the course of the last three administrations, substantially altered its concept of higher-level strategy to the needs of the modern era. This has often been obscured in debates over hearty perennials, such as whether to cut forces, cancel high-visibility weapons systems, or drop the requirement that the United States must be able to fight and win two major theater wars (MTWs) simultaneously. From the perspective of this chapter, however, a great deal of progress has been made. DoD's (and the nation's) strategy is explicitly multifaceted, as discussed here in portfolio-management terms. Attention is paid separately to current operations, recapitalization, transformation, and environment shaping. Force needs are assessed not in terms of a simplistic warfighting formula, but in terms of diverse worldwide requirements. There should be no doubt, then, about DoD's attention to the special challenges of planning under manifest uncertainty.

At the heart of those changes is the shift to capabilities-based planning of future forces, referred to above as DoD's core mission (and shown at the left in Figure 5.2).

CAPABILITIES-BASED PLANNING

Capabilities-based planning is planning, under uncertainty, that aims to provide capabilities suitable for a wide range of future challenges and circumstances while working within an economic framework. Today's defense planning, then, is about building capabilities that will be available perhaps three to 20 years from now, when future presidents, defense secretaries, and combatant commanders face the challenges of their own eras. Only sometimes will those challenges have been anticipated, and even less often will they have been planned for in detail despite all the trying. This implies that the capabilities provided to those future leaders should be designed for flexibility and adaptiveness.

Capabilities-based planning stands in contrast to what had become DoD's approach to planning, an approach based on official planning scenarios for major theater wars that not only identified adversaries, but also laid out scenario details, such as warning time and roles of allies. Figure 5.3 shows schematically the kind of scenario used. DoD's routine analysis processes had become so focused on these official scenarios, along with official databases for running official models, that the result was the virtual opposite of capabilities-based planning. It was as though the illustrative scenarios had become specifications serving to define both necessary and sufficient characteristics of the force structure. In practice, as so often happens when strategic planning processes age, the constrained analyses consistently supported current programs—i.e., they "caused no trouble."

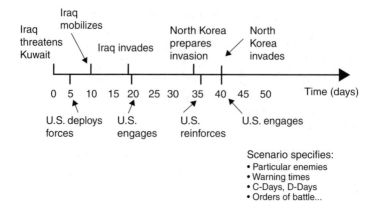

Figure 5.3—An Illustrative Threat-Based Scenario

They were not, however, useful for dealing with uncertainty or for assessing transformation concepts.[13]

It is important to emphasize that the problem with the approach was not that it identified particular threats, but that it considered only conventional-wisdom threats and, to make things worse, considered only point versions of detailed scenarios, as though the circumstances of future conflict could be predicted.

Key Features

The essence of capabilities-based planning is to deal with future uncertainty by generating "capabilities" usable for different purposes and circumstances. Its key features are

*   An emphasis on modular (building-block) capabilities usable in many ways

*   Assembly capability

---

[13]For an extensive discussion of capabilities-based planning and suggestions for its implementation, see Paul K. Davis, *Analytic Architecture for Capabilities-Based Planning, Mission-System Analysis, and Transformation*, MR-1513-OSD, RAND, 2002. Appendix A of that document lists numerous past examples of capabilities-based planning, mostly from the 1960s and 1980s.

- Goals of flexibility, adaptiveness, and robustness, rather than "optimization"
- Multiple measures of effectiveness (MOEs)
- Explicit role for judgments and qualitative assessments
- Economics of choice
- Recognition that "requirements" are the result of high-level choices that should be based on broad capabilities-based analysis.

Building blocks are central in capabilities analysis. When developing capabilities, one quickly discovers the importance of modularity: of having the capacity to take a bit of this and a bit of that, and to do something for which one had not previously planned explicitly. This approach is familiar in everyday life. Suppliers to builders, for example, do not stockpile materials fine-tuned to particular homes that may be built; rather, they stockpile bricks, mortar, and studs.

Building blocks in the military domain come in many forms and at many levels. In particular, there are multiple levels of building blocks in four dimensions:

- Units (e.g., battalions)
- Operations (or missions) and related suboperations
- Weapons systems and subsystems
- Support structures (e.g., logistics systems and, within them, individual systems such as prepositioning ships or tactical airlift).

Flexibility, adaptiveness, and robustness depend on skills in assembling building blocks for at-the-time purposes and circumstances. They are undercut by overspecialized acquisition, by not achieving the interoperability that allows the blocks to fit together easily, and by refining detailed operations plans rather than honing skills for rapid at-the-time assembly. Part of the assembly challenge is having the capacity for at-the-time tailoring—e.g., creating special hybrid units and unique types of support, rather than using only large, preexisting support structures.

The U.S. military does capabilities-based planning now at lower levels—e.g., military systems typically have specifications assuring usability in a wide variety of conditions. Similarly, lower-level operations planning tends to be quite adaptive (that is part of what makes being a young officer attractive). In contrast, higher-level operations planning is often ponderous, especially in peacetime. Although Desert Shield succeeded, the original plan had many shortcomings, and rapid plan modifications were difficult to make. Fortunately, the United States had six months before its shooting war began.

Information Technology and Mission-System Analysis

A critical issue in capabilities planning is assuring that assembly of the right capabilities can be accomplished quickly and can draw on resources that may be physically distant and that come in variously labeled packages—e.g., Army, Air Force, Navy, and Marines. At least as challenging is the task of ensuring that theater commanders will be able to draw on civilian expertise back in the United States or elsewhere when needed and to coordinate activities with those of coalition partners and nongovernmental organizations (NGOs). All of this will require excellence in the use of modern information technology, as Martin Libicki stresses in Chapter Four.

A related issue is mission-system analysis, which seeks to assure that *all* components necessary to an operation will be successful—e.g., that there will be immediately effective joint command-control; missile defense; defense suppression; reconnaissance and targeting; fire delivery; and orchestration of ground force maneuvers. Such matters are extremely important and are becoming more so.[14]

---

[14]See National Research Council, *Network Centric Naval Operations: Transitional Strategy for Emerging Operational Capabilities*, Naval Studies Board study, National Academy Press, Washington, DC, 2000; David S. Alberts, John J. Garstka, and Frederick P. Stein, *Network Centric Warfare: Developing and Leveraging Information Technology*, CCRP Series of National Defense University, Washington, DC, 1999; Paul K. Davis, James H. Bigelow, and Jimmie McEver, *Analytical Methods for Studies and Experiments on "Transforming the Force,"* DB-278-OSD, RAND, 1999; David Gompert and Irving Lachow, *Transforming U.S. Forces: Lessons from the Wider Revolution*, IP-193, RAND, 2000; and Davis, *Analytic Architecture*.

Multiple Objectives and Measures

When making assessments in capabilities analysis, multiple objectives are customary. That may seem straightforward, but defense analysis too often focuses instead on what amounts to a single objective. It is worth illustrating why this matters.

Figure 5.4 shows two ways of comparing four options: A, B, C, and D. The left panel compares them on the basis of least cost for equal effectiveness for a single measure of effectiveness, MOE 1. Perhaps this is something like the ground lost in a simulated war for a particular detailed scenario. In this comparison, option C looks best. In contrast, the right panel makes equal-cost comparisons using a range of measures (MOEs 1, 2, 3, and 4). Perhaps MOE 2 represents results for a different scenario, MOE 3 represents results for an entirely different mission, and MOE 4 assesses the relative extent of U.S. losses that would be expected over a variety of missions and scenarios. Option C may still be best with respect to MOE 1, but not by very much. As a result, its score (as indicated by shading, with lighter being better) is essentially the same as that of the other options. More importantly, option C is distinctly inferior to option D under the other measures. Overall, then, it would probably be better to choose option D. This, in miniature, is what it means to focus on flexibility and robustness rather than on optimizing (e.g., minimizing cost) for a point problem.

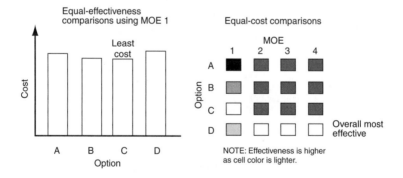

Figure 5.4—Contrasting Types of Analysis

The Concept of a Scenario Space (an Assumptions Space)

Having multiple MOEs can improve flexibility, adaptiveness, and robustness. Yet we must also recognize how sensitive force effectiveness is to highly uncertain variables often treated as if their values were known. Figure 5.5 shows how defense planning could be broadened, in two steps, from one or two threat-based point scenarios. The first step is to expand the list of name-level scenarios (i.e., scenarios specified only to the extent of giving their name, as in "China invades a unified Korea"). Recognizing this need for scope, DoD began in the mid-1990s to consider a broad range of generic threats, although most public attention still focused on threats from Iraq and North Korea.

What has not yet systematically occurred is the second step shown in Figure 5.5: for each name-level scenario, evaluate capabilities for a broad range of operational circumstances that would stress capabilities in very different ways. Ultimately, capabilities assessment requires an examination of outcomes for the entire *scenario space* (i.e., for all the combinations of factors that matter or for a truly representative distribution). This is *exploratory analysis under uncertainty.*

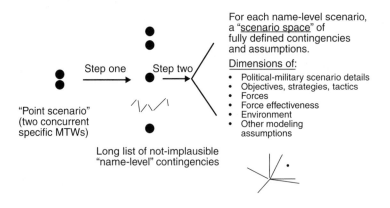

Figure 5.5—Exploratory Analysis in a Scenario Space

As the right side of Figure 5.5 indicates, it is useful to formalize this construct by recognizing that these factors can be grouped into six dimensions of scenario space:

- Political-military scenario (what is usually meant by "scenario")

- Objectives, strategies, and tactics

- Forces

- Force effectiveness (taking into account frictions and personnel quality)

- Environment

- Other modeling assumptions (e.g., feasible rates of advance and break points).

For every scenario space, an exploratory analysis covering the key uncertainties can be designed, and computers can then be used to "fly through the outcome space" to see under what assumptions war outcomes would be favorable, unfavorable, or uncertain. The purpose is to gain insight about how to avoid being in the bad regions of scenario space.[15]

To conduct an exploratory analysis, one can use the scenario-space dimensions explicitly, designing experiments to cover combinations of variables that span the relevant case space. The choice of which variables to hold constant depends on whether the application involves a military-balance assessment, an arms-control analysis, an evaluation of a new weapons system, operations planning, or something else.

Table 5.1 shows an experimental design for a hypothetical mid-1990s study assessing U.S. and allied capabilities to defeat an invasion. The abstractions, such as political-military scenario, are narrowed to specifics. In this case, the political-military scenario is represented simply by varying the time at which the United States and its ally begin mobilizing and deploying (i.e., at D–10, D–5, D, or D+5). As an-

---

[15]For more details, see Chapter Nine, "Exploratory Analysis and Implications for Modeling."

Table 5.1

Illustrative Experimental Plan: Scenario-Space Analysis of Defense Capability for a Given Name-Level Scenario

Political-military setting	Alliance reacts at C (when deployment begins) = D–10; D–5; D; D+5.
Strategies	Fixed: invasion to specific objectives; defender attempts to halt advance. One measure of outcome is where alliance is able to hold.
Forces	Enemy: 15, 20, 25, 30, or 35 divisions; 10 or 20 tactical fighter wings. Ally: 8 or 12 divisions; no significant tactical air forces. U.S. commitment: 0, 5, or 8 tactical fighter wings; 0 or 5 divisions.
Weapons systems	Ally does or does not have MLRS/DPICM.[a] U.S. does or does not buttress the ally's ground forces with reconnaissance, surveillance, and targeting information. U.S. does or does not have the BAT munition for its MLRS launchers.[b] U.S. aircraft may achieve 1, 2, 5, or 10 kills per day after air defenses are suppressed. U.S. has capability to suppress (either destroy or prevent use of) air defenses in 1, 4, or 8 days.
Environment	Normal weather.
Algorithms and other model assumptions	Attacker's nominal ground force effectiveness (based on equipment) is multiplied by 0.75 or 1 to reflect uncertainties about competence and dedication. Ally's nominal ground force effectiveness is multiplied by 0.5 or 1 to reflect uncertainties about preparation, competence, and dedication.

[a]The MLRS is a multiple-rocket launcher system that can launch a variety of munitions, one of which is abbreviated DPICMS.

[b]The MLRS can also launch the Army's Tactical Missile System (ATACM) missile, which will be able to carry brilliant anti-tank (BAT) munitions.

other example, the design includes cases in which the United States does and does not assist the ally's ground forces by providing timely reconnaissance, surveillance, and targeting information. This can have a factor-of-two effect. Overall, this analysis design would entail running 200,000 cases. This is not traditional sensitivity analysis.

My colleagues and I have used such experimental designs in studies related to NATO's defense capability, the defense of Kuwait and Saudi Arabia, and the defense of Korea. Each design was tailored to the problem at hand. In a mid-90s study, for example, the future Russian threat to Poland was quite hypothetical, and the only issue was to understand how difficult it might be for NATO to defend Poland if

Poland joined NATO. For such a study, we were careful to avoid worst-casing that postulated not only a future malevolent Russia, but also a large and supremely competent Russian army. Instead, we considered somewhat larger-than-expected Russian threats that were reasonably credible for the period under study, but did not ascribe to them advanced, U.S.-like capabilities. We also considered a range of Polish self-defense capabilities, and so on. In contrast, when studying what capabilities might be needed in the more distant future to deal with a regional peer competitor, we drew on intelligence estimates, Defense Science Board studies, and other efforts to define a range of more stressful but *plausible* (i.e., not incredible) threats— just to explore under what circumstances various U.S. capabilities would be especially valuable.

The design of such analyses can benefit from a method called "fault trees" (see Figure 5.6) that was used in a mid-1990s study that examined the defense of Kuwait and Saudi Arabia.[16] The purpose of the

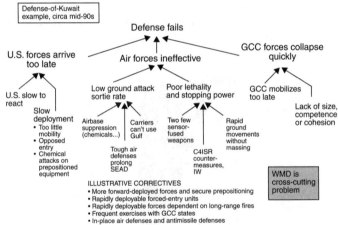

NOTE: GCC = Gulf Cooperation Council; SEAD = suppression of enemy air defenses; WMD = weapons of mass destruction; C4ISR = command, control, communications, computers, intelligence, surveillance, and reconnaissance; IW = information warfare.

Figure 5.6—Fault Tree for Defense of Kuwait and Saudi Arabia

---

[16]For a more recent study that addresses anti-access issues in some detail, see Paul K. Davis, Jimmie McEver, and Barry Wilson, *Measuring Capabilities for Interdiction: Exploratory Analysis to Inform Adaptive Strategies for the Persian Gulf*, MR-1371, RAND, 2002.

diagram, which can be created in brainstorming sessions, is to organize thinking so as to highlight the factors worth varying in analysis. Figure 5.6 does this by indicating different ways in which the United States and its allies could fail—e.g., U.S. forces could arrive too late, U.S. air forces might not be effective enough to bring about an early halt, or the local Persian Gulf–state (GCC in the figure) forces might collapse quickly because they are outnumbered and outgunned. Lower on the tree are ways these subfailures might occur, and at the bottom of the tree are natural connections to model inputs. For example, in the middle there is reference to tough air defenses prolonging SEAD (suppression of enemy air defenses) operations . In model terms, this means varying the "SEAD time" by considering different values—say, 1, 3, and 8 days.

Figure 5.6 also shows (bottom) a list of illustrative corrective measures for avoiding failed defense. Again, such lists lead to decisions about what model parameters to vary.

Figure 5.7 illustrates a "slice" through the outcome space of a theater-level simulation. Instead of seeing results for one detailed scenario, we see outcomes for a wide range of cases packaged in a way

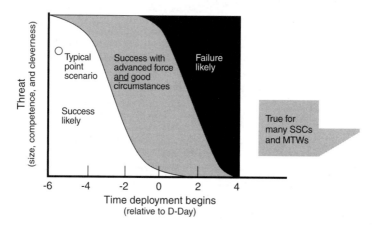

Figure 5.7—One Slice Through Outcome Space, Showing Envelopes of Capability for Defense

that tells an important story. Because we are seeing only a slice through the space, many inputs are held constant, but we do see the effects of varying threat size (y axis) and varying start time for the U.S. force deployment (x axis). Outcome is indicated by white (good), gray (uncertain), and black (likely failure). The principal point is that immediately employable force is particularly critical because fully actionable warning times may be quite short, even though strategic warning usually exists.

This depiction of analysis puts pressure on the observer to favor planning options that would put resources where they are most needed, rather than continuing to work on marginal improvements for cases in which the United States already has good capabilities. In other words, the obvious implication of such a display is to put emphasis on turning more of the shaded region to white and more of the black region to white or shaded. That is, the premium is on *early* capabilities.[17] This is in contrast to spending more money to obtain an even better outcome for scenarios already in the white region.[18]

Choices and Resource Allocation

The last topic of this chapter is how to move from a portfolio construct of overall strategy, capabilities assessment, and assessments of environment shaping and strategic adaptiveness to informing resource allocation choices. After all, capabilities-based planning cannot simply provide a blank check to prepare for any and all possibilities.[19] A portfolio framework helps, but additional methods and tools are needed, some of which already exist.

---

[17]Many options for improving *early* capabilities are discussed in Paul K. Davis, Richard Hillestad, and Natalie Crawford, "Capabilities for Major Theater Wars," in Zalmay Khalilzad and David A. Ochmanek (eds.), *Strategic Appraisal, 1997: Strategy and Defense Planning for the 21st Century*, MR-826-AF, RAND, 1997, and in Gritton et al., *Ground Forces*.

[18]As discussed by E. C. Gritton et al. (*Ground Forces for a Rapidly Employable Joint Task Force: First-Week Capabilities for Short-Warning Conflicts*, MR-1152-OSD/A, RAND, 2000), a generic version of this chart applies well in thinking about capabilities for both MTWs and SSCs (such as the Kosovo conflict).

[19]The blank-check problem is one of those raised by people who are skeptical of capabilities-based planning by "uncertainty hawks" (Carl Connetta and Charles Knight, *Dueling with Uncertainty: The New Logic of American Military Planning*, Project on Defense Alternatives, Commonwealth Institute, Cambridge, MA, 1998).

Figure 5.8 suggests that a portfolio-structured decision-support analysis should have the following inputs: multiple objectives, multiple options, many scenarios and variations (distilled from exploratory analysis), "objective" MOEs (e.g., results of simulations), multiple cost and budget measures, and subjective judgments about effectiveness. Bluntness is appropriate here about a controversial matter: Those who reject subjectivity in methodology have no place in higher-level planning, since the most important decisions are inherently subjective. Further, most allegedly objective measures derive from models with many uncertain assumptions influenced by judgments, or from data that may be a poor proxy for what is needed (e.g., Vietnam-war body-count data). The challenge is not to make things "objective," but to structure subjective judgments so that they are well defined and meaningful as part of an analysis.

Figure 5.9 is a top-level view of a desirable planning structure. The first column lists some of the policy options (these are discrete program-level options, not high-level strategy alternatives); other columns are for their different MOEs. The scorecard approach allows decisionmakers to see the component assessments, rather than forcing them to buy into any particular combining rule for overall utility.

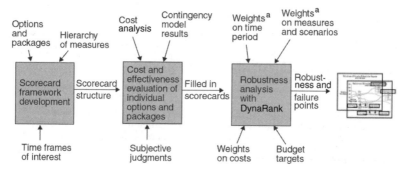

[a]Combining rules may also be nonlinear, as in taking the worst component score rather than using a weighted score.

Figure 5.8—Factors to Be Reflected in Portfolio Analysis

Option (vs. baseline)	Capabilities		Environment Shaping	Strategic Adaptiveness	Net Effect	Cost
	MTWs	SSCs				
+20 B-2s						
+1,500 SFWs						
+Allied package						
+150 UAVs						
CEC acceleration						
+1 CVBG						
More home-porting						
Many others						

NOTE: CEC = cooperative engagement capability; CVBG = carrier battle group; SFW = sensor fused weapon; UAV = unmanned aerial vehicle.

Figure 5.9—Basic High-Level Scorecard Structure

Three of the columns in this illustration correspond to the portfolio construct (capabilities, environment shaping, and strategic adaptiveness). Of these three, capabilities has two subcolumns, one for MTWs and one for SSCs, whereas environment shaping and strategic adaptiveness have none. In another application, they might have several. For other applications, there might be another column for force-management effectiveness (measuring, e.g., effects on operational tempo and ability to recruit and maintain forces). Such matters can easily be changed using a spreadsheet tool such as RAND's DynaRank.[20]

The value in any cell of the scorecard may be generated from subordinate spreadsheets that use simple models or have databases arising from more simulation or empirical work. The top-level assessment of MTW capability, for example, might be the result of numerous subordinate-level calculations for different MTWs with different assumptions, such as those about warning. Those discrete cases, in turn, would have been chosen after broad exploratory analysis in the relevant scenario space revealed the most important

---

[20]See R. J. Hillestad and Paul K. Davis, *Resource Allocation for the New Defense Strategy: The DynaRank Decision Support System*, MR-996-OSD, RAND, 1998.

factors. Still other subordinate spreadsheets and notes may elaborate on the reasoning used in subjective judgments.

Performing this type of analysis permits us to order policy options by effectiveness, cost, or cost-effectiveness. This requires a rule on how to combine the shaping, capabilities, and preparing-now components. Given such a rule, the analysis determines how to cut costs with minimal impact on effectiveness (left side of graph in Figure 5.10) or how much additional effectiveness can be achieved by buying the entire set of policy options (right side of graph).

Exploratory analysis is as essential to cost-effectiveness analysis as it is to capabilities assessment. It helps to construct different "views," which combine assumptions used in the portfolio assessment with those about the relative weights of shape, respond, and prepare now; the weights of subordinate measures such as MTW and SSC capability; and even assumptions in underlying analyses—e.g., how bad to make the worst-case scenarios. These assumptions should reflect differences in how significant people think about the issues (e.g., the weight of readiness versus modernization).

With such views established, portfolio assessment can determine how the rank orderings of options change from view to view (Figure 5.11). Options that rise to the top for all views are, by definition, ro-

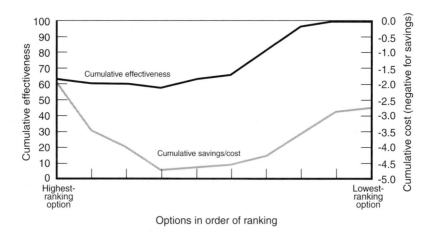

Figure 5.10—DynaRank Outputs in Cost-Effectiveness Analysis

View Emphasizing Warfighting	View Emphasizing Shaping	View Emphasizing Cost
New BRAC	25% fewer F-22s	-1 active division
Double surge sortie rates[a]	New BRAC	-1 CVBG
Allied defense package (helos, ATACMS, advisors)[b]	Allied defense package (helos, ATACMS, advisors)	25% fewer F-22s
Equip F-22s for anti-armor missions	Forward deployed wing	-2 FTWs
Rapid SEAD (HPM)	Mediterranean home-port	New BRAC
Forward deployed wing	Arsenal ship plus allied package	Forward deployed wing

NOTE: BRAC = base realignment and closure; FTW = fighter tactical wing; HPM = particular mechanism involving high-power microwave weapons.
[a]Double surge sortie rates have to do with a program that would permit temporary doubling of air force sortie rates.
[b]An allied defense package consists of specialized units and equipment that would be deployed early to help

Figure 5.11—Exploratory Analysis Showing Rank-Ordered Preferences Under Different Views

bust. Such options usually exist because big organizations have many inefficiencies that make no sense under any sensible view. In the example, all three views recognize the need for another series of base closings (a new base realignment and closure [BRAC] round). As long as the viewpoints are reasonable rather than zealous (e.g., as long as a modernization view still recognizes that shaping is significant), such analysis can help elicit agreement among people who would otherwise argue vociferously in the abstract. For example, in other work of a similar nature, the need to modernize information systems emerged as a consensus view across "stovepipe czars."

This discussion, then, has suggested how it is possible to go from the high concepts of grand strategy down to the nitty-gritty issues of economic choice using one intellectual framework. There is no guarantee that this process of working up and down the ladder of choice will be easy. But it is both feasible and desirable—given strong management, good will, and participation by senior leaders of the defense community.

Chapter Six

PLANNING THE FUTURE MILITARY WORKFORCE

Harry J. Thie

Different questions about military manpower requirements, manpower costs, and trained personnel inventory have emerged as important at various times. For example, just before World War II, the most important question was how to procure a large force immediately. After World War II, the emphasis shifted to managing a large inventory of people with military experience. Now, the emphasis is on recruiting in a highly competitive labor market. Although the broad questions remain fixed, particular aspects of them—recruiting, training, retaining, promoting, compensating, and retiring—receive more or less emphasis at particular times, depending on the nation's military, social, and economic environment. Questions and answers are shaped by many forces, including external events, societal concerns, missions, organization, technology, budget, and demographics. Specific forces at work for the past few years that affect how manpower, personnel, and training questions are asked and answered include a military end strength that is shrinking, threats changing from known to varied, a unitary mission of global conflict shifting to diverse missions within an overall policy of selective and flexible engagement, multiple unit missions replacing single unit missions, variable hierarchies replacing fixed organizational hierarchies, and a joint perspective in operational matters supplanting a service focus.

Planning the workforce is about ensuring that manpower needs are met with trained people at reasonable costs. In past years—as a result of practices from World War II through conscription and the draft-induced volunteerism that ended with Vietnam—planning the workforce was largely about determining its size: forecasting who would stay if they were currently part of it, and calculating how many new entrants would be needed each year. "Manning" the force was the mantra; "aligning" the force by numbers and grades was the goal. Planning the future force is currently shifting away from recruiting and toward overcoming the retention shortfall. Today, workers are scarce throughout the economy—not overall, but among those who are skilled and committed. Emphasis is shifting away from pure recruiting and retention strategies to strategies aimed at developing existing workforces to carry out emerging work. The goal is to develop a cadre of personnel who have the skills needed to meet the requirements of the national military strategy. Human capital accretes; it is smarter to build on what exists than to start anew.

This chapter focuses on manpower, personnel, and training. Manpower deals with the numbers and types of people needed to accomplish missions, personnel involves managing people either directly (e.g., via assignments) or through incentives (e.g., via compensation), and training and development affects knowledge, skills, and behaviors. The chapter also addresses questions about the size of the force; its grade, skill, and experience composition; and the cost and optimal methods to procure, enter, train, develop, assign, advance, compensate, and remove personnel.

To illustrate these issues, an example of how to analyze manpower and personnel policies is worked through. The specific example explores manpower, personnel, and training policy alternatives for achieving an available, qualified, stable, experienced, and motivated future force. Some policy choices can be applied servicewide; others can be applied to military units or to individual soldiers, sailors, airmen, or marines. The example illustrates controllable and uncontrollable variables involved in policy alternatives, relationships among policy choices and desired outcomes, complexity and conflicts among competing objectives, and how undesired outcomes can emerge. Frequently, the complex relationships among variables are not sufficiently considered in the process of choosing policies. As a result, what appears to be a reasonable decision to save budget dollars can have unforeseen future personnel and training consequences.

MILITARY HUMAN CAPITAL

Human capital comprises the skills, knowledge, and abilities of individuals and groups and has value inside an organization and to an organization's customers. The United States has always gained a military advantage by being able to draw on large pools of human capital.

Inside an organization, the correct skills, knowledge, and abilities lead to greater efficiency; outside an organization, they lead to greater effectiveness with customers. In the U.S. military, the combatant commanders take skills, knowledge, and abilities developed by the services and apply them to seek military effectiveness around the globe for diverse missions. The military needs a proper mix of skills and knowledge to gain internal operating efficiencies and to be effective on battlefields, however defined.

Human capital can be thought of as a "stock," much as we think of a stock of materiel. It must be built, maintained, and upgraded; left alone, it deteriorates and becomes obsolete. The next few sections review what the stock of military human capital is now, how it got that way, and what it is likely to undergo in the future, specifically:

- The historical size, source, and composition of the active military

- The present composition, characteristics, and attributes of the active military

- The future effect of the present under likely conditions.

Historical Size, Source, and Composition of the Active Force

Consider, one at a time, various characteristics of the active force: size, enlisted/officer mix, skill mix, and source of manpower. Size largely depends on external events; type of manpower and mix of occupations depend on mission, organization, and technology; and source of manpower—conscription or volunteer—depends on the size of the military relative to the size of the population.

Figure 6.1 shows the size of the active military over a 200-year period. For most of U.S. military history, the number of soldiers, sailors, airmen (after the 1920s), and marines largely depended on external

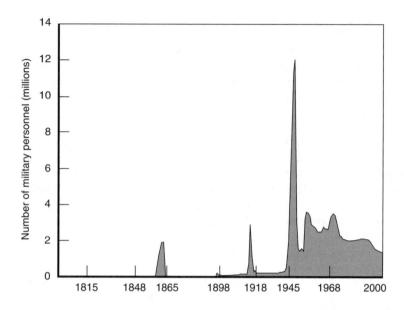

Figure 6.1—Size of Active-Duty Military, 1800–2000

events, with "bumps" in the size of the active-duty force associated with the nation's earliest wars. When the nation needed to increase the size of the military, it enlisted or conscripted recruits from the general population; when the need abated, these recruits were equally quickly separated. For example, the military increased from 28,000 in 1860 to nearly 2,000,000 by 1864; by 1866, the force had decreased to 77,000. The more recent surges in manpower appear as spikes in the data. Notice the sharp spike by 1945, as the nation mobilized for World War II and the military grew to over 12,000,000. Three years later, however, the force had shrunk to about 1,400,000, a level close to today's.

Since World War II, external events have continued to shape the size of the force—the post–World War II drawdown in the late 1940s; the Korean War in the early 1950s, with its own subsequent drawdown; the Berlin crisis, which added manpower in the early 1960s; the Vietnam conflict, with its own era of growth and drawdown. The debacle at Desert One was followed in the 1980s by the Reagan buildup, the fall of the Berlin Wall, Grenada, and Panama. In the 1990s, the breakup of the former Soviet Union, the Persian Gulf conflict, and participation in humanitarian and other nonwar operations were significant. The 1990s witnessed a sharp reduction in the size of the active military.

Figure 6.2 documents the enlisted-to-officer ratio over two centuries. During the 19th century, the ratio was rather flat, with periodic spikes; in times of conflict, the ratio tended to increase as more enlisted personnel than officers were added.

The number of enlisted personnel increased by a factor of almost six, to about 225,000, for the Spanish American War. After that war, the level fell by one-half, to about 115,000, which was a consistent level up until World War I. The "standing" active military began in this era. However, officer strength did not increase as much during this period, which accounts for the high enlisted-to-officer ratio for the first 20 years of the century. Before World War I, brawn still mattered most on the battlefield; coal-fired ships, dismounted infantry, and horse-drawn artillery required proportionally more enlisted personnel. An air force did not exist.

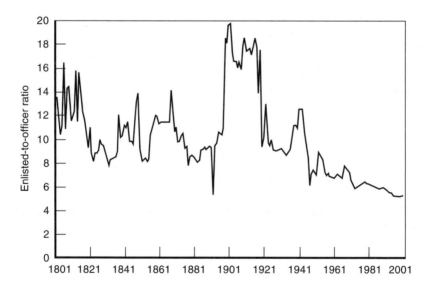

Figure 6.2—Ratio of Enlisted Personnel to Officers, 1800–2000

Since World War I, there has been a significant shift from enlisted to officer manpower. The introduction of the airplane, tank, modern steam ship, and radio shifted work toward more use of brain than brawn. New technologies tend to be "officer heavy" when first introduced, because initially they are complex and require doctrinal and organizational change. Technological innovations also initially require a larger, officer-rich support tail to provide service and supply. Since World War II, the ratio's trend has been downward, with less frequent spikes, as officers have come to represent a larger proportion of a large active military. Moreover, beginning in World War II, the need to coordinate, integrate, and sustain military forces numbering in the millions, rather than tens of thousands, has led to officers being substituted for enlisted personnel, in part to staff increasingly larger and more hierarchical organizations. These broad trends continue to the present.

The organization of work and the composition of the military force are never static; they change with mission, organization, and technology. The columns in Figure 6.3 summarize the changes in the occupational distribution of the enlisted force from 1865 to 2000.[1] The precipitous decline in jobs classified as general military is as striking as the increase in technical occupations and craftsmen.

During the early years of the military, the demand for occupational specialization was small. Almost all soldiers were infantry riflemen, with a few serving in support activities. The Navy was the first to experience the effect of the Industrial Revolution, and the shift from sails to steam was a far-reaching technological change. The Army lagged for several decades, until the World War I mobilization, but its subsequent transformation was dramatic. By 1918, the combat soldier was for the first time in a numerical minority.

Following World War II, several factors dramatically changed the occupational requirements of the services—e.g., the acceleration of weapons and military technology to include the nuclear military, the application of electronics to communications and logistics, and the

---

[1]Harold Wool and Mark Eitelberg are to be thanked for preserving much of this history. See Harold Wool, *The Military Specialist: Skilled Manpower for the Armed Forces*, The Johns Hopkins Press, MD, 1968; Mark J. Eitelberg, *Manpower for Military Occupations*, Human Resources Research Organization, VA, 1988.

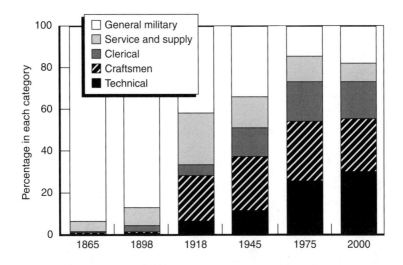

Figure 6.3—Occupational Mix, 1865–2000

emergence of missiles and air defense. Organizational structures changed to take advantage of the new armaments and processes, and there was a noticeable occupational shift from infantry, artillery, and seamanship to technicians. By the early 1980s, technical workers constituted the largest of the five separate groupings, as they do today. As of 2000, 18 percent of enlisted personnel were in a general military specialty, 35 percent were blue collar workers (service and supply workers and craftsmen), and 47 percent were white collar workers (clerical and technical workers).

The United States has used conscription and voluntary enlistment to raise manpower but has never used universal service (although that concept was hotly debated between World War II and Korea).[2] Figure 6.4 shows the active military as a percentage of the population from 1800 to 2000. The horizontal bar running across the lower part of the figure has four lightly shaded segments showing the four times (which together total only 30 out of 210 years of federal history) con-

---

[2]The term *conscription* means that certain rules are used to select a portion of the population for service. *Universal service* (or *universal military training*) means that all militarily qualified citizens must serve.

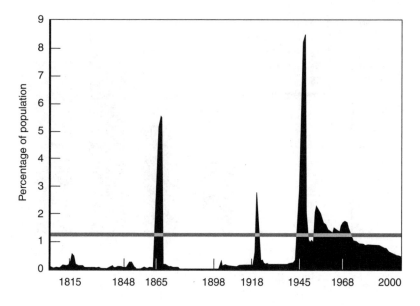

Figure 6.4—Active Military as Percentage of Population, 1800–2000

scription was used. The Civil War and World War I were both periods of wartime conscription; the first use of peacetime conscription was in 1940, shortly before World War II. The nation had a volunteer force from 1946 to 1950, but Korea saw a return to conscription. Vietnam manpower policy was dominated by conscription to meet the needs of the Army; the needs of the other services and the reserve component were met largely with volunteers (though many of these were draft induced).

Figure 6.4 also shows how the size of both the active enlisted force and the population related to the use of conscription (shown in lightly shaded part of bar) over time. The nation has always used conscription when it required an active enlisted force larger than about 1.4 percent of the population, something that has occurred only during the four periods described above. Since 1973, when the last period of conscription ended, the population has grown and the active military has shrunk. Currently, the active force represents about 0.5 percent of the population. Using the 1.4 percent as a rule of thumb means that the need for an active force of above 3.7 million would lead to conscription—a highly unlikely event in the foresee-able future. Also, conditions outlined below will most likely make the rule of thumb obsolete.

The lessons from this history are central to assessments about the future. However, the durability of these lessons cannot help but be affected by more-recent fundamental changes that must be incorpo-rated into any synthesis of the future: the greater use of civilians and reserves, and the greater education and higher aptitude of the en-listed force.

Ongoing Revolutions: Composition, Characteristics, and Attributes

Several "revolutions" now under way have import for the future. The first of these stems from the total force policy, which was about using all the manpower resources of defense. This policy was implemented in 1971 but, as Figure 6.5 suggests, did not see its defining year until 1985—the first year in which Department of Defense (DoD) civilians

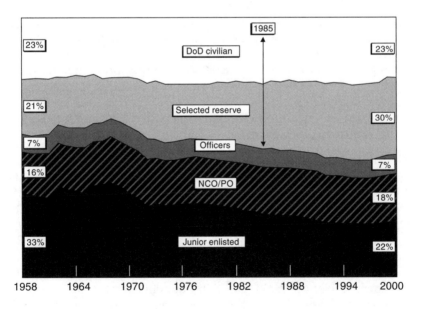

Figure 6.5—Defense Manpower Composition, 1958–2000

and selected reservists (Guard and Reserve), combined, outnumbered the active military. As of 2000, only 47 percent of total defense manpower has been active military. This is a fundamental change that needs to be central to thinking about the future stock of military human capital.

Another fundamental change took place within the active military. From 1958 on, active officers were a consistent 7 percent share of total defense manpower. However, in the enlisted category, noncommissioned officers (NCOs) and petty officers (POs) gained share—up to 18 percent of defense manpower. Civilians, reservists, and NCO/PO have, together, replaced junior enlisted (those in the grades of E1 to E4); the latter have dropped from one-third of all defense manpower in 1958 to about one-fifth in 2000. This follows directly from the changes in the nature of the military: work has become more complex and specialized, and more education and experience are required to do the work successfully.

Another dramatic change is the quality of the force. Questions remain about how best to measure quality and how much quality is really needed or affordable, given the fiscal constraints facing the military. During the post-Korean draft era and the early part of the all-volunteer force, quality (as measured by trainability) tended to be lower than it has been during the modern volunteer era. Once again, 1985 was a defining year. Figure 6.6 shows a revolution that has taken place within the enlisted force: as measured by the percentage in the highest three categories of training aptitude (Armed Forces Qualification Test [AFQT] Categories I–III), the current enlisted force, upon entry, has more ability than it ever had.

During the conscription period from 1952 to 1973, Army entrants typically had the lowest level of aptitude among all service entrants. In the early years of the all-volunteer force, aptitude levels fell significantly as the services, particularly the Army, struggled to recruit. The significant drop in the late 1970s was caused primarily by the entry test having been misnormed: the military was recruiting people who had less training aptitude than it thought. This situation changed significantly in the 1980s, with most services above 90 percent for the decade. And yet the real revolution happened in the 1990s, with all services at 97 percent and above beginning in 1991. Starting in 1985, there were 15 straight years in which at least 90 percent of all recruits

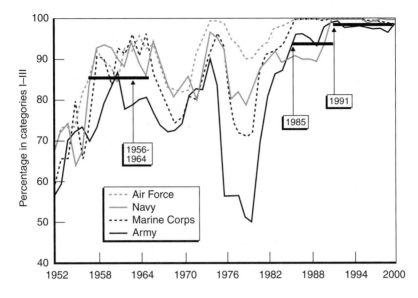

Figure 6.6—Percentage of Enlisted Accessions in Highest Three Training Aptitude Categories, 1952–2000

entering the services were in these three highest aptitude categories. And those who have entered since 1985 will make up over 95 percent of the enlisted force across all services by 2005. Where does this aptitude revolution lead? Virtually all NCOs/POs in the year 2010 (99.5 percent) will have entered since 1985. This highly trainable current and future force bodes well for those who emphasize the learning requirements of the future and the development of military human capital.

Hand in glove with the aptitude revolution is an education revolution. Officers have always been mostly college graduates, but NCOs and POs are now becoming more educated as well. In recent years, officer duties have devolved to NCOs and POs. Many types of work, from administration and paperwork to missile launching, have become sergeant and PO work—largely because of technology and a faster operational tempo. Aspects of this devolution of duties can also be seen in changing concepts of development. Training, a skill-based concept that results in an immediate ability to do certain tasks more proficiently, is slowly giving way to education as a knowledge-based enlisted force increasingly becomes a necessity for successful performance.

The enlisted force is more highly educated than in any previous era. Figure 6.7 shows the proportion of grades E6 to E9 with at least some college education for three different time periods. Fiscal year 1972 represents a force that, while not necessarily conscripted, was shaped by conscription; fiscal year 1981 represents a force shaped additionally by the early years of the volunteer force; fiscal year 1996 represents a force almost exclusively the product of the volunteer era. The figure shows that, generally, the higher the grade, the higher the educational achievement. This figure and the earlier ones show that the proportion of college graduates grew over time as well as across all grades and occupations.

Figure 6.8 shows the data by occupation (aggregated for grades E6 to E9). Even in the general military occupational group, which is the group associated with Army and Marine Corps combat skills, the proportion with at least some college is much greater than was generally believed to be achievable in the era of a conscription-shaped enlisted force.

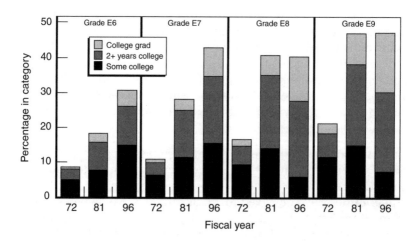

Figure 6.7—Educational Achievement for Grades E6 to E9, Selected Years

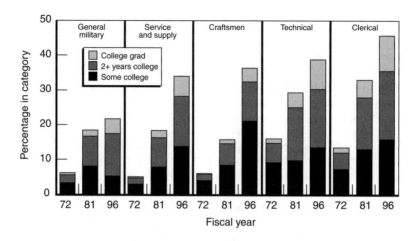

Figure 6.8—Educational Achievement for Grades E6 to E9, by Occupation, Selected Years

Looking to the Future

The near future is pretty much determined by the present and by recent history. Consider the most likely near future, in which the world of 2010 reflects today's trends—e.g., (1) the large U.S. military shrinking in size, (2) known threats becoming varied threats, (3) the unitary mission of global conflict becoming diverse missions within an overall policy of selective and flexible engagement, (4) single missions for units becoming multiple missions for units, (5) variable hierarchies replacing the fixed organizational hierarchies, (6) advanced weapons becoming integrated systems and processes, and (7) a service focus in operational matters continuing to be replaced by a joint perspective. Some speculations about more-radical excursions based on size, organization, and technology follow.

In the broadest sense, the military does what the nation asks: all missions, against all enemies, as the oath requires. Yet not all missions have to be done full time in large numbers or in all types of functional units—a distinction that differentiates active from reserve. The future military will continue to wear uniforms and, in the words of a Navy admiral, "get shot at." This differentiates the military from the defense civilian and contractor workforce (even given that the first casualty in Somalia was a defense civilian and the first in

Afghanistan was a CIA operative). The reduction of active military manpower as a proportion of all defense manpower is likely to continue. More reductions of direct defense manpower will occur as more contractors are used on and off the battlefield. Eventually, the manpower needs of the active military will be about one-third of a percent of the population, a level easily met by volunteers entering military service.

Officers "lead" in the broad sense of leadership. They set direction, align forces, and empower people. This differentiates the officer corps from the NCO and PO corps, which has evolved in its own right to be the force's managers and technicians. The experience level of the enlisted force will continue to grow as NCOs and POs continue to displace junior enlisted. Moreover, junior officers who have been managers and technicians more than leaders will begin to be supplanted by educated and experienced enlisted technicians and managers. So far, with enlisted personnel acquiring more status, their work appears to be taking on more of the hallmarks of a profession and fewer of the hallmarks of a trade. As the edge in human capital enjoyed by junior officers over senior enlisted shrinks, many issues related to the scope of the latter's responsibility, job design, status, and compensation become salient.

Two enduring characteristics—cognitive ability and conscientiousness—explain most variability in job performance. These characteristics are largely inherent in the individual and not easily changed later in life. People have them in varying levels when they enter organizations; one cannot develop, train, or educate for these characteristics except at the margin. Therefore, people have to be selected for them. The military has had and will continue to have a "select the best" strategy, expecting all entrants to be able to rise to the highest levels of responsibility. The military strives for a homogeneous entering group of high ability. As better measures of such characteristics as conscientiousness are found, the military will select for them as well. Neither all militaries around the world nor all organizations can afford such a strategy, however; instead, they select a mix of people with varied levels of these characteristics. But to get people with high levels of these characteristics, one must have appropriate selection and compensation instruments in place.

Occupational classifications derive from what work the military will be asked to do (its missions), how it structures itself to do the work (its organization), and the systems and processes it uses to accomplish the work (its technology). The competencies for military human capital change over time. Doctrine and theory for military and naval science and paradigms for leadership and management are not constants. Miniaturization, digitization, and other advances change needed military expertise. Tanks replace horses; steam replaces sail; turbines replace pistons. Is technology part of military knowledge and expertise? Certainly. Technology—how things are done—has always been part of the core knowledge of the military profession. Reskilling and upskilling will enter the lexicon of force management. The highly trainable and experienced enlisted force will be developed and redeveloped to ensure it possesses attributes critical to mission performance.

The military is likely to become smaller, more experienced, and more highly graded, with the percentage classified as general military or line category reaching a new low. These grade and skill percentages will vary by service, as they do now, but the differences will become more pronounced toward 2010. The military might evolve in a different way, however, because of varying size (smaller or larger), organizational change (outsourcing, streamlining, downgrading), and technology (user friendly or not user friendly). Based on the direction of change, the military can shrink or grow as well as compose itself of various skills and grades.

Whether military human capital will change depends on how change is defined. If it is defined as a succession of doctrinal and organizational changes in a constant-sized force, the manpower and personnel change will largely be one of composition, grade, and skill, with some manpower reductions because of productivity gains. However, if manpower is reduced to pay for new systems, what remains will be older, have a different mix of skills, and be forced to rely more on reserves and civilians. Either way, trends in manpower categorization, experience, and skill mix will be accelerated, but there will be no fundamentally new prospect.

In sum, this is what the future holds: the stock of military human capital needed will change, but in discernible directions. The active military will remain robust in size, but proportionally more defense will be provided by civilians, contractors, and selected reservists. NCOs and POs will continue to displace junior enlisted and begin to supplant junior officers. Those who enter the active military will be selected on the basis of certain enduring characteristics, such as cognitive ability and conscientiousness, for which a good measure is needed. They will be well-trained and educated. Specific knowledge and other developed attributes will change as the core of professional knowledge and experience that all military personnel must have changes with mission, organization, and technology. It is likely that career management and compensation practices will need to change. It is not likely that a revolution in military affairs (RMA), reasonably defined, will alter such trends much, but it may accelerate them.

MANPOWER AND PERSONNEL ANALYSIS

To answer questions about planning a future force, one must decide on objectives, criteria, alternatives, and measures. Models and analytic techniques can be used to relate these four elements in useful ways and to draw out consequences and tradeoffs.

The Process

The analytic process begins with the front end (more art than science), in which the problem is identified and structured. The problem first has to be stated appropriately and clearly, at which point it becomes critical that the objectives be articulated so as to spawn more-precise criteria. What is the desired outcome? Almost all objectives deal with some variant of effectiveness or cost. One part of the front end entails devising a broad, creative range of alternative policies that can be evaluated. A large part deals with sorting out ends from means from alternatives from constraints. Constantly asking "why" helps to construct a hierarchy that allows for analysis to enter a structured picture.

In the second part of the process, the analytic middle (muddle?), science replaces the art of the front end. The science does not have to be complex; logic is often sufficient and may be adequately done on the back of an envelope. This analytic middle sorts through consequences: How well do alternatives meet criteria? Models, methods, data, and qualitative assessments are brought to bear. Once the consequences of alternatives are known, tradeoffs can be made. Rarely are all objectives satisfied by one dominant alternative, so tough choices and compromises must be made when all objectives cannot be met at once.

Which objectives are more important than others? An alternative that provides more effectiveness at a lower cost is a no-brainer, but such an alternative is seldom found in the real world; and the reverse, less effectiveness at a higher cost, is seldom chosen. Alternatives that offer more effectiveness at a higher cost or a lower cost for less effectiveness or other possible combinations require hard thinking aimed at determining which alternative appears to best meet the ultimate objectives. Then, one must deal with uncertainties. What could change the assessed consequences? Specific cases can be examined or certain parameters can be judgmentally varied to see how the consequences and thus the conclusion might change. Last, what is the appetite for risk? Is it better to do nothing if there is no stomach to see the consequences through?

At this point, the back end of the analytic process is reached. Analyzing stops, and decisions or recommendations are made—which includes linking them to other problems and solutions in useful ways. Art and science give way to decision and judgment, a process that in the public sector, is not simply about selecting the "best" alternative for maximizing or minimizing criteria related to objectives, but involves consensus. What can the disparate stakeholders within DoD or across the executive and legislative branches agree to? What can be implemented?

The various parts of the manpower community go about their work differently. The personnel community, which seeks the best answer for the long term, studies the long-range, ideal effects of policy or changed parameters. This steady-state analysis applies constant rates and planning factors to see what happens in the steady state when all the transitional effects are settled out. Of course, no state is steady; transitional effects form a constant stream. But steady-state thinking is the best analytic tool for policy optimization.

The program and budget community, however, is more interested in the dynamic effects of a changed policy. What happens over a particular time horizon as rates and factors change successively? Not surprisingly, the five- to seven-year horizon of the program objectives memorandum (POM) process is frequently used. Models show the effects of policy choice projected out for about five years, but not beyond (the famous "straight-lined" from the fifth year). Program and budget analysts are more concerned with the immediate resource consequences than with long-term effectiveness issues.

And as for the managerial community, it is more interested in execution: How do we get to a chosen new policy over a period of time? What decisions have to be implemented and when if we are to gain the benefits and avoid the costs? Unfortunately, deciding on a course and implementing it are not one and the same, so tough choices often are not followed through on. The reality is a bewildering agglomeration of half-completed past policy implementations that confound not only the managerial community, but the personnel and program and budget communities as well. Personnel policy tends to accrete over time in marginal ways.

Choosing Among Alternatives, an Example

To illustrate the process just described, consider the following questions: How do specific changes in deployment, or personnel-related, policies and procedures affect

- Force readiness, particularly the availability of individuals and units for deployment?

- The level and distribution of operations tempo and its related stresses on units and individuals?

- Related outcomes, such as geographic stability, unit cohesion, and career-long job satisfaction and quality of life?

- Retention?

- Cost?

Concentrating on these questions helps in identifying objectives and alternatives—part of the front end of the process. Objectives—outcomes desired by the organization—are of extreme importance in decisionmaking. Although they are usually stated broadly, are usually poorly quantified, and may conflict with each other, their purpose is to establish what the decisionmakers consider important. Here, seven objectives have been outlined: high readiness, high geographic stability, less force stress, high unit cohesion, acceptable quality of life and career satisfaction, high retention, and lower cost. Each objective has an associated directional modifier that is useful for clarifying what the decisionmaker means.

The next part of the front end involves making these broad objectives more precise—turning them into variables that can be measured on some scale or metric. This is part of the art of analysis. One or more variables are chosen to represent each entire objective statement. Some objectives (e.g., cost) present many measurement choices; others (e.g., quality of life) seem inherently unmeasurable given the state of the art. One needs to be clear about why the specific variables and measures were chosen, because they may be assailed by those who disagree with the conclusions reached.

Table 6.1 shows the variables and measures for the seven objectives in our example.

Table 6.1

Variables and Measures for Objectives

Objective	Variables and Measures
High readiness	SORTS P-status distribution; deployable-unit distribution
High geographic stability	Time-on-station distribution
Less force stress	DEPTEMPO distribution; time away from bunk
High unit cohesion	Cross-leveling amount
Acceptable quality of life/career satisfaction	Career deployment/assignment patterns
High retention	Continuation rates
Lower cost	Cost

NOTE: SORTS (Status of Readiness and Training System) uses a numerical assessment of personnel fill to get a calculated readiness status (e.g., P1, P2). DEPTEMPO is the tempo of deployments for a unit; time away from bunk is the tempo for individuals. (DoD is in the process of making these two terms more precise.) For unit deployments, units are frequently "cross-leveled" as deployable individuals are reassigned from nondeploying to deploying units.

The last piece of the front end of the analysis entails defining policy alternatives—i.e., courses of action that, if chosen, could change the measure of an objective. For this example, policy alternatives that might apply to an entire military service were outlined, as were policy alternatives that might apply to certain units within a service and to individuals. Tables 6.2, 6.3, and 6.4 show these three alternatives sets, respectively.

Table 6.2

Policy Alternatives Applicable to an Entire Military Service

Policy	Alternative
National military strategy	More deployments; fewer deployments
Reserve component use	More; less
Active/reserve force mix	More active; more reserve
Unit basing	More dispersed; more concentrated
Proportion of operating forces (TOE/TDA[a]; ship/shore)	Higher; lower
Size of units	Larger formations; smaller formations
End strength	Higher; lower
Grade plan	Richer; leaner

[a]TOE = table of equipment; TDA = table of distribution and allowance.

Table 6.3

Policy Alternatives Applicable to Units Within a Service

Policy	Alternative
Resourcing level	Higher authorizations; lower authorizations
Manning priority	Higher; lower
Tour lengths	48 months; 36 months; 24 months; 12 months
Assignment tenure limit	6 years; 5 years; 4 years
On-deck unit system	Yes; no
P-status deployment standard	P-1; P-2; P-3
Cohesion criteria	No cross-leveling; various percentages of allowed cross-leveling
Cross-leveling rules	Local units only; same theater units only; no restrictions
Deployment priority rules	Longest time since previous unit deployment; highest proportion of deployable people; highest readiness status

Table 6.4

Policy Alternatives Applicable to Individuals

Policy	Alternative
Tour extension incentives	Strong; weak; none
Cumulative annual deployment limits	210 days; 180 days; 150 days; 120 days; 90 days
Administrative deferments	More; less
Deployment deferments	6 months; 12 months; 18 months; 24 months
Reenlistment goals	Higher; lower
Retention control points (high year of tenure)	Earlier; later
Selective reenlistment bonuses	More; fewer

Once the front end portion of the process is finished, the middle portion begins, the purpose being to determine the consequences associated with the different alternatives. In what ways do the measures or criteria change as choices are made? Here, more formal techniques are introduced. Each analysis leads to its own methods for determining the consequences of the alternatives vis-à-vis the objective criteria. Because this sample analysis was complex, a formal simulation model was built to capture all of the complicated relationships among the objectives, alternatives, measures, and policies. Any given model will only capture a subset of all the possible relationships; doing more would take more time and effort.

Figure 6.9 shows the relationships that were modeled. The figure is highly detailed, to be sure, the point being to show that many variables affect other variables. Moreover, not all possible relationships are captured. The model is complex enough to represent all those that were captured.[3]

Like all good models, this one permits sensitivity analysis—i.e., it explicitly shows how the objectives would be affected if different alternatives were chosen. In this sample case, analysis ceased at this point, and a good decision dealing with uncertainties, risks, and implementation issues followed. This case dealt with broad objectives and large-scale alternatives; much of manpower and personnel

---

[3]This model was done in conjunction with a RAND colleague, Al Robbert.

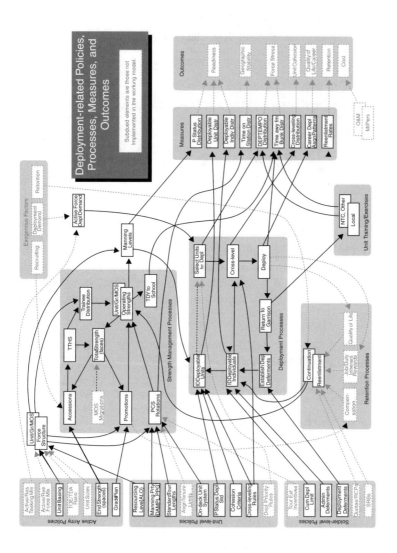

Figure 6.9—Model of Complex Relationships

analysis is narrower and more precise. While trends and broad forces do not change quickly, there is much to be learned by analyzing their impacts when seeking improvements to manpower, personnel, and training policies and processes that will increase military effectiveness and reduce costs.

Chapter Seven

THE SOLDIER OF THE 21st CENTURY

James R. Hosek

Versatility and leadership top the requirements list for the soldier of the 21st century. The future may or may not threaten a major war, but it requires the ability to fight and win one, as well as to engage in a wide variety of smaller conflicts and other operations, such as peacekeeping. The range of demands and flow of new technology call for personnel who can learn rapidly, reach high levels of competence, adapt in the face of uncertainty, and apply a variety of skills in difficult circumstances.

To obtain a versatile, well-led force, there must be a systematic approach for identifying the factors that determine versatility and leadership and for creating the organizational structures and personnel policies needed to support the desired levels of versatility and leadership. While versatility and leadership are inherently the product of policy decisions, it cannot be taken for granted that the requirements for versatility and leadership are well understood, or that the best policies for achieving those requirements are known, or that the policies are actually in place. More to the point, it is probably far more important that adaptable processes be built than that there be a single vision of future requirements and a commitment to that vision.

Adaptability's value stems from uncertainty about the scope of contingencies, the nature of security threats, the speed and range of advances in technology, and the private-sector demand for the kind of members the military would like to recruit and retain. Dynamic workforce planning models therefore have advantages over rigid, input-output planning models. Dynamic models can select policies that are robust to uncertainty and find the least-cost path to changed future requirements. The modeling technology exists, so the feasibility of using such models is not in question. What is important is how to assure that the model's data requirements are satisfied and that the model's structure supports the analysis of policy alternatives.

This chapter is not about a particular model, but about factors relevant to developing and supporting the use of dynamic models in defense manpower planning. The discussion looks to the future, to the past, and to theory. Different kinds of future forces that may affect the quantity and quality of personnel needed are described, and the experience of the all-volunteer force that bears on the services' ability to attract and manage high-quality personnel is reviewed. Among other things, this history includes a Department of Defense (DoD) willingness to conduct controlled experiments and field studies to learn about the cost and effectiveness of policy alternatives. Finally, the chapter discusses theoretical concepts underlying the structure of military compensation, a key policy instrument for meeting future manning requirements. Although the common table of basic pay has been the core of military compensation, larger pay differences across occupations and by experience will likely be needed if career lengths are to differ by occupation.

VISIONS OF THE FUTURE

To imagine the range of future needs, consider visions of future forces: the cyber soldier, the information warrior, peace operations, the rapid response force, low-manning vessels, and evolutionary change. These visions will, no doubt, change over time; they are set out here only to emphasize the diversity of requirements they imply. These visions typify a range of responses to the emergence of the new world order and the advance of technology, with its application to better defense. They are not, however, alternatives to one another: they could all occur.

Cyber Soldier

The cyber soldier belongs to a small unit whose mission is to penetrate enemy territory, engage in surveillance and reconnaissance with the assistance of advanced sensors, and call in remote-fire precision guided weapons. Cyber soldiers will need to be of high quality. The introduction of cyber units will involve organizational changes to assure smooth connections from the unit to the command and control (C2) centers. The cyber soldier concept relies on foreseeable advances in sensor technology, integrated and secure information networks, and computer software capable of tracking large numbers of targets, assigning weapons to them, and firing via remote command. The cyber soldier is entrusted with the decision to fire costly (e.g., million-dollar) weapons and can operate in a stealthy fashion, avoiding detection and capture. The technologies that enable the cyber soldier mean that greater lethality can be achieved with fewer people, with fewer casualties, and, perhaps, at a lower cost (depending on weapon cost and accuracy, as well as how correct the decisions to fire those weapons are). Thus, the cyber soldier concept could reduce the need for large ground forces. The small groups of special operators that fanned out in Afghanistan during 2001–2002, serving as spotters for bringing distant weapons to fire on Taliban and Al Qaeda opponents, were a foretaste of the cyber soldier.

Information Warrior

Enemies will employ asymmetric tactics to harm the United States. In this particular vision, a small number of hackers and terrorists may seek to disrupt information systems in the armed forces and national economy. To counteract this threat, the armed forces have a cadre of highly capable personnel, including contractors, that help develop secure systems, restore systems that have been attacked, trace the source of the attack, and assist in apprehending the attackers. In addition, there is an information warfare capability. Information warriors are up-to-date experts in hardware and software and develop a detailed knowledge of the vulnerabilities of an adversary's information infrastructure. Like pilots and doctors, information warriors have excellent private-sector opportunities (e.g., in safeguarding corporate information systems). Information warriors may be organized into their own units, much as the Air Force has organizations for space systems and missiles.

Peace Operations

Peace operations include disaster relief, humanitarian operations, peacemaking, peacekeeping, nation building, border patrol, and relationship strengthening (such as joint planning exercises and the assignment of U.S. personnel as advisors). With frequent peace operations comes the requirement for a force structure capable of handling several different small-to-medium contingencies at any given time. For some peace operations—such as disaster relief, humanitarian operations, nation building, and peacekeeping—having personnel on the ground is essential, and they need few skills or aptitudes beyond what they have today. But for other peace operations—such as those involving guerillas, urban terrain, large and well-armed adversaries, or chemical, biological, or nuclear weapons (i.e., weapons of mass destruction, or WMD)—special skills and tactics are required. Depending on the variety of peacekeeping operations needed, the services may form specialized units of personnel who are qualified in multiple skills and who take part in unit training for a diversity of threats.

Rapid Response Force

Because a rapid response can reduce the scope, risk, and cost of a major contingency, each service maintains units to deploy on short notice. These units may not require a different quantity or quality of personnel, but they will have undergone unit training and combined-unit training to maintain a high level of readiness. Current training focuses on the possibility of deployment to the next likely trouble spot. To support the rapid response units, logistics are flexible and lean. Supply and repair capabilities are efficient, with no long waits for parts or supplies crucial to the mission. The Air Force, for example, has reorganized as an expeditionary force, a change consistent with reduced overseas basing and an awareness that contingencies can occur anywhere.

Low-Manning Vessels

Labor-saving technologies will allow the services to fulfill their traditional roles and missions with fewer personnel. The Navy builds highly automated vessels that need few crew members. For every combat position eliminated, two to three fewer combat support crew members are needed. And this reduction, in turn, means a reduced number of support personnel are needed for laundry, mess, and the like. Redundant operating systems help sustain the vessel in case of attack or system failure. Crew members need to know how to operate at least one system and, often, two—e.g., automated weapons, navigation, or propulsion, and responses to system breakdown or damage from attack. Even advances in paint make a difference in the number of crew members required on older Navy ships: highly durable paints reduce the number of Gen Dets (general detail personnel) required to maintain a vessel. Other services also benefit from new technology. For instance, an increased reliance on drone vehicles for reconnaissance reduces the demand for pilots, crews, maintenance, and repairs (although it may also increase the demand for intelligence and communications personnel).

Evolutionary Change

Some variant of major theater war (MTW) is always in the set of future planning scenarios. The prospect of MTW points toward evolutionary change, a slow, formidable process that includes force modernization, the incorporation of maturing technologies, and the gradual impact of these two elements on organization and doctrine. Preparedness for major war remains the benchmark for judging military readiness. Not surprisingly, the rationale for many military assets—tanks, helicopters, aircraft, missiles, ships, submarines, artillery, military hospitals, etc.—comes from major war. Peace operations are lesser-included cases that can be handled by a subset of the forces and resources. Moreover, change can be hard to accelerate. The acquisition life cycle of new weapons is about two decades. As force modernization occurs, old equipment dating from the 1950s through the 1970s will be replaced by versions of equipment whose development began in the 1980s and 1990s. Thus, procurement over the next five to 10 years is unlikely to bring surprises in the form of wholly new equipment or systems not included in today's acquisition outlook.

Modernization involves a host of changes: digitization of the battlefield; the use of advanced information systems in logistics, administration, and medical care; and improved precision guided munitions

(PGMs), increases in stealth, improved body armor for personnel, and so forth. To many observers, the combination of advances in information technology, engineered materials, and sensors provides the foundation not just for an evolution but for a revolution in military affairs (RMA). Yet change is usually gradual and tends to lead to functions that are similar but have greater capability, a fact that has two implications for defense manpower. First, if today's personnel satisfy current military requirements, they should be adequate in the near term—i.e., the same knowledge, skills, and aptitudes are likely to be appropriate. Second, there should be enough time to change the kind of personnel or their preparation as needed. This does not necessarily mean, however, that today's personnel management and compensation policies are well suited to support such change, or even that the policies are sufficient to maintain the status quo.

Table 7.1 summarizes the different visions with respect to the need to change the organizational structure, the use of new technology, the impact on total manpower requirements, and the demand for high-quality personnel. Most changes will probably be evolutionary, yet change in technology, doctrine, or strategy might lead to radical change in manpower requirements for specific force elements.

Table 7.1

Comparing the Six Visions of the Future in Terms of Needed Changes

Vision	Organizational Change	New Technology	Manning Requirements	Personnel Quality
Cyber soldier	Yes	Yes	Decrease	High
Information warrior	Maybe	Yes	Increase	High
Peace operations	Maybe	Maybe	Same	Same
Rapid response	Yes	Maybe	Same	Same
Low-manning vessels	No	Yes	Decrease	High
Evolutionary change	Gradual	Gradual	Gradual	Gradual

EXPERIENCE OF THE ALL-VOLUNTEER FORCE

If versatility and leadership are needed in all visions of future forces, it is worthwhile to reflect on what these concepts mean. To a great extent, both depend on the quality of service members recruited and retained. In the years of the all-volunteer force, a great deal has been learned about why quality is important to military capability and how much policy action (or inaction) can influence the quality of the force. That knowledge is the background for the analysis and choices ahead.

Versatility and Leadership

Versatility is the ability to engage in multiple activities. At the individual level, training, experience, and aptitude contribute to versatility. Training provides the knowledge and skills required for certain tasks performed on duty assignments; military training typically consists of basic training, advanced individual training, and on-the-job training. Depending on the specialty's complexity, an enlisted person progresses from entry to intermediate to high skill level. The Air Force describes these as skill levels 3, 5, and 7, for example, which are analogous to apprentice, journeyman, and master levels in trade unions. As their experience increases, personnel work on different tasks, equipment, and missions in a wider range of activities, and their versatility increases. Aptitudes measured include, among others, verbal, quantitative, spatial, mechanical, and coding speed (how fast a person can assimilate new information). The U.S. military measures aptitudes with the Armed Services Vocational Aptitude Battery (ASVAB); it summarizes verbal and quantitative aptitudes in the Armed Forces Qualification Test (AFQT) score.

The concept of versatility goes beyond the individual service member. Peace operations in the 1990s often did not require units to perform missions different from their MTW missions; peace missions were mostly a subset of war missions. But the organizational versatility to handle frequent peace operations and yet maintain readiness for MTW was limited. Peace operations created organizational stress because they interfered with training and exercise programs, affected the planned rotation of personnel overseas, and sometimes reduced the quantity and quality of equipment available to nondeploying units. Moreover, there was no budgetary process for prompt funding of the services' added cost of peace operations, and the objective, scope, and duration of certain peace operations were uncertain. Over time, however, peace operations may have induced the services to become more agile and to handle such operations at lower budgetary cost and with less impact on readiness. In addition, peace operations may have provided information about the effectiveness and vulnerability of current doctrine, equipment, and training.

Because versatility depends on training, experience, and aptitude, it comes at a cost. Senior, experienced personnel cost more than junior personnel, and high-aptitude personnel, who often have better private-sector opportunities, will be bid away unless a military career offers sufficient opportunity for advancement and compensation. Thus, when the services make decisions about desired recruit quality and force experience mix, they are implicitly making decisions about versatility and cost.

Leadership skills, like other human capital, can be strengthened through training, education, and experience. In addition to having specific knowledge about an area (e.g., gunnery, logistics, medicine, intelligence), a leader should be able to identify key objectives, allocate resources efficiently toward them, foster unit cohesion, and motivate personnel to perform at high levels.[1] Allocative efficiency involves balancing marginal gains against marginal costs in a decisionmaking environment that is typically dynamic and uncertain. Poor allocative efficiency implies the leader is not making the most of versatile personnel.

Unit cohesion concerns how well a team functions as a result of its members' knowledge of one another's capabilities and commitment to a common objective.[2] In one view of combat leadership, individual performance follows from cohesion because "unit members are bonded together in their commitment to each other, the unit, and its purposes."[3] But this view does not suggest a mechanism for how cohesion is created. According to another view, cohesion will increase if

---

[1]According to William Darryl Henderson (*Cohesion: The Human Element in Combat*, National Defense University Press, Washington, DC, 1985, p. 11): "The leader must transmit organizational goals or objectives effectively from the chain of command to the small, cohesive group. Then he must lead the unit in achieving these objectives through his personal influence and technical expertise. The leader must also maintain unit cohesion by ensuring continuous organizational support and by the detection and correction of deviance from group norms. Finally, the leader assists in making or maintaining an ideologically-sound soldier by setting an example, by teaching, and by indoctrinating."

[2]This describes *task* cohesion, not *social* cohesion.

[3]Henderson, *Cohesion*, p. 23.

a leader can improve performance: "While cohesiveness may indeed lead the group to perform better, the tendency for the group to experience greater cohesiveness after successful performance may be even stronger."[4] A leader can presumably improve performance, and hence cohesion, by improved allocation of unit resources under uncertainty.

Attracting Quality Personnel

The volunteer force is premised on the ability to set military pay high enough that the supply of volunteers equals manpower requirements. Before the volunteer force, conscripts were paid below their average market wage. Moreover, even if their pay had equaled the average wage, the involuntary nature of conscription meant that a sizable portion of entering personnel would still have paid a "conscription tax"—i.e., the difference between the wage required to induce the person to enlist voluntarily and the military wage. Individuals with a high market wage or a low taste for the military had high reservation wages and therefore paid a high conscription tax. It is not surprising that first-term attrition was high among conscripts. Countries that still rely on conscription, such as Germany, Italy, and Russia, set a short mandatory term of service (a year or less). They thus have high turnover and low experience in their junior force.

The shift to an all-volunteer force in 1973 required a large increase in entry pay. Monthly pay for an enlistee rose from $144 in January 1971 to $288 in January 1972 and $307 in October 1972. As a result, the cost of first-term personnel, who made up about 50 percent of enlisted personnel, became a greater factor for a service to consider in determining personnel force size and experience mix.

The volunteer force began successfully but then faltered, in the late 1970s, as military pay fell relative to private-sector pay. This caused the services difficulty in meeting their recruiting and retention targets, and the quality of recruits declined, particularly in the Army. Lower-quality recruits had higher attrition rates and were less likely to complete training successfully. Given these circumstances, the

---

[4]Brian Mullen and Carolyn Copper, "The Relation Between Group Cohesiveness and Performance: An Integration," *Psychological Bulletin*, Vol. 115, 1994, pp. 210–227.

services and the Office of the Secretary of Defense (OSD) initiated research on whether higher-quality soldiers were cost-effective. The
research included controlled experiments on enlistment incentives
for the active and reserve forces, controlled trials that measured the
effect of quality and experience on the performance of mission-
essential tasks, and specially designed surveys and field studies
related to the relationship between experience and productivity. The
tools and methods used in this research were necessary to obtain
solid, unbiased estimates of policy alternatives that in most cases
had not been tried before and thus could not be studied using historical data.

While the research was under way, Congress boosted military pay by
26 percent between 1980 and 1982, increased recruiting resources,
and raised individual enlistment incentives. The Army and Navy introduced their "college funds" to supplement the basic educational
benefits available from the GI Bill, and all services made greater use
of enlistment bonuses. Reenlistment bonuses were increased in size
and offered to more specialties. In addition, the 1982 recession
spurred both recruiting and retention. Within a few years, these factors produced large improvements in recruit quality and the retention of experienced personnel.

Table 7.2 summarizes the results of selected analyses of personnel
productivity.[5] Of the four indicators of personnel productivity
shown—education, AFQT score, experience, and unit stability—the
first two are the foremost measures of enlisted personnel quality.
Recruits with a high school degree who also score in the upper half
of the AFQT score distribution are classified as high quality. Unit
stability means a slow turnover of personnel in the unit and hence
more experience together on average. Whereas education, AFQT
score, and experience are person-specific measures of quality, unit
stability is not.

---

[5]The table is mainly based on articles cited in John T. Warner and Beth J. Asch, "The
Economics of Military Manpower," in Keith Hartley and Todd Sandler (eds.), *Hand-
book of Defense Economics, Volume I*, Elsevier, New York, 1995, pp. 368-373, although
several other articles were also used.

Table 7.2

Factors Affecting Personnel Productivity

Output Measure	Education	AFQT Score	Individual Experience	Unit Stability
Sorties			√ (a)	
Mission capable rates	√ (b)	√ (b)	√ (a)	√ (c,d)
Maintenance downtime	√ (b,c)	√ (b,c)	√ (b)	
Multitasking			√ (e)	
Supervisor ratings			√ (f)	
Job performance tests	√ (g)	√ (g,h,i,j)	√ (k)	√ (h)

[a] A. Marcus, *Personnel Substitution and Naval Aviation Readiness*, P-3631, Center for Naval Analyses, 1982.

[b] Laura I. Junor and Jessica S. Oi, *A New Approach to Modeling Ship Readiness*, CRM 95-239, Center for Naval Analyses, 1996.

[c] S. Horowitz and A. Sherman, "A Direct Measure of the Relationship Between Human Capital and Productivity," *Journal of Human Resources*, Vol. 15, pp. 67–76, 1980.

[d] Russell W. Beland and Aline D. Quester, "The Effects of Manning and Crew Stability on the Material Condition of Ships," *Interfaces*, Vol. 21, pp. 111–120, 1991.

[e] Glenn Gotz and Richard E. Stanton, *Modeling the Contribution of Maintenance Manpower to Readiness and Sustainability*, R-3200-FMP, RAND, 1986.

[f] Mark J. Albrecht, *Labor Substitution in the Military Environment: Implications for Enlisted Force Management*, R-2330-MRAL, RAND, 1979.

[g] Thomas V. Daula and D. Alton Smith, "Are High Quality Personnel Cost Effective? The Role of Equipment Costs," *Social Science Quarterly*, Vol. 73, pp. 266–275, 1992.

[h] Barry L. Scribner, D. Alton Smith, Robert H. Baldwin, and Robert Phillips, "Are Smarter Tankers Better? AFQT and Military Productivity," *Armed Forces and Society*, Vol. 12, pp. 193–206, 1986.

[i] Bruce Orvis, Michael Childress, and J. Michael Polich, *The Effect of Personnel Quality on the Performance of Patriot Air Defense System Operators*, R-3901-A, RAND, 1992.

[j] John D. Winkler and J. Michael Polich, *Effectiveness of Interactive Videodisc in Army Communications Training*, R-3848, RAND, 1990, and Judith C. Fernandez, "Soldier Quality and Job Performance in Team Tasks," *Social Science Quarterly*, Vol. 73, pp. 253–265, 1992.

[k] C. Hammond and S. Horowitz, *Flying Hours and Crew Performance*, P-2379, Institute for Defense Analyses, 1990, and *Relating Flying Hours to Aircrew Performance: Evidence for Attack and Transport Missions*, P-2608, Institute for Defense Analyses, 1992.

As the table shows, the analyses used different measures of output. Sorties are a direct measure of current output—aircraft sorties produced per day. Mission capable rates indicate a capacity, in this case how well a ship is ready to perform its mission, where readiness depends on equipment availability and operability and personnel availability and training readiness. Maintenance downtime is an indirect measure of maintenance output; multitasking indicates the extent to which personnel with multiple-skill training differed from single-skill personnel in their ability to handle different items for repair that arrive randomly. Supervisor ratings are not tied to any specific production process; supervisors were asked to assess a person's productivity at y months (y < 48) in the first term compared with the "typical" productivity at 48 months. Job performance tests measure the capacity to perform a job such as multichannel radio equipment repair, the operation of Patriot missiles, or the operation of a tank.

In every case, the indicators of personnel quality had a positive effect on output. The results for education and AFQT vindicated the services' earlier push to increase recruit quality and confirmed what the services were reporting from field experience: high-quality personnel outperform low-quality personnel. Experience measured by years of service was also positively related to output. Since experience was a factor in all the studies, the robustness of its effect is clear. As shown and discussed below, experience levels rose throughout the 1980s and into the 1990s, increasing military capability.

After the late-1970s crisis, personnel quality improvements were nothing short of dramatic. Table 7.3 shows the percentage of recruits who were high school graduates and the percentage defined as high quality. From 1975 to 1980, the Army recruited less than 60 percent high school graduates at a time when 80 percent of 18–24 year olds had a high school degree. By 1980, only 21 percent of its recruits were high quality. By comparison, consider that the median value of the AFQT score was normed at 50 in 1980 for a nationally representative sample of the youth population. Given that 80 percent of youths were high school graduates, at least 40 percent should have been defined as high quality. The Navy's percentage of high-quality recruits was around the national average, the Marine Corps's was below average, and the Air Force's was well above average.

Table 7.3

Percentage of Recruits That Are High School Graduates and Percentage That Are High Quality, by Service and Year[a]

Service	1975	1980	1985	1990	1995	1997
Army						
High school graduate	58	52	86	94	94	90
High quality[b]	38	21[c]	49	61	64	58
Navy						
High school graduate	74	74	88	90	92	95
High quality	49	44[c]	49	53	60	61
Marine Corps						
High school graduate	47	70	90	93	95	96
High quality	32	35[c]	49	61	62	62
Air Force						
High school graduate	87	84	99	99	99	99
High quality	63	56[c]	67	84	82	77

SOURCE: *Population Representation in the Military Services, Fiscal Year 1997*, pp. D-12 and D-14.

[a]These are all non-prior service accessions.

[b]High-quality individuals are defined as those who score in the upper half of the AFQT distribution and have a high school degree.

[c]Values reflect test misnorming that led to inflated 1977–1981 scores.

By 1985, a turnaround had occurred. In the Army, Navy, and Marine Corps, the percentage of recruits with a high school degree was 5 to 10 percentage points above the national average, and the percentage of recruits that were of high quality, at 50 percent, was also above the national average. These values continued to increase into the 1990s; by 1995, the Army had 94 percent high school graduates and 64 percent high-quality recruits. The Navy and Marine Corps had over 92 and 95 percent high school graduates, respectively, and 60 and 62 percent high-quality recruits. The Air Force also made substantial gains. In 1995, 99 percent of its recruits were high school graduates and 82 percent were high quality. But recruit quality fell after 1995 because of the strong economy and the increase in college attendance, again demonstrating the need for policy action to be responsive to changes in the external environment.

Table 7.4 shows experience trends for enlisted personnel and officers. The large increase in enlisted experience allowed the services to reap substantial benefits from the higher quality of recruits: more expected years of service, higher performance during those years, and, perhaps, a greater increase in performance with experience because high-quality personnel probably learn faster. Average years of service increased by over a third for enlisted personnel and by 10 percent for officers from 1980 to 1995. Enlisted experience reached 7.4 years in 1997, versus 5.5 years in 1980, partly because of the increase in the percentage of recruits with high school degrees and the fact that their attrition was lower. In the early 1980s, the first-term attrition rate was approximately twice as high for non–high school graduates as for graduates. As the services, especially the Army, reached over 90 percent high school graduates, attrition fell and years of service increased.[6] Officers averaged 9.9 years of service in 1980 and 10.8 in 1997, indicating that an additional year of service

Table 7.4

Average Years of Service and Percent Increase in Mean Years for Enlisted Personnel and Officers

	1980	1985	1990	1995	1997
Average years of service					
Enlisted	5.5	6.0	6.8	7.4	7.4
Officers	9.9	9.9	10.4	10.7	10.8
Percent increase since 1980					
Enlisted	—	9	23	34	34
Officers	—	0	5	8	10

SOURCE: *Population Representation in the Military Services, Fiscal Year 1997*, pp. D-17 and D-27.

---

[6]In the late 1990s, Army first-term attrition was once again high, upwards of 35 percent. This was in part due to the Army's tightening of its training standards. Other causes were the more immediate accession of recruits from the delayed entry pool— i.e., recruits who would have dropped out while waiting to enter service instead dropped out during training. Increases in smoking and decreases in physical fitness also played a role.

was gained from these personnel, which is advantageous given their high costs of accession and training and long learning curves.

The gain in quality and experience was driven by systemic changes. Higher pay, bonuses, educational benefits, increased recruiting resources, improved recruiter management, and a recession led to better recruiting and retention. Higher recruit quality and higher retention rates both meant lower attrition, hence less need to recruit. This allowed the recruiting establishment to focus more on attracting high-quality recruits, which fed the positive cycle. These factors worked together fairly rapidly; much of the revolution in recruit quality occurred between 1980 and 1985. Most of the gain in high school graduates had been attained by 1985, and probably over half the gain in high-quality recruits had been attained by then.[7]

The negative cycle at the end of the 1970s was comparably rapid.[8] Both cycles reflected the potential hazards and benefits of an all-volunteer force. The late-1970s cycle destabilized the volunteer force concept, whereas the early-1980s cycle demonstrated the potential for recovery. Both episodes underscore how dependent the volunteer force is on good management, especially in compensation and recruiting. Also, even though both cycles lasted only a short time, their effects on the force quality were long lasting. Just as high-quality recruits produced the benefits described above, lower-quality recruits pointed to less military capability. They had lower pass rates in training, higher attrition and hence more unit turbulence, and lower

---

[7]In 1980, the recorded percentage of high-quality recruits was inflated by an error in test norming. Therefore, the gain in high quality from 1980 to 1985 was actually greater than shown in Table 7.3.

[8]Military/civilian pay fell throughout this period; the GI Bill, an enlistment incentive, was allowed to lapse; and the national economy improved as unemployment fell from 8.5 percent in 1975 to 5.8 percent in 1979. Recruit quality and retention rates sank, reaching perilous lows in 1980. Further, the ASVAB misnorming masked an even lower quality of recruits. The decline in recruit quality fed higher attrition, and higher attrition plus lower retention kept recruiting requirements high. Recruiting resources were not immediately increased, however, so recruiters were hard pressed to make their goals. In a scramble, they shifted more of their effort away from high-quality prospects to the easier-to-recruit segments of the market—non-graduates and those scoring in the lower half of the AFQT score distribution. As a result, although the recruiters largely succeeded in meeting their recruit quantity goals, the proportion of high-quality recruits fell.

scores on tests of skills and knowledge. The services, particularly the Army, tried to thin out low performers by tightening reenlistment standards, but a large portion of lower-quality personnel reenlisted nonetheless.

Is the conventional definition of high-quality enlisted personnel— i.e., having a high school degree and scoring in the upper half of the AFQT score distribution—too narrow? Although these two indicators are associated with high performance, research has shown (Table 7.2) that only on-the-job experience can reveal certain important but previously unobserved aspects of quality, such as effort, reliability, leadership, ability to work as part of a team, and communication skills.[9]

Information about unobserved quality can be inferred from a person's speed of promotion in the first term.[10] If, when education and AFQT are held constant, a person reaches E-4 faster than his or her peers, this might indicate the person is high quality, but it might also simply be a good random outcome. However, a person who reaches both E-4 and E-5 early is probably a high-quality individual. By analyzing promotion to E-4 and E-5, the net effect of the unobserved quality can be detected, although the individual aspects themselves cannot be identified. Empirical work suggests that unobserved quality plays a major role in accounting for the variation of quality among individuals, a role larger than that of education and AFQT.

In addition, quality and later outcomes appear to be linked. Analysis based on the extended measure of quality indicates that those who perform well in their first term stay for longer careers and reach higher ranks that have leadership responsibilities. Putting this in perspective, since education and AFQT contribute to superior performance, it is advantageous to keep these higher-quality personnel. But personnel with high AFQT scores are actually slightly more likely to leave service after the first term than are personnel with low AFQT

---

[9]Along the same lines, SAT scores predict which students will do well at elite colleges but have far less to say about subsequent earnings.

[10]Michael P. Ward and Hong W. Tan, *The Retention of High-Quality Personnel in the U.S. Armed Forces*, R-3117-MIL, RAND, 1985; James R. Hosek and Michael G. Mattock, *Learning About Quality: How the Quality of Military Personnel Is Revealed over Time*, MR-1593-OSD, RAND, 2002.

scores—an empirical fact that has been known for some time. It suggests that the civilian labor market offers somewhat better career opportunities for high-aptitude individuals than does the military, but this is speculation. The good news is that the military tends to keep personnel who perform well on duty, after controlling for AFQT score.[11]

It is worth mentioning several other issues related to the all-volunteer force that may have a place in future, dynamic models for personnel management. While these may not return as prominent issues, they have been of significant concern in the past. Specifically, critics of the volunteer force have questioned its viability given demographic trends, have decried its seemingly perverse impact on the military as a national institution, and have suggested its potential for weakening societal support for the military.

The first of these concerns—that the high accession requirements of an all-volunteer force could not be supported by the decreasing size of youth population cohorts—became moot as accession requirements fell in the early 1980s. The percentage decrease was greater than the projected percentage decline in the youth population from its high point in 1979 to its low point in 1995. The services also recruited more women.

The second concern was that the all-volunteer force would convert the military from "an organizational format that is predominately institutional to one that is becoming more and more occupational."[12] This would affect the legitimacy of and social regard for military service by replacing normative values, such as honor, duty, and country, and "esteem based on notions of service" with "prestige based on level of compensation."[13] Military personnel would no longer define their role commitment and military reference groups in

---

[11]Related work has found that with education and AFQT held constant, personnel expecting faster promotion to E-5 are more likely to reenlist—another sign of pro-selectivity (Richard Buddin, Daniel S. Levy, Janet M. Hanley, and Donald M. Waldman, *Promotion Tempo and Enlisted Retention,* R-4135-FMP, RAND, 1992.

[12]Charles C. Moskos, "Institutional and Occupational Trends in the Armed Forces," in Charles C. Moskos and Frank R. Wood (eds.), *The Military: More Than Just a Job?* Pergamon-Brassey's, New York, 1988, p.15.

[13]Moskos, "Institutional and Occupational Trends."

terms of their military peers, but instead would make comparisons to civilian occupations. The structure of compensation would shift toward salary and bonuses and away from noncash and deferred compensation.

Although the military changed under the all-volunteer concept, there is little evidence it became a weaker institution or a less capable force or was held in lower esteem by society. The volunteer concept eliminated the conscription tax and proved successful in meeting manpower requirements when pay and recruiting resources were sufficient. It is unclear whether military personnel became less likely to define themselves relative to their military role and military peers. Even under conscription, the military was a volunteer force beyond the first term of service for enlisted personnel or beyond the minimum service obligation for officers; the conversion to an all-volunteer force changed the front end. Senior personnel, those volunteering to remain in service, compare their pay and careers to those in the civilian sector as they no doubt did before the all-volunteer force.

The third concern—about an all-volunteer force weakening societal support for the military—stemmed from the observation that the fraction of the youth population serving in the military had declined. Additionally, fewer members of Congress had military experience. Table 7.5 shows enlistment figures for 18-year-olds for 1955 through 2000. In 1960, 1965, and 1970, about one in four young men entered the military. By 1980, about one in seven joined; and a decade after the Cold War, one in 12 joined. The percentage of young women entering has grown since the all-volunteer force began, but at around 2 percent, it remains small.[14] Still, it is not obvious that the decline in the percentage of young men entering the military reduced society's regard for the military or weakened Congress's resolve to keep the military strong. Fewer youth served because the volunteer force succeeded in keeping personnel longer.

---

[14]The table focuses on non-prior service enlistment, but its message would be little changed by including officers. Officers would add about 1 percentage point to the percentage of males entering service and 0.2 percentage point to the percentage of females.

Table 7.5

Enlistment Figures for 18-Year-Olds, 1955–2000

Year	18-Year-Olds (in thousands)		Non-Prior Service Accessions			Percent Accessing	
	Men	Women	Men	Women	Total	Men	Women
1955	1,074	1,068	611[a]	12[a]	623	56.9	1.1
1960	1,323	1,289	381[a]	8[a]	389	28.8	0.6
1965	1,929	1,875	406	8	414	21.0	0.4
1970	1,914	1,868	619	13	632	32.3	0.7
1975	2,159	2,097	374	36	410	17.3	1.7
1980	2,156	2,089	303	49	352	14.1	2.3
1985	1,877	1,809	259	—	297	13.8	2.1
1990	1,849	1,755	193	30	223	10.5	1.7
1995	1,796	1,710	138	29	167	7.7	1.7
2000	2,011	1,918	160	33	193	8.0	1.7

SOURCE: *Population Representation in the Military Services, Fiscal Year 1997*, pp. D-1 and D-10.

[a]Author's estimate.

Economic Theories of Compensation

Military compensation plainly is a key policy instrument for attracting and keeping high-quality personnel and for shaping the personnel force. According to a global survey of pay, "The increasing importance of human capital is transforming pay and the lives of the human resources managers who administer it. Companies see pay as their main tool for recruiting, motivating and retaining good people. All three are important."[15] Another observation: "The true value of a business (or, for that matter, of a household or a country) is often not fully reflected in the audited numbers because markets value assets that don't show up on the balance sheet. What is the key asset not shown on the balance sheet? It sounds too simple, but a good part of it is people. In today's knowledge-based economy, nothing equals the contribution of people."[16] In theory, compensation can be structured in different ways for different purposes.

[15]*The Economist,* "A Survey of Pay," May 8–14, 1999, unnumbered.

[16]Michael Milken, "From the Chairman," *Milken Institute Magazine,* First Quarter, 1999.

Military compensation includes basic pay, allowances, special and incentive pay, educational benefits, and retirement benefits.[17] Basic pay now depends solely on rank and years of service. The chief allowances are for subsistence and housing. The sum of basic pay, the subsistence allowance, the housing allowance, and the implicit tax advantage from the nontaxability of the allowances is called *regular military compensation.* Special pay supplements are associated with arduous or dangerous duty—e.g., sea pay, submarine pay, aviator continuation pay, and imminent danger pay (formerly called hazardous duty pay). Incentive pay, such as enlistment and reenlistment bonuses, is paid selectively by military occupation and changes in response to the supply of personnel. Educational benefits are available to enlisted personnel through the Montgomery GI Bill and to officers through Reserve Officers Training Corps (ROTC) scholarships and appointments to the service academies. The services supplement the GI Bill benefits with their "college funds" to attract high-quality recruits for certain military occupations. Retirement benefits do not vest until the 20th year of service, are payable immediately upon retirement from the service, and pay approximately 40 to 75 percent of basic pay depending on rank and years of service at time of retirement. There are many other elements of military compensation— uniform allowances, relocation reimbursement, and so forth—but these are more incidental in nature.[18]

The following subsections describe five theoretical perspectives on, or models of, compensation—general human capital, specific human capital, motivation of effort, initial sorting, and tournaments—and how these relate to military compensation.

General Human Capital.[19] General human capital is assumed to be equally valuable in alternative uses—for instance, as valuable in the

---

[17]A comprehensive description of military compensation and its legislative background may be found in *Military Compensation Background Papers,* 5th ed., Department of Defense, Office of Secretary of Defense, 1996.

[18]In addition, the military provides health care to service members and health care coverage to their families, and attends to the schooling of dependents (e.g., by arranging to provide it directly or by compensating local school districts to allow the children of military families based nearby to attend).

[19]The seminal contributions are Gary S. Becker, "Investment in Human Capital: A Theoretical Analysis," *Journal of Political Economy,* Vol. 70, October 1962, pp. 9–49;

military as in the private sector. Common instances of general human capital are elementary and secondary schooling, and verbal and quantitative skills. Money and equipment constitute investments in human capital, as does the individual's time. The main cost to the individual comes from forgone earnings during the time spent in school or training. Because general human capital can be used anywhere, the employer has no incentive to pay for it, and the worker bears the full cost and receives all the returns. An employer that paid for the investment could not expect to capture the returns without paying the worker a wage above his marginal value product. Such a wage would cause the worker to remain with the employer, but it would also cause the employer to lose money. Therefore, the worker bears all the cost, and the worker's subsequent wage just equals his marginal value product. Thus, in this model, the costs and returns to human capital investment are entirely the worker's, the worker receives a wage equal to marginal value product in each period, and the worker has no incentive to stay with a particular employer.

If education is taken to be an indicator of general human capital, it follows that military compensation must keep pace with market wage for those with education in order to maintain a flow of recruits. One way to judge whether compensation is keeping pace is to compare military pay with the market wage for a particular group. For instance, we can compare regular military compensation for an E-4 with the wage deciles of 22- to 26-year-old white males who are full-time year-round workers.[20] Military pay was at a value equal to the 50th percentile (median wage) in 1982, rose over the next few years to above the 60th percentile, subsided, and then rose sharply to the 70th percentile as the nation's economy slowed down and entered a recession in the early 1990s. The increase in military pay over this period thus fueled the increase in recruit quality. But from 1993 to 2000, military pay fell, relatively, and the services reported increasing difficulty in recruiting.[21]

---

and Jacob Mincer, "On-the-Job Training: Costs, Returns, and Some Implications," *Journal of Political Economy*, Vol. 70, October 1962, pp. S50–S90.

[20]Regular military compensation equals the sum of basic pay, basic allowance for subsistence, basic allowance for housing, and a tax adjustment account for the allowances not being subject to federal income tax.

[21]For further discussion, see Beth Asch, James Hosek, and John Warner, *On Restructuring Enlisted Pay*, AB-468-OSD, RAND, December 2000.

Specific Human Capital.[22] Suppose an employer can profit from a firm-specific investment in a worker if the worker remains at the firm. The only way the employer can be sure to retain the worker is to pay more than the worker can get elsewhere. The employer can do this by using part of the returns to support the increased wage. But on the margin, if the employer shares the returns but pays the full cost of the investment, the investment is unprofitable. A feasible alternative is for the employer to allow the worker to participate in the investment, sharing the returns and costs proportionately. Then the worker's wage is less than his or her opportunity wage during the investment phase and more than the opportunity wage afterwards. The employer pays part of the investment cost and afterwards receives a stream of returns equal to the difference between the worker's marginal value product and wage. Because of the sharing, the worker's wage profile is not as steep as it would be for an equal-size investment in general human capital, where the worker would bear the full cost and receive the full returns.

The specific human capital model suggests why workers at a firm who have greater seniority and who are more educated are less likely to be laid off or dismissed during a business slump. These workers tend to have more firm-specific capital invested in them. Since a worker's marginal value product exceeds his or her wage, there is room for a decrease in the marginal value product before it drops below the wage and triggers a separation. One question this model does not address is: After the investment has been made, what stops the employer from paying the worker less than promised but more than his opportunity wage? An answer stems from the concepts of repeated contracting and reputation that have been developed in game theory. With repeated contracting, the employer who wants the option of making later investments in the worker should not renege on the initial deal. If the employer damages his reputation by acting in bad faith, employees will be unwilling to deal without safeguards on their returns, the costs of which will have to be borne either by the employer directly or by the worker and then passed on to the employer as a cost of the transaction.

---

[22]The seminal contributions here are also from Becker, "Investment in Human Capital," and Mincer, "On-the-Job Training."

In military compensation, bonuses and special pay are mechanisms for rewarding investments in military-specific human capital. They are found in occupations having no direct civilian counterpart—e.g., combat arms, submariner, fighter pilot. Because bonuses and special pay encourage retention, they enable the services to get more return on their investment in military-specific human capital. Bonuses and special pay are also found in military occupations whose skills are transferable to private-sector jobs that offer more than basic pay. Because private-sector wages vary across occupations but the military uses a common basic pay table across all of them, the military must pay some occupations more to make them competitive with outside opportunities.

Motivation of Effort.[23] In this model, the employer wants the worker to exert effort, but effort is assumed to create disutility for the worker. The employer knows that a worker can be induced to exert more effort in exchange for higher future pay, but the employer cannot pay more than the worker is worth to the firm over his/her working lifetime at the firm, given the expected level of effort. Because the worker's choice of effort depends on his/her expected wage growth, the employer offers the worker a schedule of wage/effort profiles. Each worker selects the wage/effort profile that maximizes utility; higher-effort profiles generally have faster wage growth. In addition, to attract the worker, the employer must make the value of the selected wage profile at least as great as that of any alternative opportunity with a different employer. But faster wage growth cannot go on forever, because it would exceed the worker's value to the firm. Hence, if the firm is to offer steeper wage profiles to induce greater effort and thereby make the worker more valuable to the firm, the firm must also stipulate a mandatory retirement date for each wage profile.

In the military, pay growth occurs through time in service, promotion, and the year-to-year increase in expected future retirement benefits. At a given rank, the growth of time-in-service basic pay is shallow and offers little incentive for greater effort. In fact, during the first 10 or so years of service, most wage growth comes from promo-

---

[23]A key initial source is Edward P. Lazear, "Why Is There Mandatory Retirement?" *Journal of Political Economy*, Vol. 87, December 1979, pp. 1261–1284. Lazear's later reflections appear in "Personal Economics: Past Lessons and Future Directions," *Journal of Labor Economics*, Vol. 17, No. 2, pp. 199–236.

tions. But promotions are not the main focus of the effort motivation theory, which aims at effort on a given job—i.e., in the military, at a given rank. For personnel who reach 10 years of service, expected retirement benefits become an increasingly important factor in their compensation. Also, discounting causes the expected present value of retirement benefits to rise dramatically as the 20th year of service approaches. For many service members, the value of annual compensation, including the increment in expected future retirement benefits, is greater than the value of his or her output during these years—a result that fits the ideas in the incentive motivation model. The military also sets a mandatory retirement date of 30 years of service—another fit with the model.

But do expected retirement benefits actually offer a strong incentive for performance during service years 10 to 20? To reach 20 years of service at current rank, the service member must guard against a mistake or misbehavior that would result in demotion or dismissal from service. Passable behavior probably does not require much effort, so, from an organizational perspective, it is important that people *not* reach 10 to 12 years of service without having been selected for their knowledge, skills, initiative, and effort. This observation suggests the value of sorting and tournament models.

Initial Sorting.[24] Despite the information gained from résumés, job interviews, screening tests, and even handwriting analysis, employers are hard pressed to tell if a new employee is well matched to the job. Job changes are frequent among young workers; about half of all unemployment falls on workers under age 25. To some people, frequent job changes represent aimless churning within the labor market; to others, they are a sorting process. Economic models of sorting assume there is uncertainty about a worker's ability, even given observable characteristics such as education, test scores, and prior experience. Each worker has an incentive to claim high ability, especially if the employer cannot verify the claim. What the employer must do, then, is observe the worker's performance on the job and be willing to offer a contract in which higher future wages are conditional on revealed ability. Using repeated observations comparing

---

[24]Boyan Jovanovich, "Firm-Specific Capital and Turnover," *Journal of Political Economy*, Vol. 87, December 1979, pp. 1246–1260.

the worker's performance to external or internal standards, the employer can assess the worker's ability. Since assessment comes in the context of performance within the firm, ability becomes synonymous with "quality of job match."

The military does a great deal of sorting. Most officers have an initial service obligation of four years, and much of the sorting occurs after this period and during the rank of captain (O-3). That is, most officers (70 to 90 percent) continue in service after completing their service obligation but then leave service at a fairly steady rate while they are captains, say, years six to 11. About 50 percent of officer cohorts reach the O-4 promotion window around 11 to 13 years of service, and about 40 percent continue to 20 years of service (retirement eligibility). Among enlisted personnel, about 30 of every 100 accessions are lost to first-term attrition, and about half of the remaining 70 reenlist. So, about 35 percent of those in an enlisted cohort stay for a second term, and eventually about 13 percent reach 20 years of service. Those who stay tend to be personnel who have performed well relative to their peers and personnel who have a taste for the military.

Tournaments.[25] Tournament models analyze competition for promotion within a hierarchical organization. The organization is assumed to be a pyramid: the number of positions decreases as job rank increases. The employer wants the most-capable workers to ascend to positions of highest authority because high-level decisions affect productivity at all lower levels. The tournament model describes a mechanism to induce effort and sort workers efficiently. Consider a firm with two ranks, mid and high, and a worker at the mid level. The worker's incentive to compete for promotion to the high level depends on the probability of promotion and the high-level wage. The product of these two is the worker's expected wage at the high level. If the worker is a wealth maximizer, the expected wage must exceed the mid wage or the worker has no incentive to compete.

Now add a low level to the organization. A low-level worker's incentive to compete for promotion to mid level depends on the increase

---

[25]The concept of tournaments comes from Sherwin Rosen, "Prizes and Incentives in Elimination Tournaments," *American Economic Review*, Vol. 76, September 1986, pp. 701–715.

in expected wealth, which depends on the mid-level wage and the wage expected with promotion from mid to high level. Also, the low wage must be lower than the mid-level wage to create a positive incentive to compete. Now assume that the probability of promotion from mid to high level is less than that of promotion from low to mid level. This assumption accords with the job pyramid, but it is subtle because the probability of promotion depends not only on the number of higher-rank positions, but also on the rate of outflow of personnel from those positions and the firm, which in turn depends on the promotion and wage structure. It follows that the ratio of the high-level to the mid-level wage must be greater than the ratio of the mid-level to the low-level wage.[26] In other words, the wage structure is skewed by rank. The tournament model thus implies that wages should be disproportionately greater at each rank. Moreover, competing for promotion may entail exerting greater effort than otherwise and investing in human capital. In most cases, the workers compete against one another, not an external standard. To move up the promotion queue, the worker must outperform fellow workers, who are also exerting more effort. If the competition is stiff, some workers will not bother to compete. Also, if highly able workers can get by with little effort, they will do so unless they face high stakes at the higher ranks in the form of skewed pay.[27]

The military makes extensive use of promotions. Competition for them tends to induce greater effort among the competitors, and since competition favors the more able, they are the ones more likely

---

[26]The mid wage cannot be greater than the high wage. If it were, there would be no incentive for mid-level workers to compete for the high-level job. For low-level workers, the increase in expected wealth depends on mid- and high-level promotion probability and wages. Conceivably, the mid wage could be *less* than the low wage if the expected high-level wage were high enough. The second assumption rules out this possibility. This assumption is consistent with a rationality constraint: If the mid-level job required higher skills or more effort than the low-level job, qualified workers being hired from outside the firm would not choose the mid-level job unless it paid more than the low-level job.

[27]Another model is that of principal and agent (e.g., see Bengt Holmstrom, "Moral Hazard and Observability," *The Bell Journal of Economics*, Vol. 10, No. 1, Spring 1979, pp. 74–91). Typically, an efficient principal-agent contract involves the principal assigning a property right to the agent (e.g., a portion of net revenues or stock options), with the principal remaining as a residual claimant. This model does not translate easily to the military context because it is difficult to assign a property right to income or the opportunity for added wealth (stock option).

to compete. Because each rank in the military is a stepping stone to the next, the expected gain from future promotions enters current decisionmaking about whether to compete and how much effort to exert. At first glance, military compensation does not appear skewed, because basic pay does not have a prominent nonlinear increase with rank. But as mentioned earlier, after 10 years of service, the draw of retirement benefits grows much stronger each year. Since retirement benefits depend on rank at retirement, the gain associated with promotion is substantial. Thus, retirement benefits impart skew, the more so with promotion.

This does not mean retirement benefits are necessarily the best way to skew the wage structure. One could argue that a better way would be to move a large portion of military compensation from retirement benefits to current compensation to create a skewed basic pay structure.[28] And there is a definite limitation associated with using retirement benefits to create skew. The services operate their promotion systems in a way meant to provide equal opportunity for advancement regardless of one's military occupation. As a result, the expected pay grade at retirement is roughly the same across occupations. This affords little freedom to tailor career paths to specific occupations, as might be advantageous in the case of certain skills and areas (e.g., information technologists and acquisition specialists). By the same token, pay differentials across occupations can be introduced only through bonuses or special pay, neither of which counts toward increasing the size of a service member's retirement benefits.

ISSUES FOR THE FUTURE

The capability of future military forces depends on the versatility and leadership of their personnel, which, in turn, depend on the quality of not only the enlisted and officer recruits, but also the policies affecting training, experience, career development, and cohesion.

How can the military recruit and retain these high-quality personnel? The history of the all-volunteer force tells a profound story. Competitive, well-structured compensation and adequate recruiting re-

---

[28]See Beth J. Asch and John T. Warner, *A Theory of Military Compensation and Personnel Policy*, MR-439-OSD, RAND, 1994.

sources have enabled the military to attract and keep the personnel it most needs, whereas lapses in compensation and recruiting led to a manpower crisis. Moreover, a willingness to conduct formal experiments and demonstrations, as well as an ongoing program of research and analysis, was required to determine an appropriate level and structure of compensation. By managing the volunteer force well, policymakers increased quality, increased reenlistment, and increased the average career length—all of which contributed to greater military capability. The types of tools used successfully in the past can be applied to future policy alternatives. Moreover, the scope of inquiry can expand, since most past analysis focused primarily on supply issues rather than on demand (requirement) issues.

New recruiting challenges have already presented themselves. More high school graduates are choosing to attend college, shrinking the traditional recruiting pool. The number of new accessions needed has risen from levels held low during the drawdown and may rise further if force size is increased to ease the manning of peace operations, as some suggest. Private-sector wages have been rising faster for persons with some college than for those with only a high school degree, and faster for those with high aptitudes. Also, officer retention has fallen in certain areas (e.g., Air Force captains). Close monitoring and timely action are required to keep military careers competitive with private-sector opportunities, and innovative recruiting strategies are needed to align the military's recruiting strategies with the increased numbers of young people going to college and to then penetrate the two-year college market. The risk of not taking these steps is a costly loss of high-quality human capital and leadership.

Officers and enlisted personnel can expect the heightened pace of peacetime operations to continue. Service members complain of being too busy and that the unpredictability of deployments disrupts family life. Even so, those who have been deployed have somewhat higher reenlistment rates than those who have not, although extensive deployment into hostile areas can eat into this higher rate.[29] Thus, the military needs to manage the tempo of work life and the nature and frequency of deployments for all personnel.

---

[29]James R. Hosek and Mark Totten, *Does Perstempo Hurt Reenlistment? The Effect of Long or Hostile Perstempo on Reenlistment*, MR-990-OSD, RAND, 1998.

The services will also want to look at longer careers in occupations with high military-specific capital. Today's pay table is based on rank and time in service, providing most pay growth through promotions. Senior military specialists may not need a higher rank (and the command authority it provides), however, although they presumably do need incentives for performance. The pay table may have to be restructured to provide these incentives. Specialists in other areas, such as information technology, may require more-creative work environments with access to the latest technology.

Future manpower requirements will also be an issue. As future force concepts, such as the cyber soldier and information warrior, are developed, manpower will have to be brought into defense planning so that force structure assessments consider the benefits and costs of having more-experienced personnel in certain functional areas or occupations. Changes in experience mix, pressures to maintain or increase recruit quality, and private-sector wage growth may lead the military to reevaluate the structure of military compensation and military careers with respect to their cost-effectiveness in attracting, keeping, motivating, and sorting personnel.

Chapter Eight

ADAPTING BEST COMMERCIAL PRACTICES TO DEFENSE[1]

Frank Camm

Over the last decade, the Department of Defense (DoD) has sought increasingly to transform its basic approach to warfighting and the methods it uses to support warfighters.[2] As part of this effort, leaders and influential observers of DoD have repeatedly encouraged DoD to emulate "best commercial practices" (BCPs)—the practices of commercial firms that have been recognized by their peers as being the best among firms engaged in similar activities. Over the past 20 years, many successful firms have found that BCPs offer an important new source of information for improving their competitive position. In particular, they have used information on BCPs to complement and even replace more traditional forms of analysis associated with organizational innovation. Properly used, BCPs provide a rich

---

[1]Much of the material in this chapter draws on empirically based policy analysis that I have conducted at RAND with John Ausink, Laura Baldwin, Charles Cannon, Mary Chenoweth, Irv Cohen, Cynthia Cook, Jeff Drezner, Chris Hanks, Cynthia Huger, Ed Keating, Brent Keltner, Beth Lachman, Jeff Luck, Ellen Pint, Ray Pyles, Ken Reynolds, Susan Resetar, Hy Shulman, Jack Skeels, and, particularly, Nancy Moore, co-leader with me of the Project AIR FORCE project on new approaches to sourcing and contracting. Together, we have reviewed the empirical literature on identifying and implementing best commercial practices in logistics, environmental management, and sourcing-related processes. We have conducted detailed case studies on practices in over 60 commercial firms and many DoD organizations. I could not have written this chapter without the work we have done together, but I retain full responsibility for the chapter's content.

[2]For more information on this effort, see U.S. Department of Defense, *Quadrennial Defense Review Report,* Washington, DC, 30 September 2001; U.S. Congress, General Accounting Office, *Defense Reform Initiative: Organization, Status, and Challenges,* GAO/NSIAD-99-87, Washington, DC, April 1999.

database on new ideas that have worked in particular settings and on the factors underlying their success. Advocates of using BCPs in DoD argue that BCPs could serve a similar role in helping the department transform itself. That is, BCP assessment could complement other methods used to support transformation, including traditional forms of public policy analysis.

By contrast, skeptics argue that the institutional setting of DoD (and, more broadly, the federal government) is so different from the settings of commercial firms that BCPs have little to teach DoD. As my colleague, Gregory Treverton, argues, "The public and private sectors are alike in all the unimportant respects." Differences in basic values, incentives, constraints, and operating environments, as well as DoD's profoundly political setting, limit the applicability of BCPs observed in commercial firms.

This chapter describes how DoD can use BCPs to help transform activities that have appropriate commercial analogs, particularly activities in the defense infrastructure.[3] These include administrative services, generic business and personnel services, education and training, sourcing, and the elements of base operations, medical care, information services, logistics, and civil engineering that are separable from direct military operations.[4] Even where appropriate commercial analogs exist, fundamental differences between the public and private sectors require that BCPs be carefully tailored for adaptation to DoD needs. DoD has already found ways to tailor such BCPs to its peculiar needs and can do a great deal more of this in the future.

This chapter first addresses the general challenge of adapting BCPs to DoD. It then uses sourcing BCPs relevant to DoD to illustrate more concretely how to adapt BCPs to DoD's peculiar institutional setting.

----

[3]For simplicity, I speak of a monolithic DoD in search of BCPs. Of course, DoD must rely on its constituent components and agencies to find and adapt BCPs in ways that work best for them. When I speak of DoD taking any particular action, I mean a particular decisionmaker or activity within DoD acting within the constraints relevant to that part of DoD.

[4]DoD can use commercial models for other activities as well, but finding useful analogs becomes increasingly difficult as the department's core military activities are approached.

The initial overview covers four topics: (1) what BCPs are and how DoD can benefit by learning more about them; (2) the close relationship between many BCPs and operational total quality management (TQM)—i.e., TQM absorbed into day-to-day operational decision-making; (3) how DoD can identify BCPs relevant to its needs; and (4) how DoD can use formal change management techniques to adapt such BCPs to its own goals and operational environment.

Using BCPs associated with the general commercial practice called "strategic sourcing," the chapter then walks through a sequence that uses change management to adapt BCPs to DoD's needs. This sequence identifies strategic goals relevant to DoD sourcing policy, sourcing BCPs relevant to these goals and the way in which these BCPs relate to one another, DoD's recent efforts to adapt these BCPs and key barriers to more complete adaptation, and tactics DoD can use to mitigate these barriers. DoD could use a similar sequence to pursue adaptation of BCPs in any policy area.

WHAT IS A BEST COMMERCIAL PRACTICE?

BCPs are typically tied to processes—i.e., activities that transform inputs into outputs in any organization. Processes can, for example, transform strategic priorities into requirements, development resources into new products, or labor and material inputs into serviceable parts. BCPs occur in processes that use fewer inputs to yield better or more outputs faster. They make specific processes or their outputs "better, faster, and/or cheaper."

Most BCPs are more likely to occur in firms that do business with one another rather than with DoD. So, to find BCPs, DoD must typically look well beyond its traditional horizons.

Examples

Caterpillar was among the first firms recognized for world-class logistics performance. In 1990, it could fill 98 percent of all requests for parts within 48 hours, anywhere in the world. During the Persian Gulf War, Saudi Caterpillar tractors, supported by Caterpillar, were available throughout the war, whereas U.S. Army Caterpillar tractors, reliant on organic DoD support systems, were not. The specific changes in logistics and sourcing processes that brought about such world-class performance in order fulfillment and reliability are BCPs.

In 1986, the Emergency Planning and Community Right-to-Know Act (EPCRA)[5] created the toxic releases inventory (TRI), which identifies the physical volume of a list of toxic chemicals emitted by major U.S. companies each year. The TRI made many corporate executives aware, for the first time, of how their firms were affecting the environment (and how much money they were wasting as emitted chemicals). Under a variety of voluntary programs, firms committed themselves to cut emissions by an order of magnitude over three years. By implementing operational and environmental BCPs tailored to their particular industrial processes, they met their commitment without having to cut industrial production. DoD cut its TRI emissions by 50 percent over three years. It could very likely go even further.

From 1993 to 1997, AMR, the parent company of American Airlines, cut the cost of all its purchased goods and services by 20 percent (relative to inflation) without affecting performance levels. Honda cut similar costs by 17 percent from 1994 to 1997 without a performance loss. Both firms already had sophisticated purchasing programs in place. They introduced BCPs, tailored to their priorities, into their purchasing and supplier management processes to achieve these improvements; further improvement has continued in both firms as they have refined their approaches. DoD has sought savings of this magnitude primarily in incremental A-76 cost-comparison studies.[6] AMR and Honda's experiences suggest the virtues of using a much broader approach focused on process change.

Commercial Practice: Neither Monolithic nor Easy to Define

A BCP is not a *specific* best way of doing something that can be picked up and moved anywhere else. On the contrary, the first lesson

---

[5]42 U.S.C. 11001-11050, also known as Title III of SARA (Superfund Amendments and Reauthorization Act).

[6]Office of Management and Budget (OMB) Circular A-76 defines a process DoD can use to compare the costs of using public and private sources to execute a particular work scope.

from commercial practice is that the private sector accommodates an extraordinary variety of policies and practices.

What works in one place may not work in another. The best commercial firms are always trying to learn from other firms with comparable processes, but they recognize that they cannot simply emulate another firm's practice without understanding why it works. Firms look for what might work in their own setting, and when they adopt a BCP, they may use it in such a new way that it is hard to tell exactly what was learned. The fact that best practices must be *adapted* to each new setting makes them elusive; even if all commercial firms applied best practices, there would be considerable variation among them.

Some firms stand out as particularly innovative. The best firms' practices differ precisely because these firms have found different—better—policies and practices that other firms have difficulty emulating.

To complicate things further, BCPs do not stand still. The variation observed in the commercial sector reflects informal experiments that constantly test the effectiveness of doing things differently. As particular practices succeed in appropriate settings, these practices become, by definition, BCPs. They prevail as long as they continue to yield success when appropriately applied. Over time, constant innovation, imitation, and competition yield variations that work even better, constantly displacing practices once considered the best. Firms that use BCPs do not identify specific practices that they then rely on indefinitely so much as they continually seek the best practices available. A commitment to always continue this search underlies the BCPs in the best firms.

Why DoD Should Care

Global competition is driving the best commercial firms to improve every aspect of their businesses. These firms are learning how to (1) determine requirements more quickly and with greater precision to increase the firm's agility and reduce its waste, (2) integrate organic processes across functional boundaries and align those processes with the needs of customers,[7] (3) build relationships with outside sources that integrate those sources with organic processes and the buyer's customers, (4) manage these relationships to realize the buyer's and seller's expectations, and (5) pick sources that can do this.

DoD faces such challenges itself, but in a different environment. Commercial firms face competition that threatens their survival day by day. DoD operates in a more lethal environment, but one that is truly threatening only during a contingency. When DoD actually projects military force, it can expect to face opponents with access to much of the information about BCPs that DoD has. In a global setting, global commercial practices can be adapted anywhere.

Because commercial firms are learning how to perform in an increasingly turbulent, unpredictable, competitive environment, the BCPs they develop often give particular attention to managing uncertainty more effectively. With care, DoD can use BCPs to ask how better to manage the increasingly uncertain environment in which it operates. Care is required to distinguish risks whose root causes are similar for both DoD and commercial firms (such as technological innovation and the behavior of external sources) from risks unique to DoD (such as those driven by immediate military concerns or congressional politics).

As these examples illustrate, DoD can expect not only cost reductions, but also improvements in process performance and product quality and reliability.[8] What aggregate improvements BCPs will allow DoD to achieve cannot be predicted; they will depend on the particulars of the processes and products DoD addresses and on how it adapts specific commercial practices to its own institutional setting. But it is reasonable to expect that wherever DoD can find com-

---

[7]*Functions* are communities of specialists trained in similar skills, such as maintenance, financial management, or contracting. They provide skills to many different processes. *Processes* use specialists from different functions to deliver a product, such as a repaired part or a meal, to a customer. Functions tend to have an input-oriented perspective; processes tend to have an output-oriented perspective.

[8]DoD's goals reach well beyond concerns about cost, performance, quality, and reliability. As we shall see, DoD's institutional environment places high value on other goals for sourcing policies and practices. Given the priorities captured by that environment, however, BCPs are most likely to help DoD improve its costs, performance, quality, reliability, and so on. We return to this point below.

mercial analogs, it should be able to achieve significant and continuing improvements that outweigh the effort required to achieve such change. DoD can learn over time what to expect and thus specifically where to continue investing.

A BCP That DoD Uses Today: Lean Production

The book *The Machine That Changed the World* [9] did much to popularize the relevance of BCPs. It detailed how the Japanese automobile industry was outperforming its North American counterpart, which, in turn, was outperforming the European counterpart. The term *lean production* was used to explain why the performance of these industries differed, what North American industry could learn from the Japanese automobile industry, and what some BCPs were in 1990.

What did Japanese firms do right? They cut design, marketing, and production cycle times to catch errors quickly, thereby generating less wasted effort than North American firms did. They built quality into the cars to reduce the cost of after-the-fact inspections and rework, thereby slashing parts and work-in-progress inventories, which, in turn, reduced the capital investment required to produce cars. They used basic TQM tools to understand what customers wanted and then aligned all of their design, marketing, and production processes to give customers exactly that.

When RAND analysts first examined lean production, they expected to find nothing useful to DoD. What could an organization focused on warfighters learn from firms driven by commercial accountants? The answer depends on how one looks. Lean production pays particular attention to uncertainties associated with customer demand, production process performance, and the performance of external sources. When RAND analysts looked at the automobile industry, process by process, and compared the uncertainties in these processes with those in analogous processes in military logistics, they discovered that lean production offered exactly what DoD needed to

---

[9]By James P. Womack, Daniel Roos, and Daniel T. Jones, MacMillan/Rawson Associates, New York, 1990.

deal with its logistical uncertainties.[10] RAND helped the Air Force develop its first application of lean production: agile combat support (originally called "lean logistics"). The Army followed shortly thereafter, developing its velocity management, and the Marines then developed their precision logistics. Each adaptation is tailored to its specific setting in DoD.[11] None would have occurred the way it did had DoD not discovered how to learn from the experiences of the Japanese automobile industry.

What About Best Government Practice?

People in DoD tend to seek best practices elsewhere in DoD or at least in other agencies of the federal government. Benchmarking efforts in the federal government tend to focus on the government, and they suggest that cross-government learning is important.

Nevertheless, DoD ought to look as far afield as commercial firms outside DoD's traditional orbit, because these firms are experiencing a real revolution in business affairs that is likely to continue. Moreover, while defense spending is growing, it still makes up just a few percent of the U.S. economy. All else being equal, any innovation is thus many times more likely to occur outside the defense sector than within it. The likelihood is even higher for processes that are more commercial than military in character, especially those processes that make up DoD's infrastructure. If DoD can monitor commercial ideas that succeed, it can cull the best ones for its own use without having to experience the failure that some ideas, inevitably, will meet with.

In effect, BCPs help DoD focus its leadership and in-house innovation efforts on its core missions, because BCPs give it access to useful

---

[10]I. K. Cohen, John B. Abell, T. Lippiatt, *Coupling Logistics to Operations to Meet Uncertainty and the Threat (CLOUT): An Overview*, R-3979-AF, RAND, 1991; Timothy L. Ramey, *Lean Logistics: High Velocity Logistics Infrastructure and the C-5 Galaxy*, MR-581-AF, RAND, 1999.

[11]For example, agile combat support increasingly emphasizes the importance of adapting to new contingencies quickly so that the Air Force can become more "expeditionary"—i.e., can project force more quickly and reliably in a contingency. Velocity management emphasizes improvement in peacetime performance to bring Army logistics processes under control to make them more reliable and less costly.

external information about its noncore activities—i.e., those with close analogs in the commercial sector. If most technological and organizational innovations outside its core activities are highly likely to occur elsewhere, why should DoD waste its own effort and resources keeping these activities at the cutting edge of capability? BCPs offer an alternative approach, one that DoD can use if it creates and maintains core, in-house capabilities for adapting BCPs. These new capabilities would free resources and leadership efforts to focus on core activities.

That said, when an innovation enters DoD (or the rest of the government), from whatever source, it is fair game for adaptation. Adaptation of any best practice is first and foremost about change management. Much of the following discussion on implementing change applies as well to best *government* practices as to BCPs.

OPERATIONAL TOTAL QUALITY MANAGEMENT AND BCPs

As often as not, BCPs involve the application of TQM in particular settings. The ideas at the core of TQM are simple and logical: TQM offers a straightforward approach to using reliable empirical evidence to track and adjust management decisions. *Operational* TQM does this as an integral part of day-to-day management. It does not maintain a functional distinction between a "quality community" and line management.

Key Benefits of TQM: Links Between Customers and Processes, and Continuous Improvement of Resulting System

TQM seeks clear, empirically based answers to three fundamental sets of questions:[12]

• Who are the firm's customers and what do they want? If the firm has many customers, do they want different things? What can the firm do to reflect these differences in its products?

---

[12]For an eloquent demonstration of this point, see Arnold S. Levine and Jeff Luck, *The New Management Paradigm: A Review of Principles and Practices,* MR-458-AF, RAND, 1994.

- What processes does the firm use to serve its customers, and how does it coordinate these processes so that they all align with customer needs? If the firm buys inputs from external sources, how does it align these sources with its customers' needs?

- How can the firm improve? Is it serving the right customers? How can it improve its understanding of its customers' needs? How can it better coordinate and align all processes it uses to serve its customers?

Described this way, TQM sounds like simple common sense. To a large extent, it is. But such common sense focuses management's attention on (1) its customers rather than its internal constituencies (which can legitimize themselves under TQM only by serving the ultimate customer), and (2) cross-functional processes rather than the internal communities in functional divisions (which are thereby deemphasized).

TQM rejects internal standards as a basis for monitoring internal performance in favor of challenging all process owners to look for ways to improve the standard performance of each process. The logical place to look is at similar processes used elsewhere—BCPs, for example.

TQM relies on the idea that these things do not happen unless individuals do them. TQM aligns the behavior of individuals with an organization's goals. It formally recognizes the importance of stakeholders and the fact that they must participate in any process management. It then seeks rules of engagement, roles and responsibilities, metrics, and incentives that help them work toward a common purpose. In particular, it helps stakeholders involved in any process look beyond the process and understand how it can contribute to the goals of the organization as a whole. Such "common sense" demands that an organization that wants to change not only recognize what that change means for the job behavior of the individuals affected, but also prepare careful plans directly focused on how the change will affect the behavior of the individuals. These ideas demand that behavioral change lie at the heart of any organizational change induced by a decision to adapt a new practice.

TQM is most commonly associated with continuous improvement—
kaizen, in Japanese. *Kaizen* can mean taking a given process or cus-

tomer base and improving it over time—perhaps by shortening the process's cycle time or improving the firm's understanding of the customer base's latent desires. In these cases, change tends to come from the bottom, because only the individuals who understand a process's subtleties can offer useful process improvements.

More dramatic "reengineering" and strategic changes demand that an organization smash its existing processes and even seek new markets. Both of these require top-down initiative, because only by seeing the organization as a whole can one imagine a qualitatively different direction for its internal processes or its customer base. This is not what most people associate with TQM, but such distinctions may be overdrawn. In this chapter, TQM refers to the management of changes of all kinds that improve an organization's understanding of its customers, improve the processes used to serve those customers, or prepare individuals in the organization to do these things in a way that promotes the organization's goals. This definition is probably broader than the one normally used.

Implementing *kaizen* as a standard element of day-to-day management is a major change that requires commitment and sustained support from the top. Management systems throughout the organization must change; there is no *kaizen* way to implement *kaizen*. Conversely, the specific changes that implement reengineering and alternative strategic direction must come from somewhere (even if from a consultant, someone inside the organization must decide to pay attention). Radical changes to a part of an organization appear incremental to the organization as a whole—*kaizen* on a higher level. TQM provides useful principles for creating the culture that generates new ideas, be they large or small.

The best examples of the close relationship between TQM and BCPs come from looking at the ISO 9000 management standard and the U.S. Department of Commerce Malcolm Baldrige Award.[13] For both, third-party auditors use a checklist to verify that an organization

---

[13]ISO 9000 is a family of voluntary standards created and maintained by the International Standards Organizations (ISO). Organizations can be certified to ISO 9000 if they maintain a detailed set of management processes. The U.S. Congress in 1987 created the Baldrige Award to recognize U.S. organizations that best exemplify a detailed list of characteristics based on the principles of TQM.

complies with specific requirements. The lists differ, but both include the key elements of TQM and seek to know how far TQM has been integrated into day-to-day management. Both also seek to understand an organization's customers and processes, how it ensures and improves quality, and how it enables and motivates people.

DoD could use such checklists. They work best when applied by a third party, which can provide objective discipline as well as the services of a knowledgeable consultant. In fact, third-party auditors could help DoD verify whether it has adapted the critical elements of any specific BCP it might consider.

TQM Viewed with Great Suspicion by Many in DoD

Some people have heard so many different versions of TQM that it just confuses them. As quality consultants split hairs over the fine points in trying to differentiate their wares so as to gain market share, the central message gets lost in the noise. In fact, as explained above, the core ideas in TQM are simple and logical.

Other people have participated in formal efforts to implement TQM in their agencies. They have heard all the rhetoric but have seen no more performance improvement from these efforts than from their predecessors. What they remember is the decline in budget and manpower authorizations made ahead of any savings that TQM would provide, and that they lost capability when the savings did not come. Commercial firms have similarly learned that TQM works only when it goes from being a stand-alone program to an operational part of day-to-day management, which happens less often than it should. TQM must be operationally implemented to overcome this problem.

Still others, particularly those looking for new commercial ideas, observe that the term *TQM* is now largely gone from the business press. If fact, where successful, TQM has been absorbed into day-to-day management. As implementers routinely use internal management audits and align their internal organizations to the processes they use to serve customers, they mention TQM less and less. Yet ISO 9000 (and its clones[14]) has become the dominant standard that good firms use to qualify suppliers. Profitability aside, the Malcolm Baldrige Award remains the dominant U.S. measure of high management performance. Operational TQM is now so pervasive in commercial firms that it is no longer seen as separate from good management.

IDENTIFYING BCPs

To identify BCPs, an organization must learn how to look beyond its own boundaries in a new way. It must learn how to exploit the increasingly abundant information resources available on other organizations' practices. The World Wide Web is a logical first place to look for references to appropriate information, if not for the information itself. Three types of resources can be helpful:[15]

1. *Professional associations and the conferences, courses, and publications they sponsor.* These offer ideal places to track rapidly evolving BCPs and their effects. They provide information on concepts and cases, as well as a natural place to meet specific practitioners and consultants who can provide additional information about practices in specific settings.

2. *Books and journals.* The major accounting firms maintain databases on best practices and have begun to publicize their data in books.[16] More generally, books and journals offer detailed examples of best practices from an industry or academic perspective. The industry perspective typically includes hands-on detail critical to understanding the usefulness and transferability of a specific practice. The academic perspective typically puts cases in a broader context, one that is particularly useful in balancing the often over-optimistic message of the industry press. (Companies

---

[14]The automobile, aerospace, and telecommunications industries have now developed their own variations on ISO 9000: QS-9000, AS-9000, and TL-9000.

[15]Table 8.1, shown later, provides examples of items in these categories that RAND used in its work on strategic sourcing.

[16]For example, Arthur Andersen offered a comprehensive approach to adapting BCPs in Robert Hiebeler, Thomas B. Kelly, and Charles Ketterman, *Best Practices: Building Your Business with Customer-Focused Solutions,* Simon and Schuster, New York, 1998.

rarely voluntarily share information on their failures to adapt best practices.) Both perspectives are useful.

3. *Benchmarking.* A specific way to place an organization in a broader context, benchmarking typically proceeds in three stages. Stage 1, high-level benchmarking, identifies the general nature of BCPs. The resources described above focus at this level. Stage 2, quantitative benchmarking, identifies a set of metrics and compares them across organizations with similar processes. This can occur in specific studies or on an on-going basis in benchmarking networks of organizations with similar processes. Stage 3, practitioner benchmarking, allows an organization to send the people who will adapt a new practice to a place where the practice already works so they can talk to the people who make it work. Face-to-face comparisons of day-to-day operations on the best practitioner's site give an organization's own practitioners latent knowledge about how they will have to change to successfully transfer the practice that they can get in no other way.

Described in this way, the identification of BCPs is a natural aspect of market research. DoD has always conducted market research but has typically thought about it only in terms of acquisition and contracting. By contrast, all parts of the best commercial firms are becoming increasingly aware of what is happening outside their firms. Because BCPs can benefit DoD so widely, market research should interest all process managers, notably those responsible for requirements determination, organic process design, design of relationships with external sources, source selection, and ongoing performance management for internal and external sources.

Adapting BCPs for Use in DoD

The most challenging aspect of adapting a BCP is successfully transferring it into DoD—i.e., ensuring that DoD changes in a way that allows it to benefit from the BCP. BCP adaptation is thus first and foremost about managing organizational change. Any new practice will require a formal program, the goal of which will be to adapt the practice to the DoD setting and to adapt standing DoD policies and systems to support the new practice. These change-related activities present a serious challenge, no matter where the change comes from.

Formal change management systematically addresses a series of issues that are also relevant to adapting best practices:

- Who in DoD does the change affect? Do they have the same relative importance in DoD as their counterparts in the commercial world?

- Who has to change their behavior on the job? What are the best ways to induce such changes in DoD relative to the commercial source organization?

- What DoD management systems must be synchronized with the change? How do they compare to analogous management systems in the source organization?

Given the close relationship between adaptation of BCPs and change management, as well as the fact that any adaptation must ultimately support and induce a specific organizational change, DoD can best approach the challenge of adaptation itself through the lens of change management. If DoD plans for successful change management, it will also, by definition, define an effective adaptation. The two fit hand in glove.

Successful management of organizational change is in itself a BCP. As DoD adapts more commercial practices, change can become easier. In the meantime, however, change is likely to be harder in DoD than in the best commercial firms. Personnel can keep this in mind as they review material about BCPs and think about how such practices will change when they come to DoD.

Every large, complex organization faces a diverse constellation of stakeholders. Large commercial firms typically identify their shareholders, customers, employees, suppliers, and the outside community as the stakeholders relevant to their success. DoD serves taxpayers, warfighters, and military families rather than shareholders and customers. Its employees are organized differently and have different rights. It is subject to much greater external scrutiny and pressure than a typical commercial firm is; political constituencies, working through Congress or more directly, are particularly important. Because key stakeholders shape any large organizational change, DoD can expect them to alter BCPs as these practices move from any commercial organization to DoD. Such pressure could well reduce the net benefits that a BCP offers, as DoD services each stakeholder's needs.

Still, DoD can affect the balance among these stakeholders to some extent. In particular, many BCPs shift control from a functional community to a customer. For example, in a logistics setting, BCPs emphasize the availability of parts to a final user (the customer) over the efficiency of the transportation system (the functional community) used to deliver these parts. DoD has demonstrated that it can do this in selected settings.

Once DoD acts to shift authority from its functional communities to its ultimate users, DoD can accept the presence of its key stakeholders and maintain an open process in which they negotiate to shape any new commercial practice. But to succeed, DoD must guard against allowing any one stakeholder to capture the adaptation process.

Change is only as effective as the senior leadership support it can garner and sustain through the full change effort. So a successful change is typically as large as the senior leadership supporting it allows. Adaptation of a BCP may look like a large change in DoD simply because of differences between the DoD and best commercial settings. This makes senior support and proper sizing all the more important.

A common approach seeks support for a small change in one locality and uses empirical evidence of benefits from that change to engage a higher, broader level of leadership. Even with high-level support from the beginning, an incremental approach is likely to sustain the support required to make a large change and to limit the risks associated with such a change. Ways to do this include the following:

- Use carefully instrumented pilots to test BCPs and adapt them to DoD as appropriate.

- Initially choose BCPs that require the smallest adaptation to transfer them to DoD.

- Make BCPs as compatible as possible with the local DoD culture where they are received. Use waivers where they are available.

- Refrain from introducing BCPs too close to DoD's core combat-related activities so that any failures will have no more than limited effects on DoD and on the change effort itself.

Caution is important, but a proposed change must be big enough to get people's attention.

Structural Differences Between DoD and Most Best Commercial Firms

Corporate America and the major elements of DoD initially learned from one another about how to harness the myriad energies of a giant enterprise to a single purpose. Well into the 1950s, they used similar management methods to plan and operate their organizations. Since the 1950s, however, and at an accelerating rate since the 1970s, the best commercial firms have moved away from the organizational form that DoD continues to favor.[17] In particular:[18]

- While the military services and defense agencies favor strong centralized structures, best commercial firms have reduced their corporate headquarters staffs and devolved authority.

- While DoD organizations rely heavily on strong functional organizations (such as logistics, civil engineering, and financial management), best commercial firms increasingly align themselves along process lines associated with products that cut across such functional lines.

- While DoD favors clearly defined rules, roles, and responsibilities over motivation and incentives, best commercial firms rely relatively more on formal incentives to align employees with the

---

[17]The characteristics attributed to DoD here, of course, apply to the federal government as a whole.

[18]These are not the only factors that create differences between the public and private sectors. For example, DoD tends to draw a greater distinction between effectiveness (such as military capability) and efficiency (cost) goals than commercial firms do, because DoD is subject to many laws and regulations that do not affect private firms. And while DoD emphasizes procedural openness, fairness, and fraud prevention, best commercial firms are more pragmatic in their management of processes and of fraud and abuse.

organization's goals. These firms give their employees more discretion than DoD does.

These differences are real and significant, but they should not be given more importance than they warrant. DoD organizations will probably sustain their preference for directing many actions from the center and using their functional communities to do this. They will also rely more on specific rules than on incentives to align local activities with the center, and they will continue to emphasize openness, accountability, equity, and integrity. DoD must adapt any BCP to make it compatible with these priorities.[19]

To adapt a BCP, DoD must verify that relevant practices that work with commercial management systems also work with analogous DoD systems. Organizationwide management systems differ in all organizations. Because of the growing difference between DoD and the best commercial firms, the differences relevant to four types of management systems are particularly important in this context:

- *General information systems and, in particular, internal transfer prices and related decision-support information.* Prices work in qualitatively different ways in DoD and typical commercial firms.

- *Incentive and motivation systems.* Every organization has its own approach to motivating workers.

- *Workforce management systems.* DoD's need to deploy forces and its heavy reliance on a labor force with little lateral entry create workforce management challenges that the best commercial firms do not face.

- *Systems to release excess resources, particularly labor.* The federal Office of Personnel Management (OPM) and federal unions place constraints on DoD that differ from those faced by the best commercial firms, even those with strong unions.

Planning for major organizational change raises many issues similar to those associated with planning for military action. Before DoD ex-

---

[19]How best to adapt a BCP always depends on the context. The last part of this chapter illustrates this with sourcing examples.

ecutes a military action, it typically develops a detailed contingency plan. As the first day of a military campaign approaches, DoD incorporates more and more details about the actual situation to make the execution as well coordinated and free of surprises as possible. Surprises will occur, however, and the plan must adapt repeatedly as the action proceeds. But the initial plan provides enough structure to anticipate surprises and have resources in place to respond when they occur. Very similar statements could be made about how DoD develops a new weapons system, major end item, or subsystem.

DoD can think about large organizational changes in a similar way. DoD knows how to identify risks and plan against them; it can use this knowledge in planning how to adapt a BCP to its own cultural setting. Key elements of such a plan are likely to include

- A clear, succinct statement of goals, with metrics to characterize the goals. DoD can use these goal-oriented metrics to negotiate adjustments as change proceeds.

- A way to break the change into a simple, defensible set of chunks compatible with the degree of support available for the change.

- For each change, a list of the behaviors that must change on the job, barriers to these changes, and plans to overcome each barrier. These plans address appropriate roles and responsibilities, training and other resource needs, and milestones.

- A coherent endgame that ensures the change is integrated with all appropriate DoD-wide management systems and is sustainable at the end of the transition.

The natural tool to use for this monitoring is a Shewhart cycle,[20] a variation of which is shown in Figure 8.1. Such a cycle provides an integral part of a quality management system that keeps senior leadership well informed about a change's status.

---

[20]Named for Walter A. Shewhart of Bell Telephone Laboratories, it is also popularly known as a PDCA, or Plan-Do-Check-Act, cycle.

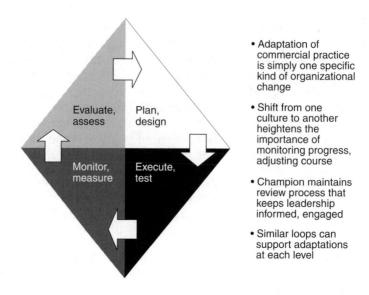

- Adaptation of commercial practice is simply one specific kind of organizational change

- Shift from one culture to another heightens the importance of monitoring progress, adjusting course

- Champion maintains review process that keeps leadership informed, engaged

- Similar loops can support adaptations at each level

Figure 8.1—A Continuous Improvement Loop Indicating Whether Adaptation Is on Track

The champion (i.e., person responsible for the change) uses the cycle to plan and design the elements of a new commercial practice, execute and thereby test this practice in DoD, monitor the test and measure the practice's performance against the stated goals of the change, and evaluate the outcomes.[21] If need be, the champion adjusts the design of the commercial practice and executes it again in the test setting. The champion includes the coalition supporting the change—i.e., the stakeholders whose organizations must alter their behavior for the change to succeed—in this loop. This gives the coalition an opportunity to approve or redirect as well.

---

[21]At RAND, we associate such a cycle with "maturation." For a discussion of maturation in the context of technological innovation, see J. R. Gebman, H. L. Shulman, and C. L. Batten, *A Strategy for Reforming Avionics Acquisition and Support*, R-2908/2-AF, RAND, 1988.

An Illustrative Example: Strategic Sourcing as a Basket of BCPs

Strategic sourcing links an organization's sources for the goods and services it uses as inputs to its corporate strategic goals. Typically, an organization identifies its customers' needs and then verifies that its sources of goods and services are tightly aligned with those needs. Every commercial firm that uses strategic sourcing customizes it to its own setting, but broadly speaking, a firm that uses strategic sourcing

- Identifies its customers' needs and translates them into measurable metrics.

- Organizes its internal processes to choose and manage sources, internal or external, accordingly.

- Develops relationships with key high-quality sources that become partnerships enabling both buyer and seller to benefit from pursuing the needs of the buyer's customers.

- Uses metrics that reflect customer priorities to measure the performance of the high-quality sources that the firm partners with.

Both buyer and seller benefit by working jointly to improve performance; joint continuous improvement lies at the heart of these partnerships.

The strategic goals relevant to strategic sourcing in DoD can be summarized as follows:[22]

- Improve military capability

- Sustain or improve safety and quality of life

- Reduce total ownership cost[23]

---

[22]These closely mirror the set—efficiency, equity, and integrity—proposed in Steven Kelman, *Procurement and Public Management*, AEI Press, Washington, 1990. Kelman inferred these by examining the rationale underlying federal procurement regulations.

[23]"Total ownership cost" is a commercial measure of all the costs associated with an activity or asset over its lifetime that DoD has begun to use. It covers all the costs of "owning" an activity or asset.

- Honor socioeconomic commitments
- Sustain the openness, equity, and integrity of the sourcing process.

With regard to military capability, the commercial analog is the value of output as measured in monetary terms. Because no one metric exists to measure military capability, this connection between the value of output and a source of inputs is more difficult to make in DoD than in the commercial sector. As for safety and quality of life, both DoD and commercial firms are concerned, but DoD is far more so. The safety of flight in a high-performance combat aircraft, for example, presents a far greater challenge than does safety assurance in most activities occurring in commercial firms. And quality of life more often applies to the workplace in commercial firms than to entire communities, as it does in DoD.

Both DoD and commercial firms also seek to cut costs. But commercial firms have far better cost accounts than DoD does and can more easily pursue comprehensive estimates of cost, such as the total ownership cost. DoD cost accounts are not even good enough to meet the standards that the Defense Contract Administration Agency (DCAA) requires of private-sector suppliers to DoD.[24] DoD needs better cost accounting procedures to go along with BCPs; perhaps they can be imported together.

DoD faces more-challenging socioeconomic goals than any commercial firm does, but commercial firms still have such goals, some self-imposed and some imposed by government regulators.[25] DoD can learn from how the best commercial firms service their socioeconomic goals, but by and large DoD will find its own way.

Finally, DoD faces more-challenging procedural openness, equity, and integrity goals than most commercial firms do. Again, DoD can

---

[24]Standard government cost accounts are typically too incomplete to allow a third party to audit them. They are also not well structured for linking total government costs to outputs or for reflecting how changes in work scope affect costs. Government accounts focus on tracking the application of congressional appropriations, not on the levels of cost relevant to management decisions.

[25]Of particular relevance to sourcing is the fact that many firms maintain goals to use small and disadvantaged businesses as sources.

learn from the way commercial firms pursue these goals. But DoD must be sensitive to its differences from the best commercial firms and verify that the best practices it imports can be adapted to the DoD setting. For example: Formal public-private competitions are far more common in DoD than in the commercial sector, because they provide the openness and equity that the federal setting demands.[26] But formal competitions can accommodate many of the sourcing practices that the best commercial firms routinely use.[27]

Under these circumstances, it may be easiest for DoD to focus its search for attractive BCPs on process changes that can enhance its capability, safety, and cost goals. It can then reflect its socioeconomic and administrative process goals as constraints inherent in the DoD institutional setting; any BCP that can enhance capability, safety, or cost goals must be compatible, when adapted, with DoD's operational socioeconomic and administrative process constraints to be useful to DoD.[28]

BCPs Relevant to DoD's Strategic Goals

Table 8.1 lists examples of the sources RAND analysts drew on to identify BCPs relevant to DoD.[29] The professional organizations

---

[26]Public-private competitions allow public and private sources to compete, in special forms of source selection, for selected government workloads. Private firms rarely use formal competitions to choose between organic and contract sources.

[27]For example, DoD can use noncost factors to compare sources, limit comparisons to preferred providers, and reward successful sources with extended contracts. The discussion below provides more detail.

[28]Such a distinction between goals and constraints does not imply that one is more important than the other. It is a natural—in fact, a necessary—part of any effort to evaluate a BCP when multiple goals or performance attributes are important.

[29]This table and the discussion here draw heavily on Ellen M. Pint and Laura H. Baldwin, *Strategic Sourcing: Theory and Evidence from Economics and Business Management,* MR-865-AF, RAND, 1997; Nancy Y. Moore et al., "Commercial Sourcing: Patterns and Practices in Facility Management," PM-667-AF, RAND, 1997; Frank Camm and Nancy Y. Moore, "Acquisition of Services in 2010: Ideas for Thinking About the Future," internal document, RAND, 1999; Nancy Y. Moore, Laura H. Baldwin, Frank A. Camm, and Cynthia R. Cook, *Implementing Best Purchasing and Supply Management Practices: Lessons from Innovative Commercial Firms,* DB-334-AF, RAND, 2002; John Ausink, Frank A. Camm, and Charles Cannon, *Performance-Based Contracting in the Air Force: A Report on Experiences in the Field,* DB-342-AF, RAND, 2001; Laura H. Baldwin, Frank A. Camm, and Nancy Y. Moore, *Federal Contract*

Table 8.1

Sources Used for Ideas on BCPs

Professional organizations, conferences, and courses	National Association of Purchasing Managers International Facility Management Association Building Owners and Managers Association Council of Logistics Management
Books	Timothy M. Laseter, *Balanced Sourcing: Cooperation ad Competition in Supplier Relationships*, Jossey-Bass for Booz-Allen & Hamilton, San Francisco, 1998
	Jordan D. Lewis, *The Connected Corporation: How Leading Companies Win Through Customer-Supplier Alliances*, Free Press, New York, 1995
	John Gattorna (ed.), *Strategic Supply Chain Alignment: Best Practice in Supply Chain Management*, Gower Publishing, Aldershot, England, 1998
	Ricardo R. Fernandez, *Total Quality in Purchasing and Supplier Management*, in Total Quality Management Series, Saint Lucie Press, FL, 1994.
Journals	*Harvard Business Review* *Sloan Management Review* *Int'l Journal of Purchasing and Material Management* *Supply Change Management Review*
Benchmarking	Arizona State University Center for Advanced Purchasing Studies Michigan State University Individual exemplar firms

shown represent commercial professionals interested in purchasing and supplier, facility, building, and logistics management. All such groups give sourcing BCPs a great deal of attention in their meetings, research programs, conferences, and courses. Arizona State and Michigan State, shown as benchmarking sources, both maintain well-known programs of research on best practices.

These sources suggest many specific BCPs for DoD to consider. A number of them are listed and defined here, after which their recent

---

Bundling: A Framework for Making and Justifying Decisions for Purchased Services, MR-1224-AF, RAND, 2001.

status in one part of DOD (the Air Force) and the potential for expanding their application in DoD are described.[30] Table 8.2 summarizes this information. Keep in mind that DoD cannot use all of these BCPs and that it must tailor those it does use for its own needs.

The specific BCPs that DoD might consider include the following:

- *Core competencies.* Identify those capabilities critical to an organization's future success or its raison d'être. These core competencies constitute an organization's unique value-added and hence cannot be outsourced. (That said, note that very few commercial firms outsource everything that lies outside their core competencies.)

- *Chief purchasing officer.* Elevate the CPO to the position of executive-level champion for purchased goods and services. CPOs own the processes that the organization uses to reach make-or-buy decisions, choose specific external sources, and manage relationships with these providers. Commercial CPOs generally do not make such decisions themselves.

- *Metrics.* Use metrics for make-or-buy decisions, source selections, or source management that promotes organizationwide, strategic goals.[31]

- *Total ownership cost.* Measure effects on cost using TOC to monetize as many factors as possible and apply them to organizationwide goals. TOC tends to allocate overhead costs to specific sourcing decisions to reflect all the direct and indirect costs relevant to a decision. Specific TOC measures are best tailored to the capabilities of an organization's cost accounts.

- *Multifunctional teams.* Develop sourcing policy decisions using multifunctional teams composed of members that have been (1) relieved of other duties, (2) trained in team processes, and

---

[30]The status of these practices in the Air Force is current as of late 2000.

[31]Such a change can have much broader effects than might first be apparent. For the Air Force, for example, it completely reframes the Air Force's current approach to determining requirements for many infrastructure activities.

Table 8.2

Summary of Openings for and Barriers to Air Force Adaptation of BCPs

BCP	Status in Air Force Today	Barriers to Further Adaptation
Identify core competencies	Does this now	Processes for choosing competencies are not aligned with Air Force strategic goals
Appoint executive-level CPO	Has this	Not effectively empowered to build strategic sourcing policy across functional lines
Use organizationwide metrics in sourcing	Is comfortable with metrics	Functional metrics not properly aligned with Air Force–wide goals
Apply total ownership cost in sourcing	Is moving in this direction	Current accounts do not support it; definition unclear
Use multifunctional teams in sourcing	Uses IPTs	Teams not yet empowered or incentivized to transcend functional priorities
Stratify supplier base	Is moving in this direction	No clear barriers but no clear metrics to reveal value easily
Use simplified acquisition	Is moving in this direction	Contracting does not consider full effects
Buy services in larger bundles	Is moving in this direction	Small business rules strongly discourage this
Use substitutes for competition	Faces strong opposition to this	CICA and small business rules strongly discourage this
Use nonprice criteria to choose sources	Is moving in this direction	Sourcing processes still require a price criterion
Reduce number of suppliers	Faces strong opposition to this	CICA and small business rules strongly discourage this
Consolidate contracts to improve leverage	Is experimenting with corporate contracts	Current data systems do not support "spend analyses" required to do this
Use performance-based statements of work	Is moving in this direction	Still learning what it means and how best to do it
Use higher skilled personnel	Is moving in this direction	Training is hard; so is handling personnel who cannot be trained

NOTE: IPT = integrated process team; CICA = Competition in Contracting Act (1984).

(3) empowered to act for their functions without consultation. The reward structures for team members should reflect the performance of the teams the members work on with respect to organizationwide goals.[32]

- *Stratified supplier base.* Use strategic criteria to stratify the supplier base. Suppliers of high-value inputs that are critical to the buyer's performance or that present other significant risks should be managed with greater care and by higher-skilled staffs than should suppliers of low-value inputs of a more generic character that present fewer risks.

- *Simplified low-priority buys.* Use automation and purchase cards to simplify low-priority buys. Automation releases personnel focused on transaction management; purchase cards further reduce transactions costs, particularly when bundled with auditing and reporting support from issuing banks.

- *Larger bundles.* Buying bundled services can allow the buyer to benefit from provider economies of scale and scope. They can also reduce transaction costs, particularly when the buyer devolves responsibility for oversight of many services to the provider.

- *Substitution of benchmarking and TQM standards for formal competition.* Benchmarking and TQM standards promote continuous improvement and make the external world more visible to the buyer. They can yield comparative information about capabilities, on a continuing basis, that buyers traditionally could only get from formal or "yardstick" competitions. By contrast, repeated competitions can impose unnecessary administrative costs and discourage long-term, joint innovation.

- *Less reliance on price.* In source selections, rely less on price and more on nonprice selection criteria. Nonprice factors can be critical to understanding total ownership costs and a source's ability to reduce them over time.

---

[32]Such a change has broad implications. It lifts decisionmaking out of a functional frame and tends to accelerate any process that depends on input from multiple functional communities (e.g., requirements determination). Inputs traditionally provided in series now occur simultaneously, with feedback from all players rather than just those downstream in a decision process.

- *Reduced number of providers.* The best buyers have cut their number of providers by an order of magnitude. Reduce the number used and select the survivors using such standards as ISO 9000 or data on past performance. Deeper investments can then be made in the remaining sources to promote joint innovations and match specific providers more effectively to emerging needs.

- *Consolidated contracts.* Consolidating contracts with remaining providers can reduce transaction costs and simplify deeper, strategic investment in a provider. It can also improve the buyer's leverage with the seller by highlighting the value of its total buy from the seller.

- *Performance-based statements of work and objectives.* Write performance-based rather than process-based statements of work and objectives—i.e., tell a provider what to do, not how to do it. This forces the buyer to think more carefully about what it values and gives providers more latitude to innovate.

- *Upgraded skill levels in purchasing organizations.* As strategic purchasing and supplier management policies grow in importance, they can no longer be managed in a back office separate from the firm's core interests. Upgrading can be paid for by simplifying small acquisitions.

In pursuing useful BCPs, DoD should not view this list simply as a menu of items it can mix and match arbitrarily. The best commercial firms find that these practices work best as an integrated package. The presence of one raises the effectiveness of the others, for several reasons:

1. Strategic sourcing relies heavily on high-level interest and carefully structured incentive systems. The latter cannot succeed without appropriate metrics. Effective buyer-seller partnerships require everyone's cooperation, and that takes support from the top.

2. Workforce upgrades are easier when funds are available from sourcing efficiencies. Automation and simplification can free up sourcing personnel. A buyer can use the savings to upgrade re-

maining personnel so that they may then plan and manage more-complex and more-creative sourcing relationships.

3. Performance-based statements of work succeed only when buyers can trust sellers enough to reduce process-oriented oversight and let providers exercise enough discretion to exploit performance-based statements of work. The right source must be in place before performance-based criteria can be used.

That said, DoD need not adopt all the suggestions to realize benefits from any one of them. Instead, DoD could recognize these synergies and verify that the mix it picks generates enough of them. This is a special challenge if DoD breaks the introduction of strategic sources into pieces to be introduced sequentially. Such a strategy would affect the realization of important synergies.

Key Barriers to DoD's Adaptation of Sourcing BCPs

DoD is already introducing some aspects of the BCPs identified above, but it has not been as aggressive about any of these practices as the best commercial firms have. In some cases, goal differences account for the differences in practice; in others, DoD can emulate BCPs much more closely. Recent Air Force experience illustrates these points:

Core competencies. DoD and the Air Force are well aware of the concept of a core competency and have begun to use it in their planning. Sourcing reviews associated with defining "core" depot activities, Defense Reform Initiative Directive (DRID) 20, and recent OMB policy based on the Federal Activities Inventory Reform (FAIR) Act of 1998 have forced DoD components to think more carefully about their core missions.[33] Unfortunately, in doing this they have relied heavily on the organic functions that currently provide services. The best commercial firms do not go this route; they handle such policy

---

[33]Congressional policy on depot use requires DoD to define the "core workload" relevant to its organic depots. DRID 20 required DoD to identify all manpower positions that could be considered for potential outsourcing via public-private competition. OMB's use of the FAIR Act requires DoD to put out for formal competition a prescribed fraction, which grows over time, of the manpower positions it has available for potential outsourcing.

at a higher level to avoid conflicts of interest with current internal providers.

Chief purchasing officer. The Air Force has a CPO, but the position lacks the authority held by CPOs in the best commercial firms. The Air Force CPO lives primarily within the acquisition community; commercial CPOs are more closely aligned with the line activities that use purchased goods and services, which gives them greater authority to work across functional boundaries in pursuit of broad, strategic organizational goals.

Metrics. Metrics of all kinds pervade the Air Force, but they tend to be designed and collected within functional organizations to meet their immediate needs. For instance, financial management focuses metrics more on managing against a plan than on responding to the needs of warfighters or their families. By contrast, BCPs explicitly align their metrics with customer needs.

Total ownership cost. DoD has been directed to start measuring TOC, using life-cycle cost as a basis. The quality of DoD cost accounts limits this effort by making it hard to trace all costs to the sourcing decisions they should influence.

Multifunctional teams. Integrated process teams (IPTs) that include members from all functions supporting a process are now a routine part of the Air Force and the rest of DoD. But these multifunctional teams are not used the same way best commercial firms use theirs. DoD team members rarely get the training on team processes that commercial team members receive, they cannot commit their functions to a decision without consultation, they are rarely managed and evaluated against specific organizationwide goals, and their members are not rewarded on the basis of such evaluations. Functional structures and the career patterns associated with them remain much more structured in DoD than in the best commercial firms, so DoD's functional organizations exercise relatively much more authority.

Stratified supplier base and simplified low-priority buys. The Air Force is moving toward stratified acquisition, which uses standard, generic contract terms to handle routine purchases and builds customized relationships with sources for strategically important inputs. Simplified acquisition and purchase cards are cutting the workload of contracting personnel associated with small transactions. A more commercial approach could reduce burdens on the functional personnel who use purchasing cards. Lightning Bolt 99-2 is a policy reform initiative that, among other things, selectively uses highly skilled teams to address complex new acquisitions of support services.[34] Overall, this effort would probably yield larger gains if the Air Force managed it against Air Force–wide goals, such as TOC, rather than metrics tied to each specific initiative.

Larger bundles. The Air Force is moving toward bundling activities and outsourcing them together. It has initiated several large, multifunctional cost comparisons for base-level services. Recent Small Business Administration (SBA) regulation requires that any federal agency bundling previously unbundled services must document the benefits that will accrue; it also limits the benefits that can be used to justify bundling.

Substitution of benchmarking and TQM standards for formal competition. The Competition in Contracting Act (CICA) of 1984 makes it hard to limit the use of competition for external-source selection. Additionally, congressional legislation and OMB Circular A-76 require that the use of public-private competition continue. DoD will have to rely heavily on competition until these directives change. Under acquisition reform, however, the Air Force is using award terms and other techniques to extend the period between competitions.

Less reliance on price. The Air Force relies increasingly on best-value competitions to choose external sources for services. These competitions all place heavy emphasis on past performance and often consider other nonprice factors. But regulations require that price remain a significant selection criterion.

Reduced number of providers. CICA limits any effort to reduce the number of sources considered in a competition or to allow offers by invitation only. But acquisition reform now allows the Air Force to "down-select" during a source selection in more or less formal ways. A down-select effectively reduces the range of competitors to those

---

[34]U.S. Air Force, SAF/AQ, *Aerospace Acquisition 2000,* April 23, 1999, available at http://www.safaq.hq.af.mil/acq_ref/bolts_99/bolt2.htm (as of October 22, 2002).

most likely to meet the government's needs. Thus, it can focus on a smaller field of offerors as it shapes the final version of any work statement.

Consolidated contracts. Contract consolidation is expanding in DoD. The Defense Logistics Agency has been writing so-called corporate contracts for over a decade, and the Air Force has several pilot corporate contracts in place and is seeking additional candidates. DoD continues to experience great difficulty in its attempts to consolidate contracts across DoD contracting organizations and across organizational lines within a provider firm.

Performance-based statements of work and objectives. The Air Force has initiated what are, in effect, over 20 successful pilots of performance-based statements of work during the last two years. This experience has revealed that knowledgeable, motivated acquisition personnel can write such statements of work in a DoD setting without much difficulty. But training remains a problem, and many noncontracting functionals and customers believe that such an approach presents more risks than rewards.

Upgraded skill levels. The Air Force strategy for contracting anticipates a smaller, more highly skilled contracting labor force. The Air Force is moving this direction but is still unclear what to do with personnel who cannot be upgraded. The Air Force has not yet extended this strategy to noncontracting personnel important to service acquisitions.

Insights from Commercial Experience on Overcoming Key Barriers

Looking across these BCPs, a number of barriers appear again and again, highlighting the importance of finding ways to ameliorate them. These include barriers to appointing an effective CPO, developing relevant metrics, using multifunctional teams or simplified acquisition, and defining requirements and performance-based statements of work. Less obviously, agreements negotiated a long time ago with competition advocates or small business advocates give them effective veto power. Some of these agreements are now reflected in laws and regulations. BCPs that can avoid these difficulties are easier to implement than those that cannot.

Most of these problems are not unique to DoD or the federal government. The best commercial firms have faced and found ways to deal with most of them. Their experience suggests that how an organization approaches strategic sourcing is often as important as what elements of strategic sourcing the organization pursues. Table 8.3 sketches the possibilities, which, in effect, illustrate how principles discussed earlier apply to the implementation of strategic sourcing BCPs.

DoD can do three things to address function-related barriers to strategic sourcing:

1. DoD can measure change in terms that transcend functional boundaries and reflect DoD-wide goals. The best commercial firms use "billets eliminated," not just "billets reviewed for potential outsourcing," to measure progress; and they use comprehensive measures of cost, not the number of items procured through a new form of contract. Such metrics are performance oriented: they tell leaders and workers what matters to the organization, not necessarily how to make detailed changes. Such an approach would encourage DoD organizations to measure costs better, thus

Table 8.3

Possible DoD Approaches to Strategic Sourcing

BCPs for Effecting Organizational Change	Implications in DoD
Use metrics relevant to parties affected to support change, justify investments, measure ultimate success, support incentives	Cost savings, billets eliminated; develop baseline, accounts that can measure these "accurately enough"
Build a coalition of parties involved	Unit commander, functionals, contracting, other support functions
Frame change to degree of senior support available	Within a major command or function and at a single base; keep as simple as possible
Have organization designated a special pilot	Attracts resources, allows policy waivers
Incentivize the parties involved	Awards, resources retained, performance reviews, protection for displaced personnel
Train personnel affected as a team	Substance of change, support tools, team process

making it easier to justify investments to support change, and would reward organizations that best promote DoD sourcing goals.

2. DoD can verify that an appropriate group of leaders, at the right level, supports change and can therefore form the core of the coalition used to plan and manage change. The coalition would include not only manpower (for A-76 actions) and contracting, but also relevant functional providers and customers of the services in question. Rapid turnover in leadership and current DoD team methods complicate coalition formation. But change metrics based on DoD-wide goals can help any group of leaders or team quickly understand the usefulness of change and make appropriate adjustments as the change evolves toward completion. In particular, such metrics can assist ultimate customers in understanding how sourcing actions can help them.

3. DoD can focus initially on smaller changes that require changes in only one organization. For example, it can pursue new sourcing practices at one base or in one functional area, but not both. As experience accumulates, an initial change can be used to build the case for broader change *if* the initial change anticipates settings for future changes and collects data relevant to future settings. Small changes limit the number of leaders who must coordinate their efforts to effect change; they also increase the likelihood that change can be completed during the leaders' limited tours of duty together.

Pilot programs are well suited to this approach. DoD has provided waivers that release many of the constraints discussed above in selected locations. Although such waivers are hard to get across the board, they can be used to establish selected beachheads, which, in turn, can supply the evidence that DoD can use to revisit the constraints.

Although performance metrics and incentives must be linked for change to be effective, there is wide scope to link performance metrics to whatever incentive system is compatible with an organization's corporate structure. DoD could use metrics like those used by the best commercial firms without changing its own incentive system much—as long as performance measures affect the incentives that DoD normally applies to the people who must change their behavior.

For example, cost-cutting goals heavily drive DoD sourcing policy. DoD can use measures of total operating cost that are as similar to those used in BCPs as its own cost accounts will allow. But it must find its own way to reward those who succeed in cutting cost. It might allow a successful organization to retain a portion of the cost savings, even if DoD needs the dollars saved more elsewhere. Or it could prominently reflect cost savings achieved in the performance reviews of the personnel involved, and use this information to affect future promotion, training, and other career management decisions.

DoD uses training to explain how people must change their behavior to make implementation successful. The best commercial firms typically use a broader approach to training, including material on effective team processes, problem solving, and the change process itself. Such training is most successful when it engages the people who will have to work together as a team to effect change (for sourcing, for example, people in contracting, manpower, and the relevant functionals, as well as the people who consume the services in question) and uses case materials tailored to the particular change in question. The case materials should reflect both specific socioeconomic and procedural factors relevant to DoD sourcing and details of commercial practice that help explain its success in the private sector.

Taken together, the BCPs discussed above point to the potential for large-scale, continuing change in DoD. It is important to remember that a similarly rich set of BCPs could be identified for practically every aspect of DoD's infrastructure activities. If DoD pursues all of these, it will enter a state that the best commercial firms increasingly take for granted: one of continuing change in which personnel have to learn to accept ongoing adjustment as a normal part of their day-to-day activities.

Change is already moving so fast and on so many fronts in DoD that many of the personnel whose behavior must change no longer understand how the changes are supposed to fit together or how to set priorities when they do not fit. These personnel do not even know who to go to for answers. Unless this state of affairs ends quickly, continuing efforts to change will overwhelm DoD personnel with "innovation fatigue" and leave them disillusioned about the possibility of progress. Unfortunately, DoD's constantly changing environment does not allow it the luxury of slowing its own change efforts. It has no choice but to learn how to live with continuing change. As DoD learns to knit together coherent packages of DoD-relevant metrics, leadership, pilots, incentives, training, and so on for each particular set of BCPs it considers adapting, it will also need to learn how to knit these packages into larger and larger programs of change. The commercial ideas offered here about how to implement individual sets of BCPs can also help DoD think about effecting change on a broader scale.

PART III. NEW TOOLS FOR DEFENSE DECISIONMAKING

INTRODUCTION TO PART III

RAND and other analysts have developed and refined a number of techniques for coping with uncertainty and making decisions that will have consequences over years, even generations. These techniques might be thought of in three broad categories: exercises, strategic products, and "groupware."

Drawing on earlier work in Europe, war-gaming for U.S. military planners was developed at the Naval War College in the late 19th century as a way of "getting into the minds" of potential military adversaries in order to develop and test alternative operational strategies.[1] In war games, the flow of events is affected by and, in turn, affects decisions made by players representing more than one "actor" or "side" that relies on less-than-perfect information. Simulations are different. Here, players represent only one actor, and some events may be determined before the game is played. Players can have incomplete and possibly misleading information—based on what sensors and human intelligence happen to provide—or they can be assumed to have complete and accurate information.

Both war games and simulations are referred to, in shorthand, as exercises. Such exercises can be conducted with educational or analytic objectives in mind: typical educational objectives include learning new lessons, reinforcing old lessons, and evaluating the understand-

---

[1] For further detail, see Peter P. Perla, *The Art of Wargaming*, Naval Institute Press, Annapolis, MD, 1990. Also see Peter P. Perla and Darryl L. Branting, "What Wargaming Is and Is Not," *Naval War College Review*, September/October 1985; and Peter P. Perla, "Games, Analyses, and Exercise," *Naval War College Review*, Spring 1987.

ing that has been gained; typical analytic objectives include developing strategy, identifying new issues, building consensus, or setting priorities. Exercises exist to test and refine human interaction, not to calculate outcomes. They explore decisionmaking by forcing players to make decisions; they achieve value by producing qualitative assessments of decisions that are made and not made and the effects of those decisions.

Exercises are generally

- Based on scenarios—i.e., credible, internally consistent, scripted events that set the scene and scope for players (although exercises can also be used to develop scenarios).

- Tolerant of some oversimplification and artificial assumptions.

- Designed by people acknowledged as experts in a particular area.

- Guided by rules and procedures to assure the logical flow of cause and effect.

Exercise play is most fruitful when participants free themselves from the constraints of "conventional wisdom" and suspend disbelief, much as they would when reading a well-written work of fiction. Getting the most out of games requires exposure of participants to a structured process of post-game analytic feedback. A well-structured exercise whose players have relevant experience and good information should yield insights about

- The feasibility of strategies, as well as their strengths and weaknesses.

- Key factors or variables that drive the results.

- The sensitivity of the results to variations in the factors or variables.

Strategic products, the second broad catgory of techniques, help evaluate the broader implications of changes in the planning environment. They come in two forms, *strategic planning*—"the evaluation and choice processes that determine how the world will be viewed, and the goals that the organization will pursue given this world view"[2]—and *strategic forecasting*. Underlying both of these is scenario-based planning.

Scenario-based planning was pioneered in the late 1960s by Royal Dutch Shell, virtually the only major oil company to anticipate the changes that would occur in the oil market in 1973–1974. Now a standard technique for long-range planning in the face of uncertainty, scenario-based planning rests on the premise that the future cannot be predicted accurately enough for good planning. Scenario-based planning rarely aims to predict; it is "a tool for ordering one's perceptions about alternative future environments in which one's decisions might be played out."[3] As one leading practitioner puts it, "The point is not so much to have one scenario that 'gets it right' as to have a set of scenarios that illuminate the major forces driving the system, their interrelationships, and the critical uncertainties."[4] Trends and key uncertainties are used to establish a range of "futures" well enough to define a manageable number of plausible, internally consistent scenarios.[5] Planners then insert themselves into each future environment and assess how their near-term decisions affected the long-term futures.

In assessing these effects, planners use common and adaptive strategies. *Common strategies* are largely independent of which specific future is anticipated; *adaptive strategies* are developed early and then executed later only if specific variations of the future ensue. Because adaptive strategies tend to be costly and risky to execute, they are developed only for selected future circumstances. And because some futures are more desirable than others, some strategies seek to improve the future while others concentrate on how to cope with the less desirable ones. In this way, defense planners help identify ac-

---

[2]Paul R. Kleindorfer, Howard C. Kunreuther, and Paul J.H. Schoemaker, *Decision Sciences: An Integrative Perspective*, Cambridge University Press, New York, 1993, p. 236.

[3]Peter Schwartz, *The Art of the Long View*, Doubleday, New York, 1991, p. 4. Also see Peter Schwartz, *The Art of Long View—Paths to Strategic Insight for Yourself and Your Company*, Bantam Doubleday Dell Publishing Group, Inc., New York, 1966.

[4]Paul J.H. Schoemaker, "How to Link Strategic Vision to Core Capabilities," *Sloan Management Review*, Fall 1992, p. 67.

[5]See, for example, Pierre Wack, "Scenarios: Shooting the Rapids," *Harvard Business Review*, November/December 1985, p. 146.

tions decisionmakers can take directly—as well as indirectly, through their influence on others.

A good defense planner will also identify a system of strategic indicators to trigger adaptive strategies, along with near-term courses of action decisionmakers may need to pursue to prepare or develop the strategies. Simply stated, the process is to develop strategies, test them, file them until needed, but exercise them periodically.[6]

In formal terms, collaboration is interaction among people that is intended to "create a shared understanding that none had previously possessed or could have come to on their own."[7] Collaboration technologies promise to improve the ability to coordinate action, share information, and understand information in order to facilitate inter- and intra-organizational teams. The following list shows three levels of collaboration; experienced defense analysts must be good at all of them.[8]

- *Level 1: Individual.* Individuals operating independently interact to selectively accommodate their own specific needs.

- *Level 2: Community of interest.* Groups of individuals exchange information in a shared community but not to achieve a common goal.

- *Level 3: Collaboration.* Individuals operate as a team to achieve a common goal by working together, sharing information, and thereby gaining new insights.

"Groupware" is software that supports the third level of collaboration. At its best, it applies the scientific method to the process of how groups use or should use analysis in making decisions. Analysis, in turn, can be considered good when it is a structured, systematic,

---

[6]On broad-based assumption-based planning and other styles of strategic planning, see Paul K. Davis and Zalmay Khalilzad, *A Composite Approach to Air Force Planning*, MR-787-AF, RAND, 1996.

[7]Michael Schrage, *No More Teams! Mastering the Dynamics of Creative Collaboration* (Doubleday, 1995), as quoted in P. A. Dargan, "The Ideal Collaboration Environment," April 2001 (available at http://www.stsc.hill.af.mil/CrossTalk/2001/apr/dargan.asp).

[8]Michael Schrage, *Shared Minds—The New Technologies of Collaboration*, Random-House, Inc., New York, 1990, as cited in P. A. Dargan.

traceable process of providing useful information to planners. This means that all data, inputs, assumptions, and methodologies are made transparent, and alternative decision paths are examined using logic chains to evaluate each one's advantages and disadvantages.

The first chapter in this part of the book is Chapter Nine, Paul Davis's "Exploratory Analysis and Implications for Modeling," in which he examines the consequences of uncertainty—not merely via standard sensitivity methods, but more comprehensively. Rather than going into excruciating detail on n^{th}-order effects, he uses a wide array of input variables (many well beyond what "experts" believe is plausible) to discover both the key uncertainties on which analysis may hinge and the primary drivers beside which all other variables pale in importance. This technique is useful primarily for studies in breadth (rather than depth), especially to gain a broad understanding of a problem area before dipping into details, or to see a forest rather than trees after detailed analysis. Hence, it is a good fit for capabilities-based planning. Davis describes techniques for doing exploratory analysis and explains how such analysis can be facilitated by multiresolution, multiperspective models (MRMPMs).

Chapter Ten, Dan Fox's "Using Exploratory Modeling," focuses on the practical issues associated with harnessing combat modeling and modern computers to explore a wide range of outcomes in order to understand the risks of engagement. In effect, he designs an experiment by identifying and then systematically varying experimental decision and risk variables to produce a range of outcomes. *Decision variables* represent policy alternatives (e.g., different levels of committed forces or alternative concepts of operations); *risk variables* (e.g., warning time) are given, not chosen. Measures of outcome may be simple (e.g., maximum kilometers that enemy forces advance) or complex (e.g., ratio of friendly to enemy losses). Combat simulation is used to create a matrix of results representing the outcomes for every combination of values for the experimental variables. Fox includes a comprehensive example that goes from designing the experiment to interpreting the results.

Stuart Starr's "Assessing Military Information Systems" is Chapter Eleven. Twenty-five years ago, Starr observes, several defense intellectuals sought to construct an ability to assess how much information systems contribute to military mission effectiveness. In line with this goal, substantial progress has been made in four areas: culture, process, tools, and experiments. Many of the principles and much of the guidance that have emerged in these areas are summarized in the revised 2002 version of *NATO Code of Best Practice for Command and Control Assessment*.[9] However, the changing geopolitical landscape poses daunting challenges for the assessment community. The contribution and impact of information systems must now be assessed in the context of not only emerging missions and complex, multi-dimensional information infrastructures ("infospheres"), but also the broader transformation of DoD itself.

Chapter Twelve is David Mussington's "The Day After Methodology and National Security Analysis." Mussington outlines the "Day After," an innovative gaming technique, developed by RAND, that examines strategic issues by playing out a scenario and then working backward to see how better decisionmaking could have improved the outcome. For this technique to work well, the scenario must be carefully designed and the testing process must be lengthy. Mussington describes how, in two concrete examples—one dealing with strategic information warfare, and one with the use of e-commerce technologies for money laundering—this approach illuminated strategy and policy questions. The most important issue in using this approach is how to remove the biases of the exercise designer or research sponsor from the scenario design or question formulation and still retain the policy relevance of the deliberations and findings. A readily usable *process* for evaluating scenario details and issue treatment is applied as an integral part of exercise development.

In the final chapter, "Using Electronic Meeting Systems to Aid Defense Decisions," Stuart Johnson explores another set of tools for improving the quality of defense deliberations. The basic problem being addressed is that, faced with complexity and uncertainty, individual planners risk becoming comfortable with familiar illusions. Moreover, there are limits to how well any one planner can imagine the future; and when planners work collectively, groupthink becomes a real risk. Johnson discusses a case in which an electronic meeting system (EMS) was used to help the Navy prepare for the 1997 Quadrennial Defense Review (QDR). Experts were first asked to

---

[9]Available at http://www.dodccrp.org/nato_supplnato.htm.

rank missions in terms of priority and likelihood (via anonymous voting, which was informed, after the fact, by group discussion). They were then asked to rank capabilities in terms of their contribution to each mission, and systems in terms of their contribution to each capability. This process resulted in a conclusion that probably would not have been recognized up front: command-and-control systems (C2) were of especial importance to naval operations and thus deserved to have their budget fenced off during the QDR process.

Chapter Nine

EXPLORATORY ANALYSIS AND IMPLICATIONS FOR MODELING

Paul K. Davis

The theme that runs through this book is that real-world strategy problems are typically beset with enormous uncertainties that should be central in assessing alternative courses of action. In the past, one excuse for downplaying uncertainty—perhaps treating it only through marginal sensitivity analysis around some "best-estimate" baseline of dubious validity—was the sheer difficulty of doing better. If analysis depended on the time it took to set up and run computer programs, then extensive uncertainty work was often ruled out. Today, however, extensive uncertainty analysis can be done with personal computers. Better software tools are needed, but existing commercial products are already powerful. There is no excuse for not doing better.

A key to treating uncertainty well is *exploratory analysis.* Its objectives are to (1) understand the implications of uncertainty for the problem at hand and (2) inform the choice of strategy and subsequent modifications. In particular, *exploratory analysis can help identify strategies that are flexible, adaptive, and robust.*[1] This chapter describes exploratory analysis, puts it in context, discusses enabling technology and theory, points to papers applying the ideas, and concludes with some challenges for those building models or developing enabling technology for modeling and simulation.

---

[1]Paul K. Davis, *Analytic Architecture for Capabilities-Based Planning, Mission-System Analysis, and Transformation,* MR-1513-OSD, RAND, 2002.

EXPLORATORY ANALYSIS

Definition

Exploratory analysis examines the consequences of uncertainty. In a sense, it is sensitivity analysis done right. Yet because it is so different in practice from what most people think of as sensitivity analysis, it deserves a separate name. It is closely related to scenario space analysis,[2] which dates back to 1983,[3] and to "exploratory modeling."[4] It is particularly useful for gaining a broad understanding of a problem domain before dipping into details. That, in turn, can greatly assist in the development and choice of strategies. It can also enhance "capabilities-based planning" by clarifying *when* (e.g., in what circumstances and with what assumptions about other factors) a given capability (e.g., an improved weapons system or enhanced command and control [C2]) will likely be sufficient or effective. This contrasts sharply with establishing a base-case scenario and an organizationally blessed model and database, and then asking, "How does the outcome for this scenario change if I have more of this capability?"

Exploratory analysis is an exciting development with a long history, including work in the 1980s and 1990s with RAND's RSAS (RAND Strategy Assessment System) and JICM (Joint Integrated Contingency Model). It is, however, only one part of a sound approach to analysis generally—a point worth pausing to emphasize.

Figure 9.1 shows how different types of models and simulations (including human games) have distinct virtues. The figure is specialized to military applications, but a more generic version applies broadly to a wide class of analysis problems. White rectangles indicate

---

[2]Paul K. Davis (ed.), *New Challenges for Defense Planning: Rethinking How Much Is Enough*, MR-400-RC, RAND, 1994.

[3]Paul K. Davis and James A. Winnefeld, *The RAND Strategic Assessment Center: An Overview and Interim Conclusions About Utility and Development Options*, R-2945-DNA, RAND, 1983.

[4]Stephen C. Bankes, "Exploratory Modeling for Policy Analysis," *Operations Research*, Vol. 41, No. 3, 1993; and Robert Lempert, Michael E. Schlesinger, and Steven C. Bankes, "When We Don't Know the Costs or the Benefits: Adaptive Strategies for Abating Climate Change," *Climatic Change*, Vol. 33, No. 2, 1996.

"good"—i.e., if a cell of the matrix is white, the type of model indicated in the left column is very effective with respect to the attribute indicated in the cell's column. In particular, analytic models (top left corner), which have low resolution, can be especially powerful with respect to their analytic agility and breadth. In contrast, they are very poor (have dark cells) with respect to recognizing or dealing with the richness of underlying phenomena, or with the consequences of both human decisions and behavior. In contrast, field experiments often have very high resolution (they may even be using the real equipment and people) and may be good or very good for revealing phenomena and reflecting human issues. They are, however, unwieldy and inappropriate for studying issues in breadth. The value of the type model for the particular purpose can often be enhanced a notch or two if the models include sensible decision algorithms or knowledge-based models that might be in the form of expert systems or artificial-intelligence agents.

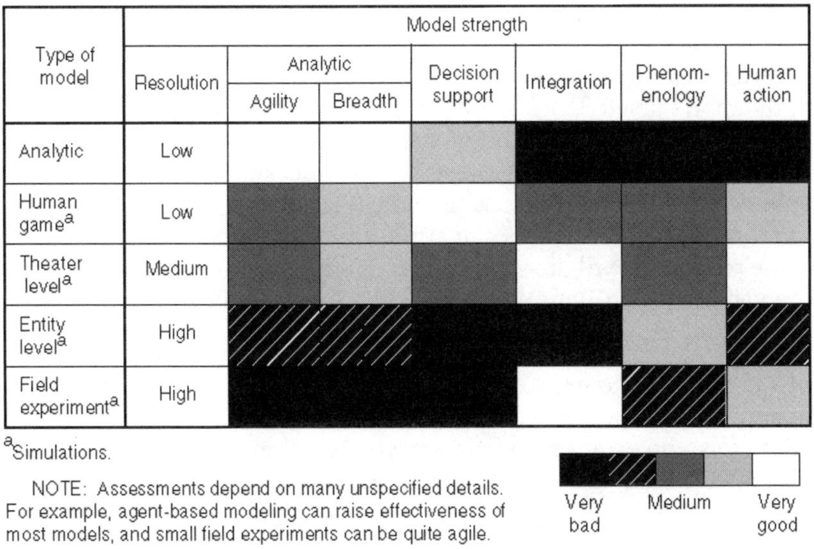

Type of model	Model strength						
	Resolution	Analytic		Decision support	Integration	Phenom-enology	Human action
		Agility	Breadth				
Analytic	Low						
Human game[a]	Low						
Theater level[a]	Medium						
Entity level[a]	High						
Field experiment[a]	High						

[a]Simulations.

NOTE: Assessments depend on many unspecified details. For example, agent-based modeling can raise effectiveness of most models, and small field experiments can be quite agile.

Very bad   Medium   Very good

Figure 9.1—Virtues of a Family of Models (Including Human Games)

Figure 9.1 is an exhortation to the Department of Defense (DoD) regarding the need to have *families of models and families of analysis*.[5] Unfortunately, it is usual for government agencies to depend more or less exclusively on a single model, which is a serious shortcoming.

Figure 9.1 reveals a niche for exploratory analysis: the top left-hand corner of the matrix, which emphasizes analytic agility and breadth of analysis. However, the technique can be used hierarchically with a suitably modularized system model. That is, one can do top-level exploration first, and then zoom in to explore in more detail—but using the same techniques—the consequences of various details within particular modules. This is easier said than done, however, especially with traditional models. Specially designed models make things much easier, as discussed in what follows.

Types of Uncertainty in Modeling

Exploratory analysis is about addressing uncertainty, but uncertainty comes in many forms. Parametric uncertainties arise from a model's inputs, from not knowing their precise values. They are not the same as structural uncertainties, which relate to questions about the form of the model itself: Does it reflect all the variables on which the real-world phenomena described by the model depend? Is the analytic form of the dependencies correct? Some uncertainties may be inherent because they represent what are called stochastic processes—the randomness of nature.[6] Some come from fuzziness or imprecision; some reflect discord among experts. Some relate to knowledge about the values of well-defined parameters; others refer to future values not yet known.

It is convenient to express uncertainties parametrically. Even when unsure about the correct form of the model, one can reflect uncertainty to some extent by having parameters that affect that form. For example, parameters may control the relative size of quadratic and exponential terms in an otherwise linear model. Or a discrete pa-

---

[5]Paul K. Davis, James H. Bigelow, and Jimmie McEver, *Analytical Methods for Studies and Experiments on "Transforming the Force,"* DB-278-OSD, RAND, 1999.

[6]The behavior of stochastic systems has a random component. Such systems are described with probabilistic equations.

rameter that is essentially a switch might determine which of a set of distinct analytic forms applies. Some parameters may apply to the fixed aspect of a model; others may apply to a random aspect. In taking this approach, one needs to keep straight how the different uncertainties come into play.[7]

Types of Exploratory Analysis

Ways to Conduct Exploratory Analysis.[8] One form of exploratory analysis is input, or parametric, exploration, which involves running models across the space of cases defined by plausible discrete values of the parameters. This is done not one at a time, as in normal sensitivity analysis, and not around some presumed base-case set of values, but, rather, for all the combinations of values defined by an experimental design. The results, which may number from dozens to hundreds of thousands or more, can be explored interactively with modern displays. Within perhaps one half-hour, a good analyst can often gain numerous important insights that were previously buried. He can understand not just which variables "matter," but when they matter. For example, he may find that outcomes are insensitive to a given parameter for the so-called base case but are quite sensitive for other plausible assumptions. That is, he may identify *when* the parameter is important. For capabilities-based planning for complex systems, this can be distinctly valuable.[9]

---

[7]See the appendix for an example that uses Lanchester equations, chosen for familiarity rather than for current usefulness.

[8]See Paul K. Davis, David C. Gompert, and Richard L. Kugler, *Adaptiveness in National Defense: The Basis of a New Framework*, IP-155, RAND, 1996; Bankes, "Exploratory Modeling"; Arthur Brooks, Steve C. Bankes, and Bart Bennett, *Weapon Mix and Exploratory Analysis: A Case Study*, DB-216/2-AF, RAND,1997; Lempert, Schlesinger, and Bankes, "When We Don't Know"; National Research Council, *Modeling and Simulation*, Vol. 9, *Technology for the United States Navy and Marine Corps, 2000–2035*, National Academy Press, Washington, DC, 1997; and Granger Morgan and Max Henrion, *Uncertainty: A Guide to Dealing with Uncertainty in Quantitative Risk and Policy Analysis*, Cambridge University Press, Cambridge, MA, 1992 (reprinted in 1998). The book by Morgan and Henrion is an excellent treatment of uncertainty in policy analysis generally.

[9]Many examples in military analysis involve warning time. Some capabilities, such as those of forward-deployed systems, are especially important only when warning time is short. If standard scenarios assume considerable warning time, such capabilities can be undervalued.

A complement to parametric exploration is probabilistic exploration, in which uncertainty about input parameters is reflected by distribution functions representing the totality of one's so-called objective and subjective knowledge. Using analytic or Monte Carlo methods, the resulting distribution of outcomes can be calculated. This can quickly give a sense for whether—all things considered—uncertainty is particularly important. In contrast to displays of parametric exploration, the output of probabilistic exploration gives little visual weight to improbable cases in which various inputs all have unlikely values simultaneously. Probabilistic exploration can be very useful for a condensed "net assessment." Note that this use of probability methods is different from using them to describe the consequences of a stochastic process within a given simulation run. Indeed, one should be cautious about using probabilistic exploration, because one can readily confuse variation across an ensemble of possible cases (e.g., different runs of a war simulation) with variation within a single case (e.g., fluctuation from day to day within a single simulated war). An unknown constant parameter for a given simulated war is no longer unknown once the simulation begins, and simulation agents representing commanders should perhaps observe and act upon the correct values within a few simulated days. Despite these subtleties, probabilistic exploration can be quite helpful.

After initial work with both parametric and probabilistic exploration, the preferred approach is *hybrid exploration*. It may be appropriate to parameterize a few key variables that are under one's control (purchases, allocation of resources, and so on) while treating the uncertainty of other variables through uncertainty distributions. Analysts might also want to parameterize a few of the principal variables characterizing the future context in which strategy must operate. In military affairs, one might parameterize assumed warning time and size of threat. There is no general procedure here; instead, the procedure should be suitable to the problem at hand. In any case, the result of such exploratory analysis can be a comprehensible summary of how known classes of uncertainty affect the problem at hand.

Consider the following examples of exploratory analysis. Figure 9.2 displays a mid-1990s parametric exploration of what is required militarily to defend Kuwait against a future Iraqi invasion by interdicting

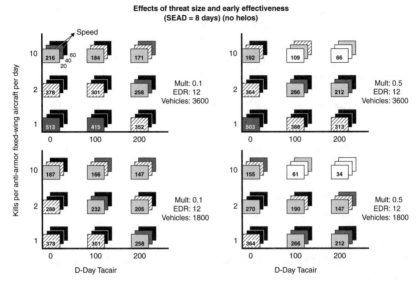

Mult.: fraction of shooters used before SEAD time; EDR: equivalent deployment rate; Vehicles: AFVs to be killed for halt.

Figure 9.2—Data View Display of Parametric Exploration

the attacker's movement with aircraft and missiles.[10] Each square in the figure represents a particular model case (i.e., a specific choice of all the input values). Taken together, the four panels summarize parametric exploration in five variables (the x, y, and z axes of each panel, one for a row of two panels, and one for a column of two panels). With four such pages, one can cover results for seven variables. The outcome of a given simulation is represented by the pattern of a given square. A white square represents a good case, in which the attacker penetrates only a few tens of kilometers before being halted. A black square represents a bad case, in which the attacker penetrates deep into the region that contains critical oil facilities. The other patterns represent in-between cases. The number in each square gives the penetration distance in kilometers.

---

[10]Paul K. Davis and Manuel J. Carrillo, *Exploratory Analysis of "The Halt Problem": A Briefing on Methods and Initial Insights,* DB-232, RAND, 1997.

To generate such results for a sizable scenario space, RAND has often used a program called Data View.[11,12,13] After running the thousands or hundreds of thousands of cases corresponding to an experimental design for parametric exploration, one explores the outcome space by choosing interactively which of the parameters to vary along the x, y, and z axes. The remaining parameters then have values shown alongside the graph. These can be changed by clicking on one of them and selecting from the menu that comes up.

Figure 9.3 shows a screen image from some recent work with Analytica on the same interdiction-of-invader-forces problem treated in Figure 9.2. In this case, the graphical display of results is more traditional. Outcome is measured along the y axis rather than by a color or pattern, and one of the independent variables is plotted along the x axis. A second variable—D-Day (the day war commences) shooters—is reflected in the family of curves. The other independent variables appear in the rotation boxes at the top. As with Data View, one changes parameter values by selecting from a menu of values. Such interactive displays allow one to "fly through the outcome space" for many independent variables (parameters), in this case nine. More parameters could have been varied interactively, but the display was still quickly interactive for the given model and computer being used (a Macintosh PowerBook G3 with 256 MB of RAM).

---

[11]This was developed at RAND in the mid-1990s by Stephen Bankes and James Gillogly.

[12]Other personal-computer tools can be used for the same purpose and the state of the art for such work is advancing rapidly. A much improved version of Data View, called CARS[TM], is under development by Evolving Logic (www.evolvinglogic.com). For those who do their modeling with Microsoft EXCEL[TM], there are plug-in programs that provide statistical capabilities and some means for exploratory analysis. Two such tools are Crystal Ball[®] (www.decisioneering.com) and Risk[®] (www.palisade.com/html/risk.html). For a number of reasons, however (visual modeling, array mathematics, etc.), my colleagues and I have in recent times most often used the Analytica[®] modeling system. Analytica is an outgrowth of the Demos system developed by Max Henrion and Granger Morgan at Carnegie Mellon University; it is marketed by Lumina (www.lumina.com).

[13]For more recent exploratory analysis work, see Paul K. Davis, Jimmie McEver, and Barry Wilson, *Measuring Interdiction Capabilities in the Presence of Anti-Access Strategies: Exploratory Analysis to Inform Adaptive Strategy in the Persian Gulf*, MR-1471-AF, RAND, 2002.

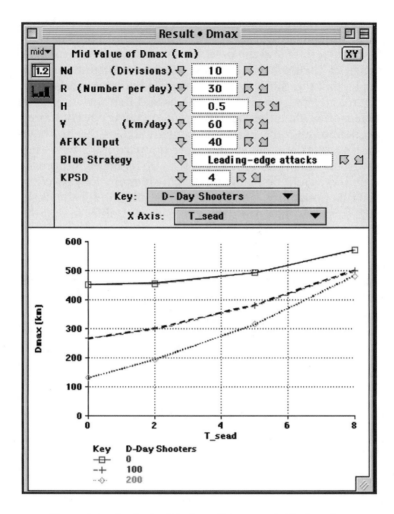

**Figure 9.3—Analytica Display of Parametric Exploration
(Simultaneous Exploration of Nine Parameters)**

So far, the examples have focused on parametric exploration. Figure 9.4 illustrates a hybrid exploration.[14] It shows the distribution of

---

[14]Paul K. Davis, David C. Gompert, Richard J. Hillestad, and Stuart Johnson, *Transforming the Force: Suggestions for DoD Strategy,* IP-179, RAND, 1998.

simulation outcomes resulting from having varied most parameter values "probabilistically" across an ensemble of possible wars, but with warning time and the delay in attacking armored columns left parametric. The probabilistic aspect of the calculation assumed, for example, that the enemy's movement rate had a triangular distribution across a particular range of values and that the suppression of air defenses would either be in the range of a few days or more like a week, depending on whether the enemy did or did not have air-defense systems and tactics that were not part of the best estimate. That is, if the enemy had some surprises up its sleeve, suppression of air defenses would be likely to take considerably longer. We represented this possibility with a discrete distribution for the likelihood of such surprises. The two curves in Figure 9.4 differ in that the one with crosses for markers assumes that interdiction of moving

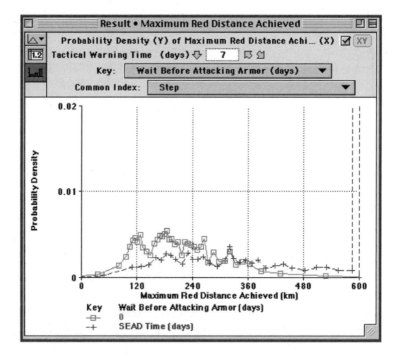

Figure 9.4—Display of "Probabilistic" Exploration

columns waits for suppression of enemy air defenses (SEAD). The other curve assumes that interdiction begins immediately because the aircraft are assumed stealthy or the defenses nonexistent.

This depiction of the problem shows in one display how widely outcomes can vary and how outcome distribution can be complex. The non-stealthy-aircraft case shows a considerable spike at the right end, where many cases pile up because, in the simulation, the attacker halts once he has reached an objective at about 600 km. Note that the mean is not a good metric: the variance is huge, and the outcome may be bimodal or even multimodal.

Advanced Concepts. The results just discussed are from analyses accomplished in recent years for DoD. Looking to the future, much more is possible with computational tools. Much better displays are possible, and, even more exciting, computational tools can be used to aid in the search process of exploration. For example, instead of "clicking" through the regions of the outcome space, tools could automatically locate portions of the space in which particular outcomes are found. Insights could be fine tuned by clicking around in that much more limited region of the outcome space. Or, if the model is itself driven by the exploration apparatus, the apparatus could search for outcomes of interest and then focus exploration on those regions of the input space. That is, the experimental design could be an output of the search rather than an input of the analysis process.

ENABLING EXPLORATORY ANALYSIS

In principle, exploratory analysis can be accomplished with any model. In practice, it becomes difficult with large and complex models. If F represents the model, it can be considered to be simply a complicated function of many variables. How can we run a computerized version of F to understand its character? If F has M inputs with uncertain values, then we could consider N values for each input, construct a full-factorial design or some properly sampled subset, run the cases, and thereby have a characterization. However, the number of such cases would grow as NM for full-factorial analysis, which quickly gets out of hand even with big computers. Quite aside from issues of setup and run time, comprehending and communicating the consequences becomes very difficult if M is large. Suppose someone asked, "Under what conditions is F less than danger_point?" Given sufficiently powerful computers and enough time, one could create a database of all the cases, after which one could respond to the question by spewing out lists of the cases in which F fell below danger_point. The list, however, might go on for many pages, perhaps even thousands. What would be done with the list? This is one manifestation of what might be called the curse of dimensionality.

It follows that—even with a perfect high-resolution model and incredibly speedy computers—abstractions, such as aggregate representations, will still be necessary. In the most usual cases, in which the high-resolution model is by no means perfect, abstractions allow analysts to ponder the phenomena in meaningful ways, with relatively small numbers of cognitive chunks to deal with. People can reason with 3, 5, or, perhaps, even 10 such cognitive chunks at a time, but not with hundreds. If the problem is truly complex, ways must be found to organize the reasoning—i.e., the problem must be decomposed. One ends up using principles of modularity and hierarchy. To head off a rejoinder commonly made at this point by aficionados of networking technology, the need for an aspect of hierarchical organization is inescapable in most systems of interest, even if the system is highly distributed and relatively nonhierarchical. Everyone can observe this when interacting with the World Wide Web.

A corollary of the need for abstractions is the need for models that use the various abstractions as inputs. It is not sufficient to display the abstractions as intermediate outputs (displays) of the ultimate detailed model. The reasons include the fact that when a decisionmaker asks a what-if question using abstractions, there is a 1:n mapping problem in translating his question into the inputs of a more detailed model. That is, the decisonmaker asks, "What if we had 25 percent more capability?" but the detailed model represents many capabilities. What assumptions about these many capabilities would correspond best to the decisionmaker's question? In contrast, a more aggregated model may already have the concept of overall capability; it can then address the decisionmaker's question directly. That is, it accepts the decisionmaker's abstractions as inputs.

Given the need for abstractions, how do we find them and how do we exploit them? The approaches fall into two groups, one for new models and the other for existing, or legacy, models.

With new models, the issue is how to design, and the options of interest are

- Design the models and model families top down so that significant abstractions are built in from the start, but do so with enough understanding of the microscopics that the top-down design is valid.[15]

- Design the models and model families bottom up, but with enough top-down insight to build in good intermediate-level abstractions from the start.[16]

- Do either or both of the above, but with designs taken from different user or theoretical perspectives.

Note that this list does not include a pure top-down or bottom-up design approach. Only seldom will either generate a good design of a complex system. Note also the idea of alternative perspectives. This recognizes that many abstractions are not unique; to the contrary, there are different ways of viewing what the key factors of the problem really are (e.g., those in combat arms typically conceive military problems differently than logisticians do).

Only sometimes is there the opportunity to design from scratch. More typically, existing models must be used (or adapted and used). Moreover, the model "families" available are often families more on the basis of assertion or hope than lineage. What does one then do? Some possibilities are as follows:

- Given existing models developed at high levels of resolution, study the model and the questions that users ask of the model to discover useful abstractions. For example, one may discover that inputs X, Y, and Z only enter the computations as the product

[15]Paul K. Davis and James H. Bigelow, *Experiments in Multiresolution Modeling (MRM)*, MR-1004-DARPA, RAND, 1998.

[16]Paul K. Davis and James H. Bigelow, *Motivated Metamodels: Synthesis of Cause-Effect Reasoning and Statistical Metamodeling*, MR-1570-AF, RAND, 2003.

XYZ. If so, then XYZ may be a natural abstraction. Or, perhaps decisionmakers ask questions in terms of concepts such as force strength or force ratio, indicating that these are significant abstractions. For mature models, the obvious place to look is the list of displays that have been added over time to provide views into the internal workings of the model.

- Apply statistical machinery to search for useful abstractions. For example, if X, Y, and Z are inputs, such machinery might test to see whether the system's behavior correlates not just with X,Y, and Z, but with XY, XZ, YZ, and XYZ. If the computation does, in fact, depend only on XYZ, that fact will show up from the statistical analysis.

- Idealize the system and develop a "formal" mathematical representation (formal in the sense of being expressed symbolically without necessarily having the intention of computing the various terms and factors) that provides hints about the model's likely behavior. For example, such a representation might be much too complex to "solve," but, if coupled with some physical reasoning and a search for postulated simplifications, it might highlight the likelihood of an overall exponential decay, or an inverse dependence on one input, or various other nonlinearities that otherwise one might think to test for. It might suggest natural *aggregation fragments*, such as the product XYZ mentioned above. In practice, this approach is most powerful if one considers the problem from different perspectives that suggest different but plausible simplifications.[17,18]

This list is less straightforward than it first appears. The first approach is perhaps a natural activity for a smart modeler/programmer who begins to study an existing program—if, and only if, he is also a believer in higher-level depictions of the problem. The second approach seems to be favored by mathematically oriented individuals who lack enough class knowledge to take the first approach, or who

---

[17]One example of a simplification is the assumption that an integral is perhaps approximately equal to a representative value of the integrand times the effective width of the integration interval, and that this width is proportional to something physically straightforward.

[18]Davis and Bigelow, *Motivated Metamodels.*

believe—based sometimes on disciplinary faith—that such statistical procedures will prove successful and that those looking for more phenomenological abstractions are fooling themselves. The third approach is a hybrid. It argues that one should use one's understanding of phenomenology, and theories of system behavior, to gain insights about the likely or possible abstractions. Only then should one crank the statistical machinery. Where it is feasible, this is the stronger approach.

Using Occam's Razor

An interesting tension arises in discussing how to form suitable abstractions. The principle of Occam's razor requires that one prefer the simplest explanation and, thus, the simplest model. Some, particularly enthusiasts of statistical approaches, tend to interpret this principle to mean that one should minimize the number of variables in a model. They tend to focus on data (natural or simulation generated) and to avoid adding variables for the purpose of "explanation" or "phenomenology" if the variables are not needed to predict the data. Instead, they prefer to "let the data speak." In contrast, subject-area phenomenologists may prefer to enrich the depiction by adding variables that provide a better picture of cause-effect chains. This, however, goes well beyond what can be supported with meager experimental data.

To not violate the Occam's Razor principle, one must remember the principle's longer form: Adopt the simplest explanation that truly explains all there is to explain—but nothing simpler! This should include phenomena that one "knows about," even if they are not clearly visible in the limited data (e.g., historical data on who won various battles with what overall attrition). I would add to this the old admonition (perhaps made first by Massachusetts Institute of Technology's Jay Forrester) to remember that to omit showing a variable one knows about may be equivalent to assuming its value to be 1 (as a multiplier) or 0.

It is sometimes useful to have a competition among approaches. For example, phenomenologists working a problem may be utterly convinced that it must be described with complex computer programs having hundreds or thousands of data elements. In such a case, it may be useful to study output behavior with a metamodel (also called a repro model and response surface).[19] In one instance with which I am familiar, such work by colleague James Bigelow showed that despite many man-years of effort building and feeding a complex ground-force model, results were strongly dominated by a single higher-level abstraction: theater-level force ratio. The implication was not that real combat is dominated only by theater-level force ratio, but, rather, that various assumptions and compromises made in developing the detailed model undercut any claims that its greater complexity and expense were adding predictive value relative to simpler models.

Although the discussion above distinguishes sharply between the case of new models and old ones, the two are connected. In essence, working with existing models should often involve sketching what the models *should* be like and how models with different resolution *should* connect substantively. That is, working with existing models may mean having to go back to design issues. If this seems suspicious, ask yourself how often you have found it easier to rederive a model and then decipher a program you have been given than to wade through the program on its own terms.

Multiresolution, Multiperspective Modeling and Model Families

Abstractions, usually aggregations, are fundamental in exploratory analysis. Finding suitable abstractions, relating them, and conducting both high-level exploratory analysis and appropriate zooming into detail are greatly facilitated if models are designed in a special way. This is the subject of multiresolution, multiperspective modeling (MRMPM). Although the subject relates most directly to new models, it is also relevant to working with legacy models in preparing for exploratory analysis.

Multiresolution modeling (MRM) is building a single model, a family of models, or both to describe the same phenomena at different levels of resolution and to allow users to input parameters at those dif-

---

[19]A metamodel is a simple model that reproduces the aggregate behavior of a more complex model, as judged by statistical comparisons over many cases.

ferent levels depending on their needs.[20] Variables at level n are abstractions of variables at level n+1. MRM has also been called variable- or selectable-resolution modeling.[21] Figure 9.5 illustrates MRM schematically. It indicates that a higher-level model (model A) itself has more than one level of resolution. It can be used with either two or four inputs. However, in addition to its own MRM features, it has input variables that can be specified directly or determined from the outputs of separate higher-resolution models (models B and C,

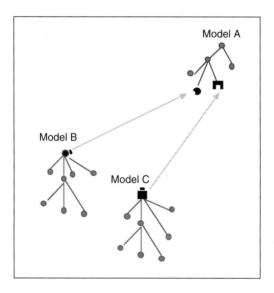

Figure 9.5—Multiresolution Family of Models

---

[20]Davis and Bigelow, *Experiments in Multiresolution Modeling.*

[21]Unfortunately, some authors use the term *multiresolution models* to mean only that there are *outputs* at different levels of detail or that a model happens to treat different phenomena asymmetrically (e.g., with detail for combat processes and a more aggregate depiction for logistics). Still other authors claim multiresolution features for models because their objects are hierarchical. The essence of multilevel resolution, as I use the term here (and as discussed in National Research Council, *Modeling and Simulation*), is having multiple levels of abstraction for key *processes,* such as attrition, movement, and communications. Achieving such MRM is quite challenging. RAND work on the subject dates back to the late 1980s.

shown as "on the side," for use when needed). In principle, one could attach models B and C in the software itself, creating a bigger model. However, in practice there are tradeoffs between doing this and keeping the more detailed models separate. For larger models and simulations, a combination single-model/family-of-models approach is desirable because it balances the needs for analytic agility and complexity management.

MRM is not enough, however, because, as noted earlier, different applications require different abstractions even if the resolution is the same—i.e., different "perspectives" are legitimate and important. Perspectives are distinguished by the conception of the system and the choice of variables; they are analogous to alternative "representations" in physics or engineering. Designing for both multiple resolution and multiple perspectives can be called MRMPM.[22]

With MRMPM models (single models or families), the concepts and predictions among levels and perspectives have to be connected (and reconciled). It is often assumed that the correct way to do this is to calibrate upward: treat the information of the most detailed model as correct and use it to calibrate the higher-level models. This, indeed, is often appropriate. The fact is, however, that the more detailed models almost always have omissions and shortcomings.[23] Models at higher levels, and from different perspectives, address some of them explicitly. Further, the different models of a family draw on different sources of information—ranging from doctrine or even "lore" on one extreme to physical measurements on a test range at the other. One class of information is not inherently better than another; it is simply different.

Figure 9.6 makes the point that members of a multiresolution model family should be *mutually* calibrated, with information flows in both directions. In the military domain, for example, low-resolution historical attrition or movement rates may be used to help calibrate more-detailed models predicting attrition and movement. This is not

---

[22]Paul K. Davis, "Exploratory Analysis Enabled by Multiresolution, Multiperspective Modeling," in Jeffrey A. Joines et al. (eds.), *Proceedings of the 2000 Winter Simulation Conference*, 2000.

[23]For example, detailed models often have a rich depiction of physical considerations but only a minimal representation of behaviors that adapt to circumstances.

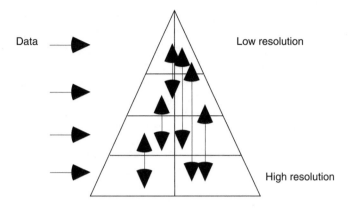

Figure 9.6—Mutual Calibration of a Family of Models

straightforward, because of the 1:n mappings. It is often done crudely, by applying an overall scaling factor (fudge factor) rather than correcting the more atomic features of the model, but it is likely to be something with which readers are familiar. However, much calibration is indeed upward. In a study using detailed order-of-battle information, for example, inputs on the number of "equivalent divisions" or "equivalent F-15 aircraft" used in abstract models can be computed from the data feeding high-resolution models. Furthermore, at least in principle, the attrition coefficients' dependence on situation (e.g., open versus wooded terrain for ground forces) should be informed by high-resolution work.

So, given their desirability, how should families of models be built? Or, given preexisting models, how "should" they relate before they are connected as software or used for mutual calibration? The first design principle may be to recognize that there are limits to what is feasible. In particular, there are limits to how well low-resolution models can be consistent with high-resolution models. *Approximation is a central concept from the outset.* Several points are especially important in thinking about this:[24]

---

[24]Davis and Bigelow, *Experiments in Multiresolution Modeling.*

- Consistency between two models of differing resolution should be assessed in the context of how the models are being used. What matters is not whether they generate the same final state of the overall system, but whether they generate approximately the same results in the application. That may be something as specific as summary graphs or rank ordering of alternatives. Another way to put this is to be practical, not theological, about how much detail is needed.

- The implications for consistency of aggregation and disaggregation processes must also be judged in context. Some disaggregation assumptions represent aggregate-level knowledge not necessarily reflected in the most detailed model.

- Comprehensive MRM is very difficult or impossible for complex modeling and simulation,[25] but having even some MRM can be far more useful than having none at all. MRM is not an all-or-nothing matter.

- The various members of an MRM family will typically be valid for only portions of the system's state space. As one moves from one region to another, valid description may require that parameter values or even the structure of the model itself be changed.

- Mechanisms are therefore needed to recognize different situations and shift models. In simulations, human intervention is one mechanism and agent-based modeling is another.[26]

- Valid MRM will often require stochastic variables represented by probability distributions, not merely mean values. Further, valid aggregate models must sometimes reflect correlations among variables that might naively be seen as probabilistically independent.

---

[25]For an excellent theoretical discussion of this, see Robert Axtell, *Theory of Model Aggregation for Dynamical Systems with Applications to Problems of Global Change*, Ph.D. dissertation, Carnegie-Mellon University (available from University Microfilms International, Ann Arbor, MI). Axtell's discussion, however, fails to emphasize the key significance of approximations. As a result, it is more pessimistic than my own work.

[26]Agent-based models include modules that represent (i.e., serve as agents for) adaptive entities, such as individual humans or groups. The basic ideas are discussed in most books dealing with "complex adaptive systems."

With these observations up front, the ideal for MRM is a hierarchical design for each MRM process, as indicated earlier, in Figure 9.5.

Models and analysis methods for exploratory analysis should have a number of characteristics. First, they should be able to reflect hierarchical decomposition through multiple levels of resolution and from alternative perspectives representing different "aspects" of a system. For example, one model might decompose a system into its organizational components, another might focus on different component processes, and yet another might follow component functions.

Less obviously, models and analysis methods should also include realistic mechanisms describing how the natural entities of the system act, react, adapt, mutate, and change. These mechanisms should reflect the relative "fitness" of the original and emerging entities for the environment in which they are operating. Many techniques are applicable here, including game theory methods and others that may be relatively familiar to readers. However, the most fruitful new approaches are those typically associated with the term *agent-based modeling*. These include submodels that act "as the agents for" specific entities—say, political leaders and military commanders or (at the other extreme) infantry privates on the battlefield. In practice, such models need not be exotic: they may correspond to some relatively simple heuristic, or intuitive, decision rules or to some well-known (though perhaps complex) operations-research algorithm. But to have such decision models is quite different from depending on scripts.

Because it is implausible that closed computer models will be able to meet the above challenge in the foreseeable future, the family of "models" should allow for human interaction—whether in human-only seminar games, small-scale model-supported human gaming, or distributed interactive simulation. This runs against the grain of much common practice, which imputes too much virtue to "closed models" that generate readily reproducible results.

The last item in the bulleted list above is often ignored in today's day-to-day work, even by good analysts who have a family of models. Often, when they seek to use models at different levels of resolution analytically, they decide on a highest-level model to be used for excursions—i.e., for examining sensitivities. They then "calibrate" this highest-level model by using one or more detailed models. For example, they might use the Brawler model of air-to-air combat between small groups of aircraft in different groupings; they would then use results of that work to calibrate the air-to-air model of a theater-level depiction, such as in the TACWAR, JICM, Thunder, or START models. This is not easy. However, the analysts would sit down, talk, draw sketches, and so on, until they gained a sense of how to go about the calibration. Ultimately, for a particular study done on a limited budget and time scale (as most are) they might use expected-value outcomes of "representative" air-to-air engagements in Brawler to set attrition coefficients in the theater-level model. This might or might not be "correct," because the relationship between the engagement level and theater level is very complex: in a real air war, there may be thousands of engagements with a wide variety of characteristics, and how to aggregate is not so clear. For example, one might imagine that 80 percent of engagements are "normal" but have little effect on relative force levels, while 20 percent of engagements are of a different character and lead to one side annihilating the other's aircraft with no losses of its own. The overall time dependence of relative force levels, then, might be dictated by the unusual, nonrepresentative engagements. However, focusing on these unusual cases in doing the calibration might outrageously exaggerate one or both of the attrition rates. The "correct" way to go about the calibration would necessarily involve explicit, study-dependent integration over classes of engagement.

Sometimes, the higher-level model inputs need to be stochastic. Figure 9.7 illustrates the concept schematically for a simple problem. Suppose that a process—for instance, one computing the losses to aircraft in air-to-air encounters—depends on five inputs: Q, X, Y, a, and b. But suppose that the outcome of ultimate interest involves many instances of that process with different values of X and Y (e.g., different per-engagement numbers of Red and Blue aircraft). An abstraction of the model might depend only on Q, a, and b (e.g., overall attrition might depend on only numbers of Red and Blue aircraft, their relative quality, and some C2 factor). If the abstraction shown is to be valid, the variable Z should be consistent with the higher-resolution results. However, if it does not depend explicitly on X and Y, then there are "hidden variables" in the problem, and Z may

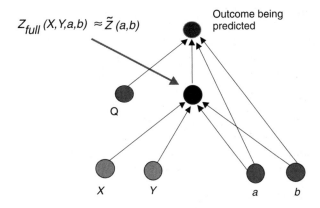

$$Z_{full}(X,Y,a,b) \approx \tilde{Z}(a,b)$$

Outcome being predicted

Q

X   Y   a   b

Figure 9.7—Input to Higher-Level Model May Be Stochastic

appear to be a random variable, in which case the predicted outcome would be a random variable. This randomness might be ignored if the distribution were narrow enough, but that might not be the case.

To compute what "should be," one would relate the probability density to a constrained integral over X and Y, appropriately weighting on the basis of likelihood and restricting the integration to regions where Z has the value of interest.

In the past, such calibrations have been rare, in significant part because analysts have lacked both theory and tools for doing things better. The "theory" part includes not having good descriptions of how the detailed model should relate to the simplified one. The tool part includes not being able to define the set of runs that should be done (representing the integral of Figure 9.7) and then to actually make those runs.

Ideally, such a calibration would be dynamic within a simulation. Moreover, it would be easy to adjust the calibration to represent different assumptions about command, control, communications, computers, intelligence, surveillance, and reconnaissance (C4ISR), as well as about tactics. We cannot do such things today, because modeling technology and practice are not up to it yet.

LESSONS FROM RECENT EXPERIENCE

Both exploratory analysis and MRM/MRMPM are relatively new concepts, but there is a growing body of examples to illustrate their practicality for addressing problems—for instance, the problem of halting an invading army using precision fires from aircraft and missiles.[27] The most recent aspects of that work included understanding in some detail how the effectiveness of such fires are affected by details of terrain, enemy maneuver tactics, certain aspects of command and control, and so on. This provided a good test bed for exploring numerous aspects of MRMPM theory.

We developed a multiresolution personal-computer model (PEM),[28] written in Analytica, to understand and extend to other circumstances the findings from entity-level simulation of ground maneuver and long-range precision fires. A major part of this work was learning how to inform and calibrate PEM to the entity-level work. There was no possibility, in this instance, of revising the entity-level model. Nor, in practice, did we have a good enough understanding of the model to construct a comprehensive calibration theory. Instead, we had to construct a new, more abstract model and attempt to impose some of its abstractions on the data from runs of the entity-level simulation in prior work, plus some special runs made for our purposes. Had we had the intermediate-level PEM several years earlier, we could have used it both to define adaptations of the entity-level model that would have generated some of the abstractions we needed and to better define the experiments conducted with the high-resolution model. Instead, we had to make do with the situation

---

[27]Our work on precision fires is discussed in Davis, Bigelow, and McEver, *Analytical Methods for Studies and Experiments*; Jimmie McEver, Paul K. Davis, and James H. Bigelow, *EXHALT: An Interdiction Model for Exploring Halt Capabilities in a Large Scenario Space*, MR-1137-OSD, RAND, 2000; Paul K. Davis, James H. Bigelow, and Jimmie McEver, *Effects of Terrain, Maneuver Tactics, and C4ISR on the Effectiveness of Long-Range Precision Fires: A Stochastic Multiresolution Model (PEM) Calibrated to High-Resolution Simulation*, MR-1138-OSD, RAND, 2000; and Davis, Bigelow, and McEver, *Effects of Terrain*. Some of this work was also used in the summer study of the Defense Science Board and is reflected in Eugene C. Gritton, Paul K. Davis, Randall Steeb, and John Matsumura, *Ground Forces for a Rapidly Employable Joint Task Force: First-Week Capabilities for Short-Warning Conflicts*, MR-1152-OSD, RAND, 2000.

[28]Davis, Bigelow, and McEver, *Effects of Terrain*.

we found ourselves in. The result is a case history with what are probably some generic lessons learned.

Figure 9.8 illustrates one aspect of our multiresolution PEM approach. The figure shows the data flow within a PEM module that generates the impact time (relative to the ideal impact time) for a salvo of precision weapons aimed at a packet of armored fighting vehicles observed by C4ISR assets at an earlier time. Other parts of the PEM combine information about packet location versus time and salvo effectiveness for targets that happen to be within the salvo's "footprint" at the time of impact in order to estimate the effectiveness of the precision weapons. For the salvo-impact-time module, Figure 9.8 shows how the PEM is designed to accept inputs as detailed as whether there is enroute retargeting of weapons, the C2 latency time, and weapon flight time. However, it can also accept more aggregate inputs, such as time from last update. If the input variable "resolution of last update calculation" is set "low," then time from last update is specified directly as input; if not, it is calculated from the lower-level inputs.

Being able to depict the problem as in Figure 9.8, and to provide users the option of what inputs to use, has proven very useful—both for analysis itself and for communicating insights to decisionmakers in communities ranging from the C4ISR community to the programming and analysis community. In particular, the work clarified how the technology-intensive work of the C4ISR acquisition community relates to higher-level strategy problems and analysis of such problems at the theater level.

Another companion piece describes how, in developing the PEM and a yet more abstract model (EXHALT) used for theater-level halt-problem analysis, we experimented with methods for dealing with the multiperspective problem.[29] Perhaps the key conclusion of this particular work is that MRMPM rather demands a building-block approach that emphasizes study-specific assembly of the precise model needed. Although we had some success in developing a closed

---

[29]Jimmie McEver, Paul K. Davis, and James H. Bigelow, "Implementing Multiresolution Models and Families of Models: From Entity Level Simulation to Personal-Computer Stochastic Models and Simple 'Repro Models,'" *SPIE 2000*, Orlando, FL, April 2000.

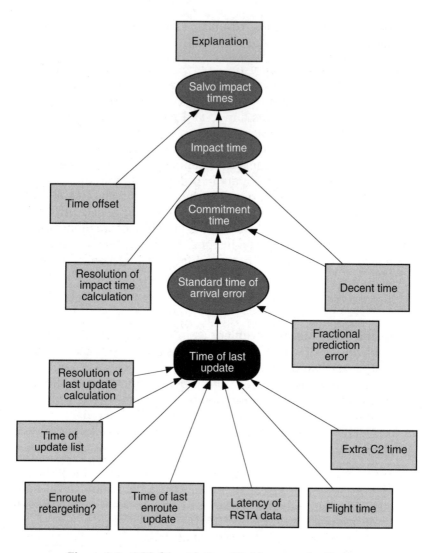

**Figure 9.8—A Multiresolution, Multiperspective Design
for Salvo-Impact-Time Module**

MRMPM model with alternative user modes representing different
demands for resolution and perspective (e.g., the switches in Figure
9.8), it proved impossible to do very much in that regard: the number

of interesting user modes and resolution combinations simply precludes being able to wire in all the relevant user modes. Moreover, the explosion of complexity occurs very quickly. Thus, despite the desire of many users to have a black-box machine that can handle all the cases and perspectives of interest, it seems a fundamental reality that at-the-time assembly from building blocks, not prior definition, is the stronger approach. This was as we expected, but even more so.

The ultimate reason for the building-block conclusion is that even in the relatively simple problem examined, the real variable trees (akin to data-flow diagrams) are bushy rather than rigorously hierarchical. Furthermore, the different legitimate perspectives can simply not all be accommodated simultaneously without making the code itself very complicated to follow. In contrast, we found it easy to construct the model needed quickly—in hours rather than days or weeks—as the result of our building-block approach, visual modeling, use of array mathematics, and strong, modular design.

As powerful as current personal computer tools are in comparison with those of past years, they are still not up to the challenge of making the building-block/assembly approach rigorous, understandable, controllable, and reproducible without unrealistically high levels of modeler/analyst discipline. Also, the search models for advanced exploratory analysis are not yet well developed. Thus, there are good challenges ahead, not just for the model builders and users, but also for the community that builds the enabling technology.

Appendix

REFLECTING UNCERTAINTY WITH PARAMETERS, AN EXAMPLE

As an example, consider a model that describes the rate at which Red and Blue suffer attrition in combat according to a Lanchester square law:

$$\frac{d\tilde{R}}{dt} = -\tilde{K}_b \tilde{B}(t) \quad \frac{d\tilde{B}}{dt} = -\tilde{K}_r \tilde{R}(t) \, ,$$

where the attrition coefficients for Red and Blue have both deterministic and stochastic parts, each of which is subject to uncertainty. The equation for Red says that the quantity of Red capability decreases in proportion to the quantity of Blue (because Blue is shooting at Red):

$$\tilde{K}_b(t) = K_{b0}\left[1 + c_b \tilde{N}_b(t; \mu, \sigma_b)\right] \quad K_{r0}\left[1 + c_r \tilde{N}_r(t; \mu, \sigma_r)\right] .$$

Here, K_{b0} and K_{r0} are average attrition rates for a given war. They may be highly uncertain (factors of 2, 3, or more), but they are constant within a war. That is, before the war, we may not know the sides' average effectivenesses, but they exist. This said, attrition will vary from battle to battle and from time period to time period within a given war. Such variation can be regarded as a stochastic process. These effects are reflected by the bracketed factors, above, where N_r and N_b are assumed to be normal random variables with means of m and standard deviations. Their parameters are also uncertain, perhaps strongly so, but it is a different kind of uncertainty than that about the average attrition for a given war.[30]

---

[30]I distinguish between deterministic uncertainty and stochastic processes, but both may be treated by the same mathematical tools, such as probability distributions. The distinction is important, however. For example, a commander discovering that his losses to attrition were three times what he expected on the first day of war—and ascribing that attrition to the unanticipated effectiveness of certain weapons—should not imagine that tomorrow is another day, that stochastic variation may result in very low attrition tomorrow, and that he therefore should continue as on the first day. Unfortunately for that commander, things won't "average out." He needs to change tactics.

So far the equations have represented input uncertainty. However, suppose that we do not know the correct equations of combat—except that, for some reason, we are convinced that the correct equations are Lanchesterian: either what aficionados call "Lanchester linear," "Lanchester square," or something in between. We could then reflect this uncertainty by rewriting the equation as

$$\frac{d\tilde{R}}{dt} = -\tilde{K}_b \tilde{B}^e(t)\tilde{R}^f(t) \quad \frac{d\tilde{B}}{dt} = -\tilde{K}_r \tilde{B}^g(t)\tilde{R}^h(t) \ .$$

Now, by treating the exponents e, f, g, and h as uncertain parameters, we can change the very structure of the model. Thus, by varying parameter values, we can explore both input and structural uncertainties in the model.

There are limits to what can be accomplished. Suppose that the correct equations of combat are indeed Lanchesterian but that the K-factors decay exponentially with time as combatants tire, lose efficiency, or husband ammunition. The consequences of different exponential decay times cannot even be explored if the phenomenon goes unrecognized. This is not an idle comment; we often do not know the underlying form of the system model: many aspects of phenomena are recognized, but not others. And they may not be observed except in unique circumstances. Despite this caveat, we can do a great deal with exploratory analysis to understand the consequences of uncertainties that can be parameterized.

Chapter Ten

USING EXPLORATORY MODELING

Daniel B. Fox

This chapter examines a way to use combat modeling that both capitalizes on the strengths of combat models and helps analysts and decisionmakers gain new insights into complex problems.

The chapter has three sections. The first of these describes the evolving defense environment, to show the need for tools that allow analysis of situations dominated by uncertainty. It also briefly discusses combat models in general and the Joint Integrated Contingency Model (JICM) in particular, covering some features of the JICM that make it especially suitable for exploratory modeling. Finally, the section compares conventional sensitivity analysis to exploratory modeling.

The second section describes how exploratory modeling is done, discussing its experimental design and its measures of outcome. It also presents a comprehensive example of applied exploratory modeling, identifying the problem and illustrating some conclusions. The third section then briefly describes exploratory modeling's key advantages.

THE NEED FOR EXPLORATORY MODELING

This book underscores the fact that the national security environment has changed dramatically and continues to change. During the Cold War, the role of U.S. military forces was to prepare for a major war in Central Europe. Other requirements—preparing to fight in Korea or in smaller-scale conflicts—were considered "lesser included cases" of the requirement for Central Europe. With the fall of the Berlin wall, the role of the U.S. military is now to prepare for a variety of contingencies, including terrorist threats. Although the nature of the future defense environment is unclear, long-term deployments to rescue "failed states" such as Afghanistan seem more likely, while having to commit forces to a major theater war (MTW) appears less so. These smaller but more likely operations are difficult to analyze. They are not amenable to many analytic tools and are dominated by uncertainties, ranging from the nature of the conflict, to the location, to the possible reactions to U.S. actions taken in response to evolving conditions.

At the same time, despite the stunning immediate aftermath of the September 11 attacks, many of these contingencies or deployments, in and of themselves, will invoke only limited national interests. The use of overwhelming force is one way to limit casualties, but sending large force deployments to problem areas stresses the rotation base of the services. The culmination of these stresses is a push for new ways of pursuing national security interests, which, in turn, creates a demand to analyze new alternatives.

Exploratory analysis is a tool to aid decisionmaking in such uncertain environments. It applies combat modeling to analytic problems in ways that have not been widely used. In particular, it uses the enormous computation capabilities of modern computers to intensively explore alternative outcomes by systematically varying assumptions. Paul Davis's Chapter Nine describes the technique in great detail. This chapter provides concrete illustrations of how this powerful technique can be used.

Given both the limitations and utility of models, it remains true that model-aided analysis says more about the analyst than about the model. It is the analyst who must judge how to represent the myriad details of the situation under study. In a nutshell, all combat models are wrong. But some, in conjunction with intelligent analysts, can be useful.

The Joint Integrated Contingency Model

The RAND-developed JICM is one such useful model. It employs modular functional submodels (some of which are listed in Figure 10.1) to manipulate the objects represented within the overall model.

Figure 10.1—JICM Functional Submodels

In JICM, one functional submodel is the simulation's strategic mobility module, which allows the analyst to set up simulation experiments that explicitly include enemy actions intended to degrade U.S. mobility. The degradation in mobility causes adjustments to the arrival of U.S. forces, which, in turn, can affect downstream theater-level outcomes.

Most theater combat models use a scenario input file that is a linear presentation of the events to be simulated.[1] By contrast, JICM uses analytic war plans that explicitly implement the major operational-level decisions of the campaign and allow the campaign to develop along alternative paths in accordance with how the simulated situation evolves. Within JICM, the war plans can query the state of the simulation and then alter actions taken by entities in the simulation

---

[1]The linear presentation generally describes the major operational events in terms of the fixed time when they are to occur in the simulation. Such events include the arrival of forces, and the timing of offensive and counteroffensive actions.

based on the results of the queries. Three examples of this kind of query are

1. If ?control[KuwaitCity]==Iraq then "do not use POMCUS"

2. If ?location[1-CAV/1-BDE]==KuwaitCity then "implement delay"

3. If (?tooth[EUSA] > 600 && ?tail[EUSA] > 800) then "begin CO"

Query 1 checks to see if Iraq has gained control of (the JICM place) Kuwait City. If so, the analytic war plans select a set of orders that does not involve attempting to use prepositioned combat equipment there. Query 2 verifies that a specific early-arriving force has arrived at Kuwait City. If so, the analytic war plans select a set of orders that implements actions to delay the advance of enemy forces in order to provide time for additional forces to arrive. Query 3 verifies that sufficient combat force and support ("tooth" and "tail") have arrived to begin the counteroffensive.

In JICM analysis, a single analytic war plan can include enough logic to react to the major operational turning points of a conflict. There is no need to create individual linear-order sequences for each alternative case to be examined.

Sensitivity Analysis and Exploratory Modeling

As is true for most models, the use of combat models typically involves some form of sensitivity analysis. In basic form, sensitivity analysis consists of three steps:

1. Establish a base case and obtain results

2. Define an alternative case by changing one or more input variables and obtain new outcomes

3. Compare the base case and alternative case, repeating steps 2 and 3 as required.

In contrast to sensitivity analysis, exploratory analysis is a more intensive process in which a range of values for a set of input variables is defined. Exploratory analysis then executes the simulation for every combination of values for all variables. Full enumeration of all possible cases can quickly mushroom to a very large number of runs.

Varying the numbers of variables and the number of values assigned to those variables produces numbers of runs for conventional sensitivity and exploratory modeling as follows:

- Conventional sensitivity: To explore sensitivity to n variables with m values each, the experiment size is 2 raised to the nth power and the number of runs is thus, e.g.,

    32 with n = 5, m = 2

    1,024 with n = 10, m = 3

    1,048,576 with n = 20, m = 4.

- Exploratory modeling: To explore an experiment with n variables with m values each, the experiment size is m^n and the number of runs is thus, e.g.,

    32 with n = 5, m = 2

    59,049 with n = 10, m = 3

    greater than a trillion with n = 20, m = 4.

Figure 10.2 shows the hours or computers needed for simulation runs. The top half of the figure shows how many hours it takes for a specified number of runs (10 to 1,000,000, across the columns) as a function of the time for each simulation run (3 to 3,000 minutes, down the rows). Networks of computers are now routinely available, so the lower half of the figure converts to an alternative metric: how many computers are needed to execute the specified number of simulations within a reasonable time limit (one week).

The number of exploratory modeling cases expands quickly as the number of variables and values rises. Such large numbers can easily tax the computation limits of even large networks of modern computers. Although most simulations are "fast" when running a single case, execution time becomes critical when exploratory modeling requires that thousands of cases be run. Thus, the art of exploratory modeling is being able to limit the analysis to the most important cases. To do so, some conventional sensitivity analysis might be used prior to the exploratory modeling in order to identify important variables in the decision space.

Number of simulation runs

Minutes per simulation run		10	100	1,000	10,000	100,000	1,000,000	
	3	1	5	50	500	5,000	50,000	
	30	5	50	500	5,000	50,000	500,000	Total hours
	300	50	500	5,000	50,000	500,000	5,000,000	
	3,000	500	5,000	50,000	500,000	5,000,000	50,000,000	
		10	100	1,000	10,000	100,000	1,000,000	
	3	1	1	1	3	30	300	Number of computers to complete simulations in 1 week (168 hours)
	30	1	1	3	30	300	3,000	
	300	1	3	30	300	3,000	30,000	
	3,000	3	30	300	3,000	30,000	300,000	

Figure 10.2—Hours or Computers Required for Simulation Runs

DOING EXPLORATORY MODELING

Apart from its dependence on the validity of the combat model itself, exploratory modeling rests on two fundamentals: experimental variables and measures of outcome.

The selection of *experimental variables* and their assigned values constitutes the experimental design for an exploratory analysis. There is no general rule for identifying the best variables or values in a given circumstance; selection depends on the nature of the problem under study and the operational experience of the analyst(s) conducting the experiment. But the ranges selected for the variables should make an analytic difference. Experimental variables come in two types. Some are quantities that can, in some sense, be controlled in the real world (e.g., the quantity of force to be applied in numbers of divisions or squadrons), whereas others represent "risks," or some uncertainty that might require some form of hedge, or "insurance."

Measures of outcome are the experimental results used to determine the relative goodness of cases. The chosen measures of outcome should be operationally meaningful to decisionmakers and, at the same time, highlight differences between the cases in the experimental design.

An example can clarify the process for and problems in conducting an exploratory analysis. Consider an exploratory analysis examining a Southwest Asia (SWA) scenario that starts with an Iraqi attack through Kuwait into Saudi Arabia. Enemy activities and allied decisions have the potential to restrict U.S. access to the theater early in the conflict. Given these potential restrictions, three different U.S. force enhancements are to be assessed.

Four of the variables in this example represent risks. Two of the four represent enemy-controlled factors (mines and chemicals), the third represents a factor controlled by U.S. allies (political access limits), and the fourth represents a risk neither fully under enemy control nor subject to U.S. choice (actionable warning time). Three additional variables represent potential U.S. force alternatives—Naval brilliant antitank (NBAT), Army brilliant antitank (ABAT), and Sea Cavalry (SCAV). These seven variables are summarized as follows:

- Mines = number of days Strait of Hormuz closed.

- Chemicals = days of effect on tactical air sortie rates and airport of debarkation (APOD) and seaport of debarkation (SPOD) unload times.

- Warning = days between day on which U.S. forces begin mobilizing (C-Day) and day on which war begins (D-Day).

- Access = base, some, less, worst, where base = NATO and Gulf Cooperation Council (GCC) access on C-Day; some = Kuwait, United Arab Emirates (UAE), and NATO on C-Day, and other GCC on D-Day; less = Kuwait, UAE, and United Kingdom (UK) on C-Day, all others except Saudi Arabia on D-Day, and Saudi Arabia on D+2; and worst = Kuwait and UK on C-Day, all others except Saudi Arabia on D-Day, and Saudi Arabia on D+4.

- NBAT = Naval-based ATACMs, 300 ship-based brilliant antitank (BAT) missiles that can be fired beginning on D-Day.

- ABAT = Ground-based BAT missile launchers stationed in the theater and 500 missiles available as soon as airlift can move missiles to the theater.

- SCAV = Sea Cavalry, ship-based attack helicopter concept providing for 1,000 sorties over the period D+0 to D+9.

A comprehensive assessment of this scenario might include an examination of various measures of outcome, but for illustrative purposes, this exposition considers only one measure—the maximum depth of penetration of enemy forces into friendly territory. Coding the measure of outcome permits rapid examination of multiple alternative cases by showing the results of several simulation experiments on a single diagram. The coding for the sample assessments is illustrated in Figure 10.3, where the darker the shading, the deeper the enemy penetration.

The encoded outcomes for 12 simulation runs are shown in Figure 10.4. Along the x axis are four different values for the access variable; along the y axis are three different values for the warning time. The values for all remaining variables are shown to the right of the illustration.

Examining Figure 10.4 in more detail highlights the fact that when there is zero warning, enemy forces penetrate deeply even under the least restrictive access constraints (no enemy mines or chemical weapons used).

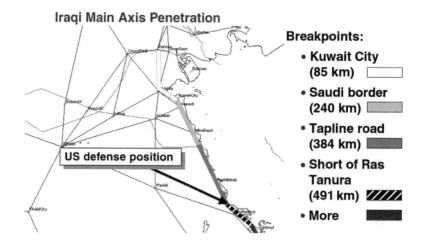

Figure 10.3—Coded Measure of Outcome

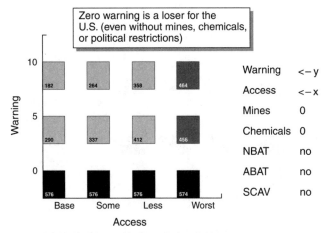

NOTE: The actual number of kilometers of
enemy penetration is shown in the lower left-
hand corner of each display box.

Figure 10.4—Exploring Access and Warning

Figure 10.5 introduces an additional display axis to augment the information of Figure 10.4. The shaded boxes appear to be stacked in sets of three; each set represents three different values of the mine variable along a z axis (drawn to allow the simultaneous presentation of more cases). Examining Figure 10.5 reinforces the previous observation that when there is zero warning time, the enemy forces are able to penetrate deeply.

Figure 10.6 replaces the mine variable on the z axis of Figure 10.5 with the chemical variable. Comparing the two suggests that chemicals may have a somewhat greater impact than mines do. Figure 10.7 directly compares mines and chemicals by moving the access variable to the z axis and putting chemicals and mines on the x and y axes. Here, warning time is five days.

Figure 10.7 makes it clearer that the outcomes tend to worsen faster as the chemical effects increase (as one moves to the right on the x axis) than they do as the mine effects increase (moving up on the y axis). That is, step increases in the chemical threat allow for greater

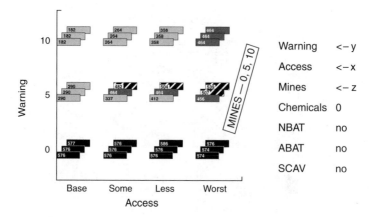

Figure 10.5—Exploring Access, Warning, and Mines

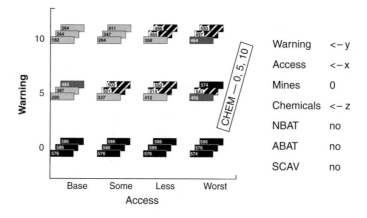

Figure 10.6—Exploring Access, Warning, and Chemicals

increases in enemy penetration than do step increases in the mine threat.

Figure 10.8 compares all three force alternatives—ABAT, SCAV, and NBAT. An examination of enemy penetration (measured in kilometers and displayed in the lower left corner of each display box) suggests that the ABAT or SCAV option restricts enemy penetration far

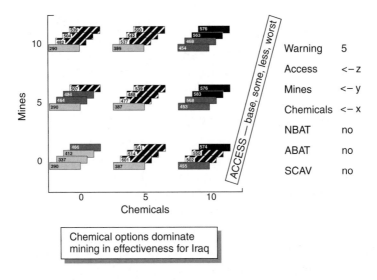

Figure 10.7—Exploring Chemicals, Mines, and Access

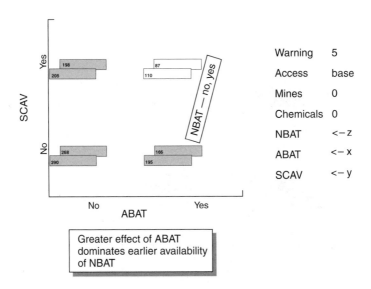

Figure 10.8—Exploring ABAT, SCAV, and NBAT

more than the NBAT option does. If the display box in the front lower left of Figure 10.8 is taken as a base case, NBAT alone reduces enemy penetration by roughly 20 km (comparing the front and rear display boxes in the lower left). ABAT alone saves 90 km (comparing the front boxes in the lower left and lower right); SCAV alone saves 80 km (comparing the front boxes in the lower left and upper left). The greater effect of ABAT offsets the earlier availability of NBAT.

Figure 10.9 illustrates how robust the ABAT and SCAV options are under the stress of enemy chemical actions. Comparing the two (i.e., comparing the three values in the display boxes in the upper left with the three values in the boxes in the lower right) suggests that they reduce enemy penetration to a similar degree.

Looking at the three values stacked along the z axis of Figure 10.9, one can see that the advantages of ABAT and SCAV are reduced when the enemy uses chemical weapons. At worst, the enemy penetrates 550 km. If both ABAT and SCAV are available (display boxes in upper right), the outcomes are substantially improved over those from either option on its own, suggesting that the two reinforce each other.

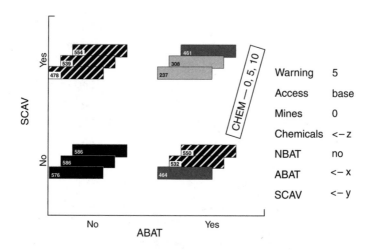

Figure 10.9—Exploring ABAT and SCAV When Chemicals Are Used

Figures 10.4 through 10.9 represent just a few of the exploratory analysis displays possible with this experimental design. In practice, any of the experimental variables can be displayed on the x, y, and z axes, and any variable not on an axis can be set to any desired value. In addition, any of the collected measures of outcome can be displayed. The figures provided here represent just one possible line of exploration through the experimental space.

THE VALUE OF EXPLORATORY MODELING

Exploratory modeling not only examines risks and force alternatives; it also can be used to test the effect of alternative theater concepts of operation (CONOPs) and alternative investments in mobility (e.g., prepositioning ashore, prepositioning afloat, and greater numbers of mobility ships or aircraft). Additionally, it permits a more extensive assessment of the U.S. force structure's robustness by making it possible to examine the many factors that might make the U.S. defense case more difficult (e.g., insufficient warning, a lack of allied contributions, unanticipated enemy strength, shortfalls in critical ammunition).

Some of JICM's features make it particularly suitable for exploratory modeling at the theater level. They include the breadth of scenarios that can be represented, the ability to address strategic mobility, and a flexible war plan system that permits many variations of the basic cases to be created.

Another advantage of exploratory modeling is that it is not limited to theater combat problems. It may be applied wherever a suitable simulation model can run all the cases in an experimental design in a reasonable time. Thus, for example, it is suitable for analyzing smaller-scale contingencies in which combat outcomes may not be the defining feature, environmental degradation, or traffic management.

Regardless of the problem to be studied, a key advantage of exploratory analysis is the ability to model both uncertainty—by using variables to represent things not under decisionmakers' control— and alternative choices. In using a model, the analyst is forced to organize all thoughts about the problem. An exploratory analysis can provide a rich illustration of the effects alternatives will have under varying circumstances, thus permitting a full appreciation of the choices.

Chapter Eleven

ASSESSING MILITARY INFORMATION SYSTEMS

Stuart H. Starr

The assessment of military information systems is an art form that has evolved substantially since the mid-1970s.[1] Until then, national security assessments generally neglected information system issues. Such systems were either assumed to be "perfect" (i.e., providing perfect information with no time delays), capable of no more than second- or third-order effects, or totally irrelevant. When they were considered, they were often treated as a "patch"—something introduced into force-on-force calculations to reflect imperfect information systems.

This chapter begins with a historical perspective on how military information systems assessment evolved. It describes the change that took place 25 years ago, which entailed a basic reengineering of the assessment process, one that involved integrating leadership, institutions, people, processes, resources, tools, research and development (R&D), and products. An initial period of innovative assessments of military information systems was followed by a hiatus in the 1980s as Department of Defense (DoD) leadership lost interest in analyzing information systems. "Paralysis through analysis" was an oft-heard criticism in the Pentagon. Budgets for military systems, including military information systems, were at historically high levels, and the Pentagon's emphasis was on acquiring military information systems, not assessing them.

---

[1]Stated more precisely, this would read "information systems in support of military operations, including systems owned and operated by nonmilitary organizations." These include command and control centers, communications, sensors, and ancillary systems (e.g., navigation).

The chapter then addresses how this attitude shifted in the early 1990s, thanks in large part to profound changes in the international scene. The Soviet Union dissolved and the Persian Gulf War provided an insight into how innovative military information systems could support contemporary warfare. Thus emerged new challenges in assessing military information systems, and hence a new information assessment process. The chapter then moves to the key principles and insights related to the assessment of information systems in the context of conventional conflict. These insights are encapsulated in the 1999 *NATO Code of Best Practice for Command and Control Assessment*,[2] a product of six years of deliberations by nine NATO nations.

The chapter concludes by summarizing the advances made in the art of assessing military information systems since the mid-1970s, and then turning to the challenges that remain, such as the development and implementation of novel assessment tools and the treatment of emerging "new world disorder" missions (i.e., coercive operations using a mix of diplomatic, informational, economic, and military resources to convince an adversary to withdraw military forces from a neighbor), and peacekeeping, homeland defense, counterterrorism, counter-weapons of mass destruction (WMD), and information operations.

HISTORICAL PERSPECTIVE

Figure 11.1 summarizes the factors that fundamentally changed how military information systems were assessed from 1975 to 1985. Key civilian and military leaders in the defense community—Robert Hermann (then assistant secretary of the Air Force for Research, Development, and Acquisition), Harry Van Trees (then principal deputy assistant secretary of defense for Command, Control, Communications, and Intelligence), Charles Zraket (then executive vice president, MITRE), and MG Jasper Welch (then director, Air Force Studies and Analyses), and others—launched a search for the "Holy Grail,"

---

[2]*NATO Code of Best Practice (COBP) on the Assessment of C2*, Research & Technology Organisation (RTO) Technical Report 9, AC/323(SAS)TP/4, Communication Group, Inc., Hull, Quebec, March 1999. (Text also available at http://www.dodccrp.org/nato_supp/nato.htm.)

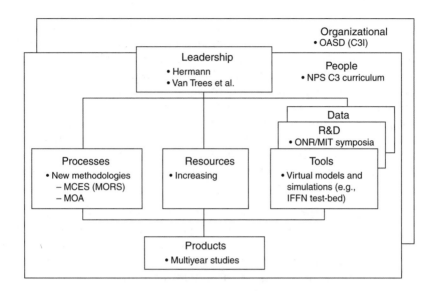

**Figure 11.1—A Business Process Reengineering Perspective of
Information Assessment (1975–1985)**

i.e., for the ability to assess the impact of C2 systems on force effectiveness.[3] They acted out of intellectual curiosity, but also because of
their emerging awareness of the importance of military information
systems in modern warfare and their need to justify budgets for military information systems to a skeptical Congress.

This initiative was helped by the creation of the office of the assistant
secretary of defense (OASD) for command, control, communications,
and intelligence (C3I), an action that brought together the disparate
DoD organizations responsible for C2, communications, intelligence,
and defense support systems (e.g., electronic warfare, navigation).
The contemporary establishment of a C3 curriculum by the Naval

---

[3]Major General Jasper A. Welch, Jr., "Command and Control Simulation—A Common
Thread," keynote address, *AGARD Conference Proceedings*, No. 268 ("Modeling and
Simulation of Avionics Systems and Command, Control and Communications
Systems"), Paris, France, October 15–19, 1979; and OSD, with the cooperation of
MITRE Corporation, C3 Division, *Proceedings for Quantitative Assessment of Utility of
Command and Control Systems*, National Defense University, Washington, DC,
January 1980.

Postgraduate School (NPS) helped create the human capital needed to assess military information systems. Finally, the Office of Naval Research (ONR) established a multiyear program with the Massachusetts Institute of Technology (MIT) to pursue R&D on information system assessment; the principals were innovators in the field of optimal control systems. Although the optimal control paradigm proved to have only limited applicability to the major issues associated with information systems, it helped address a key subset of them (e.g., the multisensor, multitarget fusion problem). The program built a vibrant community of interest that acquired a shared understanding of the problem.

Several new methods for assessing information systems consequently emerged. Workshops sponsored by the Military Operations Research Society (MORS) spawned the Modular Command and Control Evaluation Structure (MCES), a framework for defining and evaluating measures of merit for assessing information systems.[4] This framework was subsequently adapted and extended by the NATO COBP (see below).

In the mid-1980s, the "mission oriented approach" (MOA) to C2 assessment was developed and applied; its key phases are summarized in Figure 11.2.[5] The approach addresses four questions:[6]

1. What are you trying to achieve operationally?

2. How are you trying to achieve the operational mission?

3. What technical capability is needed to support the operational mission?

4. How is the technical job to be accomplished?

---

[4]Ricki Sweet et al., *The Modular Command and Control Evaluation Structure (MCES): Applications of and Expansion to C3 Architectural Evaluation*, Naval Postgraduate School, September 1986; and Ricki Sweet, Morton Metersky, and Michael Sovereign, *Command and Control Evaluation Workshop* (revised June 1986), MORS C2 MOE Workshop, Naval Postgraduate School, January 1985.

[5]David T. Signori, Jr., and Stuart H. Starr, "The Mission Oriented Approach to NATO C2 Planning," *SIGNAL*, September 1987, pp. 119–127.

[6]The questions are posed from the perspective of the friendly coalition, which subsumes operational users, military information systems architects and developers, and the science and technology community.

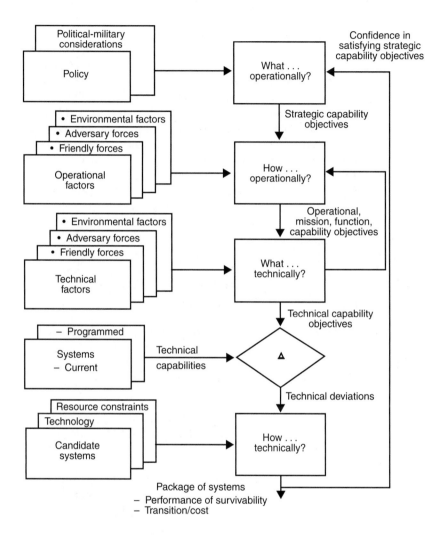

Figure 11.2—Phases of the Mission Oriented Approach

The MOA drove home the importance of assessing military information systems within the context of the missions they support. The process is implemented through top-down decomposition linking missions, functions, tasks, and systems. The "roll-up" process—in which analysts assess how candidate packages of military information systems satisfy mission objectives—remains a challenge.

One challenge of the roll-up process is understanding the performance of distributed teams of operational users under stress. To address this issue, manned simulator test-beds were developed to represent the specific weapons systems and military information systems supporting selected missions. An early example, the Theater Air Command and Control Simulation Facility (TACCSF) (originally, the Identification Friend Foe or Neutral [IFFN] test-bed), brought together teams of operators manning simulated weapons systems (e.g., airborne interceptors, high- to medium-range air defense systems) and associated military information systems (e.g., Airborne Warning and Control System [AWACS], associated ground-based C2 systems).[7] Such test-beds can flexibly assess a full range of doctrine, organization, training, materiel, leadership and education, personnel, and facilities issues associated with proposed systems-of-systems. (This combination of factors is characterized in *Joint Vision 2020*[8] by the infelicitous initialism "DOTML-PF".) Recent advances in computer science—e.g., the High Level Architecture (HLA)—have greatly helped such virtual simulations emerge and evolve.

New studies drew on these methods and tools to provide logical, systematic links between packages of military information systems and overall mission effectiveness. An early example of these products was developed as part of the NATO C3 Pilot Program in support of the Tri-Major NATO Commanders C3 Master Plan.[9]

CONTEXT FOR ASSESSING MILITARY INFORMATION SYSTEMS IN THE 21st CENTURY

Table 11.1 highlights some dramatic shifts that have occurred since the end of the Cold War. As is now commonplace to observe, the Soviet Union provided a sustained focus for intelligence gatherers and force planners during the Cold War. A few scenarios and types of

---

[7]J. E. Freeman and S. H. Starr, "Use of Simulation in the Evaluation of the IFFN Process," Paper 25, *AGARD Conference Proceedings*, No. 268 ("Modeling and Simulation of Avionics Systems and C3 Systems"), Paris, France, October 15–19, 1979.

[8]*Joint Vision 2020*, Chairman of the Joint Chiefs of Staff, Director for Strategic Plans and Policy, J5, Strategy Division, U.S. Government Printing Office, Washington, DC, June 2000.

[9]K. T. Hoegberg, "Toward a NATO C3 Master Plan," *SIGNAL*, October 1985.

Table 11.1

A New DoD Context

Area	Old	New
Threat	Relatively well-understood	New, uncertain
Missions	Established scenarios and operations	Broader range
Focus	DoD, alliance	National, coalition
Capability	Evolutionary	Revolutionary
Force	Overwhelming	Information/effects-based
Advantage	System-on-system	System-of-systems
Requirements	Relatively well-defined	Exploration/learning

operations sufficed for assessment and planning. Today's broader range of uncertain threats has made it difficult to anticipate issues and focus intelligence resources appropriately. The United States faces a variety of "new world disorder" missions, as well as the more conventional military missions (e.g., smaller-scale contingencies and major theater wars [MTWs]).

Alliances aside, DoD used to concern itself mainly with operations that involved only the U.S. military. Today's operations usually involve many other participants, such as ad hoc coalitions, various national government organizations, international organizations, and nongovernmental organizations (NGOs). Hitherto, warfighting capability evolved incrementally with the addition of each new weapons system. Now, information technology and precision weaponry may well change the nature of warfare in revolutionary ways.

Previously, success was thought to be determined by who could bring to bear overwhelming force. Today, the U.S. goal is to gather and exploit information about its adversaries so as to be able to apply the minimum force needed to achieve a specific effect, consistent with national policy. This force often transcends purely military action to include diplomatic, informational, and economic means. Advantage used to be measured in platform-centric terms—who had the best tank, ship, or plane. Today, networking sensors, C2, and weapons in a system-of-systems promise significant advantage through increased agility and more-discriminate application of force.

Finally, the stable, evolutionary environment of relatively well understood requirements has yielded to a period of experimentation and learning directed at understanding how to exploit new technologies and new concepts for competitive advantage. All told, such shifts mean a fundamentally different national security context for today's analysts, especially for those who assess information systems that play a newly critical role in force transformation. Table 11.2 highlights some of the key changes.

Analysts once could focus on ways to counter a specific threat; today, they must address capabilities that can be used in an agile manner to deal with a range of threats.[10] The stability of the threat and the evolutionary nature of military capability once permitted analysts to focus on refining established operational concepts and capabilities; today, they must explore completely new warfighting concepts, such as distributed C2 for a nonlinear battlespace. Cold War analysts could focus on the benefits of adding a new weapons system to the force mix; today's analysts must understand the fundamentals associated with networking the force or sharing information through a common relevant operational picture.

In the recent past, assessments focused on force mix/structure issues. Now, they must address *all* the elements of doctrine, organization, training, materiel, leadership and education, personnel, and

Table 11.2

New DoD Assessment Challenges

Area	Old	New
Planning	Threat-based	Capability-based
Focus	Refine established notions	Explore new possibilities
Objective	Identify benefits of incremental, new capabilities	Understand fundamentals
Assessment	Force structure	DOTML-PF
Issues	Ad hoc collection	Hierarchy of related issues
Complexity	Tractable	Exploding

---

[10]U.S. Department of Defense, *2001 Quadrennial Defense Review Report*, September 30, 2001, p. iv.

facilities (DOTML-PF). Whereas analysts used to concentrate on ad hoc issues arising in the programming and budgeting processes, they now must make systematic multilevel assessments of a comprehensive issue set.

Moreover, military information systems are themselves growing more complex. Table 11.3 highlights how emerging systems-of-systems and other integration proposals (e.g., the global information grid [GIG]) add further complexity. The challenge of assessing such systems reminds one of John Von Neumann's maxim: "A system is complex when it is easier to build than to describe mathematically."[11]

ADDITIONAL COMPLICATING AND SUPPORTING FACTORS

In assessing tomorrow's military information systems, additional factors must be considered: those that complicate the task (particular initiatives, especially by the services, and system trends) and those that can assist the analyst (such as new tools and new kinds of workshops).

Table 11.3

Simple Versus Complex Systems

Attributes	Simple Systems	Complex Systems
Number of elements	Few	Many
Interactions among elements	Few	Many
Attributes of elements	Predetermined	Not predetermined
Organization of interaction among elements	Tight	Loose
Laws governing behavior	Well-defined	Probabilistic
System evolves over time	No	Yes
Subsystems pursue their own goals	No	Yes
System affected by behavioral influences	No	Yes

SOURCE: R. Flood and M. Jackson, *Creative Problem Solving*, John Wiley, New York, 1991.

---

[11]J. Von Neumann, *Theory of Self-Replacing Automata*, University of Illinois Press, Urbana, IL, 1996.

Each service has undertaken activities to transform how it will operate.[12] The U.S. Army is transforming itself via the Stryker Brigade Combat Team (SBCT), the Future Combat System (FCS), and the Objective Force Warrior (OFW) to enhance deployability, sustainability, lethality, and survivability. These initiatives aim to dominate potential adversaries across the full conflict spectrum using information systems as the key force multiplier. The U.S. Air Force is creating an Expeditionary Aerospace Force, with enhanced responsiveness and global reach. These objectives are pursued through enhanced reach-back capability (e.g., using substantial resources in sanctuary to reduce the footprint in theater) and advanced collaboration tools (e.g., implementing the "virtual building" paradigm[13]). The U.S. Navy is pursuing the doctrine articulated in "Forward from the Sea," through the concept of network-centric warfare. Moving away from a platform-centric approach calls for the co-evolution of all the components of DOTML-PF (i.e., self-consistently modifying all aspects of the service's doctrine, organization, training, materiel, leadership and education, personnel, and facilities). A network-centric focus is promoted to enhance mission effectiveness through shared awareness and self-synchronization of the force. And, finally, the U.S. Marine Corps is using experimentation to refine "Marine Corps Strategy 21" through the innovative use of information systems to support small unit operations and urban warfare.

Information systems are perceived to be the key enablers for all these initiatives. From a joint perspective, the J-9 organization of Joint Forces Command (JFCOM) has an ambitious agenda to evaluate new joint concepts enabled by the revolution in information systems.

There is also growing interest in developing a joint, integrated information system infrastructure to underpin the operations of all missions. One aspect would be to design interoperability and security into the evolving systems-of-systems rather than treating them as add-ons. These initiatives include the Office of the Secretary of Defense (OSD)/Joint Staff efforts to have the GIG subsume the rele-

---

[12]*Service Visions*, available at http://www.dtic.mil/jv2020/jvsc.htm.

[13]Peter J. Spellman, Jane N. Mosier, Lucy M. Deus, and Jay A. Carlson, "Collaborative Virtual Workspace," *Proceedings of the International ACM SIGGROUP Conference on Supporting Group Work: The Integration Challenge*, 1997, pp. 197–203.

vant service initiatives: the Air Force's Joint Battlespace Infosphere[14] and the Army's Tactical Infosphere.[15] The systemwide initiatives would exploit the power of Web-based architectures, commercial standards and protocols, and emerging information system markup languages based on the extensible markup language (XML).

However, many of the existing assessment tools for information systems are a poor fit for this class of systems, so several joint efforts are under way to develop better ones: the Joint Warfare System (JWARS) for joint assessment and the Joint Simulation System (JSIMS) for joint training. Although these tools seek to reflect information systems explicitly (and, in several cases, to interface with operational information systems), they are still immature and largely restrict themselves to the issues associated with conventional warfare.

Over the last decade, workshops—notably those by MORS—have advanced the understanding of challenges and opportunities associated with assessing military information systems. Recent MORS workshops have sought to identify the shortfalls in the community's ability to assess the impact of information systems[16] and to formulate a plan of action to ameliorate these shortfalls.[17]

NATO CODE OF BEST PRACTICE

In 1995, NATO established Research Study Group 19 to develop a code of best practice (COBP) for assessing C2 in conventional conflict; that COBP was issued under the newly formed NATO Studies, Analysis, and Simulations (SAS) panel.[18] A follow-up effort is extending the COBP to assess C2 for operations other than war (OOTWs).

---

[14]USAF Scientific Advisory Board, *Report on Building the Joint Battlespace Infosphere, Vol. 1: Summary*, SAB-TR-99-02, December 17, 1999.

[15]Army Science Board 2000 Summer Study, "Technical and Tactical Opportunities for Revolutionary Advances in Rapidly Deployable Joint Ground Forces in the 2015–2025 Era," Panel on Information Dominance, July 17–27, 2000.

[16]Russell F. Richards, "MORS Workshop on Analyzing C4ISR in 2010," *PHALANX*, Vol. 32, No. 2, June 1999, p. 10.

[17]Cy Staniec, Stuart Starr, and Charles Taylor, "MORS Workshop on Advancing C4ISR Assessment," *PHALANX*, Vol.34, No. 1, March 2001, pp. 29–33.

[18]*NATO Code of Best Practice on the Assessment of C2.*

Figure 11.3 portrays major elements of an effective assessment process for information systems that was identified in the NATO COBP. It highlights the major steps of the assessment and the products that should be developed in it. Despite the fact that the following discussion reflects this framework, however, it should be noted that meaningful assessments of information systems rarely follow such a linear process. Recent experience suggests that the way to best fit the problem at hand is to tailor and implement a nonlinear process that iterates among these steps.

Before the assessment process begins, the first issue is who will participate. Such undertakings generally require interdisciplinary teams of individuals skilled in operations research, modeling and simulation, information systems, and operations. Extensions of the COBP to OOTW also highlights the need to include those skilled in social sciences (e.g., political science and demography). Once a team is established, the process proceeds as follows, in line with Figure 11.3:

Problem Formulation. Military information system issues are complex, poorly defined, and hard to formulate sharply—especially when used in OOTWs, where cultural and historical context must be understood. Such issues are also hard to decompose into pieces that can be analyzed individually and then brought together coherently. Worse, posing options in strictly materiel terms is rarely acceptable. Issues associated with military transformation must address all the dimensions of DOTML-PF.

Human Factors and Organizational Issues. Information systems generally support distributed teams of people operating under stress; changing these systems often leads to altered tactics, techniques, procedures, and DOTML-PF—all of which must be considered in the assessment. These issues are often difficult to assess and are the subject of ongoing research efforts.[19] Factors such as belief (e.g., morale, unit cohesion), cognitive processes (e.g., naturalistic decisionmaking), and performance modulators (e.g., fear, fatigue, and sleep deprivation) are especially challenging to address.

---

[19]William G. Kemple et al., "Experimental Evaluation of Alternative and Adaptive Architectures in Command and Control," *Third International Symposium on Command and Control Research and Technology*, National Defense University, Fort McNair, Washington, DC, June 17–20, 1997, pp. 313–321.

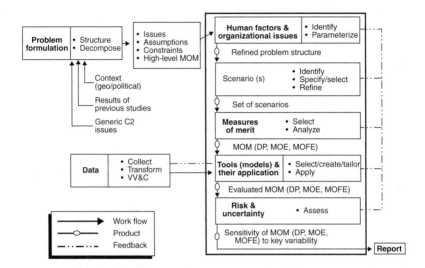

Figure 11.3—NATO COBP Assessment Methodology

Scenarios. The NATO COBP holds that military information systems can only be assessed relative to selected scenarios. Figure 11.4 identifies a scenario framework formulated in the NATO COBP; it is based on three major categories: external factors (e.g., political, military, and cultural situation), capabilities of actors (e.g., friendly forces, adversary forces, and noncombatants), and the environment (e.g., geography, terrain, and man-made structures). The challenge is to explore the scenario space rapidly and focus on its more "interesting" regions. Because military information systems are complex, looking at just one scenario is almost always a mistake. It is thus necessary to decompose the three major categories of the scenario framework, selecting a baseline scenario and interesting excursions.[20]

Measures of Merit. The NATO COBP states that no single measure exists by which the overall effectiveness or the performance of military information systems can be assessed. Drawing on prior MORS

---

[20]Stuart H. Starr, "Developing Scenarios to Support C3I Analyses," *Proceedings of the Cornwallis Group,* Pearson Peacekeeping Center, Nova Scotia, Canada, March 26–28, 1996.

External Factors	Political, military, and cultural situation	Mission objectives, mission constraints, rules of engagement	Mission tasks (e.g., military scope and intensity, joint/combined)
	National security interests		
Capabilities of Actors	• Organization, order of battle, C2, doctrine resources • Weapons, equipment • Logistics, skills, morale, etc.		
	Friendly forces	Adversary forces	Noncombatants
Environment	• Geography, region, terrain, accessibility, vegetation • Climate, weather • Civil infrastructure (e.g., transportation, telecommunications, energy generation/distribution)		

Figure 11.4—The Scenario Framework

workshops,[21] NATO recommended a multilevel hierarchy of measures of merit (MOMs), four levels of which are shown in Figure 11.5 and can be defined as follows:

- Measures of force effectiveness (MOFEs): how a force performs its mission (e.g., loss exchange ratios).

- Measures of C2 effectiveness (MOEs): impact of information systems within the operational context (e.g., the ability to generate a complete, accurate, timely common operating picture of the battlespace).

- Measures of C2 system performance (MOPs): performance of the internal system structure, characteristics, and behavior (e.g., timeliness, completeness, or accuracy).

- Dimensional parameters (DPs): properties or characteristics inherent in the information system itself (e.g., bandwidth).

Extending the NATO COBP to OOTW has demonstrated that the hierarchy of MOMs must be expanded to include measures of policy effectiveness. Since the military plays only a contributing role in such missions—ensuring that the environment is secure enough that

---

[21]Thomas J. Pawlowski III et al., *C3IEW Measures of Effectiveness Workshop*, Final Report, Military Operations Research Society (MORS), Fort Leavenworth, KS, October 20–23, 1993; and Sweet, Metersky, and Sovereign, "Command and Control Evaluation Workshop."

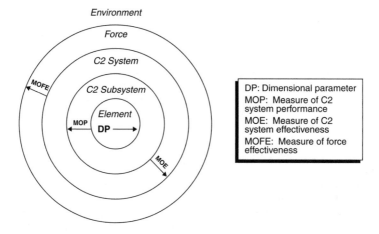

Figure 11.5—Relationships Among Classes of Measures of Merit

other organizations can function effectively—the contribution of international organizations and NGOs must be captured. Table 11.4 depicts representative MOMs for a hypothetical civil-military operations center (CMOC) that would provide the needed linkage between the military community and other organizations participating in the operation.

Historically, assessing what the MOMs at the top of the hierarchy implied for those measures at the bottom was a straightforward task. For instance, minimizing the leakage of incoming ballistic missiles creates a need for early warning to be extended and delays by military information systems to be minimized.[22] However, it is often more challenging to go "bottom-up" to estimate the effectiveness of mixes of weapons and information systems in the context of the operational scenario.

Data. At a MORS workshop in the late 1980s on simulation technology, Walt LaBerge, then principal deputy under secretary of defense (Research & Engineering), gave a presentation entitled "Without

---

[22]Signori and Starr, "The Mission Oriented Approach."

Table 11.4

Strawman MOMs for a Civil-Military Operations Center

Measures of policy effectiveness	Progress in transitioning from a failed state to a stable one (e.g., successful democratization and the ability to conduct a fair election; dealing with displaced persons and relocating displaced families)
Measures of force effectiveness	Ability of military to create and sustain a secure environment
Measures of C2 effectiveness	Quality of situational awareness and synchronization of effort
Measures of C2 performance	Ability to perform CMOC tasks and functions (e.g., time to complete a task)
Dimensional parameters	Communications (e.g., bandwidth and connectivity), automated data processing, support to personnel (e.g., quality and flexibility), collaboration tools (e.g., scalability, latency, and security)

Data We Are Nothing."[23] Unfortunately, the military's information system assessment community remains "data poor," despite repeated recommendations to establish a communitywide program to collect, transform, and verify, validate, and certify (VV&C) needed data. The problem is worse for OOTWs, because key information is controlled by NGOs (or even private corporations, such as insurance companies). Administratively, there is a need for a data dictionary/glossary at the outset of an assessment and a strategy for enhanced data management.

Tools and Their Application. Table 11.5 depicts a spectrum of assessment techniques. It discriminates among the various techniques by characterizing how they account for the systems, people, and operations/missions of interest. For example, in virtual modeling and simulation (M&S), real people are employed, interacting with simulated systems, in the context of a simulated operation. Conversely, in live M&S, real people are employed, interacting with real systems, in the context of a simulated operation. The COBP concluded that no

---

[23]*Proceedings of SIMTECH 97*, 1987–1988 (available through MORS office, Alexandria, VA).

Table 11.5

Spectrum of Assessment Techniques

Key Factors	Assessment Techniques				
	Analysis	Constructive M&S	Virtual M&S	Live M&S	Actual Operations
Typical application	Closed form, statistical	Force-on-force models; communications system models	Test-beds with humans in the loop	Command post exercises; field training exercises	After-action reports; lessons learned
Treatment of systems	Analytic	Simulated	Simulated	Real	Real
Treatment of people	Assumed or simulated	Assumed or simulated	Real	Real	Real
Treatment of operations/missions	Simulated	Simulated	Simulated	Real or simulated	Real
Resources	Relatively modest	Moderate to high	High to very high	Very high	Extremely high
Lead time to create	Weeks to months	Months to years	Years	Years	N/A
Lead time to use	Weeks to months	Weeks to months	Weeks to months	Weeks to months	N/A
Credibility	Fair to moderate	Moderate	Moderate to high	High	Very high

NOTE: M&S = modeling and simulation; N/A = not applicable.

single assessment technique would suffice for many issues of interest. A proper strategy must select and orchestrate a mix of techniques consistent with issues at hand and real-world constraints (e.g., resources, lead time). As concepts such as "information superiority" and "decision dominance" have gained interest, so has the need for tools to represent both friendly and adversary information processes. The need for discipline in applying these tools suggests that formal experimental design matrices should be employed to govern their application and support the generation of appropriate response surfaces.[24] Fast-running tools can filter down to interesting segments of solution space, at which point fine-grained tools (e.g., virtual models and simulations) can provide more-focused, in-depth assessments.

Tools that have been formally verified, validated, and accredited are, of course, preferred, but few tools have undergone such stringent quality control processes. Confidence in results thus arises when independent assessments using varying tools nonetheless reach consistent findings. As an example, to provide an initial "cut" at a complex problem, analysts are beginning to develop and employ system dynamics models. These models (e.g., the C4ISR Analytic Performance Evaluation [CAPE] family of models[25]) evolve from influence diagrams that characterize factors such as model variables, inputs, outputs, and system parameters. They capture information system performance by explicitly representing sensors of interest, aggregate aspects of C3 (e.g., explicit constraints on communications capacity; time delays experienced by C2 nodes), and the phases of the intelligence cycle. CAPE was employed in OSD's C4ISR Mission Assessment to characterize the information systems that supported the engagement of time-critical targets.[26] Figure 11.6 depicts a representative output from CAPE characterizing the sensor-to-shooter string by estimating the probability of placing time-critical targets at risk as a function of target type (i.e., range and frequency of relocation).

 Agent-based modeling represents another way to explore a solution space rapidly. It adopts a bottom-up approach to operations modeling by characterizing individual behavior (e.g., response to live or injured friendly or adversary entities; reaction to friendly or adversary objectives) and deriving emergent behavior from the resulting

---

[24]Starr, "Developing Scenarios."

[25]Jeremy S. Belldina, Henry A. Neimeier, Karen W. Pullen, and Richard C. Tepel, *An Application of the Dynamic C4ISR Analytic Performance Evaluation (CAPE) Model*, MITRE Technical Report 98W4, The MITRE Corporation, McLean, VA, December 1997.

[26]Russell F. Richards, Henry A. Neimeier, W. L. Hamm, and D. L. Alexander, "Analytical Modeling in Support of C4ISR Mission Assessment (CMA)," *Third International Symposium on Command and Control Research and Technology*, National Defense University, Fort McNair, Washington, DC, June 17–20, 1997, pp. 626–639.

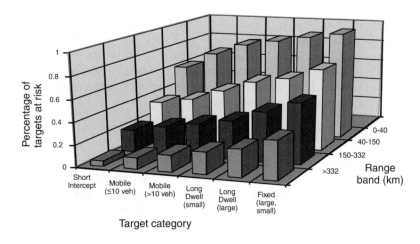

Figure 11.6—Representative CAPE Output: Targets at Risk

interactions.[27] Mana, a recent agent-based model developed by New Zealand's Defence Operational Support Establishment to prepare forces for peacekeeping operations in East Timor, has been employed to assess the risk to friendly personnel associated with alternative courses of action in OOTWs.[28]

Once the interesting parts of scenario space are identified, more-detailed simulations can explore them in greater depth. For example, to support the assessment of the time-critical target problem, the U.S. Defense Modeling and Simulation Organization (DMSO) developed Pegasus, a combination of three constructive simulations: the Extended Air Defense Simulation, Eagle, and the Navy Simulation System. JFCOM plans to use Pegasus and CAPE in its Model-Experiment-Model paradigm.

---

[27]Andrew Iiachinski, "Irreducible Semi-Autonomous Adaptive Combat (ISAAC): An Artificial-Life Approach to Land Combat," *MOR Journal*, Vol. 5, No. 3, 2000, pp. 29–46.

[28]Edward Brady and Stuart Starr, "Assessing C3I in Support of Dismounted Operations in Complex Terrain," *Proceedings of C2R&T Symposium*, NPS, Monterey, CA, June 11–13, 2002.

Other combinations are being developed that rely on virtual simulations to capture operators' response to a variety of stimuli. The Army is developing the Joint Virtual Battlespace (JVB) to assess and compare concepts proposed by contractors to implement the FCS, and the Air Force is developing the Joint Synthetic Battlespace to provide a context for acquiring a system-of-systems.

Risk and Uncertainty Assessment. The COBP notes that sensitivity analysis and risk assessment in C2 analyses often lack thoroughness because the issues are complex and the time and resources too limited. The need for and the results of sensitivity analyses should be stressed in discussions with decisionmakers. Analysts should at least test the robustness of the results against small excursions in the selected regions of scenario space. Ultimately, analysts must illuminate uncertainty, not suppress it.

Decisionmakers are also increasingly interested in getting risk-based instead of cost-benefit assessments. For example, the legislation mandating the 2001 Quadrennial Defense Review (QDR) specifically cast several questions in risk-based terms. This was echoed in the 2001 QDR itself, which introduced a new, broad approach to risk management.[29] The analysis community should also draw on the experience that financial planners and insurance actuaries have amassed in risk assessment.

This is the end of the process depicted in Figure 11.3. But, as discussed earlier, recent experience suggests that such a linear process rarely fits the needs of the situation. The last point is thus that an *iterative approach* is needed, since one pass through the assessment process is unlikely to generate meaningful answers. The first cut should be broad and shallow to identify key issues and relevant segments of scenario space, and subsequent iterations should then go narrower and deeper (drawing on suitable tools) to gain insight into key questions. Throughout this process, peer review is essential to provide adequate quality control.

------

[29] *2001 Quadrennial Defense Review Report,* Chapter VII, "Managing Risks," September 30, 2001.

ADVANCES OVER THE PAST 25 YEARS

Advances in the ability to assess military information systems are apparent in four areas. First and foremost, decisionmakers are now keenly aware that meaningful national security assessments require explicit consideration of military information systems. This awareness is apparent in recent products from the chairman of the Joint Chiefs of Staff, in which first "information superiority" and then "decision superiority" were placed at the foundation of DoD's strategic vision.[30] The easy, unknowing assumption that "information systems are perfect" is no longer acceptable.

Second, the processes for assessing military information systems have improved—a result of workshops (particularly those of MORS), individual studies (e.g., OSD's C4ISR Mission Assessment and Information Superiority Investment Strategy), and panels. Recent NATO panels have synthesized earlier efforts, promulgated COBPs, and identified the challenges associated with assessing military information systems in the context of "new world disorder" missions.

Third, considerable creativity has gone into developing new tools better suited to assessing information systems. Such advances have characterized system dynamics models (e.g., CAPE), agent-based modeling (e.g., Mana), constructive simulations (e.g., JWARS), federates of constructive simulations (e.g., Pegasus), and virtual simulations (e.g., JVB). The realization that no single tool or type of tool can adequately assess information systems has led to the creative orchestration of tools to exploit their strengths and compensate for their individual weaknesses.

Fourth, experiments that provide insights into the potential contribution of information systems to operational effectiveness are now deemed essential. New military information systems are recognized as a stimulus to new doctrine, organizations, training, leadership and education. These activities are the basis for acquiring the data and developing the models that the assessment community requires.

---

[30]See *Joint Vision 2010* and *Joint Vision 2020*, (both available at http://www.dtic.mil/jv2020).

RESIDUAL CHALLENGES: A NEW AGENDA

Despite all these advances, however, the assessment of military information systems is growing more difficult. Future missions will be much more varied than today's, yet there is great interest in an integrated system that would serve as the basis for all mission areas. And the information challenges are intermeshed with the broader transformation of the military. These changes have profound implications for the military's information system assessment community. A new agenda is needed, one with a more comprehensive analytic construct, new assessment capabilities, and a new culture/process for assessment.

A More Comprehensive Analytic Construct. The COBP makes a good start in describing how to assess a military information system. But DoD must extend it to deal with the full range of "new world disorder" missions. This will entail characterizing a broader range of scenarios, formulating new operational concepts, and deriving associated information needs. Consistent with the emerging interest in effects-based operations, the traditional hierarchy of measures of merit must be reevaluated, and new indications of operational success and failure will be needed. Finally, "soft factors," such as "sensemaking,"[31] must be represented better in community assessments.[32]

New Assessment Capabilities. DoD has historically placed great emphasis on the use of a single simulation to support major institutional decisionmaking processes (e.g., the use of TACWAR in the 1997 QDR). This is a Cold War artifact, one that is inadequate for meeting contemporary assessment needs. There is a growing need to assemble a "tool chest" that can be tailored to address the major

---

[31]Sensemaking is a process at the individual, group, organizational, and cultural level that builds on a "deep understanding" of a situation in order to deal with that situation more effectively, through better judgments, decisions, and actions (Dennis K. Leedem, *Final Report of Sensemaking Symposium*, Command & Control Research Program, OASD(C3I), Washington, DC, October 23–25, 2001 [also available at www.dodccrp.org]).

[32]David S. Alberts, John J. Garstka, Richard E. Hayes, and David A. Signori, *Understanding Information Age Warfare*, CCRP Publication Series, August 2001, p. 141.

problems of interest responsively, flexibly, and creatively. This tool chest must include a mix of exploratory tools (e.g., seminar games, influence diagrams, system dynamics models, agent-based models) that are well suited to effects-based analysis and can be used to identify and explore interesting parts of scenario space quickly and efficiently. The tool chest should also include JWARS, DoD's most recent effort to reflect military information systems and processes in a constructive simulation.

However, a tool such as JWARS will have only a supporting role to play as assessments grow narrower and deeper and thus inevitably require new virtual and live models and simulations, particularly to capture the role of the human in complex systems-of-systems. One of the associated challenges facing DoD is the development of consistent, verified databases, data dictionaries, and glossaries to link the components of the tool chest and ensure they are mutually self-consistent. This new tool chest and associated concepts of assessment will require new education and training for the assessment community.

A New Culture and Processes for Assessment. Military information system analysis must embrace a new culture of openness and cooperation that features rigorous peer review, information sharing, and collaboration across traditional organizational boundaries. In the area of transformation, new offices are emerging to stimulate the process—e.g., OSD's Office of Force Transformation and JFCOM's Project Alpha. The military information analysis community has an important role to play in linking these new entities with the traditional organizations that have been pursuing transformation (e.g., the service planning staffs and test and evaluation organizations).

Finally, with the emergence of homeland security and counterterrorism as major mission areas, additional participants must join the assessment process. These include analysts from other federal agencies, such as the new Department of Homeland Security, as well as from regional, state, and local organizations. The military analysis community must recognize that these other participants come to the problem with different frameworks and vocabularies, limited analytic tools, and little or no experience in dealing with classified information. It will take mutual education and training to forge these disparate entities into an integrated community capable of performing creative, insightful analyses of proposed information systems.

Chapter Twelve

THE "DAY AFTER" METHODOLOGY AND NATIONAL SECURITY ANALYSIS

David Mussington

The development of analytic tools to help those making national security policy is driven by the need for usable answers and the urgency of the threats facing the United States. The interaction of these two drivers has produced an array of approaches that favor insights derived from experience with international phenomena. *After all, conducting empirically valid tests of means-ends relationships in international politics is all but impossible, so implicit models must substitute for hard-to-get experimental data.* Most analysts resort to historical comparisons, reasoning via analogy, or conceptualizations that are mathematically rigorous but empirically dubious or even trivial. The "lessons of history" are said to counsel, variously, caution or haste, conservatism or aggression. Appeasement is seen as dangerous, deterrence as infallible but tenuous. Similarities between cases present and past are endlessly discussed with no firm conclusions possible or persuasive—at least as determined through analysis alone.

Decisionmakers are left with concepts and models that necessarily rest on assumptions about the international system, the decision-making and behavioral imperatives of nation-states, and the relationship of military, economic, and political power to the shaping of international outcomes. How can such broad perspectives be converted into something more immediately usable for analyzing complex international phenomena? Abstractions are inevitably gross generalizations of empirical conditions; when adapted to public policy, they are driven by the special needs of decisionmakers for a simplifying schema to understand complex conditions, and by the high level of uncertainty that characterizes political change.

One source of control (in what would otherwise be an unconstrained process) is to exploit the subject matter expertise of issue area specialists as well as rules of thumb presented by diplomatic and military *practitioners* in national security. These rules can form frameworks for understanding complex phenomena. And if these frameworks are made explicit, public policy analysis can subject them to logical and—to some extent—empirical scrutiny sensitive to temporal, technological, and political-economic factors. A setting comporting to a complex real-world international security problem can thus be represented by an abstraction based on what experts hold to be an assessment of a region, technology, or set of relationships. Yet expert-derived frames of reference are not facts, as such, but facts as implied by the conclusions and insights held by fallible human beings. Creating an environment to help this process along is what exercise designers do. Scenario designs, table-top game structures, decisionmaking simulations, and forecasts of future political-military, economic, and technological change—all of these offer tools to meet such analytic requirements. The Day After exercise methodology is one way to elicit structured expertise that channels specialist knowledge into policy dilemmas faced by decisionmakers in the short, medium, and long term.

This chapter describes this approach and shows how it was applied to real-world problems in two projects. It also discusses the value of the Day After methodology, including the special scenario design requirements necessary for successful usage.

THE METHODOLOGY IN BRIEF

A Day After exercise entails a multistage presentation of a hypothetical future, as shown in Figure 12.1. A scenario is derived from contemporary events and policy dilemmas. For design purposes, the scenario time line is divided into a future history and three steps involving actual game play, as follows.

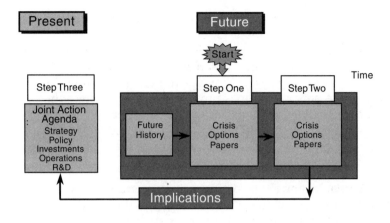

Figure 12.1—Generic Schematic of Day After Exercise Methodology

The Future History. This portion of the Day After exercise methodology is laid out on a time line that starts with the present and then offers a logical sequence of political-military, diplomatic, economic, technological, and policy-related events that identifies the key processes and actors. Background information built into the future history establishes the credibility of the event framework outlined in the next part of the exercise. The more detailed and nuanced the presentation of issues in the future history, the more the follow-on phases can unfold so as to illuminate the policy areas examined.

Step One. Step one involves a policy crisis generated by the actors, processes and entities introduced in a future history that highlights threats to entities or interests important to the United States and/or its allies. The actors are further developed by the decisions they make against a background of specific events. The scenario culminates in a definite escalation. At the end of step one, participants must collectively arrive at decisions appropriate for managing the crisis presented. They must identify the core objectives that policymakers should pursue, and they should decompose the issues entailed in adopting the favored approach to meet those objectives.

Step Two. The crisis escalates steeply in step two in a closely structured and focused evolution of the policy dilemmas and decision imperatives. Although policy responses selected by participants in step one are not directly used in the unfolding events, participants are confronted with step one decisions partially consistent with their step one deliberations. The remaining agenda of responses outlined at the onset of step two intensifies the crisis situation, in order to sharpen the policy dilemmas presented, and challenges the consensus crisis management approach selected earlier by the group. Participants must decide what actions are needed to address the situation effectively, and they must examine the likely consequences of what they decide or fail to decide.

Step Three. In step three, the participants return to the present and are asked to evaluate the situation in light of the exercise experience. Dilemmas are presented from the perspective of contemporary policy choices on the grounds that a framework of prospective actions, policy decisions, and plans could prevent or mitigate the severe conditions described in the scenario narrative. Participants are asked to seek consensus on responses and to clarify areas of pronounced disagreement. Thus, the issue agenda *following* the exercise is addressed so as to advance the identification of potential solutions.

APPLICATIONS AND EXERCISE DEVELOPMENT

The lengthy developmental process responsible for a successful exercise belies the set-piece nature of the Day After approach. Well before the exercise is run, it is tested, different scenarios and issue agendas are explored, and potential participant responses are pondered. An exercise test series helps explore a large number of scenario/issue combinations. The design process subjects this exploration to a disciplined comparative analysis, confronting possible futures with consistent questions and concepts from the perspective of participants in decisionmaking.

Many subjects and issues have been explored using this exercise methodology. Two examples are (1) strategic information warfare (SIW) and mechanisms for addressing significant infrastructure vulnerabilities and (2) electronic commerce technologies (cyberpayments) and international money laundering.

Strategic Information Warfare

Because the sponsor of the SIW exercise was the U.S. Department of Defense (DoD),[1] the focus was on information warfare (IW) as a potential impediment to the exercise of U.S. military options. Those options were themselves predicated on established plans and programs for the timely and efficient delivery of military equipment and personnel to regions designated as strategic to the protection of U.S. friends, allies, and interests. IW threats are introduced directly into existing concepts of strategic security. Although IW is characterized by unique phenomena (i.e., particular weapons and strategic utilization concepts), it is examined in a framework prestructured by well-understood political-military models.

Undertaken in 1995, the SIW Day After exercise was one of the first systematic policy development efforts to explore the potential dilemmas and decisionmaking imperatives associated with society's increasing dependence on information infrastructures. The exercise was developed at a time when basic concepts of vulnerability, crisis stability, and crisis management in the information domain were each relatively unfamiliar. To address this shortfall in rigorous and "high confidence" information warfare conceptualizations, the exercise designers created a hypothetical future in which U.S. critical information infrastructures were targeted by a foreign adversary.

The objectives of the exercise were to

- Describe and frame the concept of strategic information warfare.

- Describe and discuss the key features and related issues that characterize SIW.

- Explore the consequences of these features and issues for U.S. national security as illuminated by the exercises.

---

[1]More precisely, the project sponsor was the Office of the Secretary of Defense (OSD), and the study was defined under the auspices of RAND's National Defense Research Institute.

- Suggest analytic and policy directions for addressing elements of these SIW features and issues.[2]

SIW was framed against challenges—notably asymmetric threats to U.S. national security—deriving from post–Cold War national security imperatives. Information attacks, delivered against information infrastructures accessible via the Internet and the public telephone network, were perceived as potentially serious new vulnerabilities for U.S. military forces.[3]

The SIW exercise used a Persian Gulf scenario, with impacts in the continental United States (CONUS) and Southwest Asia. The Persian Gulf was chosen as the venue for the exercise as the result of a lengthy test series that examined four different scenarios to see which best illuminated policy and strategy issues considered analytically important by RAND researchers and the DoD sponsors. The four scenarios were as follows:[4]

- *Persian Gulf major regional contingency (circa 2000).* Iran seeks hegemony over the Persian Gulf region by overthrowing the Saudi Kingdom via an antiregime organization within Saudi Arabia. A major military crisis develops. The U.S. government decides to deploy forces as a deterrent maneuver. Iran and the local Saudi opposition conduct IW attacks on the Saudi and U.S. governments.

- *Strategic challenge by China in the Far East (circa 2005).* China makes a very aggressive move toward regional dominance. The Taiwanese government declares "independence." China conducts a robust combined-arms military operation, including the use of SIW to deter a forceful U.S. political-military response.

- *Instability in Moscow (circa 1999).* A Russian federation, ruled by a weak central government, is in thrall to several transcontinental criminal organizations (TCOs). A major fissile material diversion

---

[2]Roger C. Molander, Andrew S. Riddile, and Peter A. Wilson, *Strategic Information Warfare: A New Face of War*, MR-661-OSD, RAND, 1996, p. xii.

[3]For a detailed discussion of these issues, see *Critical Foundations: Protecting America's Critical Infrastructures*, the Report of the President's Commission on Critical Infrastructure Protection (PCCIP), Department of Commerce, Washington, DC, 1997.

[4]Molander, Riddile, and Wilson, *Strategic Information Warfare*, p. 6.

to Iran is attempted by a Russian TCO. A Russian TCO makes extensive use of offensive and defensive IW to counter opposition from the United States, several major states within the European Union (EU), and the Russian government.

- *A second Mexican revolution (circa 1998).* The Mexican government faces major challenges from the Chiapas region in southern Mexico and from antiregime movements in northern Mexico. The Mexican revolutionary movements and nongovernmental organization (NGO) allies in North America make extensive use of perception management techniques to dissuade the U.S. government from taking any forceful political, economic, or military action to shore up the beleaguered Mexican regime.

This spectrum of scenarios was adopted to explore in what contexts SIW tools, techniques, and use concepts could be studied. The Persian Gulf was selected to satisfy both the researchers' analytic judgments and the sponsors' policy development requirements,[5] for the following reasons:

- The potential of physically damaging attacks on the United States put in question the physical sanctuary of CONUS.

- A fundamental tenet of U.S. military strategy is to deploy forces to suppress would-be regional hegemons before they succeed and graduate to would-be global hegemons.

- Iran would consider a Persian Gulf scenario to be strategic warfare. Whether a regional adversary uses IW to fracture a coalition or to undermine U.S. or European domestic support for intervention, it plays a strategic game and thus forces the United States into a strategic engagement as well.

- The strategic vulnerabilities and attacks that the United States and its allies might suffer introduce the possibility that other strategic weapons (e.g., nuclear weapons) might be either brandished or used outright.

OSD's planning requirements were a major factor as well. In the end, it is hard to differentiate the scenario's timing and locale from the

---

[5]Molander, Riddile, and Wilson, *Strategic Information Warfare*, p. 8.

analytic reasons underlying scenario selection. This is to be expected where experiential data are obtained using such focused exercise techniques. The policy concepts under examination were a product of independent researcher expertise and repeated interaction with a governmental client. Interactions between clients and sponsors were deliberately structured so that the interests and priorities of the involved departments and senior decisionmakers could be understood. This understanding was then used to write the scenario, which, in turn, was iterated with the sponsor before being subjected to the test series.

Note, however, the interactive nature of the scenario choice process. The exercise tests—which used the other scenarios as well as the one ultimately selected—were each tested in a series lasting from February through June of 1995. Participant feedback on issues, exercise design, and strategy and policy concepts was integrated into each successive test. The entire process was designed to elicit the maximum participant exposure to concepts, scenario variations, and policy problems—in essence, serving as a collective exploration of policy alternatives and possible futures.

Cyberpayments and Money Laundering

The Day After exercise that focused on international money laundering and cyberpayment technologies[6] was undertaken for the U.S. Treasury's Financial Crimes Enforcement Network (FinCEN). The concern was that money launderers would use advanced payment system technologies to conceal their illicit activities.

FinCEN is an interagency clearinghouse for financial crime; it also administers reporting requirements for financial institutions under the Bank Secrecy Act.[7] Many analysts feared that the adoption by narcotics traffickers and transcontinental criminal organizations (TCO) of advanced information technologies would sharply cut the

---

[6]*Cyberpayments* is a term FinCEN coined to describe new payment system technologies that facilitate decentralized (and increasingly, peer-to-peer) value transfers analogous to the exchange of paper currency. Examples of these products include Internet-based e-cash products (such as cybercash) and stored value–type smart card instruments (such as the Visacash and Mondex products).

[7]For information about FinCEN, see http://www.ustreas.gov/fincen/.

efficacy of law enforcement's investigative tools and techniques. Such fears lent urgency to the discussions during the test series. They also opened the research sponsor to new ways of countering emerging patterns of payment system abuse.

RAND analysts, none of whom had any background in researching financial institutions or financial crime, undertook a direct and self-conscious research effort to orient themselves to the money laundering and financial crime landscape. This necessitated a close collaboration with the client and with stakeholders from the financial sector (whom the client helped identify).

The study's objectives were ambitious.[8] The main goal was to explore the dimensions and implications of potential future illicit uses of cyberpayment systems by money launderers and others seeking to conceal funds from governmental authorities so as to identify—at least in a preliminary fashion—possible law enforcement and regulatory responses.

This exercise brought together both public- and private-sector stakeholders. Indeed, FinCEN's interest in the project was driven by hopes that it could serve as a venue for interaction between the public and private sectors. The project's design and question formulation activities were helped by great cooperation from financial firms. As new technologies were anticipated in the payment system, financial industry figures argued for close coordination among state and federal regulatory agencies and private depository institutions. The Day After project served this end and helped to deepen the debate on cyberpayments and the future of payment system technologies.

The research goals of this project were to[9]

• Describe the then-current cyberpayment concepts and systems.

• Identify an initial set of cyberpayment characteristics of particular concern to law enforcement and payment system regulators.

---

[8]See Roger C. Molander, David A. Mussington, and Peter A. Wilson, *Cyberpayments and Money Laundering: Problems and Promise*, MR-965-CTI, RAND, 1998, p. 2.

[9]Molander, Mussington, and Wilson, *Cyberpayments and Money Laundering*, p. 3.

- Identify major issues that cyberpayment policies will need to address.

- Array appropriate approaches to address potential cyberpayment system abuse in a set of potential action plans.

The last goal was particularly challenging. The potential for responses to problems discovered during the exercise was clearly tied to how accurately the future of electronic payment systems was portrayed. The credibility (and longevity) of any recommendations produced by the project were contingent on good technological and market predictions.

Participants included representatives from the executive branch of the U.S. government, the cyberpayment industry, the banking industry, Congress, and academia. Exercise experiences were recorded in the test series underlying the final version of the scenario and in the final operational play itself.

The scenario selected was developed in collaboration with law enforcement officers expert in financial crime and money laundering investigations. It involved a large money laundering system that narco-traffickers used to conceal drug earnings. Funds transfers were concealed by using stored value–type smart cards for street-level drug purchases and then uploading the value into the financial system using merchant stored-value upload terminals. "Participating" store owners received a 4 percent "commission" on each of these transfers. Once the funds reached the financial system, they were electronically transferred offshore using sophisticated layering and integration techniques to hide their ultimate destination.

The scenario narrative then described the compromise of critical technologies used in the manufacture of stored value–type smart cards themselves. This created an even greater threat, one to the integrity of the U.S. and international financial systems. The final portion of the scenario involved a fictional proposal by the Mexican finance ministry to modernize its own banking infrastructure through the adoption of modern electronic banking technologies. This gave money launderers a potential opportunity to penetrate a brand new financial structure and secure unprecedented money laundering capabilities over the long term. The threats to financial system integrity motivated decisionmaking during the future history, step one, and step two.[10]

The exercise findings contained the responses of participants to such dilemmas along with a major analytic examination of those perspectives for integration into competing themes and frameworks. The action plans produced for the report were thus the product of expert assessments by third parties (exercise participants) and post hoc analysis of the deliberations by RAND analysts.

Comparison of the Two Implementations of the Methodology

A comparison of the two projects helps to illustrate the different contexts in which policy analysis interfaces with decisionmaking. In the SIW project, analysts developed scenarios in advance of their real-world appearance by extrapolating known technological trends and factoring in the continuing concerns of the national security community about potential impediments to the execution of U.S. national military strategy. Because U.S. national military strategy focuses on projecting power overseas rather than on defending the homeland, the analysis concentrated on infrastructure vulnerabilities relevant to military preparedness. Similarly, the adoption of asymmetric "counter–information infrastructure" strategies by potential adversaries would place the sanctuary of homeland into question. Hence, infrastructure concerns are related to the concern over the weakening influence of distance as a barrier to potential attacks.[11] These two concerns motivated the selection of both the scenario and the types of attacks presented.

The principal objective of the cyberpayments and money laundering study was to help facilitate a dialogue between government and private-sector personnel on a subject of near-future importance. This project involved a much more in-depth concept-creation process, one in which a community not used to thinking systematically about national strategies was introduced to wide-ranging concepts

---

[10]See Molander, Mussington, and Wilson, *Cyberpayments and Money Laundering*, Appendix B, Exercise Materials.

[11]Homeland security emerged as the preeminent national concern following the events of September 11, 2001.

through the scenario design process. The decentralized nature of law enforcement here gave rise to diverse assessments of long-term trends in criminal activity and to potential investigative counter-measures. Federal law enforcement authorities lead the anti-money laundering arena, but must collaborate with state and local law enforcement officials in individual cases. The international component of anti–money laundering law enforcement activities adds further complexity.

Concepts created in this exercise range from a listed feature set for cyberpayment instruments that defines their importance for potential misuse by money launderers, to a mechanism for tracing Internet-based electronic fund transfers.[12] Both concepts contributed to a framework that defined the technologies of importance to law enforcement and the opportunities for law enforcement to leverage these technologies to enhance investigations. An issue that emerged very quickly during this design process was the lack of clear metrics or measures for anti–money laundering techniques and strategies. Before the project, research sponsors did not appreciate how automation could help evaluate competing strategies for interdicting illicit funds movements. During the test series, this factor was proposed by the design team and emerged as a major focus of future attention for decisionmakers.[13]

Another difference between the two projects stemmed from their differing analyst-sponsor relationships. DoD has had a historically close relationship with RAND (and other independent think tanks). Thus, well-known contracting vehicles and advisory relationships existed for supporting policy analysis. FinCEN, by contrast, had never used independent third-party analysts. The analysts thus needed to foster a close working relationship with FinCEN staff during the exercise design process. Analysts and FinCEN staff had to negotiate who was to author the recommendations of the outbrief report. RAND had to preserve the independence (and peer-review quality control) of the project report's findings while showing sensitivity to the concerns of a client that feared public embarrassment if the exercise results "got out in front of" government policy.

---

[12]Molander, Mussington, and Wilson, *Cyberpayments and Money Laundering*, p. 21.

[13]Molander, Mussington, and Wilson, *Cyberpayments and Money Laundering*, p. 27.

The two exercise programs shared a public sector/private sector character. They served as environments to facilitate dialogue *and* as experimental settings in which policy concepts could be discussed, deconstructed, and critiqued. Although the Day After process hinges on bringing disparate communities of experts together, such interaction must be carefully structured to preserve its analytic independence. In the design phase of a Day After project, new concepts are created and discarded as a way of understanding a subject. Sponsors, however, may interpret such notions as indicators of the project's conclusions. As with sausage-making, the process is messy but the results are often worth the chaos of creative interaction.

The Day After and Analytic Independence

Analysis of the findings is central to the Day After methodology. The exercise designers undertake this analysis, ideally at arm's length from the research sponsor. Because sponsors are extremely engaged in exercise design, they often feel the need to "manage" the production of the report summarizing the project's deliberations and thematic insights. Yet the independence of these two items must be maintained.

A narrative report of findings, records of answers to questions, guidelines used for discussion, and concept creation is, quite appropriately, a shared enterprise; sponsors often provide note-takers and equipment to record deliberations accurately. Nevertheless, analyzing the *meaning* of the facts, insights, and conclusions of experts who interacted within a hypothetical scenario under severe time constraints remains the task of the exercise analysts. They, alone, share a conceptual understanding of the subject matter *and* an architectural knowledge of the scenario construct. Because the exercise scenario necessarily evokes real-world dilemmas, practitioners and policymakers may bring powerful preconceptions to a review of the scenario findings. The Day After method requires that the principal architects of the scenario materials act as filters, differentiating the details and nuances of the story line from the participants' responses to the story. The two projects described above evolved in ways that highlighted the importance of bias control. Both times, RAND was asked to extend the exercise results into a more in-depth examination of the subject matter. The first produced a conceptual framework for understanding the emerging IW policy environment. The second expanded issues addressed in a domestic U.S. setting into an exercise involving 27 countries from the Americas and the Caribbean.[14]

Although details differed in each case, some thematic points can be made. First, the *SIW Rising* document was prepared entirely by the design team, using traditional analytic approaches entailing brainstorming and internal RAND presentations of interim insights, followed by the drafting and redrafting of analytic concepts and models. The resulting policy framework was derived from the reports and exercise experiences achieved during other successful exercise projects. Analyzing those findings generated recurrent themes and insights that contributed to a statement about the nature of the IW setting as it may develop over the next few decades.[15]

Second, the sponsor received the report's analytic framework but not a clear "action plan" for the agency's evaluation. The sponsor already was familiar with the key concepts; many had gained support from Defense Science Board publications and other publicly available research. *SIW Rising* contributed to the policy debate by exposing senior OSD and ASD C3I (Assistant Secretary of Defense for Command, Control, Communications, and Intelligence) staff to concepts that emerged from the non–national security environment that had the potential to affect their plans and priorities.

The follow-on 26-nation cyberpayments study focused on the investigative and prosecutorial implications of money laundering using emerging payment system technologies. It required a new scenario, one that added a section on Internet gambling to the base case of potential misuse of cyberpayments technologies for the purposes of money laundering. The multijurisdictional investigative and prosecutorial nature of the money laundering problem was the focus for much of the design activity, which included employees of the

---

[14]The two reports concerned are Roger C. Molander, Peter A. Wilson, David A. Mussington, and Richard F. Mesic, *Strategic Information Warfare Rising*, MR-964-OSD, RAND, 1998; and David A. Mussington, Peter A. Wilson, and Roger C. Molander, *Exploring Money Laundering Vulnerabilities through Emerging Cyberspace Technologies*, MR-1005-OSTP/FinCEN, RAND, 1998.

[15]Molander, Wilson, Mussington, and Mesic, *Strategic Information Warfare Rising*, pp. 33–38.

Caribbean Financial Action Task Force (CFATF) and the Commonwealth Secretariat of the United Kingdom.

Because the cyberpayments exercise was meant to build a consensus action plan to address legislative, policy, and operational changes in anti–money laundering activities, its scenario had considerable political sensitivity. Thus, the scenario had to be iterated with the research sponsor to a much higher degree than usual, with considerable and detailed dialog taking place on the timing, technical description, and credibility of scenario details. In addition, the test series for the exercise entailed coordinating materials among the 26 countries participating, as well as translating game materials into Spanish.

Interaction with industry representatives provided the required details on Internet gambling and transnational electronic banking trends. Technical details in the exercise were updated with this new information, and elements from the prior exercise were also used. Scenario component reuse is a central feature of Day After scenario design; it leverages issue expertise acquired across a number of different potential projects.

The educational component of the cyberpayments exercise was much more pronounced than any other component (many Caribbean nations lacked basic familiarity with the subject matter). It was important that we educate while avoiding the perception that the Day After approach was "U.S. lecturing." Shared insights and consensus building were the clearest process objectives in the project's execution. The project achieved its objectives, with a draft agenda of priorities resulting from the meeting. In turn, model legislation to respond to many of the policy dilemmas identified within the Day After scenario was to be collaboratively developed by several participating countries. Overall, the exercise helped international dialogue; it also prepared the ground for further policy development.

THE VALUE OF THE DAY AFTER

The Day After method helps decisionmakers and policy analysts address complex subjects in an environment of hypothetical threats to policy goals and objectives. The design of scenarios in this methodology is critical, with plausibility and technical accuracy balanced against the need to focus participant attention on the key themes and analytic issues.

As noted, the Day After requires the creation of a quasi-experiment in which expert insights serve as basic facts in the context of a dynamic scenario. Assumptions that go into the scenario's future history are made as explicit as possible and then honed during repetitive testing of the exercise materials and scenario details.

The Day After methodology can frame futures that challenge analyst and research sponsor assumptions. Can a Day After scenario escape the preconceptions of the designers or the research sponsor? The answer is a qualified yes. It is possible to define scenarios and pose issue questions that challenge the presumptions of both the research sponsors and the researchers. It is not an easy task to accomplish, however, and requires a self-conscious and skilled exercise design approach.

The Day After methodology offers a mechanism for analyzing policy problems. Until now, the methodology has been applied principally to problems with a dynamic component—where technology and technological change affect the policy environment in unpredictable ways. Addressing such situations requires that maximum scope be given to exploring policy futures in order to discern thematic and issue-specific points of decision critical to the goals and/or interests of the research sponsor. This exploration feature of the Day After exercise design process differentiates it from other, more static gaming methodologies.

Lastly, the Day After method educates and raises the consciousness of participants by immersing them in an environment where they suspend disbelief and are made to challenge the views and perceptual frameworks they bring to specific problems. This forces participants to "come up to speed" quickly on complex policy problems and makes them familiar with the characteristically great uncertainty of future-oriented, technologically rich policy environments. The value of this last contribution should not be underestimated. Policymakers face difficult choices, in areas where information is hard to distinguish from advocacy. By offering a critical and rigorous process in which facts and biases are examined, the Day After methodology makes a powerful contribution to the tool kit of policy analysis.

Chapter Thirteen

USING ELECTRONIC MEETING SYSTEMS TO AID DEFENSE DECISIONS

Stuart E. Johnson

Defense decisionmaking is inevitably collaborative because it involves a range of stakeholders. The challenge is to ensure that collaboration adds value instead of producing lowest-common-denominator results.

Collaborative technologies help people develop a common perspective and make it possible to collaborate across time and space. Figure 13.1 is a matrix of collaboration, showing different combinations of time and space—from synchronous (same time, predictable) and colocated (same place) in the upper left, through asynchronous (unpredictable) and uncolocated (different place and unpredictable) in the bottom right. Illustrative collaborative tools and techniques are provided for each space-time combination.

The potential of computer-mediated communications tools for enhancing effectiveness is driving widespread interest in them. Collaboration typically disrupts existing organizational, social, computing, and network infrastructures,[1] so an organizational structure that legitimizes collaboration across hierarchical lines is a key condition of success.[2] Groupware provides a powerful vehicle for transforming

---

[1] See, for example, S. Poltrock, "Some Groupware Challenges Experienced at Boeing," available at http://orgwis.gmd.de/~prinz/cscw96ws/poltrock.html.

[2] See, for example, W. J. Orilkowski, "Learning from Notes: Organizational Issues in Groupware Implementation," *Proceedings of the ACM, Conference on CSCW '92*, 1992, pp. 362–369; B. Vadenbosch and M. M. Ginzberg, "Lotus Notes and Collaboration," *Journal of Management Information Systems*, Vol. 13, No. 3, pp. 65–81; A. S. Clarke

		Time		
		Synchronous (same, predictable)	Asynchronous	
			Predictable	Unpredictable
Space	Same place	Electronic meeting systems	Work shifts	Shared space, group calendaring
	Different places but predictable	Tele/video/ desktop conferencing	Electronic mail	Shared applications and files, collaborative writing
	Different places and unpredictable	Interactive multicast seminars, text chat	Electronic bulletin boards	Discussion databases, workflow systems

Figure 13.1—Collaboration Across Time and Space

stovepipe processes into more-integrated decisionmaking. Defense planning, in particular, can be dramatically improved.

This chapter addresses how one kind of groupware, electronic meeting systems (EMSs), can be used for simultaneous collaboration. Also included is a description of the detailed application of one EMS (Ventana Corporation's GroupSystems) to defense planning.

ELECTRONIC MEETING SYSTEMS

An EMS includes three processes that are designed to improve group productivity.[3] Table 13.1 shows these processes and some of their advantages.

(ed.), *Groupware: Collaborative Strategies for Corporate LAN's and Intranets,* Prentice Hall, Upper Saddle River, NJ, 1997; and http://copernicus.bbn.com/lab/ocsc/papers/Full.text.html.

[3]For more detail, see Jay F. Nunamaker, Jr., Robert O. Briggs, and Daniel D. Mittleman, "Electronic Meeting Systems," in David Coleman and Raman Khanna (eds.), *Groupware: Technology and Applications*, Prentice-Hall, Inc., 1995.

Table 13.1

EMS Processes and Some of Their Advantages

Process	EMS Advantages
Communication through common media (computer network, videoconference, teleconference)	Increases the number of people who can participate in a meeting through simultaneous input
Thought processes to form an action plan to accomplish a common goal (formulate, evaluate, and select or prioritize alternatives)	Generates more ideas of higher quality through various collaborative activities to generate, organize, and evaluate ideas; anonymity allows free debate on ideas
Information access to enable group members to support the thought processes using timely, accurate, and complete information	Tools can reduce information overload, increase productivity through access to a larger information base, and enhance organizational learning via electronic transcripts

An EMS focuses on group dynamics, using computer-aided parallel communications, structured and focused thought processes, and applications and tools to improve information access. Used well, an EMS can enhance defense planning by stimulating social interaction and thinking, and can accelerate strategic planning, problem solving, and the setting of priorities because its ability to exploit simultaneous input facilitates idea generation, persuasion, and decision selection.

The results produced by a decision support process depend on the participants, the leadership, and the exercise design, as well as on the underlying technology. Successful decision support exercises are those that identify and represent the problem clearly, generate and evaluate alternatives, and then select among those alternatives. An idealized flow chart of the process shows its phases:

- Define the problem

- Formulate a decision objective

- Generate decision criteria, weighting them as appropriate

- Generate alternatives

- Discuss alternatives

- Prioritize alternatives

- Rate how well each alternative meets each criterion

- Compare the scores for the alternatives and prioritize the alternatives accordingly

- Capture the pros and cons of each leading alternative for presentation to decisionmakers.

PRIORITIZING NAVAL PROGRAMS: AN EXAMPLE OF AN EMS IN USE

The Challenge

In early 1997, the Navy staff (N-8) was tasked to prepare the Navy for the first Quadrennial Defense Review (QDR). The Navy's dilemma was familiar to force planners: the Navy had developed a program in response to the defense planning guidance, and that program exceeded the *fiscal* guidance laid down by the defense secretary. Navy leadership argued to the Office of the Secretary of Defense (OSD) that it had long since eliminated the fat from its budget and requested additional funding. Simultaneously, the Navy moved to ensure that if it could *not* get additional funding, it would have the best backup plan it could devise.

In formulating its backup plan, the Navy asked the Decision Support Department (DSD) of the Naval War College to develop a methodology that would force planners to do collaborative, capabilities–based planning. DSD responded with an analytic exercise (carried out in spring 1997) that drew on decision support technologies and techniques. The results were delivered to the N-8 staff for incorporation in the Navy's input to the QDR.

The Navy's challenge was how to fit a $90 billion requirement into a fiscal guidance of $81 billion.[4] One time-honored approach would have each head of a major program element resubmit a budget that trims that program by 10 percent. This may well be the "easiest" approach in that it introduces the least stress across the organization. It

---

[4]All budget quantities are expressed in fiscal year (FY) 1997 dollars.

seems "fair," because everyone takes the same hit. But it almost always causes serious disruption from an overall planning perspective. Some programs can take a 10 percent cut with only marginal reductions in their effectiveness; others are so crippled by the cut that they might as well be eliminated.

Another common approach is to lock the heads of major programs in a room and don't let them out until they have come up with a plan that fits the budget. The problem with this approach is clear: *Program prioritization becomes subject to competition—and then compromise—among the major program sponsors.* The distortion in the resulting program is evident when one looks at the uneven capabilities that result from such bargaining.

The alternative that the Navy leadership needed was clear: *a process to prioritize programs based on capabilities that naval forces need.* This is easier said than done, however. Many capabilities go into a military force, and they can be delivered in many ways. Targets, for instance, can be struck from the sea by carrier aircraft or missiles; missiles, in turn, can be launched from a surface ship or a submarine. The DSD staff set out to design an exercise that would

- Tie program priorities to required capabilities
- Involve hands-on participation by key resource sponsors
- Be transparent to participants
- Provide a clear audit trail of results.

At the outset, the exercise design team faced the fact that program prioritization is always dangerous. Every program that has made it far enough to be in the Navy's program objectives memorandum (POM) is important; all of the programs bring some important military capability to the table. The challenge that Navy leadership laid down was as follows: programs that were multipurpose and high performing or narrow-purpose but critical to fielding key capabilities were to be identified and distinguished from programs that were narrow-purpose and whose contribution was marginal or could be covered in another way.

DSD was asked to concentrate on the investment account. True, the Navy would also look elsewhere to save money; its operations and maintenance costs refused to decline even though every year saw fewer ships in the fleet. Additional rationalization of the Navy's base structure and facilities could also save money. Nevertheless, Navy leadership felt it had a good understanding of *where* to find savings in these other accounts; it simply did not know *how* to do so. The investment account was different, however. Developing and procuring one system when another would serve much better could haunt the Navy for as long as 30 years.

Overview of Methodology

The analytic approach adapted the strategy-to-task methodology developed at RAND during the 1980s and married it to decision support technology and methods. Experts who understood U.S. national security strategy as articulated in the President's National Security Strategy and the secretary of defense's guidance to the armed services were assembled. Their understanding of this and their knowledge of activities the military had been called on to perform in the recent past would enable them to project the activities military forces would likely be asked to carry out within the foreseeable future. This, in turn, would help them judge what capabilities the Navy would need. From there, it would be a straightforward, if complex, step to determining the programs needed to field those capabilities.

The design of phase I of the exercise—through determining capabilities—is shown as a flow chart in Figure 13.2.

Once a weighted set of capability requirements has been established, the next step is to assess how well the Navy programs satisfy those weighted requirements. Figure 13.3 shows the final output as a prioritized list of major programs in the Navy's investment budget based on the contribution each makes to the weighted set of capabilities the Navy would need. The exercise flow, and the EMS's part in it, can then be described in detail.

Phase I: From Activities That Military Forces May Be Called on to Carry Out to Weighted Capability Requirements

Select the set of activities that military forces may be called on to carry out. The U.S. military responds to tasking from the national command authority that ultimately culminates in the authority of the

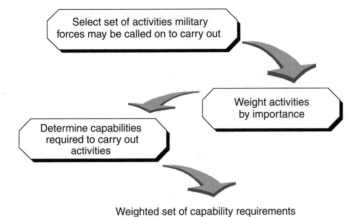

Figure 13.2—Analytic Approach, Phase I

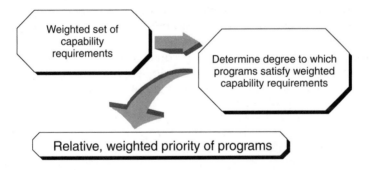

Figure 13.3—Analytic Approach, Phase II

U.S. president as commander in chief, with supplemental "advise and consent" authority resting in the U.S. Congress. Some 20 analysts (both military and civilian) from the Naval War College who were familiar with the details of the national security decisionmaking process gathered to develop a list of activities that military forces could be called on to do over the next two decades. Each analyst was asked to enter into the EMS notebook computer specific suggestions of activities with short descriptions. Each activity was displayed both on each participant's notebook computer and on a screen in the front of the room that was seen by all participants. The ability to see all the inputs limited the duplication of activities nominated and stimulated thinking.

When the participants had entered all the "activities" they could think of, the meeting facilitator led the group to review candidate activities displayed on the master screen. The group collectively examined the list, removed redundancy, and made the language more precise. The result was a long list of activities (listed in Table 13.2) that these experts felt the military could be called on to do in the foreseeable future.

A long unprioritized list is a poor foundation for making the hard choices, tradeoffs, and risk assessments that defense planners face in every Planning, Programming, and Budgeting System (PPBS) cycle. So the facilitator turned to the difficult task of prioritization.

Weight activities by importance. In the Bottom-up Review of 1993, Secretary of Defense Les Aspin had made a clear and simple judgment on the question of priorities: *The US military was to prepare to fight and win two nearly simultaneous major regional contingencies.* If the military met this standard, it could cope with other, "lesser included" contingencies. Hence, the guidance was, essentially, to prepare for the worst, and the resultant capabilities would be equal to any other challenge.

The group of experts felt that this formulation, while useful, was an oversimplification and broke down on careful examination. The devil was in the details. Some activities—e.g., maintaining a peace accord in Bosnia—turned out to be "different" cases, not "lesser included" cases. The equipment, types of units needed, and skills required were different from those of a force optimized for high-intensity conflict. Moreover, how much special attention to pay to "other" activities would have to depend on how important they were, which, the group decided, was determined both by the likelihood that the military would be called on to carry them out and the risk to U.S. national security interests were they not carried out successfully.

Militaries are constantly undertaking activities quite different from fighting a major conflict, such as maintaining a forward presence to deter aggression or monitoring international agreements. And then there are some activities—such as nuclear warfare—that are highly

Table 13.2

Missions for DoD over the Next 20 Years

Short Form	Long Form
Constabulary	Provide constabulary assistance to U.S. domestic authorities
Counterdrug	Assist U.S. civilian agencies in countering drug trafficking
Counterimmigration	Help U.S. civilian agencies interdict illegal immigration
Counterinsurgency	Protect democracies by conducting counterinsurgency
Counterproliferation	Actively support counterproliferation activities
Counterterrorism	Assist U.S. civilian agencies in countering terrorism
Crisis response	Respond to a crisis rapidly
Deter MTW	Deter a major theater war (MTW)
Deter war with peer	Deter major war with a peer competitor
Deter WMD	Deter development and use of weapons of mass destruction (WMD)
Extend deterrence	Extend deterrence and defense coverage to a friendly nation
Fight and win MTW	Fight and win a MTW
Forward engagement	Conduct forward engagement
Humanitarian ops	Conduct humanitarian relief operations
Impose U.S. will	Impose U.S. will through military intervention
Intelligence	Collect intelligence
Int'l agreements	Monitor and enforce international agreements
Limited ops	Conduct limited operations to influence a major power
Peace ops	Support and/or conduct peacekeeping operations
Protect U.S. lives	Protect U.S. lives and property (to include noncombatant evacuation operations)
Punitive strikes	Conduct limited punitive strikes
Sanctions	Enforce sanctions

unlikely but would carry serious consequences for national security if they were to happen and the United States were unprepared. Both likelihood and consequence are thus integral to assessing an activity's importance. To capture these two factors, the facilitator asked participants to assess activities against two assertions:

1. The military is likely to be called on to carry out this activity.

2. Not performing this activity successfully poses significant risks to U.S. national security.

The participants assessed each activity, one at a time, against each assertion, selecting responses ranging from strongly disagree (1) to strongly agree (5). The EMS alternative analysis module then displayed the mean, standard deviation, and range of responses for each military activity. The responses entered by participants into their notebook workstations were anonymous (although participants could compare their responses against what the group did as a whole) in order to eliminate any influence some participants might feel from others with higher rank or stronger personalities. Truly independent assessments thus were possible. Participants were encouraged to append explanations to their assessments, which, in turn, would be displayed. This yielded a much richer understanding of the results, especially any "outliers."

The responses were then binned. Activities with mean scores of 4.5 or above were placed in the Strongly Agree category, those with mean scores of 3.5 to 4.4 in the Agree category, and so on. The results are shown in Figures 13.4 and 13.5.

The facilitator then paused to review these results with the participants. Had the ensuing discussion revealed any misunderstandings of the assertions, the facilitator could have "polled" the group again once the assertions had been clarified. Repeating the poll was just a mouse-click away.

The group felt that frequency and risk were of comparable importance in evaluating activities and concluded that they should be given equal weight in a consolidated ranking (see Figure 13.6).

Note that the emerging numerical priority ranking constituted an important step beyond many strategy documents, which catalog a broad list of military missions but then implicitly concede that the next step, prioritization, is too hard, and so stop.

The group paused to reexamine whether giving equal weight to likelihood and consequence, or "criticality," was appropriate. One participant argued that because the military's job was to protect the United States and its interests from catastrophic harm, the ability to do so was the standard by which force capabilities should be judged.

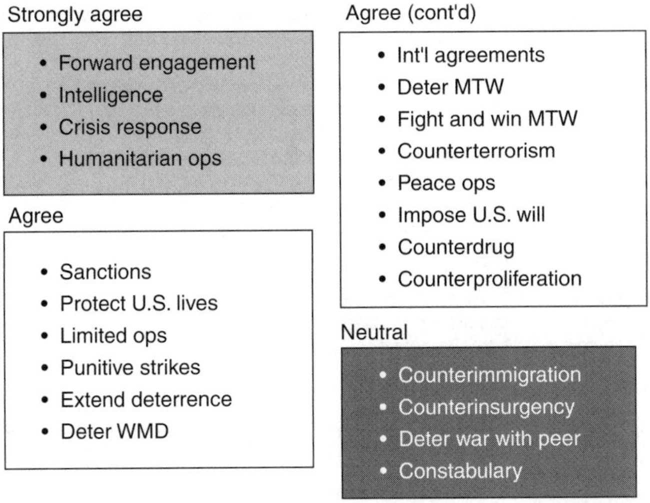

Strongly agree

- Forward engagement
- Intelligence
- Crisis response
- Humanitarian ops

Agree

- Sanctions
- Protect U.S. lives
- Limited ops
- Punitive strikes
- Extend deterrence
- Deter WMD

Agree (cont'd)

- Int'l agreements
- Deter MTW
- Fight and win MTW
- Counterterrorism
- Peace ops
- Impose U.S. will
- Counterdrug
- Counterproliferation

Neutral

- Counterimmigration
- Counterinsurgency
- Deter war with peer
- Constabulary

Figure 13.4—Responses to "The Military Is Likely to Be Called on to Carry Out This Activity"

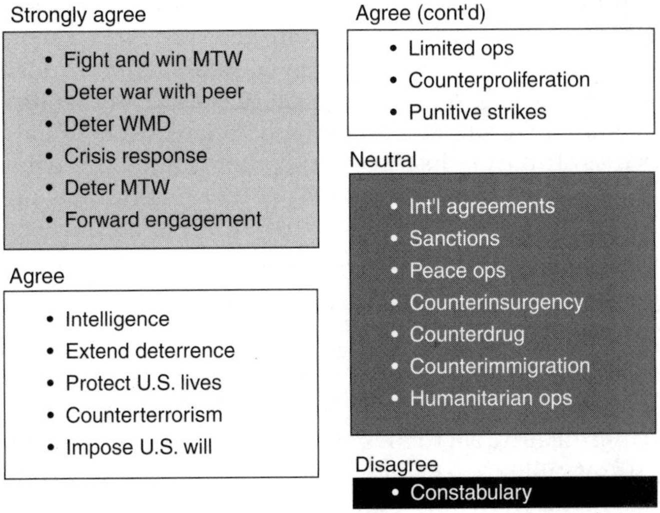

Strongly agree

- Fight and win MTW
- Deter war with peer
- Deter WMD
- Crisis response
- Deter MTW
- Forward engagement

Agree

- Intelligence
- Extend deterrence
- Protect U.S. lives
- Counterterrorism
- Impose U.S. will

Agree (cont'd)

- Limited ops
- Counterproliferation
- Punitive strikes

Neutral

- Int'l agreements
- Sanctions
- Peace ops
- Counterinsurgency
- Counterdrug
- Counterimmigration
- Humanitarian ops

Disagree

- Constabulary

Figure 13.5—Responses to "Not Performing This Activity Successfully Poses Significant Risks to U.S. National Security"

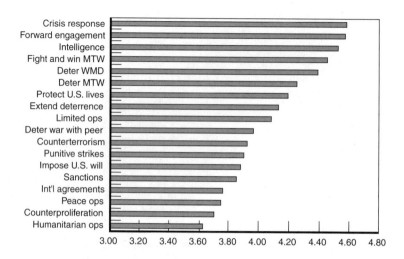

Figure 13.6—Ranking of the Importance of Military Activities

Others countered that U.S. military forces were being called on to respond to any number of situations that posed no serious threat in the short run to U.S. national security but that nonetheless required a competent response for two important reasons. First, a modest size crisis, if not checked promptly, could expand into a much larger problem. Second, the need to respond to these lesser contingencies was not going to disappear. To meet such needs, the military would be forced to strip from its forces units that would otherwise be earmarked as lead elements for any MTW that might break out. Planning deliberately for activities that must be done anyway would thus allow the military to minimize turbulence in its forces.

In this case, an equal weighting was retained. Had it not been, the EMS software would have permitted sensitivity analyses to be performed so that the group could see how priorities would change if the weighting changed. Thus, if the weighting moved to, say, 3:2, in favor of "criticality," activities that implied high-intensity warfare with a strong military (such as "deter war with a peer") would have increased modestly in importance.

Rank the relevance of naval forces in carrying out key military activities. The facilitator then asked the group to consider what naval forces could contribute to joint operations that would increase the odds of those operations succeeding. Naval forces would play an important role in most of the activities, but in some their role would be more prominent, and in others they would be less suited than the forces of another service. In some cases, naval forces would have the primary responsibility; in others, a critical role (i.e., one without which the operation would be severely hampered); in yet others, only a marginal role.

The facilitator asked participants to assess activities against two assertions:

1. This activity is likely to be performed primarily by naval forces.

2. Naval forces are critical to the performance of this activity.

After discussing the role naval forces would play in carrying out these activities, the participants entered responses into their notebook workstations. One by one, each mission was displayed, and each participant entered a response from strongly disagree (1) to strongly agree (5). Figures 13.7 and 13.8 show the results after aggregation and binning. As expected, the two responses are highly correlated, as Figure 13.9 shows.

The results of these two polls were then averaged to portray the overall "utility" of naval forces for carrying out activities the military would be called on to execute. The top 15 priorities are shown in Figure 13.10.

Determine the capabilities that naval forces will need. The prioritized list (Figure 13.10) gave the group a basis for identifying the capabilities needed and, ultimately, which programs would provide those capabilities.

As part of the 1990s effort to build a Joint Mission Essential Task List, the Navy developed its Department of the Navy (DoN) Warfare Task List, which sets out the capabilities that the Navy commits itself to maintaining in its forces. This list is reviewed and updated regularly to ensure it takes into account new capabilities that technology or new doctrine make possible. It is arranged hierarchically, which means the major categories lent themselves well to the exercise at

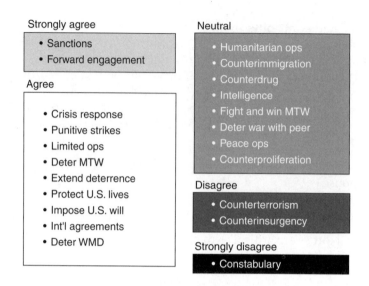

Figure 13.7—Responses to "This Activity Is Likely to Be Performed Primarily by Naval Forces"

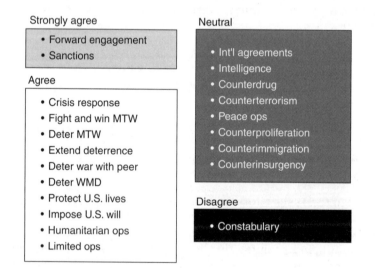

Figure 13.8—Responses to "Naval Forces Are Critical to the Performance of This Activity"

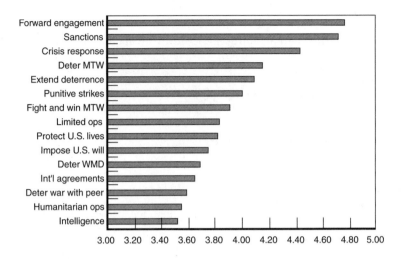

Figure 13.9—Ranking of the Relevance of Naval Forces in Carrying Out Key Military Activities

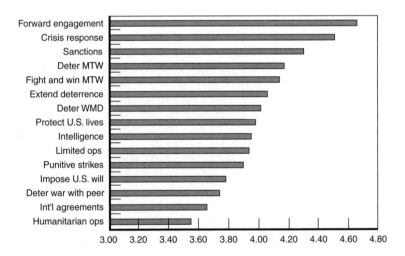

Figure 13.10—Ranking of the "Utility" of Naval Forces

hand. The DSD team preselected the following DoN warfare tasks from the list to use in arraying the various naval capabilities required:

- Airspace primacy
- Command and control of assigned U.S. and multinational forces
- Control of littoral land areas
- Fire support to forces ashore
- Forcible amphibious entry
- Forward deployed, combat-capable forces
- Gather and disseminate timely battlespace knowledge
- Precision strike
- Sub-surface primacy
- Surface primacy
- Sustained expeditionary logistics
- Theater missile defense
- Timely movement of forces and supplies by sea

One by one, each activity (e.g., fight an MTW) was displayed on the participants' screens, along with, one by one, the capabilities to be evaluated. Participants were asked to assess the contribution the capability shown made to the activity shown, the possible responses ranging from not critical (1) to highly critical (5).

The "score" for each activity-capability combination was the product of the activity's weight (shown in Figure 13.10) and the capability's degree of criticality. For example, if a participant deemed that providing theater missile defense was a capability critical (4) to the crisis response activity (4.5), the "score" for that combination would be 18 (i.e., 4 x 4.5). These scores were then summed for each capability to produce a "weighted capability requirement." A capability scored "high" on the list of weighted capabilities if it contributed disproportionately to the activities with the highest weights, or if it contributed a high value to a broad spectrum of missions. The results for the top 13 scorers are shown in Figure 13.11.

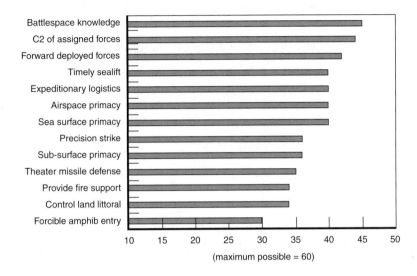

Figure 13.11—Capabilities Ordered According to Their Contribution to Weighted Activities Naval Forces Are Likely to Be Called on to Carry Out

Of particular note is the lead priority given to battlespace knowledge and effective C2. *Neither* of these two "most important" capabilities puts firepower or forces into the field. Instead, both allow the commander to understand the situation in the battlespace and to apply force or firepower more precisely and effectively.

The group singled this out as an important finding made possible by the methodology. Normally, discussions of capabilities measure effectiveness by focusing on the amount of force or, in more refined analyses, the amount of firepower a service can field. This focus biases programmatic priorities toward major weapons platforms. Because the value of battlespace knowledge and effective C2 is hard to measure and is rarely part of high-visibility programs, these two capabilities are typically put at a disadvantage when competing for resources. Even careful modeling and simulation generally understate their value. By now, most models can elevate the measure of merit to targets killed, thereby picking up the importance of such items as precision guided munitions (PGMs). But battlespace knowledge and effective C2 remain elusive capabilities to model, so they seldom are assessed in ways that give prominence to their payoff.

Phase II: Assessing the Department of the Navy Investment Program

As the last phase of the exercise, the group turned to the final task: prioritizing the Navy's investment program by assessing the largest DoN programs.[5] These 22 programs, which represented 92 percent of the total DoN investment budget, were as follows:

- New class of aircraft carriers
- F-18 E/F combat aircraft
- V-22 Osprey
- DDG-51 (with Aegis air defense system)
- Air-cushioned amphibious vessel (ACAV)
- Joint Strike Fighter (JSF)
- Lightweight 155-mm artillery piece
- Arsenal ship
- SC-21 (now the DD21) destroyer
- AV-8B V/STOL remanufacture
- F-14 upgrade
- Transport helicopter upgrades
- P-3 Orion upgrade
- Standoff precision guided machines (e.g., JSOW, JDAM)
- AIM 9X air-to-air missile
- LPD 17 amphibious transport
- Theater ballistic missile defense (TBMD)
- Surface fire support (NSFS)

---

[5]Based on the sum of procurement and 6.3 (research and development [R&D]) dollars across the 1997–2002 FYDP.

- New attack submarine (NSSN)

- Unmanned aerial vehicles (UAVs)

- Cooperative engagement capability (CEC)

- EA-6B electronic warfare aircraft

Participants were presented with a description of each program and its place in the budget. They were then asked to evaluate the contribution—from not critical (1) to highly critical (5)—that each program made to the weighted capabilities derived in phase I. As the capabilities were displayed, one by one, participants assessed the contribution the program would make to them.

The "score" assigned to each capability-program combination was the product of the capability's weight and the participant's assessment of the degree to which the program contributed to the capability. These scores were then summed for each program to produce a weighted priority list of programs in the DoN budget. Figure 13.12 shows the results.

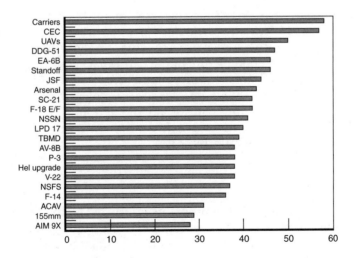

Figure 13.12—Weighted (Joint) Priority of Largest Navy Programs

A program could score high on the list of priorities if it contributed disproportionately to the capabilities with the highest weights, if it contributed at least moderately to a broad spectrum of capabilities, or if it contributed a high value to enough capabilities to push its score up. In this way, systems that contributed to a set of high-value capabilities or were important to a broad set of capabilities rose to the top.

A review of the results reveals the power of this analytic tool. The program for future carriers scored first. To be sure, it is hard to imagine a group of naval officers ranking the next generation of aircraft carriers anywhere other than first. That said, however, a carrier is a highly flexible military system, one that contributes a broad range of the required capabilities to the (weighted) military activities identified by the group.

More surprising to the naval leadership was the high priority that emerged for both CEC and UAVs. An examination of participants' entries, where they "explained" their assessments, revealed that this high priority grew out of a perception that these were critical to the high-priority capabilities they had identified earlier (see Figure 13.11). This, in turn, grew from the assessment that future military operations are likely to be carried out in an environment characterized by enemies with anti-access capabilities that include cruise and ballistic missiles. A good picture of the battlespace was judged to be critical, as well as a measure of defense—hence, the high priority assigned to the DDG-51 with its advanced air defense radar and potential to develop an anti–ballistic missile and anti–cruise missile capability. The same anti-access threat drove the robust standoff munitions buy to a high priority as well.

Other Possible Uses

This process yielded a list of programs prioritized by their contribution to the capabilities the Navy will need in the future and to the activities the Navy will likely be called on to undertake. The process provided a systematic look at the relative contribution each competing program (none of which was unimportant) might make to the naval service's future. The resulting list allowed senior Navy decisionmakers to focus on programs that ought to be fenced off as far as possible in budget deliberations. Yet this EMS technique is by no means limited to determining priorities for capabilities or programs. It could be applied to operational concepts, R&D priorities, or any decisionmaking process being conducted under conditions of uncertainty.

This book reflects the reshaping of defense analysis that went on at RAND and elsewhere after Desert Storm and the fall of communism—i.e., the movement away from a focus on the awesome predictability of the Soviet threat toward contemplation of a world that had become, if less dangerous, surely more uncertain. In place of the Cold War's one overriding potential foe, there were now numerous possible threats, so the Department of Defense (DoD) moved, haltingly, from single planning scenarios to planning for two major wars and, ultimately, to planning based not on threats or scenarios but on the capabilities needed for a fast-changing world. It is no surprise that this book, and the body of work that lies behind it, is dominated by techniques for dealing with uncertainty and, uncertainty's obverse, the explosion in information that also characterizes today's world—and tomorrow's.

In its efforts to understand and frame policy for this changing world, RAND developed new analytic techniques, such as exploratory modeling, and a wider range of its analyses became relevant, reflecting the changing nature of security. Peace and humanitarian operations, for instance, required the U.S. military to deal with not only a wide range of coalition partners, but also with private nongovernmental organizations (NGOs). The same was the case as RAND thought through the problem of protecting critical national infrastructures (such as that for information), infrastructures that are no less a national asset for being mostly in private hands.

The terrorist attacks of September 11, 2001, have now ushered in a new world, one still far from being fully apprehended by the American people or their leaders. Not only have the potential threats become still more diverse, but some of the fundamental distinctions of planning have been overturned. The United States planned—and still must plan—to project force over large distances. But it now must also deal with threats right at home. Comfortable distinctions between "foreign" and "domestic" were already being eroded by the rise of the global economy. Terrorism does not respect them at all.

The world before us will require RAND and its fellow organizations to further develop the approaches and techniques in this book. Planning will be increasingly stretched by the blizzard of uncertainty and the range of capabilities that might be needed. How much and how the U.S. military will be involved in homeland security remain to be seen, but surely the change from the world of the Cold War will be marked. Interactions defying other comfortable distinctions—those between "government" and "the private sector"—will also intensify, calling forth new ways of understanding new kinds of partnerships.

Terrorism surely is a grave threat, but it is not exclusively or even primarily a *military* threat—another manifestation of the changing nature of security. Now, as the world confounds comfortable distinctions, it also calls on a wider range of RAND analyses and impels collaborations that were infrequent before. Techniques from what used to be thought of as RAND's "domestic work" are more and more relevant to the nation's security, rather than just its well-being. RAND Health, for instance, has moved quickly to make its knowledge of medicine and health-care delivery available to those planning against biological or chemical terror. The kind of partnership between health care and national security professionals that was often discussed but seldom occurred is now happening. RAND's next volume on challenges and techniques for defense and security decisionmaking will be enriched by work from not just health, but from survey research, criminal justice and public safety, insurance and infrastructure protection, and other realms of RAND research.

Bruce W. Bennett (Ph.D., policy analysis, RAND Graduate Institute for Public Policy Analysis) is a senior analyst and professor of policy analysis at RAND. His research interests include military strategy and force planning, countering proliferation of weapons of mass destruction, Korea, and the Persian Gulf.

Nurith Berstein (Masters in public administration, Carleton University, Ottawa, Canada) is a researcher at RAND specializing in national and international security policy issues.

Frank Camm (Ph.D., economics, University of Chicago) leads research at RAND on high-level Army resource management issues associated with force structure design, logistics policy, and acquisition of combat service support services.

David S.C. Chu (Ph.D., economics, Yale University) has served in a variety of RAND and national security government posts.

Paul K. Davis (Ph.D., chemical physics, Massachusetts Institute of Technology) is a senior scientist and research leader at RAND. His research encompasses a number of areas, including strategic defense planning, future forces and force transformation, and advanced modeling and simulation. He is a professor at the RAND Graduate School; a member or former member of the Naval Studies Board of the National Research Council, the Defense Science Board, and the U.S. SALT Delegation; and author of numerous books and studies.

Daniel B. Fox (Ph.D., operations research, University of Illinois) is a senior operations research analyst at RAND. His focus is the design and application of computer simulations for analysis of complex military operations. Dr. Fox has over 30 years of experience in military operations analysis.

James R. Hosek (Ph.D., economics, University of Chicago) is a senior economist at RAND, editor-in-chief of the *RAND Journal of Economics*, RAND Graduate School professor, and former director of RAND's Defense Manpower Research Center.

Stuart E. Johnson (Ph.D., physical chemistry, Massachusetts Institute of Technology) was a senior scientist at RAND when this research was completed. He has many years of experience in defense planning and analysis at the Department of Defense, NATO headquarters, and in private industry.

Martin C. Libicki (Ph.D., city and regional planning, University of California, Berkeley) is a senior policy analyst at RAND whose areas of expertise include the application of information technology to national security.

David Mussington (Ph.D., political science, Carleton University) is a political scientist at RAND. Among his areas of expertise are critical infrastructure protection, information and technology security, and counterterrorism and cyberterrorism.

Stuart H. Starr (Ph.D., electrical engineering, University of Illinois) is the Director of Plans at The MITRE Corporation; his areas of expertise include the assessment of information systems in the context of national security missions.

Harry J. Thie (Doctorate, business administration, George Washington University) is a senior management scientist at RAND whose research explores military career management and defense organization, manpower, personnel, and training.

Gregory F. Treverton (Ph.D., economics and politics, Harvard University) is a senior policy analyst at RAND. He has worked on intelligence and on Europe for Congress, the White House and the National Intelligence Council; his current research interests also include Asia and public-private partnerships.

NATURAL STATE

NATURAL STATE

A Literary Anthology of
California Nature
Writing

Selected and Edited by Steven Gilbar
With a Foreword by David Brower

UNIVERSITY OF CALIFORNIA PRESS

Berkeley   Los Angeles   London

University of California Press
Berkeley and Los Angeles, California

University of California Press, Ltd.
London, England

Library of Congress Cataloging-in-Publication Data

Natural state : a literary anthology of California
nature writing /selected and edited by Steven Gilbar :
with a foreword by David Brower.
p.   cm.
Includes bibliographic references and index
ISBN 0–520–21208–8 (cloth : alk. paper).—
ISBN 0–520–21209–6 (pbk. : alk. paper)
1. Natural history—California.   2. Nature.
I. Gilbar, Steven.   QH105.C2N425   1998
508.794—dc 21   97–19119

508. 794

Printed in the United States of America

9   8   7   6   5   4   3   2   1

CONTENTS

THE HILLS AND VALLEYS

Foreword

This book is a feast and requires a celebration. For one thing, I have known, or am almost old enough to have known, so many of the authors: LeConte, Twain, Kerouac, Brewer, Stevenson, London, Steinbeck, Stegner, Abbey, Chase, Powell, Miller (Joaquin and Henry), Muir, and Austin—all of whom preceded me (which isn't easy). I was overwhelmed with serendipity, not to be relieved by the current host of authors who are younger (who isn't?), including John Daniel, who had learned about writing from Wallace Stegner and was fleetingly a student of mine, when as a Berkeley dropout (1931) I briefly became a visiting professor at Stanford (1982). I should take Mr. Daniel to court for overstressing my emotional stability by revealing, in matchless prose, what a desert is all about. It hurts to hold back tears when they have no place else to go.

What John McPhee, from whose *Encounters with the Archdruid* I learned who I was, writes about the seismic cross California bears renews all my old anxieties. I was born in Berkeley so close to the San Andreas that I still find fault too easily and brake for tectonic plates.

But book work, as an editor for the Sierra Club and the University of California Press, informed my Berkeley decades; and I was ready, when Ted Koppel was chairing a Stanford assembly and asked me for a couple of environmental sound bites, to conclude, "We must reform television, which is causing cerebral gridlock across America." The audience loved it. I hope the audience for this book can agree that we must also reform the Internet and Web, where electronics fail to distinguish between data and knowledge, or between surfeit and craft, or between merde (to avoid scatological alliteration) and substance.

There is no such problem with *Natural State*. The book will not cause cerebral problems; it will cure them. Moreover, it can be enjoyed indoors or out; in natural light, unencumbered by power surges; survive splashes of coffee, rain, or chardonnay; comfortably endure thermal changes on a shelf or in a knapsack, never asking to be pointed or clicked. And you can lift your eyes, when you want to, to the hills without suffering painful disintegration of the carpel tunnels or becoming roadkill on the Information Superhighway.

Add a further fussy detail: words written for a book are likely to endure in the mind, rather than perish in a landfill. There are wiser uses for land, considering that the two million Californians here when I arrived have already become thirty-two million. California wildness deserves a chance to recover, and *Natural State* lets us know why.

David Brower
Berkeley, 1997

INTRODUCTION

Calif ornia is a land of contrasts. Both the highest and lowest elevations of the lower forty-eight states are in California—and then only eighty miles apart. The hottest temperatures in the United States are found there. It has some of the world's greatest wonders, and has had some of its worst natural disasters. Naturally, this landscape has inspired prose that, like the land itself, is diverse and full of contrasts. This book aims to corral the best of it.

The special quality of California's landscape has affected all sorts of writers, not all of whom fall into the category of "nature writer" or "naturalist." Gretel Ehrlich, Barry Lopez, and David Rains Wallace, for example, have certainly made nature their special province, but they also write fiction. Then there are writers known primarily for their fiction—Henry Miller, Wallace Stegner, and Robert Louis Stevenson, to name but three—who turned to nonfiction to express their feelings about California's wild places. Also present are authors who work principally in nonfiction, such as M. F. K. Fisher, John McPhee, and John Muir. Others yet seem equally at home in both fiction and nonfiction; these include Edward Abbey, Joan Didion, and Mark Twain. Finally, there are poets, such as John Daniel, Joaquin Miller, and Gary Snyder, who have also worked in prose. Not all the pieces rounded up here are nonfiction, however. Included are selections from works of fiction by Jack Kerouac, Jack London, John Steinbeck, and others. What all the pieces by these authors have in common is good writing, which is what makes this anthology "literary," rather than a historical survey of nature writing in the state.

The constraints of space have regrettably forced the omission of much worthwhile writing. Some of the early European explorers, pioneers, and settlers left wonderfully descriptive journals about a wilder California. Writers as varied as Clarence King, Stewart Edward White, George Wharton James, Page Stegner, Judy Van Der Veer, Galen Rowell, David Wicinas, and Paul McHugh have all written memorably about the outdoors, while others, such as Jaime de Angulo, Gerald Haslam, Maxine Hong Kingston, Roy Parvin, William Saroyan, and Gary Soto, have given life and voice to the people of California, on the land and in their diverse communities. Many other important contributions could be mentioned. In order to strike a balance between classic writers and newer voices, and to provide a consistent focus on the state's natural treasures, hard choices had to be made.

The incredible biodiversity of California has not been mirrored to date by a like diversity in the cultural backgrounds of those who write about nature. Not surprisingly, most such essayists, poets, and fiction writers have been European-Americans, for they had the education and leisure required to trek through the wilderness and record their impressions. Although today some of the best writers in California are of Mexican, African, and Asian descent, these authors have usually chosen to write about their immigrant and urban experiences rather than rhapsodize about the mountains, deserts, and forests. The same is true of Native Californian writers, most of whom write about their people on the land, rather than the land itself. This situation is changing, however, and soon, no doubt, a body of "nature writing" will emerge that better reflects the cultural diversity of California's population.

Women are perhaps more adequately represented in contemporary writings about nature. Although historically they lacked not only rooms of their own, but tents as well, that has changed in the past several decades, and today women are among the best in the field.

Some years ago the Central Valley writer Gerald Haslam claimed that California has four "geo-literary" regions: the greater San Francisco Bay Area, the Heartland, the Southland, and Wilderness California. Most of the places covered in this collection are in the last region—if, that is, "wilderness" can be stretched to embrace the merely rustic and pastoral as well as the truly untamed. It does not mean places where men and women do not dwell. Simply, when we speak of wilderness, our attention is focused not on people, but on the place itself.

The book is organized around the basic landforms: mountains, hills and valleys, deserts, and coast. As a prelude, there are two California Indian myths about how the land was created. The first is an old Cahto narrative, and the second is an A-juma-wi story filtered through the modern sensibility of Darryl Babe Wilson.

Of all California's many mountain ranges, the most imposing is the Sierra Nevada. This four-hundred-mile-long wall of jagged, glacier-sculpted mountains has probably inspired more writers than any other topographical feature in the state. At the top of the list of Sierran natural wonders is surely Yosemite, represented here by Joseph LeConte experiencing its wonders for the first time, Jack Kerouac and a couple of his dharma-bum companions scaling Matterhorn Peak, Daniel Duane climbing Half Dome, and Ann Zwinger delighting in the high country's "trumpets of light." Elsewhere in the Sierra, John Muir relishes a wind storm, and Mark Twain camps out at Lake Tahoe.

Extending north and south between the Central Valley and the Pacific are the Coast Ranges. The Santa Lucia Range, for example, which is visited in a short piece by John Steinbeck, rises abruptly from the ocean to heights of almost 6,000 feet.

Other mountains, too, have heartened writers. Bordering Oregon, the Klamath Mountains (visited here by Joaquin Miller and David Rains Wallace), the Cascade Range, and the Modoc Plateau terminate the Central Valley at its north end. In the south, the valley is closed by the Transverse Ranges—so called because of their east-west lineation, which runs at an oblique angle to the northwest-southwest-trending Sierra Nevada and Coast Ranges. The Transverse Ranges comprise such mountain chains as the San Bernardinos, Santa Monicas, and Santa Ynez, as well as their interior valleys, including San Fernando, San Gabriel, and Ojai. South of the Transverse are the Peninsular Ranges— so called because most of them are in the Baja Peninsula—which include the Santa Ana and San Jacinto ranges. Isolated mountains have captured writers' hearts as well. Mount Tamalpais, for example, whose skyline and trails delight San Francisco Bay Area residents, is described here in closely observed detail by Harold Gilliam.

Wherever there are mountains, there are hills at their feet and valleys in between. Separating the Coast Ranges from the Sierra Nevada is the Great Central Valley, almost five hundred miles in length. The northern portion is known as the Sacramento Valley, and the southern the San Joaquin Valley, after the two rivers that drain them. David Mas Masumoto writes eloquently of the land that he farms near Del Rey, in the San Joaquin. Another prominent valley lies between the Transverse and Peninsular ranges: the populated Los Angeles Basin. Less great, but nonetheless dear to those who live or hike there, are the hundreds of smaller valleys and foothills throughout California. In this collection you will read about Napa Valley (Robert Louis Stevenson), Sonoma Valley (Jack London), Salinas Valley (William H. Brewer), the Altadena foothills (Hildegarde Flanner), Hemet Valley (M. F. K. Fisher), the Santa Barbara foothills (Margaret Millar), the San Rafael Wilderness (David Darlington), the Klamath Basin (Barry Lopez), and the Los Altos hills (Wallace Stegner).

California has three major deserts—the Mojave, the Colorado (or Sonoran), and the Great Basin. Each is unique and thus presents a special challenge to writers who wish to "explain" the desert. Here, the extremes of Death Valley are detailed by Edward Abbey; John Daniel and Sue Zwinger recollect memorable desert treks; Gary Paul Nabhan visits some oases in the Colorado Desert; and Mary Austin writes of the high desert of the Owens Valley.

California is delimited on the west by eight hundred miles of Pacific coastline, with its rocky headlands, bays, beaches, and offshore islands. This collection highlights various faces of this diverse margin. In the northern and central reaches we encounter the "lost coast" as it is walked by John McKinney; Russell Chatham narrates a fishing excursion on Bodega Bay; and Henry Miller describes his beloved Big Sur. Farther south, around Santa Barbara, J. Smeaton Chase and Jane Hollister Wheelwright travel on horseback on the beach, while Kem Nunn surfs the waves and Gretel Ehrlich hikes one of the Channel Islands. In the southland, T. H. Watkins and Lawrence Clark Powell reminisce about Dana Point and Malibu, respectively.

The elements—earthquakes, storms, fire—play a significant role in California. In the last section, the infamous San Andreas Fault is observed by James D. Houston and John McPhee. John Muir and Joan Didion write about the wind—a storm in the Sierra as experienced from the top of a tall tree, and a Santa Ana in Los Angeles—while Mary Austin and Jane Hollister Wheelwright describe the rain as it pours down on the Owens Valley and a Pacific beach. The aftermath of a forest fire is taken up by Margaret Millar.

Finally, in an afterword, Gary Snyder takes a broad look at California's environment and suggests ways in which it can be preserved.

I hope that this book will be kept on a nearby shelf by armchair naturalists and virtual wanderers, and in the backpacks of hikers and trekkers—to refresh and inspire them, like a dip in a cool mountain lake, and as a reminder of the "natural state" of California.

THE CREATION

Cahto Valley

The Creation

The creation myths of the Native American peoples of California have many elements in common. The following myth of the Cahto (sometimes spelled "Kato"), who inhabited Cahto and Long Valleys in Mendocino County and the upper drainage of the South Fork of the Eel River in Lake County, is a typical example. Collected in 1909 by the University of California ethnologist Pliny E. Goddard (1869–1928), it tells of the great deluge, after which Thunder, the original being, created the landscape, the animals, and humankind.

Every day it rained, every night it rained. All the people slept. The sky fell. The land was not. For a very great distance there was no land. The waters of the oceans came together. Animals of all kinds drowned. Where the water went there were no trees. There was no land.

People became. Seal, sea-lion, and grizzly built a dance-house. They looked for a place in vain. At Usal they built it, for there the ground was good. There are many sea-lions there. Whale became a human woman. That is why women are so fat. There were no grizzlies. There were no fish. Blue lizard was thrown into the water and became sucker. Bullsnake was thrown into the water and became black salmon. Salamander was thrown into the water and became hook-bill salmon. Grass-snake was thrown into the water and became steel-head salmon. Lizard was thrown into the water and became trout. . . .

"What will grow in the water?" he [the creator] asked. Seaweeds grew in the water. Abalones and mussels grew in the water. Two kinds of kelp grew in the ocean. Many different kinds grew there. . . .

"How will the water of the ocean behave? What will be in front of it?" he asked. "The water will rise up in ridges. It will settle back again. There will be sand. On top of the sand it will glisten," he said. "Old kelp will float ashore. Old whales will float ashore.

"People will eat fish, big fish," he said. "Sea-lions will come ashore. They will eat them. They will be good. Devil-fish, although they are ugly looking, will be good. The people will eat them. The fish in the ocean will be fat. They will be good.

"There will be many different kinds in the ocean. There will be water-panther. There will be stone-fish. He will catch people. Long-tooth-fish will kill sea-lion. He will feel around in the water.

"Sea-lion will have no feet. He will have a tail. His teeth will be large. There will be no trees in the ocean. The water will be powerful in the ocean," he said.

He placed redwoods and firs along the shore. At the tail of the earth, at the north, he made them grow. He placed land in walls along in front of the ocean. From the north he put down rocks here and there. Over there the ocean beats against them. Far to the south he did that. He stood up pines along the way. He placed yellow pines. Far away he placed them. He placed mountains along in front of the water. He did not stop putting them up, even way to the south.

Redwoods and various pines were growing. He looked back and saw them growing. The redwoods had become tall. He placed stones along. He made small creeks by dragging along his foot. "Wherever they flow this water will be good," he said. "They will drink this. Only the ocean they will not drink." That is why all drink, many different kinds of animals. "Because the water is good, because it is not salt, deer, elk, panther, and fishes will drink of it," he said. He caused trees to grow up along. When he looked behind himself he saw they had grown up. "Birds will drink, squirrels will drink," he said. "Many different kinds will drink. I am placing good water along the way."

Many redwoods grew up. He placed water along toward the south. He kicked out springs. "There will be springs,'" he said. "These will belong to the deer," he said of the deer-licks.

He took along a dog. "Drink this water," he told his dog. He, himself, drank of it. . . .

Tanbark oaks he made to spring up along the way. Many kinds, redwoods, firs, and pines, he caused to grow. He placed water along. . . . To make valleys for the streams he placed the land on edge. The mountains were large. They had grown. . . .

He threw salamanders and turtles into the creeks. "Eels will live in this stream," he said. "Fish will come into it. Hook-bill and black salmon will run up this creek. Last of all steel-heads will swim in it. Crabs, small eels, and day-eels will come up.

"Grizzlies will live in large numbers on this mountain. On this mountain will be many deer. The people will eat them. Because they have no gall they may be eaten raw. Deer meat will be very sweet. Panthers will be numerous. There will be many jack-rabbits on this mountain," he said.

He did not like yellow-jackets. He nearly killed them. He made blue-flies and wasps.

His dog walked along with him. "There will be much water in this stream," he said. "This will be a small creek and the fish will run in it. The fish will be good. There will be many suckers and trout in this stream."

"There will be brush on this mountain," he said. He made manzanita and white-thorn grow there. "Here will be a valley. Here will be many deer. There will be many grizzlies at this place. Here a mountain will stand. Many rattlesnakes, bull-snakes, and water snakes will be in this place. Here will be good land. It shall be a valley.

"There will be many owls here, the barking-owl, the screech-owl, and the little owl. There shall be many blue jays, grouse, and quails. Here on this mountain will be many wood-rats. Here shall be many varied robins. There shall be many woodcocks, yellow-hammers, and sapsuckers. Here will be herons and blackbirds. There will be many turtle-doves and pigeons. The kingfishers will catch fish. There will be many buzzards, and ravens. There will be many chicken-hawks. There will be many robins. On this high mountain there will be many deer," he said.

. . . The land had become good. The valleys had become broad. All kinds of trees and plants had sprung up. Springs had become and the water was flowing. . . .

"I have made a good earth, my dog," he said. "Walk fast, my dog." Acorns were on the trees. The chestnuts were ripe. The hazelnuts were ripe. The manzanita berries were getting white. All sorts of food had become good. The buckeyes were good. The peppernuts were black. The bunch grass was ripe. The grass-hoppers were growing. The clover was in bloom. The bear-clover was good. The mountains had grown. The rocks had grown. All kinds that are eaten had become good. "We made it good, my dog," he said. Fish for the people to eat had grown in the streams.

"We have come to the south now," he said. All the different kinds were matured. They started back, he and his dog. "We will go back," he said. "The mountains have grown up quickly. The land has become flat. The trout have grown. Good water is flowing. Walk fast. All things have become good. We have made them good, my dog. It is warm. The land is good.

" . . . We are about to arrive. We are close to home, my dog," he said. "I am about to get back north," he said to himself. "I am about to get back north. I am about to get back north. I am about to get back north," he said to himself.

That is all.

DARRYL BABE WILSON

Fall River Valley

Grampa Ramsey and the Great Canyon

Darryl Babe Wilson (b. 1939) was born at the confluence of Fall River and Pit River at Fall River Mills in northeastern California, "into two people": Atsuge-wi on his father's side and A-juma-wi on his mother's. He graduated from the University of California at Davis in 1992 with a major in English, and received his Ph.D. from the University of Arizona in 1997. He has spent his life preserving the oral tradition through his speaking and writing. His essays, poetry, and short fiction have appeared in numerous anthologies. This creation story first appeared in the quarterly News from Native California.

It was a summer before I kept track of time. In our decrepit automobile, we rattled into the driveway, a cloud of exhaust fumes, dust, and screaming, excited children. A half dozen ragged kids and an old black dog poured from the ancient vehicle. Confusion reigned supreme. Uncle Ramsey (after we became parents, his official title changed to "Grampa") was standing in the door of the comfortable little pine-board home just east of McArthur. Aunt Lorena was in her immaculate kitchen making coffee.

Just as quickly as we poured from the vehicle, we disappeared. There was a pervading silence. Always the crystal bowl rested on Aunt Lorena's kitchen table. Usually it held exotic, distant, tasty objects: oranges, bananas, store-bought candy! There seemed to be three hundred black, shiny eyes staring at the contents of that bowl, but we knew that we must wait for Aunt Lorena to say "when" before we could have the contents—which we instantly devoured.

I cannot remember if we had any cares. It was before I began the first grade. I didn't care if I had shoes or clothes. I didn't care about anything—except not to allow my brothers and sisters to have something that I couldn't. And when I did not know that they got something more than me, it didn't matter, really.

It seems that my "thoughts" were already focused upon some other objective. I listened to the old people. I remembered what they said, the tone of their voice, the waving of the hands. My mind registered the long silences between their choppy sentences and between their quiet words.

They spoke in our languages, A-Juma-wi and Opore-gee, and they used a very crude and stumbling English. The English words were strange. I preferred the "old language." As our lives moved into the world of the English speakers and our "old" language became less and less important and less and less used, something within the old people hesitated.

His employment as a "cowboy" came to an end when a shying horse threw him and he landed on his neck, nearly breaking it. After his days in the saddle faded, he worked on various ranches in the Fall River Valley until his retirement.

He spoke to us in Opore-gee (Dixie Valley language), giggling when the twins would say the words correctly after he explained them. We would have to go visit him many times before he would tell us a "real, not fake," story of our people and our history. During these times I took notes because a tape recorder "spooked" him; it mattered little what he was trying to say, the "ghost" inside the tape recorder affected him—he was occupied with the "ghost" instead of the lesson.

Close to the time of his "departure," he spoke of being "so old that I no longer think about the end, but think about the beginning again."

As a silent, powerful, unseen ship passing into an endless sea in the darkness, he moved into the spirit world to join his wife and others of our shattered little nation. He departed during the full moon of October 1986. Aunt Lorena preceded him by sixteen years.

Discard the rules of English kings and queens. Suspend logic. Grampa speaks as he learned to around campfires and in a distance so long ago that he claimed, "I didn't have enough good sense to listen good."

Grandfather's story:

HOW THE GREAT CANYON WAS MADE

[This canyon is between Fall River Mills and Barn, California, on the Pit River. Grandfather interchanges the names Qon and Silver-gray Fox occasionally. They are the same being in his thought.]

Qon [Silver-gray Fox] worked to make the world from a mist and a song long ago. He and Makada [Coyote] set to making things on earth. Makada was constantly trying to change things. Qon had the power to create. Makada had the power only to change things. He was always jealous because he could not create—he could only change. Qon created things. Makada always tried to change them. Qon persisted. Makada insisted. Sometimes he made a go of it. Sometimes Makada got his way. He sure was insistent, that Makada. [Smile, twinkle, and gruff giggle.]

His was the time when Qon put his place, his home—maybe you say "office"—on the Pit River/Hat Creek rim near Hogback [a small mountain]. From that place he could watch everything. This was before there was a Great Canyon, so Da-we-wewe and It-Ajuma [streams, including the Fall River and Pit River] could make it to the ocean, so salmon could come up there. Fall River and Dixie Valley are the valley drainage.

It [the office] was like an umbrella that you can look through but you could not see it—like a bubble or something but you can't see him [it]. When it rained, it did not rain in there. When it snowed, snow could not get in. Wind must go around. Storms and lightning bounced off. I don't know just how to say—as if an arch. Like a thinking or a thought or something.

I dunno. You couldn't touch it or see it. Anyhow, it was there so the Power could watch. Qon wanted everything just right. He knew he had to watch old Makada. It was bad. Qon needed help from Makada. Makada was insistent.

Qon molded earth like *wa-hach* [a form of bread made in an iron skillet without grease], flattened here, raised there. Everywhere not the same. It was when Chum-see-akoo was being made [the small area where the Hat Creek and Pit River come together and create a small peninsula in a shape like Argentina; Highway 299 East now runs through it]. Some call it Ya-nee-na. It was made. Qon wanted to name it. Makada wanted to name it. They talked. They argued.

Qon said, "Let's make some other things and get back to this place." So they did. They roamed and made *a-hew* [mountains] and *da-wi-wiwi* [streams] and *a-ju-juji* [springs]. Qon named these places. They returned to Chum-see-akoo/Ya-nee-na. Makada said, "You, brother, have named all of these other places. It is my turn to name this place right here." [A gruff giggle from Grandfather because Coyote called Silver-gray Fox "brother."]

Qon said, "No, you will call it by any name but a real name. Sometimes when you talk you don't make much sense. Let's go and make some more."

So they did. [Silver-gray Fox was in the process of making the Pit River Country into a livable place.]

Watching from a high bluff, Qon saw the insistence of Makada. He waited. Meanwhile, he forgot to make a place for the Pit River to run and drain the upper valley. He forgot to make a canyon. There was a mountain of solid rock. No canyon.

They returned to the small valley. Again they got in an argument. This time Qon give in. He give up. He got tired of arguments.

Makada called it Chum-see Akoo [Mice Valley] because he liked to eat mice. He really liked the taste of fresh mice. Today that is what we call it. Mice Valley. But what about the canyon that was filled with solid rock? The Pit River cannot run through it. The salmon must come so people can eat.

Qon looked and saw a wide spot below rock mountain. Rock mountain must be made into a canyon for Pit River. He spoke to big bass-sturgeon. "You must do this so river can run to the ocean." Sturgeon said, "Okay, but I am not strong enough to break that mountain." Qon said, 'Tomorrow I shall tell you what to do, after I think." Why did Qon have to think? I dunno.

Next day Qon said, "Go to the top of mountain [Mount Shasta] and get power." He went, then he swam back from mountain. He got back and took a run at it and hit it [the rock mountain] with his head. BANG! Again and again, BANG! It hurt. He got tired, and it hurt. Qon said, "Go back to the mountain for more power."

Meanwhile Makada was off doing something. He could not create. He was changing something. Always changing, Makada.

Sturgeon struck the mountain, BANG! again and again. Again and again. Again he got tired. Again it hurt. He went back to the mountaintop and got some more power. BANG! Old mountain rock he began to break. It got weakness. He cracked it! He got more power in a hurry. He broke it! Rocks were everywhere. Later they found some rocks clear up in Dixie [Valley]. Rocks flying everywhere. He broke through. He did it! He came out to Bo-ma-ree [Fall River Valley].

Qon said, "Good."

Meanwhile, Qon found Makada. He was up at the hot springs cooking quail eggs and looking with his head down seeing himself in the water. [Gruff giggle.] Makada always thought he was real cute.

When they came back, Makada noticed the great canyon. Qon looked at Makada. Makada looked away, with his tongue hanging sideways from his mouth, and said, "I didn't do it [make the canyon]. I was gathering quail eggs to boil in hot springs."

Looking to the rim today, you will see power [the "office"] is gone. Qon and Makada ran east up the canyon that was rushing with water [the Pit River]. There were more things to make. Maybe it was then that people were mad, but that is another story. Not for today.

We left Grampa Ramsey in possession of a "real, not fake," story. At times it seemed as if it was a story about creation in general, but it was, for the most part, a story of the Great Canyon. For this time spent with Grampa we are made richer. Richer in knowledge and understanding. Richer in language and the function of that language. Richer in the spiritual connection that binds us to the earth.

THE MOUNTAINS

Mt. Shasta

An Elk Hunt

*Joaquin Miller (1837–1913), born Cincinnatus Hiner Miller, was an eccentric,
larger-than-life poet, the self-styled "Byron of the West," who achieved great
popularity in his day but whose reputation has since melted into the mists. After
living in England for some years he retired to an estate he built in the hills of
Oakland, California. This hunting account is taken from his autobiography,*
Memorie and Rime *(1884).*

When the spring came tripping by from the south over the
chaparral hills of Shasta, leaving flowers in every footprint
as we passed, I set my face for Mount Shasta, the lightest-
hearted lad that ever mounted horse. A hard day's ride brought me to
Portuguese Flat, the last new mining camp and the nearest town to my
beloved Mount Shasta. Here I found my former partner in the Soda
Springs property, Mountain Joe, and together we went up to Mount
Shasta.

The Indian chief, Blackbeard, gave me a beautiful little valley then
known as Now-ow-wa, but now called by the euphonious name of
Squaw Valley, and I built a cabin there. As winter settled down and the
snow fell deep and fast, however, the Indians all retreated down from
out the spurs of Mount Shasta and took refuge on the banks of the

McCloud River. I nailed up my cabin and on snowshoes recrossed the fifteen miles of steep and stupendous mountains, and got down to winter at my old home, Soda Springs. But a new Yankee partner had got his grasp about the throat of things there, and instead of pitching him out into the snow I determined to give it all up and set my face where I left my heart, once more, finally and forever, with the Indians. Loaded down with arms and ammunition, one clear, frosty morning in December I climbed up the spur of Mount Shasta, which lay between me and my little valley of snow, and left the last vestige of civilization behind me. It was steep, hard climbing. Sometimes I would sink into the snow to my waist. Sometimes the snow would slide down the mountain and bear me back, half buried, to the place I had started from half an hour before. A marvel that I kept on. But there was hatred behind, there was love before—elements that have built cities and founded empires. As the setting sun gilded the snowy pines with gold I stood on the lofty summit, looking down into my unpeopled world of snow.

An hour of glorious gliding, darting, shooting on my snowshoes, and I stood on the steep bluff that girt above and about my little valley. A great, strange light, like silver, enveloped the land. Across the valley, on the brow of the mountain beyond, the curved moon, new and white and bright, gleamed before me like a drawn cimeter [*sic*] to drive me back. Down in the valley under me busy little foxes moved and shuttle-cocked across the level sea of snow. But I heard no sound nor saw any other sign of life. The solitude, the desolation, the silence, was so vast, so actual, that I could feel it—hear it. A strange terror came upon me there. And oh, I wished—how devoutly I wished I never shall forget— that I had not ventured on this mad enterprise. But I had burned my ship. It had been as impossible for me to return, tired, hungry, heartsick as I then was, as it had been for me to lay hold of the bright cold horns of the moon before me. With a sigh I tightened my belt, took up my rifle, which I had leaned against a pine, and once more shot ahead. Breaking open my cabin door, I took off my snowshoes and crept down the steep wall of snow, and soon had a roaring fire from the sweet-smelling pine wood that lay heaped in cords against the walls. Seven days I rested there, as lone as the moon in the cold blue above. Queer days! Queer thoughts I had there then. Those days left their impression clearly, as strange creatures of another age had left their footprints in the plastic clay that has become now solid stone. When the mind is so void, queer thoughts get into one's head; and they come and establish themselves and stay. I had some books, and read them all through. Here I first began to write.

On the eighth day my door darkened, and I sprang up from my work, rifle in hand. Two Indians, brave, handsome young fellows, one my best and dearest friend in all the world, stood before me. And sad tales they told me that night as I feasted them around my great fireplace. The tribe was starving over on the McCloud! The gold-diggers had so muddied and soiled the waters the season before that the annual run of salmon had failed. The Indians had for the first time in centuries no stores of dried salmon, and they were starving to death by the hundreds. And what was still more alarming, for it meant the ultimate destruction of all the Indians concerned, I was told that the natives of Pit River Valley had resolved to massacre all the settlers there. After a day's rest these two Indians, loaded with flour for the famishing tribe, set out to return. Again I was left alone, this time for nearly three weeks. The Indians returned with other young men to carry flour back to the famishing, while we who were strong and rested prepared for a grand hunt for a great band of elk which we knew wintered near the warm springs high up on the wood slopes of Mount Shasta. Perhaps I might mention here that this cabin full of provisions had remained untouched all the time of my absence. I will say further that I believe the last Indian would have starved to death rather than have touched one crumb of bread without permission. These Indians had never yet come in contact with any white man but myself. Such honesty I never knew as I found here. As for their valor and prowess, I can only point you to the Modoc battlefields, where the whole United States Army was held at bay so long nearly twenty years after, and pass on.

After great preparation, we struck out steeply up the mountain, and for three days wallowed through the snow in the dense, dark woods, when we struck the great elk trail. A single trail it was, and looked as if a saw-log had been drawn repeatedly through the snow. The bottom and sides of this trail were hard and smooth as ice. Perhaps a thousand elk had passed here. They had been breaking from one thicket of maple and other kinds of brush which they feed upon at such times, and we knew they could not have gone far through this snow, which reached above their backs. We hung up our snowshoes now and, looking to our arms, shot ahead full of delightful anticipation. At last, climbing a little hill, with clouds of steam rising from the warm springs of that region, we looked down into a little valley of thick undergrowth, and there calmly rested the vast herd of elk. I peered through the brush into the large, clear eyes of a great stag with a head of horns like a rocking chair. He was chewing his cud, and was not at all disconcerted. It is possible we were not yet discovered. More likely their numbers and strength gave them uncommon courage, and they were not to be easily frightened. I remember my two Indians looked at each other in surprise at their tranquillity. We lay there some time on our breasts in the snow, looking at them. The Indians observed that only the cows were fat and fit to kill. Some of the stags had somehow shed their horns, it seemed. There were no calves. So the Indians were delighted to know that there was yet another herd. We fell back, and formed our plan of attack at leisure. It was unique and desperate. We did not want one or two elk, or ten; we wanted the whole herd. Human life depended upon our prowess. A tribe was starving, and we felt a responsibility in our work. It was finally decided to go around and approach by the little stream, so that the herd would not start down it—their only means of escape. It was planned to approach as closely as possible, then fire with our rifles at the fattest, then burst in upon them, pistol in hand, and so, breaking their ranks, scatter them in the snow, where the Indians could rush upon them and use the bows and arrows at their backs.

Slowly and cautiously we approached up the little warm, willow-lined rivulet, and then, firing our rifles, we rushed into the corral, pistols in hand. The poor, helpless herd was on its feet in a second, all breaking out over the wall of snow, breast-high on all sides. Here they wallowed and floundered in the snow, shook their heads, and called helplessly to each other. They could not get on at all. And long after the last shot and the last arrow were spent I leisurely walked around and looked into the eyes of some of these fat, sleek cows as they lay there, up to their briskets, helpless in the snow. Of course the Indians had no sentiment in this matter. They wanted only to kill and secure meat for the hungry, and half an hour after the attack on the corral of elk they were quartering the meat and hanging it up in trees secure from the wolves. In this way they hung more than a hundred elk, not taking time to skin or dress them in any way. The tallow was heaped about our camp-fire, to be defended against the wolves at night. And such a lot of wolves as came that night! And such a noise, as we sat there feasting about the fire and talking of the day's splendid work. The next morning, loaded with tallow, my two young friends set out on the long, tedious journey to the starving camp on the McCloud River. They were going to bring the whole tribe, or at least such of them as could make the trip, and the remainder of our winter was to be spent on Mount Shasta. I was once more left alone. But as our ammunition at hand was spent, I was in great fear and in real danger of being devoured by wolves. They drew a circle around that camp and laid siege to it like an army of well-drilled soldiers. They would sit down on their haunches not twenty steps away and look at me in the most appetizing fashion. They would lick their chops, as if to say, "We'll get you yet; it's only a question of time." And I wish to put it on record that wolves, so far as I can testify, are better behaved than the books tell you they are. They snarled a little at each other as they sat there, over a dozen deep, around me, and even snapped now and then at each other's ears; but I saw not one sign of their eating or attempting to eat each other. By day they kept quiet, and only looked at me. But it was observed that each day they came and sat down a little bit closer. Night, of course, was made to ring with their howls both far and near, and I kept up a great fire.

At last—ah, relief of Lucknow!—my brave boys came back breath-less into camp. And after them for days came stringing, struggling, creeping, a long black line of withered, starving fellow-creatures. To see them eat! To see their hollow eyes fill and glow with gratitude! Ah, I have had some few summer days, some moments of glory, when the heart throbs full and the head tops heaven; but I have known no delight like this I knew there, and never shall. Christmas came and went, and I knew not when, for I had now in my careless happiness and full delight lost all reckoning of time.

Sierra Nevada

Ramblings in Yosemite

Joseph LeConte (1823–1901) was a popular professor of geology and natural history at the University of California, Berkeley. This excerpt is from A Journal of Ramblings *through the High Sierra of California (1875), written during his first journey to Yosemite as part of a university excursion party.*

JULY 30.— . . . In the afternoon we pushed on, to get our first view of Yosemite this evening, from Sentinel Dome and Glacier Point. . . . About 5 P.M. we passed a high pile of rocks, called Ostrander's Rocks. The whole trail, from Westfall's meadows to Glacier Point, is near eight thousand feet high. From this rocky prominence, therefore, the view is really magnificent. It was our first view of the peaks and domes about Yosemite, and of the more distant High Sierra, and we enjoyed it beyond expression. But there are still finer views ahead, which we must see this afternoon—yes, this very afternoon. With increasing enthusiasm we pushed on until, about 6 P.M., we reached and climbed Sentinel Dome. This point is 4,500 feet above Yosemite Valley, and 8,500 feet above the sea.

The view which here burst upon us, of the valley and the Sierra, it is simply impossible to describe. Sentinel Dome stands on the south margin of Yosemite, near the point where it branches into three canyons. To the left stand El Capitan's massive perpendicular wall; directly in front, and distant about one mile, Yosemite Falls, like a gauzy veil, rippling and waving with a slow, mazy motion; to the right the mighty granite mass of Half Dome lifts itself in solitary grandeur, defying the efforts of the climber; to the extreme right, and a little behind, Nevada Falls, with the Cap of Liberty; in the distance, innumerable peaks of the High Sierra, conspicuous among which are Clouds Rest, Mt. Starr King, Cathedral Peak, etc. We remained on the top of the dome more than an hour, to see the sunset. We were well repaid—such a sunset I never saw; such a sunset, combined with such a view, I had never imagined. The glorious golden and crimson in the west, and the exquisitely delicate diffused rose-bloom, tingeing the cloud caps of the Sierra in the east, and the shadows of the grand peaks and domes slowly creeping up the valley! I can never forget the impression. We remained, enjoying this scene, too long to think of going to Glacier Point this evening. We therefore put this off until morning, and returned to our trail about one and a half miles, to a beautiful green meadow, and there made camp in a grove of magnificent fir trees (*Albies magnifica*).

JULY 31 (SUNDAY).—I got up at peep of day this morning (I am dish-wash today), roused the party, started a fire, and in ten minutes tea was ready. All partook heartily of this delicious beverage, and started on foot to see the sunrise from Glacier Point. This point is about one and a half miles from our camp, about 3,100 feet above the valley, and forms the salient angle on the south side, just where the valley divides into three. We had to descend about eight hundred feet to reach it. We arrived just before sunrise. Sunrise from Glacier Point! No one can appreciate it who has not seen it. It was our good fortune to have an exceedingly beautiful sunrise. Rosy-fingered Aurora revealed herself to us, her votaries, more bright and charming and rosy than ever before. But the great charm was the view of the valley and surrounding peaks, in the fresh, cool morning hour and to the rosy light of the rising sun; the bright, warm light on the mountain tops, and the cool shade in the valley. The shadow of the grand Half Dome stretches clear across the valley, while its own "bald awful head" glitters in the early sunlight. To the right, Vernal and Nevada Falls, with their magnificent overhanging peaks, in full view; while directly across, see the ever-rippling, ever-swaying gauzy veil of the Yosemite Falls, reaching from top to bottom of the opposite cliff, 2,600 feet. Below, at a depth of 3,200 feet, the bottom of the valley lies like a garden. There, right under our noses, are the hotels, the orchards, the fields, the meadows, . . . the forests, and through all the Merced River winds its apparently lazy serpentine way. Yonder, up the Tenaya Canyon, nestling close under the shadow of Half Dome, lies Mirror Lake, fast asleep, her polished black surface not yet ruffled by the rising wind. I have heard and read much of this wonderful valley, but I can truly say I have never imagined the grandeur of the reality. After about one and a half hours' rapturous gaze, we returned to camp and breakfasted. I had left Glacier Point a few minutes before most of the party, as I was dishwash and had, therefore, to help cook prepare breakfast. At breakfast, I learned that two young men, Cobb and Perkins, had undertaken the foolish enterprise of going down into the valley by a canyon just below Glacier Point, and returning by 4 P.M. Think of it! 3,300 feet perpendicular, and the declivity, it seemed to me, about forty-five degrees in the canyon!

After breakfast we returned to Glacier Point and spent the whole of the beautiful Sunday morning in the presence of grand mountains, yawning chasms, and magnificent falls. What could we do better than allow these to preach to us? Was there ever so venerable, majestic, and eloquent a minister of natural religion as the grand old Half Dome? I withdrew myself from the rest of the party and drank in his silent teachings for several hours. About 1 P.M. climbed Sentinel Dome and enjoyed again the matchless panoramic view from this point, and about 2 P.M. returned to camp.

Our camp is itself about four thousand feet above the valley, and eight thousand above sea level. By walking about one hundred yards from our camp-fire, we get a most admirable view of the Sierra, and particularly a most wonderfully striking view of the unique form of Half Dome when seen in profile. I enjoyed this view until nearly time to saddle up.

Our plan is to return to Peregoy's, only seven miles, this afternoon, and go to Yosemite tomorrow morning. It is 3:30 P.M., and the young men who went down into the valley have not yet returned. We feel anxious. Will they return, or remain in the valley? Shall we remain tonight and wait for them, or go on, leading their horses, with the expectation of meeting them in the valley? We are to leave at four; we must decide soon. These discussions were cut short by the appearance of the delinquents themselves, faint with fatigue. They had been down, taken dinner, and returned. We started immediately for Peregoy's, where we arrived, 6 P.M., and camped in a grove on the margin of a fine meadow. At Peregoy's we bought a quarter of mountain mutton. We have been living on bacon and bread for some time. The voracity with which we devoured that mutton may be more easily imagined than described.

Ever since we have approached the region of the High Sierra, I have observed the great massiveness and grandeur of the clouds and the extreme blueness of the sky. In the direction of the Sierra hang always magnificent piles of snow-white cumulus, sharply defined against the deep-blue sky. These cloud-masses have ever been my delight. I have missed them sadly since coming to California, until this trip. I now welcome them with joy. Yesterday and today I have seen, in so many places, snow lying on the northern slopes of the high peaks of the Sierra.

AUGUST 1.—Yosemite today! Started as usual, 7 A.M. . . . Glorious ride this morning through the grand fir forests. This is enjoyment, indeed. The trail is tolerably good until it reaches the edge of Yosemite chasm. On the trail a little way below this edge there is a jutting point, called "Inspiration Point," which gives a good general view of the lower end of the valley, including El Capitan, Cathedral Rock, and a glimpse of Bridalveil Fall. After taking this view we began the descent into the valley. The trail winds backward and forward on the almost perpendicular sides of the cliff, making a descent of about three thousand feet in three miles. It was so steep and rough that we preferred walking most of the way and leading the horses. Poor old Mrs. Hopkins, though a heavy old lady, was afraid to ride, and therefore walked the whole way. At last, 10 A.M., we were down, and the gate of the valley is before us, El Capitan guarding it on the left and Cathedral Rock on the right, while over the precipice on the right the silvery gauze of Bridalveil is seen swaying to and fro.

We encamped in a fine forest on the margin of Bridalveil Meadow, under the shadow of El Capitan, and about one-quarter of a mile from Bridalveil Fall. Turned our horses loose to graze, cooked our midday meal, refreshed ourselves by swimming in the Merced, and then, 4:30 P.M., started to visit Bridalveil. We had understood that this was the best time to see it. Very difficult clambering to the foot of the fall up a steep incline, formed by a pile of huge boulders fallen from the cliff. The enchanting beauty and exquisite grace of this fall well repaid us for the toil. At the base of the fall there is a beautiful pool. Standing on the rocks on the margin of this pool, right opposite the fall, a most perfect unbroken circular rainbow is visible. Sometimes it is a double circular rainbow. The cliff more than six hundred feet high; the wavy, billowy, gauzy veil reaching from top to bottom; the glorious crown, woven by the sun for this beautiful veiled bride—those who read must put these together and form a picture for themselves by the plastic power of the imagination.

Some of the young men took a swim in the pool and a shower-bath under the fall. I would have joined them, but I had just come out of the Merced River. After enjoying this exquisite fall until after sunset, we returned to camp. On our way back, amongst the loose rocks on the stream margin, we found and killed another rattlesnake. This is the fourth we have killed.

Lake Tahoe

Mark Twain (1813–1890) still went by the name Samuel Clemens when he came west in 1861, where he spent a total of seven years, mostly in Nevada and California. His recollection of the period, Roughing It *(1872), has chapters on two lakes, Mono and Tahoe, that lie along the border of the two states. Mono Lake he detested; Tahoe he held to be the "fairest picture" there ever was.*

We tramped a long time on level ground, and then toiled laboriously up a mountain about a thousand miles high and looked over. No lake there. We descended on the other side, crossed the valley, and toiled up another mountain three or four thousand miles high, apparently, and looked over again. No lake yet. We sat down, tired and perspiring, and hired a couple of Chinamen to curse those people who had beguiled us. Thus refreshed, we presently resumed the march with renewed vigor and determination. We plodded on, two or three hours longer, and at last the lake burst upon us—a noble sheet of blue water lifted six thousand three hundred feet above the level of the sea, and walled in by a rim of snow-clad mountain peaks that towered aloft a full three thousand feet higher still! It was a vast oval, and one would have to use up eighty or a hundred good miles in traveling around it. As it lay there with the shadows of the mountains brilliantly photographed upon its still surface, I thought it must surely be the fairest picture the whole earth affords.

We found the small skiff belonging to the brigade boys and, without loss of time, set out across a deep bend of the lake toward the landmarks that signified the locality of the camp. I got Johnny to row—not because I mind exertion myself, but because it makes me sick to ride backward when I am at work. But I steered. A three-mile pull brought us to the camp just as the night fell, and we stepped ashore very tired and wolfishly hungry. In a "cache" among the rocks we found the provisions and the cooking utensils, and then, all fatigued as I was, I sat down on a boulder and superintended while Johnny gathered wood and cooked supper. Many a man who had gone through what I had would have wanted to rest.

It was a delicious supper—hot bread, fried bacon, and black coffee. It was a delicious solitude we were in, too. Three miles away was a sawmill and some workmen, but there were not fifteen other human beings throughout the wide circumference of the lake. As the darkness closed down and the stars came out and spangled the great mirror with jewels, we smoked meditatively in the solemn hush and forgot our troubles and our pains. In due time we spread our blankets in the warm sand between two large boulders and soon fell asleep, careless of the procession of ants that passed in through rents in our clothing and explored our persons. Nothing could disturb the sleep that fettered us, for it had been fairly earned, and if our consciences had any sins on them they had to adjourn court for that night, anyway. The wind rose just as we were losing consciousness, and we were lulled to sleep by the beating of the surf upon the shore.

It is always very cold on that lake shore in the night, but we had plenty of blankets and were warm enough. We never moved a muscle all night, but we waked at early dawn in the original positions, and got up at once, thoroughly refreshed, free from soreness, and brimful of friskiness. There is no end of wholesome medicine in such an experience. That morning we could have whipped ten such people as we were the day before—sick ones at any rate. But the world is slow, and people will go to "water cures" and "movement cures" and to foreign lands for health. Three months of camp life on Lake Tahoe would restore an Egyptian mummy to his pristine vigor and give him an appetite like an alligator. I do not mean the oldest and driest mummies, of course, but the fresher ones. The air up there in the clouds is very pure and fine, bracing and delicious. And why shouldn't it be?—it is the same the angels breathe. I think that hardly any amount of fatigue can be gathered together that a man cannot sleep off in one night on the sand by its side. Not under a roof, but under the sky; it seldom or never rains there in the summertime. I know a man who went there to die. But he made a failure of it. He was a skeleton when he came and could barely stand. He had no appetite and did nothing but read tracts and reflect on the future. Three months later he was sleeping out of doors regularly, eating all he could hold three times a day, and chasing game over mountains three thousand feet high for recreation. And he was a skeleton no longer, but weighed part of a ton. This is no fancy sketch, but the truth. His disease was consumption. I confidently commend his experience to other skeletons.

I superintended again, and as soon as we had eaten breakfast we got in the boat and skirted along the lake shore about three miles and disembarked. We liked the appearance of the place, and so we claimed some three hundred acres of it and stuck our "notices" on a tree. It was yellow-pine timberland—a dense forest of trees a hundred feet high and from one to five feet through at the butt. It was necessary to fence our property or we could not hold it. That is to say, it was necessary to cut down trees here and there and make them fall in such a way as to form a sort of enclosure (with pretty wide gaps in it). We cut down three trees apiece, and found it such heartbreaking work that we decided to "rest our case" on those; if they held the property, well and good; if they didn't, let the property spill out through the gaps and go; it was no use to work ourselves to death merely to save a few acres of land. Next day we came back to build a house—for a house was also necessary, in order to hold the property. We decided to build a substantial log house and excite the envy of the brigade boys; but by the time we had cut and trimmed the first log it seemed unnecessary to be so elaborate, and so we concluded to build it of saplings. However, two saplings, duly cut and trimmed, compelled recognition of the fact that a still modester architecture would satisfy the law, and so we concluded to build a "brush" house. We devoted the next day to this work, but we did so much "sitting around" and discussing that by the middle of the afternoon we had achieved only a halfway sort of affair which one of us had to watch while the other cut brush, lest if both turned our backs we might not be able to find it again, it had such a strong family resemblance to the surrounding vegetation. But we were satisfied with it.

We were landowners now, duly seized and possessed, and within the protection of the law. Therefore we decided to take up our residence on our own domain and enjoy that large sense of independence which only such an experience can bring. Later the next afternoon, after a good long rest, we sailed away from the brigade camp with all the provisions and cooking utensils we could carry off—borrow is the more accurate word—and just as the night was falling we beached the boat at our own landing.

If there is any life that is happier than the life we led on our timber ranch for the next two or three weeks, it must be a sort of life which I have not read of in books or experienced in person. We did not see a human being but ourselves during the time, or hear any sounds but those that were made by the wind and the waves, the sighing of the pines, and now and then the far-off thunder of an avalanche. The forest about us was dense and cool, the sky above us was cloudless and brilliant with sunshine, the broad lake before us was glassy and clear, or rippled and breezy, or black and storm-tossed, according to Nature's mood; and its circling border of mountain domes, clothed with forests, scarred with landslides, cloven by canyons and valleys, and helmeted with glittering snow, fitly framed and finished the noble picture. The view was always fascinating, bewitching, entrancing. The eye was never tired of gazing, night or day, in calm or storm; it suffered but one grief, and that was that it could not look always, but must close sometimes in sleep.

We slept in the sand close to the water's edge, between two protecting boulders, which took care of the stormy night winds for us. We never took any paregoric to make us sleep. At the first break of dawn we were always up and running foot races to tone down excess of physical vigor and exuberance of spirits. That is, Johnny was—but I held his hat. While smoking the pipe of peace after breakfast we watched the sentinel peaks put on the glory of the sun, and followed the conquering light as it swept down among the shadows and set the captive crags and forests free. We watched the tinted pictures grow and brighten upon the water till every little detail of forest, precipice, and pinnacle was wrought in and finished, and the miracle of the enchanter complete. Then to "business."

That is, drifting around in the boat. We were on the north shore. There, the rocks on the bottom are sometimes gray, sometimes white. This gives the marvelous transparency of the water a fuller advantage than it has elsewhere on the lake. We usually pushed out a hundred yards or so from shore, and then lay down on the thwarts, in the sun, and let the boat drift by the hour whither it would. We seldom talked. It interrupted the Sabbath stillness, and marred the dreams the luxurious rest and indolence brought. The shore all along was indented with deep, curved bays and coves, bordered by narrow sand beaches; and where the sand ended, the steep mountainsides rose right up aloft into space—rose up like a vast wall a little out of the perpendicular, and thickly wooded with tall pines.

So singularly clear was the water that when it was only twenty or thirty feet deep the bottom was so perfectly distinct that the boat seemed floating in the air! Yes, where it was even *eighty* feet deep. Every little pebble was distinct, every speckled trout, every hand's-breadth of sand. Often, as we lay on our faces, a granite boulder, as large as a village church, would start out of the bottom apparently, and seem climbing up rapidly to the surface, till presently it threatened to touch our faces, and we could not resist the impulse to seize an oar and avert the danger. But the boat would float on, and the boulder descend again, and then we could see that when we had been exactly above it, it must still have been twenty or thirty feet below the surface. Down through the transparency of these great depths, the water was not *merely* transparent, but dazzlingly, brilliantly so. All objects seen through it had a bright, strong vividness, not only of outline, but of every minute detail, which they would not have had when seen simply through the same depth of atmosphere. So empty and airy did all spaces seem below us, and so strong was the sense of floating high aloft in mind-nothingness, that we called these boat excursions "balloon voyages."

We fished a great deal, but we did not average one fish a week. We could see trout by the thousand winging about in the emptiness under us, or sleeping in shoals on the bottom, but they would not bite—they could see the line too plainly, perhaps. We frequently selected the trout we wanted, and rested the bait patiently and persistently on the end of his nose at a depth of eighty feet, but he would only shake it off with an annoyed manner, and shift his position.

We bathed occasionally, but the water was rather chilly, for all it looked so sunny. Sometimes we rowed out to the "blue water," a mile or two from shore. It was as dead blue as indigo there, because of the immense depth. By official measurement the lake in its center is one thousand five hundred and twenty-five feet deep!

Sometimes, on lazy afternoons, we lolled on the sand in camp, and smoked pipes, and read some old well-worn novels. At night by the campfire, we played euchre and seven-up to strengthen the mind—and played them with cards so greasy and defaced that only a whole summer's acquaintance with them could enable the student to tell the ace of clubs from the jack of diamonds.

We never slept in our "house." It never recurred to us, for one thing; and besides, it was built to hold the ground, and that was enough. We did not wish to strain it.

By and by our provisions began to run short, and we went back to the old camp and laid in a new supply. We were gone all day, and headed home again about nightfall, pretty tired and hungry. While Johnny was carrying the main bulk of the provisions up to our "house" for future use, I took the loaf of bread, some slices of bacon, and the coffeepot ashore, set them down by a tree, lit a fire, and went back to the boat to get the frying pan. While I was at this, I heard a shout from Johnny, and looking up I saw that my fire was galloping all over the premises!

Johnny was on the other side of it. He had to run through the flames to get to the lake shore, and then we stood helpless and watched the devastation.

The ground was deeply carpeted with dry pine needles, and the fire touched them off as if they were gunpowder. It was wonderful to see with what fierce speed the tall sheet of flame traveled! My coffeepot was gone, and everything with it. In a minute and a half the fire seized upon a dense growth of dry manzanita chaparral six or eight feet high, and then the roaring and popping and crackling was something terrific. We were driven to the boat by the intense heat, and there we remained, spellbound.

Within half an hour all before us was a tossing, blinding tempest of flames! It went surging up adjacent ridges—surmounted them and disappeared in the canyons beyond—burst into view upon higher and farther ridges, presently—shed a grander illumination abroad, and dove again—flamed out again, directly, higher and still higher up the mountainside—threw out skirmishing parties of fire here and there, and sent them trailing their crimson spirals away among remote ramparts and ribs and gorges, till as far as the eye could reach the lofty mountain fronts were webbed as it were with a tangled network of red lava streams. Away across the water the crags and domes were lit with a ruddy glare, and the firmament above was a reflected hell!

Every feature of the spectacle was repeated in the glowing mirror of the lake! Both pictures were sublime, both were beautiful; but that in the lake had a bewildering richness about it that enchanted the eye and held it with the stronger fascination.

We sat absorbed and motionless through four long hours. We never thought of supper, and never felt fatigue. But at eleven o'clock the conflagration had traveled beyond our range of vision, and the darkness stole down upon the landscape again.

Hunger asserted itself now, but there was nothing to eat. The provisions were all cooked, no doubt, but we did not go to see. We were homeless wanderers again, without any property. Our fence was gone, our house burned down; no insurance. Our pine forest was well scorched, the dead trees all burned up, and our broad acres of manzanita swept away. Our blankets were on our usual sand bed, however, and so we lay down and went to sleep. The next morning we started back to the old camp, but while out a long way from shore, so great a storm came up that we dared not try to land. So I baled out the seas we shipped, and Johnny pulled heavily through the billows till we had reached a point three or four miles beyond the camp. The storm was increasing, and it became evident that it was better to take the hazard of beaching the boat than to go down in a hundred fathoms of water; so we ran in, with tall whitecaps following, and I sat down in the stern sheets and pointed her head-on to the shore. The instant the bow struck, a wave came over the stern that washed crew and cargo ashore, and saved a deal of trouble. We shivered in the lee of a boulder all the rest of the day, and froze all the night through. In the morning the tempest had gone down, and we paddled down to the camp without any unnecessary delay. We were so starved that we ate up the rest of the brigade's provisions, and then set out to Carson to tell them about it and ask their forgiveness. It was accorded, upon payment of damages.

We made many trips to the lake after that, and had many a hairbreadth escape and bloodcurdling adventure which will never be recorded in any history.

JACK KEROUAC

Sierra Nevada

Climbing
Matterhorn Peak

Jack Kerouac (1922–1969) was at the center of the Beat Generation of writers that sprang up in San Francisco during the 1950s. His novel On the Road *(1957), with its energized first-person narrative and what Kerouac called "spontaneous prose," was a seminal work of that movement. His "true-story novel"* The Dharma Bums *(1958) includes the following section about a climb up Yosemite's Matterhorn Peak made by Ray Smith (Kerouac's alter ego), Henry Morley, and Japhy Ryder, a Zen-quoting free spirit modeled on the poet Gary Snyder.*

"Well here we go" said Japhy. "When I get tired of this big rucksack we'll swap."

"I'm ready now, man, come on, give it to me now, I feel like carrying something heavy. You don't realize how good I feel, man, come on." So we swapped packs and started off.

Both of us were feeling fine and were talking a blue streak, about anything, literature, the mountains, girls, Princess, the poets, Japan, our past adventures in life, and I suddenly realized it was a kind of blessing in disguise Morley had forgotten to drain the crankcase, otherwise Japhy wouldn't have got in a word edgewise all the blessed day and now I had a chance to hear his ideas. In the way he did things, hiking, he reminded me of Mike my boyhood chum who also loved to lead the way, real grave like Buck Jones, eyes to the distant horizons, like Natty Bumppo, cautioning me about snapping twigs or "It's too deep here, let's go down the creek a ways to ford it," or "There'll be mud in that low bottom, we better skirt around" and dead serious and glad. I saw all Japhy's boyhood in those eastern Oregon forests the way he went about it. He walked like he talked, from behind I could see his toes pointed slightly inward, the way mine do, instead of out, but when it came time to climb he pointed his toes out, like Chaplin, to make a kind of easier flapthwap as he trudged. We went across a kind of muddy riverbottom through dense undergrowth and a few willow trees and came out on the other side a little wet and started up the trail, which was clearly marked and named and had been recently repaired by trail crews but as we hit parts where a rock had rolled on the trail he took great precaution to throw the rock off saying "I used to work on trail crews, I can't see a trail all mettlesome like that, Smith." As we climbed the lake began to appear below us and suddenly in its clear blue pool we could see the deep holes where the lake had its springs, like black wells, and we could see schools of fish skitter.

"Oh this is like an early morning in China and I'm five years old in beginningless time!" I sang out and felt like sitting by the trail and whipping out my little notebook and writing sketches about it.

"Look over there," sang Japhy, "yellow aspens. Just put me in the mind of a haiku . . . 'Talking about the literary life—the yellow aspens.'" Walking in this country you could understand the perfect gems of haikus the Oriental poets had written, never getting drunk in the mountains or anything but just going along as fresh as children writing down what they saw without literary devices or fanciness of expression. We made up haikus as we climbed, winding up and up now on the slopes of brush.

"Rocks on the side of the cliff," I said, "why don't they tumble down?"

"Maybe that's a haiku, maybe not. It might be a little too complicated," said Japhy. "A real haiku's gotta be as simple as porridge and yet make you see the real thing, like the greatest haiku of them all probably is the one that goes 'The sparrow hops along the veranda, with wet feet,' by Shiki. You see the wet footprints like a vision in your mind and yet in those few words you also see all the rain that's been falling that day and almost smell the wet pine needles."

"Let's have another."

"I'll make up one of my own this time, let's see. 'Lake below . . . the black holes the wells make,' no that's not a haiku goddammit, you never can be too careful about haiku."

"How about making them up real fast as you go along, spontaneously?"

"Look here," he cried happily, "mountain lupine, see the delicate blue color those little flowers have. And there's some California red poppy over there. The whole meadow is just powdered with color! Up there by the way is a genuine California white pine, you never see them much any more."

"You sure know a lot about birds and trees and stuff."

"I've studied it all my life." Then also as we went on climbing we began getting more casual and making funnier sillier talk and pretty soon we got to a bend in the trail where it was suddenly gladey and dark with shade and a tremendous cataracting stream was bashing and frothing over scummy rocks and tumbling on down, and over the stream was a perfect bridge formed by a fallen snag, we got on it and lay belly-down and dunked our heads down, hair wet, and drank deep as the water splashed in our faces, like sticking your head by the jet of a dam. I lay there a good long minute enjoying the sudden coolness.

"This is like an advertisement for Rainier Ale!" yelled Japhy.

"Let's sit awhile and enjoy it."

"But you don't know how far we got to go yet!"

"Well I'm not tired!"

"Well you'll be, Tiger."

We went on, and I was immensely pleased with the way the trail had a kind of immortal look to it, in the early afternoon now, the way the side of the grassy hill seemed to be clouded with ancient gold dust and the bugs flipped over rocks and the wind sighed in shimmering dances over the hot rocks, and the way the trail would suddenly come into a cool shady part with big trees overhead, and here the light deeper. And the way the lake below us soon became a toy lake with those black well holes perfectly visible still, and the giant cloud shadows on the lake, and the tragic little road winding away where poor Morley was walking back.

"Can you see Morl down back there?"

Japhy took a long look. "I see a little cloud of dust, maybe that's him comin back already." But it seemed that I had seen the ancient afternoon of that trail, from meadow rocks and lupine posies, to sudden revisits with the roaring stream with its splashed snag bridges and undersea greennesses, there was something inexpressibly broken in my heart as though I'd lived before and walked this trail, under similar circumstances with a fellow Bodhisattva, but maybe on a more important journey. I felt like lying down by the side of the trail and remembering it all. The woods do that to you, they always look familiar, long lost, like the face of a long-dead relative, like an old dream, like a piece of forgotten song drifting across the water, most of all like golden eternities of past childhood or past manhood and all the living and the dying and the heartbreak that went on a million years ago and the clouds as they pass overhead seem to testify (by their own lonesome familiarity) to this feeling. Ecstasy, even, I felt, with flashes of sudden remembrance, and feeling sweaty and drowsy I felt like sleeping and dreaming in the grass. As we got high we got more tired and now like two true mountain climbers we weren't talking any more and didn't have to talk and were glad, in fact Japhy mentioned that, turning to me after a half-hour's silence, "This is the way I like it, when you get going there's just no need to talk, as if we were animals and just communicated by silent telepathy." So huddled in our own thoughts we tromped on, Japhy using that gazotsky trudge I mentioned, and myself finding my own true step, which was short steps slowly patiently going up the mountain at one mile an hour, so I was always thirty yards behind him and when we had any haikus now we'd yell them fore and aft. Pretty soon we got to the top of the part of the trail that was a trail no more, to the incomparable dreamy meadow, which had a beautiful pond, and after that it was boulders and nothing but boulders.

"Only sign we have now to know which way we're going, is ducks."

"What ducks?"

"See those boulders over there?"

"See those boulders over there! Why God man, I see five miles of boulders leading up to that mountain."

"See the little pile of rocks on that near boulder there by the pine? That's a duck, put up by other climbers, maybe that's one I put up myself in 'fifty-four I'm not sure. We just go from boulder to boulder from now on keeping a sharp eye for ducks then we get a general idea how to raggle along. Although of course we know which way we're going, that big cliff face up there is where our plateau is."

"Plateau? My God you mean that ain't the top of the mountain?"

"Of course not, after that we got a plateau and then scree and then more rocks and we get to a final alpine lake no biggern this pond and then comes the final climb over one thousand feet almost straight up boy to the top of the world where you'll see all California and parts of Nevada and the wind'll blow right through your pants."

"Ow . . . How long does it all take?"

"Why the only thing we can expect to make tonight is our camp up there on that plateau. I call it a plateau, it ain't that at all, it's a shelf between heights."

But the top and the end of the trail was such a beautiful spot I said: "Boy look at this . . . " A dreamy meadow, pines at one end, the pond, the clear fresh air, the afternoon clouds rushing golden . . . "Why don't we just sleep here tonight, I don't think I've ever seen a more beautiful park."

"Ah this is nowhere. It's great of course, but we might wake up tomorrow morning and find three dozen school-teachers on horseback frying bacon in our backyard. Where we're going you can bet your ass there won't be one human being, and if there is, I'll be a spotted horse's ass. Or maybe just one mountain climber, or two, but I don't expect so at this time of the year. You know the snow's about to come here any time now. If it comes tonight it's goodbye me and you."

"Well goodbye Japhy. But let's rest here and drink some water and admire the meadow." We were feeling tired and great. We spread out in the grass and rested and swapped packs and strapped them on and were rarin to go. Almost instantaneously the grass ended and the boulders started; we got up on the first one and from that point on it was just a matter of jumping from boulder to boulder, gradually climbing, climbing, five miles up a valley of boulders getting steeper and steeper with immense crags on both sides forming the walls of the valley, till near the cliff face we'd be scrambling up the boulders, it seemed.

"And what's behind that cliff face?"

"There's high grass up there, shrubbery, scattered boulders, beautiful meandering creeks that have ice in 'em even in the afternoon, spots of snow, tremendous trees, and one boulder just about as big as two of Alvah's cottages piled on top the other which leans over and makes a kind of concave cave for us to camp at, lightin a big bonfire that'll throw heat against the wall. Then after that the grass and the timber ends. That'll be at nine thousand just about."

Jumping from boulder to boulder and never falling, with a heavy pack, is easier than it sounds; you just can't fall when you get into the rhythm of the dance. I looked back down the valley sometimes and was surprised to see how high we'd come, and to see farther horizons of mountains now back there. Our beautiful trail-top park was like a little glen of the Forest of Arden. Then the climbing got steeper, the sun got redder, and pretty soon I began to see patches of snow in the shade of some rocks. We got up to where the cliff face seemed to loom over us. At one point I saw Japhy throw down his pack and danced my way up to him.

"Well this is where we'll drop our gear and climb those few hundred feet up the side of that cliff, where you see there it's shallower, and find that camp. I remember it. In fact you can sit here and rest or beat your bishop while I go rambling around there. I like to ramble by myself."

Okay. So I sat down and changed my wet socks and changed soaking undershirt for dry one and crossed my legs and rested and whistled for about a half-hour, a very pleasant occupation, and Japhy got back and said he'd found the camp. I thought it would be a little jaunt to our resting place but it took almost another hour to jump up the steep boulders, climb around some, get to the level of the cliff-face plateau, and there, on flat grass more or less, hike about two hundred yards to where a huge gray rock towered among pines. Here now the earth was a splendorous thing—snow on the ground, in melting patches in the grass, and gurgling creeks, and the huge silent rock mountains on both sides, and a wind blowing, and the smell of heather. We forded a lovely little creek, shallow as your hand, pearl pure lucid water, and got to the huge rock. . . .

At about noon we started out, leaving our big packs at the camp where nobody was likely to be till next year anyway, and went up the scree valley with just some food and first-aid kits. The valley was longer than it looked. In no time at all it was two o'clock in the afternoon and the sun was getting that later more golden look and a wind was rising and I began to think "By gosh how we ever gonna climb that mountain, tonight?"

I put it up to Japhy who said: "You're right, we'll have to hurry."

"Why don't we just forget it and go on home?"

"Aw come on Tiger, we'll make a run up that hill and then we'll go home." The valley was long and long and long. And at the top end it got very steep and I began to be a little afraid of falling down, the rocks were small and it got slippery and my ankles were in pain from yesterday's muscle strain anyway. But Morley kept walking and talking and I noticed his tremendous endurance. Japhy took his pants off so he could look just like an Indian, I mean stark naked, except for a jockstrap, and hiked almost a quarter-mile ahead of us, sometimes waiting awhile, to give us time to catch up, then went on, moving fast, wanting to climb the mountain today. Morley came second, about fifty yards ahead of me all the way. I was in no hurry. Then as it got later afternoon I went faster and decided to pass Morley and join Japhy. Now we were at about eleven thousand feet and it was cold and there was a lot of snow and to the east we could see immense snowcapped ranges and whooee levels of valleyland below them, we were already practically on top of California. At one point I had to scramble, like the others, on a narrow ledge, around a butte of rock, and it really scared me: the fall was a hundred feet, enough to break your neck, with another little ledge letting you bounce a minute preparatory to a nice goodbye one-thousand-foot drop. The wind was whipping now. Yet that whole afternoon, even more than the other, was filled with old premonitions or memories, as though I'd been there before, scrambling on these rocks, for other purposes more ancient, more serious, more simple. We finally got to the foot of Matterhorn where there was a most beautiful small lake unknown to the eyes of most men in this world, seen by only a handful of mountain-climbers, a small lake at eleven thousand some odd feet with snow on the edges of it and beautiful flowers and a beautiful meadow, an alpine meadow, flat and dreamy, upon which I immediately threw myself and took my shoes off. Japhy'd been there a half-hour when I made it, and it was cold now and his clothes were on again. Morley came up behind us smiling. We sat there looking up at the imminent steep scree slope of the final crag of Matterhorn.

"That don't look much, we can do it!" I said glad now.

"No, Ray, that's more than it looks. Do you realize that's a thousand feet more?"

"That much?"

"Unless we make a run up there, double-time, we'll never make it down again to our camp before nightfall and never make it down to the car at the lodge before tomorrow morning at, well at midnight."

"Phew."

"I'm tired," said Morley. "I don't think I'll try it."

"Well that's right," I said. "The whole purpose of mountain-climbing to me isn't just to show off you can get to the top, it's getting out to this wild country."

"Well I'm gonna go," said Japhy.

"Well if you're gonna go I'm goin with you."

"Morley?"

"I don't think I can make it. I'll wait here." And that wind was strong, too strong. I felt that as soon as we'd be a few hundred feet up the slope it might hamper our climbing.

Japhy took a small pack of peanuts and raisins and said "This'll be our gasoline, boy. You ready Ray to make a double-time run?"

"Ready. What about I say to the boys in The Place if I came all this way only to give up at the last minute?"

"It's late so let's hurry." Japhy started up walking very rapidly and then even running sometimes where the climb had to be to the right or left along ridges of scree. Scree is long landslides of rocks and sand, very difficult to scramble through, always little avalanches going on. At every few steps we took it seemed we were going higher and higher on a terrifying elevator. I gulped when I turned around to look back and see all of the state of California it would seem stretching out in three directions under huge blue skies with frightening planetary space clouds and immense vistas of distant valleys and even plateaus and for all I knew whole Nevadas out there. It was terrifying to look down and see Morley a dreaming spot by the little lake waiting for us. "Oh why didn't I stay with old Henry?" I thought. I now began to be afraid to go any higher from sheer fear of being too high. I began to be afraid of being blown away by the wind. All the nightmares I'd ever had about falling off mountains and precipitous buildings ran through my head in perfect clarity. Also with every twenty steps we took upward we both became completely exhausted.

"That's because of the high altitude Ray," said Japhy sitting beside me panting. "So have raisins and peanuts and you'll see what kick it gives you." And each time it gave us such a tremendous kick we both jumped up without a word and climbed another twenty, thirty steps. Then sat down again, panting, sweating in the cold wind, high on top of the world our noses sniffling like the noses of little boys playing late Saturday afternoon their final little games in winter. Now the wind began to howl like the wind in movies about the Shroud of Tibet. The steepness began to be too much for me; I was afraid now to look back any more; I peeked: I couldn't even make out Morley by the tiny lake.

"Hurry it up," yelled Japhy from a hundred feet ahead. "It's getting awfully late." I looked up to the peak. It was right there. I'd be there in five minutes. "Only a half-hour to go!" yelled Japhy. I didn't believe it. In five minutes of scrambling angrily upward I fell down and looked up and it was still just as far away. What I didn't like about that peak-top was that the clouds of all the world were blowing right through it like fog.

"Wouldn't see anything up there anyway," I muttered. "Oh why did I ever let myself into this?" Japhy was way ahead of me now, he'd left the peanuts and raisins with me, it was with a kind of lonely solemnity now he had decided to rush to the top if it killed him. He didn't sit down any more. Soon he was a whole football field, a hundred yards ahead of me, getting smaller. I looked back and like Lot's wife that did it. *"This is too high!"* I yelled to Japhy in a panic. He didn't hear me. I raced a few more feet up and fell exhausted on my belly, slipping back just a little. *"This is too high!"* I yelled. I was really scared. Supposing I'd start to slip back for good, these screes might start sliding any time anyway. That damn mountain got Japhy, I could see him jumping through the foggy air up ahead from rock to rock, up, up, just the flash of his foot bottoms. "How can I keep up with a maniac like that?" But with nutty desperation I followed him. Finally I came to a kind of ledge where I could sit at a level angle instead of having to cling not to slip, and I nudged my whole body inside the ledge just to hold me there tight, so the wind would not dislodge me, and I looked down and around and I had had it. *"I'm stayin here!"* I yelled to Japhy.

"Come on Smith, only another five minutes. I only got a hundred feet to go!"

"I'm staying right here! It's too high!"

He said nothing and went on. I saw him collapse and pant and get up and make his run again.

I nudged myself closer into the ledge and closed my eyes and thought "Oh what a life this is, why do we have to be born in the first place, and only so we can have our poor gentle flesh laid out to such impossible horrors as huge mountains and rock and empty space," and with horror I remembered the famous Zen saying, "When you get to the top of a mountain, keep climbing." The saying made my hair stand on end; it had been such cute poetry sitting on Alvah's straw mats. Now it was enough to make my heart pound and my heart bleed for being born at all. "In fact when Japhy gets to the top of that crag he *will* keep climbing, the way the wind's blowing. Well this old philosopher is staying right here," and I closed my eyes. "Besides," I thought, "rest and be kind, you don't have to prove anything." Suddenly I heard a beautiful broken yodel of strange musical and mystical intensity in the wind, and looked up, and it was Japhy standing on top of Matterhorn peak letting out his triumphant mountain-conquering Buddha Mountain Smashing song of joy. It was beautiful. It was funny, too, up here on the not-so-funny top of California and in all that rushing fog. But I had to hand it to him, the guts, the endurance, the sweat, and now the crazy human singing: whipped cream on top of ice cream. I didn't have enough strength to answer his yodel. He ran around up there and went out of sight to investigate the little flat top of some kind (he said) that ran a few feet west and then dropped sheer back down maybe as far as I care to the sawdust floors of Virginia City. It was insane. I could hear him yelling at me but I just nudged down at the small lake where Morley was lying on his back with a blade of grass in his mouth and said out loud "Now there's the karma of these three men here: Japhy Ryder gets to his triumphant mountaintop and makes it. I almost make it and have to give up and huddle in a bloody cave, but the smartest of them all is that poet's poet lyin down there with his knees crossed to the sky chewing on a flower dreaming by a gurgling *plage*, goddamit they'll never get me up here again."

Then suddenly everything was just like jazz: it happened in one insane second or so: I looked up and saw Japhy *running down the mountain* in huge twenty-foot leaps, running, leaping, landing with a great drive of his booted heels, bouncing five feet or so, running, then taking another long crazy yelling yodelaying sail down the sides of the world and in that flash I realized *it's impossible to fall off mountains you fool* and with a yodel of my own I suddenly got up and began running down the mountain after him doing exactly the same huge leaps, the same fantastic runs and jumps, and in the space of about five minutes I'd guess Japhy Ryder and I (in my sneakers, driving the heels of my sneakers right into sand, rock, boulders, I didn't care any more I was so anxious to get down out of there) came leaping and yelling like mountain goats or I'd say like Chinese lunatics of a thousand years ago, enough to raise the hair on the head of the meditating Morley by the lake, who said he looked up and saw us flying down and couldn't believe it. In fact with one of my greatest leaps and loudest screams of joy I came flying right down to the edge of the lake and dug my sneakered heels into the mud and just fell sitting there, glad. Japhy was already taking his shoes off and pouring sand and pebbles out. It was great. I took off my sneakers and poured out a couple of buckets of lava dust and said "Ah Japhy you taught me the final lesson of them all, you can't fall off a mountain."

"And that's what they mean by the saying, When you get to the top of a mountain keep climbing, Smith."

Mt. Tamalpais

A Mount for All Seasons

Harold Gilliam (b. 1918), a noted environmentalist, is a former staff writer and now frequent contributor to the San Francisco Chronicle. *In addition to hundreds of articles on environmental subjects, Gilliam has written sixteen books including* The Natural World of San Francisco *(1967) and* The San Francisco Experience *(1972), from which this essay on Marin County's cherished Mt. Tamalpais is taken.*

From Muir Woods, from Mill Valley, from almost any place around the base of Tamalpais, a trail network leads to all parts of the mountain, offering exploration and adventure, refreshment and renewal to all who can walk. In order to know this mountain of diverse moods, it is necessary to hike its trails in every season and every weather.

One August morning, for example, when San Francisco was dark beneath a heavy overcast, I drove to the mountain by way of Mill Valley and on the road above the town found myself in a thick fog. Switching on the windshield wipers, I continued slowly on the Panoramic Highway past Mountain Home, Bootjack, and Pantoll, then turned off for the road toward the summit, still fogbound. Suddenly I emerged from the mists and looked down on the roof of the layer of vapor, dazzling white in the sun. Below were big waves of fog, with shadows in the hollows. Slow volatile geysers rose from the crests of the waves to heights of one hundred feet or more and evaporated in the warm air above.

I parked near Rock Spring, where the sun was bright and warm. From the grove of big tanbark oaks next to the parking area came a crackling sound, as if some animal were walking among the dry leaves under the trees. I walked into the grove to investigate and was surprised to find that the trees were dripping copiously; the drops resounded as they hit the stiff brown tanbark leaves. For a moment I was puzzled as to why the trees were wet in the sun. Then it occurred to me that the fog had been in there all night, drenching the trees, and had burned off a few minutes before I arrived.

The theory was confirmed as I walked down the trail below the spring and noticed that the tawny grass in the meadow was still wet. The woods were aromatic with the smell of damp leaves in warm weather—the strong odor of the laurels, the special fragrance of live oaks and toyon and meadow grass, the Christmas-tree smell of the Douglas firs.

Rounding a bend, I came on a sight that brought me to a quick stop. There alongside the trail were several young Douglas firs still wet from the fog. From where I stood the sun was directly behind them, and every needle was bejeweled with drops of water that glistened in the morning light. Each drop reflected a different band of the spectrum, turning the sunlight into piercing reds and yellows, burning blues and purples. No Christmas tree was ever so brilliantly decked out as those Douglas firs with the fog jewelry on their needles.

The process of decoration had been a complicated one. Every drop of water had been lifted from the ocean by the moving masses of air, had been part of the great flowing fog bank, had been elevated two thousand feet above the ocean and hung with ten thousand others in resplendent array on these branches. All this elaborate preparation had taken place for a glittering display that would last only a few minutes, the interval between the lifting of the fog and the evaporation of the water particles. I had happened to come along at exactly the right time.

While I watched the spectacle began to disappear as the sun dried out each needle. The moisture passed invisibly into the air, seeming to give it a polished brilliance that sharpened the lines of trees and rocks and ridges in the sun.

The coming of the sunlight after the fog had produced an array of sounds almost as brilliant as the light on the leaves. Excited finches and sparrows twittered in the chaparral. Big jays cawed and chattered and whistled as they swooped among the live oaks. Woodpeckers beat out industrious rhythms on tree trunks. Yellow jackets buzzed and hummed in the chaparral, and from somewhere along a high wooded ridge came the scream of a red-tailed hawk. Underneath all the other sound there was a barely audible roar that might have been the imperceptible stirring of the leaves in the big Douglas firs on the ridge or perhaps even the far-off pounding of the surf along the oceanward foot of the mountain.

At a point where the trail led through a stretch of deep woods, the sunlight filtering through the canopy made patterns on the forest floor, illuminating the rich red browns of the dead leaves, and from the damp mossy bole of a big conifer a shaft of golden sunlight was raising a ghost of a vapor that drifted through the woods like an errant wisp of the vanished fog.

The same trail at another time or season is quite a different experience. The summertime hiker, the sunshine mountaineer, the fair-weather outdoorsman can participate in only a fraction of the beneficences this peak has to offer. He knows the mountain only in a time of quiescence, when the natural forces that created this magnificent parkland are at rest. To see the mountain in its full splendor, go there in fog or wind or rain; see the sun set and rise again; explore the high trails by the light of the stars and the woods in the full of the moon. Above all, to see the forces of creation at work, go at the climax of a winter storm, when the rain turns rivulets to torrents, the wind sets the groves and forests to waving and shaking, and the aroused energies of the mountain seem to radiate from the rocks themselves.

I took the trail down from Rock Spring during a rain one afternoon in November, listening to the music of the storm—the wind in the high branches overhead and the full range of tones of the moving waters. Over the mountain ten thousand springs were flowing copiously from the early storms; every gully was filled with a stream. Creeks that in August had been a mere trickle were now impassable torrents; in the larger canyons, cascades and cataracts and waterfalls shook the air with their thunder.

Light showers were falling as I strolled down the canyon between stands of big shiny-leaved madroños, through aromatic groves of laurels, past contorted live oaks arching over the trail. Outcrops of wet rock gleamed more brilliantly than they do in the brightest August sunshine. Every drop of water on the rock surface acted as a prism, both brightening the natural color and reflecting the light roundabout. Rocks that had a dull surface when dry now sparkled as if polished by a lapidary. Dun colors turned to orange and yellow; dull reds became rich ocher; outcrops of pale green serpentine were transformed into masses of shining emerald.

In the storm I became intimately aware of the force of the rushing water in sculpturing the mountain, in wearing away the rocks, in creating and deepening canyons, in depositing soil in the meadows and valleys. Consequently I noticed something that had not been evident to me before. About two hundred yards down the trail from Rock Spring, the canyon broadened to a grassy meadow. The stream, which above had been roaring over boulders in a white torrent, disappeared from view. I walked closer and found that the water had carved a miniature gorge with nearly vertical sides and was flowing six to eight feet below the level of the meadow. Here was an intriguing problem in geology. The walls of the gorge were not rock but rich alluvial soil that obviously had been deposited over a long period of time by slow-moving or still waters. I realized then that I was standing on the bed of an old lake or marsh.

At the lower end of this meadow the canyon bottom narrowed to about the width of the stream. Here, evidently, at some unknown time in the past, a landslide from the steep slopes above had blocked the stream, backing up the waters to form a lake. On the lake bed had been deposited the sediments I now saw being eroded away in the gorge. Probably in time the lake had been entirely filled with sediment and became a marsh or meadow. A flood breaching the landslide-dam would have caused the stream to flow swiftly again, rapidly cutting the gorge through the soft soil of the meadow.

At the foot of the old landslide a big Douglas fir, a century old or more, leaned precariously out over the stream, which was undermining the bank on which it stood. The curve of the trunk made me think that the tree had begun to lean about halfway in its lifetime, probably at the same time that the dam was breached and the stream began to deepen its bed. Another clue was that part of the gorge was thickly planted with relatively young Douglas firs, making a handsome wall of vegetation through the middle of the meadow. The firs were all about twenty-five feet high, indicating that they were of the same age. Evidently they had begun to grow here at the time when the stream had excavated the gorge down to the level of the new outlet and the cutting process was stabilized—perhaps thirty years ago. The gorge could not have been much older than that or its steep walls would have been eroded away long since. Such angularities do not last long in nature, and doubtless within a few more decades will disappear—along with most of the meadow.

Although I had hiked this same trail scores of times in fair weather, it had not occurred to me to look into the evolution of this meadow until I saw the full force of the flowing water during the storm and was acutely conscious of the forces that are continually creating and re-creating the landscape.

A totally different kind of experience with the mountain came one day in January, after a series of storms had been followed by a period of calm weather and tule fogs—the winter fogs that form in the cold inland valleys and move slowly westward toward the warmer ocean. From a high point in San Francisco I noticed a strange situation: instead of flowing outward through the Golden Gate as it would normally do at this time of year, the fog was flowing in from the ocean, as it would do in the summer. Wondering what could be the cause of this meteorological accident, I got in the car and headed for a grandstand view on Tamalpais. As the car climbed to the ridge above Mill Valley, through a gap in the hills I looked out to the bay and caught a quick glimpse that gave me a preview of the spectacle I was about to witness. Through Raccoon Strait, between Angel Island and Tiburon, a fog flood was pouring west. Climbing higher, I could see similar tongues flowing westward through the low saddles of the Tiburon Peninsula. There could be no doubt that this was a normal tule fog, forming inland and moving west. Yet at the same time the sea fog continued to blow in from the ocean through the Golden Gate. The two fog masses were on a collision course.

At Mountain Home, at the nine-hundred-foot elevation on Tamalpais, where the road leaves Throckmorton Ridge and turns west, I parked the car and continued up the ridge on foot, following the steep Throckmorton Trail. Here above the fog zone the sun beamed down warmly, but as I climbed to the upper part of the ridge I felt a breeze from the west—the advance guard of the fog moving in from the Pacific. The fog did not hang low on the water, as it would in the summertime, but was actually a deck of broken stratus clouds several hundred feet above the surface, as far west over the ocean as I could see.

This is the kind of fog-cloud that often heralds an approaching storm front. Actually, I learned later that there was at the time a storm center moving from the ocean across northern California and southern Oregon. I was standing at the extreme edge of the storm area, around which the air masses were moving, as they always do, in a counterclockwise direction, bringing the wind and fog and clouds to this area from the west. It was this foggy southern edge of the storm that was moving in over the coastal hills and about to collide with the westward-moving tule fogs around the bay. I hurried on up the ridge to witness what promised to be a major clash of the elements.

Higher up, I looked out on an extraordinary sight. The bay itself was almost completely covered with a thin white film of tule fog, as if wind-blown snow had drifted across the surface of a frozen lake. The hump-backed deck of the Richmond–San Rafael Bridge seemed to rest on the white expanse, and its foghorn moaned a bass dirge. Near the bridge, two ships appeared to be half sunken, the vapors level with their upper decks.

Suddenly I was startled by what appeared to be a silent explosion in a canyon directly below me. A big puff of white vapor forty feet high appeared from nowhere, rose, and drifted away. Then, at the head of an adjacent canyon, another smokelike puff appeared, boiled upward into a familiar mushroom shape, then disappeared. Responding to an old wartime reflex, I had an instinct to hit the dirt. In appearance the phenomenon was uncomfortably reminiscent of an artillery barrage.

Then, as similar "explosions" took place just at the heads of the canyons below, I realized what had happened. Masses of cool ocean air, moving in ahead of the fog and clouds, had reached the canyons above Muir Woods and Mill Valley, followed the canyons upward as if in a chute, cooled as they rose, and just below me had reached the point at which their moisture condensed into visible puffs of vapor.

I climbed on up beyond the area of "bombardment" to the summit of the East Peak of Tamalpais. Here a cold wind from the storm front was howling in from the west-northwest. I crouched on the lee side of the lookout station and gazed down across the bay. Along the near shore, the filmy fog covering the water had accumulated into drifts that buried the towns of San Rafael and Corte Madera and was flowing like driven smoke up through the foothill canyons. San Quentin on its point was half hidden in the vapors, and the channels of Corte Madera Slough gleamed up through the mists like sinuous tracings of light.

I had arrived at the summit just in time. The sea breeze, moving ahead of the fog and clouds it was carrying, had advanced over Mill Valley and across Richardson Bay and now met the edge of the advancing masses of tule fog along the Tiburon Peninsula. The forces from land and sea had come into contact, and the battle was suddenly joined on a front miles long. From the start there was little doubt as to which force was the stronger. The wind from the ocean had acquired too much momentum to be stopped by the low thin layer of tule fog from inland. The advance front of the tule fog was suddenly blunted and rolled over backwards like an ocean wave that hits a rocky cliff and rebounds. Everywhere along the battle front, in Raccoon Strait, in the passes through Tiburon Ridge, then out over the surface of the bay itself, the misty tide was turned as the tule fog began to retreat before the battering attack of the sea wind. The advance salients of tule fog seemed to rear back before the onslaught like the dismayed cavalry of Napoleon before the British fire at Waterloo.

The encounter between the two forces created an array of fantastic fog shapes such as I had never seen in many years of fog-watching. All along the battle line, the nebulous forms appeared and disappeared faster than I could keep track of them. Vapory castles quickly formed and vanished. Fog masses thrown back by the advancing west wind were broken up into swiftly moving spirals and parabolas. Steeples and pillars and vaulted arches came into being for a few moments, only to be destroyed by the wind.

The artillery barrage I had seen earlier on the mountain was repeat-ed in the valleys below on a mammoth scale. A mushroom cloud loomed over San Quentin. Over the bay's edge at Corte Madera a mass of white vapor slowly rose like a column of water, spread, and spilled over at the top in a gigantic fog fountain. Then it rose even higher and changed shape until it seemed to be a towering monolith—a vaporous

Washington Monument catching the last rays of the sun before falling back into the shaded valleys below.

Out over the bay the rout was soon complete. The filmy surface fog was swept quickly backward and piled into ridges that drifted and rolled and retreated eastward, revealing the bright surface of the water. Within twenty minutes the battle was over. Thousands of people in the valleys below had been oblivious to the spectacle going on above their heads. Looking up, they could only see that it was either foggy or clearing.

By the time the sun was about to set, the bay was cleared of all but a few pockets of tule fog along the far shores, and the sea fog was moving in force across the Marin ridges. As I left the peak numb from the cold northwest wind, I could see the giant shadow of Tamalpais stretching across the bay to Carquinez and Vallejo, twenty miles away. There was still a glow of twilight on the upper slopes as I walked back down the ridge, but in the dark valleys below, the lights of the towns and villages were shining mistily through the advancing vapors from the ocean.

To innumerable people toiling in San Francisco offices, the sight of that mountain across the Golden Gate on a clear day is always a strong temptation, but in spring the attraction becomes well nigh irresistible. One bright morning in May the pile of unfinished work on my desk was reaching the point where I could not face it without a sense of panic. The mountain was shining in the spring sun, and I made the inevitable decision—or rather, some primal instinct of self-preservation made it for me. I got in the car, headed across the bridge, took the road skirting the south side of Tamalpais, parked at Pantoll, and set out at a quick pace along the Matt Davis trail around the peak's western flank.

It was one of those bright May days when the mountain seems to vibrate with life. Birds sang lustily; the grasses were refulgent green; wildflowers, after the abundant winter rains, were spread across the grassy slopes more profusely than in any previous season in memory. Still, I was unable to exorcise the compulsions of urban living. I followed the trail from the open slopes into the woods, rounded a couple of bends, and came upon a creek cascading down a ferny ravine—a perfect spot to sit on a log and watch the light on the water. But the inner time clock was not yet unwound and kept senselessly insisting that I keep moving.

Fortunately, the spell of the falling water began to overcome the corrupt influences of civilization, and I sat on the log, observing the flowing forms of the creek as it plunged down a small precipice and glissaded over a smooth boulder into a clean pool where the surface reflected dappled sunlight upward onto the leaning bole of a big maple.

The creek flowed through a natural hillside rock garden displaying a dozen shades of green—the brownish greens of a coat of mosses draped over a big boulder like velvet, the duller green of the chain fern, the pale green of the big-leafed thimbleberry, the darker greens of the laurels above, and the brilliant spring green of the new leaves on the maple, forming a back-lighted canopy over the entire garden. The sounds were hypnotic—the high-pitched purling of the cascade, the deeper note of a fall dropping into a pool, the cawing of a jay, the exuberant chatter of a sparrow, the rustling of the leaves of maple and laurel in an occasional breeze.

When I finally got up and walked down the trail, I was able to saunter rather than trot—with only fading twinges of guilt over the wasted time. Walking brought an opening in the woods; I suddenly came upon a big sloping meadow alight with color—the bright orange of the monkey flowers, the yellow of daisies, the scarlet of the trumpet flower, and the incredible blue of masses of lupine. The field of lupine seemed to change color as I watched it. Examining the plants closely, I could see the cause of this optical illusion. Each stalk of the flower carries petals of several shades, ranging from white at the tip, through pale blue, to a vibrant purple at the base. By exposing various parts of hundreds of stalks, a breeze causes the colors to change, and the white tops in the field of blue make the entire mass seem to scintillate like wind-rippled water.

I found a good spot on a grassy slope to doze in the sun, and when I opened my eyes after a few minutes I saw directly in front of me something I had failed to notice before: a perfectly formed web about eight inches in diameter, spun between three blades of grass with such engineering skill that the three stalks moved as a unit when riffled by a breeze. The web was spread like a fisherman's net to intercept whatever game might happen through that way. An iridescent-winged insect struggled haplessly in the entanglement. In the center of the web the spider waited patiently. The spider seemed to be the villain of this production, yet he was only making his living in the legitimate way nature had provided and was no more villainous, surely, than a fisherman netting his catch. As I stood up, I startled a foot-long lizard; his back was an intricate pattern of zigzagging black and yellow designs.

I wandered through groves fragrant with the spicy scent of laurels, then continued across open grassy knolls where the ocean came into view and the sweet odors of the trailside lupine were mixed with the salt smells of the sea. After a long descent through a Douglas fir grove like a big dim chamber with pillars four feet in diameter, the trail emerged onto a high rocky point with a superb panorama of the shoreline. The waves, in lines of white surf two miles long, were curving around Duxbury Reef to the beach at Stinson, where the currents have built a sand barrier across the entrance of Bolinas Lagoon. Offshore, contrasting sharply with the vast aquamarine expanse of the ocean beyond, was a long salient of brownish water that I recognized as the ebb from the Golden Gate, a current laden with silt and sand from the streams flowing into the bay and from the Sacramento and San Joaquin, the combined waters of a dozen rivers originating near California's summit peaks from Mount Shasta to Mount Whitney.

Here on this rocky promontory a thousand feet above the sea, facing the incandescent ocean, I could almost feel the geologic heaving of the earth's crust that created this spectacle. At the foot of this mountain, slicing southward into the ocean from Bolinas Lagoon and the Olema

Valley, was the San Andreas Fault. Along the colossal rift the earth's crust has moved horizontally over the eons. Here in 1906 the land on either side of the fault slid about ten feet in opposite directions in less than a second. Before long, doubtless, it will move again.

I turned back along the trail toward civilization, with its lesser dimensions of time and space. By now it seemed to me that this day on Tamalpais had been not a retreat from duty but an advance—a salutary confrontation with the real world outside the human hive.

Crossing a high ridge with a view to the south, I spotted a red-tailed hawk riding the air currents and followed him in the binoculars as he swooped against a whirling montage of sea and mountains and sky—the wave-assaulted Marin coastline to Point Bonita, the breakers pounding the cliffs at Point Lobos, the white rows of houses where San Francisco slopes slowly up from the ocean, the eucalyptus forest on Mount Davidson, and, on the far horizon, the distant peak of Loma Prieta down the Peninsula. Then the hawk seemed to top the north tower of Golden Gate Bridge and sailed upward against a backdrop of Nob Hill skyscrapers and the observatory on Mount Hamilton, seventy miles away. I lost sight of him as he disappeared against the two massive summits of Diablo.

Trumpets of Light

Ann Zwinger (b. 1925) has written dozens of books on natural history and associated subjects. Among them are Land Above the Trees: A Guide to American Alpine Tundra *(1972) and* Run, River, Run: A Naturalist's Journey down One of the Great Rivers of the West *(1975). The following "backcountry journal" is from* Yosemite: Valley of Thunder *(1996), a book that features the photography of Kathleen Norris Cook.*

This July morning a light breeze streaks the otherwise calm surface of an alpine tarn, then dies, leaving a polished, stainless-steel skin. Yesterday my elder daughter, Susan, and I hiked eight miles into the Sierra, and twenty-five hundred feet up, into the northeast corner of the Yosemite backcountry wilderness, which brought us to this charming tarn nestled into a granite bowl at around ten thousand feet.

The sky brightens but does not heat; I enjoy earth's staging time, getting everything adjusted, ordered, before turning on the sun. By six, full sunlight stains a ridge ruddy at the far edge of the lake, reflecting in the water like warp-dyed silk. Then this July day begins with blazing trumpets of light. I've never been averse to a little glory before breakfast, and watching sunrise bestir this pond does it for me.

I suspect the real glories of Yosemite belong to the backpackers, the trudgers and trekkers, those who finish a strenuous climb and wait for their psyches to catch up, suffer a thunderstorm on an alpine fell, and most of all, let the night spirits seep into their sleep. The real glories of Yosemite belong to those who are comfortable with being uncomfortable, who know it's all right to be afraid, to be cold, wet, tired, and hungry, to be euphoric and, on occasion, ecstatic.

More than 706,000 acres, over 94 percent of the park, is managed as wilderness and can never be developed. A permit system applies to hikers and groups on horseback who plan to remain overnight, thus guaranteeing that hikers are not falling over one another or overusing one area. The park instituted a permit system because rangers counted almost five thousand campfire rings in the backcountry in 1972. The wilderness areas cope well so far with the 30 percent of the visitors who go there, perhaps because they are of a different outlook than the three million who jam into the valley and spend their time commuting between the stores at the Visitor Center and Curry Village.

Kerrick Meadow lies a little above nine thousand feet, depending on a knob here or a depression there. Laid between granite walls, the valley looks quilted in all shades of green. In this wet soil, wildflowers abound, and little apricot-colored day moths flutter up against my legs as I walk. A grasshopper with dark brown wings alights at rights angles to the sun, then ratchets off again.

Like better-known Tuolumne Meadows, Kerrick Meadow has seasonally saturated soils that maintain a water table too high for trees to grow. The meadow bears the name of James D. Kerrick, who trailed sheep here around 1880. Most of its yearly precipitation, between thirty and fifty inches, falls as snow, and the growing season seldom lasts more than nine weeks.

In the middle of Kerrick Meadow, Rancheria Creek (also probably a name used by sheepmen) flutters its way downhill on a gradual gradient. A tinsel-ribbon of water, it pauses occasionally to spread into small pools at the outside of a meander or to nibble at a bank, in no hurry to get anywhere. According to the sandy, gravelly flats alongside, its channel at high runoff sometimes widens to fifty feet. Frost heaves that make the ground expand disturb plant roots and leave bare, gravelly patches that resemble shaven spots in the lush sedge meadow that bounds the stream. These active, top layers of soil discourage plant growth and allow only the most sturdy pioneer plants, those that can withstand the thaws and freezes that unceremoniously assault their roots. These plants, like tiny daisies and lupines and bright pink pussy-paws, have many of the same adaptations as those that occupy alpine heights. They are small, close to the ground, and often densely furred with hairs.

Following the creek, Susan and I sometimes walk in a horse pack trail incised six to twelve inches below the surface. One horse concentrates more pounds per square inch and causes as much damage as twenty-five or more people. Vegetation and soil at camps where horses are tethered is impacted ten times as much as at other camps, and meadows are grazed into mud. But horse use continues because it provides easier and longer access to the backcountry.

An ominous, dark cloud to the north sits astride the valley upstream. From my perch I watch the virga, filmy veils of rain, shred down out of it. The storm crawls like a tank, filling the breadth of the canyon, scraping the granite, dragging against the ground, marching toward us with an overweening arrogance. It formed from heated air rising from the Central Valley, cooling as it rose and capturing enough moisture to form thunderheads. A grumbling muttering-in-its-beard thunder beats on the granite as if it were a tympanum, an unmistakable announcement of intent. One minute the rocks are dry, then suddenly the downpour rushes off their flanks. It rains the rest of the afternoon. It rains all night.

In the morning, watching a tent fly dry is in the same category as watching a pot boil, and the need to wait legitimizes some morning lethargy. I return to yesterday's storm-watching perch. Handfuls of moisture hang in the air, swathing everything in lingering dampness. Tiny yellow monkey flowers that would fit into a shirt button, plants maybe less than half an inch high, interweave in familial mats. The lip of each flower carries a drop of water that magnifies the red specks of its throat.

Spiny gooseberry bushes sprawl across the slope behind me, double thorns on the stems. Indians used to burn Yosemite Valley just to encourage such berry bushes to sprout, for gooseberry and other berry plants come in quicker after a burn. In more recent times, however, gooseberry and currant, shrubs of the genus *Ribes*, have been indicted as being an alternate host to white pine blister rust. Blister rust infections come in waves, usually when cool and moist conditions encourage spores to form in the gooseberry phase. For decades foresters killed gooseberries and currants to stop the spread until, in the 1960s, the rust infection was judged not to be such a threat after all. Scattered plants that escaped execution remain at higher altitudes.

While I lodgepole- and monkey-flower-watch, the sun levitates seven inches above the rock rim across the valley, and as it rises above the mists it paints sharp, clear shadows. With it comes a light breeze. I check my sleeping bag. Contrary to my pessimistic expectation of a soggy sleeping bag forever, it is dry.

Another afternoon, Susan and I hike to a higher tarn. The gravel apron around it scrunches underfoot. The water is so cold and lacking in minerals, so "pure," that no algae grow in it, no plankton, no fish.

A path crosses behind the tarn beneath its source of supply, a snowbank plastered on the scooped-out slope of granite wall a quarter mile away. Thick sedges hide threads of water that don't show up until you step into them ankle deep. At the edge of one rivulet, I spy a little half-inch tan frog with a black stripe through its eye. It hops off through skyscraper sedge—a Pacific tree frog.

After crossing the meadow, the path starts up to a divide. When it runs down again, I leave it to scramble up a bare talus slope. I intend to go only partway to a dark rocky ridge on the horizon, but it's a Pied Piper landscape, calling me through one more rock doorway, up one more rise to one more interesting plant, one more different kind of rock. I follow meekly, hypnotized, into the severe, sculptural spaces of one of my favorite places, the alpine zone.

The dark rock outcropping is so splintered into silver-dollar pieces that it clinks as I walk through it. The metamorphic hornfels shatters into smaller chips than granite, contains more minerals, and is darker and more heat absorbent than the granites, an assist to plants at cold altitudes. The outcrop is a leftover from the metamorphics that once completely covered the mountains. Surrounded above, below, and alongside by pearly gray granite, the dark rock stands out as powerfully as the clenched fist in a Rodin sculpture.

Sun shines 354 days (almost 97 percent) of the year up here, but at the same time, it can freeze any night. Wind shaves the ground like a straight razor. Precipitation drops to less than half an inch in July, with August even drier. What little moisture there is comes form melting snow.

Plants up here tend to be low cushions and mats, white phlox and pink moss campion, tiny buckwheats and little lupines, all of which withstand freezing and can photosynthesize at lower temperatures than plants of lower altitude. Lupine is heavily furred, an adaptation that lessens water loss and insulates the plant against evaporation, solar radiation, and cold. Like most alpine plants, lupines are perennials. Most annuals do not have time enough to sprout, grow, flower, and set seed in the abbreviated growing season. Many species grow for a decade or more before they store up enough energy to flower. Some reproduce by vegetative means, which gives new plants a better start and an assured source of nourishment.

Plants here take root in nearly sterile, pulverized granite, chips of feldspar, quartz bits, and sparkly flecks of mica, with not enough organic matter in it to deserve the designation of "soil." With cold temperatures and few plants, humus neither forms nor stays put on steep alpine talus slopes. Red heather, full of pink blossoms, espaliers across a rock face, preferring the acids provided by disintegrating granites. White heather nestles against a pegmatite dike full of big handsome feldspar crystals. By growing on a slight incline facing the sun, the heather receives half again more heat and light than if it grew on the flat. Creeping mats of magenta penstemons and alpine sorrel always grow along the downhill edge of rocks, capturing the runoff moisture. A dainty sandwort raises little starlike blooms with five rosy stamens hovering above five starched white petals.

Downhill, puffy patches of flake lichen tint the ground an odd and distinctive bluish-gray. Flake lichen thrives within a growing season of seven to twelve weeks and signals that this area holds snow late into the summer. Snow is more protector than growth-stopper at high altitude. On days when the wind-chill factor may drop to minus forty degrees, snow shields alpine plants from a brutal buffeting.

Upslope, narrow rivulets weep out from under a raggedy patch of snow shining like tinsel. How does a snowfield die? Rather ignominiously, I'm afraid. A beautiful expanse of pristine white snow becomes crusted with dirt and dust, its surface porous and granulated from freezing over each night, melting each day, looking like Japanese rice paper with pine needles, willow leaves, and other plant bits encased in it. These absorb enough heat to sink in a quarter inch, blackening and embedding themselves in a bezel of snow. Pink algae color teacup-sized hollows. No longer big enough to sluice a stream of icy water downhill, the snowfield drips like a dozen leaky faucets. It languishes, passing away from sun disease, a fragile Camille, a wan Traviata, a doomed Mimi, dying with operatic slowness. It goes out with neither a bang nor a whimper—just a tiny liquid tinkling, it requires the soprano of a mosquito.

As I start down, a muted clucking comes from nearby, stops, resumes. As quietly as possible, I slip out binoculars and wait. About ten feet away, close enough to see the red line above the eye, I spot a handsome male ptarmigan. About the size of a chicken, ptarmigan are an instance of Bergmann's Rule in action: creatures of cold climates tend to be larger than tropical animals, since size gives a better relationship of volume to exposed area and makes it easier to retain body heat. The bird proceeds with considerable dignity up a boulder face, snapping at flower heads, ambling up the rock to a small shady overhang. Speckled brown and white on back and wings, he blends into the dappled light under the overhang. In winter, ptarmigan turn totally white, with extravagant white pantaloons, a heavy feathering that gives extra insulation to legs and feet. Males winter above timberline, the only birds to do so in this stringent climate.

Later, after loping down a rain-greased talus slope with nothing taller in sight than I, lightning flashing and thunder banging simultaneously, a hastily donned poncho flapping, boots and pants soaked and hands stiff with cold, I finally reach a lower flat and hunker down. Just when I don't think I can get any wetter or any colder comes the hail. Stinging *petit-pois*-sized pellets insinuate themselves into every crease of my poncho, fill the puddles around my feet, and leave windrows around the rocks. What isn't already wet gets wet—soaking, irrevocably, irretrievably wet, wet from the outside and through to the other side.

At the far edge of misery a pale sun appears, not a moment too soon for this huddled mass of dripping, dirty laundry, with runny nose and squishy boots. As the last BBs of hail clear the valley, a rainbow, an incredible swatch of color, materializes against the gloomy clouds. Not your same old arch, but a rectangular banner broadcasting its blazing spectrum of color, it flutters out from under a mass of clouds in the southwest sky, undulating like northern lights.

That evening, tent pitched and trenched, clothes dry, and the comforts reestablished, I pull out the obligatory "ice-cream-and-cake-and-candle," a day-late birthday celebration for Susan: two small, slightly squashed cupcakes, one pink candle, and a packet of freeze-dried ice cream that tastes like ice cream even if it isn't cold. What's a mother for? We raise a toast of freshly filtered, very cold stream water to the pleasures of wilderness. My cup runneth over.

Waning sun, shuttered behind a pure white cloud, traces its rim with eye-blinding incandescence. Wisps of clouds radiate outward from Sawtooth Ridge like the gold rays in a baroque sculpture. Tall, dark green, narrow triangles of trees rise against a backdrop of white granite beneath a deep blue Sierran sky: unmistakably Yosemite. The sky chills to an aquamarine of limpid clarity and transparency, a cut-crystal atmosphere, before it deepens to navy blue in which stars begin to glint.

Shadows inch up the last sunlit face. With my sketchbook in my lap, I recall James D. Smillie, who published *Yellowstone to Yosemite: Early Adventures in the Mountain West* in 1872. Smillie wrote and illustrated his summer in Yosemite and with an artist's eye noted that Yosemite's granites, being so pale, are exceptionally responsive to changes in atmosphere. At sunset, he wrote that "they glow with a ruddy light, that is slowly extinguished by the upcreeping shadows of night, until the highest point flames for one moment, then dies, ashy pale, under the glory that is lifted to the sky above. Then the cold moon tips with silver those giant, sleeping forms, and by its growing light I cleared my palette, and closed the box upon my last study of the Yosemite and Sierras."

I unfold my map for the last time to check our route out tomorrow. Now its folds are worn, its edges shredded. Well used indeed. Miles calculated, elevation lines counted, meadows walked, streams crossed, heights climbed. Now, when I trace with my finger where we've been on this trip, the map lines segue into images of clumps of pines or shining tarns or mellifluous meadows. That green spot here was full of flowers and butterflies, and that blue line there was a booming waterfall, sweetened with birdsong. Those concentric ruffled circles describe the top of a dome on which I stood, those dotted blue lines the beginning of a stream that wiggled downslope.

No longer is the map two-dimensional. It is composed of height of ponderosa, breadth of valley, depth of stream, wintertime, summertime, springtime, autumntime, the vanilla smell of Jeffrey pine, the gritty feel of granite, the puckery taste of alpine sorrel, the unexpected song of a canyon wren, the senses of time, the waterfalls of the mind.

The Fourth Dimension

David Rains Wallace (b. 1945), based in Berkeley, has written nine works of natural history and two novels. One of his best books, The Klamath Knot *(1983), deals with evolution, which Wallace calls "the great myth of modern times." He explores this myth against the backdrop of the Klamath Mountains on the California-Oregon border.*

Ten years passed before I went back to the Siskiyous. During that time I walked into a number of wild places, and acquired what I thought was a fair knowledge of western mountain wilderness: of the climb from chaparral or sagebrush in the Upper Sonoran Zone; through Douglas fir, ponderosa pine, and white fir in the Transition Zone; past lodgepole pine, red fir, or Engelmann spruce in the Canadian Zone; to stunted whitebark pines and heather in the Alpine Zone. I went to a few places where there were still grizzly bear tracks as well as black bear tracks. So I didn't really expect to find much that was new when I started up the Clear Creek trail into the northern part of the high Siskiyous in June of 1979 with my down sleeping bag, gas stove, contour maps, and other sophistications. But the Siskiyous still had some things to show me.

I knew the Siskiyous are among the richest botanical areas of the

West, and I soon saw evidence of this as I followed Clear Creek upstream. Tributary ravines contained so much blossoming azalea that the forest often smelled like a roomful of fancy women, and rhododendrons were in flower on one flat bench. There were more orchids than I'd seen anywhere. California lady's slippers hung over one rivulet like tiny Japanese lanterns dipped in honey, and I found three species of coralroot, red and orange orchids that have no green leaves, lacking chlorophyll. Farther up the trail, where snow had melted recently, pink calypso orchids had just burst through the pine duff.

The forest that overshadowed these flowers was the most diverse I'd seen west of the Mississippi. Besides the Douglas fir, tan oak, madrone, golden chinquapin, and goldencup oak I had expected just east of the coastal crest, I found ponderosa pine, Jeffrey pine, sugar pine, western white pine, knobcone pine, and incense cedar. Moist ravines were full of Port Orford cedar, a lacy-foliaged tree which fluted bark like a redwood's. The diversity became confusing; it seemed I had to consult my tree field guide every few minutes.

As I climbed higher, I kept expecting this unwonted diversity to sort itself out into the usual altitudinal zones, waiting for white fir, ponderosa pine, and incense cedar to close ranks against the confusion. But it didn't happen. Douglas fir kept playing its polymorphous tricks, its foliage sometimes resembling the flattened needles of white fir, sometimes dangling like the branches of weeping spruce. I got a stiff neck looking up to see if cones hung downward, denoting Douglas fir, or stood upright, denoting white fir (or perhaps silver fir, grand fir, or noble fir, three other species found in the Klamaths).

Broad-leaved madrone and tan oak disappeared obligingly after I reached a certain altitude, but then new species appeared. I found western yew, a sturdy little tree resembling a miniature redwood, and Sadler's oak, another small tree whose serrated leaves reminded me of the chestnut oaks I'd known in the Midwest. I passed a grove of lodgepole pines, and these austere trees, which typically grow on bleak, windswept terrain, looked out of place in all the effulgent variety. The trees were sorted out somewhat according to soil conditions, but these distinctions were patchy and vague, offering cold comfort to my organizing instincts.

After two days of walking, I stood on the slopes of Preston Peak, which is 7,309 feet above sea level at its summit but seems higher as it thrusts abruptly above the forested ridges. I was surprised, on looking around at the snow-stunted trees on the glacial moraine where I stood, to find they were the same species that had accompanied me from the Klamath River: Douglas fir, ponderosa pine, incense cedar, western yew, Sadler's oak, white fir. Even goldencup oak, golden chinquapin, and bay laurel grew there at about 5,000 feet, albeit in shrubby form.

Clearly, there was something odd about the Siskiyou forest. For so many species to grow all over a mountain range simply doesn't conform to respectable western life-zone patterns. It is more like some untidy temperate deciduous forest or tropical rainforest, species promiscuously tumbled together without regard for ecological proprieties.

The high Siskiyou forest is a rare remnant of a much lusher past. Fossils of trees almost identical to those of the Siskiyous have been dug from twelve-million-year-old, Pliocene epoch sediments in what are now the deserts of Idaho and eastern Oregon. Fossils of trees not at all unlike Siskiyou species have been found in *forty*-million-year-old sediments in Alaska. In that epoch, the Eocene, a temperate forest surpassing any living today covered the northern half of this continent from coast to coast. Redwoods, pines, firs, and cedars grew with hickories, beeches, magnolias, and other hardwoods not found within a thousand miles of the Pacific Ocean today, and with ginkgoes, dawn redwoods, and other trees that don't even grow naturally in North America anymore. It is hard to imagine such a forest: it sounds like poets' descriptions of Eden. After the Eocene, though, the climate became cooler and drier; and this gradually drove the forest southward, and split it in half. Deciduous hardwoods migrated southeast, where the summer rain they needed was still available, while many conifers migrated southwest to cover the growing Rocky Mountain and Pacific Coast ranges. Ginkgoes and dawn redwoods fell by the wayside during this "long march," which has resulted in our present, relatively impoverished forests, where trees that once grew together are separated by wide prairies and plains.

There is still one area west of the Rockies, however, where rainfall and temperatures approximate the benign Eocene environment: the inner coastal ranges of southwest Oregon and northwest California, the Klamath Mountains. In the Klamaths, winters are mild enough and summers moist enough for species to grow together that elsewhere are segregated by altitude or latitude. Several species that once grew throughout the West now survive only in the Klamaths. Perched on my Siskiyou eminence, I again felt suspended over great gulfs of time. The stunted little trees and their giant relatives on the lower slopes were not a mere oddity forest where ill-assorted species came together in a meaningless jumble. They were in a sense the ancestors of all western forests, the rich gene pool from which the less varied, modern conifer forests have marched out to conquer forbidding heights from Montana to New Mexico. Looking out over the pyramidal Siskiyou ridges, I was seeing a community of trees at least forty million years old.

Later that day something hair-raising happened. There were still some patches of snow, and I had walked across one on the way to my campsite. After dinner I wandered back past that patch and found, punched deeply into each of my vibram-soled footprints, the tracks of a large bear. It probably had been foraging in Rattlesnake Meadow, heard me coming, and took the trail downhill to escape my intrusion. A simple coincidence, but it caused a sudden feeling of emptiness at the pit of my stomach, as though I were riding a fast elevator. It seemed the lesson begun ten years before was proceeding: from a realization that the world is much greater and older than normal human perception of it, to a reminder that the human is a participant as well as a perceiver in the ancient continuum of bears and forests. I was used to walking in bear tracks by this time; it was instructive to find that a bear also could walk in mine.

The Siskiyous weren't through with me. I got sick the next day for some reason, probably fatigue. I'd been living in the Midwest for three years and had grown unaccustomed to running around on mountains. It was thought-provoking to lie in the wilderness that night with the suspicion that I might have been about to have a heart attack. I had many sleepless hours to wonder why I kept going to places like the Siskiyous when so many civilized places were so much easier to get to. I'm not all *that* crazy about exercise. Wilderness areas are certainly among the most beautiful places on the planet, but I wonder if this alone is enough to explain the fascination many people feel for them, or the difficulties and real suffering they endure to reach them. I thought of Audubon, feverish and vomiting from tainted turkey meat in the trackless Ohio forest; Thoreau dragging his tuberculosis to the Minnesota frontier; Muir stumbling with frostbite across Mount Shasta's glaciers. I may have been delirious: my mind started reeling through history—tribal youths starving on mountaintops for totem visions, Taoist sages living on nettles and mushrooms in Chinese caves, Hebrew prophets eating locusts and wild honey on the Sinai peninsula, elderly Brahmins leaving comfortable estates to wander the Bengali jungle.

I wondered if my motives for going into wilderness might be more obscure, and more profound, than I had realized. While part of me was going into the mountains seeking the pleasures of exercise, self-reliance, accomplishment, and natural history, it seemed that another part was looking for things of which I had only a vague conscious awareness, as though a remote mountain or desert releases some innate human behavior, a kind of instinctive predilection for the mysterious.

So many major structures of belief have arisen at least in part from experiences in wilderness. This was to be expected with the oldest structures, such as animism and shamanism, since the entire world outside a Paleolithic camp was wilderness. But why should all the major religions of the modern world include a crucial encounter with wilderness—Moses, Jesus, and Mohammed in the desert mountains, Siddhartha in the jungle? And why should the predominant modern view of the original development of life have arisen from the five-year wilderness voyage of a Victorian amateur naturalist named Charles Darwin? There evidently is more to wilderness than meets the eye—more than water, timber, minerals, the materials of physical civilized existence. Somehow there are mental trees, streams, and rocks—psychic raw materials from which every age has cut, dammed, or quarried an invisible civilization—an imaginative world of origins and meanings—what one might call a mythology. . . .

The Klamath Mountains are an exceptionally rich storehouse of evolutionary stories, one of the rare places where past and present have not been severed as sharply as in most of North America, where glaciation, desertification, urbanization, and other ecological upheavals have been muted by a combination of rugged terrain and relatively benign climate. Klamath rocks are older than those of the California and Oregon coast ranges to the south and north or those of the Cascades in the east. They are more intricately and tortuously folded, faulted, and upthrust, forming a knot of jagged peaks and steep gorges less modified by civilization than other areas, even though they are only a day's drive from large cities. The Klamaths are not even very high as mountains go, with no peaks over ten thousand feet.

The relatively low elevation of the Klamaths, compared to the Cascades or Sierra Nevada, has caused them to be overlooked. Naturalists often say that the Klamaths are a combination of Sierra Nevada and Cascades ecosystems because the Klamaths contain species found in both other wilderness regions. This is a little like saying that a person is a combination of his brother and sister because he shares genes with both siblings. The Klamaths have a character of their own, although not perhaps as ingratiating a character as the graceful volcanic cones of the Cascades or the clean alpine country of the Sierra. There is something wizened about the Klamaths. Their canyons do not have sparkling granite walls and wide river meadows as do the U-shaped, glaciated canyons of the Sierra. Klamath canyons are preglacial, and uncompromisingly V-shaped. They've never been scoured into spaciousness by the ice flows. They seem to drop down forever, slope after forest-smothered slope, to straitened, boulder-strewn bottoms so noisy with waters and shadowed by vegetation that they may bring startling dreams and uneasy thoughts to campers.

Early explorers were stymied by these canyons. In 1828 Jedediah Smith and his party of fur trappers gave up in despair when they tried to follow the Klamath River upstream from its confluence with the Trinity River. The terrain was too rugged even for those mountain men, who had walked from Oregon to Los Angeles in search of beaver. They didn't find many beaver in Klamath Mountain rivers, which are generally too rocky and turbulent even for those ingenious rodents. The fur trappers called the Klamaths "backward," a pretty definitive judgment coming from backwoodsmen who crossed the Sierra and Cascades, not to mention the Rockies, a half-century before the railroads.

More than any other wild region I've known, the Klamaths have a venerable quality which is not synonymous with "pristine," "unspoiled," or other adjectives commonly applied to natural areas. Certainly the Klamaths are as unpolluted as any American place these days. But these adjectives imply something of the smoothness and plumpness of youth, whereas the Klamaths are marked by the wrinkles and leanness of great age. Although their peaks and high plateaus have been marked by glaciers, they are at heart preglacial mountains, with elements of flora and fauna that reach back farther into the past than any place west of the Mississippi River. The Klamaths seem so old, in fact, that I'd call them a grandparent of the Sierra and Cascades instead of a sibling.

This venerable quality is strongest in the region's National Forest wilderness areas: the Rogue River gorge and the jumbled red humps of the Kalmiopsis to the north, the jagged peaks of the high Siskiyous and Red Buttes, the huge massifs of the Marble Mountains and Salmon-Trinity Alps, the gentle but hulking summits of the Yolla Bollys to the south. (The Yolla Bollys aren't entirely within the Klamath Mountain geological province, but I include them because they're ecologically linked to the other ranges.) Wilderness in the Klamaths is still dwindling from logging and other developments, as it was when I found hiking trails so elusive in 1969, but I hope enough will eventually be protected to assure they will remain an outstanding vantage point into what I perceived during my first visit as the fourth dimension of life.

DANIEL DUANE

Sierra Nevada

Climbing Half Dome

Daniel Duane (b. 1967) has recorded his ascents of the Northwest Face of Half Dome and the Nose route on El Capitan in his first book, Lighting Out: A Vision of California and the Mountains *(1994). He has also written about surfing in* Caught Inside: A Surfer's Year on the Pacific Coast *(1996). Duane, who earned his Ph.D. in English in 1996, lives in Santa Cruz.*

No sound disturbed the natural quarry below Half Dome. In predawn light, I smeared cream cheese on a flattened onion bagel and looked out over the whole of Yosemite Valley. A surprising view from so high above, from a place I had until now only looked up to: the right wall of the valley was an ordered row of forms: Washington, Column, the Royal Arches, Yosemite Falls, the Three Brothers, and El Capitan; the left—Glacier Point, Sentinel Rock, and the Cathedral Group. Even at five A.M. the air held midsummer heat, dried sweat and dust caked my skin from the previous night's approach, and my shoulders still ached from the load. As I ate, my own stench overpowered the blandness of the bagel. I chewed slowly and looked around at the Northwest Face—there was nothing that baffled me about the wall's beauty. So out of human scale and yet so well formed, so sculpted. A vast field of fallen boulders lay along its base, like so many sculptor's shavings from a work in progress.

Nick organized the haul bag quickly, and soon we had lifted off. Half Dome wasn't so much smaller than El Cap—twenty-six pitches by comparison to thirty-two—but somehow it seemed far more manageable, less steep, and less difficult. We climbed steadily and well on familiar gray granite, deep inside corners and cracks. Perhaps because the sun didn't strike the Northwest Face until noon, and the air remained still, the wall felt like a vast and empty indoor cathedral. We ran our rope systems, made moves well within our abilities, and were soon well off the ground. Sound took on a singular quality—even with Nick a hundred feet above, every little tap of metal on stone, every scuffle of shoe, his deep breaths and occasional remarks—each and every noise echoed alone like lonely footsteps in a huge stone hall.

At a ledge a few hundred feet up, light just breaking into the sky, I prepared for my first lead of the morning. Nick sat against the rock and looked blankly out over the high country; the haul bag was perched next to him, leaning against the wall. I dismantled the pulley system and clipped the haul line into my harness to take it up with me. Then the haul bag teetered back. Nick looked up and reached for it too late, and then it was gone. Well over a hundred pounds. We both grabbed reflexively for the rope; my hand caught it and instantly slammed back against the rock and split open. The rope burned skin off my thigh as coils flipped off the ledge. The bag had a hundred and sixty-five feet to fall before it would impact my harness. Nick and I stared at each other and waited for the inevitable. I wrapped my hands around the anchor webbing and held on.

The jolt slammed me down into the ledge, then stopped. My harness had held the fall. Nick's knuckles were raw. The bag was intact. My right hand bled down into my wrist. So close to blowing the whole climb. We looked at each other in disbelief: had he forgotten to clip it to the anchor? Had I unclipped the wrong knot? It didn't matter much, and we barely spoke of the incident; we just hauled the bag back in and went on with our work.

Hours and hours of quiet climbing in the still shade; hauling, belaying, jumaring, climbing, hauling, clipping and unclipping, reclipping and untying, backing up and reorganizing, rambling up across the tower toward the wall. Alternately lost in the sheer pleasure of motion and then drifting in the emptiness of waiting. Sitting on some little ledge high over the world and just staring. I never had many thoughts at belay ledges on long climbs. I didn't ruminate on what lay below or come to new clarity about my life. The task so absorbed me and the fatigue so calmed me that I really just looked and occasionally even just saw.

We'd exchange a few words here and there about equipment or ropes or which way the route went, but I loved the feeling that very little needed saying. We'd been climbing together for a while and knew each other well. Nick had decided that cities were crowded with psychic static; he said in a pause at a ledge that high places got him above the web of noise, especially his own. And for me Half Dome, unlike El Capitan, was charted territory. My father had been here, had climbed every inch of this rock and saw it as one of his happiest experiences.

Late in the day, at pitch eight of twenty-six, Nick led out across narrow but walkable ledges and began the Robbins Traverse, where Royal Robbins had taken the first ascent team off the tower and out onto the Northwest Face. Then, with my feet in aiders, I moved as fast as I could on ancient, strange-looking bolts—fat nails driven into spread-out sheaths. Only a few of the bolts had hangers, and even those were only partially bent pieces of aluminum. The last of the bolts was so bent out of the rock it was hard to imagine much was left inside.

In the early evening we reached our bivouac ledge at pitch eleven— a thirty-foot long, three-foot wide notch formed by a massive exfoliating flake.

"Sweet, huh?" Nick said.

After a short break, we decided to fix a line or two ahead so we could get a good start in the morning. I scrambled up to where blocks lay wedged in the opening of a chimney. Stepping across them I could hear sand and pebbles drop into the chasm. Somewhere in the darkness below, light leaked in from a crack. My pitch went well—easy aid, t.c.u.'s, fixed pieces in a beautiful white corner to the left of the chimney.

I leaned back and looked about. The crack was lined with old fixed pins; the face to either side was blank. As Nick started leading the next pitch, it became clear how tired he was—too much pro, thrashing around, stepping clumsily. At last he hung from a piece and looked back down at me with a smile.

"I'm out of here," he said.

"The whole route?" I couldn't believe my ears.

"Relax, bro. Just this pitch. Let's eat." We slid back down our skinny ropes and stumbled across blocks back to the vaguely comfortable part of the ledge. Everything came out of the bag. Feet came out of sweaty, torturous rock shoes and into clean socks. No point in so much as standing up—nowhere to walk, and everything an arm's reach away. I pulled out our dinner and started getting depressed. . . . We'd bought our food in a Berkeley health food store, and had gotten on a clean fuels kick. So we had nothing but dried this, dried that, bread, cheese, nuts, seeds—nothing that felt like a fitting meal after a hard day's work.

"Dude," Nick had his head under a rock, was reaching for something. "Check it out. Treasure!" Four full cans had been abandoned by some retreating party—blueberries, clam chowder, Spaghettios, Dinosaurs with Meatballs. Stunning good fortune—the ultimate Wall Food. I couldn't believe I hadn't thought of cans before. Nick demanded the Spaghettios, so I gladly took the Dinosaurs. The fat had congealed beautifully in the top of the can and I scooped it into my mouth with an old piton. The blueberries occupied nearly an hour as we sucked then down one by one.

A red glow rose out of the horizon and Yosemite Valley three thousand feet below softened and seemed of a piece, a valley proper. The distinct monoliths fell into a pattern of overlapping slopes and walls.

Darkness filled the valley from below as the harsh white of sun on granite faded into soft, deep grays. Lights appeared, marking Curry and Yosemite Villages. Faint car headlights crawling through the trees actually looked homey and pleasant.

I'd always though that bivies up that high should be wild, dangerous, somehow violent and disorderly. Nothing could have been farther from the truth. The wind stopped and the valley's warm air rose as a soft breeze. No valley tour busses roared, no traffic honked and smoked. No sound, no wind. Just warm air. Darkness obscured the wild exposure of our perch; it seemed a natural, even exquisite place to be.

I flaked ropes between blocks to make a bed, grinning like an idiot, almost crying with pleasure at the thought of sleep. My back, legs, arms, neck, and chest burned sore; my hands were swollen, raw, and scabbed. My extra clothing filled another spot, and the tent fly filled another. When at last I lay down I felt so heavy that rolling over and dangling in the void never occurred to me as a danger. I sank into the crevice in the rocks, comfortably lodged. But for a full hour after dark, I couldn't sleep. There was too much beauty to see, too striking and unique a view, so much precious sky. A perfect place attained by perfect means, by adequate struggle. Each time I began to fade, I wanted a last look; I whispered the whole scene out loud to myself, panting lightly as I spoke, mouthing the colors, the feeling of the warmth, the unbelievable quiet and stillness and my own attendant tiredness. I told myself the whole scene again and again to remember everything.

I opened my eyes in the middle of the night, that vast wild wall just a quiet, immobile place. The full moon, out of sight behind Half Dome, washed the sweeping granite apron of Glacier Point in cold white light. And then I realized what was before me: a moonshadow of Half Dome formed in the middle of the glow, a perfect projection of its curves on the apron. It occurred to me that these mountains always etched themselves across one another by sun and by moon, by shadow, dawn and dusk, and that for that moment on that night I lay with a blessed point of view between. Soon the shadow blurred and merged with the wider brushing of moonlight; before the moon itself rose into sight from behind the dome, I had fallen asleep.

When Nick's watch alarm beeped, the sky had iced over with light and the full moon had faded. I sat up in my sleeping bag and turned so my back was against the wall and my feet off the edge. We looked about for a while, faced once again where we were. Nick fished out our ration of bagels. I drank a whole liter of water mixed with electrolyte supplements. We were slow getting moving, but when we were both well awake, stretched and warmed, we packed the terrific mess back into the haul bag and started climbing.

I felt like a fish on a line as I thrashed up our fixed ropes in a flaring chimney. For the first lead of the day, I groveled into a miserable fissure and lost confidence—aiding behind an expanding flake at the back of another chimney. I could barely turn my head around because of my helmet. Loose rock threatened to fall and kill Nick. I asked him to lower me down to clean a piece because the rope drag was stopping my upward motion.

"You can't just haul enough up?" Nick asked. "Come on, just try to haul it. It'll take forever to lower you." I looked around, already drained, worn out, tried to pull some more rope and couldn't. I got planted on a small ledge and did a full leg-press—a foot of rope came. Another press, another foot, and then I could build the anchor and relax. The day went as smoothly as the one before, and Nick and I began to talk and yell at each other, to laugh at what an absurdity it was.

We reached our bivouac—Big Sandy Ledge—at 3:30 with a storm gathering in the high mountains. We'd just dropped our gear on the ledge and sat down when three climbers popped up and hooted with delight at the sight of the approaching clouds—without bivy gear, rain gear, or food. They'd left the car at Curry Village at 9:00 A.M. that same day and had walked eight miles and climbed seventeen pitches since: bearded, sweating, psychotic superhardmen having the time of their lives.

I admitted to one of them that I thought Nick and I might be in for a wild night on the ledge—looked like a big storm coming in; lightning flashed in the distance.

"But you'll have the greatest story to tell," he said, looking around at the sky, "and the bettys'll just be like 'give me your throbbing member.'" He was gone. Up the cracks called the zigzags. For a few hours later we could hear them yelling at each other.

With hours to kill till dark we sat on the ledge and stared, peed on different terraces, looked off into the sun for hours, watched a slow changing of the day, took turns shitting into paper bags and hurling them into space. Nick didn't even clear the ledge. Quite a mess. The storm moved overhead and deep booms and cracks sent us scampering for rain gear. Lightning charged into peaks, a black curtain of rain deluged Tenaya Canyon only a half mile away. Nick giggled with nervous anticipation, apparently hoping for the thrill. We were well anchored down, had plenty of warm clothing and rain gear, and these storms rarely lasted more than a few hours. So let us have it. Blow us off the mountain.

And then the storm pulled back, just like that, and left us with a long beautiful afternoon. Sleep was again difficult because of the beauty of the night. I watched meteors, picked out constellations, leaned over to look at the valley again and again, thinking about my dad sleeping here. We woke up late, had a slow breakfast, and mosied up the zigzags. After an hour and a half, we reached Thank God Ledge, which ran left for fifty feet. I'd seen pictures of my dad on Thank God Ledge, crawling like a lowly rat. Rather undignified. I'd bet him ten dollars I'd walk the whole thing. Nick got out the camera.

I walked right out there, no sweat. Shuffling along like a man. I could swear the ledge started narrowing a bit, but I kept walking just the same. The wall was pretty vertical above and below, and the valley floor was almost four thousand feet beneath my feet, but I just put one foot in front of the other. After ten feet or so, I turned to face the wall—spread my arms out flat against it and shuffled sideways with my cheek pressed flat—just to be safe. I mean, after all, at least I was still behaving like a biped. Five feet later, I sank right down to my knees and never looked back. The hell with it. Nick shot three frames of my retreating behind.

As we approached the summit, a few tourists looked down and waved. Under great alpine peaks—snowy pinnacles in the stratosphere —the tops of Yosemite walls feel more like endings than goals, they remind you that the great part was being on the route, not, as [my friend] Aaron [Lehrman] would say, having done it. At last I scrambled up a rather mundane series of ramps and stood on top. Hikers who'd come up the cable staircase milled about. A startled teenage girl in cutoff Levis and a bikini top looked at my haggard face and said,

"Did you just come up that way?"

Great question. God, what a good question. Thank you so much for asking that question. "Well, ah, yes. Now that you mention it, I did."

She looked at me, then off the edge.

"Rad," she said. She spun on her heels and walked away, apparently having changed the channel.

On that high mesa of exfoliating granite, overweight marmots scavenged in unattended backpacks and the twenty or thirty people sitting around spoke quietly as if in a museum. A wind blew across the summit and out into the air over the valley. Kids had their pictures taken on the diving board—a thin block that stuck straight out over the abyss. Nick lay on his belly and looked over the edge back down on the route. He yelled at me to join him, but I couldn't do it—too acute a sense of gravity.

The eight miles home were all downhill, and we ran almost the whole way, fast and stumbling, trying to make the showers before closing. Down the mist trail—steep riprapping, pounding on the knees, the fabulous torrent of Nevada Falls, and the green meadow at its base— utterly unlike the surrounding plants. Vernal Falls was a wild column of water framed by moss and ferns, and its staircase trail, absolutely paved, suggested an Inca trail. At last, into the human zoo of Curry Village for showers. After washing off the whole experience, we went to the Loft Restaurant, where a Dutch milkmaiden of a girl served us hamburgers.

"Why you guys so thirsty?" she asked. "Half Dome? The Regular Route? Oh yeah, my boyfriend and I did a one-day winter ascent. It was so great."

We slept in our clean cotton T-shirts and jeans in the back of the truck. Coffee milkshakes at ten A.M., and then back to Berkeley. A Big Wall.

THE HILLS AND VALLEYS

WILLIAM H. BREWER

Salinas Valley

Into the Valley

William H. Brewer (1828–1910), as the field leader of the first California Geological Survey, headed by Josiah Dwight Whitney, traveled throughout the state during the early 1860s. His letters home were stitched together by Francis Farquhar into what would become a California classic, Up and Down California in 1860–64, *not published until 1930—seventy years after it was written, twenty years after Brewer's death.*

Monday morning, April 29, [1861,] . . . we crossed the San Luis Pass of the Santa Lucia Mountains, a pass about 1,500 or 1,800 feet high, and entered the Santa Margarita Valley. North of the Santa Lucia chain, which trends off to the northwest and ends at Monterey, lies the valley of Salinas, a valley running northwest, widening toward its mouth, and at least a hundred and fifty miles long. The valley branches above. One branch, the west, is the Santa Margarita, into which we descended from the San Luis Pass. We followed down this valley to near its junction with the Salinas River and camped at the Atascadero Ranch, about twenty-two miles from San Luis Obispo and six from the Mission of Santa Margarita.

On passing the Santa Lucia the entire aspect of the country changed. It was as if we had passed into another land and another clime. The

93

Salinas Valley thus far is much less verdant than we anticipated. There are more trees but less grass. Imagine a plain ten to twenty miles wide, cut up by valleys into summits of nearly the same level, their sides rounded into gentle slopes. The soil is already dry and parched, the grass already as dry as hay, except along streams, the hills brown as a stubble field. But scattered over these hills and in these valleys are trees every few rods—great oaks, often of immense size, ten, twelve, eighteen, and more feet in circumference, but not high; their widespreading branches making heads often over a hundred feet in diameter—of the deepest green foliage—while from every branch hangs a trailing lichen, often several feet long and delicate as lace. In passing over this country, every hill and valley presents a new view of these trees—here a park, there a vista with the blue mountains ahead. I would never tire of watching some of these beautiful places of natural scenery. A few pines were seen for several miles, with a very open, airy habit, entirely unlike any pine I have ever seen before, even lighter and airier than the Italian pines common in southern France by the Mediterranean. They cast but little shade.

Camp No. 29, Jolon Ranch, on San Antonio River

I did not write last Sunday as there was an American ranch near our camp and we borrowed some magazines, rare luxuries for camp, and I read them all day. The American who has this ranch keeps fifteen or sixteen thousand sheep. He is a very gentlemanly Virginian and was very kind to us. He says that the loss of sheep by wolves, bears, and rattlesnakes is quite an item. We are in a bear region. Three men have been killed within a year near our last camp by grizzlies.

Monday we came on here, about twenty-five miles. The day was intensely hot, and as we rode over the dry roads the sun was scorching. We crossed a ridge by a horrible road and came into the valley of the San Antonio, a small branch of the Salinas, and followed up it to this point, where we are camped on its bank. We passed but one ranch and house in the twenty-five miles. In one place, two bears had followed the road some distance the night before—their tracks were very plain in the dust. . . .

The last two days we have been exploring the hills. Yesterday, with Averill, I climbed some hills. Today he had to go to a store a few miles distant for flour, so I took a long tramp of eighteen to twenty miles alone. We got an early breakfast, and I started in the cool of the morning, with a bag of lunch, compass, canteen of water, and knife, pistol, and hammer in belt. As one is so liable to find bears and lions here, it is not well to be without arms. I pushed back over the hills and through canyons about ten miles from camp to the chain of rugged mountains west of us. I was indeed alone in the solitudes. The way led up a canyon about four miles, with high steep hills on each side, then a ridge to be crossed, from which I had a fine view, then down again and among gentle hills about three miles farther to the base of the mountains. Here a stream was crossed by pulling off boots and wading, and then up a canyon into the mountains. This last I followed as far as I considered safe, for it was just the place for grizzlies, and I kept a sharp lookout.

Here I climbed a ridge to get a view behind. The slope was very steep, the soil hot, no wind, and the sun like a furnace. I got the view and information I desired. A very rugged landscape of mountains behind, steep, rocky, black with chaparral, 3,500 to 4,000 feet high. In front was the series of ridges I had crossed; beyond, the Salinas Valley, with blue mountains on the distant eastern horizon. Some very peculiar rocky pinnacles of brown rock rose like spires near me, several hundred feet high—naked rocks. . . .

The grizzly bear is much more dreaded than I had any idea of. A wounded grizzly is much more to be feared than even a lion; a tiger is not more ferocious. They will kill and eat sheep, oxen, and horses, are as swift as a horse, of immense strength, quick though clumsy, and very tenacious of life. A man stands a slight chance if he wounds a bear, but not mortally, and a shot must be well directed to kill. The universal advice by everybody is to let them alone if we see them, unless we are well prepared for battle and have experienced hunters along. They will generally let men alone, unless attacked, so I have no serious fears of them.

Less common than bear are the California lions, a sort of panther, about the color of a lion, and size of a small tiger, but with longer body. They are very savage, and I have heard of a number of cases of their killing men. But don't be alarmed on my account—I don't court adventures with any such strangers. Deer are quite common. Formerly there were many antelope, but they are very rapidly disappearing. We have seen none yet. Rabbits and hares abound; a dozen to fifty we often see in a single day, and during winter ate many of them.

There are many birds of great beauty. One finds the representatives of various lands and climes. Not only the crow, but also the raven is found, precisely like the European bird; there are turkey-buzzards, also a large vulture something like the condor—an immense bird. Owls are very plenty, and the cries of several kinds are often heard the same night. Hawks, of various sizes and kinds and very tame, live on the numerous squirrels and gophers. I see a great variety of birds with beautiful plumage, from hummingbirds up.

But it is in reptile and insect life that this country stands preeminent. There are snakes of many species, and some of large size, generally harmless, but a few venomous. Several species of large lizards are very abundant. Salamanders and chameleons are dodging around every log and basking on every stone. Hundreds or thousands may be seen in a day, from three inches to a foot long. Some strange species are covered with horns like the horned frogs.

But insects are the most numerous. They swarm everywhere. House flies were as abundant in our tent in winter as at home in summer. Ticks and bugs get on us whenever we go in the woods. Just where we are now camped there are myriads of bugs in the ground, not poisonous, but annoying by their running over one. Last night I could scarcely sleep, and shook perhaps a hundred or two hundred out of my blankets this morning.

I shall sleep outdoors tonight—in fact, all the rest are asleep but me, and only one is in the tent. We are under some cottonwood trees, which so swarm with ladybugs that Mike yesterday counted how many he brushed off of him in an hour. They amounted to 250—but he sat still under the tree. Scorpions occur farther south and are much dreaded. The equally dreaded tarantula abounds here. It is an enormous spider, larger than a large bumblebee, and has teeth as large as a rattlesnake's. I killed one by our tent at Camp 27, and saved his teeth as a curiosity. Their holes in the ground are most ingenious.

Camp 31, Guadalupe Ranch, May 12

We left San Antonio Thursday morning, May 9, and followed up the valley a few miles, then crossed a high steep ridge over one thousand feet high, which separates the San Antonio from the Salinas, and then descended and struck down the great Salinas plain. Dry as had been the region for the last sixty or seventy miles, it was nothing to this plain.

The Salinas Valley for a hundred or more miles from the sea, up to the San Antonio hills, is a great plain ten to thirty miles wide. Great stretches are almost perfectly level, or have a very slight slope from the mountains to the river which winds through it. The ground was dry and parched and the very scanty grass was entirely dry. One saw no signs of vegetation at the first glance—that is, no green thing on the plain—so a belt of timber by the stream, from twenty to a hundred rods wide, stood out as a band of the liveliest green in this waste. The mouth of this valley opens into Monterey Bay, like a funnel, and the northwest wind from the Pacific draws up through this heated flue, with terrible force. Wherever we have found a valley opening to the northwest, we have found these winds, fierce in the afternoon. For over fifty miles we must face it on this plain. Sometimes it would nearly sweep us from our mules—it seemed as if nothing could stand its force. The air was filled with dry dust and sand, so that we could not see the hills at the sides, the fine sand stinging our faces like shot, the air as dry as if it had come from a furnace, but not so very hot—it is wonderfully parching. The poor feed and this parching wind reduced our mules in a few days as much as two weeks' hard work would. Our lips cracked and bled, our eyes were bloodshot, and skins smarting.

We stopped for lunch at a point where the mules could descend to the river. A high terrace, or bluff, skirts the present river—that is, the plain lies from 75 to 100 feet above the present river. The mules picked some scanty herbage at the base of the bluff; we took our lunch in the hot sun and piercing wind, then drove on. We pulled off from the road a mile or so at night, and stopped beneath a bluff near the river. We had slept in the open air the previous night and did so again. It runs very cold during the clear nights, yet so dry was it that no dew fell those two nights, cold as it was! The mules found some picking where you would think that a sheep or a goat would starve.

Friday we pushed on all day, facing the wind. We met a train of seven wagons, with tents and beds—a party of twenty-five or thirty persons from San Jose going to the hot springs, some on horseback. Two-thirds were ladies. A curious way for a "fashionable trip to the springs," you say, but it is the style here. They will camp there and have a grand time, I will warrant. We kept to the left bank of the river, through the Mission Soledad. Before reaching it we crossed the sandy bed of a dry creek, where the sand drifted like snow and piled up behind and among the bushes like snowbanks.

The Mission Soledad is a sorry looking place, all ruins—a single house, or at most two, are inhabited. We saw the sign up, "Soledad Store," and went in, got some crackers at twenty-five cents a pound, and went on. Quite extensive ruins surround the place, empty buildings, roofless walls of adobe, and piles of clay, once walls. It looked very desolate. I do not know where they got their water in former times, but it is dry enough now. We came on seventeen miles farther. Here we find tolerable feed and a spring of poor water, so here is a ranch.

Sorry as has been this picture, it is not overdrawn, yet all this land is occupied as "ranches" under Spanish grants. Cattle are watered at the river and feed on the plains, and scanty as is the feed, thousands are kept on this space, which must be at least four to six thousand square miles, counting way back to the Santa Lucia Mountains. The ranches do not cover all this, but cover the water, which is the same thing. We could see a house by the river every fifteen to eighteen miles, and saw frequent herds of cattle. The season is unusually dry, and the plain seems much poorer than it really is. In the spring, two months ago, it was all green, and must have been of exceeding beauty. With water this would be finer than the Rhine Valley itself; as it is, it is half desert. . . .

Yesterday I climbed the ridge southwest of camp. I ascended about 8,000 or 8,500 feet, a hard climb, and had a good view of over a hundred miles of the Salinas Valley from the Bay of Monterey to above where we last struck it, or over the extreme limits of about 130 to 150 miles, with the successive ridges beyond. Four thousand to seven thousand square miles must have been spread out before me. I have never been in a land before with so many extensive views—the wide valley, brown and dry, the green belt of timber winding through it, like a green ribbon, the mountains beyond, dried and gray at the base, and deep green with chaparral on their sides and summits, with ridge after ridge stretching away beyond in the blue distance. Then to the north, a landscape I had not seen before, with the whole Bay of Monterey in the northwest. To the west and south of me was the very rugged and forbidding chain of mountains that extends from Monterey along the coast to San Luis Obispo and there trends more easterly—the Sierra Santa Lucia.

I have found much of intense geological interest during the last two weeks. I had intended to spend at least two weeks more in this valley had we found water or feed as we expected. Not finding it, and having four weeks on our hands before the rendezvous with Professor Whitney at San Juan, I decided to push on to Monterey, which I had not intended to visit. We are now within eight or ten leagues of there—will be there in a few days. I feel now that we are indeed working north, and I long to be in San Francisco again. It is now over five months since I have attended church (Protestant), and have only had that privilege three times since I left New York.

Sunday Evening

Today has been a windier day on the plain than any other day we were on it. I am glad enough we are sheltered here in camp. Clouds of gray dust, rising to the height of five or six thousand feet, have shut out the view in the north all this afternoon, and even the hills opposite could not be seen at times, and all day they have been obscurely seen through this veil. If it is thus in May, what must it be here in July or August, as no rain will fall for at least four months yet! It was interesting yesterday, while on the peaks above, to watch the great current of air up the valley, increasing with the day until at last the valley seemed filled with gray smoke.

While speaking of the plain I forgot to mention the mirage that we had. The sun on the hot waste produced precisely the effect of water in the distance; we would see a clear lake ahead, in which would be reflected the objects on the plain. This was most marked on the dry sands near Soledad—we could see the trees at the mission mirrored in the clear surface—but it kept retreating as we advanced. The illusion was perfect. At times the atmospheric aberration would only cause objects to be distorted—wagons and cattle would appear much higher than they really were, as if seen through poor glass.

Napa Valley

The Sea Fogs

Robert Louis Stevenson (1850–1894) spent a year in California, arriving in 1879 to marry his fiancée and to improve his weak lungs. The highlight was a short honeymoon on Mount Saint Helena. That year resulted in one of the Scottish writer's most charming books, Silverado Squatters *(1883), the title referring to his visit to the abandoned Silverado Mine in Napa County.*

T he scene . . . is on a high mountain. There are, indeed, many higher; there are many of a noble outline. It is no place of pilgrimage for the summary globe-trotter; but to one who lives upon its sides, Mount Saint Helena soon becomes a center of interest. It is the Mont Blanc of one section of the Californian Coast Range, none of its near neighbors rising to one-half its altitude. It looks down on much green, intricate country. It feeds in the spring-time many splashing brooks. From its summit you must have an excellent lesson of geography: seeing, to the south, San Francisco Bay, with Tamalpais on the one hand and Mount Diablo on the other; to the west and thirty miles away, the open ocean; eastward, across the cornlands and thick tule swamps of Sacramento Valley, to where the Central Pacific Railroad begins to climb the sides of the Sierras; and northward, for what I know, the white head of Shasta looking down on Oregon. Three counties, Napa County, Lake County, and Sonoma County, march across its cliffy shoulders. Its naked peak stands nearly four thousand five hundred feet above the sea; its sides are fringed with forest; and the soil, where it is bare, glows warm with cinnabar.

Life in its shadow goes rustically forward. Bucks, and bears, and rattlesnakes, and former mining operations, are the staple of men's talk. Agriculture has only begun to mount above the valley. And though in a few years from now the whole district may be smiling with farms, passing trains shaking the mountain to the heart, many-windowed hotels lighting up the night like factories, and a prosperous city occupying the site of sleepy Calistoga; yet in the meantime, around the foot of that mountain the silence of nature reigns in a great measure unbroken, and the people of hill and valley go sauntering about their business as in the days before the flood. . . .

A change in the color of the light usually called me in the morning. By a certain hour, the long, vertical chinks in our western gable, where the boards had shrunk and separated, flashed suddenly into my eyes as stripes of dazzling blue, at once so dark and splendid that I used to marvel how the qualities could be combined. At an earlier hour, the heavens in that quarter were still quietly colored, but the shoulder of the mountain which shuts in the cañon already glowed with sunlight in a wonderful compound of gold and rose and green; and this too would kindle, although more mildly and with rainbow tints, the fissures of our crazy gable. If I were sleeping heavily, it was the bold blue that struck me awake; if more lightly, then I would come to myself in that earlier and fairier light.

One Sunday morning, about five, the first brightness called me. I rose and turned to the east, not for my devotions, but for air. The night had been very still. The little private gale that blew every evening in our cañon, for ten minutes or perhaps a quarter of an hour, had swiftly blown itself out; in the hours that followed not a sight of wind had shaken the treetops; and our barrack, for all it breaches, was less fresh that morning than of wont. But I had no sooner reached the window than I forgot all else in the sight that met my eyes, and I made but two bounds into my clothes, and down the crazy plank to the platform.

The sun was still concealed below the opposite hilltops, though it was shining already, not twenty feet above my head, on our own mountain slope. But the scene, beyond a few near features, was entirely changed. Napa Valley was gone; gone were all the lower slopes and woody foothills of the range; and in their place, not a thousand feet below me, rolled a great level ocean. It was as though I had gone to bed the night before, safe in a nook of inland mountains, and had awakened in a bay upon the coast. I had seen these inundations from below; at Calistoga I had risen and gone abroad in the early morning, coughing and sneezing, under fathoms on fathoms of grey sea-vapor, like a cloudy sky—a dull sight for the artist, and a painful experience for the invalid. But, to sit aloft one's self in the pure air and under the unclouded dome of heaven, and thus look down on the submergence of the valley, was strangely different and even delightful to the eye. Far away were hilltops like little islands. Nearer, a smokey surf beat about the foot of precipices and poured into all the coves of these rough mountains. The color of that fog ocean was a thing never to be forgotten. For an instant, among the Hebrides and just about sundown, I have seen something like it on the sea itself. But the white was not so opaline; nor was there, what surprisingly increased the effect, that breathless, crystal stillness over all. Even in its gentlest moods the salt sea travails, moaning among the weeds or lisping on the sand; but that vast fog ocean lay in a trance of silence, nor did the sweet air of the morning tremble with a sound.

As I continued to sit upon the dump, I began to observe that this sea was not so level as at first sight it appeared to be. Away in the extreme south, a little hill of fog arose against the sky above the general surface, and as it had already caught the sun, it shone on the horizon like the topsails of some giant ship. There were huge waves, stationary, as it seemed, like waves in a frozen sea; and yet, as I looked again, I was not sure but they were moving after all, with a slow and august advance. And while I was yet doubting, a promontory of the hills some four or five miles away, conspicuous by a bouquet of tall pines, was in a single instant overtaken and swallowed up. It reappeared in a little, with its pines, but this time as an islet, and only to be swallowed up once more and then for good. This set me looking nearer, and I saw that in every cove along the line of mountains the fog was being piled in higher and higher, as though by some wind that was inaudible to me. I could trace its progress, one pine tree first growing hazy and then disappearing after another; although sometimes there was none of this fore-running haze, but the whole opaque white ocean gave a start and swallowed a piece of mountain at a gulp. It was to flee these poisonous fogs that I had left the seaboard, and climbed so high among the mountains. And now, behold, here came the fog to besiege me in my chosen altitudes, and yet came so beautifully that my first thought was of welcome.

The sun had now gotten much higher, and through all the gaps of the hills it cast long bars of gold across that white ocean. An eagle, or some other very great bird of the mountain, came wheeling over the nearer pine tops and hung, poised and something sideways, as if to look abroad on that unwonted desolation, spying, perhaps with terror, for the eyries of her comrades. Then, with a long cry, she disappeared again toward Lake County and the clearer air. At length it seemed to me as if the flood were beginning to subside. The old landmarks, by whose disappearance I had measured its advance, here a crag, there a brave pine tree, now began, in the inverse order, to make their reappearance into daylight. I judged all danger of the fog was over. This was not Noah's flood; it was but a morning spring, and would now drift out seaward whence it came. So, mightily relieved, and a good deal exhilarated by the sight, I went into the house to light the fire.

I suppose it was nearly seven when I once more mounted the platform to look abroad. The fog ocean had swelled up enormously since last I saw it; and a few hundred feet below me, in the deep gap where the Toll House stands and the road runs through Lake County, it had already topped the slope, and was pouring over and down the other side like driving smoke. The wind had climbed along with it; and though I was still in calm air, I could see the trees tossing below me, and their long, strident sighing mounted to me where I stood.

Half an hour later, the fog had surmounted all the ridge on the opposite side of the gap, though a shoulder of the mountain still warded it out of our cañon. Napa Valley and its bounding hills were now utterly blotted out. The fog, sunny white in the sunshine, was pouring over into Lake County in a huge, ragged cataract, tossing treetops appearing and disappearing in the spray. The air struck with a little chill, and set me coughing. It smelt strong of the fog, like the smell of a washing-house, but with a shrewd tang of the sea salt.

Had it not been for two things—the sheltering spur which answered as a dike, and the great valley on the other side which rapidly engulfed whatever mounted—our own little platform in the canyon must have been already buried a hundred feet in salt and poisonous air. As it was, the interest of the scene entirely occupied our minds. We were set just out of the wind, and but just above the fog; we could listen to the voice of the one as to music on the stage; we could plunge our eyes down into the other, as into some flowing stream from over the parapet of a bridge; thus we looked on upon a strange, impetuous, silent, shifting exhibition of the powers of nature, and saw the familiar landscape changing from moment to moment like figures in a dream.

The imagination loves to trifle with what is not. Had this been indeed the deluge, I should have felt more strongly, but the emotion would have been similar in kind. I played with the idea, as the child flees in delighted terror from the creations of his fancy. The look of the thing helped me. And when at last I began to flee up the mountain, it was indeed partly to escape from the raw air that kept me coughing, but it was also part in play.

As I ascended the mountainside, I came once more to overlook the upper surface of the fog; but it wore a different appearance from what I had beheld at daybreak. For, first, the sun now fell on it from high overhead, and its surface shone and undulated like a great nor'land moor country, sheeted with untrodden morning snow. And next the new level must have been a thousand or fifteen hundred feet higher than the old, so that only five or six points of all the broken country below me still stood out. Napa Valley was now one with Sonoma on the west. On the hither side, only a thin scattered fringe of bluffs was unsubmerged; and through all the gaps the fog was pouring over, like an ocean, into the blue clear sunny country on the east. There it was soon lost; for it fell instantly into the bottom of the valleys, following the watershed; and the hilltops in that quarter were still clear cut upon the eastern sky.

Through the Toll House gap and over the near ridges on the other side, the deluge was immense. A spray of thin vapor was thrown high above it, arising and falling, and blown into fantastic shapes. The speed of its course was like a mountain torrent. Here and there a few treetops were discovered and then whelmed again; and for one second, the bough of a dead pine beckoned out of the spray like the arm of a drowning man. But still the imagination was dissatisfied, still the ear waited for something more. Had this indeed been water (as it seemed so, to the eye), with what a plunge of reverberating thunder would it have rolled upon its course, disemboweling mountains and deracinating pines! And yet water it was, and seawater at that—true Pacific billows, only somewhat rarefied, rolling in mid-air among the hilltops.

I climbed still higher, among the red rattling gravel and dwarf underwood of Mount Saint Helena, until I could look right down upon Silverado and admire the vapored nook in which it lay. The sunny plain of fog was several hundred feet higher; behind the protesting spur a gigantic accumulation of cottony vapor threatened, with every second, to blow over and submerge our homestead; but the vortex setting past the Toll House was too strong; and there lay our little platform, in the arms of the deluge, but still enjoying its unbroken sunshine. About eleven, however, thin spray came flying over the friendly buttress, and I began to think the fog had hunted out its Jonah after all. But it was the last effort. The wind veered while we were at dinner, and began to blow squally from the mountain summit; and by half past one, all that world of sea-fogs was utterly routed and flying here and there into the south in little rags of cloud. And instead of a lone sea-beach, we found ourselves once more inhabiting a high mountainside, with clear green country far below us, and the light smoke of Calistoga blowing in the air.

This was the great Russian campaign for that season. Now and then, in the early morning, a little white lakelet of fog would be seen far down in Napa Valley; but the heights were not again assailed, nor was the surrounding world again shut off from Silverado.

On Sonoma Mountain

Jack London (1876–1915) was one of the first great native Californian writers, having been born in San Francisco and died at his ranch in the Valley of the Moon in Sonoma County. He wrote more than twenty books, including Call of the Wild *(1903) and* Martin Eden *(1909). In one of his more obscure novels,* Burning Daylight *(1910), he wrote splendidly of the beauty of Sonoma, where the protagonist, a wealthy financier named Daylight, seeks an escape from San Francisco.*

One weekend, feeling heavy and depressed and tired of the city and its ways, he obeyed the impulse of a whim that was later to play an important part in his life. The desire to get out of the city for a whiff of country air and for a change of scene was the cause. Yet, in himself, he made the excuse of going to Glen Ellen for the purpose of inspecting the brickyard with which Holdsworthy had goldbricked him.

He spent the night in a little country hotel, and on Sunday morning, astride a saddle-horse rented from the Glen Ellen butcher, rode out of the village. The brickyard was close at hand on the flat beside the Sonoma Creek. The kilns were visible among the trees, when he glanced to the left and caught sight of a cluster of wooded knolls half a mile away, perched on the rolling slopes of Sonoma Mountain. The mountain, itself wooded, towered behind. The trees on the knolls seemed to beckon to him. The dry, early-summer air, shot through with sunshine, was wine to him. Unconsciously he drank it in in deep breaths. The prospect of the brickyard was uninviting. He was jaded with all things business, and the wooded knolls were calling to him. A horse was between his legs—a good horse, he decided, one that sent him back to the cayuses he had ridden during his eastern Oregon boyhood. He had been somewhat of a rider in those early days, and the champ of bit and crack of saddle-leather sounded good to him now.

Resolving to have his fun first and to look over the brickyard afterward, he rode up on the hill, prospecting for a way across country to get to the knolls. He left the country road at the first gate he came to and cantered through a hayfield. The grain was waist high on either side of the wagon road, and he sniffed the warm aroma of it with delighted nostrils. Larks flew up before him, and from everywhere came mellow notes. From the appearance of the road it was patent that it had been used for hauling clay to the now idle brickyard. Salving his conscience with the idea that this was part of the inspection, he rode on to the clay pit—a huge scar in a hillside. But he did not linger long, swinging off again to the left and leaving the road. Not a farmhouse was in sight, and the change from the city crowding was essentially satisfying. He rode now through open woods, across little flower-scattered glades, till he came upon a spring. Flat on the ground he drank deeply of the clear water, and looking about him, felt with a shock the beauty of the world. It came to him like a discovery; he had never realized it before, he concluded, and also, he had forgotten much. One could not sit in at high finance and keep track of such things. As he drank in the air, the scene, and the distant song of larks, he felt like a poker player rising from a night-long table and coming forth from the pent atmosphere to taste the freshness of the morn.

At the base of the knolls he encountered a tumble-down stake-and-rider fence. From the look of it he judged it must be forty years old at least—the work of some first pioneer who had taken up the land when the days of gold had ended. The woods were very thick here, yet fairly clear of underbrush, so that, while the blue sky was screened by the arched branches, he was able to ride beneath. He now found himself in a hook of several acres, where the oak and manzanita and madroño gave way to clusters of stately redwoods. Against the foot of a steep-sloped knoll he came upon a magnificent group of redwoods that seemed to have gathered about the tiny gurgling spring.

He halted his horse, for beside the spring uprose a wild California lily. It was a wonderful flower, growing there in the cathedral nave of lofty trees. At least eight feet in height, its stem rose straight and slender, green and bare, for two-thirds its length, and then burst into a shower of snow-white waxen bells. There were hundreds of these blossoms, all from the one stem, delicately poised and ethereally frail. Daylight had never seen anything like it. Slowly his gaze wandered from it to all that was about him. He took off his hat, with almost a vague religious feeling. This was different. No room for contempt and evil here. This was clean and fresh and beautiful—something he could respect. It was like a church. The atmosphere was one of holy calm. Here man felt the prompting of nobler things. Much of this and more was in Daylight's heart as he looked about him. But it was not a concept of his mind. He merely felt it without thinking about it at all.

On the steep incline above the spring grew tiny maidenhair ferns, while higher up were larger ferns and brakes. Great, moss-covered trunks of fallen trees lay here and there, slowly sinking back and merging into the level of the forest mould. Beyond, in a slightly clearer space, wild grape and honeysuckle swung in green riot from gnarled old oak trees. A gray Douglas squirrel crept out on a branch and watched him. From somewhere came the distant knocking of a woodpecker. This sound did not disturb the hush and awe of the place. Quiet woods' noises belonged there and made the solitude complete. The tiny bubbling ripple of the spring and the gray flash of squirrel were as yardsticks with which to measure the silence and motionless repose.

"Might be a million miles from anywhere," Daylight whispered to himself.

But ever his gaze returned to the wonderful lily beside the bubbling spring.

He tethered the horse and wandered on foot among the knolls. Their tips were crowned with century-old spruce trees, and their sides clothed with oaks and madroños and native holly. But to the perfect redwoods belonged the small but deep canyon that threaded its way among the knolls. Here he found no passage out for his horse and he returned to the lily beside the spring. On foot, tripping, stumbling, leading the animal, he forced his way up the hillside. And ever the ferns carpeted the way of his feet, ever the forest climbed with him and arched overhead, and ever the clean joy and sweetness stole in upon his senses.

On the crest he came through an amazing thicket of velvet-trunked young madroños, and emerged on an open hillside that led down into a tiny valley. The sunshine was at first dazzling in its brightness, and he paused and rested, for he was panting from the exertion. Not of old had he known shortness of breath such as this, and muscles that so easily tired at a stiff climb. A tiny stream ran down the tiny valley through a tiny meadow that was carpeted knee high with grass and blue and white nemophila. The hillside was covered with mariposa lilies and wild hyacinth, down through which his horse dropped slowly, with circumspect feet and reluctant gait.

Crossing the stream, Daylight followed a faint cattle trail over a low, rocky hill and through a wine-wooded forest of manzanita, and emerged upon another tiny valley, down which filtered another spring-fed meadow-bordered streamlet. A jackrabbit bounded from a bush under his horse's nose, leaped the stream, and vanished up the opposite hillside of scrub oak. Daylight watched it admiringly as he rode on to the head of the meadow. Here he startled up a many-pronged buck, that seemed to soar across the meadow, and to soar over the stake-and-rider fence, and, still soaring, disappeared in a friendly copse beyond.

Daylight's delight was unbounded. It seemed to him that he had never been so happy. His old woods training was aroused, and he was keenly interested in everything—in the moss on the trees and branches; in the bunches of mistletoe hanging in the oaks; in the nest of a wood rat; in the watercress growing in the sheltered eddies of the little stream; in the butterflies drifting through the rifted sunshine and shadow; in the blue jays that flashed in splashes of gorgeous color across the forest aisles; in the tiny birds, like wrens, that hopped among the bushes and imitated certain minor quail-calls; and in the crimson-crested woodpecker that ceased its knocking and cocked its head on one side to survey him. Crossing the stream, he struck faint vestiges of a wood-road, used, evidently, a generation back, when the meadow had been cleared of its oaks. He found a hawk's nest on the lightning-shattered tipmost top of a six-foot redwood. And to complete it all, his horse stumbled upon several large broods of half-grown quail, and the air was filled with the thrum of their flight. He halted and watched the young ones "petrifying" and disappearing on the ground before his eyes, and listening to the anxious calls of the old ones hidden in the thickets.

"It sure beats country places and bungalows at Menlo Park," he communed aloud, "and if ever I get the hankering for country life, it's me for this every time."

The old wood-road led him to a clearing, where a dozen acres of grapes grew on wine-red soil. A cow path, more trees and thickets, and he dropped down a hillside to the southeast exposure. Here, poised above a big forested canyon, and looking out upon Sonoma Valley, was a small farmhouse. With its barn and outhouses it snuggled into a nook in the hillside, which protected it from west and north. It was the erosion from this hillside, he judged, that had formed the little level stretch of vegetable garden. The soil was fat and black, and there was water in plenty, for he saw several faucets running wide open.

Forgotten was the brickyard. Nobody was at home, but Daylight dismounted and ranged the vegetable garden, eating strawberries and green peas, inspecting the old adobe barn and the rusty plough and barrow, and rolling and smoking cigarettes while he watched the antics of several broods of young chickens and the mother hens. A foot trail that led down the wall of the big canyon invited him, and he proceeded to follow it. A water pipe, usually above ground, paralleled the trail, which he concluded led upstream to the bed of the creek. The wall of the canyon was several hundred feet from top to bottom, and so magnificent were the untouched trees that the place was plunged in perpetual shade. He measured with his eye spruces five and six feet in diameter and redwoods even larger. One such he passed, a twister that was at least ten or eleven feet through. The trail led straight to a small dam where was the intake for the pipe that watered the vegetable garden. Here, beside the stream, were alders and laurel trees, and he walked through fern-brakes higher than his head. Velvety moss was everywhere, out of which grew maidenhair and gold-back ferns.

Save for the dam, it was a virgin wild. No axe had invaded, and the trees died only of old age and stress of winter storm. The huge trunks of those that had fallen lay moss-covered, slowly resolving back into the soil from which they sprang. Some had lain so long that they were quite gone, though their faint outlines, level with the mould, could still be seen. Others bridged the stream, and from beneath the bulk of one monster half a dozen younger trees, overthrown and crushed by the fall, growing out along the ground, still lived and prospered, their roots bathed by the stream, their upshooting branches catching the sunlight through the gap that had been made in the forest roof.

Back at the farmhouse, Daylight mounted and rode on away from the ranch and into the wilder canyons and steeper steeps beyond. Nothing could satisfy his holiday spirit now but the ascent of Sonoma Mountain. And here on the crest, three hours afterward, he emerged, tired and sweaty, garments torn and face and hands scratched, but with sparkling eyes and an unwonted zestfulness of expression. He felt the illicit pleasure of a schoolboy playing truant. The big gambling table of San Francisco seemed very far away. But there was much more than illicit pleasure in his mood. It was as though he were going through a sort of cleansing bath. No room here for all the sordidness, meanness, and viciousness that filled the dirty pool of city existence. Without pondering in detail upon the matter at all, his sensations were of purification and uplift. Had he been asked to state how he felt, he would merely have said that he was having a good time; for he was unaware in his self-consciousness of the potent charm of nature that was percolating through his city-rotted body and brain—potent, in that he came of an abysmal past of wilderness dwellers, while he was himself coated with the thinnest rind of crowded civilization.

There were no houses in the summit of Sonoma Mountain, and, all alone under the azure California sky, he reined in on the southern edge of the peak. He saw open pasture country, intersected with wooden canyons, descending to the south and west from his feet, crease on crease and roll on roll, from lower level to lower level, to the floor of Petaluma Valley, flat as a billiard table, a cardboard affair, all patches and squares of geometrical regularity where the fat freeholds were farmed. Beyond, to the west, rose range on range of mountains cuddling purple mists of atmosphere in their valleys, and still beyond, over the last range of all, he saw the silver sheen of the Pacific. Swinging his horse, he surveyed the west and north, from Santa Rosa to Mount St. Helena, and on to the east, across Sonoma Valley, to the chaparral-covered range that shut off the view of Napa Valley. Here, partway up the eastern wall of Sonoma Valley, in range of a line intersecting the little village of Glen Ellen, he made out a scar upon a hillside. His first thought was that it was the dump of a mine tunnel, but remembering that he was not in gold-bearing country, he dismissed the scar from his mind and continued the circle of his survey to the southeast, where, across the waters of San Pablo Bay, he could see, sharp and distant, the twin peaks of Mount Diablo. To the south was Mount Tamalpais, and, yes, he was right, fifty miles away, where the draughty winds of the

Pacific blew in the Golden Gate, the smoke of San Francisco made a low-lying haze against the sky.

"I ain't seen so much country all at once in many a day," he thought aloud.

He was loath to depart, and it was not for an hour that he was able to tear himself away and take the descent of the mountain. . . .

Instead of returning to the city on Monday, Daylight rented the butcher's horse for another day and crossed the bed of the valley to the eastern hills. . . . On through the chaparral he went, following faint cattle trails and working slowly upward till he came out on the divide and gazed down into Napa Valley and back across to Sonoma Mountain.

"A sweet land," he muttered, "an almighty sweet land."

Salinas Valley

Flight

John Steinbeck (1902–1968), the Nobel Prize–winning writer best known for The Grapes of Wrath *(1939), was born and raised in the Salinas Valley— the "long valley" along the Salinas River in central California—where he set much of his fiction. The following is excerpted from the short story "Flight" in the collection* The Long Valley *(1938), about nineteen-year-old Pepé Torres, who, after killing another man in a knife fight, flees from his farm on Monterey's wild coast into the foothills of the Santa Lucia Mountains.*

It was the first dawn when he rode up the hill toward the little canyon which let a trail into the mountains. Moonlight and day-light fought with each other, and the two warring qualities made it difficult to see. Before Pepé had gone a hundred yards, the outlines of his figure were misty; and long before he entered the canyon, he had become a grey, indefinite shadow.

Mama stood stiffly in front of her doorstep, and on either side of her stood Emilio and Rosy. They cast furtive glances at Mama now and then.

When the grey shape of Pepé melted into the hillside and disap-peared, Mama relaxed. She began the high, whining keen of the death wail. "Our beautiful—our brave," she cried. "Our protector, our son is gone." Emilio and Rosy moaned beside her. "Our beautiful—our brave, he is gone." It was the formal wail. It rose to a high piercing whine and subsided to a moan. Mama raised it three times and then she turned and went into the house and shut the door.

Emilio and Rosy stood wondering in the dawn. They heard Mama whimpering in the house. They went out to sit on the cliff above the ocean. They touched shoulders. "When did Pepé come to be a man?" Emilio said.

"Last night," said Rosy. "Last night in Monterey." The ocean clouds turned red with the sun that was behind the mountains.

"We will have no breakfast," said Emilio. "Mama will not want to cook." Rosy did not answer him. "Where is Pepé gone?" he asked.

Rosy looked around at him. She drew her knowledge from the quiet air. "He has gone on a journey. He will never come back."

"Is he dead? Do you think he is dead?"

Rosy looked back at the ocean again. A little steamer, drawing a line of smoke, sat on the edge of the horizon. "He is not dead," Rosy explained. "Not yet."

Pepé rested the big rifle across the saddle in front of him. He let the horse walk up the hill and he didn't look back. The stony slope took on a coat of short brush so that Pepé found the entrance to a trail and entered it.

When he came to the canyon opening, he swung once in his saddle and looked back, but the houses were swallowed in the misty light. Pepé jerked forward again. The high shoulder of the canyon closed in on him. His horse stretched out its neck and sighed and settled to the trail.

It was a well-worn path, dark soft leaf-mould earth strewn with broken pieces of sandstone. The trail rounded the shoulder of the canyon and dropped steeply into the bed of the stream. In the shallows the water ran smoothly, glinting in the first morning sun. Small round stones on the bottom were as brown as rust with sun moss. In the sand along the edges of the stream the tall, rich wild mint grew, while in the water itself the cress, old and tough, had gone to heavy seed. The path went into the stream and emerged on the other side. The horse sloshed into the water and stopped. Pepé dropped his bridle and let the beast drink of the running water.

Soon the canyon sides became steep and the first giant sentinel redwoods guarded the trail, great rounded trunks bearing foliage as green and lacy as ferns. Once Pepé was among the trees, the sun was lost. A perfumed and purple light lay in the pale green of the underbrush. Gooseberry bushes and blackberries and tall ferns lined the stream, and overhead the branches of the redwoods met and cut off the sky.

Pepé drank from the water bag, and he reached into the flour sack and brought out a black string of jerky. His white teeth gnawed at the string until the tough meat parted. He chewed slowly and drank occasionally from the water bag. His little eyes were slumberous and tired, but the muscles of his face were hard set. The earth of the trail was black now. It gave up a hollow sound under the walking hoofbeats.

The stream fell more sharply. Little waterfalls splashed on the stones. Five-fingered ferns hung over the water and dripped spray from their fingertips. Pepé rode half over in his saddle, dangling one leg loosely. He picked a bay leaf from a tree beside the way and put it into his mouth for a moment to flavor the dry jerky. He held the gun loosely across the pommel.

Suddenly he squared in his saddle, swung the horse from the trail, and kicked it hurriedly up behind a big redwood tree. He pulled up the reins tight against the bit to keep the horse from whinnying. His face was intent and his nostrils quivered a little.

A hollow pounding came down the trail, and a horseman rode by, a fat man with red cheeks and a white stubble beard. His horse put down its head and blubbered at the trail when it came to the place where Pepé had turned off. "Hold up!" said the man and he pulled up his horse's head.

When the last sound of the hooves died away, Pepé came back into the trail again. He did not relax in the saddle any more. He lifted the big rifle and swung the lever to throw a shell into the chamber, and then he let down the hammer to half cock.

The trail grew very steep. Now the redwood trees were smaller and their tops were dead, bitten dead where the wind reached them. The horse plodded on; the sun went slowly overhead and started down toward the afternoon.

Where the stream came out of a side canyon, the trail left it. Pepé dismounted and watered his horse and filled up his water bag. As soon as the trail had parted from the stream, the trees were gone and only the thick brittle sage and manzanita and chaparral edged the trail. And the soft black earth was gone, too, leaving only the light tan broken rock for the trail bed. Lizards scampered away into the brush as the horse rattled over the little stones.

Pepé turned in his saddle and looked back. He was in the open now: he could be seen from a distance. As he ascended the trail the country grew more rough and terrible and dry. The way wound about the bases of the great square rocks. Little grey rabbits skittered in the brush. A bird made a monotonous high creaking. Eastward the bare rock mountaintops were pale and powder dry under the dropping sun. The horse plodded up and up the trail toward a little V in the ridge which was the pass.

Pepé looked suspiciously back every minute or so, and his eyes sought the tops of the ridges ahead. Once, on a white barren spur, he saw a black figure for a moment, but he looked quickly away, for it was one of the dark watchers. No one knew who the watchers were, nor where they lived, but it was better to ignore them and never to show interest in them. They did not bother one who stayed on the trail and minded his own business.

The air was parched and full of light dust blown by the breeze from the eroding mountains. Pepé drank sparingly from his bag and corked it tightly and hung it on the horn again. The trail moved up the dry shale hillside, avoiding rocks, dropping under clefts, climbing in and out of old water scars. When he arrived at the little pass he stopped and looked back for a long time. No dark watchers were to be seen now. The trail behind was empty. Only the high tops of the redwoods indicated where the stream flowed.

Pepé rode on through the pass. His little eyes were nearly closed with weariness, but his face was stern, relentless, and manly. The high mountain wind coasted sighing through the pass and whistled on the edges of the big blocks of broken granite. In the air, a red-tailed hawk sailed over close to the ridge and screamed angrily. Pepé went slowly through the broken jagged pass and looked down on the other side.

The trail dropped quickly, staggering among broken rock. At the bottom of the slope there was a dark crease, thick with brush, and on the other side of the crease a little flat, in which a grove of oak trees grew. A scar of green grass cut across the flat. And behind the flat another mountain rose, desolate with dead rocks and starving little black bushes. Pepé drank from the bag again, for the air was so dry that it encrusted his nostrils and burned his lips. He put the horse down the way, starting little stones that rolled off into the brush. The sun was gone behind the westward mountain now, but still it glowed brilliantly on the oaks and on the grassy flat. The rocks and the hillsides still sent up waves of the heat they had gathered from the day's sun.

Pepé looked up to the top of the next dry withered ridge. He saw a dark form against the sky, a man's figure standing on top of a rock, and he glanced away quickly, not to appear curious. When a moment later he looked up again, the figure was gone.

Downward the trail was quickly covered. Sometimes the horse floundered for footing, sometimes set his feet and slid a little way. They came at last to the bottom where the dark chaparral was higher than Pepé's head. He held up his rifle on one side and his arm on the other to shield his face from the sharp brittle fingers of the brush.

Up and out of the crease he rode, and up a little cliff. The grassy flat was before him, and the round comfortable oaks. For a moment he studied the trail down which he had come, but there was no movement and no sound from it. Finally he rode out over the flat, to the green streak, and at the upper end of the damp he found a little spring welling out of the earth and dropping into a dug basin before it seeped out over the flat.

Pepé filled his bag first, and then he let the thirsty horse drink out of the pool. He led the horse to the clump of oaks, and in the middle of the grove, fairly protected from sight on all sides, he took off the saddle and the bridle and laid them on the ground. The horse stretched his jaws sideways and yawned. Pepé knotted the lead rope about the horse's neck and tied him to a sapling among the oaks, where he could graze in a fairly large circle.

When the horse was gnawing hungrily at the dry grass, Pepé went to the saddle and took a black string of jerky from the sack and strolled to a oak tree on the edge of the grove, from under which he could watch the trail. He sat down in the crisp dry oak leaves and automatically felt for his big black knife to cut the jerky, but he had no knife. He leaned back on his elbow and gnawed at the tough strong meat. His face was blank, but it was a man's face.

The bright evening light washed the eastern ridge, but the valley was darkening. Doves flew down from the hills to the spring, and the quail came running out of the brush and joined them, calling clearly to one another.

Out of the corner of his eye Pepé saw a shadow grow out of the bushy crease. He turned his head slowly. A big spotted wildcat was creeping toward the spring, belly to the ground, moving like thought.

Pepé cocked his rifle and edged the muzzle slowly around. Then he looked apprehensively up the trail and dropped the hammer again. From the ground beside him he picked an oak twig and threw it toward the spring. The quail flew up with a roar and the doves whistled away. The big cat stood up for a long moment; he looked at Pepé with cold yellow eyes, and then fearlessly walked back into the gulch.

The dusk gathered quickly in the deep valley. Pepé muttered his prayers, put his head down on his arm, and went instantly to sleep.

The moon came up and filled the valley with cold blue light, and the wind swept rustling down from the peaks. The owls worked up and down the slopes looking for rabbits. Down in the brush of the gulch a coyote gabbled. The oak trees whispered softly in the night breeze.

Pepé started up, listening. His horse had whinnied. The moon was just slipping behind the western ridge, leaving the valley in darkness behind it. Pepé sat tensely gripping his rifle. From far up the trail he heard an answering whinny and the crash of shod hooves on the broken rock. He jumped to his feet, ran to his horse, and led it under the trees. He threw on the saddle and cinched it tight for the steep trail, caught the unwilling head and forced the bit into the mouth. He felt the saddle to make sure the water bag and the sack of jerky were there. Then he mounted and turned up the hill.

It was velvet dark. The horse found the entrance to the trail where it left the flat and started up, stumbling and slipping on the rocks. Pepé's hand rose up to his head. His hat was gone. He had left it under the oak tree.

The horse had struggled far up the trail when the first change of dawn came into the air, a steel greyness as light mixed thoroughly with dark. Gradually the sharp snaggled edge of the ridge stood out above them, rotten granite tortured and eaten by the winds of time. Pepé had dropped his reins on the horn, leaving direction to the horse. The brush grabbed at his legs in the dark until one knee of his jeans was ripped.

Gradually the light flowed down over the ridge. The starved brush and rocks stood out in the half light, strange and lonely in high per-spective. Then there came warmth into the light. Pepé drew up and looked back, but he could see nothing in the darker valley below. The sky turned blue over the coming sun. In the waste of the mountainside, the poor dry brush grew only three feet high. Here and there, big out-croppings of unrotted granite stood up like mouldering houses. Pepé relaxed a little. He drank from his water bag and bit off a piece of jerky. A single eagle flew over, high in the light.

Without warning Pepé's horse screamed and fell on its side. He was almost down before the rifle crash echoed up from the valley. From a hole behind the struggling shoulder, a stream of bright crimson blood pumped and stopped and pumped and stopped. The hooves threshed on the ground. Pepé lay half stunned beside the horse. He looked slowly down the hill. A piece of sage clipped off beside his head and another crash echoed from side to side of the canyon. Pepé flung himself frantically behind a bush.

He crawled up the hill on his knees and one hand. His right hand held the rifle up off the ground and pushed it ahead of him. He moved with the instinctive care of an animal. Rapidly he wormed his way toward one of the big outcroppings of granite on the hill above him. Where the brush was high he doubled up and ran, but where the cover was slight he wriggled forward on his stomach, pushing the rifle ahead of him. In the last little distance there was no cover at all. Pepé poised and then he darted across the space and flashed around the corner of the rock.

He leaned panting against the stone. When his breath came easier he moved behind the big rock until he came to a narrow split that offered a thin section of vision down the hill. Pepé lay on his stomach and pushed the rifle barrel through the slit and waited.

The sun reddened the western ridges now. Already the buzzards were settling down toward the place where the horse lay. A small brown bird scratched in the dead sage leaves directly in front of the rifle muzzle. The coasting eagle flew back toward the rising sun.

Pepé saw a little movement in the brush far below. His grip tightened on the gun. A little brown doe stepped daintily out on the trail and crossed it and disappeared into the brush again. For a long time Pepé waited. Far below he could see the little flat and the oak trees and the slash of green. Suddenly his eyes flashed back at the trail again. A quarter of a mile down there had been a quick movement in the chaparral. The rifle swung over. The front sight nestled in the V of the rear sight. Pepé studied for a moment and then raised the rear sight a notch. The little movement in the brush came again. The sight settled on it. Pepé squeezed the trigger. The explosion crashed down the mountain and up the other side, and came rattling back. The whole side of the slope grew still. No more movement. And then a white streak cut into the granite of the slit and a bullet whined away and a crash sounded up from below. Pepé felt a sharp pain in his right hand. A sliver of granite was sticking out from between his first and second knuckles and the point protruded from his palm. Carefully he pulled out the sliver of stone. The wound bled evenly and gently. No vein nor artery was cut.

Pepé looked into a little dusty cave in the rock and gathered a handful of spider web, and he pressed the mass into the cut, plastering the soft web into the blood. The flow stopped almost at once.

The rifle was on the ground. Pepé picked it up, levered a new shell into the chamber. And then he slid into the brush on his stomach. Far to the right he crawled, and then up the hill, moving slowly and carefully, crawling to cover and resting and then crawling again.

In the mountains the sun is high in its arc before it penetrates the gorges. The hot face looked over the hill and brought instant heat with it. The white light beat on the rocks and reflected from them and rose up quivering from the earth again, and the rocks and bushes seemed to quiver behind the air.

Pepé crawled in the general direction of the ridge peak, zigzagging for cover. The deep cut between his knuckles began to throb. He crawled close to a rattlesnake before he saw it, and when it raised its dry head and made a soft beginning whirr, he backed up and took another way. The quick grey lizards flashed in front of him, raising a tiny line of dust. He found another mass of spider web and pressed it against his throbbing hand.

Pepé was pushing the rifle with his left hand now. Little drops of sweat ran to the ends of his coarse black hair and rolled down his cheeks. His lips and tongue were growing thick and heavy. His lips writhed to draw saliva into his mouth. His little dark eyes were uneasy and suspicious. Once when a grey lizard passed in front of him on the parched ground and turned its head sideways he crushed it flat with a stone.

When the sun slid past noon he had not gone a mile. He crawled exhaustedly a last hundred yards to a patch of high sharp manzanita, crawled desperately, and when the patch was reached he wriggled in among the tough gnarly trunks and dropped his head on his left arm. There was little shade in the meager brush, but there was cover and safety. Pepé went to sleep as he lay and the sun beat on his back. A few little birds hopped close to him and peered and hopped away. Pepé squirmed in his sleep and he raised and dropped his wounded hand again and again.

The sun went down behind the peaks and the cool evening came, and then the dark. A coyote yelled from the hillside. Pepé started awake and looked about with misty eyes. His hand was swollen and heavy; a little thread of pain ran up the inside of his arm and settled in a pocket in his armpit. He peered about and then stood up, for the mountains were black and the moon had not yet risen. Pepé stood up in the dark. The coat of his father pressed on his arm. His tongue was swollen until it nearly filled his mouth. He wriggled out of the coat and dropped it in the brush, and then he struggled up the hill, falling over rocks and tearing his way through the brush. The rifle knocked against stones as he went. Little dry avalanches of gravel and shattered stone went whispering down the hill behind him.

After a while the old moon came up and showed the jagged ridgetop ahead of him. By moonlight Pepé traveled more easily. He bent forward so that his throbbing arm hung away from his body. The journey uphill was made in dashes and rests, a frantic rush up a few yards and then a rest. The wind coasted down the slope rattling the dry stems of the bushes.

The moon was at meridian when Pepé came at last to the sharp backbone of the ridgetop. On the last hundred yards of the rise no soil had clung under the wearing winds. The way was on solid rock. He clambered to the top and looked down on the other side. There was a draw like the last below him, misty with moonlight, brushed with dry struggling sage and chaparral. On the other side the hill rose up sharply and at the top the jagged rotten teeth of the mountain showed against the sky. At the bottom of the cut the brush was thick and dark.

Pepé stumbled down the hill. His throat was almost closed with thirst. At first he tried to run, but immediately he fell and rolled. After that he went more carefully. The moon was just disappearing behind the mountains when he came to the bottom. He crawled into the heavy brush feeling with his fingers for water. There was no water in the bed of the stream, only damp earth. Pepé laid his gun down and scooped up a handful of mud and put it in his mouth, and then he spluttered and scraped the earth from this tongue with his fingers, for the mud drew at his mouth like a poultice. He dug a hole in the stream bed with his fingers, dug a little basin to catch water; but before it was very deep his head fell forward on the damp ground and he slept.

The dawn came and the heat of the day fell on the earth, and still Pepé slept. Late in the afternoon his head jerked up. He looked slowly around. His eyes were slits of wariness. Twenty feet away in the heavy brush a big tawny mountain lion stood looking at him. Its long thick tail waved gracefully, its ears were erect with interest, now laid back dangerously. The lion squatted down on its stomach and watched him.

Pepé looked at the hole he had dug in the earth. A half inch of muddy water had collected in the bottom. He tore the sleeve from his hurt arm, with his teeth ripped out a little square, soaked it in the water, and put it in his mouth. Over and over he filled the cloth and sucked it.

Still the lion sat and watched him. The evening came down, but there was no movement on the hills. No birds visited the dry bottom of the cut. Pepé looked occasionally at the lion. The eyes of the yellow beast drooped as though he were about to sleep. He yawned and his long thin red tongue curled out. Suddenly his head jerked around and his nostrils quivered. His big tail lashed. He stood up and slunk like a tawny shadow into the thick brush.

A moment later Pepé heard the sound, the faint far crash of horses' hooves on gravel. And he heard something else, a high whining yelp of a dog.

Pepé took his rifle in his left hand and he glided into the brush almost as quietly as the lion had. In the darkening evening he crouched up the hill toward the next ridge. Only when the dark came did he stand up. His energy was short. Once it was dark he fell over the rocks and slipped to his knees on the steep slope, but he moved on and on up the hill, climbing and scrabbling over the broken hillside.

When he was far up toward the top, he lay down and slept for a little while. The withered moon, shining on his face, awakened him. He stood up and moved up the hill. Fifty yards away he stopped and turned back, for he had forgotten his rifle. He walked heavily down and poked about in the brush, but he could not find his gun. At last he lay down to rest. The pocket of pain in his armpit had grown more sharp. His arm seemed to swell out and fall with every heartbeat. There was no position lying down where the heavy arm did not press against his armpit.

With the effort of a hurt beast, Pepé got up and moved again toward the top of the ridge. He held his swollen arm away from his body with his left hand. Up the steep hill he dragged himself, a few steps and a rest, and a few more steps. At last he was nearing the top. The moon showed the uneven sharp back of it against the sky.

Pepé's brain spun in a big spiral up and away from him. He slumped to the ground and lay still. The rock ridgetop was only a hundred feet above him.

The moon moved over the sky. Pepé half turned on his back. His tongue tried to make words, but only a thick hissing came from between his lips.

When the dawn came. Pepé pulled himself up. His eyes were sane again. He drew his great puffed arm in front of him and looked at the angry wound. The black line ran up from his wrist to his armpit. Automatically he reached in his pocket for the big black knife, but it was not there. His eyes searched the ground. He picked up a sharp blade of stone and scraped at the wound, sawed at the proud flesh and then squeezed the green juice out in big drops. Instantly he threw back his head and whined like a dog. His whole right side shuddered at the pain, but the pain cleared his head.

In the grey light he struggled up the last slope to the ridge and crawled over and lay down behind a line of rocks. Below him lay a deep canyon exactly like the last, waterless and desolate. There was no flat, no oak trees, not even heavy brush in the bottom of it, And on the other side a sharp ridge stood up, thinly brushed with starving sage, littered with broken granite. Strewn over the hill there were giant outcroppings, and on the top the granite teeth stood out against the sky.

The new day was light now. The flame of the sun came over the ridge and fell on Pepé where he lay on the ground. His coarse black hair was littered with twigs and bits of spider web. His eyes had retreated back into his head. Between his lips the tip of his black tongue showed.

He sat up and dragged his great arm into his lap and nursed it, rocking his body and moaning in his throat. He threw back his head and looked up into the pale sky. A big black bird circled nearly out of sight, and far to the left another was sailing near.

He lifted his head to listen, for a familiar sound had come to him from the valley he had climbed out of; it was the crying yelp of hounds, excited and feverish, on a trail.

Pepé bowed his head quickly. He tried to speak rapid words but only a thick hiss came from his lips. He drew a shaky cross on his breast with this left hand. It was a long struggle to get to his feet. He crawled slowly and mechanically to the top of a big rock on the ridge peak. Once there, he arose slowly, swaying to his feet, and stood erect. Far below he could see the dark brush where he had slept. He braced his feet and stood there, black against the morning sky.

There came a ripping sound at his feet. A piece of stone flew up and a bullet droned off into the next gorge. The hollow crash echoed up from below. Pepé looked down for a moment and then pulled himself straight again.

His body jarred back. His left hand fluttered helplessly toward his breast. The second crash sounded from below. Pepé swung forward and toppled from the rock. His body struck and rolled over and over, starting a little avalanche. And when at last he stopped against a bush, the avalanche slid slowly down and covered up his head.

Spirits of the Valley

Mary Frances Kennedy Fisher (1908–1992) was raised in Whittier, California. She later lived in France for extended periods, and spent the last twenty years of her life in a house built for her in a vineyard in Glen Ellen, California. Acclaimed in particular for her writing on culinary subjects, she is admired for her fine prose styling. Her more than twenty books include The Art of Eating *(1954),* Among Friends *(1971), and* Stay Me, Oh Comfort Me: Journals and Stories, *1933–1941 (1993), which includes a recollection of her years near Hemet, written in 1984, of which the following is an excerpt.*

Some people believe that it is a fortunate thing if a person can live in a real valley instead of on flat open land, and they may well be right. For some sixteen years, from 1940 on, I lived most of the time on ninety acres of worthless land southeast of the little town of Hemet in southern California, and they were fine magical ones, important in the shaping of many people besides me, perhaps because Hemet Valley was a true one in every sense. At its far eastern end rose the high mountains that separated coastal land from desert, and our little town lay almost as near their base as Palm Spring did on their other side. Mount San Jacinto loomed on the north; to the south, high rocky hills rolled toward the Mexican border, and westward the valley opened gently, as any proper valley should, toward broad coastal flats and the far Pacific Ocean.

My husband, Dillwyn Parrish, and I bought our land for almost nothing: it was haunted, for one thing, and completely untillable. And we lived there intensely until he died three years later, according to medical schedule, of Buerger's disease. Then I stayed on, through another marriage and two little daughters, who spent their first years there with me after I divorced their father. When the oldest was going on six, we moved to my family ranch near Whittier to live with Father after Mother died. I worked half-time on his newspaper and ran the household, and as often as possible (weekends, vacations) we went back to Hemet to the little ranch house in the wild rocky hills.

It became clear that I could not raise two growing females there alone, where I had decided to remain. Now and then I found someone to repair storm damage and so on, but finally it seemed wise to sell the place. I felt thankful for everything I had learned there, and when I said it was no longer mine, I withdrew forever from it, even though ashes of my love and my mother may still blow from under some of its great rocks. I know the wind still sings over the Rim of the World and always will.

Tim (my husband was always called that by people who loved him, which meant everyone) named our ranch Bareacres, after a character in *Vanity Fair* who had several marriageable daughters and countless acres of barren land. He managed to sell the land, bought a string of pearls and a husband for each girl, and he and Lady Bareacres lived penniless but happy ever after, as I remember.

Certainly our land was bare! It rose in rough steep hills, with one deep canyon that split it down from the Rim of the World, its horizon, to the wide dead riverbed that was its northern boundary. A thin little road track went up from the valley floor, past our house and on up past the trickle of our only spring, to a deserted old ranch on the Rim of the World. There was a big sturdy redwood tank at the spring and a handful of stubby cottonwoods, and down nearer our house in the canyon, dry except for an occasional mud puddle from the underground trickle, stood a few tall eucalyptus trees. The rest of the place was covered with great harsh boulders, some of them bigger than a house. On the flat top of an enormous rock above the spring, two oblong tubs had been chipped out centuries ago, and we were told that sick Indians were brought there to lie in the hot sun while soothing water was poured over them, water that we found was heavy with lithium.

In front of the house, which stood about a thousand feet up off the wide dry riverbed that separated us from Hemet Valley, the land was steep but with fewer big rocks, almost like a meadow, covered with sage and mesquite and low cactus. Across the riverbed, northward, between us and Mount San Jacinto, lay the flat valley land, rich with apricot orchards. It was neatly laid out with roads and little houses here and there, but we could see only a general kind of lush carpet, flowery in spring, then green, and then winter-silver. Hemet was westward, invisible.

Our narrow dirt road went straight across the riverbed and up to the valley floor to meet Crest Drive, which curved the whole length of the valley. Directly opposite us, a small grove of eucalyptus trees grew down the slope where Fredrika van Benschoten had a little orange orchard along Crest, and in that grove the Squawman, who had left his land for us to find, had a correct Navaho house built for his bride. It was of adobe, one room and wide closet and a corner hearth, and it was so heavily plastered that there were no hard corners or lines but a softness to everything under the thick whitewash, as if it were a robe to be worn, firm and protecting but with no part of it to cut or hurt or rub against. The floor was of dark crude tile. The beams across the low ceiling were slender eucalyptus trunks. There was a kind of kitchen in the closet whose wall came up only to eye height, and Freda had piped cold water to a small sink. There was no toilet, and since the Squawman had not made an outhouse, I decided the grove was answer enough.

I spent much time in the squaw house, mostly after Tim died. I wrote a couple of books there. I never slept there, strange to say, but would go down from Bareacres in the mornings. I always took a thermos of broth or a cool drink, and about 11:00 I'd go out and look up across the riverbed and see my home there, sometimes with my two little girls waving from the west terrace, with a neighbor to watch them until I got back. The trees Tim and I had planted back of the house and down into the canyon were thriving: sycamores, eucalyptus, tough cottonwoods.

When Tim and I bought the place, with a veteran's bonus of $2,000 plus $225 we borrowed (we were dead broke after his illness made us leave Switzerland in 1938 when World War II got under way), it was flatly undesirable, even according to the realtor who showed it to us. It had been owned by a shady fellow said to be a degraded government Indian trader, an army officer, whose Navaho woman followed him to Hemet Valley. He bought what we called Bareacres twenty years later, but she, of course, did not live there, so her relatives unwillingly came from New Mexico and built her a decent house across the riverbed from Freda's grove.

Because of strict caste laws, the Navaho was not only called a lost member of her own tribe but could not have anything to do with the local Indians, the Sobodans, who were beneath her social level. It must have been very lonely for her. The Squawman, as he was always scornfully called, had a lot or some or a few valuable Indian artifacts, depending on who was talking about him to us, and most of them were gone when his body was found in the house and a clean bullet hole showed in the south window. Perhaps it was robbery? Navaho are good shots, we were told. The little house in Freda's grove was empty, with not even a blanket or cup left. Nobody knew "anything." Up on the hill across the dead riverbed the air blew through the unlocked door of the Squawman's house. Everything in it was stolen, gradually and without real harm . . . no vandalism, no ugly dirt, no mischievous fires. It was haunted, for sure.

It looked empty and welcoming when Tim and I first saw it in the kind January sunlight, and we stepped into it past the bullet hole as if it had been waiting. We rented an airy little house near Moreno, toward Riverside, and came every day over the Jack Rabbit Trail around the base of the mountain with two old carpenters Tim found. We shifted a few walls around and screened the long front porch that was held up by six trunks of cedar trees that Indians had brought from Mexico, it was said, for the Squawman. . . .

[Our friend] Arnold knew more about native desert plants than anyone I ever heard of, and while he was the caretaker up at the Ramona Bowl it was a kind of secret paradise for botanists and crackpot gardeners who came to watch him plant the unplantables and whom he in turn watched like a hawk, because they almost always tried to steal some of his cuttings. It was a game they all played, and Arnold reported every sneaky trick, every artful dodge, of this unending tournament of trickery among the famous people who came to watch him. He turned weeds into jewels, for sure.

After Tim died, Arnold buried the little tin box of clinkers [Tim's ashes] under an enormous hanging rock. I said, "Let's go up to the Rim of the World and let the winds catch them," but he said, "Nope," and simply walked off. I knew it was all right, and went back to Bareacres and waited, and when he came back, we had a good nip of whiskey. . . .

That is the way Bareacres is, of course. I am told that the fine pure air that first drew us there, half mountain and half desert, is now foul with smog and that the rich carpet of fruit trees we looked down on is solid with RVs and trailer parks. One block on Main Street is now in the *Guinness Book of World Records,* or maybe it is *Ripley's Believe It or Not:* something like 182 banks and savings-and-loan offices on that sleepy little stretch of sidewalk! And there are almost a hundred doctors, most of them connected with "convalescent homes" of varying status and opulence. And Crest Drive is lined with million-dollar villas, with the subdivision where Bareacres was (a "ninety-acre hell of red-hot rocks and rattlesnakes," as one New Yorker described it to us after a lost weekend there) the most snobbish and stylish area between Palm Springs and Los Angeles.

That is the way it is, I say, and I do not grieve or even care, any more than I did when Arnold went up the hill with the little box. I have taken and been given more than can ever be known that is heartwarming and fulfilling forever from that piece of wild haunted untillable land we named Bareacres for a time. No doubt roads have been cut into it and rocks have been blasted away, but I know that the contours cannot change much in a few hundred years in that country. And meanwhile the ghosts are there, even of the sick sad Indians who went to lie in the magic lithium waters of the spring, and even of the poor Squawman with a bullet in his heart, and of my own mother who loved the place . . . they are all there to cleanse and watch over it. They, and many more of us, keep an eye on things so that time itself can stay largely unheeded, as anyone will know who spends more than a few minutes in country like Bareacres.

There are many pockets of comfort and healing on this planet, and I have touched a few of them, but only once have I been able to stay as long and learn and be told as much as there on the southeast edge of Hemet Valley.

B A R R Y   L O P E Z

Klamath Basin

A Reflection
on White Geese

Barry Lopez (b. 1945) grew up in the San Fernando Valley in southern California and lives today in the Cascade Mountains of Oregon. The author of such important works of natural history as Arctic Dreams *(1986), which won the National Book Award, and* Of Wolves and Men *(1978), he has been called one of "the leading contemporary spokesman for an ethical revaluation of our ecological behavior." "A Reflection of White Geese" appeared originally as a magazine piece with photographs by Frans Lanting, and was republished in* Crossing Open Ground *(1988).*

I slow the car, downshifting from fourth to third, with the melancholic notes of Bach's sixth cello suite in my ears—a recording of Casals from 1936—and turn east, away from a volcanic ridge of black basalt. On this cool California evening, the land in the marshy valley beyond is submerged in gray light, while the far hills are yet touched by a sunset glow. To the south, out the window, Venus glistens, a white diamond at the horizon's dark lapis edge. A few feet to my left is lake water—skittish mallards and coots bolt from the cover of bulrushes and pound the air furiously to put distance between us. I am chagrined, and slow down. I have been driving like this for hours—slowed by snow in the mountains behind me, listening to the cello suites—driving hard to get here before sunset.

I shut the tape off. In the waning light I can clearly see marsh hawks swooping over oat and barley fields to the south. Last hunts of the day. The eastern sky is beginning to blush, a rose afterglow. I roll the window down. The car fills with the sounds of birds—the nasalized complaints of several hundred mallards, pintails, and canvasbacks, the slap-water whirr of their halfhearted takeoffs. But underneath this sound something else is expanding, distant French horns and kettledrums.

Up ahead, on the narrow dirt causeway, I spot Frans's car. He is here for the same reason I am. I pull up quietly and he emerges from his front seat, which he has made into a kind of photographic blind. We hug and exchange quiet words of greeting, and then turn to look at the white birds. Behind us the dark waters of Tule Lake, rippled by a faint wind, stretch off north, broken only by occasional islands of hardstem bulrush. Before us, working methodically through a field of two-row barley, the uninterrupted inquiry of their high-pitched voices lifting the night, are twenty-five thousand snow geese come down from the Siberian and Canadian Arctic. Grazing, but alert and wary in this last light.

Frans motions wordlessly to his left; I scan that far eastern edge of Tule Lake with field glasses. One hundred thousand lesser snow geese and Ross's geese float quietly on riffles, a white crease between the dark water and the darkening hills.

The staging of white geese at Tule Lake in northern California in November is one of the most imposing—and dependable—wildlife spectacles in the world. At first one thinks of it only as a phenomenon of numbers—it's been possible in recent years to see as many as three hundred thousand geese here at one time. What a visitor finds as startling, however, is the great synchronicity of their movements: long skeins of white unfurl brilliantly against blue skies and dark cumulonimbus thunderheads, birds riding the towering wash of winds. They rise from the water or fall from the sky with balletic grace, with a booming noise like rattled sheets of corrugated tin, with a furious and unmitigated energy. It is the *life* of them that takes such hold of you.

I have spent enough time with large predators to know the human predilection to overlook authority and mystery in the lives of small, gregarious animals like the goose, but its qualities are finally as subtle, its way of making a living as admirable and attractive, as the grizzly bear's.

Geese are traditional, one could even say conservative, animals. They tend to stick to the same nesting grounds and wintering areas, to the same migration routes, year after year. Males and females have identical plumage. They usually mate for life, and both sexes care for the young. In all these ways, as well as in being more at ease on land, geese differ from ducks. They differ from swans in having proportionately longer legs and shorter necks. In size they fall somewhere between the two. A mature male lesser snow goose (*Chen caerulescens*), for example, might weigh six pounds, measure thirty inches from bill to tail, and have a wingspan of three feet. A mature female would be slightly smaller and lighter by perhaps half a pound.

Taxonomists divide the geese of the Northern Hemisphere into two groups, "gray" and "black," according to the color of their bills, feet, and legs. Among black geese like Canada geese and brandt they're dark. Snow geese, with rose-pink feet and legs and pink bills, are grouped with the gray geese, among whom these appendages are often brightly colored. Snow geese also commonly have rust-speckled faces, from feeding in iron-rich soils.

Before it was changed in 1971, the snow goose's scientific name, *Chen hyperborea*, reflected its high-arctic breeding heritage. The greater snow goose (*C. c. atlantica*)—a larger but far less numerous race of snow goose—breeds in northwestern Greenland and on adjacent Ellesmere, Devon, and Axel Heiburg islands. The lesser snow goose breeds slightly farther south, on Baffin and Southampton islands, the east coast of Hudson Bay, and on Banks Island to the west and Wrangel Island in

Siberia. (Many people are attracted to the snow goose precisely because of its association with these little-known regions.)

There are two color phases, finally, of the lesser snow goose, blue and white. The combined population of about 1.5 million, the largest of any goose in the world, is divided into an eastern, mostly blue-phase population that winters in Texas and Louisiana, and a western, white-phase population that winters in California. (It is the latter birds that pass through Tule Lake.)

The great numbers of these highly gregarious birds can be misleading. First, we were not certain until quite recently where snow geese were nesting, or how large their breeding colonies were. The scope of the problem is suggested by the experience of a Canadian biologist, Angus Gavin. In 1941 he stumbled on what he thought was a small breeding colony of lesser snow geese, on the delta of the McConnell River on the east coast of Hudson Bay—14,000 birds. In 1961 there were still only about 35,000 birds there. But a 1968 survey showed 100,000 birds, and in 1973 there were 520,000. Second, populations of arctic-breeding species like the snow goose are subject to extreme annual fluctuations, a boom-and-bust cycle tied to the unpredictable weather patterns typical of arctic ecosystems. After a series of prolonged winters, for example, when persistent spring snow cover kept birds from nesting, the Wrangel Island population of snow geese fell from 400,000 birds in 1965 to fewer than 50,000 in 1975. (By the summer of 1981 it was back up to 170,000.)

The numbers in which we see them on their wintering grounds are large enough to be comforting—it is hard at first to imagine what would threaten such flocks. Snow geese, however, face a variety of problems. The most serious is a striking loss of winter habitat. In 1900 western snow geese had more than 6,200 square miles of winter habitat available to them on California's Sacramento and San Joaquin rivers. Today, ninety percent of this has been absorbed by agricultural, industrial, and urban expansion. This means ninety percent of the land in central California that snow geese once depended on for food and shelter is gone. Hunters in California kill about twenty percent of the population each year and leave another four to five percent crippled to die of starvation and injuries. (An additional two to three percent dies each year of lead poisoning, from ingesting spent shot.) An unknown number are also killed by high-tension wires. In the future, geese will likely face a significant threat on their arctic breeding grounds from oil and gas exploration.

The birds also suffer from the same kinds of diseases, traumatic accidents, and natural disasters that threaten all organisms. Females, for example, fiercely devoted to the potential in their egg clutches, may choose to die of exposure on their nests rather than abandon them in an unseasonable storm.

In the light of all this, it is ironic that the one place on earth a person might see these geese in numbers large enough to cover half the sky is, itself, a potential threat to their existence.

The land now called Tule Lake National Wildlife Refuge lies in a volcanic basin, part of which was once an extensive 2,700-square-mile marshland. In 1905 the federal government began draining the area to create irrigated croplands. Marshland habitat and bird populations shrank. By 1981 only fifty-six square miles of wetland, two percent of the original area, was left for waterfowl. In spite of this reduction, the area, incredibly, remains an ideal spot for migratory waterfowl. On nearly any given day in the fall a visitor to the Klamath Basin might see more than a million birds—mallards, gadwalls, pintails, lesser scaups, goldeneyes, cinnamon teals, northern shovelers, redheads, canvasbacks, ruddy ducks; plus western and cackling Canada geese, white-fronted geese, Ross's geese, lesser snow geese, and whistling swans. (More than 250 species of birds have been seen on or near the refuge, and more than 170 nest here.)

The safety of these populations is in the hands of a resident federal manager and his staff, who must effectively balance the birds' livelihood with the demands of local farmers, who use Tule Lake's water to irrigate adjacent fields of malt barley and winter potatoes, and waterfowl hunters, some of whom come from hundreds of miles away. And there is another problem. Although the Klamath Basin is the greatest concentration point for migratory waterfowl in North America, caring well for birds here is no guarantee they will fare well elsewhere along the flyway. And a geographic concentration like this merely increases the chance of catastrophe if epidemic disease should strike.

The first time I visited Tule Lake I arrived early on a fall afternoon. When I asked where the snow geese were congregated I was directed to an area called the English Channel, several miles out on the refuge road. I sat there for three hours, studying the birds' landings and takeoffs, how they behaved toward each other on the water, how they shot the skies overhead. I tried to unravel and to parse the dazzling synchronicity of their movements. I am always struck anew in these moments, in observing such detail, by the way in which an animal slowly reveals itself.

Before the sun went down, I drove off to see more of the snow goose's landscape, what other animals there might be on the refuge, how the land changed at a distance from the water. I found the serpentine great blue heron, vivacious and melodious flocks of red-winged blackbirds, and that small, fierce hunter, the kestrel. Muskrats bolted across the road. At the southern end of the refuge, where cattails and bulrushes give way to rabbit brush and sage on a volcanic plain, I came upon mule deer, three does and four fawns standing still and tense in a meandering fog.

I found a room that evening in the small town of Tulelake. There'd not been, that I could recall, a moment of silence all day from these most loquacious of geese. I wondered if they were mum in the middle of the night, how quiet they were at dawn. I set the alarm for 3 A.M.

The streets of Tulelake are desolate at that hour. In that odd stillness —the stillness of moonlit horses standing asleep in fields—I drove out into the countryside, toward the refuge. It was a ride long enough to hear the first two movements of Beethoven's Fifth Symphony. I drove in a light rain, past white farmhouses framed by ornamental birches and weeping willows. In the 1860s this land was taken by force from the Modoc Indians; in the 1940s the government built a Japanese internment camp here. At this hour, however, nearly every landscape has a pervasive innocence. I passed the refuge headquarters—low shiplapped buildings, white against a dark ridge of basalt, facing a road lined with Russian olives. I drove past stout, slowly dying willows of undetermined age, trees that mark the old shore line of Tule Lake, where it was before the reclamation project began.

The music is low, barely audible, but the enthusiasm in some of the strong passages reminds me of geese. I turn the tape off and drive a narrow, cratered road out into the refuge, feeling the car slipping sideways in the mud. Past rafts of sleeping ducks. The first geese I see surge past just overhead like white butterflies, brushing the penumbral dimness above the car's headlights. I open the window and feel the sudden assault of their voices, the dunning power of their wings hammering the air, a rush of cold wind and rain through the window. In a moment I am outside, standing in the roar. I find a comfortable, protected place in the bulrushes and wait in my parka until dawn, listening.

Their collective voice, like the cries of athletic young men at a distance, is unabated. In the darkness it is nearly all there is of them, but for an occasional and eerie passage overhead. I try to listen closely: a barking of high-voiced dogs, like terriers, the squealing of shoats. By an accident of harmonics the din rises and falls like the cheering of a crowd in a vast stadium. Whoops and shouts; startled voices of outrage, of shock.

These are not the only voices. Cackling geese pass over in the dark, their cries more tentative. Coyotes yip. Nearby some creature screeches, perhaps a mouse in the talons of a great horned owl, whose skipping hoots I have heard earlier.

A gibbous moon shines occasionally through a wind-driven overcast. Toward dawn the geese's voices fall off suddenly for a few moments.

The silence seems primordial. The black sky in the east now shows blood red through scalloped shelves of cloud. It broadens into an orange flare that fades to rose and finally to the grays of dawn. The voices begin again.

I drive back into Tulelake and eat breakfast amid a throng of hunters crowding the tables of a small cafe, steaming the windows with their raucous conversation.

Bob Fields, the refuge manager, has agreed to take me on a tour in the afternoon. I decide to spend the morning at the refuge headquarters, reading scientific reports and speaking with biologist Ed O'Neill about the early history of Tule Lake.

O'Neill talks first about the sine qua non, a suitable expanse of water. In the American West the ownership of surface water confers the kind of political and economic power that comes elsewhere with oil wells and banks. Water is a commodity; it is expensive to maintain and its owners seek to invest the limited supply profitably. A hunting club that keeps private marshland for geese and ducks, for example, will do so only as long as they feel their hunting success warrants it. If the season is short-ened or the bag limit reduced by the state—the most common ways to conserve dwindling waterfowl populations—they might find hunting no longer satisfying and sell the marsh to farmers, who will turn it into cropland. Real estate speculators and other landowners with substantial surface-water rights rarely give the birds that depend on their lands a second thought when they're preparing to sell. As O'Neill puts it, "You can't outweigh a stack of silver dollars with a duck."

The plight of western waterfowl is made clearer by an anomaly. In the eastern United States, a natural abundance of water and the closure of many tracts of private land to hunting provide birds with a strong measure of protection. In the West, bird populations are much larger, but water is scarcer and refuge lands, because they are largely public, remain open to hunting.

By carefully adjusting the length of the hunting season and the bag limits each year, and by planting food for the birds, refuge managers try to maintain large bird populations, in part to keep private hunting clubs along the flyway enthusiastic about continuing to provide additional habitat for the birds. Without the help of private individuals, including conservation groups that own wetlands, the federal and state refuge systems simply cannot provide for the birds. . . .

Some birds, the snow geese among them, have adapted to shortages of food and land. Deprived of the rootstocks of bulrushes and marsh grasses, snow geese in the West have switched to gleaning agricultural wastes and cropping winter wheat, a practice that has spread to the Midwest, where snow geese now feed increasingly on rice and corn. A second adjustment snow geese have made is to linger on their fall migrations and to winter over farther north. That way fewer birds end up for a shorter period of time on traditional wintering grounds, where food is scarcer each year.

As we spoke, O'Neill kept glancing out the window. He told me about having seen as many as three hundred thousand white geese there in years past. With the loss of habitat and birds spreading out now to winter along the flyway, such aggregations, he says, may never be seen again. He points out, too, looking dismayed and vaguely bitter, that these huge flocks have not been conserved for the viewer who does not hunt, for the tourist who comes to Tule Lake to see something he has only dreamed of.

We preserve them, principally, to hunt them.

In broad daylight I was able to confirm something I'd read about the constant, loud din of their voices: relatively few birds are actually vocalizing at any one time, perhaps only one in thirty. Biologists speculate that snow geese recognize each other's voices and that family units of three or four maintain contact in these vast aggregations by calling out to one another. What sounds like mindless chaos to the human ear, then, may actually be a complex pattern of solicitous cries, discretely distinguished by snow geese.

Another sound that is easier to decipher in daylight is the rising squall that signals they are leaving the water. It's like the sustained hammering of a waterfall or a wind booming in the full crowns of large trees.

One wonders, watching the geese fly off in flocks of a hundred or a thousand, if they would be quite so arresting without their stunning whiteness. When they fly with the sun behind them, the opaque white of their bodies, the white of water-polished seashells, is set off against grayer whites in their tail feathers and in their translucent, black-tipped wings. Up close these are the dense, impeccable whites of an arctic fox. Against the grays and blues of a storm-laden sky, the whiteness has a surreal glow, a brilliance without shadow.

I remember watching a large flock rise one morning from a plowed field about a mile distant. I had been watching clouds, the soft, buoyant, wind-blown edges of immaculate cumulus. The birds rose against much darker clouds to the east. There was something vaguely ominous in this apparition, as if the earth had opened and poured them forth, like a wind, a blizzard, which unfurled across the horizon above the dark soil, becoming wider and higher in the sky than my field of vision could encompass, great swirling currents of birds in a rattling of wings, one fluid recurved sweep of ten thousand passing through the open spaces in another, counterflying flock, while beyond them lattice after lattice passed like sliding walls, until in the whole sky you lost your depth of field and felt as though you were looking up from the floor of the ocean through shoals of fish.

At rest on the water the geese drank and slept and bathed and preened. They reminded me in their ablutions of the field notes of a Hudson Bay trader, George Barnston. He wrote of watching flocks of snow geese gathering on James Bay in 1862, in preparation for their annual two-thousand-mile, nonstop thirty-two-hour flight to the Louisiana coast. They finally left off feeding, he wrote, to smooth and dress their feathers with oil, like athletes, biding their time for a north wind. When it came they were gone, hundreds of thousands of them, leaving a coast once "widely resonant with their petulant and incessant calls" suddenly as "silent as the grave—a deserted, barren, and frozen shore."

Barnston was struck by the way snow geese do things together. No other waterfowl are as gregarious, certainly no other large bird flies as skillfully in such tight aggregations. This quality—the individual act beautifully integrated within the larger movement of the flock—is provocative. One afternoon I studied individual birds for hours as they landed and took off. I never once saw a bird on the water move over to accommodate a bird that was landing nor a bird ever disturbed by another taking off, no matter how tightly they were bunched. In no flight overhead did I see two birds so much as brush wing tips. Certainly they must; but for the most part they are flawlessly adroit. A flock settles gently on the water like whiffling leaves; birds explode vertically with compact and furious wing beats and then stretch out full length, airborne, rank on rank, as if the whole flock had been cleanly wedged from the surface of the water. Several thousand bank smoothly against a head wind, as precisely as though they were feathers in the wing of a single bird.

It was while I sat immersed in these details that Bob Fields walked up. After a long skyward stare he said, "I've been here for seven years. I never get tired of watching them."

We left in his small truck to drive the narrow causeways of Tule Lake and the five adjacent federal refuges. Fields joined the U.S. Fish and Wildlife Service in 1958, at the age of twenty-two. His background is in range biology and plant ecology as well as waterfowl management. Before he came to Tule Lake in 1974, to manage the Klamath Basin refuges, he worked on the National Bison Range in Montana and on the Charles Sheldon Antelope Range in Nevada.

In 1973 a group of visitors who would profoundly affect Fields arrived at Tule Lake. They were Eskimos, from the Yukon-Kuskokwim delta of Alaska. They had come to see how the geese populations, which they depend on for food, were being managed. In the few days they were together, Fields came to understand that the Eskimos were appalled by the waste they saw at Tule Lake, by the number of birds hunters left crippled and unretrieved, and were surprised that hunters took only the breast meat and threw the rest of the bird away. On the other hand, the aggregations of geese they saw were so extensive they believed someone was fooling them—surely, they thought, so many birds could never be found in one place.

The experience with the Eskimos—Fields traveled north to see the Yukon-Kuskokwim country, and the Eskimos returned to Tule Lake in 1977—focused his career as had no other event. In discussions with the Eskimos he found himself talking with a kind of hunter he rarely encountered anymore—humble men with a respect for the birds and a sense of responsibility toward them. That the Eskimos were dumbstruck at the number of birds led him to more sobering thoughts: if he failed here as a refuge manager, his failure would run the length of the continent.

In the years following, Fields gained a reputation as a man who cared passionately for the health and welfare of waterfowl populations. He tailored, with the help of assistant refuge manager Homer McCollum, a model hunting program at Tule Lake, but he is candid in expressing his distaste for a type of hunter he still meets too frequently—belligerent, careless people for whom hunting is simply violent recreation; people who trench and rut the refuge's roads in oversize four-wheel-drive vehicles, who are ignorant of hunting laws or who delight in breaking them as part of a "game" they play with refuge personnel.

At one point in our afternoon drive, Fields and I were watching a flock of geese feeding in a field of oats and barley on the eastern edge of the refuge. We watched in silence for a long time. I said something about the way birds can calm you, how the graceful way they define the sky can draw irritation right of you. He looked over at me and smiled and nodded. A while later, still watching the birds, he said, "I have known all along there was more to it than managing the birds so they could be killed by some macho hunter." It was the Eskimos who gave him a sense of how a hunter should behave, and their awe that rekindled his own desire to see the birds preserved.

As we drove back across the refuge, Fields spoke about the changes that had occurred in the Klamath Basin since the federal reclamation project began in 1905. Most of the native grasses—blue bench wheat grass, Great Basin wild rye—are gone. A visitor notices foreign plants in their place, like cheatgrass. And introduced species like the ring-necked pheasant and the muskrat, which bores holes in the refuge dikes and disrupts the pattern of drainage. And the intrusion of high-tension power lines, which endanger the birds and which Fields has no budget to bury. And the presence of huge pumps that circulate water from Tule Lake to farmers in the valley, back and forth, back and forth, before pumping it west to Lower Klamath Refuge.

It is over these evolving, occasionally uneasy relationships between recent immigrants and the original inhabitants that Fields keeps watch. I say goodbye to him at his office, to the world of bird poacher, lead poisoning, and politically powerful hunting and agricultural lobbies he deals with every day. When I shake his hand I find myself wanting to thank him for the depth with which he cares for the birds, and for the intelligence that allows him to disparage not hunting itself but the lethal acts of irresponsibility and thoughtless people.

I still have a few hours before I meet Frans for dinner. I decide to drive out to the east of the refuge, to a low escarpment which bears the carvings of Indians who lived in this valley before white men arrived. I pass by open fields where horses and beef cattle graze and cowbirds flock after seeds. Red-tailed hawks are perched on telephone poles, watching for field rodents. A light rain has turned to snow.

The brooding face of the escarpment has a prehistoric quality. It is secured behind a chain link fence topped with barbed wire, but the evidence of vandals who have broken past it to knock off souvenir petroglyphs is everywhere. The castings of barn owls, nesting in stone pockets above, are spread over the ground. I open some of them to see what the owls have been eating. Meadow voles. Deer mice.

The valley before me has darkened. I know somewhere out there, too far away to see now, long scarves of snow geese are riding and banking against these rising winds, and that they are aware of the snow. In a few weeks Tule Lake will be frozen and they will be gone. I turn back to the wall of petroglyphs. The carvings relate, apparently, to the movement of animals through this land hundreds of years ago. The people who made them made their clothing and shelters, even their cooking containers, from the lake's tule reeds. When the first white man arrived—Peter Ogden, in 1826—he found them wearing blankets of duck and goose feathers. In the years since, the complex interrelationships of the Modoc with this land, largely unrecorded to begin with, have disappeared. The land itself has been turned to agriculture, with a portion set aside for certain species of birds that have passed through this valley for no one knows how many centuries. The hunters have become farmers, the farmers landowners. Their sons have gone to the cities and become businessmen, and the sons of these men have returned with guns, to take advantage of the old urge, to hunt. But more than a few come back with a poor knowledge of the birds, the land, the reason for killing. It is by now a familiar story, for which birds pay with their lives.

The old argument, that geese must be killed for their own good, to manage the size of their populations, founders on two points. Snow goose populations rise and fall precipitously because of their arctic breeding pattern. No group of hunters can "fine-tune" such a basic element of their ecology. Second, the artificial control of their numbers only augments efforts to continue draining wetlands.

We must search in our way of life, I think, for substantially more here than economic expansion and continued good hunting. We need to look for a set of relationships similar to the ones Fields admired among the Eskimos. We grasp what is beautiful in a flight of snow geese rising against an overcast sky as easily as we grasp the beauty in a cello suite; and intuit, I believe, that if we allow these things to be destroyed or degraded for economic or frivolous reasons we will become deeply and strangely impoverished.

I had seen little of my friend Frans in three days. At dinner he said he wanted to tell me of the Oostvaardersplassen in Holland. It has become a major stopover for waterfowl in northern Europe, a marsh that didn't even exist ten years ago. Birds hardly anyone has seen in Holland since the time of Napoleon are there now. Peregrine falcons, snowy egrets, and European sea eagles have returned.

I drive away from the escarpment holding tenaciously to this image of reparation.

Tehachapi Mountains

In Condor Country

David Darlington (b. 1951) is a freelance writer based in Berkeley, California, who has published widely on natural history. His book In Condor Country *(1987) traces the efforts made to save the California condor from extinction.*

It is early in the morning and we are near the top of a mountain. Along the shoulders of the road, hunters appear and disappear; their fluorescent orange hats and coats take shape and then diminish in the fog, the visual equivalent of clanging buoys. Visibility perhaps extends to one hundred feet. Rain and wind have drawn a maze of channels on the windshield of the pickup, although it is September—officially too early for rain in California. Nevertheless, water falling from the sky is beating a steady snare-drum roll on the camper top. I sit under it in the back, bouncing on the tire wells with Eben [McMillan]; we face each other across a chilly atmosphere that makes faint clouds of our breath.

The truck is climbing a badly rutted dirt road toward the summit. Granite extrusions and Ponderosa pines pass within a foot of the windows. Eben stares out at them as he rocks from side to side, gripping the edges of his ridged steel seat. He wears a bent gray felt cowboy hat and a navy blue windbreaker. In the early light his eyes seem as cold as the air; when Eben takes his glasses off and isn't squinting in the sun, his eyes reveal their true color, which is the color of ice.

On top of the mountain, seven cars sit facing a billboard in a full-bore gale. Rain comes in horizontally up here; we get out of the truck, and I have to pull my hat low on my head to prevent it from flying away. Just downhill, a park ranger is pulling a gigantic pump hose toward an outhouse from a light green truck. Thoroughly soaked, he smiles up at us. The pines around him are white bark and Jeffrey; lightning has transformed the trunk of one into an upside-down U, but the tree is still living.

The billboard says:

The California condor, a rare and endangered species fully protected by state law, can be seen from this point. Adult birds may
be identified by their large size, black color with orange head, and
by the triangular white patch on the underside of each wing. The
condor has an average wing-spread of nine feet, the longest of any
North American land bird. Riding favorable air currents, it can soar
and glide for more than one hour at a time in steady flight. From
June through October one or more condors may usually be seen
soaring in the vicinity of this observation site. Help protect and
preserve this vanishing species.

Los Padres National Forest
U.S. Department of Agriculture

On clear days, the view from this spot encompasses great vistas of brown cliffs, blue ridges bordering the Cuyama River, and the multi-colored patchwork of farms in the San Joaquin Valley. Today the view is about what you'd get from inside an oxygen tent. Nevertheless, Eben insists on walking the narrow trail to the lookout to make sure that no one from our proposed party is out there looking for condors. "They'd have to be crazy to be out there," he allows, "but birders are crazy."

The path to the lookout is covered with asphalt and lined with granite rocks. No one—not even a birder—is out there. We return to the parking lot, and Eben confers with several of the people sitting in the cars. Satisfied that we've found everyone we're going to find, he climbs back into the truck, but this time we ride in front, with heat and other humans, back down the mountain to a wide place in the road, which Eben has designated a meeting spot.

The mountain is Mount Pinos—at nine thousand feet, the highest peak in the Tehachapis. If you look at the major mountain ranges of California on a map, they form a kind of horseshoe: the open end of the shoe is in the north; the eastern prong is the Sierra Nevada; the Coast Ranges constitute the wing to the west. The southern segment of the shoe—the part you might grip if you aimed to pitch all these mountains toward a stake somewhere in, say, the USSR—is made up of the Transverse Ranges (including the Tehachapis), which run east-west six-ty miles north of the Los Angeles basin. To some ways of thinking, these mountains are the true barrier between northern and southern California: dry, rugged country of sandstone and chaparral where time-worn cliffs loom like parapets in a Pleistocene animals' Alamo—the last refuge of the California condor.

Once a year Eben leads a condor watch for the National Audubon Society's Golden Gate chapter (one that has broken with the organiza-tion's leadership and rejected captive breeding). The traditional site for the event is Mount Pinos and the traditional time is late September—calving season on the cattle ranches in the foothills of the Tehachapis. Many of the calves are stillborn, and about one cow in ten will fail to survive the ordeal of childbirth; the result on enormous grazing tracts like the Hudson, Snedden, and San Emidio ranches (especially when combined with the effects of the first week of deer hunting season) is a landscape littered with carcasses and afterbirth—and, as a consequence, condors. . . .

It was a gray, dank day that made the barren brown early-autumn land-scape seem oppressive—even emptier than usual. As we traveled through it, the normal complement of natural phenomena was performed by the local fauna. A golden eagle tearing at a squirrel carcass on the side of the road allowed the car to come unusually close, then took off and flew alongside us, its huge wings flapping just feet from the car. "This time of year you see things like that," Eben said. "The mammals go underground and the migrating eagles get pretty hungry." Farther on, an enormous fuzzy spot was crossing the road—a tarantula, as it turned out. Eben: "They claim that the ones we see are more than twenty years old. They're looking for a female and that's why they're out traveling. This is a high-mortality time of year for them. The pepsis wasp is a leavening factor on spider populations. They call it the tarantula hawk—it paralyzes the tarantula, then lays its eggs on it. The larvae tunnel inside and develop there. There are hundreds of different kinds of pepsis wasp, and each one uses a different spider."

The highway lost its straightness now, bending into big curves as it climbed through humped yellow hills of increasing steepness. I noted the onset of the dizzy euphoria that accompanies entry into foothills. To the west, the craggy ridges of the Caliente Mountains seemed to be stacked on top of one another, receding into the distance under a low, dark gray sky that matched the color of the road.

We pass by our campground at Valle Vista. A couple of miles farther is the Los Padres National Forest sign, surrounded now by cars and people. The cars are laden with equipment; cameras, lenses, tripods, telescopes. One license plate says BIRDIN. . . .

Eben's entrance into the scene as usual stimulates a minor stir. He is the eccentric old man, the colorful sage, the back country guru. His effect on this group of amateur naturalists is that of a magnet on iron filings. As people greet him he grins amiably, shaking various right hands with his left. One man says, "This is my fourth trip down here and I haven't seen a condor yet."

Eben says "Well, you'll see one today."

"You heard him," the man tells the others.

The view from this lookout offers a roadside panorama of condor country, a powerful dose of the immensity of America. Steep red and white cliffs descend from both right and left to frame a section of dull brown foothills, gentle in comparison with the cliffs. There are distant dirt roads and cattle trails traversing the tops of open ridges, and immense brown sandstone rocks in the middle of the landscape. Beyond these hills stretches the San Joaquin Valley, a flat quilt of green and brown squares—those that are irrigated and those that are plowed. Away to the northwest the hills go white, or almost pink, like tortured flesh—the southern end of the Temblors, a forbidding no man's land that appears to be suffocating in some sort of haze. To the southeast, the Tehachapis are faintly blue on the horizon when they're visible at all; the fitful storm clouds come and go, obscuring sections of the entire picture, occasionally reducing our field of vision to the bare brown hillsides immediately before us. . . .

Noon. Eric [Caine, a birder,] announces, "There's a pair of condor at five o'clock. They're circling. They're gonna get up above the horizon in about thirty seconds." He looks at his watch, then back at the black dots in the distance. "They just hit. Took 'em eighteen seconds."

"Where are you talking about?"

"In the flat beyond Lone Tree there's a red and white tower. Not the Purina one, though. Above it there's a line of white clouds superimposed on the gray. The birds are just to the right of it."

"Oh, yeah!"

"Oh, they're huge!"

"Those are condor," Eric says. "Two adults."

"I just lost them over Brush Mountain."

Eric says, "They'll be back, and they might be close." . . .

Four P.M. The air is filled with a gusty drizzle. Someone says, "There's something big above Lone Tree. It's being chased by two smaller birds."

"Condor!" cries Eben. "Flex-glide!"

"What I'm seeing ain't in a flex-glide," says Eric.

"Well," says Eben, "I can't see so good."

"Condor," confirms Eric, studying the speck. "Coming our way."

The bird is cruising in leisurely loops, like a toy boat circling in an eddy. When it enters the foreground below us, still too distant for its white wingpatches to be visible, it turns, banks, and rises. Now it does go into the flex-glide, dipping its wings and suddenly soaring behind the ridge to our left. Having tired of the social scene, I climb the clay embankment on the other side of the road, slip through the barbed-wire fence, and set off in the direction where the condor disappeared.

The warm wind is blowing now; the rain has stopped. I tie my coat around my waist and ascend a hill of oak and foxtail. Beyond the ridge that borders the road is a broad brown and yellow valley with gigantic outcroppings of pockmarked rocks. The surrounding hillsides are bare, eroded; but on the higher hills the bush takes over—green manzanita, chaparral. Behind these foothills four ridges recede, becoming bluer as they grow more distant. There are flat banks of fog in the far valleys and stacks of gray clouds on the horizon. A black dot rises from the ridgeline; I raise my glasses and it leaps into close-up: the condor, its white patches clearly visible against the black, widespread wings.

The bird banks and rises in lazy circles, another smaller raptor behind it, and I realize for the umpteenth time how regal raptors are on their rounds; it has to do with how little effort they seem to expend, how steady their bearing is, how unchallenged their place in the sky. As advertised, this particular condor is steady to the point of an aeronautic appearance; it looks like a glider or Piper Cub with wings supported by solid struts. Nevertheless, the fingerlike pinion feathers seem to express an attitude of relatedness; they're spread the way your fingers would be if you were shooing something away from you—an air of utter independence.

After a lengthy period of circling, the bird comes to earth on the valley floor, a few hundred yards from a cluster of farm buildings. I watch through the binoculars for a while, but the condor doesn't move, so I keep on hiking. There are lots of brightly colored wildflowers in the barren-looking landscape—purple asters with yellow centers, scarlet buglers being visited by iridescent hummingbirds. I find the big brown rocks in the valley to be filled with caves, and I crawl inside one to get out of the rain—which has, not surprisingly, resumed. Eventually, though, opting for view, I climb the exterior of the cliff in a fine misting shower. When I get to the tip, I look up and am startled to see the condor above me.

The bird seems to be scrutinizing me (I remember Ken Brower's line: "When man and condor meet today, it is with a glance of mutual appraisal, each to see whether the other is yet extinct"). What, I wonder, do you say when you're finally face-to-face with an absolute—the biggest bird in North America, the embodiment of all endangered species, a messenger from the living to the dead. I don't say anything; I stand in the rain with upturned face, a lone earthling rooted to a rock, regarding the hovering form of extinction. This condor is an anomaly, I know; a living incarnation of mortality. Spinning high in the air above me, framed against storm clouds, with warm sheets of water blowing between us, it seems a specter. It occurs to me that this spooky creature has on a hell of a Halloween costume: a skeleton suit and a jack-o'-lantern head, a vivid uniform for a vulture. The decoration alone would set it apart from any other bird, and the temptation to assign it symbolic status is irresistible. But as I watch it, the condor doesn't strike me as a symbol of extinction so much as a totem for North America itself. It's because of the coloring, somehow—red, white, and black is a morbid heraldry for a once-promising continent, a land that's been dying since 1492, a place that harbors the exotics of the earth and in doing so drives its native inhabitants into oblivion.

In spite of this, the condor does not appear gloomy; it seems polite, tolerant, curious. After a moment, having witnessed enough of me and my perambulations, it dips its wings and glides away. I glass it in profile and see the naked head extended, held slightly lower than the rest of the horizontal body in the sulky demeanor of vultures. It disappears in the direction of the lookout, and soon I hear distant, excited voices wafting across the sodden landscape: "Hey!" "Hey!" then a second of silence and, finally, cheers and clapping.

For those of us raised far away from wilderness—in places populated solely by domesticated animals, with untamed ones glimpsed only in books or on television—there's something miraculous about seeing them in the wild. The first time I saw a bear in the woods, I couldn't believe there was something so big that nobody owned, fed, or kept on a leash. The self-sustaining ability of nature seems a marvel, though it's literally the oldest thing in the world. Similarly, seeing the condor here where it "belongs" is simultaneously remarkable and mundane. I was actually surprised by how natural it seemed; there were no trumpets, no soundtrack music, no caustic debate, no fee of admission. The condor seemed unaware of its celebrity or of the controversy that surrounds it. It was just a big black and white bird flying around in a quiet canyon. To be sure, its size and bearing distinguish it from any other animal you might imagine; but, for me, the most extraordinary thing about the condor was the fact that it was free.

San Joaquin Valley

Winter's Fog

David Mas Masumoto (b. 1954) is a third-generation Japanese-American peach and grape farmer, a freelance writer, and a farm activist. After graduating from the University of California at Berkeley in 1976 he earned a master's degree in community development from UC Davis. This selection is from his 1995 "chronicle of four seasons on my family farm," Epitaph for a Peach.

On cold winter nights I step out into our porch to check the thermometer. It has not changed much all day, ranging between a cold in the low thirties to a high in the mid-forties with a damp, biting fog blanketing the valley farmlands. From my porch I hear the tap-tap-tap of dewdrops trickling down the barren branches, falling and landing on the damp leaves below. I can feel the cold on my cheeks and the warmth of our home's wood stove still within my sweater.

Beyond me the vines and peach trees change seasons too. I think of the past year and the decisions I would have altered, modifications I can plan for in the coming season. Yet no matter what new course I may choose, a natural rhythm remains. I know the vines and trees will still be pruned soon, as they have been for generations.

The fog continues to roll in. Where it's heading I do not know. It passes in front of the porch like a shifting cloud. If I stare at it long enough, it seems that I start to move instead. I imagine our farmhouse cutting through the gray mist like a lost ship, my porch transformed into the bridge. I lean against the rail and peer into the drifting fog as my vessel heads into the night.

I sail on, the thermometer the only instrument on board. I like watching the gradual temperature changes, the measurement of a cold front moving in or the dramatic drop in readings with the loss of sunlight. Several years ago an arctic blast moved into the valley like a silent wolf. For days it hunted, freezing oranges and killing trees. I monitored its progress on my thermometer, recording historic low temperatures—dropping below twenty and never rising above freezing even in sunshine. Farmers could do little except watch. We only had our thermometers to help us verify what we already knew.

But a thermometer enables me to see the wild. The arctic wolf of that winter came alive in the dropping mercury. During the summer a different creature ventures into our valley—the searing heat that stays above one hundred degrees into the evening hours. My senses feel the extremes and my thermometer enables me to process the impression like a series of snapshots. The wild is seen.

A naturalist may disagree, claiming that agriculture tames the wild and farmers manipulate their world to disable the beast of nature. Judging by my last year trying to save a peach, though, I'd say that gives us farmers too much credit. On a farm, much more is out of control than is in control. I fool myself when I call myself master of my farm. My thermometer reveals my impotence, for I cannot even consistently predict a day's highs or lows.

The fog carries a deep, penetrating cold with it. It doesn't take long before I'm chilled to the bone, especially when I'm in the fields, walking in the damp grass. Once my boots and pants get wet, I have only hours before my legs grow numb. At night, while standing on my porch deck, I feel the fog invade my clothes, infiltrating the layers, announcing itself with my involuntary shiver.

I return inside, where I can watch the fog sail past our large windows. We have few curtains in our house, most of our windows are bare. From the inside I can see the panorama of the farm. I am exposed to the wild nature beyond the glass. I've spent hours in front of the windows, watching storms march in from the west and wind blow rain and hail onto the porch. I can witness the sun rise and set on the mountains that ring the valley, study the ripples of August heat rising from the earth, and feel the glass warm against my skin.

The exchange is reciprocal, especially during the winter. The cold easily permeates the interiors, chilling the house and forcing me to wear sweaters even inside. The intrusion is welcomed though, the season a natural cadence I feel within, a natural clock I respond to.

The change of season connects me with the surrounding wild, a wild I work within. I grow crops from the earth and have discovered that the best soil is also wild. This past year I have learned that productivity is little more than managed chaos, wildness the source of fertility.

In the fog I can hear the voices of farmers before me. Once I believed their old stubborn ways had no place in the progressive world of modern farming. But now they sing of traditions that have a place in my winter season more than ever.

Two wind socks flutter in the shifting fog. In Japanese, the wind is called *kami*, with an honorific *sama* often added. Wind is respected and revered, *kamisama* becomes a spirit that's alive. I can see that spirit in a wind sock, the energy captured for a moment in a dance of colors, then released as the tail flaps and waves.

Even in winter there is life on the farm. I feel something sacred, a meaning added to my work and my peaches and grapes. I feel connected with the universe. The world of nature and human nature are my teachers, showing and not telling me the secrets of the wild and sacred. From my porch deck I sail into a new world. Discoveries loom in the fog, opportunities inhabit this wilderness. It is a sacred place for myself and my family because I can call this farm home.

Altadena foothills

A Vanishing Land

Hildegarde Flanner (1899–1987), poet, playwright, and essayist, was also an early environmentalist. She moved to southern California soon after graduating from the University of California at Berkeley in 1923. The following is taken from A Vanishing Land, *a booklet written in the 1950s that came out of her experience of having lived thirty-six years in one suburban garden in the foothills of Altadena. "From there," she wrote, "I was closely aware of what was going on in the valley and the coastal plain below. We were within reach of the smog and often affected by it." In 1962 she moved to Napa Valley.*

When I first came to live in southern California, around 1925, I was looked upon as a foreigner from Indiana, so much was the lack of nativity formerly noticed by born Californians. I had not been here long before I saw how desirable it would have been, in a country whose character was equally strange and absorbing to me, to be bred and born in the grain of mountain, desert, palm, and semi-tropic. My family came here for the same comfortable and aesthetic reason that has always turned midland and prairie Americans toward the coast. We came to live in a choice landscape in a choice climate. As a child in Indiana I had known the northern forests, where summer evenings brought the enchantment of fireflies and the cold unrolling song of the whippoorwill, and where the squally lakes held quiet shallows for slender rushes and my light canoe. Yet the Middle West had never offered the satisfactions we found here in southern California, where it is difficult to locate a dull view and where the weather is so easygoing and bohemian as to make the exotic out-of-doors a free and informal conservatory for daily living. To own a small piece of earth endowed with fine scenery in an amiable climate, this was what we came for and what, before long, we obtained. Since that time I have lived in the same garden in the foothills above the city of Pasadena. Eleven miles away the tall city hall of Los Angeles is visible on a clear day.

Western sensitivities, like western mockingbirds, are sometimes given to intoxicated utterance, and rather like the mockingbirds, to a certain defensiveness also, as if such extravagance anticipated a rebuke. When it comes to writing about the western earth, this makes for a sort of self-consciousness, a sense of being watched; or is it only that we are watching ourselves be cautious? Yet if we have anything here that could be called a tradition, it lies simply in appreciation of the earth, an appreciation that is perhaps captive but neither hysterical nor insincere. The person to whom a modest and genuine identity with the scene is important must wait for that relationship to overtake him, for he will never discover it by pursuit. Romantic enthusiasm comes quickly, but insight into the unexpected delicacies and extremities of the dry western earth, a taste for its arid cryptic literalness, and the excitement of its antiquity where the massive inner centuries have left their tracks in view, such familiarity comes only with living close enough to the earth and long enough, and under the touch of its very physical and poetic spirit of place. The attachment which has made the westerner seem naive or very regional is not so hard to tolerate if it is recollected that to live here is in a way a challenge, at least for those who stop to think of it. As a nation with the habit of going west, more and more of us have reached the last barrier. It is a fascinating barrier of mountain, desert, and ocean, and it is also psychological because it is unfamiliar and final. Our material and gainful energies can soon be at ease, but our minds turn in more slowly, inquisitive though they may be to create. Of the influence we encounter we make not one but many images of the earth, and gradually through that possessiveness we learn to be at home.

Now after years of living with the western earth I believe that I have learned some of its native truths, not profound, it may be, but possibly better than profound, the kind that accumulate personal human meanings, which relate one to environment. For instance, it is of the nature of things here that sunlight seems to be absorbed by what it shines on and to last over in a contained state so that objects then are bright from inside out with a long-deposited glow, an old mineral light that is like no other reflection in other climates as it falls into the eye and slips into the mind. It is an ordinary phenomenon of matter, light, color, and drought, and one notes it as fact, not as fantasy, not because there is any desire to be mystified. Explained or unexplained, it gives ocular pleasure. Also it soon comes to one here that, because of some desert discipline nature has known, ethereal things may be strong and enduring, like the frosty-white flowers of the yucca in whose reality we feel no difference of degree compared with the harsh hot boulders the plant grows among. And when I burn eucalyptus in my fireplace (a tree, like myself, not indigenous but long since deeply settled), the smell of the smoke is not merely a woody pungence to my sense, it carries an image of life. And when a bird sings at night in my own garden, garrulous and exaggerated though he may be, his meaning is plain and simple, for it is about this land I have come to love, and its spirit. Yet love alone is not all. If assurance of identity has overtaken me through the years, it comes lately with disturbed concern and in company with the amazements, the losses, and the pressures of progress and change. Today I can see with melancholy that time and too many other things have passed this way since I came to live above the valley near the foot of the mountains. Most difficult to accept, even the earth itself is altered. That which overtakes me now, threatens to become a memory. Southern California, as I have known it, is a vanishing land. . . .

The first aggressive dream of California, that of the Spanish centuries, was a tough, hard-hitting dream mingled of avarice, valor, and fable. That dream has by now had a good many lives, always including something of "where life is better." It has taken on new burdens and new boasts and is full of the commotion of success. Southern California, always alluring in its character of hope, so typical of the West and the frontier, has, until recently, had more to offer to vacationers than to workers. Now, in this small area between the mountains and the ocean, the Californian dream has built, in a few thickly crowded years, a concentration of industry valued annually at five billion dollars, including the nation's third largest concentration of petroleum processing, while the dream rides to work and to pleasure in one of the world's largest mobs of automobiles, on a network of recently built and already antiquated freeways.

To these very considerable realities, and because of them, something else had been added to our land, our lives, and our times, something that baffles and evades final definition yet is itself unpleasantly actual. Let me describe, as I fondly observe it, the scene over which this enigma has thrown a shadow.

The mountains that stand across the northern side of the Los Angeles basin are not among the most spectacular in the state. They lack the huge loft of the Sierra Nevada, they do not have the fossil-like, handsome satanic look of antiquity seen on the slopes of the Panamint, they do not glow with all the hyacinth and magenta that burn the San Jacinto in the desert evening, nor do they take cloud shadows with the ghostly elegance of the lifeless hills at the head of the Coachella Valley. Yet choose a good morning to see them from the edge of the mesa looking up the Arroyo Seco, on the land first settled by the founders of the city of Pasadena, and you will see why people have been glad to live where the abrupt and sheltering range of the San Gabriel Mountains could be seen. Locally we call them the Sierra Madre, and beneath their close, tough, and dwarfish forest of dark chaparral the long sweep of their variable undershape is clearly visible. They are noble enough, but not beyond the scale of human feelings. The psalmist who said "From whence cometh my help" was not looking at an Alp. The ocean and ages out of which they rose have perished, but our mountains are with us, with cold sweet water in their granite veins. They show their inner structure, as western mountains do, in pale, delineating streaks and angles of clear rocky strength which leave their mounting and descending pyramidal patterns in the mind. Between the scenic semicircle of this range on the north and the Pacific on the south are Los Angeles and its attendant cities lying in a large landscape of idyllic forms in hill and valley well colored with winter's greens or the dark yellows of summer.

There are sometimes mornings that are clear, still, and soft. From the foothills above Pasadena I can see for sixty miles or more, at least as far as a Mt. Santiago in Orange County, at whose foot years ago Madam Modjeska, the renowned Polish actress, made an Arcadian home in a grove of oaks. Closer at hand the hills of El Monte and La Puente stand, and the San Jose hills below Covina, and on the coast the Long Beach headlands, and out in the Pacific show the two heights of Catalina Island. Much nearer through the vast lens of the morning I can see a part of the complex aesthetic detail of the San Gabriel Valley. Cities, scenery, boulevards, and trees make a design of such textural charm as to suggest the quality of a Hokusai print, an intimate distance of green precisions in which a host of hills are floating and made darkly distinct with froth of dissolving mist at their feet. Clustered buildings appear in spots of colored emphasis, and thousands of palms and deodars add vertical and verdant steeples. All this delights the eye, the mind, the heart, with romantic geometries and the pride of home. But not for long. Gradually all those remarkable harmonies and differences of texture fade and flatten, while a horizon of spectral murk advances and takes the valley from below and to the east, flows up arroyos, climbs the foothills, surrounds and fills my own garden, and goes on west along the mountains, obscuring them from sight behind a mobile, drifting wall. Although I live less than a mile from the mountains, they are repeatedly lost to view, and the scene I knew for years in clean bright air can most often now be observed only as a dim copy of the original. . . .

It is asking too much of the vigorous present to be plaintive over what it destroys. Yet is not for plaintive reasons that memory fits together the fragments scattered in the velocity of progress. If there are things too good to lose, then in some way the pleasures of possessing them must be protected. As conservation, memory is only a frail force, but fanatic. No least little pearly grit of desirable recollection escapes it. And so it is I happen to recall the patch of modest nievitas. They were growing in the brief grass of the season where a side road led from the highway toward the foothills. It started to rain and the odor of rain on earth rose in the air. Nievitas are very small flowers noticeable only because they grow companionably in fresh white crowds. On that day as the rain came on, slowly at first and scattered, the large drops here and there pecked at a flower spike which quickly began to bob and nod. As the rain increased, the show of spattered pecking and the bobbing flowers took on a faster pace and all through the colony was that continual ripple of nodding and straightening flowers. It was a diminutive spectacle and the little nievitas are over-dainty on their thin hirsute stems, yet they are flowers too fine to forget, for they provided for me this gently animated scene. On that corner of the crossroad something has now been built, a place to eat or buy gas or sell real estate, it could not matter which. No roots of any kind will grow there again. I have a true concern to keep this fragile recollection of an ephemeral thing very clear. In the shelter of memory, as long as these words may last, those small white flowers, bending in the spring rain and rising, are safe in a vanishing land.

I cannot say as I look back when or quite how it was that the mountain above my home with its tenacious chaparral and lean granite ceased to be the remote profile of the unknown and became the familiar form below which a human life has taken what shape it has, touched in many ways by the life in the mountain above. It was the angry whine of the puma heard one evening from the distance, or the thrash of storm wind as it came savagely down, or the way the naked stones stop the full moon as it floats up, or the gleaming of a flock of pure white pigeons flying into the blue mountain, or over the years a hundred other things, that gave uncanny intimations and certainties beyond bare stone and altitude, until finally the hard light in the high rocks glowed more warmly, as if words had been spoken and a meaning given. And once on a green afternoon of winter I followed the trail in Rubio or Las Flores Canyon and found proof that a mountain is not a towering monument of solitude and time but a small and perfect gift for a moment of exquisite pleasure. On the moist bank and close to see were ferns no broader than a squirrel's foot, and tiny pointed flowers and fruits of moss on little slopes of velvet, and in a frail fungus goblet one diamond, one drop of brilliant rain, a deep drink for Oberon of the mountains. The spell cast by the sylvan weathers that made this pretty thing lay on my mind as I went home, and lies there still.

A dull haze now comes between me and the mountain. The great form that had been so explicit is often dim or not seen at all. A continuity is broken, a symbol is threatened, and the thought of home itself is altered and confused.

It was something so different from the present that one remembers, only to find that the telling evaporates in the busy realism of our day. Yet the difference is real also, and memory tries to assess it with no illusions and no elegiac foolishness, wanting only to keep faith with the fragrant groves and with a valley whose light was beneficent and clear, so clear that the least stem of filaree or pannicle of wild oat was set apart from the rest in thin flake of truth like the mica that drops from a stone. And that long summer view of dry brown Californian earth stretching in peace under native oak and sycamore—it is sad to love this landscape as much as we still do, since love like that will now be always thinking of the end.

It is not too strange that our occasional bright days are haunted days, haunted not by the past but by the future, and the future begins to feel as finished and fatalistic as the past. On these uncommon days when the weather itself seems intuitive, the future is physically visible. I can see it from the loud freeway as my car carries me to an elevation. There

below me lies my valley. Everything is terribly clear, sharp, and veridi-
cal, big things are plain and portentous, little things plain as old bright
bones, all seen as it must be, quickly, but seen for miles, and everything
splitting intensely into a million of itself in precise excess of infatuated
destiny. Revelation, prophecy, history, change, and progress, what dazed
and dim figures they are, moving confounded among their works in a
vanishing land.

Los Altos Hills

Remnants

We are a remnant people in a remnant country. We
have used up the possibilities inherent in the youth of
our nation; the new start in a new place with new vision
and new hope. . . . We have come, or are coming fast,
to the end of what we were given.

Wendell Berry

*Wallace Stegner (1909–1993) was long identified with Stanford University,
where he taught for many years and where a writing fellowship bears his
name. His award-winning fiction, essays, biographies, and histories display his
love and concern for the West, both that which has vanished and that of the
present. In 1983 he collaborated with nature photographer Eliot Porter on*
American Places, *where "Remnants" first appeared.*

Nearly every morning a coyote works the pasture beyond our
yard fence. He comes up out of the woods that fill the little
canyon to the south—woods out of sight from our windows,
under the roll of the hill—and quarters the field, hunting under the
unpastured grass now matted by the rains. He is as pointed as an arrow;
his plume, carried straight out behind his lean shape, feathers him for
swift accuracy. His nose is long and sharp, his ears are alert, his head is

always turning while nose, ears, and eyes appraise some tenuous signal. His sonar is tuned to the slightest stir of a mouse among the grass roots, a gopher turning in its sleep underground, a cricket uncrossing its legs. Every so often he points, stiffens, lifts one trembling front paw, quivers, flattens, and pounces. His paws hold down whatever he has caught, his nose probes under them. Generally there is nothing there, and he goes back to his restless search. Occasionally, he digs, never very hopefully or very long. And even while digging, even while preparing to pounce, he is never for more than a second or two unaware of our house a hundred feet away. He gives us long stares, with his head turned from whatever a moment ago preoccupied him. He watches us to see if we have moved.

Perhaps he sees our shapes beyond the glass; perhaps he sees no more than the morning reflected there. Perhaps he hears faint murmurs of the "Today Show" or "Good Morning America" or the "CBS Morning News" that we take with our breakfast coffee. Over the years we have watched many things out these bedroom windows—pygmy nuthatches at the bird feeder, quail pecking in coveys among the grass, deer standing on their hind legs to browse the pyracantha berries, a red-tailed hawk sitting in a pasture oak getting warm enough to fly. But the coyotes are new. We have seen them only in the last year or two. Perhaps they have been driven in from the Pacific side of the Coast Range by drouth or some drastic shutting off of a food supply.

Whatever brought them, whether they came as refugees or, like most of us, in search of better economic opportunities, they are now here in numbers. On nights of big moons they hunt through the woods and pastures and close up to the houses scattered through the hills. When one catches something, or wishes he could catch something, or grows furious that he has not caught something, his yell goes up and is answered from a half dozen different directions. That chilling blood-cry makes my wife shiver and recall stories about Siberian wolves. It also starts every dog within two miles to asserting his territory. Dobermans, police dogs, Airedales, bull terriers, basset hounds, beagles, short-haired pointers, Labradors, St. Bernards, Kerry blues, mutts big and small all declare their solidarity of domestic protectiveness and unease when they hear the wild summons from out under the moon.

Watching this morning coyote scrounge for mice and crickets in the pasture, bold at the very doors of the suburbs, I am reminded of a story Robert Frost used to tell about meeting on a train a young man who, questioned about what he did for a living, admitted that he was an exterminator. "Ha!" said the poet, interested. "Tell me. What can you exterminate?" The exterminator grew embarrassed. "Confidentially," he said, "nothing."

Wouldn't it be nice to think so! This coyote, a member of a species that has been shot, trapped, poisoned, and chased with dogs for as long as his kind and the human kind have known one another, would seem to corroborate the exterminator's pessimism. He survives; there is a modus vivendi. Nobody is setting out poison, I hear no shooting among the hills. The professors, electronics executives, and engineers from Silicon Valley who live around here don't keep sheep or chickens. An old enemy has come to seem harmless, even attractive. We point him out to visitors, who are charmed. We crowd to the windows to watch him pounce on the matted grass. We cock our ears to his yelling in the moonlight, and smile, glad he is out there, and making it.

The coyote is to native American folklore what the fox was to the fabulists of the Old World. Trickster, demigod, he is very smart and never careless, bold but not brash. If he had an escutcheon, his motto would be *Non timeo sed caveo*. Like the wolf, he has a family and pack life that comforts and assists him in a hard world, but he can get along without it when he needs to. He is fast, shifty, good at running, good at hiding out, nocturnal when he has to be, diurnal when he chooses. Like the buzzard, he can eat anything. Content with small blessings—a lamb here, a chicken there—he will make do on mice and crickets when better is not available. And he seems to know that he is safer here among the engineers and executives in their thickening subdivisions than he used to be over on the other side of the range, where ranchers carry rifles in the racks of their pickups and the Fish and Game people, when not prevented by environmentalist outrage, drop from airplanes pieces of meat laced with 1080. The coyote finds our suburb a peach bowl, and has happily adapted himself.

But he is a special case, and in the end even he may prove to be not exempt from the consequences of sharing the earth with *Homo sapiens.* Many other local species, including some that the coyote was evolved to prey on, are already fading as my breath fades on our windowpane. In the thirty-two years we have lived in this house in these Coast Range foothills we have watched it happen. Helped it happen.

The marriage of people to a place may be close and considerate, and it may be hardly more than sanctioned rape. It may arise from choice, chance, or necessity, like human marriages. In practice, arranged marriages work out about as often as romantic elopements—a good thing, too, for not many of us can choose the place we live in. We can love a well-lived-in place even when it is essentially unlovable. I have seen a black girl, brought to a Vermont lake for the summer, grieve for the hot days in Harlem when a hydrant would be opened. If a place is a real place, shaped by human living, and not a thing created on a speculator's drawing board and stamped on a landscape like a USDA stamp on a side of beef, it will interact with the people who live in it, and they with it. The trouble is that places work on people very slowly, but people work on places with the single-minded ruthlessness of a beaver at a cottonwood tree. Occasionally they make the desert blossom as the rose, as the Mormons are fond of saying. As often, they simply make deserts.

Europeans and their American descendants did not set out to live with this continent, learn its rules and its moods, love, honor, and obey it. They set out to "tame" or "conquer" or "break" the wilderness. They imposed their old habits on the new land, they "improved," as in homesteads, they "developed," as in towns. They replaced, destroyed, and polluted, they bent the earth and all its native forms of life to the satisfaction of their own needs. The process was dramatized in North and

South America, and later in Australia, but it is not peculiarly American or Australian. I have read that in Sicily, that island which was a kind of dry run for the American melting pot, colonized by Greeks, Carthaginians, and Romans, invaded by Visigoths, Normans, and God knows who else, there is not now a single tree or shrub of the varieties that clothed the island in the sixth century B.C. People have come close to altering the whole biotic community, animals and plants alike. And though blood oranges and olives may be an improvement on some things that used to grow there, what once grew there is lost forever and its importance simply cannot be determined now.

Changes will occur whether we intend them or not. We cannot leave one footprint in a new country, pass through it with horses or mules, careen our *Golden Hind* on its empty beach, without bringing in our luggage or our pockets, in our infested hair or clothes, in our garbage, in the dung of our animals and the sputum of our sick and the very dirt under our fingernails, things which were not there before, and whose compatibility with the native flora and fauna is utterly unknown. That is why the patriot who tucked an American flag into a moon capsule could have spoiled everything for the exobiologists eager to determine whether any life existed on the moon. Here on earth, the conservationists who created our national wilderness system knew from the beginning that by this date, wilderness in America is an approximation only. There is no such thing as a true, pure, unmodified wilderness in the entire world. The Greenland glaciers are layered with particulate pollution, Antarctic penguins have DDT in their livers. A wind blowing across Seattle or Portland carries the taint of man in the Montana backwoods.

As naturally as ants herd aphids, we encourage the plants that feed or pleasure us, and extirpate those that don't. We cut forests, impound rivers, plow grasslands, seal millions of acres under sterile concrete, pump out fossil water, change climates to some degree. Planted crops go wild, wild crops are sprayed or crowded out, and changed plant communities encourage the ascendancy or the elimination of animal species. In mining our habitat, we destroy the habitat of whole biotic communities. We commit multiple genocide, we create population explosions. Ecology, a science hardly two generations old, has begun to teach us something about cause and consequence: that is the earth speaking, trying to state its case for survival. But experience might have taught us much sooner.

My family were homesteaders in southern Saskatchewan during World War I. In every acre we could plow, we planted wheat. One consequence, unforeseen and not understood, was that the gophers—"flickertails," Richardson's spermophiles—throve incontinently. They came from miles of bald prairie to feast on our wheat, and stayed to dig burrows and raise families. For their convenience we had dammed a coulee and created a waterhole. Lovely. A land of milk and honey.

I spent my summers trying to exterminate them. They multiplied faster than my traps, poisons, .22, and buckets for drowning them out could reduce them. By replacing buffalo grass with wheat we had touched off a population explosion beyond our containing. The creatures that preyed on gophers—the weasels, ferrets, badgers, hawks, coyotes, shrikes, and gopher snakes—multiplied too, though more slowly, and I killed them too, though in smaller numbers, not knowing they were my allies. Nothing availed. Everything gained on us. Then came a dry cycle, the wheat failed three summers in succession, and we were driven out. The drouth that defeated us also defeated the legions of creatures we had baited into life by tampering with their environment. Once we were gone, the prairie should have settled back into something like its natural populations in their natural balances, except. Except that we plowed up two hundred acres of buffalo grass, and had imported Russian thistle—tumbleweed—with our seed wheat. For a season or two, some wheat would volunteer in the fallow fields. Then the tumbleweed would take over, and begin to roll. We homesteaded a semiarid steppe and left it nearly a desert.

Not deliberately. We simply didn't know what we were doing. People in new environments seldom do. Their only compulsion is to impose themselves and their needs, their old habits and old crops, upon the new earth. They don't look to see what the new earth is doing naturally; they don't listen to its voice.

Ours was short-grass prairie. Historically the tall-grass variety east of the 100th meridian did better. It is changed, but it is no desert; there is probably no more fertile farmland in the world. Nevertheless, much was lost. As white settlement advanced from the Mississippi to the Missouri and beyond, prairie flowers did not grow older hour by hour. They got plowed up and grazed off. Where once big bluestem and switchgrass and Indian grass grew as high as a horse, and flowers snagged in the stirrups of a rider, we have made cities, towns, shopping centers, parking lots, feed lots, highways, and fields of corn, sorghum, and soybeans. The old species are gone or only precariously hanging on. As Aldo Leopold discovered, almost the only places where the native plants could sustain and reproduce themselves were the fenced rights of way of railroads, protected from both plows and grazing animals. Those accidental preserves are now beyond price, precious to biologists trying to reconstruct the vanishing prairie biota, and more precious to all of us than we may realize.

Obviously not all human tinkering is thoughtless, nor is all of it destructive. People coming to a new world take back the new plants and animals that native peoples have domesticated. American potatoes, tomatoes, maize, turkeys, and tobacco literally revolutionized the eating and living habits of the world, and vastly increased its carrying capacity of *Homo sapiens.* A wave of green revolution rushed eastward from our shores from the sixteenth century on. Before too long, Englishmen were smoking, and were eating a bird they called a turkey, and the Italian cuisine was being enlarged by tomatoes and the maize that Italians still call *gran turco,* apparently under the impression that it came from the Near East. By the eighteenth century there were representations of corn leaves in Chinese art.

But there was a reverse process, too. Settlers brought in seeds and cuttings and some of them had the messianic enthusiasm of Johnny

Appleseed. Read in the letters between Thomas Jefferson and John Bartram the eagerness with which intelligent people experimented with Old World plants in the New World. So far as I know, neither Jefferson nor Bartram introduced any killing pests into America, but their sort of experimentation conducted indiscriminately elsewhere has produced a history of ecological trauma, an elaborate industry of biological study and control, and the beginnings of a public concern that is sometimes sentimental but is indispensable.

Cause begets consequences, in nature as in logic. We understand that in its cruder manifestations—kill off the hawks and coyotes and you will be swamped periodically by rodents—but the subtler relationships, the web of small tensions and accommodations and standoffs that make for ecological health, we have hardly begun to appreciate.

How could the Spaniards have known (and what would they have cared, being hot for the riches of Cíbola?) that the horses they brought to the New World would find some parts of it horse heaven, and that the multiplying get of escaped studs and mares would transform the life of whole nations of Indians, and hence of the whites who fought them? How could they possibly have foreseen that after the conquest was over and the Indians crushed, the merest remnants of the wild horse herds would become a cause of contention among western ranchers who want to make dog food of them, animal lovers determined to save them, and federal land managers uncertain which course to follow?

Why didn't Captain James Cook stop to think, before he released goats in the Hawaiian Islands, that goats are very destructive and very adaptable, and that the islands contained no predators to hold them in check? Why couldn't he have predicted that the goats would defy efforts to control them, and two centuries after their release would still be peeking at tourists around the crags of Waimea Canyon?

Could the prospectors who turned burros loose in the Grand Canyon country have known that burros are as durable and tenacious as goats, and as destructive of their range? Would they have done anything if they had realized that one day the feral burros would threaten the existence of the desert bighorn and the desert range itself? And how should we respond to the tender-hearted and tender-minded people who block the National Park Service and the Bureau of Land Management from applying the only management tactic—shooting a lot of burros—that will have any effect?

Cause and consequences occur in many combinations. It is one kind of mistake to shoot all the millions of passenger pigeons, or cut down all the sandalwood trees in Hawaii to provide incense for Chinese joss houses. It is another to import European chestnuts or Dutch elms, each carrying its endemic disease, into a continent whose native chestnuts and elms have no resistance to those diseases. Florida must find a way to deal with the water hyacinths it planted in an ill-advised hour. Virginia must somehow clear its woods of the engulfing Japanese honeysuckle that it first brought in to stabilize railroad embankments. Hawaii, a group of islands almost as much altered by exotics as Sicily, finds itself at war with plants such as lantana, a garden flower elsewhere, a weed in the islands; and with animals like the mongoose, imported to prey on rats, which has become as much a nuisance as the rats themselves.

Considerations such as these are the ABC's of our growing environmental consciousness. We are a weed species, and wherever we go we crowd out natives and carry with us domesticated species that may become weeds in the new environment. What we destroy we often do not intend to harm. What we import, we import with the best intentions. But I find myself wondering, as I watch this coyote who has survived all our direct attacks on him and our indirect attacks on his habitat, why we should have had to repeat so much dreary history on the San Francisco Peninsula in the years since World War II, why we seem to have learned so little since Segesta and Agrigento were metropolises twenty-five hundred years ago.

When we moved into them, the Peninsula foothills back of Stanford University seemed to us as untouched as New South Wales must have seemed to Captain Cook. Actually they were far from virginal. White men have been here for two hundred years, and as a consequence the pastures are a mixture of native plants and of runaways from hayfields and ranch yards. Some—shooting stars, poppies, lupines, blue-eyed grass, tarweed—are surely natives. Others—wild oats, filaree, ryegrass, burclover—are just as surely Europeans naturalized. I don't know whether needlegrass, screwgrass, foxtail grass, and yellow star thistle are natives or not. They ought to be, else why are their seeds armored to withstand a climate that is rainless seven months of the year, and so cunningly equipped to attach themselves to any fur, sock, or trouser cuff that happens by? In cursing these plants for what they do to my dog's feet, ears, and tear ducts, I may be cursing intrusive weeds, but more likely I am objecting to species that have more right here than I do. If I don't like what grows here, why did I move in? Why do I stay? And in trying to eradicate them I am being both human and futile, for they are at least as indestructible as the coyote.

The woods are more native than the pastures, for trees and shrubs must survive not simply a season, but cycles of seasons, and not many exotics have the genes to make it without human help. These live oaks, blue oaks, white oaks, buckeyes, and bay laurels, with their understory of toyon and poison oak, gooseberry and blackberry and elderberry, maidenhair and lady fern, must have grown in pretty much these proportions, in these same creek bottoms and on these same north-facing slopes, since the Ohlone Indians used to gather acorns here; but I never see "wild plums" blooming in the ravines without suspecting that the rootstock of hill apricot orchards has gone wild and adapted itself.

As for the wildlife that we found—the foxes, raccoons, opossums, skunks, wood rats, jackrabbits, cottontails, gophers, moles, voles, field mice, lizards and skunks and newts and toads and tree frogs, gopher snakes and rattlesnakes and king snakes and ring-necked snakes, hawks and owls and buzzards and quail and the layered populations of songbirds, both winterers and summer dwellers—it must have been much the same, perhaps with a few mountain lions, bears, and eagles, when this land was a Spanish grant. And bobcats. There had to be bobcats where there were so many gophers and mice and quail, and I know there are still bobcats because I have seen their pug tracks around a spring. But I have never seen a bobcat in the flesh in all the years we have lived here. That puts the bobcat in a special class, more durable than most of the nocturnals and small predators, perhaps as durable as the coyote.

In any case, changes that had taken place before our coming did not trouble us, and had not seriously damaged the hills. We accepted our surroundings as if they had just been smoothed and rounded and peopled by the hand of God, and we tried to keep them as we found them. Nevertheless, we disturbed them a great deal, occasionally for good, sometimes neutrally, often for ill.

We disturbed them simply because we were *Homo fabricans*. We built structures, we brought water to a dry hilltop, we planted exotic trees, shrubs, flowers, fruits, and vegetables, we brought in our domesticated animals and birds. And everything we established, even our garbage cans and our compost heap, sent out urgent messages to impoverished species that were barely holding their own in the pastures and ravines. Because we were one of only three or four houses in a wide area, we had the impact of pioneers.

Some of our installations were gestures of friendship: bird feeders and sugar-water suppers. But our inadvertent invitations were accepted as eagerly as our deliberate ones. A dozen species could have sued us for creating attractive nuisances. From every direction things converged on our island of artificial green. We brought on population explosions of several kinds, and then had to deal with them or submit to them.

Sometimes the consequences of our invasion pleased us. The linnets and Bewick's wrens that found nesting places in our carport were welcome, and we were troubled only when our car desolated a nest. The golden-crowned sparrows that roosted by dozens in the *Eucalyptus globulus* with which I screened the watertank were even more welcome, for through the winter and spring they sweetened the air with their tremulous, plaintive, three-note call. Ditto for the mockingbirds that made our pyracantha hedge their own. Ditto for the deer that came to dine on pyracantha berries, crabapples, roses, and anything else they found. Having to choose between a garden and the deer, we would have chosen the deer, though we might have forgotten that if we had not grown the garden the deer would not be there. Because of the open pasture next to us, we did not drive away the meadowlarks, or haven't yet.

We did not much mind the raccoons, foxes, opossums, and skunks that were enticed by our garbage cans and our little clutch of bantam hens. I grumbled, but not excessively when the coons tipped over garbage cans and pried off the lids and left me with a lot of wilted lettuce, coffee grounds, and bloody butcher paper to clean up. As for the bantams, they could look after themselves; they were not the soft touch that other hens would have been. They could fly like pheasants, they roosted high in the oaks. They laid their eggs in hidden places. Any coon or possum or fox that got a meal off them deserved it. One by one they disappeared, but meanwhile we had these bandit coons looking in our windows at night, and sometimes, sitting in my study, I could watch a pair of foxes come up onto my deck and groom themselves, apparently unable to see or smell me where I sat, six feet away, behind the glass. Once or twice a skunk gave it to the dog cold turkey, but that was a permanent harm neither to the dog nor to us. In fact, it taught each of our dogs in turn how to behave himself, and not to rush out all bravado and teeth when something stirred in the yard.

And the frogs. Where do frogs come from on a dry hill a mile from any spring or creek, in a climate where for half the year it simply cannot rain? Nevertheless, the week we built a fishpond, they were there, and homesteaded it happily, and filled it with their slimy eggs that turned in spring to pollywogs. Every night, in season, they conducted love concerts that could drown out conversations even inside the house. Stamp on the patio bricks and they fell silent so suddenly, from such a crescendo of noise, that the stillness rang like quinine in the ears, the sort of silence I have heard nowhere else except in the middle of the Amazon jungle.

Even a peacock moved in on us—arrived one morning by air, discovered the dog's dish with some leftover kibbles in it, and stayed. He stayed for three years, roosting ceremonially in the live oaks and making hopeless, fantastic, love to the cat, and on spring nights drowning out even the frogs with his piercing call for a peahen.

Country living, the Peaceable Kingdom. But that was only one side of it. Being human, we found some forms of life more attractive than others. We believed in weeds and pests, and they found us like fulfilled prophecy.

Gophers, not the Richardson's spermophiles of my boyhood but a surlier, more underground race, tunneled in from the dry pastures to enjoy our tomatoes and tulip bulbs and gnaw on the sweet rootlets of our cherry trees. Snakes followed them. We did not mind the gopher snakes and king snakes, in fact were glad to have them, as well as the tiny ring-necked snakes that lived under damp patches of leaves and fed on angleworms. But rattlesnakes dozing on our doormat made my wife nervous, and so we applied the human remedy, the remedy my family had found in Saskatchewan for any unwanted life. We killed them, as we killed gophers when we could catch them, and mice when they got too thick, and wood rats when they nested in the storage cupboards. In this we had the enthusiastic cooperation of our Siamese cat, an efficient killer but indiscriminate. He not only kept the mice and gophers on their toes, he decimated the lizards, got his share of linnets and sparrows and wrens, salvaged the cedar waxwings and robins that got drunk on fermented berries and tried to fly through the plate glass, and brought in, on special occasions, such rarer game as squirrels, and once a jackrabbit bigger than he was. All this in spite of our canned cat food and our precautions, our shuttings-in and our bells.

As with mammals, so with insects. We did not like to spray, for that meant undoing friend and foe alike. So we had ants, and with the ants, aphids. We had whiteflies and mealybugs and red spiders and thrips. We had leaf miners and twig borers and oak-leaf caterpillars. And especially we had earwigs and sowbugs. It is not a pleasure to a husbandman to find his strawberries infested with sowbugs. They eat their way into a succulent berry like hyenas into the body of a dead elephant. As for earwigs, they make lace of citrus leaves, and one spring they found the clematis vine over the entrance such a beautiful place to breed in that when I shook the vine I was showered with hundreds of crawling, pincered, vicious little bodies. Shuddering, I cut off the vine at the ground, dragged its infested tangle into the driveway, threw gasoline on it, and set it afire. Then I went downtown and bought snail, earwig, and sowbug poisons. Having played Tempter, I found that I had to play God in self-defense.

We have not been alone. There have been other gods before us and after us. In our first years here, though we had neighbors within a comfortable half mile, we could see not a single light at night except stars and moon and the glow on the sky above the valley conurbia. There was a great healing in that darkness that is not present now. Now we look out on constellations of lights, nebulae spiraling up hillside roads called Way and Lane and Drive. We see white dwarfs, but few black holes. The security lights of some neighbors burn into our windows all night long—perhaps to scare away the coyotes. Many yards are surrounded by chain-link fences to keep the deer out. On Saturday nights our walls and ears pound with the hard rock blasting from decks where the young are holding parties. The weeds, of whom we were among the first, have closed in.

And the life forms that we tempted, enjoyed, struggled against, loved? Alas.

It has been years since I had to go out into the moonlight, drawn by the barking of the dog, and rescue from carport or lumber pile an opossum that, lifted upon to a safe oak limb, plays possum for a while and then creeps away. I am not philosophical about cleaning up garbage spilled by a neighbor's dalmatian, as I was when the coons used to spill it. It is years since I heard that muscular rush into the dark as the dog charged and the coon fled. No foxes have groomed themselves in the light beyond my study window for a decade, and we would have thought the foxes gone for good if we had not seen, just the other day, a survivor out in the coyote's pasture hunting ground, walking as it were in the coyote's tracks and pouncing on the same mice or insects. If I thought installing bantam hens would bring them back in force, I would call on some henhouse tomorrow.

Nowadays, few skunks come by to drink out of our fishpond and teach our dog manners. The bloom of enveloping scent now rarely spreads and lingers in our bedroom when one walks around the house. There has not been a rattlesnake on our doormat for a decade and a half, and even gopher and king snakes are getting so scarce that when I see one in the road I get out and carry it off into the grass where it will not get run over. Sometimes I bring one home and make it welcome on our turf, but so far as I can see, none has stayed. Either neighbors kill them, or they find that the neighborhood cats have so thinned out the gophers and mice that there is nothing here to live on. It is a rare spring, nowadays, when even a single gopher kicks out his piles of dirt, making his underground beeline toward our garden.

The trees are tougher, and the native species may survive all our efforts to replace them with exotics. Development has brought water mains into the hills, and except in drouth years such as 1976 and 1977, there is plenty of Sierra water for the nursery plants and trees that new householders instantly set out. For a while, at least, this semi-desert may blossom as the rose. On the other hand, what one sees around old homesteads is likely to be native, reinforced by the Monterey pines, eucalyptus, pepper trees, and oleanders that have adapted to this climate; and that may be what surrounds us all a generation from now. The genes that were evolved for these hills have a way of asserting themselves whenever a fifty-year freeze or hundred-year drouth teaches local gardeners humility. Clear away the corpses of the exotics, and you find in the duff underneath them the sturdy oak seedlings, the sprays of poison oak, the insistent coyote-brush.

But also—and this should have been just as predictable—nursery escapees with the toughness to survive. Around the place where I once had a flowering peach (I cut it down because I couldn't control the peach-leafcurl) there is a stubborn patch of lippia that each season spreads a foot or two in every direction before the summer drouth slows it down. Around the basin of my new lime tree is a patch of crabgrass that I know will be even more stubborn. Both those patches came from the same nursery, an inadvertent bonus. Like the wild oats and the bur-clover, they may be part of tomorrow's pasture. If the pasture is there.

There is no reason to expect it will be. The town's policies are friendly to subdividers. In suburbs such as this, people with a tenderness for the earth seldom get elected to town councils or appointed to planning commissions. Their sentiments are seen as interfering with profits and growth. The towns are run by people who see land as a commodity. James Fenimore Cooper once described this tendency as the defeat of Principle by Interest. Whatever it is, I observe with foreboding that every individual who has held and left the post of town manager in our suburb has left it to become a developer.

So the pasture is likely to go, and with it will go much that has made our thirty years here a long delight, a continual course in earth-keeping. All around it the bulldozers are at work tearing up the hills for new houses—twelve here, thirty-one there, fifteen across the gully. That may be the reason why we see coyotes where we never used to see them, and why the one fox we have seen in years was in that same field. There may literally be no other place for them, or for the deer that in these winter months herd up in bunches of eighteen or twenty and come and go through our yard, sliding through our sagging barbed wire fences as smoothly as swallows hit a hole in a barn. What we see out of our bed-room windows may be only the remnants, deceptively numerous because concentrated in this one patch of open space.

There are, thank God, other centers—Stanford's Jasper Ridge preserve, Palo Alto's Foothill Park, various parcels held as open space by the Mid-Peninsula Regional Park District—where the wild things can keep a foothold. But all of those places are close to developed areas, all are near roads, and the creatures which live in them are regularly exposed to their greatest natural enemy, the automobile. And here is another observation that sours my ruminations: we have lived on our country road for thirty-two years. In that time, though I have seen hundreds of animals crossing the road, I never hit one. Yet the road is rarely without its flattened carcass, skunk or opossum or raccoon or snake. If I can miss these things, driving the road several times a day every day of the week, why can't other drivers? I have to assume that they try not to miss but to hit them, that they are like some trigger-happy neighbors we have had through the years—the policeman who sat on his patio in pajamas on Sunday mornings and popped off quail and towhees with a .38 revolver, the Texas lady who kept a loaded .22 in her kitchen and blazed away out the door at anything passing through.

We live among the remnants. Feral housecats, as efficient at hunting as the foxes, opossums, and raccoons, and more efficient at breeding—and constantly replenished by hit-and-run owners who drop them off in the country and drive away—have almost cleaned out the gophers, and I suppose the mice as well. That means that most of the animals who depend on that food supply couldn't make a living now even if we restocked the area with them. Even if there were enough food, the other hazards would be fatal. The last pair of great horned owls went several years ago, both of them apparently indirect victims of the poisoned carrots that some neighbor put out for the gophers. Both came to die in our yard. As one of them squatted in the patio, panting with open beak in the full sun, I passed my hand across above him to cut off the sun from his blinded eyes, and watched the slit of pupil widen instantly in the shadow, a miraculously controlled lens shutter, before the fierce yellow eyes went out. It wasn't quite what Aldo Leopold saw as the green fire went out of the eyes of a dying wolf, but it carried something like the same message, and it shook me.

Remnants. The pair of red-tails that we have known for a long long time still nest in the eucalyptus at the south edge of the pasture, but I don't expect, ever again, to be sitting in the patio talking to a visitor and see one of them come over at thirty feet, struggling with a four-foot gopher snake and very close to crashing. The visitor, a New York editor, accused me of staging that episode to plug California living. If I could stage it now, I probably would, knowing that the snake is in danger of starving to death anyhow, or of having his head crushed by somebody who can't see that he wears no rattles on his tail.

THE DESERT

Desert Walking

*John Daniel (b. 1948) was a student of Wallace Stegner at Stanford, where
Daniel later taught for a number of years. A widely published poet, he has also
written nature essays infused with a poetic consciousness, such as this recollection of a desert ramble published in* The Trail Home: Nature, Imagination,
and the American West *(1992).* Looking Back: A Son's Memoir *was published in 1996. Daniel lives with his wife in the foothills of Oregon's Coast
Range.*

My friend John, whom I've known since childhood, entered a
Vedic monastic order after college and spent ten years as a
renunciate monk in southern California, cut off from his
former life and the outside world. In those years he studied rigorously
and meditated four to five hours a day. When he decided to emerge
from isolation, he bought a four-wheel-drive pickup and started traveling to desert places in California and Arizona. He camped and hiked,
usually alone, for days and sometimes weeks at a time. It was in the
desert that he felt closest to the mystery of being. The created universe,
as I understand his belief, is in reality a vibration, a single tone struck in
the beginning from Spirit. Alone in the quiet of stone and sand, my
friend listens for the sound of all that is.

John and I argue when we see each other. We have never hiked together in the desert, possibly never will—there's a good chance we would drive each other crazy. But I listen to him. There's much in his religion that seems strange to me, but I respect his search, I respect his discipline, and I understand him when he talks about the desert. I too keep going there. Something in its silences keeps calling me. I see a little farther there. Religion is from *religare*, to tie back. Walking freely in desert emptiness, I learn a little more of what it is that I am tied to.

The lowering sun was still much too hot, my neck and arms already burned, I wondered why I had driven eight hundred miles for this. I had done a lot of backpacking, but all in mountains, the Sierra Nevada and Oregon Cascades, among lakes and flowery high meadows, in conifer woods as comfortable as old clothes. This was different. This was glaring knife-edged boulders strewn down barren slopes, clumps of wizened and eaten prickly pear, a scattering of stunted pines. This was the rank green scummy pool by which I'd dropped my pack, miserably heavy with five gallons of city water, and now sat panting in disgust, waiting for the sun to dive behind the Panamint crest.

The beautiful is a dangerous idea. Once inside it, it's hard to see out. I knew the High Sierra was beautiful, with its tumbling runnels and glacial brilliance and green expanses—but this oven of a desert gorge? This stark prison I had worked so hard to enter, scattering lizards, chucking rocks at the braying goomered burro who'd stood in my way? It was like spending years reading Wordsworth, page after lovely page, and suddenly hitting William Carlos Williams. Is this *poetry?* These fractured lines, these bare *things?* Unadorned in the rhetoric of green?

But the place was working on me, of course, even as I sat there. Even in my sunburned weariness I felt its freshness. By sundown I was admiring how pinyon roots jam right in rock crevices, how their stiff limbs creak in a rise of wind. The land's red and yellow mineral streaking glowed in the last light. Death Valley cooled in pale haze below me.

Two frogs started to chirp at dusk—they liked this place just fine, and kept telling me. A cool wash of moonlight, the stones radiant with hoarded warmth, a little wind at work, And next morning, as I hiked on, the canyon took me in. Narrowing, it played a slow winding rhythm between sheer walls, each turn a gateway to the unknown. I climbed dry waterfalls, clattered across loose gravel, slogged through sand, and kept on walking, winding in and out of light and shadow, breeze and stillness, following the scent of sun-warm stone and the bright piping of a bird I never saw.

Driving Highway 140 southeast from the Warner Mountains in Oregon, you pass from pine forest down into Deep Creek Canyon, where the slopes are studded with the squat green flame-shapes of junipers. The canyon dumps you out into open basin and range, a few trees fringing the higher ground. They grow sparser as you drive on, deeper into the Great Basin, until topping out on Doherty Rim you see a wind-beaten clump on the left, and way off to the right there's a single flat-crowned juniper—the final tree.

Somehow, by bird or rat or stormwind, a seed arrived in the right place at the right time. In a crevice among lichen-crusted scabrocks, possibly shaded by a clump of sage, it found just enough moisture for just enough time to elaborate its roots and begin to rise, imperceptibly through the seasons, alone in a high dryland sea. Beyond that tree, except for the planted poplars of an occasional ranch, it's nothing but small sage and rabbit-brush, crumbling crops of volcanic rock, nothing but the long contours of the open land, all the many miles to the Pine Forest Mountains of Nevada.

Desert presents itself in particularities. Thirty miles across wavering flats, Shiprock stands in stillness. A coyote lopes along a ridge and disappears. Deep in a canyon, one cottonwood flares yellow against pink stone. A silvery luminescence next to my foot takes shape as *frog* on gray limestone. Above me on a ledge, one clump of cactus has unfurled its papery burgundy flowers. A raven croaks—part of me waits all day to hear it again. The parched hillside I've been climbing reveals a small band of aspens huddled in a crease of land where a clear spring rises.

The eye moves from point to point, thing to particular thing, great and small. The mind can take its time, surrounding what it wonders at without distraction, and each object takes on heightened life. Maybe that's why my own life feels brightened in the desert. I too am here, a singularity myself, as improbably rightful as the one juniper, the clear spring, the sundown glow that flares the canyon walls and dies away.

As I walk up a canyon, I move toward source and seeing. Each twisting turn, each dry chute I climb opens the way a little farther. When the canyon forks, I hesitate. I have to choose one way. On steep sections my hands and feet work in concert—I have purpose. I am focused ahead, I ascend as if toward an astonishing secret at the canyon's origin. If I'm allowed to climb far and high enough, the walls that have been confining me may lower themselves. The sky broadens, surrounding me slowly, openness on my shoulders. I see the canyon that led me here winding away below. I see parts of neighboring canyons, spires of stone, buttes and mesas, blue mountains ranging away on the world's curve. The secret may be the rock I'm sitting on. Or it may be out there somewhere, in the complication of the carved land.

As I walk down a canyon, the tendency of the entire land collects me. I was alone on the dry flat where I started, but as little walls channel the sandy wash, company appears. Bunchgrass may be the first. A single flower shouts blue. The sand is damp, and after a while water is trickling beside me, sloshing around my boots, and the walls have shouldered higher. Willows trail their limbs in the current. Cottonwoods tremble in a breeze I can't feel. Swallows chatter overhead, where the blue sky has been squeezed thin by stone expanses only the sun can climb. Along their base, other humans left markings long ago. Like me. Like the grasses and the willows, the swallows and the cottonwoods, they followed the voice of steady changefulness, the fluent voice that says, *I am the one who sings through stone. I called you here. I know the way.*

Brown boulders the size of houses choke the mouth of a side canyon, jagged-edged, lighter colored where they split away, not long ago, from the upper walls. A forty-foot spire has sheared from the wall and dropped straight down, implanting itself among the riverbank cottonwoods whose contortions bear witness to brutal floods. Titanic violence composes this serenity I come for. These monolithic walls are splitting, sliding, crumbling to sand. The canyon is scouring deeper. I miss a lot, visiting for a dot of time, a week, a human life.

Any wilderness speaks silently of time, but time is nowhere clearer than in desert canyons. Descending millions of years through solid sand dunes, red mud mires, the rippled bottoms of ancient seas, here I walk in time, dwarfed by the mute magnitude of eons. Here, along with other newcomers—wren, cottonwood, lizard—I am swallowed in the long story of Earth. I walk in a stillness like no other, and though I don't hear what John hears, the sound of all that is, I feel it close. I imagine walking deeper than I can, down to the black stone that cooled from fiery torrents when the planet's face was red and flowing. And I dream deeper still, of entering the original fire itself, where if I lost myself I might for just one instant grasp the puzzle of being, my mind in its last speck of time might ride the leaping arc from nothingness to solid worlds.

The answers to the biggest questions are hard to come by, even in the desert. Bruce, my frequent hiking partner, is a molecular biologist. He studies the minute workings of life, and he tells me it's very much a mystery how life became alive. It's simply unknown to the bright minds and prodigious equipment of science how nucleic acids began to replicate themselves, how the translation of RNA into proteins evolved, and how these baffling developments came to be incorporated within a cell membrane. Once you have the cell, says Bruce, it's not too hard—

though it took another two billion years—to get to the elaboration of complex life forms. Once you have the cell.

The startling fact is that a rock-and-water planet came to life. Nothing is more apparent, and nothing is less understood. Unlike many of his colleagues, Bruce doesn't scorn this idea that life may have originated from spores that arrived in meteors. Given how little is known, he says, no plausible theory can be dismissed. He will entertain any explanation with the bounds of nature, any explanation short of God. Bruce is a scientist. He doesn't care much for religion.

"But what if God is nothing outside nature," I'm arguing tonight. "What if God is in nature, is nature, and evolution is God's way of being born?"

"Why do you have to call it God?" he says. "Listen. Matter is so subtle and so incredibly complex it doesn't *need* to be dressed up with divinity."

I can't refute that. I'm not sure I want to refute it. We look at the fire, drinking our brandy, and after a while I wander off to my sleeping bag. Staring at the brink of cliff straight overhead, silhouetted against stars, I'm unsettled. *Nothing, something. No-life, life.* We're looking at the same thing, neither of us can explain it, and we make different leaps of faith. Being is so extraordinary I can only call it divine. We see contrariwise and we see the same. What we see, we love.

The bumpy shadows on the cliff brink are bothering me. I'm worried that one of the less subtle acts of matter might flatten me in the night, and so I drag my sleeping bag farther under the overhang, a little closer to the fire, a little closer to where Bruce is sleeping. Tomorrow we'll talk more. We'll walk on up the canyon, and we'll both keep our eyes open.

This heat is *palpable*, it's pressing solid, almost seems to hold me upright as I lurch and stumble with my load. I'm not hot, I'm *wired*. I'm dancing with the bees around pink cactus blooms, the stones a bright dry river passing under. Somewhere along this big bajada there's a canyon mouth, there's cool rock shade, there's a place to drop this water tank I've packed for miles—a water tank myself, of course, a pouch of ancient sea traipsing on two legs through a hundred twelve degrees of blessed sun. Is this what evolution had in mind when that lungfish flopped out on the shore? Am I the avant-garde, the pioneer? I'm a fool, I'm way outside my depth. I'm stumbling like a drunkard here where stones and cactus, everything but bees holds still in heat, I'm crazy with bright clarity—those peaks across the valley close enough to touch, to drink, to swallow whole and keep on walking, as this lit vastness swallows me.

First it was soft hail beads, falling thickly, bouncing off the red sandstone, sliding down the angled slabs, jumping on the ground as if alive. Then papery flakes, with wind, thinning now to fine sugar specks. The silent storm fills the wash, gray and blind and steadily sifting down.

The snow terraces itself on ledges, sticks in delicate scallops on steeper surface. The busy pines and junipers are forested with it. Yuccas gather it in, each of them holding a loose ball, their straight yellow spines sticking through. Each tree and shrub, alive and dead, gracefully accepts the snow. I hear it ticking on the rocks. Water drips from the overhang. My fire flutters.

Waiting out a snowstorm under a dripping ledge is not what I expected. I had hoped to be miles farther by now, miles closer to the canyons I came to see. But the canyons will be there tomorrow. They'll be there for a long time. A destination sets you in motion, but once you're moving here, what's important is where you are. That's what I keep forgetting out there among cars and books and jobs. I forget this presentness. I need this slowing down—to open outward, to be still, to gather in what comes as the yuccas gather their globes of snow.

After breakfast Bruce and I eat a few mushrooms and set out to explore the little canyon where we've camped. It's a hot morning. The stream collects in several deep tanks, clear and green, and Bruce can't resist.

Scientists need to relax. They lead intense lives, one eye screwed to the microscope, the other scanning for the next grant—and hoping for a glimpse of the wild Nobel. I leave him splashing, a goofy grin on his face, and continue upcanyon.

A fly drones under a tree. Ambling along, I'm clothed in the heat of the day. Nothing changes really. Rocks don't turn to jelly, visions don't boil from the sky. Mind emerges from its usual cave, infusing the body, and with all our senses you remember—*yes, this is how it is.* The tree, the droning fly, everything is only more itself. Climbing the slope of bitter-brush, I smooth my hands along the canyon wall, press my cheek to its coolness, inhale its ancient smell.

From the earth will I cry unto thee, when my heart is overwhelmed: lead me to the rock that is higher than I. It's more than I can comprehend, almost more than my heart can bear, this beauty we are born to. All this earth, and we alive in it, to walk here, to touch this solid truth. . . . *Being is its own answer . . .*

On up the canyon, hiking with a boy's happiness, I'm thinking about the sixties. We were kids in a new car, revving the engine, driving way too fast. But what we glimpsed was real, the realest thing we'd ever seen. I remember me and John standing in the light rain with blankets on our shoulders, shivering half the night in a field as we tried to speak our sense of sacredness, how near it was. How near. He followed the glimpse to a monastery and out again. I followed into the world and into words. We both followed to the desert, and we're still following.

Bruce catches up, refreshed and laughing. He's been watching me, amused at how my head's been rotating angle to angle as I've walked, as if I were some yellow-capped root. Ridiculous, I tell him. I've been immersed in important thoughts, oblivious to outward things. His vision must be affected.

We stop for a small lunch, walk again, and after a few turns of canyon we arrive where we didn't know we were heading. We're standing in a pool looking up a tall waterslide cut so deeply into stone it forms a chamber, a cool grotto crossed above our heads by a slanting arch. The smooth sculpted walls rise past the arch to a crack of blue sky far above, and the green shimmer of the water we have stirred fills the chamber—wavering sheens of light alive on our bodies, our faces, around and above us, intermingling on the surfaces of stone.

I follow a necessity older than my conscious choice, older than my life or any life, a way worked out through ages between the tendencies of rain and rock. Where the walls lift high, I cannot leave. My freedom is to follow, my confinement my opportunity. In the light or sun, I move forward in my human way. I walk a while in the open hold of land. Wind and water, the beautiful blind carving—none of it for me, yet there's room. I'm walking, and the way is clear.

I used to hope for a monumental discovery in the desert. Around each canyon bend, above each dry waterfall, up the shadowy passage of a side canyon, I longed for something I had never seen—an undisturbed Indian village, the eyes of a cougar, a visible spirit. What I really longed for was a vision, a flash of knowing in whose light I would understand my life and death, and all the hieroglyphic forms of nature.

I've walked some desert miles now, and I'm beginning to think that vision is not a sudden kind of thing. Maybe it's a progress, a slow gathering of small seeings. Maybe it has to be. Walking a canyon sometimes I'll stop, vowing to look up so intensely at a certain thing—a purple flower, a sandstone spire—that its entire being will come clear to me. I stare, but my mind grows weary. The flower's language is untranslatable. I could stare until I fell to bones at the base of that rock tower, and still its sheer, water-stained surface would thwart me. Maybe, as the greatest friend and lover of these canyons insisted, its meaning *is* its surface. It stands in its peculiar form, unlike any other spire in the desert, in the universe, a monument to nothing but itself.

And so I walk again. The canyon keeps on going, and ordinary wonders mark its way. A cactus grows in a dead juniper. A small dinosaur rests on a rock. Rippling water goes orange in the late sun. The canyon keeps on winding, part shadow and part sun, revealing itself before me as it closes behind. What I see I touch with my awareness, the only light I have, and enough. I walk. And a good place to end my walk is the impassable overhang that finally blocks my way, to lie curled in its cool shade with the few ferns that live there, listening to a slow drip of water. The way I came, the way I will return, is waiting when I'm ready. And winding on above me is the canyon I will never climb, winding deep among the bluffs and spires, winding on through distant ranges, through the wilderness of scattered stars.

Here, where I come to get away from people, there are people who come with me. They travel the canyons too, their faces drifting in and out of my awareness—my wife, my mother and my brother, Bruce the scientist, John with this gray head listening, all my closest friends. As my mind quiets here, I see them lit with a certain still clarity, and I sense that all of us are living a forgotten story, acting perfectly ourselves, as perfectly as the stones are stones, as perfectly as the water flows. The story is close around me here, and it's never closer than in fall, when the cottonwoods turn yellow-gold against the red rock walls.

The story those trees tell is the same story sunset tells, the glad and fearful story, the story I'm alive to learn. Sunset tells it grander—you can see how vast and old it is, how other stories all form part of it, all end in that rich light. But you can't touch the sunset. You can't stand next to it or lean against it. With their trunks and limbs, their leaves that stir in the least of winds, cottonwoods bring the story down from sky and place it here, close to us, in ground.

There are graceful ones that rise in a few gentle curves of trunk. There are those with two trunks, or three, or four. There are trees that circle upon themselves in corkscrew loops. There are bowed and twisted trees, trees that wander along the ground like blind beggars, trees that dive down into sand and lift upward again. And there is one tree I've seen that grows sideways out of a silt shelf and arches back above the shelf to bury its broken crown at the bottom of the canyon wall. Its crumbling bark exposes cracked and riddled grain, and for part of its contorted length the tree is split clear open, filled with stones and dead leaves caught from the crushing floods. Along its great body it still raises a few living limbs, small trees themselves, flagged with the bright leaves of its kind.

If we didn't hide our histories inside us, we'd see our own lives as we see the trees. We'd see how some of us rise true and easily, how some are bent or split from their beginnings. We'd see where we were chafed or broken, where love failed or never was, where love returned. We'd see where troubles beset us, how we bent and twisted beneath their weight, how we've grown as we've been able to grow and never have stopped growing, branching form the single source, how in our bodies' heaviness we touch the air and tremble—how each of us, in one peculiar unlikely way, rises in the light.

Death Valley

Edward Abbey (1927–1989) was both a novelist and a nature writer whose work brought into bold relief the conflict between civilization and nature, whether in his anarchic novel The Monkey Wrench Gang *(1975) or his classic testament to the Sonoran Desert,* Desert Solitaire *(1968). This essay is from* The Journey Home *(1977).*

Summertime

From Daylight Pass at 4,317 feet we descend through Boundary Canyon and Hell's Gate into the inferno at sea level and below. Below, below . . . beneath a sea, not of brine, but of heat, of shimmering simmering waves of light and a wind as hot and fierce as a dragon's breath.

The glare is stunning. Yet also exciting, even exhilarating—a world of light. The air seems not clear like glass but colored, a transparent, tinted medium, golden toward the sun, smoke-blue in the shadows. The colors come, it appears, not simply from the background, but are actually present in the air itself—a vigintillion microscopic particles of dust reflecting the sky, the sand, the iron hills.

On a day in June at ten o'clock in the morning the thermometer reads 114 degrees. Later in the day it will become hotter. But with humidity close to zero such heat is not immediately unpleasant or even uncomfortable. Like the dazzling air, the heat is at first somehow intoxicating—one feels that grace and euphoria that come with just the right ration of Old Grandad, with the perfect allowance of music. Sunlight is magic. Later will come. . . . Yes, out of the car and standing hatless under the sun, you begin to feel the menace in this arid atmosphere, the malignancy within that silent hurricane of fire.

We consider the dunes, the sea of sand. Around the edges of the dunes grow clumps of arrowweed tall as corn shocks, scattered creosote shrubs bleached out and still, a few shaggy mesquite trees. These plants can hardly be said to have conquered the valley, but they have in some way made a truce—or found a point of equilibrium in a ferocious, inaudible struggle between life and entropy. A bitter war indeed: The creosote bush secretes a poison in its roots that kills any other plant, even its own offspring, attempting to secure a place too near; in this way the individual creosote preserves a perimeter of open space and a monopoly of local moisture sufficient for survival.

We drive on to the gas station and store at Stovepipe Wells, where a few humans huddle inside beneath the blast of a cold-air blower. Like other mammals of the valley, the human inhabitants can endure its summer only by burrowing deep or by constructing an artificial environment—not adaptation but insulation, insularity.

Sipping cold drinks, we watch through the window a number of desert sparrows crawl in and out of the grills on the front of the parked automobiles. The birds are eating tourists—bugs and butterflies encountered elsewhere and smashed, baked, annealed to the car radiators. Like the bears of Yellowstone, the Indians of Arizona, and roadside businessmen everywhere, these birds have learned to make a good thing off passing trade. Certainly they provide a useful service; it's a long hot climb out of here in any direction, and a clean radiator is essential.

The Indians of Death Valley were cleverest of all. When summer came they left, went up into the mountains, and stayed there until it was reasonable to return—an idea too subtle in its simplicity for the white man of today to grasp. But we too are Indians—gypsies anyhow—and won't be back until September.

Furnace Creek, September 17. Again the alarming descent. It seemed much too hot in the barren hills a mile above this awful sinkhole, this graben (for Death Valley is not, properly understood, a valley at all), this collapsed and superheated trench of mud, salt, gravel, and sand. Much too hot—but we felt obliged to come back once more.

A hard place to love, Death Valley. An ugly place, bitter as alkali and rough, harsh, unyielding as iron. Here they separate the desert rats from the mice, the hard-rock prospectors from the mere rock hounds.

Cactus for example. There is none at all on the floor of the valley. Too dry or too brackish or maybe too hot. Only up on the alluvial fans and the side canyons a thousand feet above sea level do we find the first stunted and scrubby specimens of cholla and prickly pear and the pink-thorned cottontop—poor relation of the barrel cactus.

At first glance, speeding by car through this valley that is not a valley, one might think there was scarcely any plant life at all. Between oases you will be impressed chiefly by the vast salt beds and the immense alluvial fans of gravel that look as hostile to life as the fabled seas of the moon.

And yet there is life out there, life of a sparse but varied sort—salt grass and pickleweed on the flats, far-spaced clumps of creosote, saltbush, desert holly brittlebush, and prickly poppy on the fans. Not much of anything, but a little of each. And in the area as a whole, including the surrounding mountains up to the eleven-thousand-foot summit of Telescope Peak, the botanists count a total of nine hundred to a thousand different species, ranging from microscopic forms of algae in the salt pools to limber pine and the ancient bristlecone pine on the peaks.

But the first impression remains a just one. Despite variety, most of the surface of Death Valley is dead. Dead, dead, deathly—a land of jagged salt pillars, crackling and tortured crusts of mud, sunburnt grav-

el bars the color of rust, rocks and boulders of metallic blue naked even
of lichen. Death Valley is Gravel Gulch.

Telescope Peak, October 22. To escape the heat for a while, we spend the
weekend up in the Panamints. (Summer still baking the world down
below, far below, where swirls of mud, salt, and salt-laden streams lie
motionless under a lake of heat, glowing in lovely and poisonous shades
of auburn, saffron, crimson, sulfurous yellow, dust-tinged tones of white
on white.)

Surely this is the most sterile of North American deserts. No matter
how high we climb it seems impossible to leave behind the influence of
aridity and anti-life. At 7,000 feet in this latitude we should be entering
a forest of yellow pine, with grassy meadows and freshwater brooks. We
are farther north than Santa Fe or Flagstaff. Instead there are only the
endless barren hills, conventional in form, covered in little but shattered
stone. A dull monotonous terrain, dun-colored, supporting a few types
of shrubs and small, scattered junipers.

From 7,000 to 9,000 feet we pass through a belt of more junipers and
a fair growth of pinyon pines. Along the trail to Telescope Peak—at
10,000 feet—appear thin stands of limber pine and the short, massive,
all-enduring bristlecone pine, more ancient than the Book of Genesis.
Timberline.

There is no forest here. And fifty or sixty airline miles to the west
stands the reason why—the Sierra Nevada Range, blocking off the sea
winds and almost all the moisture. We stand in the rain shadow of that
still higher wall.

I walk past three wild burros. Descendants of lost and abandoned
prospectors' stock, they range everywhere in the Panamints, multiplying
freely, endangering the survival of the native bighorn sheep by tres-
passing on the latter's forage, befouling their springs. But the feral burros have their charm too. They stand about a hundred feet from the
trail watching me go by. They are quite unafraid, and merely blink their
heavy eyelashes like movie starlets when I halt to stare at them.

However, they are certainly not tame. Advance toward them and they trot off briskly.

The bray of the donkey is well known. But these little beasts can make another sound even more startling because so unexpected. Hiking up some arid canyon in the Panamints, through what appears to be totally lifeless terrain, you suddenly hear a noise like a huge dry cough behind your shoulder. You spring ten feet forward before daring to look around. And see nothing, nothing at all, until you hear a second cough and scan the hillsides and discover far above a little gray or black burro looking down at you, waiting for you to get the hell out of its territory.

I stand by the cairn on the summit of Telescope Peak, looking out on a cold, windy, and barren world. Rugged peaks fall off southward into the haze of the Mojave Desert; on the west is Panamint Valley, the Argus Range, more mountains, more valleys, and finally the Sierras, crowned with snow; to the north and northwest the Inyo and White mountains; below lies Death Valley—the chemical desert—and east of it the Black Mountains, the Funeral Mountains, the Amargosa Valley, and farther mountains, wave after wave of wrinkled ridges standing up from the oceanic desert sea until vision gives out somewhere beyond the curving rim of the world's edge. A smudge hangs on the eastern horizon, suggesting the presence of Death Valley's counterpart and complement, the only city within one hundred miles: Las Vegas: Glitter Gulch West.

Echo Canyon, November 30. A hard place to love. Impossible? No, there were a few—the prospectors, the single-blanket, jackass prospectors who wandered these funeral wastes for a century dreaming of what? Sudden wealth? Not likely. Not Shorty Borden, for example, who invested eight months of his life in building by hand a nine-mile road to his lead and silver diggings in Hanaupah Canyon. Then discovered that even with a road it would still cost him more to transport his ore to the nearest smelter than the ore itself was worth.

Echo Canyon. We are deep into the intricacies of the Funeral

Mountains. Named not simply for their proximity to Death Valley, but also for shape and coloration: lifeless escarpments of smoldering red bordered in charcoal, the crags and ridges and defiles edged in black and purple. A primeval chaos of faulted, uplifted, warped, and folded dolomites, limestones, fanglomerates of mud, sand, and gravel. Vulcanism as well: vesiculated andesite, walls embellished with elegant mosaics of rose and yellow quartz. Fool's gold—pyrite—glittering in the black sand, micaceous shales glinting under black light, veins of pegmatite zigzagging and intersecting like an undeciphered script across the face of a cliff; the writing on the wall: "God Was Here." Shallow caves, holes in the rock, a natural arch, and the canyon floor littered with boulders, deep in coarse gravel.

Nowhere in Echo Canyon can I find the slightest visible trace of water. Nevertheless, it must be present under the surface, at least in intermittent or minute amounts, for here and there stand living things. They look dead but are actually dormant, waiting for the resurrection of the rain. I mean the saltbush, the desert fir, the bladderweed, a sprinkling of cottontop cactus, the isolated creosote bush. Waiting.

You may see a few lizards. In sandy places are the hoofprints of bighorn sheep, where they've passed through on their way from the high parts of the range to the springs near Furnace Creek. Sit quite still in one spot for an hour and you might see a small gray bird fly close to look you over. This is the bird that lives in Echo Canyon.

The echoes are good. At certain locations, on a still day, one clear shout will create a series of overlapping echoes that goes on and on toward so fine a diminuendo that the human ear cannot perceive the final vibrations.

Tramp far enough up Echo Canyon and you come to a ghost town, the ruins of a mining camp—one of many in Death Valley. Deep shafts, a tipple, a rolling mill largely intact, several cabins—one with its inside walls papered with pages from the *Literary Digest*. Half buried in drifted sand is a rusted model-T Ford without roof or motor, a child's tricycle, a broken shovel.

Returning through twilight, I descend the narrow gorge between flood-polished walls of bluish andesite—the stem of the wine glass. I walk down the center of an amphitheater of somber cliffs riddled with grottoes, huge eyesockets in a stony skull, where bats hang upside down in the shadows waiting for night.

Through the opening of the canyon I can see the icy heights of Telescope Peak shining under the cloud-reflected light of one more sunset. Scarlet clouds in a green sky. A weird glow pervades the air through which I walk; it vibrates on the canyon walls, revealing to me all at once a vision of the earth's slow agony, the convulsive grinding violence of a hundred thousand years. Of a million years. I write metaphorically, out of necessity. And yet it seems impossible to believe that these mountains, old as anything on the surface of the planet, do not partake in some dim way of the sentience of living tissue. Geologies: From these rocks struck once by lightning gushed springs that turned to blood, flesh, life. Impossible miracle. And I am struck once again by the unutterable beauty, terror, and strangeness of everything we think we know.

Furnace Creek, December 10. The oasis. We stand near the edge of a grove of date palms looking eastward at the soft melting mudhills above Texas Spring. The hills are lemon yellow with dark brown crusts on top, like the frosting on a cake. Beyond the hills rise the elaborate, dark, wine-red mountains. In the foreground, close by, irrigation water plunges into a pool, for which it is diverted into ditches that run between rows of date palms.

The springs of Furnace Creek supply not only the palms but also the water needs of the hotel, the motel (both with swimming pools), Park Service headquarters and visitor center, an Indian village, and two large campgrounds. I do not know the output of these springs as measured in gallons per minute. But I do know that during the Christmas and Easter holidays there is enough water available to serve the needs of ten thousand people. Where does it come from? From a natural reservoir in the base of the bleak, fatally arid Funeral Mountains. A reservoir that may be joined to the larger underground aquifers beneath the Amargosa and Pahrump valleys to the east.

This does not mean that the Furnace Creek portion of Death Valley could support a permanent population of ten thousand drinking, back-scrubbing, hard-flushing suburbanites. For the water used here comes from a supply that may have required twenty thousand years to charge; it is not sustained by rainfall—not in a country where precipitation averages two inches per year.

That's the mistake they made in central Arizona—Tucson and Phoenix—and are now making in Las Vegas and Albuquerque. Out of greed and stupidity, but mostly greed, the gentry of those cities overexpanded their investment in development and kept going by mining the underground water supply. Now that the supply is dwindling, they set up an unholy clamor in Congress to have the rest of the nation save them from the consequences of their own folly. Phoenix might rise again from ashes—but not, I think, from the sea of sand that is its likely destiny.

There are about two hundred springs, all told, within the boundaries of Death Valley National Monument, counting each and every tiny seep that produces any flow at all. None except those in the northeast corner of the park are comparable to the springs at Furnace Creek. In addition to the springs, there are the heavily saline, undrinkable waters of Salt Creek, Badwater, and the valley floor itself.

All this water is found in what meteorologists believe to be the hottest place on earth, year in and year out hotter than the Sahara, the Great Karroo, the Negev, the Atacama, the Rub' al-Khali ("Empty Quarter") of Arabia, or the far-outback-of-beyond in central Australia. The world's record is held by Libya, where a temperature of 136 degrees Fahrenheit was once recorded at a weather station called Azizia. Death Valley's high so far is a reading of 134 degrees at Furnace Creek. But Azizia has been unable to come near repeating its record, while temperatures at Furnace Creek consistently exceed the mean maximums for Azizia by ten percent. And Badwater, only twenty miles south of Furnace Creek, is on the average always 4 degrees hotter. It follows that on the historic day when the thermometer reached 134 at Furnace Creek, it was probably 138 at Badwater. But there was nobody around at Badwater that day (July 10, 1913).

Official weather readings are made from instruments housed in a louvered wooden box set five feet above the ground. In Death Valley the temperature on the surface of the ground is ordinarily fifty percent higher than in the box five feet above. On a normal summer's day in Death Valley, with the thermometer reading 120 degrees Fahrenheit, the temperature at ground surface is 180.

Curiosities: There are fish in the briny pools of Salt Creek, far out on the hottest, bleakest, saltiest part of the valley floor—the inch-long cyprinodon or pupfish. There is a species of soft-bodied snail living in the Epsom salts, Glauber's salt, and rock salts of Badwater. There are fairy shrimp in the *tinajas* or natural cisterns of Butte Valley in the southwest corner of the park: estivating beneath the clay most of the year, they wriggle forth to swim, rejoice, and reproduce after that rarest and most wonderful of Death Valley events, a fall of rain.

More curiosities: Blue herons enter the valley in winter; also trumpeter swans; grebes, coots, and mallards can by seen in the blue ponds of Saratoga Springs; and for a few weeks in the fall of one year (1966) a real flamingo made its home among the reeds that line the shore of the sewage lagoon below Park Village. Where this flamingo came from no one could say; where it went the coyotes most likely could testify. Or perhaps the lion.

A lean and hungry mountain lion was observed several times that year during the Christmas season investigating the garbage cans in the campgrounds. An old lion, no doubt—aging, possibly ill, probably retired. In short, a tourist. But a lion even so.

But these are mere oddities. All the instruments agree that Death Valley remains the hottest place on earth, the driest in North America, the lowest in the Western Hemisphere. Of all deathly places the most deadly—and the most beautiful.

Badwater, January 19. Standing among the salt pinnacles of what is called the Devil's Golf Course, I heard a constant tinkling and crackling noise—the salt crust expanding in the morning sun. No sign of life out there. Experimentally I ventured to walk upon, over, among the pinnacles. Difficult, but not impossible. The formations are knee-high, white within but stained yellow by the dusty winds, studded on top with sharp teeth. Like walking on a jumble of broken and refrozen slabs of ice: At every other step part of the salt collapses under foot and you drop into a hole. The jagged edges cut like knives into the leather of my boots. After a few minutes of this I was glad to return to the security of the road. Even in January the sun felt uncomfortably hot, and I was sweating a little.

Where the salt flats come closest to the base of the eastern mountains, at 278 feet below sea level, lies the clear and sparkling pool known as Badwater. A shallow body of water, surrounded by beds of snow-white alkali. According to Death Valley legend the water is poisonous, containing traces of arsenic. I scooped up a handful and sampled it in my mouth, since the testing of desert waterholes has always been one of my chores. I found Badwater lukewarm, salty on the tongue, sickening. I spat it out and rinsed my mouth with fresh water from my canteen.

From here, the lowest point in all the Americas, I gaze across the pale lenses of the valley floor to the brown out-wash fan of Hanaupah Canyon opposite, ten miles away, and from the canyon's mouth up and up and up to the crest of Telescope Peak with its cornices of frozen snow 11,049 feet above sea level. One would like to climb or descend that interval someday, the better to comprehend what it means. Whatever it means.

I have been part of the way already, hiking far into Hanaupah Canyon to Shorty Borden's abandoned camp, up to that loveliest of desert graces, a spring-fed stream. Lively, bubbling, with pools big enough and cold enough, it seemed then, for trout. But there are none. Along the stream grow tangles of wild grapevine and willow; the spring is choked with watercress. The stream runs for less than a mile before disappearing into the sand and gravel of the wash. Beyond the spring, upcanyon, all is dry as death again until you reach the place where the canyon forks. Explore either fork and you find water once more—on the right a little waterfall, on the left in a grottolike glen cascades sliding down through chutes in the dark blue andesite. Moss, ferns, and flowers cling to the damp walls—the only life in this arid wilderness. Almost no one ever goes there. It is necessary to walk for many miles.

Devil's Hole, February 10. A natural opening in the desert floor; a queer deep rocky sinkhole with a pond of dark green water at the bottom. That pond, however, is of the kind called bottomless; it leads down and down through greener darker depths into underwater caverns whose dimensions and limits are not known. It might be an entrance to the subterranean lakes that supposedly lie beneath the Funeral Mountains and the Amargosa Valley.

The Park Service has erected a high steel fence with locked gate around the hole. Not to keep out tourists, who only want to look, but to keep out the aqualung adventurers who wish to dive in and go all the way down. Within the past year several parties of scuba divers have climbed over and under the fence anyway and gone exploring down in that sunless sea. One party returned to the surface one man short. His body has not been found yet, though many have searched. If supposition is correct, the missing man may be found someday wedged in one of the outlets of Furnace Creek springs.

Death Valley has taken five lives this year—one by water, two by ice, and two by fire. A hiker slipped on the glazed snow of the trail to Telescope Peak and tumbled a thousand feet down a steep pitch of ice and rock. His companion sent for help; a member of a professional mountaineering team, climbing down to recover the victim, also fell and was also killed.

Last summer two young soldiers from the Army's nearby Camp Irwin went exploring in the desert off the southwest corner of Death Valley. Their jeep ran out of gas, they tried to walk home to the base. One was found beside the seldom-traveled desert road, dead from exhaustion and dehydration. The body of the other could not be found, though two thousand soldiers hunted him for a week. No doubt he wandered off the trail into the hills seeking water. Absent without leave. He could possibly be still alive. Maybe in a forgotten cabin up in the Panamints eating lizards, waiting for some war to end.

Ah to be a buzzard now that spring is here.

The sand dunes, March 15. At night I hear tree toads singing in the tamarisk along the water channels of Furnace Creek Ranch. The days are often windy now, much warmer, and rain squalls sail north through the valley, obscuring both sky and sun. The ground squirrels scamper from hole to hole in the mud hills, the Gambel's quail swoop in flocks low over the ground, alight, and run in unison through the brush, calling to one another. Tawny coyotes stand bold as brass close to the road in broad daylight and watch the tourists drive by. And the mesquite thickets, black and lifeless-looking since last fall, have assumed a delicate tinge of spring green.

Death Valley's winter, much too lovely to last, is nearly over.

Between winds and storms I walk far out on the dunes. How hot and implacably hostile this sea of sand appeared last June when we saw it for the first time. Then it seemed to be floating in heat waves, which gathered among the dunes and glistened like pools of water, reflecting the sky.

I bear for the highest of the dunes, following the curving crests of the lesser dunes that lead toward it. On the way I pass a few scraggly mesquite trees, putting out new leaves, and a number of creosote shrubs. No other plants are deep-rooted enough to survive in the sand,

and these too become smaller and fewer as I advance and the dunes rise higher. On the last half mile to the topmost point there is no plant life whatsoever, although in the sand I find the prints of ravens, coyotes, mice, lizards. The sand is firm, rippled as the seashore, and virginal of human tracks; nobody has come this far since the last windstorm a few days ago.

Late in the afternoon I reach the summit of the highest dune, two hundred feet above the valley floor. Northward the sand drops abruptly away to smaller dunes, mud flats, a scatter of creosote and mesquite—and what looks to be, not a mirage, but a pond of real water encircled by the dunes.

Glissading down the hill of sand, climbing another, and down the far side of that, I come to the margin of the pool. The sandy shore is quick, alive, and I sink ankle deep in the mud as I bend to taste the water and find it fresh, cool, with hardly a trace of salt—fit to drink. The water must be left over from the recent rain.

I struggle out of the wet sand onto the dunes. Here I'll make camp for the evening. I scoop a hole in the sand, build a tiny fire of mesquite twigs, and sear a piece of meat on the flaming coals. Mesquite makes excellent fuel—burns with a slow hot flame, touching the air with a nutsweet fragrance, and condenses as it burns to a bed of embers that glow and glimmer like incandescent charcoal. Fire is magic, a purifying and sanctifying magic, and most especially a mesquite fire on a sand dune at evening under desert skies, on the shore of a pool that gleams like polished agate, like garnet, like a tiger's eye.

The sun goes down. A few stray clouds catch fire, burn gold, vermillion, and driftwood blue in the unfathomed sea of space. These surrounding mountains that look during the day like iron—like burnt, mangled, rusted iron—now turn radiant as a dream. Where is their truth? A hard clean edge divides the crescent dunes into black shadow on one side, a phosphorescent light on the other. And above the rim of the darkening west floats the evening star.

SUSAN ZWINGER

Colorado Desert

Overlooking Carrizo Gorge

Susan Zwinger (b. 1947) is an author and naturalist whose fiction, poetry, and scholarly articles have been featured in numerous magazines and journals. Following the tradition of her mother, Ann Zwinger, she has also written several books about her wilderness journeys, including Still Wild, Always Wild: A Journey into the Desert Wilderness of California *(1997), from which this piece is excerpted.*

I gaze out from Carrizo Gorge above Interstate 8 and piece together the new Sonoran wilderness where I will hike and backpack over the next two weeks. On foot, I will cover sixty miles of the pristine yet long-traveled desert sands. It's the edges and borders and ecotones that drive me wild. I need to know how the Mexican Sonoran melts into the United States' Sonoran, how the Peninsular Mountains of coastal California melt into the Sonoran Desert floor, and how Anza-Borrego State Park flows into its adjacent wild lands: Carrizo Gorge Wilderness, 15,700 acres of deep canyons; the Jacumba Wilderness, 33,670 acres of rugged waterless mountains; and the Coyote Mountains, 17,000 acres of outrageously colored rock.

Far to the north, the cobalt ridge of the Santa Rosa Mountains entices me to backpack deep into an ancient Cahuilla village in Rockhouse Canyon. Closer to me stand the Fish Creek Mountains, full of pure gypsum, and the Coyote Mountains, with their sediments of a six-million-year-old sea. In between the Carrizo Badlands: I ache to explore their four-hundred-foot cones of gold, red, green, and purple remnants of marine reefs, lake deposits, and ancient Colorado River deltas. Within the badlands, I will tromp along with mastodons, early llamas, horses, tapirs, and saber-toothed tigers, or hang with giant sloths— twenty thousand years too late.

The Sonoran Desert is the youngest North American desert, having existed for only the last twelve thousand years. It stretches from 23 degrees north in Baja California, Mexico, to 35 degrees north on the border with Arizona. Mostly lying in Mexico, it spills over the U.S. border with its lush variety of bizarre life forms—twenty-foot-tall cacti, raucous carrion-eating birds, wily reptiles, and plants endemic only to the southernmost edge of the United States. As a subtropical desert, it tends to have a greater number of species than do the more temperate desert habitats

I have driven fifteen hundred miles from my rainy home in Washington State, longing for the Sonoran's magic—life forms and weather distinctly different form those found in any other desert. Here, the unique pattern of rainfall creates the largest cactus in the world— the saguaro, strange trees with green bark; the palo verde; and bizarre forms of the lily family, the yucca and nolina. Long, gentle winter rains from the coast and the shorter more intense summer rains from the southeast make possible the outlandish ocotillo, the eight-foot-high teddy bear cholla, the fragrant desert lavender shrub, and the elephant tree with its water-swelled, rhinoceros-skinned trunk and lemon-smelling leaves.

I throw my worn-out army poncho, Therm-a-Rest mattress, and twenty-seven-year-old sleeping bag on the sandy, dry ground because I want to wake with the breath of the Sonoran in my nostrils. In the damp morning or after rain, odors of incredible intensity emanate from desert plants that have evolved volatile oils to prevent desiccation: vivid lemons, pungent pines, lavender, mint, sage, rosemary, creosote, and intoxicating earth smells.

It is early February, and Carrizo Gorge Overlook is an ideal place for my exploration to begin. Below me, dropping three thousand feet down, the In-ko-pah, Carrizo, and Bow Willow Gorges look like arid crevices of rock boulders. I know that a hike up from the bottom of Bow Willow will reveal hidden palm oases, waterfalls, and cool pools after a rain, yet because of this barren view I don't believe it yet. This overlook straddles the transition between the peninsular zone's moist mountain climate and the dramatic Sonoran Desert. I stand at the serrated knife-edge of two ecosystems and their exceptionally rich variety of species. Last night I slept half a mile back from this escarpment under lush old madroñas, huge manzanitas with thick trunks, and deep green oak trees. Yet here, the lush foliage of ocean cliffs dovetails with the scrub of desert floor: *Ephedra viridis* (bright green Mormon tea), desert scrub oak, rabbit brush, sage, and oval-leaved buckwheat. Nuttall's woodpecker, scrub jay, and chickadee of the mountain chaparral mix air waves with Cooper's hawk, turkey vulture, and a magnificent eagle with a flashing golden head.

To the east-northeast, the whiter-than-white Salton Sea shimmers below sea level. Far to the southeast, Picacho Peak Wilderness drops toward the Colorado River; I plan to go there next. To the southeast, the Mexican border's steep mountain terrain, the Jacumba Wilderness, sinks from high coastal mountains on the west to sea level in a matter of miles. The U.S. Border Patrol sits outside the waterless wilderness and waits for thirsty illegal aliens.

Directly below me is the infamous Carrizo Corridor. I stare at this barren—or so it seems from up here—desert strip, which was an obvious route for Native Americans traveling by foot between the interior and the coast. Because they knew how to listen to the desert, what to eat, where to look for water, and sought the guidance of shamans, the ancestors of the Cahuilla would pass through with relative ease, taking notice of the great beauty around them.

Beauty, however, was not the preoccupation of the first Europeans who passed through this rugged, "impenetrable" topography. Here, where less than an inch of rain per year may fall and the temperature day after day may soar to 108 degrees, thousands of soldiers, miners, settlers, Spanish friars, snake oil peddlers, outlaws, and dreamers crossed this dry expanse, passing from palm grove to palm grove, spring to spring. Their bodies, composed of 92 percent water, would be incapacitated by a 2 percent water loss; at 8 percent loss they were dead. Death from dehydration is awful, slow, and torturous, with swollen tongue and hallucinations.

I imagine each of these Native Americans and European travelers leaving a different colored ribbon behind them in their wanderings. Then, in my mind's eye, I add the silver cross-hatching of railroad, the powder blues and pale greens of 1930s Chevys along old Route 99, and the strong reds, dark greens, and blacks of sport utility vehicles on State Route 2. Their intersections weave an intricate crochet of hope, intent, and culture.

Many of the threads, however, end abruptly—explorer or pioneer fallen, desiccated hands outreached toward springs, men slumped over fried radiators, miners picked clean by coyotes, ill-prepared pioneers carried off in the guts of vultures. Just so much dried, bleached detritus on the desert pavement.

Bow Willow Gorge to Carrizo Gorge Overlook

Before dawn the next morning I drive an hour, through the dramatic Jacumba boulders and into the bottom of Bow Willow Gorge in Anza-Borrego State Park. Soon after dawn, there on the Sonoran Desert floor, I look up again to the Carrizo Gorge Overlook where I stood yesterday and have a burning desire to make my way up there on foot— four thousand feet above. I want to know intimately, increment by increment, plant by plant, how such an enormous ecological-altitudinal change unfolds.

At the lower end, Bow Willow Wash begins as a groggy, quarter-mile-wide, deep sand arroyo where creosote and mesquite are half buried in the debris of the last flash flood. Shiny black phainopeplas—cardinal-shaped, obsidian-black birds—start up from their bushes like black holes in the air.

At thirteen hundred feet the day is heating up: no shade and no sign of water. It is my first day back in the desert. I feel anxious. To take my mind off my hot feet, I notice the bright chartreuse and red balls of mistletoe beginning to bloom in the dull brown shrubs. Dripping with sweat, miserably hot, I hear a sudden swell of bird chirruping.

One hundred feet below me, the shrub down in the arroyo appears gray in color. Now that I am closer I see its color is bright green. Water? The first surface water has appeared where there has been no water for almost a year. It has instantly created a stream habitat: water beetles and algae asleep for months have sprung to life. The multitude of desert seeds, such as chia, sleeping dry and "dead" for years, have swollen and surrounded themselves with sticky mucilage to protect the life within them as they sprout. The boulders suddenly are slick with algae strands which undulate in the current. Water striders, insects which walk on surface tension, have suddenly found water where water was not. Bird volume has increased tenfold.

I am down there in an instant. On my hands and knees, armpit-deep, I plunge my whole skull in. Cold water goes up my nose, down my neck. Cold desert water!

Cooled down, finally, I scramble with all four limbs up through shed-sized boulders and native palms. I watch the water pulse below me through eight-foot-tall carrizo reeds. Bow Willow Canyon narrows darkly; on its steep sides, talus teeters straight up for hundreds of feet. I scramble, up and down, over and through these great stone slabs. A pearly gray California tree frog sits perfectly camouflaged on the quartz monzonite stone; I have heard their lovely Ukrainian choir at dusk.

At sixteen hundred feet, something is happening to the vegetation—the higher I climb, the more plants come into bloom. A Costa's hummingbird zaps by me at impossible velocity, stopping where it finds a solid profusion of red-orange tube flowers—a chuparosa shrub, *Justicia californica.*

At seventeen hundred feet, I discover something amazing.

Mountain chaparral—a sugar bush, deep and shiny green like manzanita—which grows at thirty-five hundred feet in the coastal mountain transition zone, appears down here at seventeen hundred feet. I am in a classic ecotone, a transition between one ecosystem and another. In the middle of the steep canyon, rock pools, cool temperatures, and tall reeds have created a microclimate.

After the dry, pricking tans of the desert arroyo, suddenly I'm walking into a Technicolor land of the living. I find a misted hanging rock garden next to a seven-foot waterfall lush with chuparosa, desert apricot, desert rockpea, water-logged mosses, a California cloak fern, *Notholaena californica.* Ferns are supposed to exist in moist forests, yet here they are in glorious desert conditions. I strip off my pack, stinky bandanna, and boots, then lie back in the waterfall's spray and dibble my toes in the lucid brown pool. Up close to my eyeballs, ferns studded with water have sprung from cracks in solid stone. To protect themselves from summer's harsh heat, they grow furry white hairs on top and exude wax underneath.

Paradise at eighteen hundred feet. The next twenty-two hundred feet promise to be a bleak boulder-scramble. Wisdom is the better part of desert travel. This is as far as I'm going.

Colorado Desert

The Palms in Our Hands

Gary Paul Nabhan (b. 1952) is an ethnobiologist, plant ecologist, and author who has devoted his career to advocating the preservation of desert plants and the lifestyles of native desert people. In Gathering the Desert *(1985) he wrote about a dozen of the more than 425 edible wild species found in the Sonoran (Colorado) Desert, including the palm tree.*

Around Palm Springs, California, half of the sixty thousand residents are over sixty years old. In August, the asphalt running in to the various retirement subdivisions drives the thermometer up over 170 degrees. The pavement is so hot, you can fry a snowbird's egg on it—if you can find one. Most of the old birds who stay year-round stay inside during the summer. They may take a couple of showers a day to stay fresh. Many of them pay Southern California Edison a thousand dollars a month or more to keep their air conditioners running straight through the summer.

Outside, there is little shade you can sit under. Carports or porches, if those can be considered "outside." A eucalyptus in the backyard, perhaps. A couple of lollipop-shaped citrus trees or an African sumac, though they are seldom manicured so that you can fit a warm body beneath their canopies. The Hollywood junipers in the front may throw a shadow on the wall, but they don't shade a soul.

Then there are the palms. All the planned adult communities have broad streets lined with widely spaced palms. They are lucrative commodities in the landscape-nursery industry of southern California, sold by the foot, hauled by truck, and propped up in yards as if a motion picture studio were making an instant oasis movie right there in the new neighborhood. Introduced date palms are placed in strategic locations, but they usually have a big puddle of irrigation water at their bases which keeps folks from sitting beneath them. And there are the lines of native palms, the shorter "California fan palms" with petticoats of dead fronds trimmed halfway down their stout trunks, interspersed every sixty feet with tall, slender "Mexican skydusters." Landscape architects love how these two variants of *Washingtonia filifera* "rise out of the bare earth" on the curbs of urban boulevards, either in monotonous rows "for cadence" or singly, "like an exclamation point." They are planted in these subdivisions to make each landowner feel that he is living within his very own "oasis paradise." Yet these palms are stuck out on the side of the street where hardly anyone walks. Separated from one another by irrigated lawns of empty space, each throws a tiny oval shadow down on the ground. Torn from their evolutionary history of being densely clustered with other palms of various ages, each is as lonesome as a fish out of school.

When the more speculative subdivisions dry up economically, the faucets close, and the flow of water from some subterranean aquifer slows. The billboard showing a life of leisure played out beneath a palm grove cracks in the wind, then blows over. On one abandoned boulevard near Palm Springs, a starved *Washingtonia* finally curls down, fronds gone, dead growth tip touching the dust. The whole plant makes a big, sad U. It looks like a lean-legged ostrich hiding its head in the ground.

Nearby, a speculator leaves his office—a mobile trailer—and heads into town for a noonday drink. Parking his air-conditioned Oldsmobile, he locks the doors and walks, sweating, across the superheated paved lot. A palm silhouette shaped of menthol-green neon lights the window of the entrance to the Oasis Tap, promising paradise and lunch inside. His arms quiver and he makes a quiet grunt while pulling open the heavy door. Coldness rushes out. He enters. He can hardly see anything except for the flashing lights of the electric Coors ski-slope sign on the far wall. He takes off his sunglasses and his eyes adjust to the dimly lit tavern. He is glad to have taken refuge in this little electrically simulated oasis, away from business, bright lights, and the blazing sun. He finds a stool. Perspiration cools quickly on his arm.

"Whatchou guys been up to, huh? Hey," he pants, "gimme a cold one. Hey, what they got on the tube today? Are the Padres gonna let the Goose pitch today? Is that game on? What time is it anyway?"

He reaches for the icy Coors in front of him and takes the first gulp. A chill hits his chest. He gasps. Staring at the TV, still sweating, he can't see a single Padre.

He never walks out of the Oasis Tap.

Three women ascend from a hole in a mound near their house as the shade begins to side up the Sonoran *barranca* slope. It is after four on a June afternoon. They have been in the shelter of their *huki* since eleven or so. The two younger women joke while casually stripping palm fiber for the rectangular-shaped *petaca* baskets that they will begin the next day. The older woman, plaiting a new palm sombrero for her husband, is quiet, thoughtful. The last double-weave sombrero like this one lasted her husband for four years; his newer, store-bought plastic fiber hat hardly weathered seven months of his constant use. So she starts twilling its roundish crown, working down toward the pliant brim, and tomorrow will weave back to the top and tie it in. It will take several days of work for something that most people now buy at the store. But then again, having a durable hat is important. It is all that stands between her husband and the scorching sun on these June days when he has to work long hours to prepare his fields for the rainclouds that will soon cross central Sonora.

By noon on most days since early May, she has been retreating with the other women into the huki, a semi-subterranean shelter where a roof of logs, palm fronds, dirt, and brush covers a shallow excavation into a hillside. There, with her bare feet on the earthen floor, she hums quietly to herself while weaving, or giggles at the jokes the other two make about the men. There, in the musky dark, the frond fibers of the Sonoran palmetto, *Sabal uresana*, remain moist and workable. There, too, she has a break after helping her husband do the milking, after making breakfast and cheese, after sweeping the house and the ramada. Her thoughts are her own in the huki. Although she continues to work, the shadowy solitude somehow restores her freshness.

Huki. Perhaps it means "basket-house," or possibly "menstrual hut." Whatever the derivation, it is an ancient word among the Uto-Aztecan languages, and *huki* is a term still shared by Mountain Pima, Cahitan, and a few Warihio in Sonora and adjacent Chihuahua. The structures remain in use in the foothills of the sierras of east-central Sonora, but most hukis have fallen into abandonment in the lowlands. South of 30 degrees latitude, and below 1,000 meters in elevation in eastern Sonora, the Sonoran palmetto has been among the major weaving fibers for utility baskets, hats, sleeping mats, and other household articles for centuries. Two other palm species, beargrass, sotol, and agaves are also woven into baskets or cordage, but their association with the huki is not as strong.

Sonoran palmetttos are used for myriad purposes. The fronds are employed for thatching the sides and roofs of Warihio and Pima homes, ramadas, and A-frame shelters. Sections of the trunks serve as uprights and crossbeams in houses. Whole lengths are stacked up to make corrals. The hearts of palm seedlings are infrequently roasted and eaten like agave hearts. Yet this practice apparently has not been too intensive or widespread in Sonora during recent times. The density and areal extent of certain palm stands in fairly accessible areas suggest that they have escaped overexploitation. *Sabal uresana* grows in extensive stands near

Opodepe, Onavas, Sevepa, Mazocahui, and other ancient pueblos in central Sonora, well within reach of where thousands of people have lived for centuries. Perhaps only "surplus" palm hearts were used in years when there was an abundance of young plants resulting from the beneficial effects of burning the palmetto oases and savannas. Piman speakers are well aware that the whole palm dries up if the bud is used. Palm fronds are too important to let a whole plant be lost in just one meal.

Palms may have appeared as far north as central California more than seventy million years ago, based on reports of pollen similar to that of *Sabal* and *Washingtonia* found in Late Cretaceous sediments. Fossilized imprints of palm fronds have been found embedded in Californian limestone strata twenty-five to thirty feet below the present surface of the ground. Sometime less than five million years ago other tropical plants such as wild figs began to drop out of sight of these northern palms as summer rains decreased and winter temperatures lowered. For some reason, the *Washingtonia filifera* palms have persisted in more northerly, winter rainfall–dominated localities than those of *Sabal uresana* and *Erythrea* palms in Baja California or in Sonora. By themselves, the northern palms are considered relicts left over from earlier climates that were more favorable for your average palm.

They too may have been occasionally extirpated on a local basis from small canyons within their range by floods, freezes, borers, droughts, or disease. Later they could have been dispersed to some of the same sites again as seeds in the feces of wandering coyotes. For periods prior to human habitation of the continent, *Washingtonia* palms had already earned the status of survivor, persisting in areas over long stretches of time, through varying climates, while other early-established plants were lost from the region's flora.

After people came upon palms in the western Sonoran Desert, it must have been difficult for them to conceive of a life in which these palms were absent. Before A.D. 1500, there may have been a period of a couple of centuries when *Washingtonia* lined the shores of prehistoric

Lake Cahuilla in the Salton basin, if Richard Felger's hypothesis is correct. Prehistoric Indians harvested nearly forty species of plant and animal foods along the shores of Lake Cahuilla, and contemporary palm oases are situated close to this ancient shoreline. These shady oases would have been ideal sites for processing such foods, and many bedrock mortars used for grinding are found in the washes running through them. Virtually every palm oasis in southern California has prehistoric pottery or petroglyphs associated with it. Scratched and painted glyphs tell us of giants, big-horned animals, and solar visions dreamed by our antecedents. Under the tallest palm in North America dreams grew large.

The Aguas Calientes group of Cahuilla Indians at Palm Springs tells a story about the creation of the first palm. As Francisco Patencio recalled, it began when one of the head men realized that his life as one of the People was about done, and that he should prepare to go:

> The man wanted to benefit his people, so he said, I am going to be a palm tree. There are no palm trees in the world. My name shall always be Palm. From the top of the earth to the end of the earth my name shall be Palm. So he stood up very straight and very strong and very powerful, and soon the bark of the tree began to grow around him. And so he passed from the sight of his people.
>
> Now the people were settled all about the country in many places but they all came to Indian Wells to eat the fruit of the palm tree. The meat of the fruit was not very large, but it was sweet like honey, and was enjoyed by everybody—animals and birds too. The people carried the seed to their homes and palm trees grew from this seed in many places. The palm trees in every place came from the first palm tree, but, like the people who change in customs and language, the palms often were somewhat different . . . all, every one of them, came from this first palm tree, the man who wanted to benefit his people.

The benefits? Food from buds, flowers, and fruit. The fruit are produced on as many as thirty-one stalks per tree, with each fruit cluster weighing from five to twenty pounds. Fiber for sandals, skirts, trays, and baskets. Petioles for spoons and bows. Fronds for thatched ramadas. Wood for innumerable needs. The pithy wood from the branches of the palm fruit clusters was used as tinder when fires were started by friction-spinning. Home, hearth, cloth, food, and fiber—the palm was to the Desert Cahuilla what the bison was to the historic Sioux.

The Cahuilla and other tribes probably dispersed palms to other canyons, both unintentionally like the coyotes and intentionally like the Early People. Stands high in the San Jacinto Mountains have been traced back to Cahuilla plantings. The seeds are easy to germinate in moist soils, and young plants, carefully transported, could have been transplanted. *Washingtonia* palms, now found at the Papago oasis of Quitovac, Sonora, may have arrived on that scene in historic times via aboriginal trade routes. It could have easily been maintained there where western Papagos continue to transplant, burn, and irrigate various plants much the same way historic Cahuilla did.

Palm seed gets around, whether in guts of wildlife, in human guts, or in human hands.

In truth, the fate of various palms has been in our hands for centuries. Humans have longed changed the age structure of "wild" palm stands by increasing the frequency of burning and by management practices such as irrigation and clearing of ground-covering plant litter. Go to nearly any palm stand in Baja California, Sonora, or Arizona and you will see some blackened trunks that are the evidence of fires, often ones intentionally initiated by local residents. In 1909, botanist Parish saw that "it is almost impossible to find mature indigenous palms from which the leaves have not been repeatedly burned." Such torched oases have irked many a purist naturalist wishing to visit palms in their presumed natural state, with long skirts of fronds tapering down toward the ground. Instead they see charred, bared trunks that are ugly as plucked chickens.

However ugly they may have looked, only a small percentage of plants died in each oasis fire set by historic Indians. At the same time, brush, debris, and competing plants were killed back. Water and nutrients were freed. Ecologist Richard Vogl estimates that Indian-managed oases were burned nearly every four years, and each fire stimulated a subsequent bumper crop of fruit to be produced. In one of his study sites, palms surviving a burn averaged twenty-one stalks of fruit after a fire, as opposed to twelve in the unburned control. Following a fire, fruit are so abundant that the surplus falling to the open ground may produce thousands of new seedlings. These bumper crops attract birds and larger mammals, some of whom were hunted. The fires also improve the nutritional value of oasis understory plants such as saltgrass and rushes.

If you live within a palm oasis for any period of time, you find reasons to burn, to clear away dead fronds and the creatures associated with them. Early Anglo-American naturalists claimed that the Cahuilla had spiritual reasons for burning oases—because dry fronds were the hiding place of spirits, or to offer fire to the dead and to send messages to departed friends. Cahuilla have also offered much more mundane reasons for setting fires in the palms near where they lived. Patencio remembered that "the bugs that hatched on top of the palm trees made the fruit sick, and no fruit came. After the trees were set afire and burned, the bugs were killed and the trees gave good fruit." Long after the Cahuilla began such a practice, the USDA undertook studies which confirmed that periodic burning is the most effective way to eliminate scale and spider mite pests, thereby increasing palm fruit harvests.

There are other motives for burning dried fronds. They get in the way of harvesters, and fallen ones provide shelter for rodents and other camp-robbers. Wasps and yellow jackets often hang their nests among drooping fronds, and fires dispel them as well.

Such human modifications of palm populations probably began in prehistoric times, but the palms remained reproductive. All ages of one or two palm species could be seen clustered together in canyons where springs or seeps fed them, forming oasis microhabitats that sheltered cultures from the extremes of the open desert environment. . . .

In April, 1782, the soldier-explorer Pedro Fages encountered two small oases of *Washingtonia filifera* around pools of water as his party traveled northwest out of the Imperial Valley. Numerous palm springs such as these had been used by the Kumeyaay ancestors since at least A.D. 1000. Yet one of the spots that Fages visited was singled out in the next century as the southern Palm Springs, owing to its accessibility to a foot trail that grew into the Butterfield Stage and Overland Mail Line.

Another, northern Palm Springs grew from campsite to stagestop to artists' colony to resort to unwieldy retirement community in less than a century. But it was the southern site that was more frequently visited earlier. In the 1840s, the Mormon Battalion recorded twenty to thirty native palms at this southerly oasis. These palms did not survive for more than a decade.

In 1833, Dr. W. P. Blake of the Pacific Railway Survey unknowingly stopped at the same site that the Franciscans and Mormons had camped on in earlier years. He commented upon the destruction left in the wake of careless Forty-niners:

> Three or four palm trees, each about thirty feet high, are standing on the bank from which the springs issue. They are much injured by fire and persevering attacks of emigrants who have cut down many of the finest of the group, as if determined that the only trees that grace the sandy avenue of the Desert, and afford a cool place for the Springs, should be destroyed.

Just five years later, J. M. Farwell rode the Butterfield Line to the southern Palm Springs:

> This place takes its name from a species of palm trees which formerly grew here, and which within a few years were standing, as I saw the trunks as they lay upon the ground, and the stumps

from which they were cut. . . . It was bright moonlight while we remained here, and the beauty and singularity of the scene will not soon fade from my memory.

Recalling these events a century later, historian E. I. Edwards lamented that the "picturesque oasis [had been] stripped of its crowning glory. The palm trees had been cut down. All of them." At the time of his visit to the site in 1959, "only one isolated stump remained as a visible reminder of the palms." Two other trunk fragments were uncovered within a mound of dirt. The springs had become seasonally dry.

In the meantime, the northern town of Palm Springs prospered. By the mid-1880s, Anglo-American settlers had begun to build irrigation ditches from other springs to support agricultural development. These ditches later fed not farms but urban landscaping. There are perhaps more cultivated palms today in *the* Palm Springs—the northern one—than in all the historic canyons of Alta California. Something different from mainstream agriculture developed—a myth of idyllic oasis life. Here in the Perfect Land, you could live and breathe and, if you were so inclined, plant a backyard orchard. The *San Bernardino Weekly* ran this notice of a land auction in October 1887:

> Invest at Palm Springs, where there is NO FROST! NO HEAVY WINDS! NO FOG! THE HOME OF THE BANANA, DATE AND ORANGE! Only spot in California where frost, fog and windstorms are absolutely unknown. . . . Best Opportunity for Men of Moderate Means.

Plans for the Perfect Land were, at that time, built on the presumption of Perfect Access to Water. Such perfect access remained in the bush, never quite coming securely into hand. Anglos and the Aguas Calientes branch of the Cahuilla Indians fought over water rights for three decades. During the 1894–1905 drought, agriculture in the valley almost turned belly-up under the hot, dry sky. But the government finally led the Indians into a complex settlement that returned to them certain water rights plus a checkerboard of land tracts in Palm Valley that they could then lease to non-Indians for ninety-nine-year periods.

Most of the Aguas Calientes families joined in the rush for the Perfect Deal and soon became prominent developers. Aguas Calientes descendants now have interest in condominiums, tract housing, hotels, and unrestricted bingo-game bonanzas. Once posing for tourist photos in bedouin garb on the backs of camels, welcoming visitors to the "New Araby," some of the Aguas Calientes people have turned their drome-daries in for Mercedeses.

This is not to say that agriculture failed to develop in the region. On the contrary, southeastern California is among the four richest agricultural zones in the United States. Yet the natural attributes that once attract-ed men of modest means to the area are now largely gone. The air is often dull gray in color, a stifling haze. Highway signs reading "Day-light Test Area" and "Keep headlights on for the next 50 miles" perplex unacquainted travelers. Surface water resources are overallocated. Groundwater overdraft per year has become so great that it would take decades without pumping to return the water table to its pre-1900 lev-els. The Coachella Valley's groundwater quality has also worsened. High levels of total dissolved salts, boron, fluoride, and sulfates severe-ly constrain the future uses of this resource.

Is there negative feedback between southern California's Idyllic Oasis myth and natural oases left in the region? At first it appears as if the Coachella Valley's prosperity simply allows more people to appreci-ate the native oases—many are now protected, and they are elegantly interpreted at the Palm Springs Museum by enthusiastic, competent naturalists. It is believed that the number of palms in southern Cali-fornia canyons may be on the upswing. Most of these canyons are above the valley, in the zone of groundwater recharge, so that they are mini-mally affected by groundwater pumping on the plains below.

But it is the oasis as a unique microenvironment that has suffered, through fire suppression, exclusion of Native American gardening, and locally within the valley, changing water relations. Less than four hundred hectares of native palm oasis habitat persist in the wilds of the American Southwest.

Ecologist Richard Vogl has eloquently written of how "empty" southern Californian palm stands feel today:

> The original oases were largely open and foot-worn, free of accumulated plant debris. Springs were clear and impounded water holes were maintained for bathing and washing. In addition, hand-dug channels shunted water to small garden patches. Today's oases are usually cluttered and choked with plant accumulations, springs are silted in or taken over by emergent aquatic plants, and unimpeded streams tumble down to sink into the desert floors.
>
> Oases formerly smelled of charred wood, camp fires, burned grass, and moist soil, occasionally interrupted by cooking food. In some instances, oases could be smelled before they were seen. Today's oases take on the more subtle odors of the existing vegetation, they smell of willows, of mule fat, or of desert lavender, but seldom of smoke, char and fire.

Years of fire suppression allow the buildup of tinder to the extent that when a fire does occur, it damages many more palms. Similarly, there have always been flash floods in southern California, but their frequencies and intensities have changed with urbanization. At Willow Hole near Palm Springs, twenty-one palms were evident in 1961. A 1969 flash flood, intensified by the amount of runoff rapidly dumped into washes from a paved housing development upstream, downcut the wash running through Willow Hole, dropping the water table there by six meters. By 1983, only nine palms were left, all scattered along the edge of surrounding dunes, where moisture bleeds out of their sandy shoulders.

Not too far away, the celebrated Thousand Palms oasis sits beside a series of sedimentary hills. Its three groves look fine from the summits of these hills. But when you meander under the palms you see that a number of them have been saved by supplemental water provided to them by a trickle irrigation system. It is like seeing someone fed intravenously, knowing that he might not survive without this lifeline. The smallest of the three groves, Powell Palms, has been particularly vulnerable to arroyo downcutting and water table droppage over the last decade. Groundwater use at nearby housing developments can only aggravate this situation.

It has become clear that no oasis is an island unaffected by surrounding land uses and abuses. Northeast of Palm Springs in the Mohave Desert, the National Park Service created Joshua Tree National Monument to preserve palm and yucca stands. Groundwater consumption in nearby fields and military bases has caused a five-meter drop in the groundwater over the last four decades. Spring-fed pools dried up in the Oasis of Marah (Twenty-nine Palms) over a decade ago. To avoid desiccation of the tourist attraction there, the wild *Washingtonia*, the National Park service is running a pipeline up to the palms to keep them irrigated. With what? Pumped groundwater.

Somewhere within this rapidly changing scene, a man emerged who truly loved palm oases, as they have been and should be. Randall Henderson was born in the late 1880s in Ohio, but by the end of World War I he was firmly planted in the deserts of southern California. From 1920 up until his death on the Fourth of July 1970, Henderson visited eighty-eight native palm oases in Alta California and Arizona, and no less than eight oases in Baja California. Using a hand-held counter, he individually tallied the number of *Washingtonia* palms in natural habitats north of the border (11,000) as well as some 4,500 of the estimated 18,000 palms of three species found within the first eighty kilometers south of the international boundary.

His quest for understanding the context of palms took him into remote areas with the likes of renowned botanist Liberty H. Bailey and the Pai-Pai Indians, seasoned oasis dwellers. The astonishing amount of information that he published on oases in his twenty-one years as editor of *Desert* magazine continues to dwarf that contributed by any trained scientist. His notes and photos form a baseline from which we can record change in their habitats. His compulsiveness for counting palms did not, however, diminish his wonder that any are able to grow in such an arid environment: "I have never ceased to be amazed and delighted at the paradox of palms growing wild in the desert, for this tree must have abundant water at its shallow roots."

What Henderson recognized is that much of the natural elegance of palms has to do with their specificity to certain kinds of places, their geological, hydrological, and microclimatic conditions. Most of the California palm oases are situated where springs and seeps well up at fault lines, such as the San Andreas, that are part of tectonic-plate intersection. Hillside seeps caused by water outflow from exposed geological strata provide habitats for palms in Fishtail Canyon in the Kofa Mountains of Arizona and in Horseshoe Palms in the Indio Hills of California. Where water bubbles up on floodplains or in canyons due to impervious bedrock reaching the surface, oases such as Pushwalla Palms are formed. These islands of greenery float like mirages on the edge of sand seas surrounding the Salton Sea and Colorado River delta. Their beauty is in part due to contrast with their surrounding environment. Oases cannot occur just anywhere, for the natural habitats within which palms can persist for centuries are few and far between. Once established, the palms help create soil conditions and a buffered microclimate that encourage future generations of palms.

Henderson detailed the uniqueness of nearly every oasis he visited and pointed out differences and similarities with others nearby. Late in life, he became greatly disturbed that each oasis was rapidly becoming like every other in southern California, that suburbanization was making the landscape more homogenous. The town of Palm Desert that he founded in 1948 currently houses more than 11,000 people. It now suffers from the same trappings that most post–World War II instant cities do.

One thing eventually saddened Henderson even more than the cancerous growth in his own backyard; it was the repercussions from a stripped-down jalopy that he adapted in the 1930s to drive down sandy washes during his oasis explorations. His modest homemade contraption became the prototype for the modern dune buggy.

When he realized what destruction off-road vehicles would cause, he retired from tourist-oriented *Desert* magazine in 1958 and poured his energies into the Desert Protective Council. He had hoped to put constraints on the all-terrain vehicles that were flooding the Mohave and Sonoran Deserts, but he was too late to turn the tide. By the time he died there were an estimated five million off-road vehicles in the United States. Many of their western owners had access to Henderson's earlier publications on how to get to remote places, including oases. For a conservationist loving tranquillity, it was the equivalent of creating a Frankenstein. In his last days, he wondered when society would realize that it was "time to see what could be done about tooting auto horns, badly muffled exhausts, blatant radios . . . and the prattle of garrulous and ill-tempered humans."

Traveling over a wide washboard road on the edge of Laguna Salada, Paul Mirocha and I inadvertently ended up at one of Henderson's favorite oases, Guadalupe Canyon. We had missed the ill-defined intersections with two roads leading toward more northerly canyons in the Sierra Juarez of Baja California. Our road was considerably better than the winding course of dry arroyo that Henderson had used as a path, but still it rattled our kidneys. When we reached sight of the first palms, we stopped in the middle of the road, emptied the truck cab and ourselves, and watched the sun go down behind the Sierras.

We were relieved to reach any oasis by sunset, let alone one where we turned out to be the only visitors. Not that we were the only people evident, for caretaker Arturo Loya Espinosa lives half a kilometer upstream from where we camped. We heard his dogs and chickens all night. He rents out primitive huts and camping spaces with fire pits, charges fees to enter the swimming pool and hot springs, and rakes up beer cans and plastic bags after visitors leave. He knows where the ancient fire pits are, and the bedrock mortars, the petroglyphs. He also knows the way to a cave containing clay ollas and palm sandals, but he won't take anyone there. He concedes that there is virtually no place near the oasis that you can go without finding evidence of human activities, camping debris, ancient or otherwise.

Yet palms, not public paraphernalia, dominated the habitat and consumed our attention. The last light glinted off the Virgin of Guadalupe, a rock outcrop high above us. We sat down amidst a dense clump of *Washingtonia* and *Brahea* palms.

What music to wash the road-roar out of our ears! The flower stalks drooped down like streamers, rattling in the wind against the half-burned miniskirts of old fronds. From the background noise of the canyon bottom below, the rush and bubble of spring water wafted in. I looked up: a quarter moon, the Virgin, and the free flight of western yellow bats leaving their roosts beneath the fronds.

As an inky darkness steeped into the canyon, my eyes worked harder. On a bench across the arroyo bottom, several hundred palms of all ages gathered around seeps. Arrowweed, carrizo reeds, screwbeans, and saltgrass grew in their shadows. Climbing down across the mineral-rich stream and up toward the bench, I found raccoon and skunk tracks in the mud. The best find, though, was as I approached the heart of the palm stand. There, in the ashes below a fire-tumbled giant, were palm seedlings. Scattered around in the darkness, there were densely toothed new palm sprouts and seedlings of various sizes and ages, manelike hairs emanating from their young, tender fronds. They were growing in the protection of their elders, where the earth gave freely of its waters. They would offer to future generations the chance to see an oasis as it should be, where it should be.

THE COAST

Gaviota Coast Trails

J. Smeaton Chase (1864–1923) emigrated to Los Angeles from England in 1890. He traveled throughout California, and wrote half a dozen books about its natural wonders. In California Coast Trails *(1913) he recounts his 1911 horseback trip up the coast, including his adventure on the Gaviota coast, south of Point Conception.*

The coast road from this point west for ten or twelve miles is little more than a track, and that of the roughest kind, quite impossible for wheeled vehicles. There was a fence across the path, and a notice was posted that travelers must take the beach. I rode down to the shore, but when I saw that a little farther on the tide was washing up to the base of the cliffs I turned back, found a way through the fence, and trespassed on my way.

The country hereabout is monotonous and unattractive. Low undulating hills run for mile on mile, treeless, and scanty even of brush, and the cañons are dry and shadeless. We marched some miles before finding water, and I resolved to camp at the first creek I should see. At last I came to one, which afforded good pasturage also; and, dismounting, I led Chino down toward the beach, where I noticed a little bench of green grass at the mouth of the cañon and on the very edge of the shore sand.

Here the expedition narrowly escaped disaster. The inwash of the tide, meeting the water of the creek, had formed an area, a sort of pit, of quicksand. This we had to cross in order to reach the beach, and in a moment, without warning, I was up to my middle, and Chino, following close behind, plunged in beside and almost upon me. On the instant I threw myself backward, and tried to work myself out, but the sand clogged me as if it were liquid lead, and I could not reach back with my hands to where the solid ground would give me support. Chino, meanwhile, was struggling desperately but helplessly, the heavy saddle-bags and other articles of his load weighing him down so that he was already half covered.

By great good fortune the cañon wall was nearby, not over eight feet away. It was of weathered rock, soft and shaley, and I though that if I could anyhow work over to it I could get grip enough on it to support myself. It seemed an impossible thing to do, with the fatal sand clasping and weighing me down, but I attempted it.

I remember that, as I struggled, a horror of the commonplace sunlit evening flashed over me and, with it, the thought that no one would ever know what had happened to me, for there would be no trace, no clue. That horrible sand would close over me, the sun would shine on the spot, the roar of waves would go on unbroken; I should simply cease to be. I think I wondered whether there would not be any way of telling my friends; but I am not sure whether that thought came then, or in thinking it over afterward.

All this can only have taken a very short time, during which I was struggling to reach the rocky wall. At last my fingers scraped the rock, and gradually I was able to draw myself backward to firm ground. Then I ran round by the solid beach sand, crossing the creek, and came back to Chino. He had stopped struggling, but lay over on his side, and had sunk so that one of the saddle-bags was quite out of sight. Blood, too, was spattered all about him.

Coming as close as was safe behind him, I gradually loosened as much of his load as I could reach. Then I caught his rope and tried to get him to exert himself. For some time he made no move, and I thought he must have broken his off-side foreleg on a half-buried snag of dead wood that projected above the sand. Again and again I tried to get him to move, but he still lay on his side, drawing great gasping breaths, and I about decided I should have to shoot him where he lay. But I made a last effort, shouting and hauling at him with all my strength, until I literally forced him to bestir himself: when, putting my last ounce into it, I pulled and shouted, refusing to allow him to relax his efforts for a moment and gradually working his head round somewhat toward where I stood. With a final wild spasm he scrambled up onto the dry, hard sand and stood snorting and trembling pitifully, bespattered with blood and utterly exhausted.

I was vastly relieved to find that the blood was coming from his mouth and nostrils. He had broken some small blood vessel in his first struggles. I took off the saddle and led him carefully over to a grassy spot, where I washed out his mouth and then gave him a thorough rubbing down; and within half an hour I had the satisfaction of seeing my staunch companion of so many days and nights feeding with equanimity and even enthusiasm.

The incident was sufficiently dangerous to give me a lesson in caution, as well as cause for hearty thankfulness. There was not the slightest hint of treachery in the appearance of the sand, but thereafter I went warily in all doubtful places. I ransacked my rescued saddle-bags and made a rare supper to celebrate the adventure. As the bags were strongly made, and waterproofed, the contents had not been much damaged. Then I ran up my sleeping tent, in view of the fog which I could see advancing from the sea. I chose a place on a little shelf of dry sand, sheltered by the angle of the cañon wall, and apparently above high-water mark by a safe though narrow margin. Then in the dusk I gathered a pile of driftwood and made a royal fire, by which I sat until long after dark, listening with more than usual enjoyment to the tinkle of Chino's bell and the manifold voices of the sea.

There seemed that night to be an unusual variety in the sound of the surf. Intervals of dramatic silence were broken suddenly by roars as if huge bodies of water were being dropped from some great height. Then would come a long, sibilant swish, which, after subsiding to rippling murmurs, ended smartingly with a *thump, fortissimo*. Occasionally, in the midst of a long whisper there would come a smart clap, followed by little quarrelings, and shudderings, and sighs, almost of human quality of tone. The ordinary sounds of the breakers, the steady pound, boom, and clatter, pound, boom, and clatter, seemed not to be in evidence.

The entertainment was so interesting that it drew me down to the water's edge. When I passed beyond the light of the fire, I found a new fascination in the pale sea-flame that hovered and raced up and down my quarter mile of beach as the rollers broke in ghostly phosphorescence. Then a steamer, three or four miles out, passed on her way upcoast, her lights shining genially across the black void of water. I fancied that some lover and lass, leaning together over the bulwarks, might be watching my twinkling beacon, and I went back and threw on another log to brighten the blaze, in the hope that the beam might stimulate my swain to some urgency, or some pretty fancy, that should bring a happy climax to his wooing.

When at last I felt in mood to turn in, I noticed that the tide had made a long advance toward my tent; but I felt sure that it was close upon its turn and that I could hold my ground. Still, as there seemed just a possibility of trouble, I did not undress to my usual camping limit, but got into my blankets partly dressed, and soon fell asleep. I suppose I had slept about half an hour when I awoke with an uneasy feeling that the water was coming too near. Looking out, I saw that the stronger waves were sending their fans of foam quietly up to within a few feet of me, leaving a very slight rise of beach before they would wash against and undermine my little shelf of sand. There seemed to be still a "sporting chance" that I should be safe, and I lay down again; but the thought of awaking next time to find myself swamped and the tent collapsing over me was so annoying that I could not sleep and resolved to move.

To go farther back was impossible, for the stream ran only a few yards behind me, so I gathered an armful of my traps and made a bolt in the darkness across the creek, which was already flooding with seawater, and found a level place among the grass near my horse. I had to make two more flights to and fro to bring over the rest of my belongings, and then, too disgusted to set up the tent again, I made a windbreak of the saddle-bags, rolled myself up in the blankets, and finally got to sleep. My last glance across at the red embers of the fires showed an ambitious wave in the act of washing it out of existence.

In spite of mishaps, the place was so attractive, in its close proximity to the sea and its complete retirement, that I decided to remain for another day. The swallows that haunted the cliffs made the pleasantest of company, flying happily about me, and pursuing the sand flies almost into the coffee. The weather, too, supplied the one desirable thing, namely, shade, which the camp otherwise lacked; for the fog of the night, lifting but not passing off all day, afforded a delightful temperature, with restful tones of color. It is so that I best love the sea. Its grandeur, its significance, its solemnity, are far more felt than "'neath the all revealing sun"; and the water itself, deeply, darkly clear, seems more aqueous and elemental.

There was an unusual number of seabirds hereabouts, and in a walk down the beach I came upon the rocky point which was their home. Hundreds of them sat ranked in demure hierarchy, the shags, who were the most numerous, taking the lowest place, then the white-backed gulls, and, presiding over all with an air of burlesque dignity, a dozen or so pelicans. At my approach the whole company took flight, and in a moment "the winged air was darkened with plumes." The clatter of wings was bewildering as they circled once or twice and then streamed off to settle on the belt of kelp which here forms a floating reef unbroken for mile on mile. The flight of the pelican is a wonderful exhibition of ease in motion. I was never tired of watching them gliding in file, smooth, swift, and silent, with no movement of wing for great distances. If ever men attain to such perfection of aeronautics (though that is impossible), I mean to sell my belongings, to my boots, if necessary, and purchase the magic machine.

Returning from my walk, I almost stepped upon a rattlesnake that lay coiled among the driftwood which I had been drawing upon for my fire. He was not a large one, and the calendar in his tail marked only four changes of skin; but I judged that he must die. Mr. Muir, I remember, deprecates killing these creatures, and says that, having once put one to death, he felt himself "degraded by the killing business, farther from heaven." On the other hand, I recalled that when, on the island called Melita, a viper bit the shipwrecked apostle in the hand, he unceremoniously "shook off the beast into the fire." My little reptile was a potential evil-doer also, and on the whole I saw no reason for trying to better such a notable example as that of St. Paul.

At evening the cloud curtain to the south lifted a little from the horizon, and one of the islands of the Channel Group shone out like a great jewel in the light of the setting sun. It was very beautiful, and rather solemn—the slow lifting of the veil; the magic of the revelation; the silent passage through tone on tone of ethereal color until, when the sun had sunk, the distant isle stood marked in soft dense purple on a glowing belt of yellow, the only object between gray cloud and gray of sea. Then came the gradual lowering of the veil again over all. There was something unearthly in the quiet color-action, as if an angel had managed the heavenly display. Indeed, perhaps one had.

Malibu

Where the Mountains Meet the Sea

Lawrence Clark Powell (b. 1906) was Chief Librarian (1944–1961) and Dean of the School of Library Services (1960–1966) at UCLA. He is also the author of a number of books about his life, his travels, and literature, including the following selection from The Little Package (1964), *about his days living in Malibu in the late 1950s and 1960s.*

My boyhood and youth were nourished by the San Gabriels and the San Bernardinos, which ranges wall out the desert from southern California. It was not until I went to work at UCLA and moved near to the campus that allegiance was transferred to the Santa Monicas, a less spectacular range that rises in Hollywood and extends fifty miles to a marine ending at Point Mugu.

From living in Beverly Glen, I came to love the surrounding range of chaparral, oak, and sycamore. It was a good place for our sons to live as boys, and now that they are grown to manhood they find their subconscious minds full of memories of their mountain boyhood.

Although . . . I discovered the westernmost part of the range in the poems of Madeleine Ruthven, it was not until a decade later, in 1944, that I came actually to know this remote area. At war's end my friend Gordon Newell, the sculptor, acquired land on the north slope of the mountains, overlooking Seminole Hot Springs, and it served me as a kind of retreat from too much city. From driving and walking and talking to Newell, I came to know and love his land and the sea of chaparral that enislanded it. The north slope of the Santa Monicas is green the year round from springs, one of which he had deepened and rock-lined, so that it was an unfailing source of cold water, even in the driest summer. Through the years I watched him quarry honey-colored flagstone, sift and sack leaf-mold, breed Nubian goats, keep bees, carve wood, and cut stone, while his wife Emelia fashioned delicate jewelry and airy mobiles, and their children thrived in a kind of twentieth-century Theocritean idyll.

It takes time to assimilate the essences of a land. When after years of residence in Inyo County Mary Austin wrote *The Land of Little Rain*, her publishers wanted her to move around the country, writing similar books about other places of residence. Her reply was that it would take her ten years in a locale to be able to evoke its spirit, as indeed she did later for Arizona–New Mexico in *The Land of Journeys' Endings*.

Thus, although we moved to the Malibu, in the seaward lee of the Santa Monicas, as recently as 1955, I brought to the land years of slow-growing knowledge and deepening love for this country "where the mountain meets the sea"; and I was ready to write about it not as a stranger. In fact, it was this long background of reading and seeing that motivated our move—that and the feeling we have always had for the seashore. Plus something else, instinctive, mysterious, and right.

So it was a kind of magnetic homecoming, this move to the Malibu, and now our leisure time is divided between shoreline walks and mountain drives.

On this coast the seasons merge imperceptibly into each other. When the rainy season is regular, then it is easier to know the time of year. When drought comes, how is one to know summer and fall for winter and spring? By the stars to be sure, and the position of the sun—those heavenly clockworks that transcend earthly times of wet and dry.

In the late autumn the evening wears Vega like a blue-white diamond. Arcturus has set long before the sun. Capella comes up over the mountain, brightest of the northernmost stars, and toward midnight, when Sirius is well risen, there directly below it, just above the horizon, appears the sky's number-two glitterer, the southern star Canopus, never rising high enough to get beyond the city's atmosphere, which lends it a baleful light.

The sun, which in summer sets behind the mountain, has moved out to sea, dropping from sight at the point where San Nicolas Island lies, if we were high enough to see it. See it we did from the crest of the mountains, on one of the day's-end drives that conclude our otherwise stay-at-home Sundays, lying between Santa Barbara Rock and the Santa Cruz–Anacapa conjunction, eighty miles out, dark whale on the blue sea, never to be seen from shoreline.

Living on the Malibu one can choose between many peaceful things to do—stay at home and read or write or garden and other chores, or just sit; or drive in the hills; or walk on the beach. There is choice too among the hill drives—whether it be up the Decker Road along Mulholland, and down the Arroyo Sequit to the sea again, or up Little Sycamore Canyon on the Yerba Buena Road, over Triunfo Pass with a view to Lake Sherwood, then down past the lake, through Hidden Valley, over the hills and down Long Grade Canyon to Camarillo and the coast highway; or west from Little Sycamore along narrow roads leading into cul-de-sacs, where one sees foxes and hawks, and water flowing out of rock face—all of this within fifty miles of Los Angeles, unknown to the millions.

In the autumn of 1955, when the first of two fires swept over the mountains from the valley, leaped the crest of Boney Ridge, and devoured the forest of red shanks which graced that mountain's southern slope, we feared a long bareness for the burned flanks. Winter rains brought a myriad of flowers in places where the sun had not penetrated for years, and then in the spring we rejoiced to see rise from the base of the burned chaparral delicate new growth. The fire had not proved mortal; though ten years would be needed for the forest to recover.

Summer's flowers succeeded spring's pinks and blues and whites— orange monkey flower, red gooseberry, and larkspur, and the purple sage, bee heaven on earth—while the arroyos became *seco* and sand choked the creek mouths.

By summer the winter's creek wood had all been gathered, and the gleaning was again of plank wood cast up by the sea, that and shells and fragments to serve as gravel on the garden paths. All these years I had remembered the crushed abalone shells with which Una and Robinson Jeffers graveled their paths at Tor House, and now I began to strew our walks with shells and bones and jeweled bits from the seashore.

The Chumash who dwelled here were jewelry makers, and the Southwest Museum [in Los Angeles] preserves examples of their neck-laces of tide-line treasures. Now I see why. The wash of water renders all things smooth, and after high tide recedes one finds the bench strewn with beautiful fragments. Westward I walk, stooping, picking, filling a cloth bag, until it becomes leaden and the way back weary. And when at last I empty it out on the path at home, the scattering irides-cences and pearly bits—blue black of mussel, flesh pink of cowrie, pur-ple of abalone—make a display Tiffany's should envy, and I am moved to acquire a polishing wheel, a cutter and a borer, a ball of cord, and become a necklace maker. The abalone shells of this coast were prized by the Hopis far to the east, who ground them for dye tincture. These Mollusca are rarely exposed by even the lowest tide, seeking the safety of deeper water, and even then skin divers need powerful leverage to pry them loose, and woe to the man whose hand is caught. Freshly caught and sauteed in butter they are delicious, and their shells remain forever beautiful.

Indians are buried everywhere from Mugu Lagoon to Malibu Creek. Every bulldozing operation brings their bones and artifacts to light, as one did just across Broad Beach Road from us—a dozen huddled skeletons, four or five hundred years old, taking no notice of their noisy resurrection. Our geranium garden, falling to Encinal Creek, is sure to be a burying ground, the diggers tell us. Mary Austin writes of the residue of personality that always haunts a place once inhabited by man. Jeffers's poetry is full of these hauntings. But I cannot say that I have encountered spirits here on the Malibu. Perhaps the diesels drive them away. I have no fear of them, however. The Chumash were a gentle people, living on shellfish, roots, and acorn meal. We who are carnivorous may leave a different residue. Sometimes I wonder who will follow us here, and what they will make of our artifacts—books and disks and Scriptos and, less tangible though perhaps more lasting, our love for this marine mountainscape called the Malibu.

Along the Malibu there has been good aftermath of the storm, and the coast has been gathering manna. Mushrooms and other edible fungi rose overnight, and lived briefly in the light of day before consummating a buttery union in the skillet. Mustard greens likewise had a short life span before they too yielded up on the stove. Last year's stalks were rooted out by the wind and spilled like skeletons against the fences, to make room for the new growth now in its head-high yellow prime.

Mussels also are in season—no delicacy, true, but few meals are more satisfying than a mess of them, gathered at ebb tide in the twilight, then steamed open and dunked in lemon butter, salty, sandy, tough little guys, tasting of kelpy iodine, an atavistic feast linking us with our predecessors on this coastal shelf, who gave names to many of the places, from Anacapa and Hueneme to Mugu, Malibu, and Topanga.

Now we know why they inhabited the lagoons at the creek mouths, for when the rainy runoff swells these *arroyos secos* to savage streams, the rivers break their summer sand bars and run to the sea, bearing treasure to the tidelanders. We live on the cliff by the estuary of Encinal Creek, and at the height of the storm, when we went down with shovels to divert ravenous runoffs, we saw the little watercourse, long barred from union with the ocean and held in stagnant continence, changed to a torrent and raging out of the Santa Monicas to an eager consummation with the sea.

The Pacific was belying its name, roiled up for a mile offshore, windblown, coffee-colored, perilous to all but its native denizens—and I doubt they were pleased with the turmoil. We dwell on an open coast, with few shelters for small craft, and the shoreline is that seen by Cabrillo, Drake, Vancouver, and Dana, and in our day by the crews of purse seiner, tuna clipper, and tanker. The Catalina and Santa Barbara channels afford scant protection from southwesterlies, and the islands themselves are mostly steep and forbidding on both their leeward and windward sides.

Life on the Malibu is richest at the creek mouths, the Chumash knew; and so did we, after the storm was over and the runoff from the mountain washed upon the beaches. What a haul of firewood for the gleaning! We envy our neighbors the Brents, whose open fireplace will take logs up to ten feet in length. Ours is only twenty-four inches wide, which means that sawing, chopping, and splitting must follow gleaning and hauling.

It is years since the hills received such a scouring, yielding logs and stumps, burned roots, and rotting branches of oak, sycamore, red shank, and chamisal, much of it smashed to fireplace length in its fall down the stream beds, and sculptured into beautiful shapes.

The sea itself casts up wood, smoothed by wind and wave—empty packing cases of water chestnuts from Hong Kong and ammunition boxes from navy vessels, flawed planks of pine, Douglas fir, oak, and redwood, cast overboard from lumber schooners, flotsam, corks from fishermen's nets, an occasional Japanese glass float, battered lobster traps, and sundry jetsam not worth its salt.

The first step is to cache the wet wood and let it dry, before carrying it up the path to the cliff top. If one posts his pile with a sign reading, "Blest be he who leaves my logs; curst be he who steals my sticks," he is certain to find it when he returns, and just half its weight.

The joy of gathering beach wood is matched by that of burning it, although an occasional twinge is felt, like eating one's pet rabbit, when a shaft of skin-smooth chaparral is reduced to silvery ash. This wild wood's smoke has its own smells, different from those of domestic firewood—oak and walnut perfumy, eucalyptus acrid, orange bittersweet, and juniper like incense—and unless it has been submerged a long while, it does not burn with a blue flame. One twelve-foot length of a 2-by-4 was difficult to identify. From its weight and grain and color I called it oak. When I began to saw it, I realized my error. The fragrance was like the interior of our clothes closet. Cedar! The smoke from its burning was even sweeter. Once I found a broken mast or boom, stamped with Chinese characters. On sawing, it proved to be camphor wood, so pungent that I kept a section of it in my clothes closet.

Characteristic of this coast is the offshore wind that blows after dark, very faintly, a mere breath of mountain air suspiring delicately toward the sea, bearing smells of sun-warmed brush and stream bed with smoke from our chimney, ghosts of the beach wood, drifting down over the dark sand and water, residue of fire, liberated energy, sweeter far than incense of cathedral.

Now winter's constellations are risen high, Sirius ruling the zenith and fiery Canopus, describing his short arc above the southern horizon. In the west the lighthouse opens like an eye, then closes, leaving the night darker than before. In the east, when it is very clear, the Point Vicente light can be seen on the Palos Verdes and, nearer, the light buoy off Point Dume. These smells and sights assure one that one can leave the world to the wakeful and seek one's bed, with the final thought that another storm will find us in the wood business.

Big Sur

When he moved to Big Sur in 1944, Henry Miller (1891–1980) had already achieved some notoriety with the publication in the 1930s of his Paris novels, including Tropic of Cancer *(1934). Ensconced atop Partington Ridge, he became the center of an artists' colony and continued to write—and to paint. His book of ramblings about California,* Big Sur and the Oranges of Hieronymous Bosch—*from which this excerpt is taken—was published in 1957.*

It was twelve years ago on a day in February that I arrived in Big Sur—in the midst of a violent downpour. Toward dusk that same day, after a rejuvenating bath outdoors at the hot sulphur springs (Slade's Springs), I had dinner with the Rosses in the quaint old cottage they then occupied at Livermore Edge. It was the beginning of something more than a friendship. It would be more just, perhaps, to call it an initiation into a new way of life.

It was a few weeks after this meeting that I read Lillian Bos Ross's book *The Stranger.* Till then I had been only a visitor. The reading of this "little classic," as it is called, made me more than ever determined to take root here. "For the first time in my life," to quote Zande Allen's words, "I felt to home in the world I was borned in."

Years ago our great American poet Robinson Jeffers began singing of this region in his narrative poems. Jack London and his friend George Stirling made frequent visits to Big Sur in the old days; they came on horseback, all the way from the Valley of the Moon. The general public, however, knew almost nothing of this region until 1937 when the Carmel–San Simeon highway, which skirts the Pacific for a distance of sixty miles or more, was opened up. In fact, until then it was probably one of the least known regions in all America.

The first settlers, mountain men mostly, of hardy pioneer stock, came around 1870. They were, as Lillian Ross puts it, men who had followed the buffalo trails and knew how to live on meat without salt. They came afoot and on horseback; they touched ground which no white man had ever set foot on before, not even the intrepid Spaniards.

So far as is known, the only human beings who had been here before were the Esselen Indians, a tribe of low culture which had subsisted in nomadic fashion. They spoke a language having no connection with that of other tribes in California or elsewhere in America. When the padres came to Monterey, around 1770, these Indians spoke of an ancient city called Excelen which was theirs but of which no vestiges have ever been found.

But perhaps I should first explain where the Big Sur region is located. It begins not far north of the Little Sur River (Malpaso Creek) and extends southward as far as Lucia, which, like Big Sur, is just a pinpoint on the map. Eastward from the coast it stretches to the Salinas Valley. Roughly, the Big Sur country comprises an area two to three times the size of Andorra.

Now and then a visitor will remark that there is a resemblance between this coast, the South Coast, and certain sections of the Mediterranean littoral; others liken it to the coast of Scotland. But comparisons are vain. Big Sur has a climate of its own and a character all its own. It is a region where extremes meet, a region where one is always conscious of weather, of space, of grandeur, and of eloquent silence. Among other things, it is the meeting place of migratory birds coming from north and south. It is said, in fact, that there is a greater variety of birds to be found in this region than in any other part of the United States. It is also the home of the redwoods; one encounters them on entering from the north and one leaves them on passing southward. At night one can still hear the coyote howling, and if one ventures beyond the first ridge of mountains one can meet up with mountain lions and other beasts of the wild. The grizzly bear is no longer to be found here, but the rattlesnake is still to be reckoned with. On a clear, bright day, when the blue of the sea rivals the blue of the sky, one sees the hawk, the eagle, the buzzard soaring above the still, hushed canyons. In summer, when the fogs roll in, one can look down upon a sea of clouds floating listlessly above the ocean; they have the appearance, at times, of huge iridescent soap bubbles, over which, now and then, may be seen a double rainbow. In January and February the hills are greenest, almost as green as the Emerald Isle. From November to February are the best months, the air fresh and invigorating, the skies clear, the sun still warm enough to take a sun bath.

From our perch, which is about a thousand feet above the sea, one can look up and down the coast a distance of twenty miles in either direction. The highway zigzags like the Grand Corniche. Unlike the Riviera, however, here there are but few houses to be seen. The old-timers, those with huge landholdings, are not eager to see the country opened up. They are all for preserving its virginal aspect. How long will it hold out against the invader? That is the big question.

The stretch of scenic highway referred to earlier was cut through at enormous expense, literally blasted out of the mountainside. It now forms part of the great international highway which will one day extend from the northern part of Alaska to Tierra del Fuego. By the time it is finished the automobile, like the mastodon, may be extinct. But the Big Sur will be here forever, and perhaps in the year A.D. 2000 the population may still number only a few hundred souls. Perhaps like Andorra and Monaco, it will become a Republic all its own. Perhaps the dread invaders will not come from other parts of this continent but from across the oceans, as the American aborigines are said to have come. And if they do, it will not be in boats or in airplanes.

And who can say when this region will once again be covered by the waters of the deep? Geologically speaking, it is not so long ago that it rose from the sea. Its mountain slopes are almost as treacherous as the icy sea in which, by the way, one scarcely ever sees a sailboat or a hardy swimmer, though one does occasionally spot a seal, an otter, or a sperm whale. The sea, which looks so near and so tempting, is often difficult to reach. We know that the Conquistadores were unable to make their way along the coast, neither could they cut through the brush which covers the mountain slopes. An inviting land, but hard to conquer. It seeks to remain unspoiled, uninhabited by man.

Often, when following the trail which meanders over the hills, I pull myself up in an effort to encompass the glory and the grandeur which envelops the whole horizon. Often, when the clouds pile up in the north and the sea is churned with whitecaps, I say to myself: "This is the California that men dreamed of years ago, this is the Pacific that Balboa looked out on from the Peak of Darien, this is the face of the earth as the Creator intended it to look." . . .

Here at Big Sur, at a certain time of the year and certain time of the day only, a pale blue-green hue pervades the distant hills; it is an old, nostalgic hue which one sees only in the works of the old Flemish and Italian masters. It is not only the tone and color of distance abetted by the magic fall of light, it is a mystic phenomenon, or so I like to think, born of a certain way of looking at the world. It is observable in the work of the older Breughel, for one. Strikingly present in the painting called "The Fall of Icarus," in which the peasant with his plough dominates the foreground, his costume just as enchanting and obsessional as the enchanting and obsessive sea far below him.

There are two magic hours of the day which I have only really come to know and wait for, bathe in, I might say, since living here. One is dawn, the other sunset. In both we have what I like to think of as "the true light"—the one cold, the other warm, but both creating an ambiance of super-reality, or the reality behind reality. At dawn I look out to sea, where the far horizon is painted with bands of rainbow tints, and then at the hills that range the coast, ever entranced by the way the reflected light of dawn licks and warms the "backs of the drugged rhinoceroses." If there is a ship in sight the sun's bent rays give it a gleam and sparkle which is utterly dazzling. Once can't tell immediately that it is a ship; it seems more like the play of northern lights.

Toward sundown, when the hills in back of us are flushed with the other "true light," the trees and scrub in the canyons take on a wholly different aspect. Everything is brush and cones, umbrellas of light—the leaves, boughs, stalks, trunks standing out separate and defined, as if etched by the Creator Himself. It is then one notices rivers of trees catapulting down the slopes! Or are they columns of soldiers (hoplites) storming the walls of the canyon? At any rate, at this hour one experiences an indescribable thrill in observing branches, between the leaves. It is no longer earth and air, but light and form—heavenly light, celestial form. When this intoxicating reality reaches its height the rocks speak out. They assume more eloquent shapes and forms than the fossils of prehistoric monsters. They clothe themselves in vibrant-colored raiment glittering with metallic residues.

Fall and winter are the best times to get the "revelation," for then the atmosphere is clear, the skies more full of excitement, and the light of the sun, because of the low arc it describes, more effective. It's at this hour, after a light rain, that the hills are ringed with fuzzy trails which undulate with the undulating golds of the hills. Turning a bend, the hill before you stands out like the coat of an Airedale seen through a magnifying glass. So hoary does it look that one scans the horizon in search of a shepherd leaning against his crook. Memories of olden times return, the leavings of childhood reading: illustrations from story books, first gleanings of mythology, faded calendars, the chromos on the kitchen wall, bucolic prints on the walls of the man who extracted your tonsils. . . .

If we don't always start from Nature we certainly come to her in our hour of need. How often, walking the barren hills, I've stopped to examine a twig, a dead leaf, a fragrant bit of sage, a rare flower that has lingered on despite the killing heat. Or stood in front of a tree studying the bark, as if I had never before noticed that trunks are covered with bark, and that the bark as well as the tree itself leads its own life.

It's when the lupine has run its course, as well as the bluebonnets and the wildflowers, when the foxtails are no longer a menace to the dogs, when there is no longer a riot and profusion assailing the senses, that one begins to observe the myriad elements which go to make up Nature. (Suddenly, as I put it down now, Nature seems like a strange new word to me. What a discovery man made when he found the word, just one, to embrace this indescribable thesaurus of all enveloping life!) . . .

There are . . . times when I seem to be in what I can only call an autodidactic mood. At such times I am instructing myself in the art of seeing with new eyes. I may be in a painting phase or getting ready to enter one. (These phases come over me like a sickness.) I will be on the Angulo trail, facing the gigantic ten-gallon rock at Torre Canyon, with a dog on either side of me . . . and look and look and look at a blade of grass, a deep shadow in the fold of a hill, a deer standing motionless, no bigger than a speck, or turn my gaze upon the churning lace which the sea makes around a clump of rock, or that white collar of foam which fastens itself to the flanks of the "diplodoci," as I sometimes call the half-submerged beastlike mountains that rise up out of the ocean bed to bask in the sun. It's quite true, as Lynda Sargent used to say, that the Santa Lucia range is hermaphroditic. In form and contour the hills and mountains are usually feminine, in strength and vitality masculine. They look so very ancient, especially in the early morning light, and yet they are, as we know, only newly risen. The animals have done more to them than man, fortunately. And the wind and rain, the sunlight and moonlight, still more. Man has known them only a short while, which accounts perhaps for the pristine quality which they still preserve.

If it be shortly after sunup of a morning when the fog has obliterated the highway below, I am then rewarded with a spectacle rare to witness. Looking up the coast toward Nepenthe, where I first stayed (then only a log cabin), the sun rising behind me throws an enlarged shadow of me into the iridescent fog below. I lift my arms as in prayer, achieving a wing-span no god ever possessed, and there in the drifting fog a nimbus floats about my head, a radiant nimbus such as the Buddha himself might proudly wear. In the Himalayas, where the same phenomenon occurs, it is said that a devout follower of the Buddha will throw himself from a peak—"into the arms of Buddha." . . .

When first I beheld this wondrous region I thought to myself—"Here I will find peace. Here I shall find the strength to do the work I was made to do."

Back of the rise which overshadows us is a wilderness in which scarcely anyone ever sets foot. It is a great forest and game reserve intended to be set apart forever. At night one feels the silence all about, a silence which begins far back of the ridge and which creeps in with the fog and the stars, with the warm valley winds, and which carries in its folds a mystery as deep as the earth's own. A magnetic, healing ambiance. The advent of city folk, with their cares and worries, is pure dissonance. Like the lepers of old, they come with their sores. Whoever settles here hopes that he will be the last invader. The very look of the land makes one long to keep it intact—the spiritual reserve of a few bright spirits.

Of late I have come to take a different view of it. Walking the hills at dawn, or at dusk, looking over the deep canyons or seaward toward the far horizon, absorbed in reveries, drowned in the awesome beauty of it all, I sometimes think how wonderful will be the day when all these mountainsides are filled with habitations, when the slopes are terraced with field, when flowers burst forth everywhere, not only wildflowers planted by human hands for human delectation. I try to imagine what it may be like a hundred, five hundred, years hence. I picture villas dotting the slopes, and colossal stairways curving down to the sea where boats lie at anchor, their colorful sails unfurled and flapping listlessly in the breeze. I see ledges cut into the sharp flanks of the cliffs, to give purchase to chapels and monasteries suspended between heaven and earth, as in Greece. I see tables spread under brilliant awnings (as in the time of the Doges), and wine flowing into golden goblets, and over the glitter of gold and purple I hear laughter, laughter like pearling rapids, rising from thousands of jubilant throats. . . .

Yes, I can visualize multitudes living where now there are only a few scattered families. There is room here for thousands upon thousands to come. There would be no need for Jake to deliver food and mail three times a week. There would be ways and means undreamed of today. It could happen, in fact, in a very few years from now. What we dream is the reality of tomorrow.

This place can be a paradise. It is now, for those who live it. But then it will be another paradise, one in which all share, all participate. The only paradise, after all.

Peace and solitude! I have had a taste of it, even here in America. Ah, those first days on Partington Ridge! On rising I would go to the cabin door and, casting my eyes over the velvety, rolling hills, such a feeling of contentment, such a feeling of gratitude was mine that instinctively my hand went up in benediction. Blessings! Blessings on you, one and all! I blessed the trees, the birds, the dogs, the cats. I blessed the flowers, the pomegranates, the thorny cactus. I blessed men and women everywhere, no matter on which side of the fence they happened to be.

That is how I like to begin each day. A day will begun, I say. And that is why I choose to remain here, on the slopes of the Santa Lucia, where to give thanks to the Creator comes natural and easy. Out yonder they may curse, revile, and torture one another, defile all the human instincts, make a shambles of creation (if it were in their power), but here, no, here it is unthinkable, here there is abiding peace, the peace of

God, and the serene security created by a handful of good neighbors living at one with the creature world, with noble, ancient trees, scrub and sagebrush, wild lilacs and lovely lupine, with poppies and buzzards, eagles and hummingbirds, gophers and rattlesnakes, and sea and sky unending.

T. H. WATKINS

Dana Point

The Sundown Sea

*T. H. Watkins (b. 1936) was born in Loma Linda, where he spent his sum-
mers at the beach; these experiences are eloquently recounted in* On the Shore
of the Sundown Sea *(1973). Widely published in the fields of history and the
environment, Watkins was for many years associated with* American
Heritage *and* Wilderness *magazines.*

You ran, dog at your side, not just to keep warm or for the simple
joy of it, but because you wanted to take advantage of every
secret moment of this time. Your parents had not forbidden
these unsupervised expeditions; they simply did not know about them,
and you wanted to keep it that way. God knew, it was dangerous enough
a business, clambering barefoot over rocks polished by centuries of
beating surf, made slick, smooth, and wet. One slip, and you could
break an arm or leg, or even crack your skull. And if you were injured as
far out on those rocks as you frequently ventured, you could lay immo-
bilized until the tide returned and the sea washed your body away—and
no one to know where you were. If you thought about it, it could all be
pretty frightening—but of course you did not think about it. Your step
was sure and unhesitant, your confidence boundless, your good luck
remarkable.

And it was worth it, for this rocky landscape, stripped of the sea which kept it hidden for most of the day, vibrated with a secret, mysterious, unimaginable life that creeped and crawled in its pools, its dark nooks and crannies, like a population straight out of dream. Where else but out of the mists of dream could a hermit crab have been spawned? Barely an inch in length, he scrabbled and lurched among the rocks, seeking an unoccupied shell to inhabit; without it, he was a pitiful, helpless creature, his pink lower body curled under his torso like a tiny coil of rope; with it, he lurched along as before—quite as helpless, but at least granted the illusion of security. Starfish, too, were dreamlike, inching through life on those impossible arms, changing colors to match their surroundings, their mouths a tiny slit in the bottom center of their bodies, where mouths had no business being. And more: crabs, pink ones the size of dinner plates with pincers that could hurt, if not maim; mottled yellow ones as broad as the palm of your hand, little sand-colored ones no larger than your thumbnail; mussels and sea-snails clustered on the sides of rocks, extensions of the stone itself, immobile, hiding from the light, waiting for the return of the tide and their real world; the occasional landlocked ray trying to hide itself behind a rock in a tide pool, and once in a while a smelt or a rock fish, or a gang of herring that had become similarly trapped; nearly invisible sea worms that squiggled along the bottom of pools like miniature snakes; and, most wondrous of all, the rainbow-colored anemones, half-animal, half-flower, lurking in rock crannies with poison at the heart of their beauty. Over it all the ubiquitous gulls wheeled and screamed, small shadows of death that harvested what they could of that abundance of life.

You were entranced, utterly. Leaping from rock to rock, tide pool to tide pool, you poked and probed and watched everything you could watch. Lying on your belly at the edge of a particularly rich pool, you would be driven by the small boy's insatiable need to know, to understand, to experience—in short, to meddle. You would take out your little tin shovel from the sand bucket and use it to stir up a sleeping ray, if you could reach him. You would use it to stroke the petals of a crimson anemone, shuddering as the petals convulsed in an attempt to draw the shovel into its maw; thus you discovered that beauty could be a trap—a very large thing to learn at so young an age. You would seek out a large crab and toy with it until in its rage and fear it gripped the shovel firmly. You would then lift it out of the pool and dump it in your bucket, captured, helpless to escape the mindless cruelty of your curiosity. For you it was a game, for him a death struggle.

No matter how often or how long you visited this secret world, the potential for surprise was never absent—and it could sometimes be a large surprise indeed. Once you discovered the body of a sea lion stranded on the edge of a tide pool far out among the rocks. You came upon it suddenly, unexpectedly, while crawling over the lip of a rock, and at first you thought it was alive. But no; the gulls had already been at its eyes. It was a huge mound of blue-black flesh, perhaps six or seven feet from nose to tail. You poked at the still resilient flesh with your shovel—gingerly, and a little fearfully. This was not your first dramatic encounter with death; after all, you had watched gulls hammering and picking at still-living crabs, a grisly and unforgettable spectacle. But never before had you realized the sheer power of a force that could destroy even this human-sized creature, leaving it to be picked at by gulls and crabs and whatever other scavengers there were who did the sea's bone-cleaning. To stand too close to it was to stand too close to your own end. You left it finally, left if for the sea that would reclaim it in a few hours.

Perhaps it was nothing more complicated than your stomach-clock sounding an alarm for food, but you always seemed to know when it was time to head back to camp. You dumped whatever creatures you might have in your bucket back into their tide pool and scrambled back across the rocks to the beach where your dog would be waiting (she possessed no measurable interest in tide pools or slippery rocks). Running along the beach (when did you not run?) you stopped now and then to scoop up a few shells, for you had to have some reasonable excuse for your long absence. *Where in the world have you been? Shells?* you could say, holding out your bucket. *I've been collecting shells.* The answer would suffice, for there was neither danger nor mystery in shell-collecting.

Mystery and danger were the very elements of a small boy's life then—certainly the elements of this small boy's life. A ten- or eleven-year-old boy is the essential Romantic, a creature riveted by wonder most of the time, driven by the need to challenge the very heart of life the rest of the time, a confused and confusing mix of Don Quixote, Tarzan, and Neil Armstrong. Parents sometimes mistake his dreamy-mindedness for stupidity, his daredevil antics for willful attempts to gray the hair of his elders. Not so. He is simply doing what his genes have programmed him to do, which is to learn the mystery and test the danger of life. Most of us get over this, sooner or later; we acquire wisdom and caution, become bank managers or real estate salesmen or book writers, ultimately reaching that point in life when we are certain that all the mysteries have been learned, all the dangers tested. Others are not so fortunate, but they are to be pitied, not censured.

There was both danger and mystery enough in my world by the sundown sea—more than enough, more than could be learned, or tried. Take the mystery of the Sound, for instance. I have only heard it three times in my life, and those three times when I was a boy, but the memory of it has not diminished since, and I think I will be remembering it when my nerveless fingers are plucking at my last coverlet. The first time was pure accident, as discoveries usually are. Involved in my usual afternoon wave-chasing, I selected a towering devil of a wave to ride; it may have been twelve feet or more from base to crest, and definitely was not the sort of wave to try to ride. I realized my mistake almost immediately, but even then it was too late to do anything about it, for I was caught in its curl and would have to ride it out. The lip of the wave curved over my head, and for one brief instant I found myself in a long, green translucent tunnel that stretched forty or fifty feet on either side of me. That moment was when I heard the Sound, a high, hollow, almost metallic keening that cut through the outside roar of the surf until it was all that could be heard. It seemed to come from a great distance, like a cry out of the ancestral night, then swept over me and moved on just as the wave seized my helpless body and plunged it through the water and into the sand, where I gouged out a good-sized trench. The Sound could not have lasted for more than two seconds, but when I finally surfaced I was certain that I had been privileged to experience one of the essential mysteries. I tried again and again over the years to re-create the circumstances of that moment, but was able to do so only twice, each time as much by accident as by design. I suppose the phenomenon could be explained away by various acoustical laws having to do with decibels and the Doppler effect, but I remain as convinced today as I was then that I had heard nothing less than the voice of the sea itself.

There were other things to know, less intense, perhaps, but no less wondrous in their own right. Not far from the point where the rocks and the tide pools lay was the canyon that Salt Creek had cut into the bluffs on its way to the sea (it was no more than an outsized gulch, of course, but it served my purposes to think of it as a canyon). Salt Creek was just a trickle by normal creek standards, but this was sandstone country—even the soil was little more than well-packed sand—and the canyon it had cut into the bluffs was deep and narrow and dark, running perhaps two hundred and fifty or three hundred yards back to the Coast Highway, and filled with a strange mix of coast chaparral, ice plant, Scotch broom, wild mustard, and occasional clusters of iridescent ferns in little dells where the creek had formed pools. And there were caves. The first time I ventured into the canyon, I counted seven open caves, ranging in size and shape from a nichelike hole that could barely shelter a child to a commodious little cavern that could have held half a dozen adults or more. How they got there I had no idea, whether carved by wind and weather, by Indians (although I found no bones, no skulls, no pottery shards to suggest it), or by those who followed. I immediately peopled them with all manner of types from my imagination, not excluding pirates, and fancied myself the first person to see them in generations. . . .

As anyone who has ever watched the adventures of Jacques Yves Cousteau (or even those of Lloyd Bridges) must know by now, one of the most compelling wonders of the sea is not what is on it or around it, but what is under it. I found some of that wonder in my tide pool explorations, but only that part which the sea itself chose to reveal. To know it truly, you had to enter the undersea world without passport and explore it on your own. My expeditions along these lines were fairly limited, I have to admit. It was not yet an age when the aqua-lung was standard equipment for weekend hobbyists (nor could I have afforded one, in any case), and I had to make do with the basics, which were pretty basic: one rubber face mask that always seemed to leak just a little, one pair rubber flippers that never fit quite right, one plastic snorkel which I never did learn how to use properly. This was skin diving just one step removed from skin, but it was enough to give me at least partial entrance into a world I could not otherwise have known, that dim, green world where light entered in slanting, mote-filled rays, where rocks that were gray or black in the sunlight took on a spectrum of shadings from some dark rainbow, where dangling kelp became a coral jungle, murky, tangled, and dangerous, where the bottom sand was impossibly white, impossibly smooth, where the commonest fish acquired a mystery and dimension that transcended everything you had always believed you knew about fish.

In time, I took possession of a spring-powered aluminum speargun, one of the most deadly looking instruments man has devised since the invention of the crossbow. As my mother took pains to remind me, it was deadly, capable of piercing the midsection of a fully grown man at a distance of several feet—*under* water. I promised faithfully never to aim it at the midsection of a fully grown man, or even a half-grown man, and with my face mask, my flippers, and my snorkel I entered the water as a Mighty Hunter of the Deep.

What a fraud that pose was. In the two summers I sported around with that speargun, I did not fire it once at any living target. It was not as if I had never killed fish before. I had killed hundreds. Standing at the gunwales of a deep-sea boat, I had cheerfully hauled in barracuda, shovel-nosed sharks, sand sharks, halibut, sculpin, and once—almost—a sea bass so huge it bent my rod double before carrying my tackle back to the deep. Sitting in a rowboat on a lake, I had caught sacks full of bluegill, crappie, sunfish, and bass. Tramping the bouncing stream of Bear Creek in the San Bernardino Mountains, I had put limits of trout in my creel. Leaning on the rail of the pier at Newport Beach during the no-limit seasons of the mackerel run, I had pulled in dozens of the shining, muscular beasts, then gutted them, cleaned them, and beheaded them with the aplomb of an Elizabethan executioner. No, I was a fully accredited fish killer of no little experience.

But I could not kill a fish swimming under water, nor did I ever try. It puzzled me then, and it has puzzled me periodically since, although I think now that I may be close to an answer. It was not that I was incompetent, and therefore afraid to try my skill. I had practiced assiduously, and was good—well, adequate. It was not that the fish were beautiful, particularly (although they were beautiful, as only a creature in his nautical environment can be beautiful). It certainly was not that I had an aversion to killing: I had done enough of that, God knows. It was a kind of fear, I think the fear of an alien in a world that neither welcomes him nor understands him. I could be tolerated as an observer, perhaps, but the moment I chose to kill, or try to kill, I would have chosen to become part of that world, to accept it on its own terms, to be fully vulnerable to all the laws which governed it, unto death itself. And some part of me must have known, or suspected, that the attempt could destroy me, for it was not my world. It would never be my world.

So I did not kill fish under water. And in the process of not killing fish, and questioning why, I must have gained a hint, however subconscious, of a very important truth: that the mysteries we explore in the world around us (or below us) very often turn out to be mysteries within ourselves, that the challenge to test and know is a challenge to test and know ourselves first, the world second. I came much closer to realizing this truth the day I climbed Dana Point.

My father and I and a friend and his two boys had been out in Dana Cove all afternoon, diving for abalone (paradox: I would strip abalone from their rocks with a tire iron, but I could not kill fish). After we had paddled back to the beach where our two families waited for us, my father's friend suggested that the five of us men (or so he called us) try climbing the old hand-and-knee trail etched into the leeward face of the point, which rose straight above us like a wall. I was then, and am now, terrified of any significant height, and the idea appalled me. I assumed that my father felt the same, since to the best of my knowledge, in my presence or otherwise, he had never climbed anything higher than a ten-foot ladder, solidly planted. Yet he accepted the idea, for reasons which I still believe were not entirely rational. The man who suggested it was his friend. The friend was blond, brown, muscular, and agile, while my father was black-haired, red more often than brown, generally slender (although he filled out nicely in later years), and stiff in his movements when not in the water. The friend was a back-slapping extrovert, while my father chewed his meditative cud. The suggestion was unmistakably made as a kind of challenge, and I suppose there was nothing my father could do but accept it, pride being the heedless thing it is.

Normally, my mother would have raised holy hell at any such idea, and I looked to her with a hopeful heart. But she was a very smart wife, and knew when to shut up. She said nothing. The thought of objecting personally, myself, never entered my mind. How could I shame my father? We climbed Dana Point.

Possibly because I was the smallest of the bunch—and therefore the most easily caught in the case of a violent backslide—I was put in the head of the line, with my father behind me, and behind him the other two boys and their father. We had only about 130 feet to climb, but I never traveled so long a distance in my life. The first fifty or sixty feet were not so bad, for they were up a little ravine that was blocked off left and right as if it were a tunnel; I could see only ahead of me or behind me, neither of which views were particularly alarming. Then the ravine ended, and I ventured out on the surface of the cliff itself. This was not good, for the higher I climbed, the more a sense of proportion I acquired. Height developed real meaning, because I could look off the left edge of the trail and see below me the rocks and surf of the beach, which became smaller and smaller the more I scraped and scrambled up the cliff. At one point, perhaps seventy or eighty feet up, I looked over the side and saw my mother, who waved unenthusiastically, a pinched and worried look on her face. I froze momentarily, for I had never seen my mother from such a height. She was a doll, an ant, and I knew suddenly, inarguably, that I was going to fall. I only prayed that I might land smack on my head, to keep the pain brief.

"C'mon, Tommy, let's get going." Behind me, my father's face was as shriveled and white as I was sure my own must be. But behind him, the two boys waited impatiently, fearlessly, as brainless as their father who had insisted on this whole business. I moved on, somehow, knowing perfectly well that at any moment I would make a fatal slip, or the ledge would give way beneath me, or a monstrous rock would crash down on me from above, punching me into the abyss where the waves made spiderweb patterns on the sand.

Suddenly, before I knew it, I was at the top. Above and to the left of me was the little wooden observation tower. One more series of carved footholds and I was over the edge, standing safe in the middle of several square feet of flat ground. Behind me, my father popped over the edge with a relieved and only slightly hysterical laugh, and after him came the two boys and their father, all laughing, as if they were ready to do it again. The idiots.

Standing there, both feet spread wide, the wind in my hair, looking down on the miniature cove, I felt huge, Olympian. In spite of myself, I had met my fear and survived it. I had come to a working compromise with one of my deepest personal mysteries, for I knew as I stood there that my fear had been a very real and reasonable one, and should have been respected. I did not regret climbing Dana Point; I may even have celebrated it. But I knew that I would never do it again.

A Certain Moment

Russell Chatham (b. 1939), a native of San Francisco, began fishing, painting, and writing at an early age. His essays have appeared in such publications as the Atlantic *and* Esquire. *His books include* Dark Waters *(1988) and* The Angler's Coast *(1990), from which this essay about bass fishing in Marin County's Tomales Bay is taken.*

The fisherman's day began before daylight. Roads were lightly iced where water had seeped from a rain earlier in the week, and a dense tule fog hugged the valleys. Eaves were white with frost in San Anselmo, and the vague predawn light showed Fairfax utterly deserted. The landscape surrounding the rest of the drive lay pristine beneath a silver mantle: White's Hill, San Geronimo Valley, Samuel P. Taylor State Park, Tocaloma, and, finally, the Olema Grade, giving rise at its crest to the full sweep of Inverness Ridge and Tomales Bay, where the fisherman was going after striped bass.

Near the town of Point Reyes Station the road branched left, and at White House Pool steelhead fishermen were beginning to gather. Beyond Inverness Park, past Willow Point, the road skirted the bay, and the angler pulled onto a wide shoulder. As he stepped from the car and walked to the water's edge, ice and frost crunched beneath his feet.

Dawn was breaking and the brittle air hung still, with mingled scents of the marsh and wet farmland. Except for the distant rumble of the sea at Point Reyes and the intermittent call of a mallard out on the nearby moor, the landscape was silent. Over the water itself a light mist spiraled gently toward a clear azure sky in which the morning star was quickly dimming.

A light eight-foot boat soon sat ready at the water's edge. There had been a choice in launching locations: here, to fish the morning high water without having to row for an hour first, or down at the Golden Hind dock, which later would be convenient—necessary, actually—on the minus tide when it was time to come in. The fisherman had chosen the former, deciding to come ashore at the yacht club or wherever he could, then walk back to his car.

The rod was strung, a momentarily appealing fly tied on, and the tackle set on the seat, tip over the stern. In minutes the trim El Toro was rhythmically disturbing the surface with a wake of foam and bubbles. Ahead, behind his back, the fisherman heard the cries of water birds as they took flight. He chose a likely area on the flooding water and drifted with the tide, casting at random. An hour passed. There were baitfish everywhere, and when the sun had risen well in the sky, little Bonaparte's gulls started fluttering and diving to feed. Several bass surfaced but on such widely divergent tangents that it was useless to try to discover a pattern. All he could do was fish the vicinity and hope.

The day grew sublime, one that winter sometimes offers as counterpoint. The cloudless air was pure, almost fragile, the temperature hovering in the sixties. Earlier it had been cold enough for wispy sheets of ice to form against the shoreline, but now the sun was at its winter zenith. The angler had reason for remaining confident even though the morning's initial enthusiasm had long waned. In previous weeks he'd caught enough fish so that, as the hour or tide changed, he could always recall a success during conditions similar to the present moment. Nearby, a flock of bluebills circled, set their wings, and alighted. The myriad bay ducks—scoter, mud hen, bufflehead, goldeneye, ruddy—

were moving continually, and it was impossible to distinguish between their rings and those made by surfacing bass. Overhead, great Vs of pintails whistled, and once, very high, he saw geese.

Low water would be at sundown. The tide, which had started to fall at noon, ran rapidly. Wind blew against tide, causing the boat to drift at an angle across the bay, rather than with either wind or tide alone. By casting to one side and then the other as the boat moved, great swaths of water were probed. Assuming an average cast to be seventy feet, each pass ate up a ribbon of territory a hundred and forty feet wide. Using a floating head and dark streamer, the angler confined his drifts to areas no more than four feet deep, as the stripers seemed to maintain this level while the tide fell.

All during the afternoon he found nothing, and his casts occasionally failed to straighten, causing irritation. The flats had not produced as they should have and the tide was steadily drying them up. As he turned to watch a backcast fling spray into the afternoon sun he knew it was time to move. The sun was lowering against the peninsula and soon the short twilight of winter would gather.

The angler had thought of a particular oyster bed during the morning but not as the last resort it had now become. He'd fully expected to catch fish at intervals throughout the outgoing tide, then move to the bed on the low water. He knew the cove near the fence held bass on a minus tide when the broad expanse to the south was completely dry. As he rowed from near the yacht club over to Millerton Point, the breeze died and the air became icy still as it had been at dawn. The many birds so obvious earlier could no longer be seen clearly and the shoreline was becoming indistinct behind a bluish haze through which only an occasional light sparkled. The earth was immersing itself into the pearly liquid of dusk. Exposed shoreline crackled and Inverness Ridge loomed black, its forest of ancient pine standing in sharp contrast to the sensual, easy slopes of the hills to the east. In the distance a chain saw whined, and behind Inverness thin columns of smoke eased skyward as night began to fall.

The oyster fence lent a certain definition to the otherwise undefined basin where the angler hoped to fish. Like sentinels, the long row of slender eucalyptus poles stretched to the north, guarding vulnerable crustaceans against the appetites of the many large bat rays that inhabited the cove. In places the fence suffered the disrepair of time, which gave it a particular attraction.

Nearing the stakes, the fisherman carefully drew his oars back through the locks after a final stroke, which sent the little boat surging forward. The boat drifted slowly on the glassy water, then stopped. Picking up the fly rod, he took the slender bucktail from the cork grip, dropped it over, and watched it vanish into the green, past the faintly reflected rose sky. Downward thrusts laid a pattern of loose monofilament in the boat. A tentative false cast followed before the rod hissed a clean delivery eighty feet toward the fence. As the fly settled he imagined its descent into dimness. The next cast straightened several yards to the right of the first, beginning a radius that would eventually strike all the water.

When nearly half of the second cast was recovered, he saw a boil behind the fly. Had the surface not been still it would have gone unnoticed; in fact, so subtle was this evidence of a missed strike that it was at once undeniable and unbelievable. The fish had stayed deep; cruising, it had arced beneath the bait, making the surface well up in a restrained convulsion. The disturbance has scarcely dissipated when the next cast was formed of slow, mannered loops that slid smoothly forward, back, then far forward to the bass again. Sensing the lethargy of the season, the angler slowed the retrieve, inducing several more passes. Near the boat the line tightened, but when he struck there was nothing. He began to strip in line for another cast.

It seemed inevitable that the line should pull up again as it just had, but his first strip met with solid resistance and the long rod curved fully, its tip low. Momentarily unbalanced, at the top if his vision he saw the water open and churn, then bulge as the fish moved off. Loose line, which had been coiled haplessly in the boat, snapped against the guides until it was taut to the reel, then released in spasms as the bass surged away. Fifty yards of line hummed under the strain of the fish's pulsing attempts to free itself as it circled widely. The boat returned and moved with the bass, but even so, recovered line was soon lost. This was the linear fight of the shallows. When the fish ran, the rod plunged but came back as the reel gave line until the run ceased. Then the rod went down again as line went back onto the spool.

Soon the bass was thrashing nearby, turning, boring down and away. It seemed so dark, its green back glistening, its stripes sharply defined. It thrust its tail, sending a crescent of water over the angler. In a moment the striper lay motionless off the transom. But it dived beneath the boat and then away in a tight arc, which brought it to the surface again a few feet out. This time, in a quick succession of moves, the fisherman took the leader in his left hand, set the rod down, grabbed the hook shank with his right, clamped his left on the fish's jaw, and, using this paralyzing grip, lifted twenty pounds of striped bass over the gunwale.

There was still enough light in the afterglow to have fished longer, but he didn't. It had been a difficult day, and this was, he thought, its proper conclusion. He snipped the leader and wound in his line.

The sky was pale lemon toward the ocean, and a light was on at the oyster company. Stars were coming out strongly above, and Inverness glimmered from across the bay as the angler started the long row back. Settling into the rhythm of it, he glanced behind him to look at the fish, but saw first a three-quarter moon rising over the gently rolling hills to the east. In the magic, almost colorless light, the bass glinted from the bow, its lifeless form stretched over coils of rope. He felt mutely accused and melancholy over this complicated yet unplanned death. The perfect eye, which moments earlier had guided the fatal chase, no longer saw. But the decision was final, the memory forever etched; he had done as he would do, and in the morning would perhaps arise again before dawn to begin another day of fishing.

Tapping the Source

Kem Nunn (b. 1948) attracted critical attention in 1984 with his first novel, Tapping the Source, *set mostly in the surf culture of Orange County's Huntington Beach. The following scene, however, is set at an isolated beach near Santa Barbara's Hollister Ranch, where the novel's protagonist, Ike, is taken by his friend, Preston. Nunn's latest novel is* The Dogs of Winter *(1997).*

The night was filled with the song of insects, the earthy scents of grass and sage, the damp salt smell of the sea. The moon lit the road and threw a silver light upon the blades of grass, the polished rails of the boards. They walked for what seemed to Ike a long time. His arms ached and each felt about a foot longer when they finally put everything down. They rolled the bags out between the roots of some thick trees on the side of a hill. The ground fell away into darkness, more trees. The moon was straight overhead now. In the distance Ike could hear the sound of surf. . . .

In the morning Ike saw that the hillside was higher and steeper than he had guessed in the night. A clump of trees obscured the view directly in front of them, but off to the left the ground dropped away to reveal other hills, great patches of mustard and wildflowers, green grass and dark trees, and below it all, the sea.

The beaches here were different from those Ike had gotten used to. The beaches in Huntington were wide and flat, colors kept to a minimum. Here the scenery was wild, the colors lush, varied. Long lines of hills rolled toward the sea then broke into steep tumbling cliffs, patchworks of reds and browns. Below the cliffs were thin white crescents and rocky points that reached into the Pacific. There were no traffic noises here, no voices. There were only the calls of the birds, the breeze in the grass, and the surf cracking far below them.

They pulled on trunks and wet suits in the crisp morning air. They knelt on the rocky soil beneath the trees and waxed their boards. The smells of rubber and coconut mixed with the smells of the earth and grass. "We'll get some morning glass," Preston told him. "Surf till ten or eleven, then back here for some food and sleep, surf again around sunset."

They stashed the bags and gear and started down the slope. . . . When they had cleared the trees, they stopped and looked down. "Look at that," Preston told him, and he did: the unmarked crescent of white sand, the rocky point, the perfect liquid lines waiting to be ridden, and he figured that perhaps he knew after all why they had come. He touched Preston's arm as they started down. "Thanks," he said. "Thanks for bringing me." Preston just laughed and led the way, and his laughter rang among the hills.

They entered the water near the middle of the crescent-shaped beach. Ike followed Preston, and when they had pushed through the shore break, Preston angled his board toward the point. Ahead of them the horizon was a straight blue line. The sun sparkled on the water and the water was like glass, smooth and clear so you could look down and see small schools of fish and tendrils of seaweed reaching for the sun. Soon they were paddling over shoulders, the waves lifting and lowering them, and Ike could feel his heart beginning to thump against the deck of his board. He had never paddled out this far or been in waves like these.

At last Preston dug his legs into the water and drew himself up to straddle the board. Ike did the same and together they looked very far away. . . .

"This is what it's all about," Preston said. "You know, there used to be places like this all up and down the coast. Surf 'em with your friends. They're gone now. Fucking developers. People. Fuckers'll all drown in their own garbage before it's over, wait and see." He seemed a little winded from the paddle, as if it was something he had not done in a long time. He swung his arms and rolled his thick neck, then squinted out to sea as the next outside set began to build. Ike forgot about the coastline and began to paddle. It looked like they were still too far inside, but Preston called him back: "Just stick with me, hot shot; set up like I tell you to."

Ike did set up as Preston told him. The set was moving past them now and Preston began paddling hard to the left, paddling closer toward the center of the peaks. Ike paddled after him. As each wave reached them it lifted them high into the air and as it passed there was fine white spray blown back from the lip and there were rainbows caught in the spray. Suddenly Preston turned to him and shouted: "Your wave, ace. Dig for it."

Ike swung the board around and began to paddle and almost at once, without time for a second thought, he was in the grip of the wave. He could hear Preston yell behind him. He could hear the wind and a funny kind of swishing sound. He gripped his rails and swung himself up and there he was, at the top, the wave a great moving hill beneath him, and he was amazed at the height, amazed at how different this was from the short, steep faces he had ridden at Huntington. He was dropping and picking up speed. His stomach rose in his chest. The wave face grew steeper, a green wall that went on forever. The board pushed against his feet. There was a feeling of compression, as if he stood on the floor of a speeding elevator. And then it was over. He made a bit of a turn at the bottom, come to a dead stop. He left the deck as if catapulted, skidded once on his face and stomach before going under, and that was when the whole Pacific Ocean came down on top of him. He had no idea of where he was in relation to the surface. His head filled with salt water. He could feel the leash that connected his ankle to his board dragging him beneath the water. He tried to relax, to go limp, but what he kept seeing was the way Preston would find his body, bloated and discolored, half eaten by crabs, caught between the rocks. He began to claw with both hands, to fight for the surface, and suddenly he was there, the sea a mass of swirling white water all around him, the sunlight dancing in the foam, and he was sucking in great lungfuls of air and blinking the salt out of his eyes and marveling at the beauty of the sky. . . .

They surfed until the sun was overhead and Ike's arms were so weary he could barely lift them out of the water. But he had begun to catch waves, to paddle for them, make the drop, the turn. He was also beginning to see that the wipe-outs wouldn't kill him, not these waves, not today.

They did as Preston had suggested, surfed until noon then returned to the camp, where they ate canned peaches and drank water, slept in the shade of the trees with the hills and ocean spread out below them. Near sunset they surfed again. The water passed like polished glass beneath their boards. Once Ike turned to see Preston sitting on his board maybe fifty yards away. The sea was dark and all around him slivers of sunlight shimmered and vanished like darting schools of fish. On the horizon, the sun had begun to melt, had gone red above a purple sea. The tide was low and the waves turned crisp black faces toward the shore while trails of mist rose from their feathering lips in fine golden arcs. The arcs rose into the sky, spreading and then falling back into the sea, scattering their light across the surface like shards of flames. There was a cyclical quality in all of this, in the play of light, in the movement of the swell. It was an incredible moment and he felt suddenly that he was plugged into all, was part of it in some organic way. The feeling created an awareness of a new set of possibilities, a new rhythm. He wanted to laugh, or to shout. He put his hand in the air and waved at

Preston across the dark expanse. It was a crazy kind of wave—done with the whole arm, his hand swinging at the end of it, full of childish exuberance. And as he watched, Preston raised his own arm and waved back. . . .

By midmorning Ike was alone with the waves. . . . The morning, the surf, could not have been more perfect. A clean swell, three to five feet out of the southwest. Paper-thin walls with long workable faces turned toward the sun. While he surfed, a school of porpoise arrived to join him for a time in the waves, passing in a leisurely fashion, slapping at the water with their bodies, calling to one another with strange sounds. They passed so close he could have reached them in a single stroke. A group of pelicans cruised by in formation, their bodies within inches of the sea. They circled the point and passed him once more, this time just inside the lineup, actually skimming along the faces of the waves, the last bird just ahead of the falling crest so it was like they were surfing, at play on the empty point, and he joined them in the waves, letting jewel-strung faces slip beneath his board, carving lines out of crisp morning glass.

He did not have to rush, to worry about beating anybody back outside, or watch for someone dropping in on him. He could paddle out slowly, take as much pleasure in watching the empty liquid lines as he did in riding them. It was something he had not fully appreciated on his first visit, how surfing was not just about getting rides. It struck him this morning that what he was doing was not separated into different things. Paddling out, catching rides, setting up. Suddenly it was all one act, one fluid series of motions, one motion even. Everything coming together until it was all one thing: the birds, the porpoise, the leaves of seaweed catching sunlight through the water, all one thing and he was one with it. Locked in. Not just tapping the source, but of the source.

Channel Islands

Santa Rosa

Gretel Ehrlich (b. 1946) is usually associated with Wyoming, the setting of her best-known book, the acclaimed The Solace of Open Spaces *(1985). However, she grew up in Santa Barbara, where she continues to live part of the year, and of which she has written, as in this essay about neighboring Santa Rosa Island.*

Green, no one here remembers when it started. Maybe three days ago, after seven months of brown. "It comes on like blindness," one of the cowboys says. "One day the green puts your eyes out, and you didn't even see it coming." I'm standing on the mountainous top of Santa Rosa island off the Santa Barbara coast. Out across the channel waters—white-capped, big-swelled, and shark-glutted —I can see, on the California mainland, the ridge where my house is perched. From there, the view down a canyon perfectly frames Santa Rosa. It is as if this marine shard were the missing half of the land where I live, the other side of my green mind. Santa Rosa island is shaped like a four-pointed star plucked in the middle and dropped. The east and west arms reach for the shore of the next islands in the chain. They were once linked together in a sixty-mile-long island: now the passages between them are cross-currented, choppy, wild, and dangerous, churning gyres rotating counterclockwise, mixing warm water into the cold and bathing the islands in clear seas. At 53,000 acres, Santa Rosa is the second largest of the eight Channel Islands and has been run as a cattle ranch for almost a hundred years by the Vail and Vickers families. Plunging down a rough dirt track in the Vails' battered pickup truck, we go east toward Bechers Bay, the steep land splaying out into broad coastal grasslands. Two foxes, endemic to the island, pounce on a field mouse, oblivious to our passing, reminding me that the four northern islands—Anacapa, Santa Cruz, Santa Rosa, and San Miguel—are sometimes called the Galapagos of the Northern Hemisphere.

We pass a stand of Torrey pines. Tall and thin-limbed, they are pruned by the raging winds that have driven some people on this island crazy. We cross a creek, and the land grows broader. Salt grass tightens its hold on sandy coastal bluffs as a hard northwesterly wind surges our way. Below us the bay is held by a wide curve of sand where snowy plovers nest, and to the southeast a stream widens into a freshwater estuary where egrets and herons prance and stalk, performing their near-motionless ballets. As we descend to the lee side of the island, a feeling of calm engulfs me.

Islands remind us of our intrinsic solitude, yet they usually stand in relationship to a greater body of land and so also teach us about relatedness, just as the islands in a Japanese garden must rest in harmony with the garden.

In our travels we are lured to islands, as if crossing their watery boundaries will endow us with a more vivid sense of ourselves set apart from the maddening fray. But once there, the plangent wholeness of the place blossoms forth: grasses, flowers, birds, trees, streams, animals all distinguished by having gotten there and survived, having been bound together by the frame of limited space.

We follow a long narrow barranca called the Wreck because the British ship *Crown of England* went aground here in 1894. Swales of green flatten out near shore as waves break with sharp reports, as if to say: "Home at last. I have come such a long way."

Near a set of sorting corrals for cattle, a meandering stream is still mostly dry, and a single tree's tortured trunk twists upward from bedrock.

"There never was much in the way of vegetation in this canyon," foreman Bill Wallace tells me, "and after last year's floods, even that was swept away."

We cross the creek and follow the coast west to a beach where cattle take their morning rest on the sand. At low tide, eelgrass is swept up on brown rock, and jade green waves break like windowpanes on the bare bones of the island.

Beyond, a black ridge bends down to the sea, and from around its snout a plug of fog spews continually, never coming onto land.

Another day, the green has intensified. "Who needs a damned watch around here?" one of the men says. "The grass grows an inch every minute."

The southwest coast of the island is paradisiacal. Accordioned by a winter storm in Hawaii, I am on my favorite part of the island, China Camp, once an abalone camp of Chinese fishermen. A set of corrals and a small two-room cabin on the coastal plain overlook the ocean.

"Used to camp here when we were gathering," Russ Vail says. "I've traveled around some, and I guess this is one of the most beautiful spots in the world," he adds quietly, then looks west toward San Miguel. "The other one is next door."

As we come down off the mountain, hundreds, maybe even thousands, of western meadowlarks fly up, land, and throw their heads back in ecstatic song. This whole island is musical, a meadowlark orchestra.

Now the thick roll of fog that pulled past black rock yesterday twists overhead, and I feel as if I were riding a sea turtle, a great green back floating in mist. Waves that are lapis and foam break through the fog at the fringes of this tiny universe, and a seal observes me from the trough between sets of waves.

In Arlington Canyon we come across the site of Phil Orr's camp. An archaeologist with the Santa Barbara Museum of Natural History, Orr did research on early man here on Santa Rosa for twenty years, from 1947 to 1967.

"He was a little crazy," Al Vail says, bemused. "Lived in a cave, fed the damned foxes, and spent years looking around for bones."

Orr theorized that hunter-gatherers lived on these islands as long ago as 35,000 years, though current thinking dates humans here to less than a third of that. Before those people, there were dwarf mammoths, giant mice, sea otters, and flightless geese. Even though the geology of the West is relatively new, the island seems old, having weathered continuous habitation by animals and humans for more years than we know.

Down by the shore Arlington Creek empties out into another estuary loaded with ducks. Huge beams from a wrecked boat are strewn in grass, and an elephant seal, his face and neck scarred from a lifetime of fighting, is slumped across a hummock of kelp, dead.

Fog billows over us and San Miguel disappears. An island may represent apartness and isolation, but that too is only an aspect of its stepping-stone unity with the whole. How do you know you are apart if you do not know there is something other—other islands, a mainland?

When Juan Cabrillo sailed into the Santa Barbara Channel in 1542, the Chumash people greeted him in their plank canoes, called *tomols*. They called what we know as Santa Rosa by the named Wi'ma—driftwood.

Each island had its own dialect, and the island tribes remained distinct from the Chumash who lived in villages along the mainland from Malibu to San Simeon.

They thought of the channel as a stream to step over. "I make a big step," one Chumash islander song goes. "I am always going over to the other side. I always jump to the other side, as if jumping over a stream of water. I make a big step."

With these words, sung in Santa Rosa island dialect, the Fox Dance began, the participants moving in a circle from fire to fire taking up offerings of *islay*, wild cherries. At the end, when the fox dancer whirled around and around under his weighted headdress, another song was such in Cruzeño—the language of Santa Cruz island: "March! There comes the swell of the sea, and the wood tick is drowning."

There were many dances—the Swordfish, Barracuda, Arrow, and Skunk, and the haunting chant of the Seaweed Dance: "I walk moving my brilliance and feathers. I will always endure in the future. . . . "

But they did not endure. They were gone—moved to the mainland—by 1817.

"There are many ghosts on this island," Nita Vail, Al's daughter, tells me.

On Bechers Bay is the main ranch house, the oldest standing house in Santa Barbara County, built in 1865. It is plain and rickety.

When I slept there, the winds seized and shook it, and two elegant Torrey pines outside the door swayed with the house's shaking.

Behind the house two red barns are still standing, but the original bunkhouse is gone. An old cook named Henry fell asleep with a cigarette in bed, burning it down, with himself and his dog in it. For years afterward the Vails said they could hear Henry walking around, clanking pots and pans in the middle of the night.

All afternoon we stroll luxuriant Lobos Canyon, one of the deepest and most unusual barrancas of them all. Year-round springs feed watercress, reeds, and sedge grasses. A snipe flies up as I splash through the stream, and an orange-crowned warbler sings in a small tree. As we tunnel down, the canyon walls grow taller; they are sheaves of sandstone, carefully etched with fine lines as if music had been written on them, the notes erased by wind. Here and there shallow caves have been smoothed out by the island's hard winds, and in one amphitheater, a long tooth of rock hangs down from the roof of a cave, as if from the roof of some orange giant's mouth.

Downstream. More green: reeds, grasses, ferns, Toyon—California holly—and willows grow tall, and even the colonies of lichen on boulders stand up as if starched. A forty-foot-high wall is feathered into delicate filaments that look like the underside of a mushroom, sunsplashed and edible.

"I would like to die here," Nita says, "except I love this canyon so much, I'd want to stay alive to savor it."

As would I.

Lost Coast

John McKinney (b. 1956), award-winning nature writer, conservationist, and Los Angeles Times *hiking columnist, is the author of several walking guides as well as* A Walk Along Land's End: Discovering California's Unknown Coast *(1995), a narrative of a journey inspired by J. Smeaton Chase's 1912 trek. A native of southern California, the author has long been active in the effort to save the region's and the state's environment.*

It doesn't get any wilder than this.

California has a very long coastline, and millions of acres of wilderness, but it has only one wilderness coast.

The Lost Coast.

A day's walk north of Fort Bragg I'm greeted by towering shoreline cliffs, rising abruptly like volcanoes from the sea. I get just a glimpse of the two-thousand-foot-high cliffs before the morning mist turns to heavy fog and the coast is lost to my view. The Lost Coast is so rough—rougher even than Big Sur's coast—that it even thwarted California's highway engineers; much to their frustration, they were compelled by geography to route the Coast Highway inland more than twenty miles.

The Lost Coast is black sand beaches strewn with patterns of driftwood and the sea's debris, a mosaic of small stones. On grassy blufftops, sheep and cows turn tail to angry winds blowing in from Siberia and the Bering Sea. Canyon mouths fill with fog, nourishing the redwoods within.

Abandoned barns and failed fences record the efforts of settlers who tried, but failed, to tame this land. Nowhere is the Lost Coast blighted by transmission lines, oil wells, power plants, RV parks, or fast-food franchises.

As traced on the map, the Lost Coast's northern boundary is the Eel River in Humboldt County, its southern boundary Usal Beach in Mendocino County. Much of the Lost Coast is in public ownership as part of the King Range National Conservation Area in the north and Sinkyone Wilderness State Park in the south.

But "Lost Coast" is not a place name found on any map.

Except mine.

One January, a few years back, I served as volunteer ranger/campground host for Sinkyone Wilderness State Park. I cared for a couple of horses, gave directions to the very few visitors who braved the rain and miserable park road to get to the coast, read and wrote in the ranch house that serves as the park's visitor center on those days when it rained hard, and wandered the trails on those days when it rained less. I hiked all the Lost Coast's trails, mapped the territory, then supervised production of a map called "Trails of the Lost Coast."

The word *lost* on a map has long been a call of the wild to me. Lost Palms Oasis and Lost Horse Mine in the Mojave Desert, Lost Valley in Big Sur, and Lost Lake in the High Sierra are just a few of the lost places I've found.

A fifty-five mile footpath—Lost Coast Trail—traverses the Lost Coast. To reach the trailhead, from Wages Creek Beach outside the hamlet of Rockport, where I camped in a private campground, I must walk seven miles along the beaches and bluffs, then another seven miles up Usal Road. The road, a muddy thoroughfare not pictured on most maps, hasn't changed much since Jack London and his wife, Charmian, drove it in a horse-drawn carriage on a trip to Eureka in 1911, or since

J. Smeaton Chase rode it in 1912. I'm not surprised that after two hours of hiking the road, not a single car has passed me.

Usal Road, with a couple of name changes, follows the crest of the ocean fronting Lost Coast peaks. It doesn't offer much in the way of coastal views, but winds through some wild country. Chase followed roads the length of the Lost Coast. He and I will part company, so to speak, at Usal Beach, where I will join the Lost Coast Trail, a pathway of late 1980s vintage.

"Actual, rosy, purple-blotched foxgloves, such as I last saw in the lanes of Surrey and Devon," he exults.

Chase, two decades removed from an England he would never see again, was understandably nostalgic. But for what exactly? The Britain of his youth? Would Chase have enjoyed a 1912 ride around Britain's coast more, or less, than his ride along California's? Would he have been inspired by Mother England's tidy fields and hedgerows or appalled by the motorcars, mines, mills, and other manifestations of the Industrial Age?

As I walk Usal Road, maybe there's a better question to ponder: Would I—or a reborn Joseph Smeaton Chase—better enjoy a modern-day adventure along land's end in Britain or in California?

These days about 80 percent of Californians and a like percentage of Brits live within thirty miles of coast. But while sharing a common proximity to the ocean, we do not share a common coastal view. In England, the coast is where one gets rid of things—power plants, resorts, gun emplacements, oil refineries, sewage plants—presumably to keep the interior looking pastoral. We Californians, while guilty of placing (more than) our share of horrors on the coast, attempt to locate the worst of our architectural and ecological atrocities some distance inland.

In Britain, the Countryside Commission, so successful at preserving the nation's hills and dales, has not had similar success along the coast. In California, the Coastal Commission has waged a foot-by-foot battle for public access and the preservation of beauty, but its legal powers end a quarter mile inland.

At several locales along Britain's coast, I've felt myself a witness to the last gasp of an empire. Fortress Britain, whose castellated coast has long been a defense against barbarians, is still repelling invaders, this time with ramparts of uglification. Walking Britain's coast left me with the impression of a nation looking inward, determined to take care of its own.

We Californians, by contrast, appear worried what people sailing in from the Pacific Rim will think when they see our coast. And we seem to care not a whit what other Americans, or anyone arriving from the East, will see as they cross the interior on their way to the coast.

After his brief look backward to Britain, Chase looks ahead. He tells us for the first time that he always planned to finish his ride by November 1, and that he has but ten days or so to make the Oregon line.

Despite the rude and crude Californians met during the latter part of this journey, despite witnessing the great tracts of land laid waste by lumbermen, Chase is as plucky, as indefatigable, as ever as he rides the Lost Coast. His "There-will-always-be-a-California" point of view is as unshakable as the "There-will-always-be-an-England" belief held by generations of traveling scribes.

I arrive at Usal Camp on the banks of Usal Creek, select a campsite (I can choose from among fifteen sites in the fifteen-site camp), and set up my tent. Sunset draws near, though I know this only by consulting the moist face of my watch, not by any glimpse of the day star, which has been absent all day.

I follow Usal Creek to its mouth at Usal Beach, a dramatic, dark sand-and-gravel strand backed by tall cliffs whose tops are lost in the fog. Scattered at the base of the eroded cliffs are huge boulders. Such rocks falling from the bluffs make me glad Lost Coast Trail stays atop the bluffs rather than below them.

Usal Beach is not a friendly place. Not only do huge rocks rain on the beach, but huge rogue waves frequently surprise-attack the shore. The surf pounds offshore rock pillars, socks Usal Creek in the mouth.

However, these adverse conditions that discourage even walking Usal Beach did not discourage capitalists of a hundred years ago.

During the 1890s, Captain Robert Dollar regularly navigated his steamship, *Newsboy,* in and out of the treacherous doghole port of Usal in order to transport logs sawn by the Usal Redwood Company. The aptly named Dollar went on to greater fame as founder of the Dollar Steamship Line, later the President Line. The sawmill closed in 1900, and Usal became a near–ghost town, largely because the timber in these parts was inferior. The redwoods' timber prospects looked good to the loggers, but the tall trees never yielded board-feet commensurate to their great size, and produced a lesser grade of lumber. Nevertheless, Georgia Pacific Company resumed logging after World War II and continued until 1986, when, after cutting down most of the trees, it sold its land to the park. In 1969, the company burned Usal to the ground, to avoid what it termed "liability problems."

I lug some driftwood back to my camp and, after much coaxing, get the wet wood to burn. When the fire offers more heat than smoke, I put my pot of macaroni and cheese on the fire. As my hands and face warm and my damp clothes dry, my thoughts turn from California's wettest land to its driest.

After Chase finished his long coastal ride, he began exploring the desert, wrote desert books, moved to Palm Springs and married. No doubt after an upbringing in the England damp, and his excursion along this coast, he was ready to live out his remaining days where it was warm and dry.

The Lost Coast is said to have two seasons: six months of rain and six months of fog. It's very foggy again today. The ocean below and the sky above are a single shade of gray. The tall grass covering the coastal slopes and the Douglas fir that border the meadowland are dripping. Lost Coast Trail is muddy, and populated by so many earthworms that the earth itself seems alive and wiggling.

I enter Dark Canyon, a rainforest-like environment of bay laurels draped with moss, maple, and alder. The fog lingers in this canyon, so that the land never seems to dry. The fog tarries too in Anderson and Northport gulches. The Lost Coast's canyons and gulches, from Usal to Bear Harbor, were logged not so many years ago, but the fog softens the scars, hides the stumps. Wrapped in mist, the forest is healing.

Along Little Jackass Creek grows one of the few surviving old-growth redwood groves, the Sally Bell Grove, named for the last full-blooded Sinkyone. She survived a massacre of her people to become a woman of strong will and strong medicine.

Near the grove, I hail state park ranger John Jennings, an easygoing mustachioed fellow who has patrolled here almost since the beginning. "Here" is Sinkyone Wilderness State Park; "the beginning" was in 1975, when the state park opened.

He spent the afternoon finding and cleaning up a marijuana garden, he reports. The grower had harvested his plants, but not his trash, and Jennings hauled away beer bottles and a hammock. "A lot of trash for just two plants."

While the marijuana industry here is small-scale compared to elsewhere in Humboldt County, the weed and its growers nevertheless invade the state park.

The Lost Canyon is part of the so-called Emerald Triangle, the name given to an area of Humboldt, Mendocino, and Trinity counties where many a marijuana garden grows. Indeed, the sinsemilla flourishes.

In the good old days of 1960s and 1970s, big growers harvested huge fortunes—crops of hundreds of plants grew along the Lost Coast on such places as the banks of the Mattole River and Ettersburg. But growers have fallen on hard times, particularly on the coastwood side of the isosceles. The CAMP (Campaign Against Marijuana Plants), complete with helicopter surveillance and trucks full of heavily armed men running through the woods, has been effective in reducing the number of growers. So have stiffer jail sentences and fines, not to mention confiscation and forfeiture of their land.

Now growers have taken up guerrilla gardening—cultivating perhaps a half dozen, sometimes only one or two, plants in dispersed locations on public land. Still, a single sinsemilla plant is a cash crop for several thousand dollars, making it worth the risk to many.

As a peace officer—a term that better describes his job than that of his city cop counterparts—Jennings must protect the Lost Coast from the locals, who, like the native Sinkyone who preceded them, could be said to be a family-oriented loosely organized tribal group that lives off the land. But many locals are attracted to the Lost Coast because it's long been a place for people to escape tax collectors, the criminal justice system, and most conventional forms of personal and social responsibility.

"John, there are three seasons," Jennings tells me.

"No way, John. You told me two the last time I was here: the foggy season and the rainy season."

"That's the weather. The humans around here observe three seasons: hunting season, fishing season, and growing season."

These three seasons make it rough for Jennings in a park designated "wilderness." A wilderness is by definition off-limits to vehicles, which severely restricts what locals call "traditional uses" of the land.

"Traditional uses" is a motto that plays well with the conservative board of supervisors and county government, but in practice is quite different. Traditional wood gathering means four-wheeling it up to a tree and chain-sawing what you need. Traditional fishing is backing up to the river and fishing off the back of a truck. Traditional hunting is blasting at critters from a pickup trucks. Traditional agriculture is planting pot on public land.

In the minds of many locals, the gun is an integral part of the coastal system, and they want to solve these traditional problems in their traditional manner.

Problem: Too few steelhead

Solution: Shoot the sea lions

Problem: Too few trout

Solution: Shoot the merganser ducks

Problem: Too few quail to shoot

Solution: Shoot the bobcats

Problem: Too few deer to shoot

Near sunset—or more precisely, about when the sun sets, since I have not glimpsed the orb all day—I reached Wheeler, where some cement foundations mark what was a company town, from 1950 to 1960. Near the ruins grow spearmint, alyssum, and other domestic plants gone wild. During the Lost Coast's logging decade, diesels hauling 120,000 pounds of logs thundered along Usal Road from Wheeler, a modern town of thirty families, with electricity and phones.

Wheeler, one of the last company towns (and maybe the newest ghost town) on the California coast, was established by the Wheeler family. The Wheelers renamed Jackass Creek "Wolf Creek," probably so they could call their business Wolf Creek Timber Company rather than Jackass Creek Timber Company, no doubt preferring to name their company after a predator rather than a nitwit.

One of mapmaking's great joys is choosing geographical names among contenders. I figured that Jackass Creek was so named before the Wheelers and their timber company came, so Jackass Creek it should be henceforth, and Jackass Creek it is on my Lost Coast Map.

I pitch my tent by Jackass Creek beneath two large redwoods. The redwoods remind me that tomorrow I will visit a very special stand of the tall trees—the J. Smeaton Chase Grove, a grove that I named for my trail companion.

From Wheeler, I ascend steep switchbacks, then wind through a grassland at the edge of a forest. Among the blue-eyed grass and monkey flowers are the foxgloves so beloved by Chase.

I reach Duffy's Gulch, a garden of rhododendrons, head-high ferns, and vines climbing redwoods to the sky. Splashing color about the gulch are Indian paintbrush, dandelions, huckleberry, Douglas iris, Calypso orchid, and some bright red poison oak. The trees in J. Smeaton Chase Grove are towering thousand-year-old redwoods, some ten feet in diameter, surrounded by a multitude of ferns—sword, lady, five-finger, and woodwardia.

Doubtless Chase would have frowned at me for naming a grove for him. He was a modest man (far more photographs of his horse survive than of him) and in *California Coast Trails* wrote of the vanity of naming groves of the tallest living things for men of questionable stature.

But Chase also wrote of the rest that comes with an eternal sleep in the woods: "Every good man loves the woodland, and even if our concerns keep us all our lives out of our heritage we hope to lie down at last under the quiet benediction of slow-moving branches." . . .

It is a miracle the redwoods of J. Smeaton Chase Grove escaped the ax and saw, I think as I tramp under ever gloomier skies to Bear Harbor, the main port for southern Humboldt and northern Mendocino counties from the 1860s to the turn of the century. This onetime timber shipping point isn't much more than a mile from the grove's virgin redwoods. . . .

It begins to rain and I decide not to stop at Railroad Creek trail camp, but to push on for the relative comfort of Needle Rock Ranch House. Just offshore, a strange cloud formation, like a blackened teapot, pours water from the ocean onto the land.

An hour's walk in the rain (a relief, actually, from the incessant fog,) brings me to the ranch house, a combination visitor center/hostel, where I unpack my things. . . .

The dark clouds vanish and the rain ceases. I step out onto the porch to see the sun, low over the water, struggling against the gloom. An isolated, lone eucalyptus shines ghostly white against the dark, storm-tossed sea.

It is this special, brooding light that intrigued the great Catholic theologian Thomas Merton when he visited here and talked of establishing a monastery for Trappist monks. He thought the Lost Coast shores around Needle Rock an ideal location for a life of prayer and contemplation—high praise indeed for one who believed so strongly in the power of physical silence and seclusion. . . .

Above the roar of the breakers I hear what sounds like the crack of a bat meeting a baseball, like someone taking batting practice on the bluffs. I walk up the coast one hundred, two hundred yards, following my ears until I spot an amazing sight. Two bull Roosevelt elk paw the ground, lower their heads, butt antlers. Around them, grazing on the bluffs, are two dozen females, by all outward appearances utterly disinterested in the result of this combat.

Again and again the elk circle, feint, clash. From a distance they look evenly matched, but up close it's apparent that a young bull, strong but outweighed, is challenging an older bull. No blood is drawn. This is more ritual, than actual, combat.

Roosevelt elk are enchanted-looking creatures, with chocolate-brown faces and necks, tan bodies, and dark legs. The California natives look like a cross between a South American llama and a deer. In truth, the elk are more awesome when they butt heads than when they call. I always figured elk had a majestic call, a trumpet to arms, but these Roosevelts have a funny little call more like the wee-wee of a pig than the bugle of a powerful thousand-pound elk.

The younger bull may successfully challenge his elder next year or the year after, but this evening the older bull, with his fuller antlers and more clever moves, and still very much in his prime, is a sure bet to keep his harem. Sunset (the first I've seen in days) casts an orange glow over the clifftop combatants, like a floodlight on a stage. When the light finally fades and darkness falls, the duel ends.

Dark shapes gather together, protection against the enemies of the night, but if the elk intend to be inconspicuous they had better stop eating. The ruminants tear at the grass, an aggressive munching, like a lion ripping into a kill.

The next morning I hike up Whale Gulch on the Lost Coast Trail, leaving behind the state park and entering King Range National Conservation Area. Its one of the wettest spots in America, with over a hundred inches of rain annually, but today the weather seems most indecisive. Black clouds hover offshore to my left, the sun rises over the King Range to my right. The radio in the ranch house predicted a 50 percent chance of showers.

Soon after the boundary between state park and U.S. Bureau of Land Management territories, I cross another boundary, the line between Mendocino and Humboldt counties. The county line is another boundary of sorts—the fortieth parallel of latitude.

The change in latitude heralds a change in attitude.

In the sharp morning light, the land shows its scars. The King Range is chain saw country, Utah with fog. The magnificent coast is visible, and files of Douglas fir, but so also are clear-cut ridges, overgrazed slopes, and silted streams. Some of this land looks like the "Before Rehabilitation" pictures in the Boy Scouts' Soil and Water Conservation merit badge pamphlet.

I think of yet another boundary I've crossed—this one wholly in my mind. After all this coast walking, I've decided there are three Californias: Smog Land, Fog Land, and Log Land. This beginning of BLM land, this fortieth parallel, this Mendocino-Humboldt county line: this is clearly the start of Log Land.

As I climb Chemise Mountain the vegetation changes. Most of the firs have been logged, and it's tan oak and madrone that cling to the steep hillsides. Near the top of Chemise Mountain is some chemise (greasewood), as well as chaparral bushes and lots of manzanita; the presence of drought-resistant plants only a mile or so from a thick rainforest is truly bizarre. The difference in ecology has to do with elevation. Chemise Mountain, at 2,596 feet, is about two thousand feet higher than the rainforest. I enjoy the view from atop the mountain: King's Peak, the dominant promontory to the north, a half dozen ridges of the Sinkyone to the south, Shelter Cove on the coast far below. The view doesn't last long; it closes like a storm window.

As I descend Chemise Mountain Trial toward the coast, the weather has decided to be—indecisive. The sun warming the King Range from the east meets the storm brewing on the western horizon, and the result is neither rain nor sun but a dense fog.

Here on these very steep slopes, exposed to the full fury of Pacific storms, the firs grow grotesque, their massive trunks short and twisted. Only the patter of condensed fog dripping from the branches breaks the silence.

I hurry through the dark, spooky forest. The reason for my hustle down the knee-jarring decline is that I have an appointment with Point No Pass on the beach below at precisely 2:53 P.M., and I must not be late. Such punctuality is critical because rounding the aptly named point is only possible at a rare minus tide, which, luckily for me, happens to occur this afternoon. If I can't round Point No Pass and walk the beach to Shelter Cove, I will have to ascend this brutal slope of Chemise Mountain and hike over the crest of the King Range to continue north.

About a quarter mile from the beach I reach the end of Chemise Mountain Trail; it's been buried by a landslide, as if a giant bulldozer has scraped the side of the mountain. I slip-slide on feet and butt through the slide zone, hoping the mountain doesn't slide with me to the sea. When I reach the beach, I walk a mile to Point No Pass and, thanks to my watch and tide table, am able to round the point and reach Shelter Cove. . . .

An elderly couple walks the black sand beach patrolled by swifts and swallows and . . . I can't believe my eyes . . . trucks and off-road vehicles. . . . Rifles hang in gun racks in the cabs of the passing pickup trucks, fishing poles in the beds behind them. The Lost Coast locals are ever ready to practice their traditional hunting and fishing techniques.

The beach, twenty-five miles from Shelter Cove to the mouth of the Mattole River, is the longest roadless stretch in California. Something of the thrill of knowing this, of walking this coast, is diminished when, road or not, vehicles are permitted on the beach for the first three and a half miles.

Dodging cars and trucks, I walk the beach to Gitchell Creek, just beyond the boundary, separating beaches that allow vehicles from beaches that forbid them. Just in case one of the locals decides to practice some traditional drunk driving on the beach tonight, I pitch my tent behind a massive log that seems guaranteed to stop even a tank.

As I gather driftwood for my evening fire, I nearly step on a rattlesnake. As lethargic a creature as I've ever seen, the timber rattler manages one flick of the forked tongue at me before uncoiling itself from a piece of wood and crawling deeper into the woodpile. I manage to work up some sympathy for a snake in such a cold and wet part of the world. The Lost Coast belongs to amphibians, not reptiles.

The next morning I'm off into the fog, and in a few miles reach Buck Creek, where a steep trail leaves the beach and climbs into the King Range. This is my only chance to leave the beach and hike along the crest of the King Range. But now that I've left civilization—and vehicles—behind, I want to stick with the beach.

And a magnificent beach it is—rock, pebbles, and coarse black sand strewn with great logs, as if the sea, not the land, had been logged. And water, water, everywhere; the ocean, deep and wide and restless on my left, the fog all around me, creeks trickling, waterfalls tumbling from the rainforest above to the beach below. High above me, at the limits of vision, where the green slope meets the gray sky are seeps and springs nurturing hanging wildflower gardens, scattered like Easter eggs in the forest.

After a long day, I make another beach camp, another driftwood fire, at Cooksie Creek. Then back to the beach the next morning.

I hear the residents of Sea Lion Rocks before I see them—two dozen Steller's sea lions. A mile beyond the big creatures is the abandoned Punta Gorda lighthouse. In 1911, after several ships were wrecked on the rocks and reefs of the Lost Coast, a lighthouse was built a mile south of Punta Gorda, a name meaning "massive point."

The mouth of the Mattole River, a complication of gravel bars, marks the northern end of the Lost Coast. Seagulls and osprey circle above me as I watch the harbor seals bob in the tidal area where the river meets the ocean. I look back into the mist at the King Range, at slopes that seem so much steeper than the angle of repose, and that are kept from collapsing into the sea only by some hidden force deep within the earth.

It is not really the coast that is lost, but ourselves. If we cannot find the coast because of the smoke of our cities, the walls we build to keep one another out, the industries we run that run us, it is surely we who are lost.

We all need one place on the map, one place in our hearts that is lost. In a wild place, lost from the mean streets, we can find ourselves, our best selves. A place that is peaceful, for prayer and for contemplation, is good; a place that is wild, for challenge and confrontation, is better; and a place that is both peaceful and wild, for the love of life and the lust of living, is best.

EARTH, WIND, RAIN, AND FIRE

San Andreas Fault

Continental Drift

James D. Houston (b. 1933) is California born and educated. He has taught writing for a many years and has written several novels, a collection of short stories, and several works of nonfiction. The following is the prologue to his 1978 novel Continental Drift.

From high above, say gazing down from one of our tracking satellites, he can see it plain as an incision, a six-hundred-mile incision some careless surgeon stitched up across the surface of the earth. It marks the line where two great slabs of the earth's crust meet and grind together. Most of North America occupies one of these slabs. Most of the Pacific Ocean floats on the other. A small lip of the Pacific slab extends above the surface, along America's western coastline, a lush and mountainous belt of land not as much a part of the rest of the continent as it is the most visible piece of that slab of crust which lies submerged. The line where these two slabs, or plates, meet is called the San Andreas Fault. It cuts south from San Francisco, past San Jose, underneath the old San Juan Bautista Mission, on down behind Los Angeles, and back under water again at the Gulf of California.

The Pacific plate, he will tell you, is creeping north and west at about two inches per year, an example of the movement geologists call continental drift. Our globe, which appears to be divided into continents and bodies of water, is actually a patchwork of these vast plates, all floating around in a kind of subterranean pudding. What it resembles most is a badly fractured skull. From time to time the towns and cities along the fault line have been jiggled or jolted by temblors large and small, when sections of it buckle or lock, and then unbend, release, or settle. There are people who predict that one day the ultimate quake is going to send a huge chunk of California sliding into the ocean like Atlantis. They foresee this as one of the worst disasters in the history of the civilized world. They sometimes add that in a land as bizarre and corrupt as California is reputed to be, such a fate has been well earned.

Montrose Doyle will tell you all that is poppycock. Both the physics and the prophecy. He will tell you that the earth's crust is three hundred miles thick, whereas the fault line only cuts down for thirty of those miles. He will tell you that if anything is going to undo this piece of coast it will be the accumulated body weight of all the people who have been moving into his part of the world at a steady rate since 1849. But it won't be the San Andreas. He has made it his business to find out what he can about this creature, because he owns fifty-five acres of orchard and grazing land that border it. He grew up on this ranch, will probably die here, and during his forty-six years he has seldom felt more than a tic across the earth's skin, an infrequent shiver in the high cupola which serves as his personal antenna and seismograph.

Montrose has studied with fascination the photographs of rotundas upended in the streets of San Francisco during the famous quake of 1906. He has corresponded with experts. And he has escorted visitors over to Hollister, twenty-five miles east of where his own house stands. An otherwise neat and orderly farm town, Hollister happens to be gradually splitting in two, because it sits in the fracture zone, like an Eskimo village caught on a cracking ice floe. By following cracks you can trace the subtle power of the fault as it angles under the town, offsetting sidewalks and curbstones and gutters, an effect most alarming in the house of a chiropractor which you pass soon after entering Hollister from the west. One half of a low concrete retaining wall holding back the chiropractor's lawn has been carried north and west about eight inches. The concrete walkway is buckling. Both porch pillars lean precariously toward the coast. In back, the wall of his garage is bent into a curve like a stack of whale's ribs. The fact that half his doomed house rides on the American plate and the other half rides the Pacific has not discouraged this chiropractor from maintaining a little order in his life. He hangs his sign out front, he keeps his lawn well mowed and the old house brightly, spotlessly painted.

One afternoon Montrose leaned down to talk with a fellow in Hollister who was working on the transmission of a Chevy pickup. The curb his truck stood next to had been shattered by the ageless tension of those two slabs of earth crust pulling at each other. Five inches had opened in the curb, like a little wound, and someone had tried to fill it with homemade concrete, and that had started to split.

Monty said, "Hey!"

The grease-smeared face emerged, irritably. It was hot. The man said, "Yeah?"

"Hey, doesn't the fault line run through this part of town?"

"The what?"

"The San Andreas . . ."

"Oh, that damn thing." The man waved his wrench aimlessly. "Yeah, she's around somewhere," and he slid back out of sight underneath his pickup.

Montrose regards that man with fondness now. He voiced Monty's own attitude pretty well, which is to say, none of this really troubles him much. Is he a fatalist? Yes. And no. He anticipates. Yet he does not anticipate. What he loves to dwell on—what he savors so much during those trips to Hollister—is that steady creep which, a few million years hence, will put his ranch on a latitude with Juneau, Alaska. He admires the foresight of the Spanish cartographers who, in their earliest maps, pictured California as an island. Sometimes late at night, after he has been drinking heavily, he will hike out to his fence line and imagine that he can feel beneath his feet the dragging of the continental plates, and imagine that he is standing on his own private raft, a New World Noah, heading north, at two inches per year.

Most of the time he doesn't think about it at all. It is simply there, a presence beneath his land. If it ever comes to mind during his waking hours, he thinks of it as just that, a presence, a force, you might even say a certainty, the one thing he knows he can count on—this relentless grinding of two great slabs which have been butting head-on now for millennia and are not about to relax.

San Andreas Fault

The San Andreas Discrepancy

John McPhee (b. 1931) is one of the most highly regarded writers in America, whose books on a wide variety of subjects usually first appear as essays in the New Yorker. *Over the span of fifteen years McPhee explored the San Andreas Fault with Eldridge Moores, a tectonist at the University of California, Davis; the result was* Assembling California *(1993), a historical and geological cross-section of the state.*

arther north [of Los Angeles], it loses, for a while, its domestic charm. Almost all water disappears in a desert scene that, for California, is unusually placed. The Carrizo Plain, only forty miles into the Coast Ranges from the ocean at Santa Barbara, closely resembles a south Nevada basin. Between the Caliente Range and the Temblor Range, the San Andreas Fault runs up this flat, unvegetated, linear valley in full exposure of its benches and scarps, its elongate grabens and beheaded channels, its desiccated sag ponds and dry deflected streams. From the air, the fault trace is keloid, virtually organic in its insistence and its creep—north forty degrees west. On the ground, standing on desert pavement in a hot dry wind, you are literally entrenched in the plate boundary. You can see nearly four thousand years of motion in the bed of a single intermittent stream. The bouldery brook, bone dry, is fairly straight as it comes down the slopes of the Temblor Range, but the San Andreas has thrown up a shutter ridge—a sort of sliding wall—that blocks its path. The stream turns ninety degrees right and explores the plate boundary for four hundred and fifty feet before it discovers its offset bed, into which it turns west among cobbles and boulders of Salinian granite.

You pass dead soda ponds, other offset streams. The (gravel) road up the valley is for many miles directly on the fault. Now and again, there's a cattle grid, a herd of antelope, a house trailer, a hardscrabble ranch, a fence stuffed with tumbleweed, a pump in the yard. A daisy wheel turns on a tower. Down in the broken porous fault zone there will always be water, even here.

With more miles north come small adobes, far apart, each with a dish antenna. And with more miles a handsome spread, a green fringe, a prospering ranch with a solid house. The fault runs through the solid house. And why should it not? It runs through greater San Francisco.

Of the two most direct routes from southern to northern California, always choose the San Andreas Fault. If you have adequate time, it beats the hell out of Interstate 5. Nearly always, some sort of road stays right in the fault zone. Like a water-level route through rough country, the fault is a place to find gentle grades and smooth ground. When the fault makes minor turns, they are nothing compared to the bends of a river. With more distance north, the desert plain yields to hay meadows and then to ever lusher country, until vines are standing in the fault-trace grabens and walnuts climb the creaselike hills. Ground squirrels appear, and then ever larger flocks of magpies, and then cottonwoods, and then oaks in thickening numbers, and velure pastures around horses with nothing to do. In age and rock type, the two sides of the fault are as different as two primary colors. Strewn up the west side are long-transport gabbroic hills and deracinated ranges of exotic granite. Just across the trough is Franciscan melange—stranger, messier, more interesting to Moores.

Near Parkfield, you cross a bridge over the San Andreas where Cholame Creek runs on the fault. The bridge has been skewed—the east end toward Chihuahua, the west end toward Mt. McKinley. Between Cholame and Parkfield, plate-shattering ruptures have occurred six times since 1857, an average of one every twenty-two years, and the probability that another will occur before 2003 has been reckoned at ninety-eight percent. Thirty-four people live in Parkfield. If the population is ever to increase, seismologists will be the first to know it, for the valley here is wired like nowhere else. Parkfield has attracted earthquake-prediction experts because the brief interval time on this segment of the fault suggests that if they monitor this place they may learn something before they die. Also, the Parkfield segment has—in Moores's words—"relatively simple fault geometry." And the last three earthquakes have had a common epicenter and have been of equal magnitude.

An average of one plate-shattering earthquake every twenty-two years works out to 45,000 per million years. The last big Parkfield event was in 1966. It broke the surface for eighteen miles. Words on the town's water tower say "Parkfield, Earthquake Capital of the World, Be Here When It Happens." The actual year doesn't matter much. The instrumentation of Parkfield assumes that a shock is imminent. Its purpose is not to confirm the calculated averages but to develop a technology of sensing—within months, days, hours, or minutes—when a shock is coming. Even a minute's warning, or five minutes', or an hour's, let alone a day's, could (in highly populated places) save many lives and much money. Accordingly, the Cholame Valley around Parkfield—between Middle Mountain, in the north, and Gold Mountain, to the south—has been equipped with several million dollars' worth of strain gauges, creepmeters, earth thumpers, laser Geodimeters, tiltmeters, and a couple of dozen seismographs. It is said that the federal spending has converted the community from Parkfield to Porkfield. Some of the seismographs are in holes half a mile deep. Experience suggests that rocks creep a little before they leap. The creepmeters are sensitive to tens of millionths of an inch of creep.

If ever there was a conjectural science, it is earthquake prediction, and as research ramifies, the Tantalean goal recedes. The maximum stress on the San Andreas Fault—the direction of maximum push—turns out to be nearly perpendicular to the directions in which the fault sides move, like a banana peel's horizontal slip when pressure comes upon it from above. A fault that moves in such a manner must be weak enough to slide—must be, in a sense, lubricated. Among other things, the pressure of water in pores of rock in the walls of the fault has been mentioned as a lubricant, and so has the sudden release of gases that may result from shaking. Such mechanisms would tend to randomize earthquakes, diminishing the significance of mounting strains and temporal gaps. Those who practice earthquake prediction will watch almost anything that might contribute to the purpose. A geyser in the Napa Valley inventively named Old Faithful seems to erupt erratically both before and after large earthquakes that occur within a hundred and fifty miles—an observation that is based, however, on records kept for scarcely twenty years. In 1980, the United States Geological Survey began monitoring hydrogen in soils. Two years later, near Coalinga, about twenty miles northeast of Parkfield, the hydrogen in the soil was suddenly fifty times normal. It appeared in bursts, and such bursts became increasingly numerous in April 1983. In May 1983, a 6.5 earthquake occurred on a thrust fault under Coalinga. Releases of radon are watched. So are patterns and numbers of microquakes, especially those that are known as the Mogi doughnut. In the mid-1960s, a Japanese seismologist noticed on his seismograms that microquakes occurring in the weeks before a major shock sometimes formed rings around the place that became the epicenter. Mogi's doughnut is a wonderful clue, but—like hydrogen bursts and radon releases—before most major shocks it fails to appear.

People who live in earthquake country will speak of earthquake weather, which they characterize as very balmy, no winds. With prescient animals and fluctuating water wells, the study of earthquake weather is in a category of precursor that has not attracted funds from the National Science Foundation. Some people say that well water goes down in anticipation of a temblor. Some say it goes up. An ability to sense imminent temblors has been ascribed to snakes, turtles, rats, eels, catfish, weasels, birds, bears, and centipedes. Possible clues in animal behavior are taken more seriously in China and Japan than they are in the United States, although a scientific paper was published in *California Geology* in 1988 evaluating a theory that "when an extraordinarily large number of dogs and cats are reported in the 'Lost and Found' section of the *San Jose Mercury News*, the probability of an earthquake striking the area increases significantly."

Earthquake prediction has taken long steps forward on the insights of plate tectonics but has also, on occasion, overstepped. Until instrumentation is reliably able to chart a developing temblor, predictors obviously have a moral responsibility to present their calculations shy of the specific. The mathematical equivalent of a forked stick will produce such absurdities as the large earthquake that did not occur as predicted in New Madrid, Missouri, on December 2, 1990. A USGS geologist and a physicist in the United States Bureau of Mines whose research included (among other things) the study of rocks cracking in a lab predicted three great earthquakes for specific dates in the summer of 1981, to take place in the ocean floor near Lima. The largest—9.9—was to be twenty times as powerful as any earthquake ever recorded in the world. A few hundred thousand Peruvians were informed that they would die. Nothing happened.

If you set stakes in a straight line across a valley glacier and come back a year later, you will see the curving manner in which the stakes have moved. If you drive fence posts in a straight line across the San Andreas Fault and come back a year later, almost certainly you will see a string line of fence posts—unless your fence is in the hundred miles north of the Cholame Valley. There the line will be offset slightly, no more than an inch or two. Another year after that a little more; and so forth. In its 740 miles of interplate abrasion, the San Andreas Fault is locally idiosyncratic, but nowhere more so than here in the Central

Creeping Zone. Trees move, streams are bent, sag ponds sag. In road asphalt, echelon fractures develop. Slivers drop as minigrabens. Scarplets rise. The fault is very straight through the Central Creeping Zone. It consists, however, of short (two to six miles), stepped, parallel traces, like the marks made on ice by a skater. Landslides occur frequently in the Central Creeping Zone, obscuring the fresh signatures of the creep.

"The creep is relatively continuous for 170 kilometers here and seems to account for nearly all of the movement," Moores remarked. "Creep is rare. Most fault movement is punctuated. The creep produces numerous small earthquakes. There are actual 'creep events,' wherein as much as five hundred meters of the fault zone will experience propagating creep in one hour." There were many oaks and few people living in the creep zone. The outcrops on the Pacific side of the fault sparkled with feldspar and mica—the granitic basement of the Gabilan Range. More than three thousand feet in elevation and close against the fault trace, the Gabilan Range creeps, too.

Jumping and creeping, the San Andreas Fault's average annual motion for a number of millions of years has been thirty-five millimeters. The figure lags significantly behind the motion of the Pacific Plate, whose travels, north by northwest, go a third again as fast. In the early days of plate tectonics, this incongruous difference was discovered after the annual motion of the Pacific Plate was elsewhere determined. The volcanic flows that crossed the San Andreas and were severed by the fault had not been carried apart at anything approaching the rate of Pacific motion. This became known as the San Andreas Discrepancy. If the Pacific Plate was moving so much faster than the great transform fault at its eastern edge, the rest of the motion had to be taken up somewhere. Movements along the many additional faults in the San Andreas were not enough to account for it. Other motions in the boundary region were obviously making up the difference.

With the development of hot-spot theory (wherein places like Hawaii are seen as stationary and deeply derived volcanic penetrations of the moving plates) and of other refinements of data on vectors in the lithosphere, the history of the Pacific Plate became clearer. About three and a half million years ago, in the Pliocene Epoch, the direction in which it was moving changed about eleven degrees to the east. Why this happened is the subject of much debate and many papers, but if you look at the Hawaiian Hot Spot stitching the story into the plate, you see, at least, that it did happen: there is an eleven-degree bend at Pliocene Oahu.

The Pacific Plate, among present plates the world's largest, underlies about two-thirds of the Pacific Ocean. North-south, it is about eight thousand miles long, and east-west, it is about six thousand miles wide. What could cause it to turn? Various events that occurred roughly three and a half million years ago along the Pacific Plate margins have been nominated as the cause. For example, the Ontong-Java Plateau, an immense basaltic mass in the southwest Pacific Ocean, collided with the Solomon Islands, reversing a subduction zone (it is claimed) and jamming a huge slab of the Pacific Plate under the North Fiji Plateau. The slab broke off. Suddenly released from the terrific drag on its southwest corner, the rest of the great northbound plate turned eleven degrees to the northeast. A number of coincidental collisions along the plate's western margin may have contributed to the change in vector. Additional impetus may have been provided by the subduction of a defunct spreading center at the north end of the plate. The extra weight of the spreading center, descending, may have tugged at the plate and given it clockwise torque. Whatever the cause, it's not easy to imagine a vehicle that weighs 345 quadrillion tons suddenly swerving to the right, but evidently that is what it did.

The tectonic effect on North America was something like the deformation that results when two automobiles sideswipe. Between the Pacific and North American Plates, the basic motion along the San Andreas Fault remained strike-slip and parallel. But as the Pacific Plate sort of jammed its shoulder against most of California a component of compression was added. This resulted in thrust faults and accompanying folds—anticlines and synclines. (Petroleum migrated into the anticlines, rose into their domes, and was trapped.)

Earlier—about five million years before the present—the ocean spreading center known as the East Pacific Rise had propagated into North America at the Tropic of Cancer, splitting Baja off the rest of the continent and initiating the opening of the Gulf of California. (By coincidence, the walls of the Red Sea, which much resembles the Gulf of California, parted at the same time.) The splitting off of Baja was accompanied by very strong northward compression, which raised, among other things, the Transverse Ranges above Los Angeles, at the great bend of the San Andreas. That the Transverse Ranges were rising compressionally had been obvious to geologists long before plate tectonics identified the source of the compression. But not until the late 1980s did they come to see that compression as well as strike-slip motion accompanies the great fault throughout its length, as a result of the slight shift in the direction of the Pacific Plate three and a half million years ago. All these compressional aspects taken together—anticlines, synclines, and thrust faults in a wide swath from one end of California almost to the other—account for some of the missing motion in the San Andreas Discrepancy. The Los Angeles basin alone has been squeezed about a centimeter a year for two million two hundred thousand years. The sites of Laguna Beach and Pasadena are fourteen miles closer together than they were 2.2 million years ago. This has happened an earthquake at a time. For example, the Whittier Narrows earthquake of 1987 lessened the breadth of the Santa Monica Mountains and raised the ridgeline.

The Whittier Narrows hypocenter was in a deeply buried fault in a young anticline. Such faults tend to develop about ten miles down and gradually move toward the surface. Northward for five hundred miles, young anticlines on the east side of the San Andreas Fault are similar in nature—the products of deep successive earthquakes. Most are recently discovered, and many more, presumably, remain unknown. They make very acute angles with the fault, like the wake of a narrow boat. When a temblor goes off like a hidden grenade, geologists often have not suspected the existence of the fault that has moved. The 6.5 earthquake at Coalinga in 1983 was that kind of surprise. It increased the elevation of the ridge above it by more than two feet.

In 1892, a pair of enigmatic earthquakes shook Winters, which is near Davis, in the Great Central Valley. Evidently, the earthquakes occurred on the same sort of blind thrust that is under Coalinga, but the Winters thrust is of particular interest because it is east of the Coast Ranges and fifty miles from the San Andreas. Yet it is apparently a product of the newly discovered folding and faulting that everywhere shadow the great fault. The Central Valley of California is about the last place in the world where virtually any geologist would look for an Appalachian-style fold-and-thrust belt. Without shame, Moores sketches one on a map of California; it goes up the west side of the valley almost all the way from the Tehachapi Range to Red Bluff and reaches eastward as far as Davis. He and his Davis colleague Jeff Unruh have been out looking for tectonic folds in the surreally flat country surrounding the university. This is a game of buff even beyond the heightened senses of the blind. They have found an anticline—an arch with limbs spread wide for many miles and a summit twenty-five feet high. They call it the Davis Anticline. It is a part of what Moores likes to describe as "the Davis campus fold-and-thrust belt." He is having fun, but the folds are not fictions. The anticline at Davis has developed in the past hundred thousand years. It is rising ten times as fast as the Alps.

On perhaps the weirdest geologic field trip I have ever been invited to observe, he and Unruh went out one day looking for nascent mountains in the calm-water flatness of the valley. There were extremely subtle differentiations. Moores said, "We are looking here on the surface for something that is happening five kilometers down—blind thrusts. Compressional stress extends to the center of the valley."

"Topography doesn't happen for nothing," Unruh said. "Soil scientists have long recognized that these valley rises are tectonic uplifts. Soils are darker in basinal areas. There's a fault-propagation fold in this part of the valley."

Moores later wrote to me:

> We continue to gather evidence. We have seen two seismic profiles that show a horizontal reflection, presumably a fault, that extends all the way from the Coast Ranges to the Sacramento River. Jeff has been working at stream gradients. The rationale is that where there is a sharp change in gradient on a flood plain there is a reason, and the reason here is uplift. The analysis fits the two areas of acknowledged uplift west of Davis pretty well, and seems to indicate a new north-trending zone of uplift that goes right through Davis itself. Maybe there was a reason why the Patwin Indians selected this particular spot on the banks of Putah Creek for this village, after all. It was a high spot in a swamp, and it was high because it is coming up!

The compressive tectonism associated with the plate boundary contributes to the total relative plate motion, but not much: the overall average is less than a centimeter a year. And that does not nearly close the numerical gap. Surprisingly, the rest of the missing motion seems to come from the Basin and Range, the country between Reno and Salt Lake City, wherein the earth's crust has been stretching out and breaking into blocks, which float on the mantle as mountains. The stretching has increased the width of the region by sixty miles in a few million years. Very-long-baseline interferometry has shown that the Basin and Range is spreading about ten millimeters a year in a direction west-northwest. This supplies enough of the total plate-boundary motion between the Gulf of California and Cape Mendocino to make up the difference in the San Andreas Discrepancy. If some Pacific Plate motion is coming from Utah, Utah is part of the plate boundary.

The westernmost range of the Basin and Range Province is the Sierra Nevada, which has risen on a normal fault that runs along the eastern base of the mountains. The fault has experienced enough earth-quakes to give the mountains their exceptional altitude. The most recent great earthquake there was in 1872. In a few seconds, the mountain range went up three feet. In the same few seconds, the Sierra Nevada also moved north-northwest twenty feet. That would help to fill in anybody's discrepancy.

Sierra Nevada

A Wind-Storm
in the Forest

John Muir (1838–1914) came with his family from Scotland to Wisconsin when he was eleven. He traveled to California in 1868. In 1889 he began, with Robert Underwood Johnson, a campaign to establish a national park that would include the Yosemite Valley; as a result of their efforts the Yosemite, Sequoia, and General Grant National Parks were established. Muir's careful field journals became the basis of descriptive essays of the area, which in turn resulted in his first book, The Mountains of California *(1894), from which this depiction of a storm in the Yuba River Valley is taken.*

The mountain winds, like the dew and rain, sunshine and snow, are measured and bestowed with love on the forests to develop their strength and beauty. However restricted the scope of other forest influences, that of the winds is universal. The snow bends and trims the upper forests every winter, the lightning strikes a single tree here and there, while avalanches mow down thousands at a swoop as a gardener trims out a bed of flowers. But the winds go to every tree, fingering every leaf and branch and furrowed bole; not one is forgotten; the Mountain Pine towering with outstretched arms on the rugged buttresses of the icy peaks, the lowliest and most retiring tenant of the dell; they seek and find them all, caressing them tenderly, bending them in lusty exercise, stimulating their growth, plucking off a leaf or limb as required, or removing an entire tree or grove, now whispering and cooing through the branches like a sleepy child, now roaring like the ocean; the winds blessing the forests, the forests the winds, with ineffable beauty and harmony as the sure result.

After one has seen pines six feet in diameter bending like grasses before a mountain gale, and ever and anon some giant falling with a crash that shakes the hills, it seems astonishing that any, save the lowest thickset trees, could ever have found a period sufficiently stormless to establish themselves; or, once established, that they should not, sooner or later, have been blown down. But when the storm is over, and we behold the same forests tranquil again, towering fresh and unscathed in erect majesty, and consider what centuries of storms have fallen upon them since they were first planted,—hail, to break the tender seedlings; lightning, to scorch and shatter; snow, winds, and avalanches, to crush and overwhelm,—while the manifest result of all this wild storm-culture is the glorious perfection we behold; then faith in Nature's forestry is established, and we cease to deplore the violence of her most destructive gales, or of any other storm-implement whatsoever.

There are two trees in the Sierra forests that are never blown down, so long as they continue in sound health. These are the Juniper and the Dwarf Pine of the summit peaks. Their stiff, crooked roots grip the storm-beaten ledges like eagles' claws, while their lithe, cord-like branches bend round compliantly, offering but slight holds for winds, however violent. The other alpine conifers—the Needle Pine, Mountain Pine, Two-leaved Pine, and Hemlock Spruce—are never thinned out by this agent to any destructive extent, on account of their admirable toughness and the closeness of their growth. In general the same is true of the giants of the lower zones. The kingly Sugar Pine, towering aloft to a height of more than 200 feet, offers a fine mark to storm-winds; but it is not densely foliaged, and its long, horizontal arms swing round compliantly in the blast, like tresses of green, fluent algae in a brook; while the Silver Firs in most places keep their ranks well together in united strength. The Yellow or Silver Pine is more frequently overturned than any other tree on the Sierra, because its leaves and branches form a larger mass in proportion to its height, while in many places it is planted sparsely, leaving open lanes through which storms may enter with full force. Furthermore, because it is distributed along the lower portions of the range, which was the first to be left bare on the breaking up of the ice-sheet at the close of the glacial winter, the soil it is growing upon has been longer exposed to post-glacial weathering, and consequently it is in a more crumbling, decayed condition than the fresher soils farther up the range, and therefore offers a less secure anchorage for the roots.

While exploring the forest zones of Mount Shasta, I discovered the path of a hurricane strewn with thousands of pines of this species. Great and small had been uprooted or wrenched off by sheer force, making a clean gap, like that made by a snow avalanche. But hurricanes capable of doing this class of work are rare in the Sierra, and when we have explored the forests from one extremity of the range to the other, we are compelled to believe that they are the most beautiful on the face of the earth, however we may regard the agents that have made them so.

There is always something deeply exciting, not only in the sounds of winds in the woods, which exert more or less influence over every mind, but in their varied waterlike flow as manifested by the movements of the trees, especially those of the conifers. By no other trees are they rendered so extensively and impressively visible, not even by the lordly tropic palms or tree-ferns responsive to the gentlest breeze. The waving of a forest of the giant Sequoias is indescribably impressive and sublime, but the pines seem to me the best interpreters of winds. They are mighty waving goldenrods, ever in tune, singing and writing wind-music all their long century lives. Little, however, of this noble tree-waving and tree-music will you see or hear in the strictly alpine portion of the forests. The burly Juniper, whose girth sometimes more than equals its height, is about as rigid as the rocks on which it grows. The slender lash-like sprays of the Dwarf Pine stream out in wavering ripples, but the tallest and slenderest are far too unyielding to wave even in the heaviest gales. They only shake in quick, short vibrations. The Hemlock Spruce, however, and the Mountain Pine, and some of the tallest thickets of the Two-leaved species bow in storms with considerable scope and gracefulness. But it is only in the lower and middle zones that the meeting of winds and woods is to be seen in all its grandeur.

One of the most beautiful and exhilarating storms I ever enjoyed in the Sierra occurred in December 1874, when I happened to be exploring one of the tributary valleys of the Yuba River. The sky and the ground and the trees had been thoroughly rain-washed and were dry again. The day was intensely pure, one of those incomparable bits of California winter, warm and balmy and full of white sparkling sunshine, redolent of all the purest influences of the spring, and at the same time enlivened with one of the most bracing wind-storms conceivable. Instead of camping out, as I usually do, I then chanced to be stopping at the house of a friend. But when the storm began to sound, I lost no time in pushing out into the woods to enjoy it. For on such occasions nature has always something rare to show us, and the danger to life and limb is hardly greater than one would experience crouching deprecatingly beneath a roof.

It was still early morning when I found myself fairly adrift. Delicious sunshine came pouring over the hills, lighting the tops of the pines and setting free a stream of summery fragrance that contrasted strangely with the wild tones of the storm. The air was mottled with pine-tassels and bright green plumes, that went flashing past in the sunlight like birds pursued. But there was not the slightest dustiness, nothing less pure than leaves, and ripe pollen, and flecks of withered bracken and moss. I heard trees falling for hours at the rate of one every two or three minutes; some uprooted, partly on account of the loose, water-soaked condition of the ground; others broken straight across, where some weakness caused by fire had determined the spot. The gestures of the various trees made a delightful study. Young Sugar Pines, light and feathery as squirrel-tails, were bowing almost to the ground; while the grand old patriarchs, whose massive boles had been tried in a hundred storms, waved solemnly above them, their long, arching branches streaming fluently on the gale, and every needle thrilling and ringing and shedding off keen lances of light like a diamond. The Douglas Spruces, with long sprays drawn out in level tresses, and needles massed in a gray, shimmering flow, presented a most striking appearance as they stood in bold relief along the hilltops. The madroños in the dells, with their red bark and large glossy leaves tilted every way, reflected the sunshine in throbbing spangles like those one so often sees on the rippled surface of a glacier lake. But the Silver Pines were now the most impressively beautiful of all. Colossal spires 200 feet in height waved like supple goldenrods chanting and bowing low as if in worship, while the whole mass of their long, tremulous foliage was kindled into one continuous blaze of white sun-fire. The force of the gale was such that the most steadfast monarch of them all rocked down to its roots with a motion plainly perceptible when one leaned against it. Nature was holding high festival, and every fiber of the most rigid giants thrilled with glad excitement.

I drifted on through the midst of this passionate music and motion, across many a glen, from ridge to ridge; often halting in the lee of a rock for shelter, or to gaze and listen. Even when the grand anthem had swelled to its highest pitch, I could distinctly hear the varying tones of individual trees,—Spruce, and Fir, and Pine, and leafless Oak,—and even the infinitely gentle rustle of the withered grasses at my feet. Each was expressing itself in its own way,—singing its own song, and making its own peculiar gestures,—manifesting a richness of variety to be found in no other forest I have yet seen. The coniferous woods of Canada, and the Carolinas, and Florida, are made up of trees that resemble one another about as nearly as blades of grass, and grow close together in much the same way. Coniferous trees, in general, seldom possess individual character, such as is manifest among oaks and elms. But the

California forests are made up of a greater number of distinct species than any other in the world, And in them we find, not only a marked differentiation into special groups, but also a marked individuality in almost every tree, giving rise to storm-effects indescribably glorious.

Toward midday, after a long, tingling scramble through copses of hazel and ceanothus, I gained the summit of the highest ridge in the neighborhood, and then it occurred to me that it would be a fine thing to climb one of the trees to obtain a wider outlook and get my ear close to the Aeolian music of its top-most needles. But under the circumstances the choice of a tree was a serious matter. One whose instep was not very strong seemed in danger of being blown down, or of being struck by others in case they should fall; another was branchless to a considerable height above the ground, and at the same time too large to be grasped with arms and legs in climbing, while others were not favorably situated for clear views. After cautiously casting about, I made choice of the tallest of a group of Douglas Spruces that were growing close together like a tuft of grass, no one of which seemed likely to fall unless all the rest fell with it. Though comparatively young, they were about 100 feet high, and their lithe, brushy tops were rocking and swirling in wild ecstasy. Being accustomed to climb trees in making botanical studies, I experienced no difficulty in reaching the top of this one, and never before did I enjoy so noble an exhilaration of motion. The slender tops fairly flapped and swished in the passionate torrent, bending and swirling backward and forward, round and round, tracing indescribable combinations of vertical and horizontal curves, while I clung with muscles firm braced, like a bobolink on a reed.

In its widest sweeps my tree-top described an arc of from twenty to thirty degrees, but I felt sure of its elastic temper, having seen others of the same species still more severely tried—bent almost to the ground indeed, in heavy snows—without breaking a fiber. I was therefore safe, and free to take the wind into my pulses and enjoy the excited forest from my superb outlook. The view from here must be extremely beautiful in any weather. Now my eye roved over the piny hills and dales as over fields of waving grain, and felt the light running in ripples and broad swelling undulations across the alleys from ridge to ridge, as the shining foliage was stirred by corresponding waves of air. Oftentimes these waves of reflected light would break up suddenly into a kind of beaten foam, and again, after chasing one another in regular order, they would seem to bend forward in concentric curves, and disappear on some hillside, like sea-waves on a shelving shore. The quantity of light reflected from the bent needles was so great as to make whole groves appear as if covered with snow, while the black shadows beneath the trees greatly enhanced the effect of the silvery splendor.

Excepting only the shadows there was nothing somber in all this wild sea of pines. On the contrary, notwithstanding this was the winter season, the colors were remarkably beautiful. The shafts of the pine and libocedrus were brown and purple, and most of the foliage was well tinged with yellow; the laurel groves, with the pale undersides of their leaves turned upward, made masses of gray; and then there was many a dash of chocolate color from clumps of manzanita, and jet of vivid crimson from the bark of the madroños, while the ground on the hillsides, appearing here and there through openings between the groves, displayed masses of pale purple and brown.

The sounds of the storm corresponded gloriously with this wild exuberance of light and motion. The profound bass of the naked branches and boles booming like waterfalls; the quick, tense vibrations of the pine-needles, now rising to a shrill, whistling hiss, now falling to a silky murmur; the rustling of laurel groves in the dells, and the keen metallic click of leaf on leaf—all this was heard in easy analysis when the attention was calmly bent.

The varied gestures of the multitude were seen to fine advantage, so that one could recognize the different species at a distance of several miles by this means alone, as well as by their forms and colors, and the way they reflected the light. All seemed strong and comfortable, as if really enjoying the storm, while responding to its most enthusiastic greetings. We hear much nowadays concerning the universal struggle for existence, but no struggle in the common meaning of the word was manifest here; no recognition of danger by any tree; no deprecation but rather an invincible gladness as remote from exultation as from fear.

I kept my lofty perch for hours, frequently closing my eyes to enjoy the music by itself, or to feast quietly on the delicious fragrance that was streaming past. The fragrance of the woods was less marked than that produced during warm rain, when so many balsamic buds and leaves are steeped like tea; but, from the chafing of resiny branches against each other, and the incessant attrition of myriads of needles, the gale was spiced to a very tonic degree. And besides the fragrance from these local sources there were traces of scents brought from afar. For this wind came first from the sea, rubbing against its fresh, briny waves, then distilled through the redwoods, threading rich ferny gulches, and spreading itself in broad undulating currents over many a flower-enameled ridge of the coast mountains, then across the golden plains, up the purple foothills, and into these piny woods with the varied incense gathered by the way.

Winds are advertisements of all they touch, however much or little we may be able to read them, telling their wanderings even by their scents alone. Mariners detect the flowery perfume of land-winds far at sea, and sea-winds carry the fragrance of dulse and tangle far inland, where it is quickly recognized, though mingled with the scents of a thousand land-flowers. As an illustration of this, I may tell here that I breathed sea-air on the Firth of Forth, in Scotland, while a boy; then was taken to Wisconsin, where I remained nineteen years; then, without in all this time having breathed one breath of the sea, I walked quietly, alone, from the middle of the Mississippi Valley to the Gulf of Mexico, on a botanical excursion, and while in Florida, far from the coast, my attention wholly bent on the splendid tropical vegetation about me, I suddenly recognized a sea-breeze, as it came sifting through the palmettos and blooming vine-tangles, which at once awakened and set free a thousand dormant associations, and made me a boy again in Scotland, as if all the intervening years had been annihilated.

Most people like to look at mountain rivers, and bear them in mind; but few care to look at the winds, though far more beautiful and sublime, and though they become at times about as visible as flowing water. When the north winds in winter are making upward sweeps over the curving summits of the High Sierra, the fact is sometimes published with flying snow-banners a mile long. Those portions of the winds thus embodied can scarce be wholly invisible, even to the darkest imagination. And when we look around over an agitated forest, we may see something of the wind that stirs it, by its effects upon the trees. Yonder it descends in a rush of waterlike ripples, and sweeps over the bending pines from hill to hill. Nearer, we see detached plumes and leaves, now speeding by on level currents, now whirling in eddies, or, escaping over the edges of the whirls, soaring aloft on grand, upswelling domes of air, or tossing on flame-like crests. Smooth, deep currents, cascades, falls, and swirling eddies, sing around every tree and leaf, and over all the varied topography of the region with telling changes of form, like mountain rivers conforming to the features of their channels.

After tracing the Sierra streams from their fountains to the plains, marking where they bloom white in falls, glide in crystal plumes, surge gray and foam-filled in boulder-choked gorges, and slip through the woods in long, tranquil reaches—after thus learning their language and forms in detail, we may at length hear them chanting all together in one grand anthem, and comprehend them all in clear inner vision, covering the range like lace. But even this spectacle is far less sublime and not a whit more substantial than what we may behold of these storm-streams of air in the mountain woods.

We all travel the milky way together, trees and men; but it never occurred to me until this storm-day, while swinging in the wind, that trees are travelers, in the ordinary sense. They make many journeys, not extensive ones, it is true; but our own little journeys, away and back again, are only little more than tree-wavings—many of them not so much.

When the storm began to abate, I dismounted and sauntered down through the calming woods. The storm-tones died away, and, turning toward the east, I beheld the countless hosts of the forests hushed and tranquil, towering above one another on the slopes of the hills like a devout audience. The setting sun filled them with amber light, and seemed to say, while they listened, "My peace I give unto you."

As I gazed on the impressive scene, all the so-called ruin of the storm was forgotten, and never before did these noble woods appear so fresh, so joyous, so immortal.

Los Angeles

The Santa Ana

Joan Didion (b. 1934), a native of the Sacramento Valley, is an esteemed writer of essays and fiction, including the novels River Run *(1963) and* Play It as It Lays *(1970). She lived for many years in the Los Angeles area, and much of her nonfiction is about life there. This piece, originally published in the* Saturday Evening Post, *was collected in* Slouching Towards Bethlehem *(1968).*

There is something uneasy in the Los Angeles air this afternoon, some unnatural stillness, some tension. What it means is that tonight a Santa Ana will begin to blow, a hot wind from the northeast whining down through the Cajon and San Gorgonio Passes, blowing up sandstorms out along Route 66, drying the hills and the nerves to the flash point. For a few days now we will see smoke back in the canyons, and hear sirens in the night. I have neither heard nor read that a Santa Ana is due, but I know it, and almost everyone I have seen today knows it too. We know it because we feel it. The baby frets. The maid sulks. I rekindle a waning argument with the telephone company, then cut my losses and lie down, given over to whatever it is in the air. To live with the Santa Ana is to accept, consciously or unconsciously, a deeply mechanistic view of human behavior.

I recall being told, when I first moved to Los Angeles and was living on an isolated beach, that the Indians would throw themselves into the sea when the bad wind blew. I could see why. The Pacific turned ominously glossy during a Santa Ana period, and one woke in the night troubled not only by the peacocks screaming in the olive trees but by the eerie absence of surf. The heat was surreal. The sky had a yellow cast, the kind of light sometimes called "earthquake weather." My only neighbor would not come out of her house for days, and there were no lights at night, and her husband roamed the place with a machete. One day he would tell me that he had heard a trespasser, the next a rattlesnake.

"On nights like that," Raymond Chandler once wrote about the Santa Ana, "every booze party ends in a fight. Meek little wives feel the edge of the carving knife and study their husbands' necks. Anything can happen." That was the kind of wind it was. I did not know then that there was any basis for the effect it had on all of us, but it turns out to be another of those cases in which science bears out folk wisdom. The Santa Ana, which is named for one of the canyons it rushes through, is a *foehn* wind, like the *foehn* of Austria and Switzerland and the *hamsin* of Israel. There are a number of persistent malevolent winds, perhaps the best known of which are the mistral of France and the Mediterranean sirocco, but a *foehn* wind has distinct characteristics: it occurs on the leeward slope of a mountain range and, although the air begins as a cold mass, it is warmed as it comes down the mountain and appears finally as a hot dry wind. Whenever and wherever a *foehn* blows, doctors hear about headaches and nausea and allergies, about "nervousness," about "depression." In Los Angeles some teachers do not attempt to conduct formal classes during a Santa Ana, because the children become unmanageable. In Switzerland the suicide rate goes up during the *foehn*, and in the courts of some Swiss cantons the wind is considered a mitigating circumstance for crime. Surgeons are said to watch the wind, because blood does not clot normally during a *foehn*. A few years ago an Israeli physicist discovered that not only during such winds, but for the ten or twelve hours which precede them, the air carries an unusually high ratio of positive to negative ions. No one seems to know exactly why that should be; some talk about friction, and others suggest solar disturbances. In any case the positive ions are there, and what an excess of positive ions does, in the simplest terms, is make people unhappy. One cannot get much more mechanistic than that.

Easterners commonly complain that there is no "weather" at all in southern California, that the days and the seasons slip by relentlessly, numbingly bland. That is quite misleading. In fact the climate is characterized by infrequent but violent extremes; two periods of torrential subtropical rains which continue for weeks and wash out the hills and send subdivisions sliding toward the sea; about twenty scattered days a year of the Santa Ana, which, with its incendiary dryness, invariably means fire. At the first prediction of a Santa Ana, the Forest Service flies men and equipment from northern California into the southern forests, and the Los Angeles Fire Department cancels its ordinary non-firefighting routines. The Santa Ana caused Malibu to burn the way it did in 1956, and Bel Air in 1961, and Santa Barbara in 1964. In the winter of 1966–67 eleven men were killed fighting a Santa Ana fire that spread through the San Gabriel Mountains.

Just to watch the front-page news out of Los Angeles during a Santa Ana is to get very close to what it is about the place. The longest Santa Ana period in recent years was in 1957, and it lasted not the usual three or four days but fourteen days, from November 21 until December 4. On the first day 25,000 acres of the San Gabriel Mountains were burning, with gusts reaching 100 miles an hour. In town, the wind reached Force 12, or hurricane force, on the Beaufort Scale; oil derricks were toppled and people ordered off the downtown streets to avoid injury from flying objects. On November 22 the fire in the San Gabriels was out of control. On November 24 six people were killed in automobile accidents, and by the end of the week the *Los Angeles Times* was keeping a box score of traffic deaths. On November 26 a prominent Pasadena attorney, depressed about money, shot and killed his wife, their two sons, and himself. On November 27 a South Gate divorcee, twenty-two, was murdered and thrown from a moving car. On November 30 the San Gabriel fire was still out of control, and the wind in town was blowing eighty miles an hour. On the first day of December four people died violently, and on the third the wind began to break.

It is hard for people who have not lived in Los Angeles to realize how radically the Santa Ana figures in the local imagination. The city burning is Los Angeles's deepest image of itself; Nathanael West perceived that, in *The Day of the Locust*; and at the time of the 1965 Watts riots what struck the imagination most indelibly were the fires. For days one could drive the Harbor Freeway and see the city on fire, just as we had always known it would be in the end. Los Angeles weather is the weather of catastrophe, of apocalypse, and, just as the reliably long and bitter winters of New England determine the way life is lived there, so the violence and the unpredictability of the Santa Ana affect the entire quality of life in Los Angeles, accentuate its impermanence, its unreliability. The wind shows us how close to the edge we are.

Great Basin Desert

Nurslings of the Sky

Mary Austin (1868–1934) moved to California after graduating from college in Illinois in 1888, and soon moved to the high desert country of the Owens River Valley in Inyo County, between Death Valley and the eastern base of the Sierra Nevada. She would memorialize the region in her first and most endur-ing book (of thirty-five), The Land of Little Rain *(1903), in which this essay appeared.*

Choose a hill country for storms. There all the business of the weather is carried on above your horizon and loses its terror in familiarity. When you come to think about it, the disastrous storms are on the levels, sea or sand or plains. There you get only a hint of what is about to happen, the fume of the gods rising from their meet-ing place under the rim of the world; and when it breaks upon you there is no stay nor shelter. The terrible mewings and mouthings of a Kansas wind have the added terror of viewlessness. You are lapped in them like uprooted grass; suspect them of a personal grudge. But the storms of hill countries have other business. They scoop watercourses, mature the pines, twist them to a finer fibre, fit the firs to be masts and spars, and, if you keep reasonably out of the track of their affairs, do you no harm.

They have habits to be learned, appointed paths, seasons, and warnings, and they leave you no doubt about their performances. One who builds his house on a waterscar on the rubble of a steep slope must take chances. So they did in Overtown who built in the wash of Argus water, and at Kearsarge at the foot of a deep, treeless swale. After twenty years Argus water rose in the wash against the frail houses, and the piled snows of Kearsarge slid down at a thunder peal over the cabins and the camp, but you could conceive that it was the fault of neither the water nor the snow.

The first effect of cloud study is a sense of presence and intention in storm processes. Weather does not happen. It is the visible manifestation of the Spirit moving itself in the void. It gathers itself together under the heavens; rains, snows, yearns mightily in wind, smiles; and the Weather Bureau, situated advantageously for that very business, taps the record on his instruments and going out on the street denies his God, not having gathered the sense of what he has seen. Hardly anybody takes account of the fact that John Muir, who knows more of mountain storms than any other, is a devout man.

Of the high Sierras choose the neighborhood of splintered peaks about the Kern and Kings river divide for storm study, or the short, wide-mouthed cañons opening eastward on high valleys. Days when the hollows are steeped in a warm, winey flood the clouds came walking on the floor of heaven, flat and pearly gray beneath, rounded and pearly white above. They gather flock-wise, moving on the level currents that roll about the peaks, lock hands and settle with the cooler air, drawing a veil about those places where they do their work. If their meeting or parting takes place at sunrise or sunset, as it often does, one gets the splendor of the apocalypse. There will be cloud pillars miles high, snow-capped, glorified, and preserving an orderly perspective before the unbarred door of the sun, or perhaps more ghosts of clouds that dance to some pied piper of an unfelt wind. But be it day or night, once they have settled to their work, one sees from the valley only the blank wall of their tents stretched along the ranges. To get the real effect of a mountain storm you must be inside.

One who goes often into a hill country learns not to say: What if it should rain? It always does rain somewhere among the peaks; the unusual thing is that one should escape it. You might suppose that if you took any account of plant contrivances to save their pollen powder against showers. Note how many there are deep-throated and bell-flowered like the penstemons, how many have nodding pedicels as the columbine, how many grow in copse shelters and grow there only. There is keen delight in the quick showers of summer cañons, with the added comfort, born of experience, of knowing that no harm comes of a wetting at high altitudes. The day is warm; a white cloud spies over the cañon wall, slips up behind the ridge to cross it by some windy pass, obscures your sun. Next you hear the rain drum on the broad-leaved hellebore, and beat down the mimulus beside the brook. You shelter on the lee of some strong pine with shut-winged butterflies and merry, fiddling creatures of the wood. Runnels of rainwater from the glacier-slips swirl through the pine needles into rivulets; the streams froth and rise in their banks. The sky is white with cloud; the sky is gray with rain; the sky is clear. The summer showers leave no wake.

Such as these follow each other day by day for weeks in August weather. Sometimes they chill suddenly into wet snow that packs about the lake gardens clear to the blossom frills, and melts away harmlessly. Sometimes one has the good fortune from a heather-grown headland to watch a rain-cloud forming in mid-air. Out over meadow or lake region begins a little darkling of the sky—no cloud, no wind, just a smokiness such as spirits materialize from in witch stories.

It rays out and draws to it some floating films from secret cañons. Rain begins, "slow dropping veil of thinnest lawn"; a wind comes up and drives the formless thing across a meadow, or a dull lake pitted by the glancing drops, dissolving as it drives. Such rains relieve like tears.

The same season brings the rains that have work to do, ploughing storms that alter the face of things. These come with thunder and the play of live fire along the rocks. They come with great winds that try the pines for their work upon the seas and strike out the unfit. They shake down the avalanches of splinters from sky-line pinnacles and raise up sudden floods like battle fronts in the cañons against towns, trees, and boulders. They would be kind if they could, but have more important matters. Such storms, called cloud-bursts by the country folk, are not rain, rather the spillings of Thor's cup, jarred by the Thunderer. After such a one the water that comes up in the village hydrants miles away is white with forced bubbles from the wind-tormented streams.

All that storms do to the face of the earth you may read in the geographies, but not what they do to our contemporaries. I remember one night of thunderous rain made unendurably mournful by the houseless cry of a cougar whose lair, and perhaps his family, had been buried under a slide of broken boulders on the slope of Kearsarge. We had heard the heavy detonation of the slide about the hour of the alpenglow, a pale rosy interval in a darkling air, and judged he must have come from hunting to the ruined cliff and paced the night out before it, crying a very human woe. I remember, too, in that same season of storms, a lake made milky white for days, and crowded out of its bed by clay washed into it by a fury of rain, with the trout floating in it belly up, stunned by the shock of the sudden flood. But there were trout enough for what was left of the lake next year, and the beginning of a meadow about its upper rim. What taxed me most in the wreck of one of my favorite cañons by cloud-burst was to see a bobcat mother mouthing her drowned kittens in the ruined lair built in the wash, far above the limit of accustomed waters, but not far enough for the unexpected. After a time you get the point of view of gods about these things to save you from being too pitiful.

The great snows that come at the beginning of winter, before there is yet any snow except the perpetual high banks, are best worth while to watch. These come often before the late bloomers are gone and while the migratory birds are still in the piney wood. Down in the valley you see little but the flocking of blackbirds in the streets, or the low flight of mallards over the tulares, and the gathering of clouds behind Williamson. First there is a waiting stillness in the wood; the pine-trees creak although there is no wind, the sky glowers, the first rock by the water borders. The noise of the creek rises insistently and falls off a full note like a child abashed by sudden silence in the room. This changing of the stream tone following tardily the changes of the sun on melting snows is most meaningful of wood notes. After it runs a little trumpeter wind to cry the wild creatures to their holes. Sometimes the warning hangs in the air for days with increasing stillness. Only Clark's crow and the strident jays make light of it; only they can afford to. The cattle get down to the foothills and ground-inhabiting creatures make fast their doors. It grows chill, blind clouds fumble in the cañons; there will be a roll of thunder, perhaps, or a flurry of rain, but mostly the snow is born in the air with quietness and the sense of strong white piñons softly stirred. It increases, is wet and clogging, and makes a white night of midday.

There is seldom any wind with first snows, more often rain, but later, when there is already a smooth foot or two over all the slopes, the drifts begin. The late snows are fine and dry, mere ice granules at the wind's will. Keen mornings after a storm they are blown out in wreaths and banners from the high ridges sifting into the cañons.

Once in a year or so we have a "big snow." The cloud tents are widened out to shut in the valley and an outlying range or two and are drawn tight against the sun. Such a storm begins warm, with a dry white mist that fills and fills between the ridges, and the air is thick with form-less groaning. Now for days you get a hint of the neighboring ranges until the snows begin to lighten and some shouldering peak lifts through a rent. Mornings after the heavy snows are steely blue, two-edged with cold, divinely fresh and still, and these are times to go up to the pine borders. There you may find floundering in the unstable drifts "tainted wethers" of the wild sheep, faint from age and hunger; easy prey. Even the deer make slow going in the thick fresh snow, and once we found a wolverine going blind and feebly in the white glare.

No tree takes the snow stress with such ease as the silver fir. The star-whorled, fan-spread branches droop under the soft wreaths—

droop and press flatly to the trunk; presently the point of overloading is reached, there is a soft sough and muffled drooping, the boughs recover, and the weighting goes on until the drifts have reached the midmost whorls and covered up the branches. When the snows are particularly wet and heavy they spread over the young firs in green-ribbed tents wherein harbor winter loving birds.

All storms of desert hills, except wind storms, are impotent. East and west of the Sierras they rise in nearly parallel ranges, desertward, and no rain breaks over them, except from some far-strayed cloud or roving wind from the California Gulf, and these only in winter. In summer the sky travails with thunderings and the flare of sheet lightnings to win a few blistering big drops, and once in a lifetime the chance of a torrent. But you have not known what force resides in the mindless things until you have known a desert wind. One expects it at the turn of the two seasons, wet and dry, with electrified tense nerves. Along the edge of the mesa there it drops off to the valley, dust devils begin to rise white and steady, fanning out at the top like the genii out of the fisherman's bottle. One supposes the Indians might have learned the use of smoke signals from these dust pillars as they learn most things direct from the tutelage of the earth. The air begins to move fluently, blowing hot and cold between the ranges. Far south rises a murk of sand against the sky; it grows, the wind shakes itself, and has a smell of earth. The cloud of small dust takes on the color of gold and shuts out the neighborhood, the push of the wind is unsparing. Only man of all folk is foolish enough to stir abroad in it. But being in a house is really much worse; no relief from the dust, and a great fear of the creaking timbers. There is no looking ahead in such a wind, and the bite of the small sharp sand on exposed skin is keener than any insect sting. One might sleep, for the lapping of the wind wears one to the point of exhaustion very soon, but there is dread, in open sand stretches sometimes justified, of being over blown by the drift. It is hot, dry, fretful work, but by going along the ground with the wind behind, one may come upon strange things in its tumultuous privacy. I like these truces of wind and heat that the desert makes, otherwise I do not know how I should come by so many acquaintances with furtive folk. I like to see hawks sitting daunted in shallow holes, not daring to spread a feather, and doves in a row by the prickle-bushes, and shut-eyed cattle, turned tail to the wind in a patient doze. I like the smother of sand among the dunes, and finding small coiled snakes in open places, but I never like to come in a wind upon the silly sheep. The wind robs them of what wit they had, and they seem never to have learned the self-induced hypnotic stupor with which most wild things endure weather stress. I have never heard that the desert winds brought harm to any other than the wandering shepherds and their flocks. Once below Pastaria Little Pete showed me bones sticking out of the sand where a flock of two hundred had been smothered in a bygone wind. In many places the four-foot posts of a cattle fence had been buried by the wind-blown dunes.

It is enough occupation, when no storm is brewing, to watch the cloud currents and the chambers of the sky. From Kearsarge, say, you look over Inyo and find pink soft cloud masses asleep on the level desert air; south of you hurries a white troop late to some gathering of their kind at the back of Oppapago; nosing the foot of Waban, a woolly mist creeps south. In the clean, smooth paths of the middle sky and highest up in air, drift, unshepherded, small flocks ranging contrarily. You will find the proper names of these things in the reports of the Weather Bureau—cirrus, cumulus, and the like—and charts that will teach by study when to sow and take up crops. It is astonishing the trouble men will be at to find out when to plant potatoes, and gloze over the eternal meaning of the skies. You have to beat out for yourself many mornings on the windy headlands the sense of the fact that you get the same rainbow in the cloud drift over Waban and the spray of your garden hose. And not necessarily then do you live up to it.

Santa Barbara

The Storm

Jane Hollister Wheelwright (b. 1905) wrote about growing up on the historic 39,000-acre Hollister Ranch, a land of mountains, mesas, arroyos, and seacoast in Santa Barbara County, in The Ranch Papers: A California Memoir *(1988). She and her daughter, Lynda Wheelwright Schmidt, both of whom were Jungian analysts, collaborated on* The Long Shore: A Psychological Experience of the Wilderness *(1991).*

A deluge during the night made planning for the day useless. By morning two inches of rain had fallen; as the forecast had pre dicted, a two-inch sheet of water laid out on 39,000 acres. In the middle of the morning, over leisurely cups of coffee, I thought of my good luck the day before in escaping back to the ranch in mid-afternoon despite the prevailing dark and forbidding mood. I also relished revisioning the scene encountered on the way, especially the Mexican cattle gathered on the mesas in all their odd shapes and colors—many more than in the early morning. Some of them were milling in bunches on the road in continuous restless movements. Others seemed even more vigorous than in the morning: now grabbing at food on the trot, rudely pulling grass up by the roots and quickly, neatly, nibbling yellow mustard flowers. They were demonstrating what had happened to the yellow effect on the range that year. Individual animals taking their stand on the road held their own against me, making butting gestures at the car.

The last of the cattle from high back country over the home canyon poured down the precipitous fronting hills, high tailing it through the heavy sage, kicking, jumping, sliding. Like the others in the early morning they were wildly, dangerously playful. They were also moving to the mesas where the great blue herons had gone the day before in anticipation of rain. These birds always knew; they were truly reliable weather forecasters.

In the night, rain and wind slapped against the board and batten of the superintendent's little house. The eucalyptus over our heads whirled round in violent, erratic, mad dances. Distant breakers and still more distant thunder added to the confusion. Rain, wind, and breakers combined their fury in a roaring turmoil throughout the night. There was some comfort in this pandemonium, for without a doubt it ensured a good year of plenty for beasts, plants, and man.

Listening to the storm gave me time to reminisce about our seacoast. The breakers, whatever their intensity, are indicators of the state of things. They also convey messages from distant lands—taking up the pressures from foreign storms thousands of miles away to spend them against our cliffs. The ocean limits the surrounding elements with its one mighty voice. So alive, it is like a faithful companion, a protector in the night. The power of the moon, too, had been reflected in the wide tidal swings.

That night, violence was only a variation on the theme—the ocean's other side. It comforted me in my snug hideout, promoting sleep.

The rain finally ceased by daybreak. But the minus tide would not turn from its extra high until late morning, so there was no use venturing out. The superintendent advised against a ride because the horse could never make it on the soaked trails. Reluctant to offer advice, he said in a near whisper: "Let the ground settle itself down a bit before riding to the beach." The ground had a life of its own? A familiar note—animism perhaps—but it seemed more like the natural feeling of a man intimate with the place.

Later in the day, being impatient, I had decided to go ahead on horseback and find out what he meant. The oozing ground, swollen and shifting in the saturating water, was treacherously undermined. Old Roan slipped and slid, his feet going in four directions at times. It was strange to see a horse so helpless. The old feelings of terra firma, the solid reliability taken for granted, all that one associates with the ground underfoot, were no more. There were no little islands of safety. That was my first conscious encounter with hostile land. It reminded me of bottomless bogs and quicksand experienced long ago in small estuaries formed by our larger creeks. I looked back with more awareness to the day our Indian pony sank to her belly, my brother and I hauling on the reins, forcing her to fight her way out. We were too young to fully grasp the horror of that predicament.

I could not remember having experienced a quarter of a mile like this—and it was all because I wanted a safe ride on the beach. The earth clung in masses to my shoes, sticking in heavy lumps of adobe we called "gumbo mud." I nearly gave up.

The ocean was not much more inviting. It churned and swirled and reared. Muddy runoff had turned it to a light dull brown. Mud still flowed from every stream, out of every culvert and indentation in the land. It streamed out of scalloped crests topping the banks as hundreds of tiny streams seeped down their fronts.

A broad continuous band of yellow foamed as breakers and swells piled up. There was not a square inch of quiet water anywhere; the tide had turned only because the tide book said it would. Nevertheless there was a thin telltale strip of raised sand, no longer reached by the waves. Storm pressures were still driving up the water. In all this turmoil, the small snipe scuttled along the ebb of the surf, scratching whatever was left exposed, hustling just out of reach of the incoming waves. A natural law was in control; they were tiny atoms of order within the unruly, law-breaking elements.

To the west the sky was heavy gray with ominous black masses of clouds directly in the line of our progress. A cold and wettish wind came from that quarter like a spear thrust. Was a second storm brewing? Better not think about it. There was the blue sky to the south and east, which promoted wishful thinking for one bent on a long ride.

White cotton clouds hovered over the range, but they were rolled back on themselves by the wind. Down the coast, eastward and as far as the rounded green hills of the Alegria Canyon, the background was gray and almost blotted out. The perfect, almost rounded hilltops that always so pleased the senses now stood out sharply green against the gray.

Earlier storms had denuded the beach at the headlands. There was nothing but rock underfoot, and the deluge of the night before had scraped them clean. The exposed ledge, which extended from the high yellow earth banks until it dipped out of sight in the wild water, had a curious, chipped look, as though leveled off by chisel strokes. Centuries of wave action had done that.

Old Roan preferred the ledge to the sand dune, into which he tended to sink. He sniffed suspiciously at the smaller deposits in the rock. With frank disapproval he cleared them in wide, unexpected lunges. He spooked at the tiny earth slides from above and shied at every insignificant pebble rolling down the bank. He had a special distaste for the minute cave-ins on the small sandy banks of streams traversing the beach. His jumping and snorting finally got to me, infecting me with uneasy feelings and foreboding. The horse seemed particularly focused on something in the high, saturated cliffs. He continually pulled away from them. Landslides? Strangely he did not fuss at all at the piles of debris and mounds of kelp on the shining, slippery rock underfoot, nor did he mind the splashing waves.

Old Roan never stopped trying to double back for home and get out of the situation. He had more sense that I, who exerted all possible pressure to keep him moving forward. On hindsight, I am sure he was wary of the black horizon that should have been disturbing me.

Around the next headland, and past more rock ledges, we edged along a narrow pass against the bank where the waves were still smashing at the bits of white sand that were left there. Underfoot it was soft but not impassable; but Old Roan only snorted louder than ever.

Suddenly, the cold wind in our faces doubled in force, and with no warning clouds blacked out the sun and everything around us. Single fat raindrops fell in the bitter stinging cold, and then came the downpour. My mackintosh, which was made for fishing, not riding, only came to my knees. The horse slowed to a standstill in spite of my forcing. We endured for some minutes—then somehow the rain was no longer wet. It had turned into large hailstones that bounced off both of us.

Pandemonium hit the breakers. The streams of water flowing out of banks swelled to twice what they had been, new ones broke out everywhere and from places never before even associated with water. Breakers darkened into deep brown with the mud. The earth, rocks, water, and mud broke loose as though there were no moorings left in the world. Over it all were the wild cries of shorebirds. The drenching continued, intermittently relieved by hail. My shoes filled with water and my jeans were soaked from the knees down. The horse dripped water; his ears drooped dejectedly.

There was one alternative to our predicament: turn back and try to reach home. But I was not in my right mind; this was perhaps my last chance to face out a storm—to indulge in what few people ever feel anymore.

Horses in pasture back their rumps into a storm when it drives too hard; it is warmer that way. It was, and Old Roan calmed down a little. We hugged the bank to escape the whipping wind despite the eerie sense that something high up should not be trusted. Old Roan's suspicious behavior had undermined me—or possibly my own sensitivity was sharpening. Without the slightest warning a torrent broke out at our feet where it didn't belong. Old Roan recoiled and so did I. A long, wide, solid streak rushed across the clean gray sand into the yellow ocean foam. That kind of mud contamination of the ocean and beach confuses a lifelong sense of difference between sand and earth, in spite of their common origin.

We would have done better on the sheltered side of the next headland. Where we stood was too much in line with the gale, but to move at all was arduous. The horse seemed to agree with me; it was better to stay put, in spite of the beating.

The wait gave me time to register a mixture of feelings. There was first the foolish one for not having noted the black warnings in the west; but over and above that was the exhilaration that came from bearing out the crisis to its end. To be undefeated—so far—felt good. The sense of having endured in so wild a situation made me part of nature, part of life. It was a chance to look out at nature from inside her. It was reassuring, too, to find out once more that a bitter cold soaking does no real harm. I was able also to forget for a while the endless manmade devices in one's daily city life that are designed to prevent one from being fully alive. Overall was the need to experience the violence of the wild once more, perhaps for the last time, and, if possible, take at least some of it with me.

The drenching may have lasted half an hour and was followed, again with no warning, by a blazing hot, glaring sun. The shorebirds, particularly the killdeer and the willets, which had been screeching throughout the squall, were suddenly silenced. A solitary great blue heron still faced the direction of the storm, but this time with his neck pulled in. Snipe flew low over the foam. Many tiny beach flies stung me. The impact of their minute, solid bodies had the force of hailstones. They swarmed out of nowhere to be in the hot sun that was playing on the steaming banks.

From time to time black clouds gathered threateningly to the west, announced by alarmed cries of the birds. Now that the storm had subsided, I could look around, and the wetting no longer mattered because of the heat.

Red-winged blackbirds were already dotting the sand. They were out of place, like the vultures I had seen once on the beach at La Paz. Their conspicuous markings and shrub-loving characteristics did not fit that setting. They were like people flocking to the beach on an unexpectedly sunny day in winter. The glistening green-black birds, with their startling red wing spots edged in yellow, sang ineffectually and incongruously against the breakers. Their songs were an odd contrast to the killdeer alarums—thin and shrill, synchronized and percussive. White gulls were flying low over my head in a slow, relaxed, orderly formation, enjoying the hot sun and the sudden quiet.

It was already past noon. In the east, great white clouds followed in force. One dark rain cloud, apparently in the process of releasing some of its load, loomed up again in the west like a gigantic hand. The thick wrist rose on the horizon and the fingers reached into the clear blue sky. It was the mysterious signal to Elijah: "*Behold, there ariseth a little cloud out of the sea like unto a man's hand. The heaven was black with clouds and wind, and there was a great rain.*" We were directly in its path yet still in the hot sun. The atmosphere was clear, the visibility nearly perfect. Like a magnet the clarity of the air drew close what was around us—the oil platform stood out clearly. Visibility also heralds a storm; yet what about the thorough scrubbing we had just had!

Beyond the San Augustine Canyon's cove, the headland had melted into a confusion of yellow earth—into shifts and slides loosened by the saturating water. One mass that had slipped was still leaning on the cliff face. Caves, cracks, and holes opened high up in the precarious jumble. Piles of earth were strewn over the sand. Old bench marks from ancient ocean levels on the cliff still barely showed. Much of the coastline had been chewed off and washed out to sea. All in all, as on land, it gave off a sense of impermanence and insecurity.

Old familiar sand dunes normally piled high against banks and cliffs were gone, leaving only small sand deposits here and there in crevices and corners out of reach of the onslaught of waves. The cement flume for the pipes laid out to sea for oil and gas was exposed, forming a barrier across the beach. Two days earlier it had been out of sight, submerged.

Flocks of godwit, their light brown color warm in the sun against the white and gray of the other birds, were maneuvering on the beach. The warm color tucked under their brown wings blazed into red when they flew. Cousins of the curlew, they stalked around like miniature storks with their necks pulled in.

We continued on up the beach in the direction of Point Conception nearly as far as Little Cojo Cove. Large rocks stuck out of the sand and shallow water in a strange wild alignment. Old Roan once more sniffed and snorted and tried to turn back. His fear unnerved me. The minus tide, by now receded to its low ebb, left the tall, glistening black rocks boldly silhouetted. No longer just the remains of an ancient submerged rock stratum, they seemed to fulfill a mysterious purpose. Black shapes, strangely reminiscent of the eerie menhirs of Brittany, jutted from the flattened breakers. Ocean water churned white at their bases. The largest rock of all, a boulder, was set apart from the series. It barely surfaced, its bald top glistening. To this Old Roan said no, and he circled around it warily, snorting loudly. He would not be forced. For such a stable, sensible horse, his fear and distrust of the rock surprised me. But I was sympathetic—it was indeed the head of a submerged monster.

Looking for giant limpets I dismounted and examined another rock in the shallow water. I had to reach the rock in the infrequent intervals between the biggest waves. Climbing up, holding the reins with my free hand, I caught several limpets before they clamped down with their forty-pound thrust. The knapsack for the shells somehow had to be kept from falling into the water. It was a balancing stunt on the slippery surface, made more so by thousands of tiny jets of water from sea anemones. There was always the danger of being washed off. The suspicious roan knew I was out of my head. His complaints were continuous. Each breaking wave sent him swinging round and round the rock. The deep water splashed over most of the rock and welled up to his cinch band. He could have reared, falling back on his reins, and broken free, leaving me to walk the seven miles home.

But by then we had both had enough. As we set out for home, relief showed in every movement of my horse. His ears pricked forward and there was a spring in his gait. His anticipation of home promised a long, peaceful journey for me. My only concern lay in the threat from the black cloud looming in the distance and moving toward us. The visibility again increased suddenly. Small details in the superstructure of the oil platform brightened. Out at sea, a freighter's bow and stern were visible. Its middle section appeared as though it were below the water, meaning the ship was beyond the horizon.

The rain cloud to the west came inexorably toward us, but, by some undeserved luck, it came only as far as the breaker line at our feet and then quickly veered back out to sea. It swung back and forth a second and a third time. Its abortive charges gave me, finally, some feeling of community.

The willets refused to fly away unless we came right up to them. They seemed only mildly afraid of us. In flight they revealed striking black and white markings—broad black velvet appliqued to a background of white. The few times they left the sand they flew in long sweeps over the breakers and came in to land not far in front of us. They always kept in the same flight pattern. Finally, at the end of the cove, they doubled back and settled in peace behind us.

At three, and right on time, I heard the familiar relaxed jiggedy-jog of the orange-colored train, "The Daylight," as it slipped over the rail joints. When it came into sight without the usual fanfare and fuss, it looked caught by surprise. Its engine sounded a very long dragged-out "Ooo-oo" at each crossing. It chugged along languidly for a crack train; it seemed to belong there, and did not jar the feeling of the coast in the slightest. The noises it made recalled my childhood when we had no other way of telling time, and the sound of a whistle in the distance meant we were hopelessly late for lunch.

Puffy mounds of pure white foam, left by the outgoing tide, skidded slightly on the wet sand as we approached the home canyon. But behind us, our constant companion was the great black hand of rain, looming against the surrounding sky of clear bright blue. Its wrist still resting on the western horizon, the long, dark fingers of the hand now stretched directly overhead, angling across and far down the coast in the high wind. Out at sea, rain fell at intervals in dark, thick, slanting streaks from the cloud's fingers.

The afternoon sun was low in the west, lighting up the mist upon rows of churning breakers, like charging herds of phantom horses, their manes flowing in the wind. The mist had refracted the light in a way that intensified and magnified everything. The softening effect of the mist enhanced the brilliant green of the long, thin fringe of grass topping the cliffs and banks.

Over to the east, there were a few low-lying black and troubled clouds. The hand never left us. Overhead its fingers continued to stretch from out of the west and veer seaward. Far out to sea, a few clouds, lit by the sun, piled up gracefully like miniature castles and small towers. The shapes were delicate whirlwinds that pirouetted; otherwise, the sky was cloudless. Dark green seaweed showed in the minus tide, and streamers of green brightened the brown kelp. The sparkling foam bubbled and popped on the sand as the sun lowered almost to the sea's horizon. The foam scudded a bit in the slight wind; some of it slid out on the tide. In it were yellow and pink and green lights that shone like diamonds.

By five o'clock it was quiet enough to hear the small birds in the brush on the low banks. Only the breakers stirred. All else was serene in the long shadows. The horizontal evening light brought out the white of the churning water, making it glow in the mist that was blown out to sea from the turmoil.

Big shorebirds were very much in evidence. Waiting as though performing a stately dance, they jutted their necks out and back like East Indian dancers. Among them were round-bodied black turnstones, black and white with long black vests. The little snipe, shining white and no longer so drab as they had appeared in the stormy overcast, were busy pecking their supper.

Creeks tumbled out of the large culverts under the track's right-of-way. By then I was walking to get the stiffness out of my bones, so in order to cross and stay dry I had to remount Old Roan each time we came to a stream. My saddle was weighted down with a sack of abalone shells, and my knapsack had to be treated gently, because it was full of frail shells. With my stiffness, mounting became a chore. After the first sprightly move toward home, Old Roan resumed his jumping each time a pebble rolled down the cliff. He grunted at the few tiny mudballs and cave-ins made by the streams rushing across the sand to meet the incoming tide. At each crossing he lowered his muzzle, sniffed at the water, groaned, and sighed miserably. But as yet, no complaints about the ocean. Apparently he was not going to forgive me for the morning's huddle against the cliff.

One last look to the west in the path of the setting sun revealed miles of churning breakers, their mist and foam lifted high. It was a lovely vista, tender and luminous, and infinite. The broad band of moving white water along the breaker line swept gracefully with the curve of the coast. It extended all the way to the sun, which now rested on the water. Breaker beyond breaker beyond breaker were topped, softened and lighted.

We were ushered around the last headland by the few remaining rays of the sun not yet lost to the sea's depths. They were exactly at the point of being cut off by the horizon, but in the last moment the rays lit the small, smooth pebbles scattered over the wet sand, making each one a tiny lantern in the black. The shore was carpeted with softly glowing lights, like those of fireflies.

It was dark on land where we climbed up at the home canyon. The big clouds behind the sentinel hills of the Bulito were a mysterious smoke color. They were massed and softened at first sight, and rounded. In no time, they took on something of the seashells below them, more salmon than pink.

It was hard to let go of the sight in order to open the stiff gate at the tracks, but I had to hurry because black night was about to descend. Twilight is very brief at this latitude.

A last look at the sea was barely possible but essential. The familiar abalone colors had surfaced and the sea had calmed. It was as though it were content at last to be put to bed by night.

The drama that was there that day was something to talk about; yet, paradoxically, there was a stronger need to be silent. It was too personal a matter to discuss, and the others sensed this when I reached the house. The superintendent merely said, "We thought about you during the cloudburst." No questions were asked. They somehow knew the experience on the beach was part of a personal farewell to the land of my beginning.

Santa Barbara

After the Fire

Margaret Millar (1914–1994) was one of the premier suspense writers of her day. She was also an active environmentalist, and the author of a nonfiction paean to birding, The Birds and the Beasts Were There *(1967), which contains this description of the aftermath of the devastating Coyote fire in the hills above Santa Barbara.*

Fire . . . is a natural condition of life in the chaparral regions of southern California, and an essential condition if vegetation is to remain young and vigorous. Without an occasional clearing out, the underbrush gets so thick and high that deer and other mammals can't penetrate it and ground-dwelling birds have trouble foraging. When this happens the chaparral, normally rich in wildlife, becomes incapable of supporting its usual share. Fire occurring at twenty- to twenty-five-year intervals is a benefit, a cleaning-out of dead and diseased wood and groundcover. (Before any nature lover sets off into the hills with a pack of matches, it should be noted that more frequent fires result in the destruction of chaparral, and its conversion to a different and less interesting type of vegetation.)

Some forty or more plant species are grouped together under the name chaparral. Chaparral is the Spanish word for scrub oak; it also means a short, stocky person, and perhaps this gives, to someone who has never seen it, a better idea of chaparral. Chaparral is short, stocky, tough vegetation, capable of withstanding a yearly drought of six months or more.

Throughout the centuries a number of ways have evolved for chaparral plants to survive burning. Some, like green-bark ceanothus, sprout new leaves directly from the "dead" stumps. Some have woody crowns or burls at ground level, like toyon, or underground, like Eastwood manzanita, which is back to full size in a few years. Others have seeds with a hard coat that must be split open by fire, or else soft-coated seeds which need very high temperatures to trigger their internal chemistry. Among the plants with seeds requiring fire in order to germinate are some of the most dominant and important in the chaparral group of this region—chamise, big berry manzanita, laurel sumac, hoary leaf ceanothus, big pod ceanothus, sugar bush, and lemonade bush. All but chamise are frequently used in cultivated gardens.

After the Coyote fire I hiked around the burned areas, observing as a bird watcher, not a botanist. But I couldn't help noticing that greenery started to reappear almost as soon as the earth had cooled. This applied especially to a certain vine, rather similar to a grapevine, which spread along the ground, as lush a green as ever graced a rain forest, and wrapped its tendrils around the blackened stumps of trees and shrubs. This was chilicothe, or wild cucumber. Its appearance had been neither delayed nor hastened by the fire, by the rain that followed, or by any external circumstances at all. When its cycle of growth was ready to begin again, it began: everything necessary for the complete process— leaves, flowers, fruit, seeds—was contained in a giant tuber buried underground.

An example of the chilocothe's self-containment and independence of the outside world was accidentally provided by the local Botanic Garden. To show the public the size of the tubers, one weighing about fifty pounds was dug up and placed in the information center. At Christmas time it started sprouting, and within the next few weeks it went through its entire growth cycle while in a display case. Again the following year, still in the display case, it grew leaves and tendrils, it flowered and fruited and went to seed. It was only during this second cycle that the tuber becomes noticeably smaller and wrinkled as its water content decreased.

The emergence of the chilicothe was unimportant as far as food or shelter for wildlife was concerned. Yet it appeared to be a signal for the forest to come alive again. After a December rainfall of four and a half inches, oaks that looked ready for the woodpile and seemed to be still standing only because nobody had leaned against them, suddenly burst out with a cluster of leaves here, and a cluster there. No two trees re-foliated in quite the same way. These native oaks are accustomed to fires and make strong comebacks, as do the sycamores. Not so the pines, which lack the regenerative powers of the other species. The pines that looked dead were dead. Although a few of them put out new needles at the top, these soon withered and dropped, and nothing further happened.

Such debility on the part of the tree itself must, in order to account for the species' survival through centuries of periodic fires, be compensated for by the durability of the seed or the seed's protective device. Some pines, such as Bishop, knobcone, and to a certain extent Monterey, are equipped with closed cones which open and drop their seeds only when exposed to very high temperatures. There is a stand of Bishop pines near Santa Barbara which passers-by assume to be a state or county planting because the trees are all exactly the same size. The actual reason is that the seeds all germinated after the same fire.

During the Coyote fire the eucalyptus trees, especially the most widely planted variety, blue gum, burned very quickly. This was partly because of their natural oil content, which caused a great deal of black smoke, and partly because they were very dry. The deep underground water which carried many large trees through the summer drought was unavailable to the shallow-rooted eucalyptus. But their comeback was also quick. In fact, the adaptation of these imports from Australia to

California fire provided one of the oddest sights of the spring and summer. Normally, eucalyptus leaves grow like other leaves, out of branches and twigs. When the branches and twigs, however, were consumed by fire, the leaves grew instead out of the trunk of the tree. They looked like telephone poles which had suddenly started to sprout leaves from top to bottom.

Certain trees took a long time to show signs of regeneration. These included the redwoods in the center of the Botanic Garden and the olive trees on the slopes of a canyon adjoining the Botanic Garden. The grove had been planted for the commercial milling of oil in the 1880s, about the time the first daily newspaper was established in Santa Barbara and the first free library and reading room was opened. The olive oil project was abandoned when cheap Mexican labor became scarce. One of the methods used to keep the workers on the job would be frowned on by present-day union officials; whenever the braceros gave evidence of wanting a siesta, a barrel of wine, carried on a donkey-drawn sled, passed between the rows of trees, and the braceros were bribed with booze on a considerably more generous scale than the British seamen with once-a-day grog.

This olive grove, left untended for years and with a heavy growth of underbrush between the trees, was severely damaged by the fire. The underbrush was the main reason for the destruction, not, as some people believed, the oil content of the wood or leaves. When I walked through the area a week after the fire ended, all the trees looked dead, and continued to do so for a long time. Yet on a visit in mid-January, sixteen months after the fire, I noticed that nearly every blackened stump was showing some greenery at the base. The heavy rains in November and December had caused the various kinds of grasses to grow thick and tall, and there were birds everywhere: house finches, white-crowned sparrows, golden-crowned sparrows, and lesser gold-finches foraged in flocks, with the sparrows providing the dinner music, assisted by two or three invisible wrentits. The brown towhees took part with an occasional chink, reminding me of grade school monotones who are allowed to accompany their musical classmates by "playing" percussion pie plates or cake tins. Dozens of quail, securely hidden, ticked and talked, discussing the intruder among themselves without bothering to lower their voices. They made it plain that they considered me a yark and a kookquat; since I didn't know what a yark or a kookquat was, I couldn't very well contradict them.

The same visit provided an unexpected bonus, a pair of black-chinned sparrows, male and female, resting on the burned branch of an olive tree. These birds are normally seen only during the late spring and summer in stands of chamise-dominant chaparral in the mountains or foothills. Finding them in January near the city limits was highly irregular. Perhaps the Coyote fire had something to so with their appearance, since the species is known to be partial to burn areas where the new vegetation is only half grown.

On my next visit to the olive grove in mid-July, most of the trees gave evidence that they would recover completely in time. Branches growing out of the woody crown were as long as six feet and covered with silver-green leaves.

Even without the braceros and the wine wagon to keep them on the job, there will someday be another crop of olives for the white-crowned sparrows, robins, and California thrashers.

The forest was turning green again. For residents of the fire areas the change was gradual. For those who only visited from time to time it was incredibly fast and far, from death to life. At the higher altitudes the white-bark ceanothus had a fresh growth of the tough, wiry stems and sharp spikes that kept predators away from such guests as the green-tailed towhee and the mountain quail. Closer to sea level the green-bark ceanothus was performing a similar function for the lazuli bunting and California quail, the wrentit and lark sparrow.

Soon manzanita apples would again be ripening for the cedar waxwings, toyon berries for the purple finches, and mistletoe for the phainopeplas. Oak buds were already appearing for the band-tailed pigeons, and there was promise of a fresh crop of chaparral currants for the hermit thrushes, mountain cherries for the Townsend solitaires, nightshade for the grosbeaks. Through the picture window beside my chair I watched the mountains recover from the fire, each day bringing a new patch of green that turned to violet when the sun set.

As each day of recovery came and went, and each new flight of birds landed on the ledge to feed, I was continually reminded of a letter John Keats sent to a friend in 1817.

"The setting Sun will always set me to rights," he wrote, "or if a Sparrow come before my Window I take part in its existence and pick about the Gravel."

GARY SNYDER

Afterword

Coming into the Watershed

Gary Snyder (b. 1930) is a native Californian who grew up in the Pacific
Northwest but returned to do graduate work at the University of California at
Berkeley in East Asian languages. After some years in Japan he returned in
1969 to build a homestead in the Sierra foothills and teach at UC Davis. His
poetry collections include Turtle Island, *awarded the 1975 Pulitzer Prize, and*
what may be his chief work, Mountains and Rivers without End *(1996). In*
1990 Snyder and his neighbors formed the Yuba Watershed Institute, which
comanages 1,800 acres of timberland with the Bureau of Land Management
near Nevada City. This essay, first presented as a talk for the California
Studies Center at California State University–Sacramento as part of their
1992 conference "Dancing at the Edge," was published in A Place in Space
(1995).

I had been too long in the calm Sierra pine groves and wanted to
hear surf and the cries of sea birds. My son Gen and I took off one
February day to visit friends on the north coast. We drove out of
the Yuba River canyon and went north from Marysville—entering that
soulful winter depth of pearly tule fog—running alongside the Feather

River and then crossing the Sacramento River at Red Bluff. From Red Bluff north the fog began to shred, and by Redding we had left it behind. As we crossed the mountains westward from Redding on Highway 299 we paid special attention to the transformations of the landscape and trees, watching to see where the zones would change and the natural boundaries could be roughly determined. From the Great Valley with its tules, grasses, valley oak, and blue oak we swiftly climbed into the steep and dissected Klamath range with its ponderosa pine, black oak, and manzanita fields. Somewhere past Burnt Ranch we were in the redwood and Douglas fir forests—soon it was the coastal range. Then we were descending past Blue Lake to come out at Arcata.

We drove on north. Just ten or fifteen miles from Arcata, around Trinidad Head, the feel of the landscape subtly changed again—much the same trees, but no open meadows, and a different light. At Crescent City we asked friends just what the change between Arcata and Crescent City was. They both said (to distill a long discussion), "You leave 'California.' Right around Trinidad Head you cross into the maritime Pacific Northwest." But the Oregon border (where we are expected to think "the Northwest" begins) is still many miles farther on.

So we had gone in that one afternoon's drive from the Mediterranean-type Sacramento Valley and its many plant alliances with the Mexican south, over the interior range with its dry pine-forest hills, into a uniquely Californian set of redwood forests, and on into the maritime Pacific Northwest: the edges of four major areas. These boundaries are not hard and clear, though. They are porous, permeable, arguable. They are boundaries of climates, plant communities, soil types, styles of life. They change over the millennia, moving a few hundred miles this way or that. A thin line drawn on a map would not do them justice. Yet these are the markers of the natural nations of our planet, and they establish real territories with real differences to which our economies and our clothing must adapt.

On the way back we stopped at Trinidad Head for a hike and a little birding. Although we knew they wouldn't be there until April, we walked out to take a look at the cliffs on the head where tufted puffins nest. For tufted puffins, this is virtually the southernmost end of their range. Their more usual nesting ground is from southeastern Alaska through the Bering Sea and down to northern Japan. In winter they are far out in the open seas of the North Pacific. At this spot, Trinidad, we could not help but feel that we touched on the life realm of the whole North Pacific and Alaska. We spent that whole weekend enjoying "liminality," dancing on the brink of the continent.

I have taken to watching the subtle changes of plants and climates as I travel over the West. We can all tell stories, I know, of the drastic changes we have noticed as we ranged over this or that freeway. This vast area called "California" is large enough to be beyond any one individual's ability (not to mention time) to travel over and to take it all into the imagination and hold it clearly enough in mind to see the whole picture. Michael Barbour, a botanist and lead author of *California's Changing Landscapes*, writes of the complexity of California: "Of the world's ten major soils, California has all ten. . . . As many as 375 distinctive natural communities have been recognized in the state. . . . California has more than five thousand kinds of native ferns, conifers, and flowering plants. Japan has far fewer species with a similar area. Even with four times California's area, Alaska does not match California's plant diversity, and neither does all of the central and northeastern United States and adjacent Canada combined. Moreover, about 30 percent of California's native plants are found nowhere else in the world."

But all this talk of the diversity of California is a trifle misleading. Of what place are we speaking? What is "California"? It is, after all, a recent human invention with hasty straight-line boundaries that were drawn with a ruler on a map and rushed off to an office in D.C. This is another illustration of Robert Frost's line, "The land was ours before we were the land's." The political boundaries of the western states were established in haste and ignorance. Landscapes have their own shapes and structures, centers and edges, which must be respected. If a relationship to a place is like a marriage, then the Yankee establishment of a jurisdiction called California was like a shotgun wedding with six sisters taken as one wife.

California is made up of what I take to be about six regions. They are of respectable size and native beauty, each with its own makeup, its own mix of bird calls and plant smells. Each of these propose a slightly different lifestyle to the human beings who live there. Each led to different sorts of rural economies, for the regional differences translate into things like raisin grapes, wet rice, timber, cattle pasture, and so forth.

The central coast with its little river valleys, beach dunes and marshes, and oak-grass-pine mountains is one region. The great Central Valley is a second, once dominated by swamps and wide shallow lakes and sweeps of valley oaks following the streams. The long mountain ranges of the Sierra Nevada are a third. From a sort of Sonoran chaparral they rise to arctic tundra. In the middle elevations they have some of the finest mixed conifer forests in the world. The Modoc plateau and volcano country—with its sagebrush and juniper—makes a fourth. Some of the Sacramento waters rise here. The fifth is the northern coast with its deep interior mountains—the Klamath region—reaching (on the coast) as far north as Trinidad Head. The sixth (of these six sisters) consists of the coastal valleys and mountains south of the Tehachapis, with natural connections on into Baja. Although today this region supports a huge population with water drawn from the Colorado River, the Owens Valley, and the great Central Valley, it was originally almost a desert.

One might ask, What about the rest? Where are the White Mountains, the Mojave Desert, the Warner Range? They are splendid places, but they do not belong with California. Their watersheds and biological communities belong to the Great Basin or the lower Colorado drainage, and we should let them return to their own families. Almost all of core California has a summer-dry Mediterranean climate with (usually) a fairly abundant winter rain. More than any thing else, this rather special type of climate is what gives our place its fragrance of oily aromatic herbs, its olive-green drought-resistant shrubs, and its patterns of rolling grass and dark forest.

I am not arguing that we should instantly redraw the boundaries of the social construction called California, although that could happen some far day. But we are becoming aware of certain long-range realities, and this thinking leads toward the next step in the evolution of human citizenship on the North American continent. The usual focus of attention for most Americans is the human society itself with its problems and its successes, its icons and symbols. With the exception of most Native Americans and a few non-natives who have given their hearts to the place, the land we all live on is simply taken for granted—and proper relation to it is not considered a part of "citizenship." But after two centuries of national history, people are beginning to wake up and notice that the United States is located on a landscape with a severe, spectacular, spacy, wildly demanding, and ecstatic narrative to be learned. Its natural communities are each unique, and each of us, whether we like it or not—in the city or countryside—lives in one of them.

Those who work in resource management are accustomed to looking at many different maps of the landscape. Each addresses its own set of meanings. If we look at land ownership categories, we get (in addition to private land) the Bureau of Land Management, national forest, national park, state park, military reserves, and a host of other public holdings. This is the public domain, a practice coming down from the historic institution of the commons in Europe. These lands, particularly in the arid West, hold much of the water, forest, and wildlife that are left in America. Although they are in the care of all the people, they have too often been managed with a bent toward the mining or logging interests and toward short-term profits.

Conservationists have been working since the 1930s for sustainable forestry practices and the preservation of key blocks of public land as wilderness. They have had some splendid success in this effort, and we are all indebted to the single-minded dedication of the people who are behind every present-day wilderness area that we and our children walk into. Our growing understanding of how natural systems work brought us the realization that an exclusive emphasis on disparate parcels of land ignored the insouciant freeness of wild creatures. Although individual islands of wild land serving as biological refuges are invaluable, they cannot by themselves guarantee the maintenance of natural variety. As biologists, public managers, and the involved public have all agreed, we need to know more about how the larger-scale natural systems work, and we need to find "on-the-ground" ways to connect wild zone to wild zone wherever possible. We have now developed the notion of biological corridors or connectors. The Greater Yellowstone Ecosystem concept came out of this sort of recognition. Our understanding of nature has been radically altered by systems theory as applied to ecology, and in particular to the very cogent subdisciplines called island biogeography theory and landscape ecology.

No single group or agency could keep track of grizzly bears, which do not care about park or ranch boundaries and have necessary, ancient territories of their own that range from late-summer alpine huckleberry fields to lower-elevation grasslands. Habitat flows across both private and public land. We must find a way to work with wild ecosystems that respects both the rights of landowners and the rights of bears. The idea of ecosystem management, all the talk now in land management circles, seems to go in the right direction. Successfully managing for the ecosystem will require as much finesse in dealing with miners, ranchers, and motel owners as it does with wild animals or bark beetles.

A "greater ecosystem" has its own function and structural coherence. It often might contain or be within a watershed system. It would usually be larger than a county, but smaller than a western U.S. state. One of the names for such a space is "bioregion."

A group of California-based federal and state land managers who are trying to work together on biodiversity problems recently realized that their work could be better accomplished in a framework of natural regions. Their interagency "memorandum of understanding" calls for us to "move beyond existing efforts focused on the conservation of individual sites, species, and resources . . . to also protect and manage ecosystems, biological communities, and landscapes." The memorandum goes on to say that "public agencies and private groups must coordinate resource management and environmental protection activities, emphasizing regional solutions to regional issues and needs."

The group identified eleven or so such working regions within California, making the San Francisco Bay and delta into one, and dividing both the Sierra and the valley into northern and southern portions. (In landscapes as in taxonomy, there are lumpers and splitters.) Since almost 50 percent of California is public domain, it is logical that the chiefs of the BLM, the Forest Service, California Department of Fish and Game, California Department of Forestry, State Parks, the Federal Fish and Wildlife Service, and such should take these issues on, but that they came together in so timely a manner and signed onto such a far-reaching plan is admirable.

Hearing of this agreement, some county government people, elected officials, and timber and business interests in the mountain counties went into a severe paranoid spasm, fearing—they said—new regulations and more centralized government. So later in the fall, an anonymous circular made its way around towns and campuses in northern California under the title "Biodiversity or New Paganism?" It says that "California Resource Secretary Doug Wheeler and his self-appointed bioregional soldiers are out to devalue human life by placing greater emphasis on rocks, trees, fish, plants, and wildlife." It quotes me as having written that "those of us who are now promoting a bioregional consciousness would, as an ultimate and long-range goal, like to see this continent more sensitively redefined, and the natural regions of North America—Turtle Island—gradually begin to shape the political entities within which we work. It would be a small step toward deconstruction of America as a superpower into seven or eight natural nations—none of which have a budget big enough to support missiles." I'm pleased to say I did write that. I'd think it was clear that my statement is not promoting more centralized government, which seems to be a major fear, but these gents want both their small-town autonomy and the military-industrial state at the same time. Many a would-be westerner is a rugged individualist in rhetoric only, and will scream up a storm if taken too far from the government tit. As Mark Reisner makes clear in *Cadillac Desert*, much of the agriculture and ranching of the West exists by virtue of a complicated and very expensive sort of government welfare: big dams and water plans. The real intent of the circular (it urges people to write the state governor) seems to be to resist policies that favor long-range sustainability and the support of biodiversity, and to hold out for maximum resource extraction right now.

As far as I can see, the intelligent but so far toothless California "bioregional proposal" is simply a basis for further thinking and some degree of cooperation among agencies. The most original part is the call for the formation of "bioregional councils" that would have some stake in decision making. Who would be on the bioregional council is not spelled out. Even closer to the roots, the memorandum that started all this furor suggests that "watershed councils" would be formed, which, being based on stream-by-stream communities, would be truly local bodies that could help design agreements working for the preservation of natural variety. Like, let's say, helping to preserve the spawning grounds for the wild salmon that still come (amazingly) into the lower Yuba River gravel wastelands. This would be an effort that would have to involve a number of groups and agencies, and it would have to include the blessing of the usually development-minded Yuba County Water Agency.

The term "bioregion" was adopted by the signers to the Memorandum on Biological Diversity as a technical term from the field of biogeography. It's not likely that they would have known that there were already groups of people around the United States and Canada who were talking in terms of bioregionally oriented societies. I doubt they would have heard about the first North American Bioregional Congress held in Kansas in the late eighties. They had no idea that for twenty years communitarian ecology-minded dwellers-in-the-land have been living in places they call "Ish" (Puget Sound and lower British Columbia) or "Columbiana" (upper Columbia River) or "Mesechabe" (lower Mississippi) or "Shasta" (northern California), and all of them have produced newsletters, taken field trips, organized gatherings, and at the same time participated in local politics.

That "bioregion" was an idea already in circulation was the bad, or good, luck of the biodiversity agreement people, depending on how you look at it. As it happens, the bioregional people are also finding "watershed councils" to be the building blocks of a long-range strategy for social and environmental sustainability.

A watershed is a marvelous thing to consider: this process of rain falling, streams flowing, and oceans evaporating causes every molecule of water on earth to make the complete trip once every two million years. The surface is carved into watersheds—a kind of familial branching, a chart of relationship, and a definition of place. The watershed is the first and last nation whose boundaries, though subtly shifting, are unarguable. Races of birds, subspecies of trees, and types of hats or rain gear often go by the watershed. For the watershed, cities and dams are ephemeral and of no more account than a boulder that falls in the river or a landslide that temporarily alters the channel. The water will always be there, and it will always find its way down. As constrained and polluted as the Los Angeles River is at the moment, it can also be said that in the larger picture that river is alive and well under the city streets, running in giant culverts. It may be amused by such diversion. But we who live in terms of centuries rather than millions of years must hold the watershed and its communities together, so our children might enjoy the clear water and fresh life of this landscape we have chosen. From the tiniest rivulet at the crest of a ridge to the main trunk of a river approaching the lowlands, the river is all one place and all one land.

The water cycle includes our springs and wells, our Sierra snowpack, our irrigation canals, our car wash, and the spring salmon run. It's the spring peeper in the pond and the acorn woodpecker chattering in a snag. The watershed is beyond the dichotomies of orderly/disorderly, for its forms are free, but somehow inevitable. The life that comes to flourish within it constitutes the first kind of community.

The agenda of a watershed council starts in a modest way: like saying,

"Let's try and rehabilitate our river to the point that wild salmon can successfully spawn here again." In pursuit of this local agenda, a community might find itself combating clear-cut timber sales upstream, water-selling grabs downstream, Taiwanese drift-net practices out in the North Pacific, and a host of other national and international threats to the health of salmon.

If a wide range of people will join in on this effort—people from timber and tourism, settled ranchers and farmers, fly-fishing retirees, the businesses and the forest-dwelling new settlers—something might come of it. But if this joint agreement were to be implemented as a top-down prescription, it would go nowhere. Only a grass-roots engagement with long-term issues can provide the political and social stability it will take to keep the biological richness of California's regions intact.

All public land ownership is ultimately written in sand. The boundaries and management categories were created by Congress, and Congress can take them away. The only "jurisdiction" that will last in the world of nature is the watershed, and even that changes slightly over time. If public lands come under greater and greater pressure to be opened for exploitation and use in the twenty-first century, it will be the local people, the watershed people, who will prove to be the last and possibly most effective line of defense. Let us hope it never comes to that.

The mandate of the public land managers and the Fish and Wildlife people inevitably directs them to resource concerns. They are proposing to do what could be called "ecological bioregionalism." The other movement, coming out of the local communities, could be called "cultural bioregionalism." I would like to turn my attention now to cultural bioregionalism and to what practical promise these ideas hold for fin-de-millennium America.

Living in a place—the notion has been around for decades and has usually been dismissed as provincial, backward, dull, and possibly reactionary. But new dynamics are at work. The mobility that has characterized American life is coming to a close. As Americans begin to stay put, it may give us the first opening in over a century to give participatory democracy another try.

Daniel Kemmis, the mayor of Missoula, Montana, has written a fine little book called *Community and the Politics of Place* (Norman: University of Oklahoma Press, 1990). Mr. Kemmis points out that in the eighteenth century the word *republican* meant a politics of community engagement. Early republican thought was set against the federalist theories that would govern by balancing competing interests, devise sets of legalistic procedures, maintain checks and balances (leading to hearings held before putative experts) in place of direct discussion between adversarial parties.

Kemmis quotes Rousseau: "Keeping citizens apart has become the first maxim of modern politics." So what organizing principle will get citizens back together? There are many, and each in its way has its use. People have organized themselves by ethnic background, religion, race, class, employment, gender, language, and age. In a highly mobile society where few people stay put, thematic organizing is entirely understandable. But place, that oldest of organizing principles (next to kinship), is a novel development in the United States.

"What holds people together long enough to discover their power as citizens is their common inhabiting of a single place," Kemmis argues. Being so placed, people will volunteer for community projects, join school boards, and accept nominations and appointments. Good minds, which are often forced by company or agency policy to keep moving, will make notable contributions to the neighborhood if allowed to stay put. And since local elections deal with immediate issues, a lot more people will turn out to vote. There will be a return of civic life.

This will not be "nationalism" with all its dangers, as long as sense of place is not entirely conflated with the idea of a nation. Bioregional concerns go beyond those of any ephemeral (and often brutal and dangerous) politically designated space. They give us the imagination of "citizenship" in a place called (for example) the great Central Valley, which has valley oaks and migratory waterfowl as well as humans among its members. A place (with a climate, with bugs), as Kemmis says, "develops practices, creates culture."

Another fruit of the enlarged sense of nature that systems ecology and bioregional thought have given us is the realization that cities and suburbs are a part of the system. Unlike the ecological bioregionalists, the cultural bioregionalists absolutely must include the cities in their thinking. The practice of urban bioregionalism ("green cities") has made a good start in San Francisco. One can learn and live deeply with regard to wild systems in any sort of neighborhood—from the urban to a big sugar-beet farm. The birds are migrating, the wild plants are looking for a way to slip in, the insects in any case live an untrammeled life, the raccoons are padding through the crosswalks at 2:00 A.M., and the nursery trees are trying to figure out who they are. These are exciting, convivial, and somewhat radical knowledges.

An economics of scale can be seen in the watershed/bioregion/city-state model. Imagine a Renaissance-style city-state facing out on the Pacific with its bioregional hinterland reaching to the headwaters of all the streams that flow through its bay. The San Francisco/valley rivers/Shasta headwaters bio-city region! I take some ideas along these lines from Jane Jacobs's tantalizing book *Cities and the Wealth of Nations* (New York: Random House, 1984), in which she argues that the city, not the nation-state, is the proper locus of an economy, and then that the city is always to be understood as being one with the hinterland.

Such a non-nationalistic idea of community, in which commitment to pure place is paramount, cannot be ethnic or racist. Here is perhaps the most delicious turn that comes out of thinking about politics from the standpoint of place: anyone of any race, language, religion, or origin is welcome, as long as they live well on the land. The great Central Valley region does not prefer English over Spanish or Japanese or Hmong. If it had any preference at all, it might best like the languages it heard for thousands of years, such as Maiduor Miwok, simply because it's used to them. Mythically speaking, it will welcome whoever chooses to observe the etiquette, express the gratitude, grasp the tools, and learn the songs that it takes to live there.

This sort of future culture is available to whoever makes the choice, regardless of background. It need not require that a person drop his or her Buddhist, Jewish, Christian, animist, atheist, or Muslim beliefs but simply add to that faith or philosophy a sincere nod in the direction of the deep value of the natural world and the subjecthood of nonhuman beings. A culture of place will be created that will include the "United States," and go beyond that to an affirmation of the continent, the land itself, Turtle Island. We could be showing Southeast Asian and South American newcomers the patterns of the rivers, the distant hills, saying, "It is not only that you are now living in the United States. You are living in this great landscape. Please get to know these rivers and mountains, and be welcome here." Euro-Americans, Asian Americans, African Americans can—if they wish—become "born-again" natives of Turtle Island. In doing so we also might even (eventually) win some respect from our native American predecessors, who are still here and still trying to teach us where we are.

Watershed consciousness and bioregionalism is not just environmentalism, not just a means toward resolution of social and economic problems, but a move toward resolving both nature and society with the practice of a profound citizenship in both the natural and the social worlds. If the ground can be our common ground, we can begin to talk to each other (human and nonhuman) once again.

> California is gold-tan grasses, silver-gray tule fog,
> olive-green redwood, blue-gray chaparral,
> silver-hue serpentine hills.
> Blinding white granite,
> blue-black rock sea cliffs.
> —Blue summer sky, chestnut brown slough water, steep purple city
>   streets—hot cream towns. Many colors of the land, many colors
>   of the skin.

Abbey, Edward. *The Best of Edward Abbey*. San Francisco: Sierra Club Books, 1988.

———. *Confessions of a Barbararian: Selections from the Journals of Edward Abbey, 1951–1989*. Boston: Little, Brown, 1994.

———. *The Journey Home: Some Words in the Defense of the American West*. New York: E. P. Dutton, 1977.

Austin, Mary. *The Flock*. Boston: Houghton Mifflin, 1906.

———. *Isidro*. Boston: Houghton Mifflin, 1905.

———. *The Land of Little Rain*. Boston: Houghton Mifflin, 1903.

Brewer, William H. *Up and Down California in 1860*. Edited by Francis P. Farquhar. New Haven: Yale University Press, 1930; repr. Berkeley: University of California Press, 1940.

Chase, J. Smeaton. *California Coast Trails*. Boston: Houghton Mifflin, 1913.

———. *California Desert Trails*. Boston: Houghton Mifflin, 1919.

———. *Yosemite Trails*. Boston: Hougton Mifflin, 1911.

Chatham, Russell. *The Angler's Coast*. Livingston, Mont.: Clark City Press, 1990.

———. *Dark Waters*. Livingston, Mont.: Clark City Press, 1988.

Daniel, John. *All Things Touched by Wind*. Anchorage: Salmon Run Press, 1994.

———. *Common Ground*. Lewiston, Idaho: Confluence Press, 1988.

———. *The Trail Home: Nature, Imagination, and the American West*. New York: Pantheon Books, 1992.

Darlington, David. *Angels' Visits: An Inquiry into the Mystery of Zinfandel*. New York: Henry Holt, 1992.

———. *In Condor Country.* Boston: Houghton Mifflin, 1987.

———. *The Mojave: A Portrait of the Definitive American Desert.* New York: Henry Holt, 1996.

Didion, Joan. *Play It as It Lays.* New York: Farrar, Straus & Giroux, 1970.

———. *Run River.* New York: Ivan Obolensky, 1963.

———. *Slouching Towards Bethlehem.* New York: Farrar, Straus & Giroux, 1968.

Duane, Daniel. *Caught Inside: A Surfer's Year on the California Coast.* New York: North Point Press, 1996.

———. *Lighting Out: A Vision of California and the Mountains.* St. Paul: Graywolf Press, 1994.

Ehrlich, Gretel. *Islands, the Universe, Home.* New York: Viking Press, 1991.

———. *The Solace of Open Spaces.* New York: Viking Press, 1985.

Fisher, M. F. K. *Last House: Reflections, Dreams, and Observations, 1943–1991.* New York: Pantheon Books, 1995.

———. *Stay Me, Oh Comfort Me: Journal and Stories, 1933–1941.* New York: Pantheon Books, 1993.

———. *To Begin Again: Stories and Memoirs, 1908–1929.* New York: Pantheon Books, 1992.

Flanner, Hildegarde. *At the Gentle Mercy of Plants: Essays and Poems.* Santa Barbara: John Daniel, 1986.

———. *Brief Cherishing: A Napa Valley Harvest.* Santa Barbara: John Daniel, 1985.

———. *A Vanishing Land.* Portola Valley, Calif.: No Dead Lines, 1980.

Gilliam, Harold. *Creating Carmel: An Enduring Vision.* Salt Lake City: Peregrine Smith Books, 1992.

———. *Island in Time: The Point Reyes Peninsula.* San Francisco: Sierra Club Books, 1962.

———. *The San Francisco Experience.* New York: Doubleday, 1972.

Goddard, Pliny E. "The Creation." *University of California Publications in American Archaeology and Ethnology* 184, no. 2 (1909). Reprinted in *Folk Tales of the North American Indians,* edited by Stith Thompson. North Dighton, Mass.: JG Press, 1995.

———. *Indians of the Southwest.* New York: American Museum of Natural History, 1913.

Houston, James D. *California Heartland: Writing from the Great Central Valley* (with Gerald Haslam). Santa Barbara: Capra Press, 1978.

———. *Californians: Searching for the Golden State.* New York: Alfred A. Knopf, 1982.

———. *Continental Drift.* New York: Alfred A. Knopf, 1978.

———. *In the Ring of Fire: A Pacific Basin Journey.* San Francisco: Mercury House, 1997.

———. *Running West.* New York: Crown Publishers, 1989.

Kerouac, Jack. *Big Sur.* New York: Viking Press, 1962.

———. *The Dharma Bums.* New York: Viking Press, 1958.

———. *On the Road.* New York: Viking Press, 1957.

———. *Selected Letters, 1940–1956.* Edited by Ann Charters. New York: Viking Press, 1995.

LeConte, Joseph. *Autobiography.* Edited by William Dallam Arms. New York: D. Appleton, 1903.

———. *A Journal of Ramblings Through the High Sierra of California by the "University Excursion Party."* San Francisco: Frances & Valentine, 1875.

London, Jack. *Burning Daylight.* New York: Macmillan, 1910.

———. *Jack London's California: The Golden Poppy and Other Writings.* Edited by Sol Noto. New York: Beaufort Books, 1986.

——— *Novels and Stories.* Library of America, 2 vols. New York: Literary Classics of the United States, 1982.

———. *The Valley of the Moon.* New York: Macmillan, 1913.

Lopez, Barry. *Crossing Open Ground.* New York: Scribner's, 1988.

———. *Crow and Weasel.* New York: Random House, 1991.

———. *Field Notes: The Grace Notes of the Canyon Wren.* New York: Alfred A. Knopf, 1994.

———. *Of Wolves and Men.* New York: Scribner's, 1978.

Masumoto, David Mas. *Country Voices: An Oral History of a Japanese-American Family Farm Community.* Del Rey, Calif.: Inaka Countryside Publications, 1987.

———. *Epitaph for a Peach: Four Seasons on My Family Farm.* San Francisco: HarperCollins West, 1995.

———. *Harvest Son.* New York: W. W. Norton, 1998.

McKinney, John. *A Walk Along Land's End: Discovering California's Unknown Coast.* San Francisco: HarperCollins West, 1995.

———. *Walking the California Coast: One Hundred Adventures Along the California Coast.* San Francisco: HarperCollins West, 1994.

———. *Walking California's State Parks.* San Francisco: HarperCollins West, 1994.

McPhee, John. *Assembling California.* New York: Farrar, Straus & Giroux, 1993.

Millar, Margaret. *The Birds and the Beasts Were There.* New York: Random House, 1967.

Miller, Henry. *The Air-Conditioned Nightmare.* New York: New Directions, 1945.

———. *Big Sur and the Oranges of Hieronymous Bosch.* New York: New Directions, 1957.

———. *The Henry Miller Reader.* Edited by Lawrence Durrell. New York: New Directions, 1959.

Miller, Joaquin. *Memorie and Rime.* New York: Funk & Wagnals, 1884.

———. *Life Amongst the Modocs: Unwritten History.* London: Bentley, 1873.

Muir, John. *The Mountains of California.* New York: Century, 1894.

———. *My First Summer in the Sierra.* Boston: Houghton Mifflin, 1911.

———. *The Yosemite.* New York: Century, 1912.

Nabhan, Gary Paul. *The Desert Smells like Rain: A Naturalist in Papago Indian Country.* San Francisco: North Point Press, 1982.

———. *Gathering the Desert.* Tucson: University of Arizona Press, 1985.

———. *The Geography of Childhood (Why Children Need Wild Places)* (with Stephen Trimble). Boston: Beacon Press, 1994.

Nunn, Kem. *The Dogs of Winter.* New York: Scribner's, 1997.

———. *Pomona Queen.* New York: Pocket Books, 1992.

———. *Tapping the Source.* New York: Delacorte Press, 1984.

Powell, Lawrence Clark. *California Classics: The Creative Literature of the Golden State.* Los Angeles: Ward Ritchie Press, 1971.

———. *Fortune and Friendship: An Autobiography.* New York: Bowker, 1968.

———. *The Little Package.* New York: World, 1964.

Snyder, Gary. *Mountains and Rivers Without End.* Washington, D.C.: Counterpoint, 1996.

———. *A Place in Space: Ethics, Aesthetics, and Wilderness.* Washington, D.C.: Counterpoint, 1995.

———. *The Practice of the Wild.* New York: Farrar, Straus & Giroux, 1990.

Stegner, Wallace. *American Places* (with Page Stegner). New York: E. P. Dutton, 1983.

———. *American West as Living Space.* Ann Arbor: University of Michigan Press, 1987.

———. *Angle of Repose.* New York: Doubleday, 1971.

———. *Where the Bluebird Sings to the Lemonade Springs: Living and Writing in the West.* New York: Random House, 1992.

Steinbeck, John. *The Grapes of Wrath.* New York: Viking Press, 1939.

———. *The Long Valley.* New York: Viking Press, 1938.

———. *The Pastures of Heaven.* New York: Brewer, 1932.

———. *To a God Unknown.* New York: Ballou, 1933.

———. *Tortilla Flat.* New York: Covici, Friede, 1935.

Stevenson, Robert Louis. *Silverado Journal.* Edited by J. E. Jordan. San Francisco: Book Club of California, 1954.

———. *The Silverado Squatters.* London: Chatto & Windus, 1883.

Twain, Mark. *Autobiography.* 2 vols. New York: Harper, 1924.

———. *Roughing It.* New York: Harper & Bros., 1906.

Wallace, David Rains. *Bulow Hammock: Mind in a Forest.* San Francisco: Sierra Club Books, 1989.

———. *The Klamath Knot: Explorations of Myth and Evolution.* San Francisco: Sierra Club Books, 1972.

———. *The Untamed Garden and Other Personal Essays.* Columbus: Ohio State University Press, 1986.

Watkins, T. H. *On the Shore of the Sundown Sea.* San Francisco: Sierra Club Books, 1973.

———. *Time's Island: The California Desert.* Salt Lake City: Gibbs Smith, 1989.

———, ed. (with Patricia Byrnes). *The World of Wilderness: Essays on the Power and Purpose of Wild Country.* Boulder, Colo.: Roberts Rinehart, 1995.

Wheelwright, Jane Hollister. *The Long Shore: A Psychological Experience of the Wilderness* (with Lynda Wheelwright Schmidt). San Francisco: Sierra Club Books, 1991.

———. *The Ranch Papers: A California Memoir.* San Francisco: Lapis Press, 1988.

Wilson, Darryl Babe. "Grampa Ramsey and the Great Canyon." In *Blue Dawn, Red Earth: New Native American Storytellers,* edited by Clifford E. Trafzer. New York: Doubleday, 1996.

———. "Before There Was Something, There Was Nothing: The Creation." In *The Sound of Rattles and Clappers: A Collection of New California Indian Writing,* edited by Greg Sarris. Tucson: University of Arizona Press, 1994.

Zwinger, Ann. *A Desert Country near the Sea: A Natural History of the Cape Region of Baja California.* New York: HarperCollins, 1983.

———. *Land Above the Trees: A Guide to American Alpine Tundra.* New York: Harper & Row, 1972.

———. *Run, River, Run: A Naturalist's Journey Down One of the Great Rivers of the American West.* New York: HarperCollins, 1972.

———. *Yosemite: Valley of Thunder.* New York: HarperCollins, 1996.

Zwinger, Susan. *Stalking the Ice Dragon: An Alaskan Journey.* Tucson: University of Arizona Press, 1991.

———. *Still Wild, Always Wild: A Journey into the Desert Wilderness of California* (with photographs by Jeff Garton). San Francisco: Sierra Club Books, 1997.

ACKNOWLEDGMENTS

"Death Valley," from *The Journey Home* by Edward Abbey. © 1977 by Edward Abbey. Used by permission of Dutton Signet, a division of Penguin Books USA Inc. and Don Congdon Associates, Inc.

"Into the Valley," from *Up and Down California in 1860–1864* by William H. Brewer, edited by Francis Farquhar. © 1949 by The Regents of the University of California. Reprinted by permission of the University of California Press.

"A Certain Moment," from *Angler's Coast* by Russell Chatham. © by Russell Chatham. Reprinted by permission of Clark City Press, 1990.

"Desert Walking," from *The Trail Home* by John Daniel. © 1992 by John Daniel. Reprinted by permission of Pantheon Books, a division of Random House, Inc.

"In Condor Country," from *In Condor Country* by David Darlington. © 1987 by David Darlington. Reprinted by permission of Frederick Hill Associates Literary Agency.

"The Santa Ana," from "Los Angeles Notebook," in *Slouching Towards Bethlehem* by Joan Didion. © 1968 and renewed by Joan Didion. Reprinted by permission of Farrar, Straus & Giroux, Inc.

"Climbing Half Dome," © 1994 by Daniel Duane. Reprinted from *Lighting Out* with the permission of Graywolf Press, St. Paul, Minnesota, and Ellen Levine Literary Agency.

"Santa Rosa" reprinted by permission from the July/August 1996 issue of *Islands* magazine. © 1966 by Islands Publishing Company. All rights reserved.

"Spirits of the Valley" reprinted from *Stay Me, Oh Comfort Me* by M. F. K.

Fisher. © 1992 by M. F. K. Fisher. Reprinted by permission of Pantheon Books, a division of Random House, Inc., and Lescher & Lescher, Ltd.

"A Vanishing Land, " from *A Vanishing Land* by Hildegarde Flanner. © 1980 by John Monhoff. Reprinted by permission of John Monhoff and No Dead Lines.

"A Mount for All Seasons," from *The San Francisco Experience* by Harold Gilliam. © 1972 by Harold Gilliam. Used by permission of Doubleday, a division of Bantam Doubleday Dell Publishing Group, Inc.

"Continental Drift," from *Continental Drift* by James D. Houston. © 1988 by James D. Houston. Reprinted by permission of author.

"A Reflection on White Geese," from *Crossing Open Ground* by Barry Lopez. © 1988 by Barry Holstun Lopez. Reprinted by permission of Sterling Lord Literistic, Inc.

"Climbing Matterhorn Peak," from *The Dharma Bums* by Jack Kerouac. © 1958 by Jack Kerouac, renewed by Stella Kerouac and Jan Kerouac. Used by permission of Viking Penguin, a division of Penguin Books USA Inc.

"Lost Coast" (abridged). Reprinted by permission of author.

"The San Andreas Discrepancy," from *Assembling California* by John McPhee. © 1993 by John McPhee. Reprinted by permission of Farrar, Straus & Giroux, Inc., and Macfarlane Walter & Ross, Toronto.

"Winter's Fog," from *Epitaph for a Peach* by David Mas Masumoto. © 1995 by David Mas Masumoto. Reprinted by permission of HarperCollins Publishers, Inc.

"After the Fire," from *The Birds and Beasts Were There* by Margaret Millar. © 1967 by Margaret Millar, renewed 1995 by The Margaret Millar Charitable Remainder Unitrust u/a 1/12/82. Reprinted by permission of Harold Ober Associates Incorporated.

"Big Sur," from *Big Sur and the Oranges of Hieronymus Bosch* by Henry Miller. © 1957 by New Directions Publishing Corp. Reprinted by permission of New Directions Publishing Corp.

"The Palms in Our Hands," from *Gathering the Desert* by Gary Paul Nabhan. © 1985 by Gary Paul Nabhan. Reprinted by permission of the University of Arizona Press.

"Tapping the Source" by Kem Nunn. Reprinted by permission of author.

"Where the Mountains Meet the Sea," from *The Little Package* by Lawrence Clark Powell. © 1964 by Lawrence Clark Powell. Reprinted by permission of author.

"Remnants" by Wallace Stegner. From *American Places* by Wallace Stegner;

originally published in *Country Journal,* December 1979. © 1979 by Wallace Stegner. Reprinted by permission of Brandt & Brandt Literary Agents, Inc.

"Flight," from *The Long Valley* by John Steinbeck. © 1938, renewed © 1966 by John Steinbeck. Used by permission of Viking Penguin, a division of Penguin Books USA Inc.

"The Fourth Dimension," from Chapter One (abridged) of *The Klamath Knot* by David Rains Wallace. © 1972 by Sierra Club Books. Reprinted by permission of Sierra Club Books.

"The Sundown Sea," © 1973 by T. H. Watkins. Reprinted by permission of author.

"The Storm," © 1988 by Jane Wheelwright Hollister. Reprinted by permission of author.

"Grampa Ramsey and the Great Canyon" first appeared in *News from Native California* (Malcolm Margolin, editor) and was collected in *Blue Dawn, Red Earth* (Clifford E. Trafzer, editor), published by Doubleday, 1996. Reprinted by permission of author.

"Trumpets of Light," excerpt from *Yosemite: A Valley of Thunder* by Ann Zwinger. © 1996 by Tehabi Books, Inc. Reprinted by permission of Tehabi Books.

"Overlooking Carrizo Gorge," excerpt from *Still Wild, Always Wild* by Susan Zwinger. © 1997 by Susan Zwinger. Reprinted by permission of Sierra Club Books.

Designer:	Nola Burger
Compositor:	Integrated Composition Systems, Inc.
Text:	10/15 Janson
Display:	Janson and Futura Heavy
Printer and Binder:	BookCrafters, Inc.